Ken Howland
April, 1974

THE WRITINGS OF
JONATHAN SWIFT

AUTHORITATIVE TEXTS

BACKGROUNDS

CRITICISM

NORTON CRITICAL EDITIONS

⇒⇒ A NORTON CRITICAL EDITION ⇐⇐

THE WRITINGS OF JONATHAN SWIFT

AUTHORITATIVE TEXTS
BACKGROUNDS
CRITICISM

⇒⇒⇐⇐

Edited by
ROBERT A. GREENBERG
QUEENS COLLEGE

WILLIAM BOWMAN PIPER
RICE UNIVERSITY

W · W · NORTON & COMPANY · INC · *New York*

W. W. NORTON & COMPANY, INC.
also publishes

THE NORTON ANTHOLOGY OF ENGLISH LITERATURE
edited by M. H. Abrams et al.

THE NORTON ANTHOLOGY OF POETRY
edited by Arthur M. Eastman et al.

WORLD MASTERPIECES
edited by Maynard Mack et al.

THE NORTON READER
edited by Arthur M. Eastman et al.

THE NORTON FACSIMILE OF
THE FIRST FOLIO OF SHAKESPEARE
prepared by Charlton Hinman

and the NORTON CRITICAL EDITIONS

FIRST EDITION

Library of Congress Cataloging in Publication Data
Swift, Jonathan, 1667–1745.
    The writings of Jonathan Swift.

    (A Norton critical edition)
    Bibliography: p.
    I. Greenberg, Robert A., ed. II. Piper, William
Bowman, 1927–
PR3722.G7   828′.5′09   72-7038
ISBN 0-393-04283-9
ISBN 0-393-09415-4 (pbk.)

PRINTED IN THE UNITED STATES OF AMERICA

1 2 3 4 5 6 7 8 9 0

Contents

Backgrounds

Criticism

Preface

The purpose of this volume is to make as accessible as possible to the modern reader the best and most characteristic writings of Jonathan Swift. It contains his essential masterpieces, *Gulliver's Travels* and *A Tale of a Tub*, and a wide selection of his other work in prose and poetry. By including a number of the impressive if unpleasant poems Swift wrote after 1729, poems traditionally excluded from collections of his writings, it offers the reader a more substantial and, we believe, more accurate representation of Swift's achievement from virtually the beginning of his career to the end. Except for the *Travels*, which we have placed first, the writings are separated into prose and poetry; and in each category they have been arranged in generally chronological sequence. Our policy has been to avoid excerpts and wherever possible to give Swift complete; the *Journal to Stella*, an unavoidable exception to this policy, is, we hope, sufficiently represented to convey the quality of the whole of that remarkable record. We have also brought together in a supplementary section a variety of contemporary materials—correspondence, anecdotes, literary texts—which throw light on Swift and on the literary and social context within which he worked. And we have included, finally, a selection of modern critical essays in the hope, not of exhausting the issues they raise about Swift and his work, but of bringing these issues into prominence through the medium of spirited commentary and analysis. A further sense of the wealth and diversity of modern discussions of Swift can be found in the annotated bibliography that closes this volume.

Editorial notes have been provided to clarify verbal complexities, topical references, and other details that may prove elusive to the modern reader. In a few of them we have referred the reader on to standard editions of Swift: to the *Prose Works*, edited by Herbert Davis; to the *Poems*, edited by Harold Williams; and to the *Tale*, edited by A. C. Guthkelch and D. Nichol Smith. These editorial notes are signaled throughout the book by arabic numbers and appear at the feet of the appropriate pages—except in the case of three works: the *Tale*, the *Battel*, and the *Fragment*. Swift added many footnotes and marginal notes of his own to these works; and since all of his additions have been exactly rendered, it seemed best to place our notes in a body immediately following the *Fragment* (pp. 415–420). Swift's own notes, here and elsewhere, are indicated, as they were commonly indicated in the editions he oversaw, by asterisks, swords, parallel bars, and other such symbols.

The texts for the *Travels* and other works we have derived primarily from the Faulkner edition of the works, first published in Dublin with Swift's knowledge in 1735. However, our text for the *Tale* and its two companions, the *Battel* and the *Fragment*, which was not incorporated into any formal edition of Swift's works until after 1750, comes primarily from Swift's augmented edition of 1710. Establishing texts of certain of the poems was a difficult task; and in three instances—"Baucis and Philemon," "The Progress of Beauty," and "Verses on the Death"—we have relied heavily on the great modern edition by Harold Williams. This was made possible by permission of the Clarendon Press, which we herewith acknowledge. In general, we have arrived at our texts with the idea of presenting, in the case of each work, a reading as close as possible to Swift's own freshest and fullest creative intention. We have indicated our textual decisions in the notes whenever that seemed useful or advisable.

In composing this book, we have benefited from the facilities and holdings of the Paul Klapper Library of Queens College; and we have enjoyed the help of a number of people: Mrs. Monika Orr and Mr. Richard Perrine of the Rice University Library; Mrs. Catherine Veninga and Miss Eileen Coumont, graduate assistants in the Rice University English Department; and Professors Paul Hunter, Ronald Paulson, and Monroe K. Spears. Particular thanks are due Emily Garlin of W. W. Norton & Co., Inc., for her response to the complexities of eighteenth-century typography.

The Text of
Gulliver's Travels

CAPT. LEMUEL GULLIVER
Splendide Mendax. Hor.

VOLUME III.

Of the AUTHOR's

WORKS.

CONTAINING,

TRAVELS

INTO SEVERAL

Remote Nations of the WORLD.

In Four PARTS, *viz.*

I. A Voyage to LIL-
LIPUT.

II. A Voyage to BROB-
DINGNAG.

III. A Voyage to LA-

PUTA, BALNIBARBI,
LUGGNAGG, GLUBB-
DUBDRIB and JAPAN.

IV. A Voyage to the
COUNTRY of the
HOUYHNHNMS.

By *LEMUEL GULLIVER*, firſt a Surgeon,
and then a CAPTAIN of ſeveral SHIPS.

———— *Retroq;*
Vulgus abhorret ab his.

In this Impreſſion ſeveral Errors in the *London* and *Dublin*
Editions are correƈted.

DUBLIN:

Printed by and for GEORGE FAULKNER, Printer
and Bookſeller, in *Eſſex-Street*, oppoſite to the
Bridge. MDCCXXXV.

A Letter

from Capt. Gulliver, to his Cousin Sympson

I hope you will be ready to own publickly, whenever you shall be called to it, that by your great and frequent Urgency you prevailed on me to publish a very loose and uncorrect Account of my Travels; with Direction to hire some young Gentlemen of either University to put them in Order, and correct the Style, as my Cousin *Dampier*[1] did by my Advice, in his Book called, A *Voyage round the World*. But I do not remember I gave you Power to consent, that any thing should be omitted, and much less that any thing should be inserted: Therefore, as to the latter, I do here renounce every thing of that Kind; particularly a Paragraph about her Majesty the late Queen *Anne*, of most pious and glorious Memory; although I did reverence and esteem her more than any of human Species. But you, or your Interpolator, ought to have considered, that as it was not my Inclination, so was it not decent to praise any Animal of our Composition before my Master *Houyhnhnm*: And besides, the Fact was altogether false; for to my Knowledge, being in *England* during some Part of her Majesty's Reign, she did govern by a chief Minister; nay, even by two successively; the first whereof was the Lord of *Godolphin*, and the second the Lord of *Oxford*; so that you have made me *say the thing that was not*. Likewise, in the Account of the Academy of Projectors, and several Passages of my Discourse to my Master *Houyhnhnm*, you have either omitted some material Circumstances, or minced or changed them in such a Manner, that I do hardly know mine own Work. When I formerly hinted to you something of this in a Letter, you were pleased to answer, that you were afraid of giving Offence; that People in Power were very watchful over the Press; and apt not only to interpret, but to punish every thing

[1] William Dampier (1652-1715), a noted explorer whose books on travel were widely read. Swift may have patterned some of Gulliver's traits after him.

IV

which looked like an *Inuendo* (as I think you called it.) But pray,
how could that which I spoke so many Years ago, and at above five
Thousand Leagues distance, in another Reign, be applyed to any
of the *Yahoos*, who now are said to govern the Herd; especially, at
a time when I little thought on or feared the Unhappiness of living
under them. Have not I the most Reason to complain, when I see
these very *Yahoos* carried by *Houyhnhnms* in a Vehicle, as if these
were Brutes, and those the rational Creatures? And, indeed, to avoid
so monstrous and detestable a Sight, was one principal Motive of
my Retirement hither.

Thus much I thought proper to tell you in Relation to your
self, and to the Trust I reposed in you.

I do in the next Place complain of my own great Want of
Judgment, in being prevailed upon by the Intreaties and false
Reasonings of you and some others, very much against mine own
Opinion, to suffer my Travels to be published. Pray bring to your
Mind how often I desired you to consider, when you insisted on
the Motive of *publick Good*; that the *Yahoos* were a species of
Animals utterly incapable of Amendment by Precepts or Examples:
And so it hath proved; for instead of seeing a full Stop put to all
Abuses and Corruptions, at least in this little Island, as I had
Reason to expect: Behold, after above six Months Warning, I cannot learn that my Book hath produced one single Effect according
to mine Intentions: I desired you would let me know by a Letter,
when Party and Faction were extinguished; Judges learned and upright; Pleaders honest and modest, with some Tincture of common
Sense; and *Smithfield* blazing with Pyramids of Law-Books; the
young Nobility's Education entirely changed; the Physicians banished; the Female *Yahoos* abounding in Virtue, Honour, Truth and
good Sense; Courts and Levees of great Ministers thoroughly
weeded and swept; Wit, Merit and Learning rewarded; all Dis-
gracers of the Press in Prose and Verse, condemned to eat nothing
but their own Cotten, and quench their Thirst with their own Ink.
These, and a Thousand other Reformations, I firmly counted upon
by your Encouragement; as indeed they were plainly deducible
from the Precepts delivered in my Book. And, it must be owned
that seven Months were a sufficient Time to correct every Vice
and Folly to which *Yahoos* are subject; if their Natures had been
capable of the least Disposition to Virtue or Wisdom: Yet so far
have you been from answering mine Expectation in any of your

Letters; that on the contrary, you are loading our Carrier every Week with Libels, and Keys, and Reflections, and Memoirs, and Second Parts; wherein I see myself accused of reflecting upon great States-Folk; of degrading human Nature, (for so they have still the Confidence to stile it) and of abusing the Female Sex. I find likewise, that the Writers of those Bundles are not agreed among themselves; for some of them will not allow me to be Author of mine own Travels; and others make me Author of Books to which I am wholly a Stranger.[2]

I find likewise, that your Printer hath been so careless as to confound the Times, and mistake the Dates of my several Voyages and Returns; neither assigning the true Year, or the true Month, or Day of the Month: And I hear the original Manuscript is all destroyed, since the Publication of my Book. Neither have I any Copy left; however, I have sent you some Corrections, which you may insert, if ever there should be a second Edition: And yet I cannot stand to them, but shall leave that Matter to my judicious and candid Readers, to adjust it as they please.

I hear some of our Sea-*Yahoos* find Fault with my Sea-Language, as not proper in many Parts, nor now in Use. I cannot help it. In my first Voyages, while I was young, I was instructed by the oldest Mariners, and learned to speak as they did. But I have since found that the Sea-*Yahoos* are apt, like the Land ones, to become new fangled in their Words; which the latter change every Year; insomuch, as I remember upon each Return to mine own Country, their old Dialect was so altered, that I could hardly understand the new. And I observe, when any *Yahoo* comes from *London* out of Curiosity to visit me at mine own House, we neither of us are able to deliver our Conceptions in a Manner intelligible to the other.

If the Censure of *Yahoos* could any Way affect me, I should have great Reason to complain, that some of them are so bold as to think my Book of Travels a meer Fiction out of mine own Brain; and have gone so far as to drop Hints, that the *Houyhnhnms*, and *Yahoos* have no more Existence than the Inhabitants of *Utopia*.

Indeed I must confess, that as to the People of *Lilliput*, *Brobdingrag*, (for so the Word should have been spelt, and not

---

[2] The immediate success of the *Travels* inspired several publishers to issue keys and continuations; none came from Swift.

erroneously *Brobdingnag*) and *Laputa*; I have never yet heard of
any *Yahoo* so presumptuous as to dispute their Being, or the Facts
I have related concerning them; because the Truth immediately
strikes every Reader with Conviction. And, is there less Probability
in my Account of the *Houvhnhnms* or *Yahoos*, when it is manifest
as to the latter, there are so many Thousands even in this City,
who only differ from their Brother Brutes in *Houyhnhnmland*, because they use a Sort of a *Jabber*, and do not go naked. I wrote for
their Amendment, and not their Approbation. The united Praise
of the whole Race would be of less Consequence to me, than the
neighing of those two degenerate *Houyhahnms* I keep in my Stable;
because, from these, degenerate as they are, I still improve in some
Virtues, without any Mixture of Vice.

Do these miserable Animals presume to think that I am so far
degenerated as to defend my Veracity; *Yahoo* as I am, it is well
known through all *Houyhnhnmland*, that by the Instructions and
Example of my illustrious Master, I was able in the Compass of
two Years (although I confess with the utmost Difficulty) to remove that infernal Habit of Lying, Shuffling, Deceiving, and
Equivocating, so deeply rooted in the very Souls of all my Species;
especially the *Europeans*.

I have other Complaints to make upon this vexatious Occasion; but I forbear troubling myself or you any further. I must
freely confess, that since my last Return, some Corruptions of my
Yahoo Nature have revived in me by conversing with a few of your
Species, and particularly those of mine own Family, by an unavoidable Necessity; else I should never have attempted so absurd a
Project as that of reforming the *Yahoo* Race in this Kingdom; but, I
have now done with all such visionary Schemes for ever.

April 2, 1727.

The Publisher
to the Reader

The author of these Travels, Mr. *Lemuel Gulliver*,[1] is my antient and intimate Friend; there is likewise some Relation between us by the Mother's Side. About three Years ago Mr. *Gulliver* growing weary of the Concourse of curious People coming to him at his House in *Redriff*, made a small Purchase of Land, with a convenient House, near *Newark*, in *Nottinghamshire*, his native Country; where he now lives retired, yet in good Esteem among his Neighbours.

Although Mr. *Gulliver* were born in *Nottinghamshire*, where his Father dwelt, yet I have heard him say, his Family came from *Oxfordshire*; to confirm which, I have observed in the Church-Yard at *Banbury*, in that County, several Tombs and Monuments of the *Gullivers*.

Before he quitted *Redriff*, he left the Custody of the following Papers in my Hands, with the Liberty to dispose of them as I should think fit. I have carefully perused them three Times; The Style is very plain and simple; and the only Fault I find is, that the Author, after the Manner of Travellers, is a little too circumstantial. There is an Air of Truth apparent through the whole; and indeed the Author was so distinguished for his Veracity, that it became a Sort of Proverb among his Neighbors at *Redriff*, when any one affirmed a Thing, to say, it was as true as if Mr. *Gulliver* had spoke it.

By the Advice of several worthy Persons, to whom, with the Author's Permission, I communicated these Papers, I now venture to send them into the World; hoping they may be, at least for some time, a better Entertainment to our young Noblemen, than the common Scribbles of Politicks and Party.

---

[1] Gulliver's initial name carries perhaps a Biblical resonance: see Proverbs 31 for the wise counsel of King Lemuel.

This Volume would have been at least twice as large, if I had not made bold to strike out innumerable Passages relating to the Winds and Tides, as well as to the Variations and Bearings in the several Voyages; together with the minute Descriptions of the Management of the Ship in Storms, in the Style of Sailors: Likewise the Account of the Longitudes and Latitudes; wherein I have Reason to apprehend that Mr. *Gulliver* may be a little dissatisfied: But I was resolved to fit the Work as much as possible to the general Capacity of Readers. However, if my own Ignorance in Sea-Affairs shall have led me to commit some Mistakes, I alone am answerable for them: And if any Traveller hath a Curiosity to see the whole Work at large, as it came from the Hand of the Author, I will be ready to gratify him.

As for any further Particulars relating to the Author, the Reader will receive Satisfaction from the first Pages of the Book.

RICHARD SYMPSON

Contents

x

PART IV: A Voyage to the Country of the Houyhnhnms

PART I

A VOYAGE TO LILLIPUT

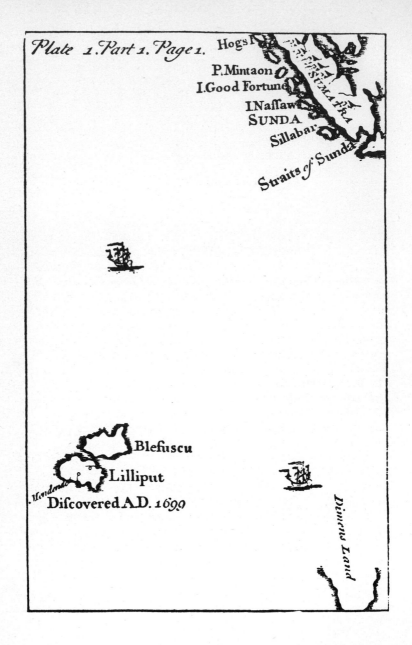

CHAPTER I

The Author giveth some Account of himself and Family; his first Inducements to travel. He is shipwrecked, and swims for his Life; gets safe on shoar in the Country of Lilliput; is made a Prisoner, and carried up the Country.

My Father had a small Estate in *Nottinghamshire*; I was the Third of five Sons. He sent me to *Emanuel-College* in *Cambridge*, at Fourteen Years old, where I resided three Years, and applied my self close to my Studies: But the Charge of maintaining me (although I had a very scanty Allowance) being too great for a narrow Fortune; I was bound Apprentice to Mr. *James Bates*, an eminent Surgeon in *London*, with whom I continued four Years; and my Father now and then sending me small Sums of Money, I laid them out in learning Navigation, and other Parts of the Mathematicks, useful to those who intend to travel, as I always believed it would be some time or other my Fortune to do. When I left Mr. *Bates*, I went down to my Father; where, by the Assistance of him and my Uncle *John*, and some other Relations, I got Forty Pounds, and a Promise of Thirty Pounds a Year to maintain me at *Leyden*:[1] There I studied Physick two Years and seven Months, knowing it would be useful in long Voyages.

Soon after my Return from *Leyden*, I was recommended by my good Master Mr. *Bates*, to be Surgeon to the *Swallow*, Captain *Abraham Pannell* Commander, with whom I continued three Years and a half, making a Voyage or two into the *Levant* and some other Parts. When I came back, I resolved to settle in *London*, to which Mr. *Bates*, my Master, encouraged me; and by him I was recommended to several Patients. I took Part of a small House in the *Old Jury*; and being advised to alter my Condition, I married Mrs. *Mary Burton*, second Daughter to Mr. *Edmond Burton*, Hosier, in

[1] The University of *Leyden*, important as a center for the study of medicine.

3

Newgate-street, with whom I received four Hundred Pounds for a Portion.

But, my good Master *Bates* dying in two Years after, and I having few Friends, my Business began to fail; for my Conscience would not suffer me to imitate the bad Practice of too many among my Brethren. Having therefore consulted with my Wife, and some of my Acquaintance, I determined to go again to Sea. I was Surgeon successively in two Ships, and made several Voyages, for six Years, to the *East* and *West-Indies*; by which I got some Addition to my Fortune. My Hours of Leisure I spent in reading the best Authors, ancient and modern; being always provided with a good Number of Books; and when I was ashore, in observing the Manners and Dispositions of the People, as well as learning their Language; wherein I had a great Facility by the Strength of my Memory.

The last of these Voyages not proving very fortunate, I grew weary of the Sea, and intended to stay at home with my Wife and Family. I removed from the *Old Jury* to *Fetter Lane*, and from thence to *Wapping*, hoping to get Business among the Sailors; but it would not turn to account. After three Years Expectation that things would mend, I accepted an advantageous Offer from Captain *William Prichard*, Master of the *Antelope*, who was making a Voyage to the *South-Sea*. We set sail from *Bristol*, *May* 4th, 1699 and our Voyage at first was very prosperous.

It would not be proper for some Reasons, to trouble the Reader with the Particulars of our Adventures in those Seas: Let it suffice to inform him, that in our Passage from thence to the *East-Indies*, we were driven by a violent Storm to the North-west of *Van Diemen's* Land. By an Observation, we found ourselves in the Latitude of 30 Degrees 2 Minutes South. Twelve of our Crew were dead by immoderate Labour, and ill Food; the rest were in a very weak Condition. On the fifth of *November*, which was the beginning of Summer in those Parts, the Weather being very hazy, the Seamen spyed a Rock, within half a Cable's length of the Ship; but the Wind was so strong, that we were driven directly upon it, and immediately split. Six of the Crew, of whom I was one, having let down the Boat into the Sea, made a Shift to get clear of the Ship, and the Rock. We rowed by my Computation, about three Leagues, till we were able to work no longer, being already spent with Labour while we were in the Ship. We therefore trusted ourselves to the Mercy of the Waves; and in about half an Hour the Boat was overset by a sudden Flurry from the North. What became of my Companions in the Boat, as well as of those who escaped on the Rock, or were left in the Vessel, I cannot tell; but conclude they were all lost. For my own Part, I swam as Fortune directed me, and was pushed forward by Wind and Tide. I often let my Legs drop, and could feel no Bottom; But when I was almost gone, and able to struggle no longer, I found myself within my Depth; and by this Time the Storm was much abated. The Declivity was so small, that I walked near a Mile before I got to the Shore, which I conjectured was about Eight o'Clock in the Evening. I then advanced forward near half a Mile, but could not discover any Sign of Houses or Inhabitants; at least I was in so weak a Condition, that I did not observe them. I was extremely tired, and with that, and the Heat of the Weather, and about half a Pint of Brandy that I drank as I left the Ship, I found my self much inclined to sleep. I lay down on the Grass, which was very short and soft; where I slept sounder than ever I remember to have done in my Life, and as I reckoned, above Nine Hours; for when I awaked, it was just Day-light. I attempted to rise, but was not able to stir: For as I happened to lie on my Back, I found my Arms and Legs were strongly fastened on each Side to the Ground; and my Hair, which was long and thick, tied down in the same Manner. I likewise felt several slender Ligatures across my Body, from my Armpits to my Thighs. I could only look upwards; the Sun began to grow hot, and the Light offended my Eyes. I heard a confused Noise about me, but in the Posture I lay, could see nothing except the Sky. In a little time I felt something alive moving on my left Leg, which advancing gently forward over my Breast, came almost up to my Chin; when bending my Eyes downwards as much as I could, I perceived it to be a human Creature not six Inches high,[2] with a Bow and Arrow in his Hands, and a Quiver at his Back. In the mean time, I felt at least Forty more of the same Kind (as I conjectured) following the first. I was in the utmost Astonishment, and roared so loud, that they all ran back in a Fright; and some of them, as I was afterwards told, were hurt with the Falls they got by leaping from my Sides upon the Ground. However, they

[2] The scale of Lilliput to Gulliver's world is generally one to twelve. If this creature is a typical Lilliputian, then Gulliver is somewhat under six feet tall.

soon returned; and one of them, who ventured so far as to get a full Sight of my Face, lifting up his Hands and Eyes by way of Admiration, cryed out in a shrill, but distinct Voice, *Hekinah Degul:* The others repeated the same Words several times, but I then knew not what they meant. I lay all this while, as the Reader may believe, in great Uneasiness; At length, struggling to get loose, I had the Fortune to break the Strings, and wrench out the Pegs that fastened my left Arm to the Ground; for, by lifting it up to my Face, I discovered the Methods they had taken to bind me; and, at the same time, with a violent Pull, which gave me excessive Pain, I a little loosened the Strings that tied down my Hair on the left Side; so that I was just able to turn my Head about two Inches. But the Creatures ran off a second time, before I could seize them; whereupon there was a great Shout in a very shrill Accent; and after it ceased, I heard one of them cry aloud, *Tolgo Phonac;* when in an Instant I felt above an Hundred Arrows discharged on my left Hand, which pricked me like so many Needles; and besides, they shot another Flight into the Air, as we do Bombs in *Europe;* whereof many, I suppose, fell on my Body, (though I felt them not) and some on my Face, which I immediately covered with my left Hand. When this Shower of Arrows was over, I fell a groaning with Grief and Pain; and then striving again to get loose, they discharged another Volly larger than the first; and some of them attempted with Spears to stick me in the Sides; but, by good Luck, I had on me a Buff Jerkin, which they could not pierce. I thought it the most prudent Method to lie still; and my Design was to continue so till Night, when my left Hand being already loose, I could easily free myself: And as for the Inhabitants, I had Reason to believe I might be a Match for the greatest Armies they could bring against me, if they were all of the same Size with him that I saw. But Fortune disposed otherwise of me. When the People observed I was quiet, they discharged no more Arrows: But by the Noise increasing, I knew their Numbers were greater; and about four Yards from me, over-against my right Ear, I heard a Knocking for above an Hour, like People at work; when turning my Head that Way, as well as the Pegs and Strings would permit me, I saw a Stage erected about a Foot and a half from the Ground, capable of holding four of the Inhabitants, with two or three Ladders to mount it: From whence one of them, who seemed to be a Person of Quality, made me a long Speech, whereof I understood not one Syllable. But I should have mentioned, that before the principal Person began his Oration, he cryed out three times *Langro Dehul san*: (these Words and the former were afterwards repeated and explained to me.) Whereupon immediately about fifty of the Inhabitants came, and cut the Strings that fastened the left side of my Head, which gave me the Liberty of turning it to the right, and of observing the Person and Gesture of him who was to speak. He appeared to be of a middle Age, and taller than any of the other three who attended him; whereof one was a Page, who held up his Train, and seemed to be somewhat longer than my middle Finger; the other two stood one on each side to support him. He acted every part of an Orator; and I could observe many Periods of Threatnings, and others of Promises, Pity and Kindness. I answered in a few Words, but in the most submissive Manner, lifting up my left Hand and both my eyes to the Sun, as calling him for a Witness; and being almost famished with Hunger, having not eaten a Morsel for some Hours before I left the Ship, I found the Demands of Nature so strong upon me, that I could not forbear shewing my Impatience (perhaps against the strict Rules of Decency) by putting my Finger frequently on my Mouth, to signify that I wanted Food. The *Hurgo* (for so they call a great Lord, as I afterwards learnt) understood me very well: He descended from the Stage, and commanded that several Ladders should be applied to my Sides, on which above an hundred of the Inhabitants mounted, and walked towards my Mouth, laden with Baskets full of Meat, which had been provided and sent thither by the King's Orders upon the first Intelligence he received of me. I observed there was the Flesh of several Animals, but could not distinguish them by the Taste. There were Shoulders, Legs, and Loins shaped like those of Mutton, and very well dressed, but smaller than the Wings of a Lark. I eat them by two or three at a Mouthful; and took three Loaves at a time, about the bigness of Musket Bullets. They supplyed me as fast as they could, shewing a thousand Marks of Wonder and Astonishment at my Bulk and Appetite. I then made another Sign that I wanted Drink. They found by my eating that a small Quantity would not suffice me; and being a most ingenious People, they slung up with great Dexterity one of their largest Hogsheads; then rolled it towards my Hand, and beat out the Top; I drank it off at a Draught, which I might well do, for it hardly held half a Pint, and tasted like a

small Wine of *Burgundy*, but much more delicious. They brought
me a second Hogshead, which I drank in the same Manner, and
made Signs for more, but they had none to give me. When I had
performed these Wonders, they shouted for Joy, and danced upon
my Breast, repeating several times as they did at first, *Hekinah
Degul*. They made me a Sign that I should throw down the two
Hogsheads, but first warned the People below to stand out of the
Way, crying aloud, *Borach Mivola*; and when they saw the Vessels
in the Air, there was an universal Shout of *Hekinah Degul*. I confess I was often tempted, while they were passing backwards and
forwards on my Body, to seize Forty or Fifty of the first that came
in my Reach, and dash them against the Ground. But the Remembrance of what I had felt, which probably might not be the worst
they could do; and the Promise of Honour I made them, for so I
interpreted my submissive Behaviour, soon drove out those Imaginations. Besides, I now considered my self as bound by the Laws of
Hospitality to a People who had treated me with so much Expence
and Magnificence. However, in my Thoughts I could not sufficiently wonder at the Intrepidity of these diminutive Mortals, who
durst venture to mount and walk on my Body, while one of my
Hands was at Liberty, without trembling at the very Sight of so
prodigious a Creature as I must appear to them. After some time,
when they observed that I made no more Demands for Meat, there
appeared before me a Person of high Rank from his Imperial
Majesty. His Excellency having mounted on the Small of my Right
Leg, advanced forwards up to my Face, with about a Dozen of his
Retinue; And producing his Credentials under the Signet Royal,
which he applied close to my Eyes, spoke about ten Minutes, without any Signs of Anger, but with a kind of determinate Resolution;
often pointing forwards, which, as I afterwards found, was towards
the Capital City, about half a Mile distant, whither it was agreed
by his Majesty in Council that I must be conveyed. I answered
in few Words, but to no Purpose, and made a Sign with my Hand
that was loose, putting it to the other, (but over his Excellency's
Head, for Fear of hurting him or his Train) and then to my own
Head and Body, to signify that I desired my Liberty. It appeared
that he understood me well enough; for he shook his Head by way
of Disapprobation, and held his Hand in a Posture to shew that
I must be carried as a Prisoner. However, he made other Signs to
let me understand that I should have Meat and Drink enough, and

very good Treatment. Whereupon I once more thought of attempting to break my Bonds; but again, when I felt the Smart of their Arrows upon my Face and Hands, which were all in Blisters, and many of the Darts still sticking in them; and observing likewise that the Number of my Enemies encreased; I gave Tokens to let them know that they might do with me what they pleased. Upon this, the *Hurgo* and his Train withdrew, with much Civility and chearful Countenances. Soon after I heard a general Shout, with frequent Repetitions of the Words, *Peplom Selan*, and I felt great Numbers of the People on my Left Side relaxing the Cords to such a Degree, that I was able to turn upon my Right, and to ease my self with making Water; which I very plentifully did, to the great Astonishment of the People, who conjecturing by my Motions what I was going to do, immediately opened to the right and left on that Side, to avoid the Torrent which fell with such Noise and Violence from me. But before this, they had dawbed my Face and both my Hands with a sort of Ointment very pleasant to the Smell, which in a few Minutes removed all the Smart of their Arrows. These Circumstances, added to the Refreshment I had received by their Victuals and Drink, which were very nourishing, disposed me to sleep. I slept about eight Hours as I was afterwards assured; and it was no Wonder; for the Physicians, by the Emperor's Order, had mingled a sleeping Potion in the Hogsheads of Wine.

It seems that upon the first Moment I was discovered sleeping on the Ground after my Landing, the Emperor had early Notice of it by an Express; and determined in Council that I should be tyed in the Manner I have related, (which was done in the Night while I slept) that Plenty of Meat and Drink should be sent me, and a Machine prepared to carry me to the Capital City.

This Resolution perhaps may appear very bold and dangerous, and I am confident would not be imitated by any Prince in *Europe* on the like Occasion; however, in my Opinion it was extremely Prudent as well as Generous. For supposing these People had endeavoured to kill me with their Spears and Arrows while I was asleep; I should certainly have awaked with the first Sense of Smart, which might so far have rouzed my Rage and Strength, as to enable me to break the Strings wherewith I was tyed; after which, as they were not able to make Resistance, so they could expect no Mercy.

These People are most excellent Mathematicians, and arrived to a great Perfection in Mechanicks by the Countenance and Encouragement of the Emperor, who is a renowned Patron of Learning. This Prince hath several Machines fixed on Wheels, for the Carriage of Trees and other great Weights. He often buildeth his largest Men of War, whereof some are Nine Foot long, in the Woods where the Timber grows, and has them carried on these Engines three or four Hundred Yards to the Sea. Five Hundred Carpenters and Engineers were immediately set at work to prepare the greatest Engine they had. It was a Frame of Wood raised three Inches from the Ground, about seven Foot long and four wide, moving upon twenty two Wheels. The Shout I heard, was upon the Arrival of this Engine, which, it seems, set out in four Hours after my Landing. It was brought parallel to me as I lay. But the principal Difficulty was to raise and place me in this Vehicle. Eighty Poles, each of one Foot high, were erected for this Purpose, and very strong Cords of the bigness of Pack thread were fastened by Hooks to many Bandages, which the Workmen had girt round my Neck, my Hands, my Body, and my Legs. Nine Hundred of the strongest Men were employed to draw up these Cords by many Pullies fastned on the Poles; and thus in less than three Hours, I was raised and slung into the Engine, and there tyed fast. All this I was told; for while the whole Operation was performing, I lay in a profound Sleep, by the Force of that soporiferous Medicine infused into my Liquor. Fifteen hundred of the Emperor's largest Horses, each about four Inches and a half high, were employed to draw me towards the Metropolis, which, as I said, was half a Mile distant.

About four Hours after we began our Journey, I awaked by a very ridiculous Accident; for the Carriage being stopt a while to adjust something that was out of Order, two or three of the young Natives had the Curiosity to see how I looked when I was asleep; they climbed up into the Engine, and advancing very softly to my Face, one of them, an Officer in the Guards, put the sharp End of his Half-Pike a good way up into my left Nostril, which tickled my Nose like a Straw, and made me sneeze violently: Whereupon they stole off unperceived; and it was three Weeks before I knew the Cause of my awaking so suddenly. We made a long March the remaining Part of the Day, and rested at Night with Five Hundred Guards on each Side of me, half with Torches, and half with Bows and Arrows, ready to shoot me if I should offer to stir. The next Morning at Sunrise we continued our March, and arrived within two Hundred Yards of the City-Gates about Noon. The Emperor, and all his Court, came out to meet us; but his great Officers would by no Means suffer his Majesty to endanger his Person by mounting on my Body.

At the Place where the Carriage stopt, there stood an ancient Temple, esteemed to be the largest in the whole Kingdom; which having been polluted some Years before by an unnatural Murder, was, according to the Zeal of those People, looked upon as Prophane, and therefore had been applied to common Uses, and all the Ornaments and Furniture carried away. In this Edifice it was determined I should lodge. The great Gate fronting to the North was about four Foot high, and almost two Foot wide, through which I could easily creep. On each Side of the Gate was a small Window not above six Inches from the Ground: Into that on the Left Side, the King's Smiths conveyed fourscore and eleven Chains, like those that hang to a Lady's Watch in *Europe*, and almost as large, which were locked to my Left Leg with six and thirty Padlocks. Over against this Temple, on the other Side of the great Highway, at twenty Foot Distance, there was a Turret at least five Foot high. Here the Emperor ascended with many principal Lords of his Court, to have an Opportunity of viewing me, as I was told, for I could not see them. It was reckoned that above an hundred thousand Inhabitants came out of the Town upon the same Errand; and in spight of my Guards, I believe there could not be fewer than ten thousand, at several Times, who mounted upon my Body by the Help of Ladders. But a Proclamation was soon issued to forbid it, upon Pain of Death. When the Workmen found it was impossible for me to break loose, they cut all the Strings that bound me; whereupon I rose up with as melancholy a Disposition as ever I had in my Life. But the Noise and Astonishment of the People at seeing me rise and walk, are not to be expressed. The Chains that held my left Leg were about two Yards long, and gave me not only the Liberty of walking backwards and forwards in a Semicircle; but being fixed within four Inches of the Gate, allowed me to creep in, and lie at my full Length in the Temple.

CHAPTER II

The Emperor of Lilliput, *attended by several of the Nobility, comes to see the Author in his Confinement. The Emperor's Person and Habit described. Learned Men appointed to teach the Author their Language. He gains Favour by his mild Disposition. His Pockets are searched, and his Sword and Pistols taken from him.*

When I found myself on my Feet, I looked about me, and must confess I never beheld a more entertaining Prospect. The Country round appeared like a continued Garden; and the inclosed Fields, which were generally Forty Foot square, resembled so many Beds of Flowers. These Fields were intermingled with Woods of half a Stang,[1] and the tallest Trees, as I could judge, appeared to be seven Foot high. I viewed the Town on my left Hand, which looked like the painted Scene of a City in a Theatre.

I had been for some Hours extremely pressed by the Necessities of Nature; which was no Wonder, it being almost two Days since I had last disburthened myself. I was under great Difficulties between Urgency and Shame. The best Expedient I could think on, was to creep into my House, which I accordingly did; and shutting the Gate after me, I went as far as the Length of my Chain would suffer; and discharged my Body of that uneasy Load. But this was the only Time I was ever guilty of so uncleanly an Action; for which I cannot but hope the candid Reader will give some Allowance, after he hath maturely and impartially considered my Case, and the Distress I was in. From this Time my constant Practice was, as soon as I rose, to perform that Business in open Air, at the full Extent of my Chain; and due Care was taken every Morning before Company came, that the offensive Matter should be carried off in Wheel-barrows, by two Servants appointed for that Purpose.

[1] A quarter of an acre.

I would not have dwelt so long upon a Circumstance, that perhaps at first Sight may appear not very momentous; if I had not thought it necessary to justify my Character in Point of Cleanliness to the World; which I am told, some of my Maligners have been pleased, upon this and other Occasions, to call in Question. When this Adventure was at an End, I came back out of my House, having Occasion for fresh Air. The Emperor was already descended from the Tower, and advancing on Horseback towards me, which had like to have cost him dear; for the Beast, although very well trained, yet wholly unused to such a Sight, which appeared as if a Mountain moved before him, reared up on his hinder Feet: But that Prince, who is an excellent Horseman, kept his Seat, until his Attendants ran in, and held the Bridle, while his Majesty had Time to dismount. When he alighted, he surveyed me round with great Admiration, but kept beyond the Length of my Chains. He ordered his Cooks and Butlers, who were already prepared, to give me Victuals and Drink, which they pushed forward in a sort of Vehicles upon Wheels until I could reach them. I took these Vehicles, and soon emptied them all; twenty of them were filled with Meat, and ten with Liquor; each of the former afforded me two or three good Mouthfuls, and I emptied the Liquor of ten Vessels, which was contained in earthen Vials into one Vehicle, drinking it off at a Draught; and so I did with the rest. The Empress, and young Princes of the Blood, of both Sexes, attended by many Ladies, sate at some Distance in their Chairs; but upon the Accident that happened to the Emperor's Horse, they alighted, and came near his Person; which I am now going to describe. He is taller by almost the Breadth of my Nail, than any of his Court; which alone is enough to strike an Awe into the Beholders. His Features are strong and masculine, with an *Austrian* Lip, and arched Nose, his Complexion olive, his Countenance erect, his Body and Limbs well proportioned, all his Motions graceful, and his Deportment majestick.[2] He was was then past his Prime, being twenty-eight Years and three Quarters old, of which he had reigned about seven, in great Felicity, and generally victorious. For the better Convenience of beholding him, I lay on my Side, so that my Face was parallel to his, and he stood but three Yards off: However, I have

[2] Swift intended the Emperor to represent George I, who reigned 1714-1727. Swift's description is a calculated irony since George was gross and unattractive.

had him since many Times in my Hand, and therefore cannot be deceived in the Description. His Dress was very plain and simple, the Fashion of it between the *Asiatick* and the *European*; but he had on his Head a light Helmet of Gold, adorned with Jewels, and a Plume on the Crest. He held his Sword drawn in his Hand, to defend himself, if I should happen to break loose; it was almost three Inches long, the Hilt and Scabbard were Gold enriched with Diamonds. His Voice was shrill, but very clear and articulate, and I could distinctly hear it when I stood up. The Ladies and Courtiers were all most magnificently clad, so that the Spot they stood upon seemed to resemble a Petticoat spread on the Ground, embroidered with Figures of Gold and Silver. His Imperial Majesty spoke often to me, and I returned Answers, but neither of us could understand a Syllable. There were several of his Priests and Lawyers present (as I conjectured by their Habits) who were commanded to address themselves to me, and I spoke to them in as many Languages as I had the least Smattering of, which were *High* and *Low Dutch*, *Latin*, *French*, *Spanish*, *Italian*, and *Lingua Franca*; but all to no purpose. After about two Hours the Court retired, and I was left with a strong Guard, to prevent the Impertinence, and probably the Malice of the Rabble, who were very impatient to croud about me as near as they durst; and some of them had the Impudence to shoot their Arrows at me as I sate on the Ground by the Door of my House; whereof one very narrowly missed my left Eye. But the Colonel ordered six of the Ringleaders to be seized, and thought no Punishment so proper as to deliver them bound into my Hands, which some of his Soldiers accordingly did, pushing them forwards with the Butt-ends of their Pikes into my Reach: I took them all in my right Hand, put five of them into my Coat-pocket; and as to the sixth, I made a Countenance as if I would eat him alive. The poor Man squalled terribly, and the Colonel and his Officers were in much Pain, especially when they saw me take out my Penknife: But I soon put them out of Fear; for, looking mildly, and immediately cutting the Strings he was bound with, I set him gently on the Ground, and away he ran. I treated the rest in the same Manner, taking them one by one out of my Pocket; and I observed, both the Soldiers and People were highly obliged at this Mark of my Clemency, which was represented very much to my Advantage at Court.

Towards Night I got with some Difficulty into my House, where

I lay on the Ground, and continued to do so about a Fortnight; during which time the Emperor gave Orders to have a Bed prepared for me. Six Hundred Beds of the common Measure were brought in Carriages, and worked up in my House; an Hundred and Fifty of their Beds sown together made up the Breadth and Length, and these were four double, which however kept me but very indifferently from the Hardness of the Floor, that was of smooth Stone. By the same Computation they provided me with Sheets, Blankets, and Coverlets, tolerable enough for one who had been so long enured to Hardships as I.

As the News of my Arrival spread through the kingdom, it brought prodigious Numbers of rich, idle, and curious People to see me; so that the Villages were almost emptied, and great Neglect of Tillage and Houshold Affairs must have ensued, if his Imperial Majesty had not provided by several Proclamations and Orders of State against this Inconveniency. He directed that those, who had already beheld me, should return home, and not presume to come within fifty Yards of my House, without Licence from Court; whereby the Secretaries of State got considerable Fees.

In the mean time, the Emperor held frequent Councils to debate what Course should be taken with me; and I was afterwards assured by a particular Friend, a Person of great Quality, and who was as much in the *Secret* as any; that the Court was under many Difficulties concerning me. They apprehended my breaking loose; that my Diet would be very expensive, and might cause a Famine. Sometimes they determined to starve me, or at least to shoot me in the Face and Hands with poisoned Arrows, which would soon dispatch me: But again they considered, that the Stench of so large a Carcase might produce a Plague in the Metropolis, and probably spread through the whole Kingdom. In the midst of these Consultations, several Officers of the Army went to the Door of the great Council Chamber; and two of them being admitted, gave an Account of my Behaviour to the six Criminals above-mentioned; which made so favourable an Impression in the Breast of his Majesty, and the whole Board, in my Behalf, that an Imperial Commission was issued out, obliging all the Villages nine hundred Yards round the City, to deliver in every Morning six Beeves, forty Sheep, and other Victuals for my Sustenance; together with a proportionable Quantity of Bread and Wine, and other Liquors: For the due Payment of which his Majesty gave Assignments upon his Treasury. For this Prince lives chiefly upon his own Demesnes; seldom, except upon great Occasions raising any Subsidies upon his Subjects, who are bound to attend him in his Wars at their own Expence. An Establishment was also made of Six Hundred Persons to be my Domesticks, who had Board-Wages allowed for their Maintenance, and Tents built for them very conveniently on each side of my Door. It was likewise ordered, that three hundred Taylors should make me a Suit of Cloaths after the Fashion of the Country: That, six of his Majesty's greatest Scholars should be employed to instruct me in their Language: And, lastly, that the Emperor's Horses, and those of the Nobility, and Troops of Guards, should be exercised in my Sight, to accustom themselves to me. All these Orders were duly put in Execution; and in about three Weeks I made a great Progress in Learning their Language; during which Time, the Emperor frequently honoured me with his Visits, and was pleased to assist my Masters in teaching me. We began already to converse together in some Sort; and the first Words I learnt, were to express my Desire, that he would please to give me my Liberty; which I every Day repeated on my Knees. His Answer, as I could apprehend, was, that this must be a Work of Time, not to be thought on without the Advice of his Council; and that first I must *Lumos Kelmin pesso desmar lon Emposo*; that is, *Swear a Peace with him and his Kingdom*. However, that I should be used with all Kindness; and he advised me to acquire by my Patience and discreet Behaviour, the good Opinion of himself and his Subjects. He desired I would not take it ill, if he gave Orders to certain proper Officers to search me; for probably I might carry about me several Weapons, which must needs be dangerous Things, if they answered the Bulk of so prodigious a Person. I said, his Majesty should be satisfied, for I was ready to strip my self, and turn up my Pockets before him. This I delivered, part in Words, and part in Signs. He replied, that by the Laws of the Kingdom, I must be searched by two of his Officers: That he knew this could not be done without my Consent and Assistance; that he had so good an Opinion of my Generosity and Justice, as to trust their Persons in my Hands: That whatever they took from me should be returned when I left the Country, or paid for at the Rate which I would set upon them. I took up the two Officers in my Hands, put them first into my Coat-Pockets, and then into every other Pocket about me, except my two Fobs, and another secret Pocket which I had no Mind should be searched, wherein I had some little Necessaries of no Consequence to any but my self. In one of my Fobs there was a Silver Watch, and in the other a small Quantity of Gold in a Purse. These Gentlemen, having Pen, Ink, and Paper about them, made an exact Inventory of every thing they saw; and when they had done, desired I would set them down, that they might deliver it to the Emperor. This Inventory I afterwards translated into *English*, and is Word for Word as follows.

Imprimis, In the right Coat-Pocket of the *Great Man Mountain* (for so I interpret the Words *Quinbus Flestrin*) after the strictest Search, we found only one great Piece of coarse Cloth, large enough to be a Foot-Cloth for your Majesty's chief Room of State. In the left Pocket, we saw a huge Silver Chest, with a Cover of the same Metal, which we, the Searchers, were not able to lift. We desired it should be opened; and one of us stepping into it, found himself up to the mid Leg in a sort of Dust, some part whereof flying up to our Faces, set us both a sneezing for several Times together. In his right Waistcoat-Pocket, we found a prodigious Bundle of white thin Substances, folded one over another, about the Bigness of three Men, tied with a strong Cable, and marked with black Figures; which we humbly conceive to be Writings; every Letter almost half as large as the Palm of our Hands. In the left there was a sort of Engine, from the Back of which were extended twenty long Poles, resembling the Pallisado's before your Majesty's Court; wherewith we conjecture the *Man Mountain* combs his Head; for we did not always trouble him with Questions, because we found it a great Difficulty to make him understand us. In the large Pocket on the right Side of his middle Cover, (so I translate the Word *Ranfu-Lo*, by which they meant my Breeches) we saw a hollow Pillar of Iron, about the Length of a Man, fastened to a strong Piece of Timber, larger than the Pillar; and upon one side of the Pillar were huge Pieces of Iron sticking out, cut into strange Figures; which we know not what to make of. In the left Pocket, another Engine of the same kind. In the smaller Pocket on the right Side, were several round flat Pieces of white and red Metal, of different Bulk: Some of the white, which seemed to be Silver, were so large and heavy, that my Comrade and I could hardly lift them. In the left Pocket were two black Pillars irregularly shaped: we could not, without Difficulty, reach the Top of them as we stood at the Bottom of his Pocket: One of them was covered, and seemed all of a

Piece; but at the upper End of the other, there appeared a white
round Substance, about twice the bigness of our Heads. Within each
of these was inclosed a prodigious Plate of Steel; which, by our
Orders, we obliged him to shew us, because we apprehended they
might be dangerous Engines. He took them out of their Cases, and
told us, that in his own Country his Practice was to shave his Beard
with one of these, and to cut his Meat with the other. There were
two Pockets which we could not enter: These he called his Fobs;
they were two large Slits cut into the Top of his middle Cover, but
squeezed close by the Pressure of his Belly. Out of the right Fob
hung a great Silver Chain, with a wonderful kind of Engine at the
Bottom. We directed him to draw out whatever was at the End of
that Chain; which appeared to be a Globe, half Silver, and half of
some transparent Metal: For on the transparent Side we saw certain strange Figures circularly drawn, and thought we could touch
them, until we found our Fingers stopped with that lucid Substance. He put this Engine to our Ears, which made an incessant
Noise like that of a Water-Mill. And we conjecture it is either some
unknown Animal, or the God that he worships: But we are more
inclined to the latter Opinion, because he assured us (if we understood him right, for he expressed himself very imperfectly) that he
seldom did any Thing without consulting it. He called it his Oracle,
and said it pointed out the Time for every Action of his Life. From
the left Fob he took out a Net almost large enough for a Fisherman, but contrived to open and shut like a Purse, and served him
for the same Use: We found therein several massy Pieces of yellow
Metal, which if they be of real Gold, must be of immense Value.

Having thus, in Obedience to your Majesty's Commands, diligently searched all his Pockets; we observed a Girdle about his
Waist made of the Hyde of some prodigious Animal; from which,
on the left Side, hung a Sword of the Length of five Men; and on
the right, a Bag or Pouch divided into two Cells; each Cell capable
of holding three of your Majesty's Subjects. In one of these Cells
were several Globes or Balls of a most ponderous Metal, about the
Bigness of our Heads, and required a strong Hand to lift them: The
other Cell contained a Heap of certain black Grains, but of no
great Bulk or Weight, for we could hold about fifty of them in the
Palms of our Hands.

This is an exact Inventory of what we found about the Body
of the *Man Mountain*; who used us with great Civility, and due

Respect to your Majesty's Commission. Signed and Sealed on the fourth Day of the eighty ninth Moon of your Majesty's auspicious Reign.[3]

Clefren Frelock, Marsi Frelock.

When this Inventory was read over to the Emperor, he directed me to deliver up the several Particulars. He first called for my Scymiter, which I took out, Scabbard and all. In the mean time he ordered three thousand of his choicest Troops, who then attended him, to surround me at a Distance, with their Bows and Arrows just ready to discharge: But I did not observe it; for my Eyes were wholly fixed upon his Majesty. He then desired me to draw my Scymiter, which, although it had got some Rust by the Sea-Water, was in most Parts exceeding bright. I did so, and immediately all the Troops gave a Shout between Terror and Surprize; for the Sun shone clear, and the Reflexion dazzled their Eyes, as I waved the Scymiter to and fro in my Hand. His Majesty, who is a most magnanimous Prince, was less daunted than I could expect; he ordered me to return it into the Scabbard, and cast it on the Ground as gently as I could, about six Foot from the End of my Chain. The next Thing he demanded was one of the hollow Iron Pillars, by which he meant my Pocket-Pistols. I drew it out, and at his Desire, as well as I could, expressed to him the Use of it, and charging it only with Powder, which by the Closeness of my Pouch, happened to escape wetting in the Sea, (an Inconvenience that all prudent Mariners take special Care to provide against) I first cautioned the Emperor not to be afraid; and then I let it off in the Air. The Astonishment here was much greater than at the Sight of my Scymiter. Hundreds fell down as if they had been struck dead; and even the Emperor, although he stood his Ground, could not recover himself in some time. I delivered up both my Pistols in the same Manner as I had done my Scymiter, and then my Pouch of Powder

[3] This search and listing, like many of the details in the first voyage, refer to the conflict between Tories and Whigs in the first quarter of the eighteenth century. Though Swift began as a Whig, he joined with the Tories in 1710, a connection he never abandoned. In a general sense, he is here satirizing Whig suspicions and investigations of their opponents; in particular, he is probably alluding to an investigation in 1715 of the Earl of Oxford and Viscount Bolingbroke. Both were leaders of the Tories, and Swift's close friends. Gulliver in Bk. I often stands for Oxford or Bolingbroke, and occasionally (as here) for both.

and Bullets; begging him that the former might be kept from Fire; for it would kindle with the smallest Spark, and blow up his Imperial Palace into the Air. I likewise delivered up my Watch, which the Emperor was very curious to see; and commanded two of his tallest Yeomen of the Guards to bear it on a Pole upon their Shoulders, as Dray-men in *England* do a Barrel of Ale. He was amazed at the continual Noise it made, and the Motion of the Minute-hand, which he could easily discern; for their Sight is much more acute than ours: He asked the Opinions of his learned Men about him, which were various and remote, as the Reader may well imagine without my repeating; although indeed I could not very perfectly understand them. I then gave up my Silver and Copper Money, my Purse with nine large Pieces of Gold, and some smaller ones; my Knife and Razor, my Comb and Silver Snuff-Box, my Handkerchief and Journal Book. My Scymiter, Pistols, and Pouch, were conveyed in Carriages to his Majesty's Stores; but the rest of my Goods were returned me.

I had, as I before observed, one private Pocket which escaped their Search, wherein there was a Pair of Spectacles (which I sometimes use for the Weakness of my Eyes) a Pocket Perspective, and several other little Conveniences; which being of no Consequence to the Emperor, I did not think my self bound in Honour to discover; and I apprehended they might be lost or spoiled if I ventured them out of my Possession.

CHAPTER III

The Author diverts the Emperor and his Nobility of both Sexes, in a very uncommon Manner. The Diversions of the Court of Lilliput *described. The Author hath his Liberty granted him upon certain Conditions.*

My Gentleness and good Behaviour had gained so far on the Emperor and his Court, and indeed upon the Army and People in general, that I began to conceive Hopes of getting my Liberty in a short Time. I took all possible Methods to cultivate this favourable Disposition. The Natives came by Degrees to be less apprehensive of any Danger from me. I would sometimes lie down, and let five or six of them dance on my Hand. And at last the Boys and Girls would venture to come and play at Hide and Seek in my Hair. I had now made a good Progress in understanding and speaking their Language. The Emperor had a mind one Day to entertain me with several of the Country Shows; wherein they exceed all Nations I have known, both for Dexterity and Magnificence. I was diverted with none so much as that of the Rope-Dancers, performed upon a slender white Thread, extended about two Foot, and twelve Inches from the Ground. Upon which, I shall desire Liberty, with the Reader's Patience, to enlarge a little.

This Diversion is only practised by those Persons, who are Candidates for great Employments, and high Favour, at Court. They are trained in this Art from their Youth, and are not always of noble Birth, or liberal Education. When a great Office is vacant, either by Death or Disgrace, (which often happens) five or six of those Candidates petition the Emperor to entertain his Majesty and the Court with a Dance on the Rope; and whoever jumps the highest without falling, succeeds in the Office. Very often the chief Ministers themselves are commanded to shew their Skill, and to convince the Emperor that they have not lost their Faculty. *Flimnap*, the Treasurer, is allowed to cut a Caper on the strait Rope, at least an Inch higher than any other Lord in the whole Empire. I have seen him do the Summerset several times together, upon a Trencher fixed on the Rope, which is no thicker than a common Packthread in *England*. My Friend *Reldresal*, principal Secretary for private Affairs, is, in my Opinion, if I am not partial, the second after the Treasurer; the rest of the great Officers are much upon a Par.

These Diversions are often attended with fatal Accidents, whereof great Numbers are on Record. I my self have seen two or three Candidates break a Limb. But the Danger is much greater, when the Ministers themselves are commanded to shew their Dexterity: For, by contending to excel themselves and their Fellows, they strain so far, that there is hardly one of them who hath not received a Fall; and some of them two or three. I was assured, that a Year or two before my Arrival, *Flimnap* would have infallibly broke his Neck, if one of the *King's Cushions*, that accidentally lay on the Ground, had not weakened the Force of his Fall.

There is likewise another Diversion, which is only shewn before the Emperor and Empress, and first Minister, upon particular Occasions. The Emperor lays on a Table three fine silken Threads of six Inches long. One is Blue, the other Red, and the third Green. These Threads are proposed as Prizes, for those Persons whom the Emperor hath a mind to distinguish by a peculiar Mark of his Favour. The Ceremony is performed in his Majesty's great Chamber of State; where the Candidates are to undergo a Tryal of Dexterity very different from the former; and such as I have not observed the least Resemblance of in any other Country of the old or the new World. The Emperor holds a Stick in his Hands, both Ends parallel to the Horizon, while the Candidates advancing one by one, sometimes leap over the Stick, sometimes creep under it backwards and forwards several times, according as the Stick is advanced or depressed. Sometimes the Emperor holds one End of the Stick, and his first Minister the other; sometimes the Minister has it entirely to himself. Whoever performs his Part with most Agility, and holds out the longest in *leaping* and *creeping*, is rewarded with the Blue-coloured Silk; the Red is given to the next, and the Green to the third, which they all wear girt twice round about the Middle; and you see few great Persons about this Court, who are not adorned with one of these Girdles.[1]

The Horses of the Army, and those of the Royal Stables, having been daily led before me, were no longer shy, but would come up to my very Feet, without starting. The Riders would leap them over my Hand as I held it on the Ground; and one of the Emperor's Huntsmen, upon a large Courser, took my Foot, Shoe and all; which was indeed a prodigious Leap. I had the good Fortune to divert the Emperor one Day, after a very extraordinary Manner. I desired he would order several Sticks of two Foot high, and the Thickness of an ordinary Cane, to be brought me; whereupon his Majesty commanded the Master of his Woods to give Directions

---

[1] The previous four paragraphs convey Swift's estimate of the court of George I. Flimnap represents Robert Walpole, the Whig leader; Reldresal, probably Walpole's successor in 1717; the "King's Cushion," the King's mistress who helped Walpole return to office (1721) after his "fall." The colored threads correspond to the Orders of the Garter, the Bath, and the Thistle.

accordingly; and the next Morning six Wood-men arrived with as many Carriages, drawn by eight Horses to each. I took nine of these Sticks, and fixing them firmly in the Ground in a Quadrangular Figure, two Foot and a half square; I took four other Sticks, and tyed them parallel at each Corner, about two Foot from the Ground; and then I fastened my Handkerchief to the nine Sticks that stood erect; and extended it on all Sides, till it was as tight as the Top of a Drum; and the four parallel Sticks rising about five Inches higher than the Handkerchief, served as Ledges on each Side. When I had finished my Work, I desired the Emperor to let a Troop of his best Horse, Twenty-four in Number, come and exercise upon this Plain. His Majesty approved of the Proposal, and I took them up one by one in my Hands, ready mounted and armed, with the proper Officers to exercise them. As soon as they got into Order, they divided into two Parties, performed mock Skirmishes, discharged blunt Arrows, drew their Swords, fled and pursued, attacked and retired; and in short discovered the best military Discipline I ever beheld. The paralled Sticks secured them and their Horses from falling over the Stage; and the Emperor was so much delighted, that he ordered this Entertainment to be repeated several Days; and once was pleased to be lifted up, and give the Word of Command; and, with great Difficulty, persuaded even the Empress her self to let me hold her in her close Chair, within two Yards of the Stage, from whence she was able to take a full View of the whole Performance. It was my good Fortune that no ill Accident happened in these Entertainments; only once a fiery Horse that belonged to one of the Captains, pawing with his Hoof struck a Hole in my Handkerchief, and his Foot slipping, he overthrew his Rider and himself; but I immediately relieved them both: For covering the Hole with one Hand, I set down the Troop with the other, in the same Manner as I took them up. The Horse that fell was strained in the left Shoulder, but the Rider got no Hurt, and I repaired my Handkerchief as well as I could: However, I would not trust to the Strength of it any more in such dangerous Enterprizes.

About two or three Days before I was set at Liberty, as I was entertaining the Court with these Kinds of Feats, there arrived an Express to inform his Majesty, that some of his Subjects riding near the Place where I was first taken up, had seen a great black Substance lying on the Ground, very oddly shaped, extending its

Edges round as wide as his Majesty's Bedchamber, and rising up
in the Middle as high as a Man. That it was no living Creature,
as they at first apprehended; for it lay on the Grass without Motion,
and some of them had walked round it several Times: That by
mounting upon each others Shoulders, they had got to the Top,
which was flat and even; and, stamping upon it, they found it was
hollow within: That they humbly conceived it might be something
belonging to the *Man-Mountain*; and if his Majesty pleased, they
would undertake to bring it with only five Horses. I presently knew
what they meant; and was glad at Heart to receive this Intelligence.
It seems, upon my first reaching the Shore, after our Shipwreck, I
was in such Confusion, that before I came to the Place where I
went to sleep, my Hat, which I had fastened with a String to my
Head while I was rowing, and had stuck on all the Time I was
swimming, fell off after I came to Land; the String, as I conjecture,
breaking by some Accident which I never observed, but thought my
Hat had been lost at Sea. I intreated his Imperial Majesty to give
Orders it might be brought to me as soon as possible, describing
to him the Use and the Nature of it: And the next Day the Wag-
goners arrived with it, but not in a very good Condition; they had
bored two Holes in the Brim, within an Inch and a half of the Edge,
and fastened two Hooks in the Holes; these Hooks were tyed by a
long Cord to the Harness, and thus my Hat was dragged along for
above half an *English* Mile: but the Ground in that Country being
extremely smooth and level, it received less Damage than I expected.

Two Days after this Adventure, the Emperor having ordered
that Part of his Army, which quarters in and about his Metropolis,
to be in a Readiness, took a fancy of diverting himself in a very
singular Manner. He desired I would stand like a *Colossus*, with my
Legs as far asunder as I conveniently could. He then commanded
his General (who was an old experienced Leader, and a great Patron
of mine) to draw up the Troops in close Order, and march them
under me; the Foot by Twenty-four in a Breast, and the Horse by
Sixteen, with Drums beating, Colours flying, and Pikes advanced.
This Body consisted of three Thousand Foot, and a Thousand
Horse. His Majesty gave Orders, upon Pain of Death, that every
Soldier in his March should observe the strictest Decency, with regard to my Person; which, however, could not prevent some of the
younger Officers from turning up their Eyes as they passed under
me. And, to confess the Truth, my Breeches were at that Time in

so ill a Condition, that they afforded some Opportunities for
Laughter and Admiration.

I had sent so many Memorials and Petitions for my Liberty,
that his Majesty at length mentioned the Matter first in the Cabinet, and then in a full Council; where it was opposed by none, except *Skyresh Bolgolam*, who was pleased, without any Provocation,
to be my mortal Enemy. But it was carried against him by the
whole Board, and confirmed by the Emperor. That Minister was
Galbet, or Admiral of the Realm; very much in his Master's Confidence, and a Person well versed in Affairs, but of a morose and
sour Complection. However, he was at length persuaded to comply;
but prevailed that the Articles and Conditions upon which I should
be set free, and to which I must swear, should be drawn up by himself. These Articles were brought to me by *Skyresh Bolgolam* in
Person, attended by two under Secretaries, and several Persons of
Distinction. After they were read, I was demanded to swear to the
Performance of them; first in the Manner of my own Country, and
afterwards in the Method prescribed by their Laws; which was to
hold my right Foot in my left Hand, to place the middle Finger of
my right Hand on the Crown of my Head, and my Thumb on the
Tip of my right Ear. But, because the Reader may perhaps be
curious to have some Idea of the Style and Manner of Expression
peculiar to that People, as well as to know the Articles upon which
I recovered my Liberty; I have made a Translation of the Whole
Instrument, Word for Word, as near as I was able; which I here
offer to the Publick.

GOLBASTO MOMAREN EVLAME GURDILO SHEFIN MULLY ULLY
GUE, most Mighty Emperor of *Lilliput*, Delight and Terror of the
Universe, whose Dominions extend five Thousand Blustrugs, (about
twelve Miles in Circumference) to the Extremities of the Globe:
Monarch of all Monarchs: Taller than the Sons of Men; whose
Feet press down to the Center, and whose Head strikes against the
Sun: At whose Nod the Princes of the Earth shake their Knees;
pleasant as the Spring, comfortable as the Summer, fruitful as
Autumn, dreadful as Winter. His most sublime Majesty proposeth
to the *Man-Mountain*, lately arrived at our Celestial Dominions,
the following Articles, which by a solemn Oath he shall be obliged
to perform.

First, The *Man-Mountain* shall not depart from our Dominions, without our Licence under our Great Seal.

Secondly, He shall not presume to come into our Metropolis, without our express Order; at which time, the Inhabitants shall have two Hours Warning, to keep within their Doors.

Thirdly, The said *Man-Mountain* shall confine his Walks to our principal high Roads; and not offer to walk or lie down in a Meadow, or Field of Corn.

Fourthly, As he walks the said Roads, he shall take the utmost Care not to trample upon the Bodies of any of our loving Subjects, their Horses, or Carriages; nor take any of our said Subjects into his Hands, without their own Consent.

Fifthly, If an express require extraordinary Dispatch; the *Man-Mountain* shall be obliged to carry in his Pocket the Messenger and Horse, a six Days Journey once in every Moon, and return the said Messenger back (if so required) safe to our Imperial Presence.

Sixthly, He shall be our Ally against our Enemies in the Island of *Blefuscu,* and do his utmost to destroy their Fleet, which is now preparing to invade Us.

Seventhly, That the said *Man-Mountain* shall, at his Times of Leisure, be aiding and assisting to our Workmen, in helping to raise certain great Stones, towards covering the Wall of the principal Park, and other our Royal Buildings.

Eighthly, That the said *Man-Mountain* shall, in two Moons Time, deliver in an exact survey of the Circumference of our Dominions, by a Computation of his own Paces round the Coast.

Lastly, That upon his solemn Oath to observe all the above Articles, the said *Man-Mountain* shall have a daily Allowance of Meat and Drink, sufficient for the Support of 1728 of our Subjects; with free Access to our Royal Person, and other Marks of our Favour. Given at our Palace at *Belfaborac* the Twelfth Day of the Ninety-first Moon of our Reign.

I swore and subscribed to these Articles with great Chearfulness and Content, although some of them were not so honourable as I could have wished; which proceeded wholly from the Malice of *Skyresh Bolgolam* the High Admiral: Whereupon my Chains were immediately unlocked, and I was at full Liberty: The Emperor himself, in Person, did me the Honour to be by at the whole Ceremony. I made my Acknowledgments, by prostrating myself at his Majesty's Feet: But he commanded me to rise; and after many gracious Expressions, which, to avoid the Censure of Vanity, I shall not repeat; he added, that he hoped I should prove a useful Servant, and well deserve all the Favours he had already conferred upon me, or might do for the future.

The Reader may please to observe, that in the last Article for the Recovery of my Liberty, the Emperor stipulates to allow me a Quantity of Meat and Drink, sufficient for the Support of 1728 *Lilliputians.* Some time after, asking a Friend at Court how they came to fix on that determinate Number; he told me, that his Majesty's Mathematicians, having taken the Height of my Body by the Help of a Quadrant, and finding it to exceed theirs in the Proportion of Twelve to One, they concluded from the Similarity of their Bodies, that mine must contain at least 1728 of theirs, and consequently would require as much Food as was necessary to support that Number of *Lilliputians.* By which, the Reader may conceive an Idea of the Ingenuity of that People, as well as the prudent and exact Oeconomy of so great a Prince.

CHAPTER IV

Mildendo, the Metropolis of Lilliput, described, together with the Emperor's Palace. A Conversation between the Author and a principal Secretary, concerning the Affairs of that Empire. The Author's Offers to serve the Emperor in his Wars.

The first Request I made after I had obtained my Liberty, was, that I might have Licence to see *Mildendo,* the Metropolis;

which the Emperor easily granted me, but with a special Charge
to do no Hurt, either to the Inhabitants, or their Houses. The
People had Notice by Proclamation of my Design to visit the Town.
The Wall which encompassed it, is two Foot and an half high, and
at least eleven Inches broad, so that a Coach and Horses may be
driven very safely round it; and it is flanked with strong Towers at
ten Foot Distance. I stept over the great *Western* Gate, and passed
very gently, and sideling through the two principal Streets, only in
my short Waistcoat, for fear of damaging the Roofs and Eves of
the Houses with the Skirts of my Coat. I walked with the utmost
Circumspection, to avoid treading on any Stragglers, who might
remain in the Streets, although the Orders were very strict, that all
People should keep in their Houses, at their own Peril. The Garret
Windows and Tops of Houses were so crowded with Spectators,
that I thought in all my Travels I had not seen a more populous
Place. The City is an exact Square, each Side of the Wall being five
Hundred Foot long. The two great Streets which run cross and divide it into four Quarters, are five Foot wide. The Lanes and Al-
leys which I could not enter, but only viewed them as I passed, are
from Twelve to Eighteen Inches. The Town is capable of holding
five Hundred Thousand Souls. The Houses are from three to five
Stories. The Shops and Markets well provided.

The Emperor's Palace is in the Center of the City, where the
two great Streets meet. It is inclosed by a Wall of two Foot high,
and Twenty Foot distant from the Buildings. I had his Majesty's
Permission to step over this Wall; and the Space being so wide
between that and the Palace, I could easily view it on every Side.
The outward Court is a Square of Forty Foot. and includes two
other Courts: In the inmost are the Royal Apartments, which I was
very desirous to see, but found it extremely difficult; for the great
Gates, from one Square into another, were but Eighteen Inches
high, and seven Inches wide. Now the Buildings of the outer Court
were at least five Foot high; and it was impossible for me to stride
over them, without infinite Damage to the Pile, although the Walls
were strongly built of hewn Stone, and four Inches thick. At the
same time, the Emperor had a great Desire that I should see the
Magnificence of his Palace: But this I was not able to do till three
Days after, which I spent in cutting down with my Knife some of
the largest Trees in the Royal Park, about an Hundred Yards distant from the City. Of these Trees I made two Stools, each about

three Foot high, and strong enough to bear my Weight. The People having received Notice a second time, I went again through the City to the Palace, with my two Stools in my Hands. When I came to the Side of the outer Court, I stood upon one Stool, and took the other in my Hand: This I lifted over the Roof, and gently set it down on the Space between the first and second Court, which was eight Foot wide. I then stept over the Buildings very conveniently from one Stool to the other, and drew up the first after me with a hooked Stick. By this Contrivance I got into the inmost Court; and lying down upon my Side, I applied my Face to the Windows of the middle Stories, which were left open on Purpose, and discovered the most splendid Apartments that can be imagined. There I saw the Empress, and the young Princes in their several Lodgings, with their chief Attendants about them. Her Imperial Majesty was pleased to smile very graciously upon me and gave me out of the Window her Hand to kiss.

But I shall not anticipate the Reader with farther Descriptions of this Kind, because I reserve them for a greater Work, which is now almost ready for the Press; containing a general Description of this Empire, from its first Erection, through a long Series of Princes, with a particular Account of their Wars and Politicks, Laws, Learning, and Religion; their Plants and Animals, their peculiar Manners and Customs, with other Matters very curious and useful; my chief Design at present being only to relate such Events and Transactions as happened to the Publick, or to my self, during a Residence of about nine Months in that Empire.

One Morning, about a Fortnight after I had obtained my Liberty, *Reldresal*, Principal Secretary (as they style him) of private Affairs, came to my House, attended only by one Servant. He ordered his Coach to wait at a Distance, and desired I would give him an Hour's Audience; which I readily consented to, on Account of his Quality, and Personal Merits, as well as of the many good Offices he had done me during my Sollicitations at Court. I offered to lie down, that he might the more conveniently reach my Ear; but he chose rather to let me hold him in my Hand during our Conversation. He began with Compliments on my Liberty; said, he might pretend to some Merit in it; but, however, added, that if it had not been for the present Situation of things at Court, perhaps I might not have obtained it so soon. For, *said he,* as flourishing a Condition as we appear to be in to Foreigners, we labour under two mighty Evils; a violent Faction at home, and the Danger of an Invasion by a most potent Enemy from abroad. As to the first, you are to understand, that for above seventy Moons past, there have been two struggling Parties in this Empire, under the Names of *Tramecksan*, and *Slamecksan*, from the high and low Heels on their Shoes, by which they distinguish themselves.

It is alledged indeed, that the high Heels are most agreeable to our ancient Constitution: But however this be, his Majesty hath determined to make use of only low Heels in the Administration of the Government, and all Offices in the Gift of the Crown; as you cannot but observe; and particularly, that his Majesty's Imperial Heels are lower at least by a *Drurr* than any of his Court; (*Drurr* is a Measure about the fourteenth Part of an Inch.) The Animosities between these two Parties run so high, that they will neither eat nor drink, nor talk with each other. We compute the *Tramecksan*, or High-Heels, to exceed us in Number; but the Power is wholly on our Side. We apprehend his Imperial Highness, the Heir to the Crown, to have some Tendency towards the High-Heels; at least we can plainly discover one of his Heels higher than the other; which gives him a Hobble in his Gait.[1] Now, in the midst of these intestine Disquiets, we are threatened with an Invasion from the Island of *Blefuscu*, which is the other great Empire of the Universe, almost as large and powerful as this of his Majesty.[2] For as to what we have heard you affirm, that there are other Kingdoms and States in the World, inhabited by human Creatures as large as your self, our Philosophers are in much Doubt; and would rather conjecture that you dropt from the Moon, or one of the Stars; because it is certain, that an hundred Mortals of your Bulk, would, in a short Time, destroy all the Fruits and Cattle of his Majesty's Dominions. Besides, our Histories of six Thousand Moons make no Mention of any other Regions, than the two great Empires of *Lilliput* and *Blefuscu*. Which two mighty Powers have, as I was going to tell you, been engaged in a most obstinate War for six and thirty Moons

---

[1] The High-Heels stand for the Tories, or high-church party; the Low-Heels for the Whigs, or low-church party. George I favored the Whigs; the Prince of Wales (afterwards George II) indicated favor to both parties, hence his hobble.

[2] As Lilliput is England, so Blefuscu is France. England and France were the principal opponents in the War of the Spanish Succession (1701-1713), in progress at the time of Gulliver's adventure.

past. It began upon the following Occasion. It is allowed on all Hands, that the primitive Way of breaking Eggs before we eat them, was upon the larger End: But his present Majesty's Grandfather, while he was a Boy, going to eat an Egg, and breaking it according to the ancient Practice, happened to cut one of his Fingers. Whereupon the Emperor his Father, published an Edict, commanding all his Subjects, upon great Penalties, to break the smaller End of their Eggs. The People so highly resented this Law, that our Histories tell us, there have been six Rebellions raised on that Account; wherein one Emperor lost his Life, and another his Crown. These civil Commotions were constantly fomented by the Monarchs of *Blefuscu*; and when they were quelled, the Exiles always fled for Refuge to that Empire. It is computed, that eleven Thousand Persons have, at several Times, suffered Death, rather than submit to break their Eggs at the smaller End. Many hundred large Volumes have been published upon this Controversy: But the Books of the *Big-Endians* have been long forbidden, and the whole Party rendred incapable by Law of holding Employments.[3] During the Course of these Troubles, the Emperors of *Blefuscu* did frequently expostulate by their Ambassadors, accusing us of making a Schism in Religion, by offending against a fundamental Doctrine of our great Prophet *Lustrog*, in the fifty-fourth Chapter of the *Brundrecal*, (which is their *Alcoran*.) This, however, is thought to be a meer Strain upon the Text: For the Words are these; *That all true Believers shall break their Eggs at the convenient End*: and which is the convenient End, seems, in my humble Opinion, to be left to every Man's Conscience, or at least in the Power of the chief Magistrate to determine. Now the *Big-Endian* Exiles have found so much Credit in the Emperor of *Blefuscu's* Court; and so much private Assistance and Encouragement from their Party here at home, that a bloody War hath been carried on between the two Empires for six and thirty Moons with various Success; during which Time we have lost Forty Capital Ships, and a much greater

---

[3] Swift is referring to three related conflicts: (1) that originally between England and Rome, during which Henry VIII issued an "Edict" denying Papal authority; (2) that within England, between Roman Catholics (Big-Endians) and Protestants (Little-Endians), which resulted in the execution of Charles I, the forced exile of James II, and the imposing of restrictions on native Catholics; and (3) that between Protestant England and Catholic France, during which France harbored Catholic exiles, and was accused of plotting against England.

Number of smaller Vessels, together with thirty thousand of our best Seamen and Soldiers; and the Damage received by the Enemy is reckoned to be somewhat greater than ours. However, they have now equipped a numerous Fleet, and are just preparing to make a Descent upon us: And his Imperial Majesty, placing great Confidence in your Valour and Strength, hath commanded me to lay this Account of his affairs before you.

I desired the Secretary to present my humble Duty to the Emperor, and to let him know, that I thought it would not become me, who was a Foreigner, to interfere with Parties; but I was ready, with the Hazard of my Life, to defend his Person and State against all Invaders.

CHAPTER V

The Author by an extraordinary Stratagem prevents an Invasion. A high Title of Honour is conferred upon him. Ambassadors arrive from the Emperor of Blefuscu, and sue for Peace. The Empress's Apartment on fire by an Accident; the Author instrumental in saving the Rest of the Palace.

The Empire of *Blefuscu,* is an Island situated to the North North-East Side of *Lilliput,* from whence it is parted only by a Channel of eight Hundred Yards wide. I had not yet seen it, and upon this Notice of an intended Invasion, I avoided appearing on that Side of the Coast, for fear of being discovered by some of the Enemies' Ships, who had received no Intelligence of me; all intercourse between the two Empires having been strictly forbidden during the War, upon Pain of Death; and an Embargo laid by our Emperor upon all Vessels whatsoever. I communicated to his Majesty a Project I had formed of seizing the Enemies' whole Fleet; which, as our Scouts assured us, lay at Anchor in the Harbour ready to sail with the first fair Wind. I consulted the most experienced Seamen, upon the Depth of the Channel, which they had often plummed; who told me, that in the Middle at high Water it was seventy *Glumgluffs* deep, which is about six Foot of *European* Measure; and the rest of it fifty *Glumgluffs* at most. I walked to the North-East Coast over against *Blefuscu*; where, lying down behind a Hillock, I took out my small Pocket Perspective Glass, and viewed the Enemy's Fleet at Anchor, consisting of about fifty Men of War, and a great Number of Transports: I then came back to my House, and gave Order (for which I had a Warrant) for a great Quantity of the strongest Cable and Bars of Iron. The Cable was about as thick as Packthread, and the Bars of the Length and Size of a Knitting-Needle. I trebled the Cable to make it stronger; and for the same Reason I twisted three of the Iron Bars together, bending the Extremities into a Hook. Having thus fixed fifty Hooks to as many Cables, I went back to the North-East Coast, and putting off my Coat, Shoes, and Stockings, walked into the Sea in my Leathern Jerkin, about half an Hour before high Water. I waded with what Haste I could, and swam in the Middle about thirty Yards until I felt the Ground; I arrived at the Fleet in less than half an Hour. The Enemy was so frighted when they saw me, that they leaped out of their Ships, and swam to Shore; where there could not be fewer than thirty thousand Souls. I then took my Tackling, and fastning a Hook to the Hole at the Prow of each, I tyed all the Cords together at the End. While I was thus employed, the Enemy discharged several Thousand Arrows, many of which stuck in my Hands and Face; and besides the excessive Smart, gave me much Disturbance in my Work. My greatest Apprehension was for my Eyes, which I should have infallibly lost, if I had not suddenly thought of an Expedient. I kept, among other little Necessaries, a Pair of Spectacles in a private Pocket, which, as I observed before, had escaped the Emperor's Searchers. These I took out, and fastened as strongly as I could upon my Nose; and thus armed went on boldly with my Work in spight of the Enemy's Arrows; many of which struck against the Glasses of my Spectacles, but without any other Effect, further than a little to discompose them. I had now fastened all the Hooks, and taking the Knot in my Hand, began to pull; but not a Ship would stir, for they were all too fast held by their Anchors; so that the boldest Part of my Enterprize remained. I therefore let go the Cord, and leaving the Hooks fixed to the Ships, I resolutely cut with my Knife the Cables that fastened

the Anchors; receiving above two hundred Shots in my Face and
Hands: Then I took up the knotted End of the Cables to which my
Hooks were tyed; and with great Ease drew fifty of the Enemy's
largest Men of War after me.

The *Blefuscudians*, who had not the least Imagination of what
I intended, were at first confounded with Astonishment. They had
seen me cut the Cables, and thought my Design was only to let the
Ships run a-drift, or fall foul on each other: But when they per-
ceived the whole Fleet moving in Order, and saw me pulling at the
End; they set up such a Scream of Grief and Dispair, that it is al-
most impossible to describe or conceive. When I had got out of
Danger, I stopt a while to pick out the Arrows that stuck in my
Hands and Face, and rubbed on some of the same Ointment that
was given me at my first Arrival, as I have formerly mentioned. I
then took off my Spectacles, and waiting about an Hour until the
Tyde was a little fallen, I waded through the Middle with my
Cargo, and arrived safe at the Royal Port of *Lilliput*.

The Emperor and his whole Court stood on the Shore, expecting
the Issue of this great Adventure. They saw the Ships move forward in a large Half-Moon, but could not discern me, who was up
to my Breast in Water. When I advanced to the Middle of the
Channel, they were yet more in Pain because I was under Water
to my Neck. The Emperor concluded me to be drowned, and that
the Enemy's Fleet was approaching in a hostile Manner: But he
was soon eased of his Fears; for the Channel growing shallower
every Step I made, I came in a short Time within Hearing; and
holding up the End of the Cable by which the Fleet was fastened, I
cryed in a loud Voice, *Long live the most puissant Emperor of Lilliput!* This great Prince received me at my Landing with all possible Encomiums, and created me a *Nardac* upon the Spot, which is
the highest Title of Honour among them.

His Majesty desired I would take some other Opportunity of
bringing all the rest of his Enemy's Ships into his Ports. And so
unmeasurable is the Ambition of Princes, that he seemed to think
of nothing less than reducing the whole Empire of *Blefuscu* into a
Province, and governing it by a Viceroy; of destroying the *Big-Endian* Exiles, and compelling that People to break the smaller End of
their Eggs; by which he would remain sole Monarch of the whole
World. But I endeavoured to divert him from this Design, by
many Arguments drawn from the Topicks of Policy as well as Jus-

tice: And I plainly protested, that I would never be an Instrument of bringing a free and brave People into Slavery: And when the Matter was debated in Council, the wisest Part of the Ministry were of my Opinion.

This open bold Declaration of mine was so opposite to the Schemes and Politicks of his Imperial Majesty, that he could never forgive me: He mentioned it in a very artful Manner at Council, where, I was told, that some of the wisest appeared, at least by their Silence, to be of my Opinion; but others, who were my secret Enemies, could not forbear some Expressions, which by a Side-wind reflected on me. And from this Time began an Intrigue between his Majesty, and a Junta of Ministers maliciously bent against me, which broke out in less than two Months, and had like to have ended in my utter Destruction. Of so little Weight are the greatest Services to Princes, when put into the Balance with a Refusal to gratify their Passions.

About three Weeks after this Exploit, there arrived a solemn Embassy from *Blefuscu*, with humble Offers of a Peace; which was soon concluded upon Conditions very advantageous to our Emperor; wherewith I shall not trouble the Reader. There were six Ambassadors, with a Train of about five Hundred Persons; and their Entry was very magnificent, suitable to the Grandeur of their Master, and the Importance of their Business. When their Treaty was finished, wherein I did them several good Offices by the Credit I now had, or at least appeared to have at Court; their Excellencies, who were privately told how much I had been their Friend, made me a Visit in Form. They began with many Compliments upon my Valour and Generosity; invited me to that Kingdom in the Emperor their Master's Name; and desired me to shew them some Proofs of my prodigious Strength, of which they had heard so many Wonders; wherein I readily obliged them, but shall not interrupt the Reader with the Particulars.

When I had for some time entertained their Excellencies to their infinite Satisfaction and Surprize, I desired they would do me the Honour to present my most humble Respects to the Emperor their Master, the Renown of whose Virtues had so justly filled the whole World with Admiration, and whose Royal Person I resolved to attend before I returned to my own Country. Accordingly, the next time I had the Honour to see our Emperor, I desired his general Licence to wait on the *Blefuscudian* Monarch, which he was pleased to grant me, as I could plainly perceive, in a very cold Manner; but could not guess the Reason, till I had a Whisper from a certain Person, that *Flimnap* and *Bolgolam* had represented my Intercourse with those Ambassadors, as a Mark of Disaffection, from which I am sure my Heart was wholly free. And this was the first time I began to conceive some imperfect Idea of Courts and Ministers.[1]

It is to be observed, that these Ambassadors spoke to me by an Interpreter; the Languages of both Empires differing as much from each other as any two in *Europe*, and each Nation priding itself upon the Antiquity, Beauty, and Energy of their own Tongues, with an avowed Contempt for that of their Neighbour: Yet our Emperor standing upon the Advantage he had got by the Seizure of their Fleet, obliged them to deliver their Credentials, and make their Speech in the *Lilliputian* Tongue. And it must be confessed, that from the great Intercourse of Trade and Commerce between both Realms; from the continual Reception of Exiles, which is mutual among them; and from the Custom in each Empire to send their young Nobility and richer Gentry to the other, in order to polish themselves, by seeing the World, and understanding Men and Manners; there are few Pers ns of Distinction, or Merchants, or Seamen, who dwell in the Maritime Parts, but what can hold Conversation in both Tongues; as I found some Weeks after, when I went to pay my Respects to the Emperor of *Blefuscu*, which in the Midst of great Misfortunes, through the Malice of my Enemies, proved a very happy Adventure to me, as I shall relate in its proper Place.

The Reader may remember, that when I signed those Articles upon which I recovered my Liberty, there were some which I disliked upon Account of their being too servile, neither could any thing but an extreme Necessity have forced me to submit. But being now a *Nardac*, of the highest Rank in that Empire, such Offices were looked upon as below my Dignity; and the Emperor (to do him Justice) never once mentioned them to me. However, it was not long before I had an Opportunity of doing his Majesty,

[1] Gulliver's capture of the fleet has reference to the Treaty of Utrecht, which, effected by the Tories, ended the war with France. Claims of Gulliver's "disaffection" echo Whig claims that the Treaty was too generous to France, while the fact that Gulliver's was a naval victory reflects the Tory contention that the Treaty preserved England's mastery of the seas. Here again, Gulliver stands for the Tory leaders, Oxford and Bolingbroke.

at least, as I then thought, a most signal Service. I was alarmed at Midnight with the Cries of many Hundred People at my Door; by which being suddenly awaked, I was in some Kind of Terror. I heard the Word *Burglum* repeated incessantly; several of the Emperor's Court making their Way through the Croud, intreated me to come immediately to the Palace, where her Imperial Majesty's Apartment was on fire, by the Carelessness of a Maid of Honour, who fell asleep while she was reading a Romance. I got up in an Instant; and Orders being given to clear the Way before me; and it being likewise a Moonshine Night, I made a shift to get to the Palace without trampling on any of the People. I found they had already applied Ladders to the Walls of the Apartment, and were well provided with Buckets, but the Water was at some Distance. These Buckets were about the Size of a large Thimble, and the poor People supplied me with them as fast as they could; but the Flame was so violent, that they did little Good. I might easily have stifled it with my Coat, which I unfortunately left behind me for haste, and came away only in my Leathern Jerkin. The Case seemed wholly desperate and deplorable; and this magnificent Palace would have infallibly been burnt down to the Ground, if, by a Presence of Mind, unusual to me, I had not suddenly thought of an Expedient. I had the Evening before drank plentifully of a most delicious Wine, called *Glimigrim*, (the *Blefuscudians* call it *Flunec*, but ours is esteemed the better Sort) which is very diuretick. By the luckiest Chance in the World, I had not discharged myself of any Part of it. The Heat I had contracted by coming very near the Flames, and by my labouring to quench them, made the Wine begin to operate by Urine; which I voided in such a Quantity, and applied so well to the proper Places, that in three Minutes the Fire was wholly extinguished; and the rest of that noble Pile, which had cost so many Ages in erecting, preserved from Destruction.

It was now Day-light, and I returned to my House, without waiting to congratulate with the Emperor; because, although I had done a very eminent Piece of Service, yet I could not tell how his Majesty might resent the Manner by which I had performed it: For, by the fundamental Laws of the Realm, it is Capital in any Person, of what Quality soever, to make water within the Precincts of the Palace. But I was a little comforted by a Message from his Majesty, that he would give Orders to the Grand Justiciary for passing my Pardon in Form; which, however, I could not obtain.

And I was privately assured, that the Empress conceiving the
greatest Abhorrence of what I had done, removed to the most
distant Side of the Court, firmly resolved that those Buildings
should never be repaired for her Use; and, in the Presence of her
chief Confidents, could not forbear vowing Revenge.[2]

CHAPTER VI

Of the Inhabitants of Lilliput; *their Learning, Laws,
and Customs. The Manner of Educating their Children.
The Author's Way of living in that Country. His Vindication of a great Lady.*

Although I intend to leave the Description of this Empire
to a particular Treatise, yet in the mean time I am content to
gratify the curious Reader with some general Ideas. As the common
Size of the Natives is somewhat under six Inches, so there is an
exact Proportion in all other Animals, as well as Plants and Trees:
For Instance, the tallest Horses and Oxen are between four and
five Inches in Height, the Sheep an Inch and a half, more or less;
their Geese about the Bigness of a Sparrow; and so the several
Gradations downwards, till you come to the smallest, which, to my
Sight, were almost invisible; but Nature hath adapted the Eyes
of the *Lilliputians* to all Objects proper for their View: They see
with great Exactness, but at no great Distance. And to show the
Sharpness of their Sight towards Objects that are near, I have been
much pleased with observing a Cook pulling a Lark, which was not
so large as a common Fly; and a young Girl threading an invisible
Needle with invisible Silk. Their tallest Trees are about seven
Foot high; I mean some of those in the great Royal Park, the
Tops whereof I could but just reach with my Fist clinched. The

---

[2] The Empress here represents Queen Anne, and her response seems to
relate to Anne's reaction to Swift's earlier work, *A Tale of a Tub,* which
she thought coarse and disrespectful to religion. Her "revenge" was to
limit Swift's chances of preferment within the Church of England.

other Vegetables are in the same Proportion: But this I leave to the Reader's Imagination.

I shall say but little at present of their Learning, which for many Ages hath flourished in all its Branches among them: But their Manner of Writing is very peculiar; being neither from the Left to the Right, like the *Europeans*; nor from the Right to the Left, like the *Arabians*; nor from up to down, like the *Chinese*; nor from down to up, like the *Cascagians*; but aslant from one Corner of the Paper to the other, like Ladies in *England*.

They bury their Dead with their Heads directly downwards; because they hold an Opinion, that in eleven Thousand Moons they are all to rise again; in which Period, the Earth (which they conceive to be flat) will turn upside down, and by this Means they shall, at their Resurrection, be found ready standing on their Feet. The Learned among them confess the Absurdity of this Doctrine; but the Practice still continues, in Compliance to the Vulgar.

There are some Laws and Customs in this Empire very peculiar; and if they were not so directly contrary to those of my own dear Country, I should be tempted to say a little in their Justification. It is only to be wished, that they were as well executed. The first I shall mention, relateth to Informers. All Crimes against the State, are punished here with the utmost Severity; but if the Person accused make his Innocence plainly to appear upon his Tryal, the Accuser is immediately put to an ignominious Death; and out of his Goods or Lands, the innocent Person is quadruply recompensed for the Loss of his Time, for the Danger he underwent, for the Hardship of his Imprisonment, and for all the Charges he hath been at in making his Defence. Or, if that Fund be deficient, it is largely supplyed by the Crown. The Emperor doth also confer on him some publick Mark of his Favour; and Proclamation is made of his Innocence through the whole City.

They look upon Fraud as a greater Crime than Theft, and therefore seldom fail to punish it with Death: For they alledge, that Care and Vigilance, with a very common Understanding, may preserve a Man's Goods from Thieves; but Honesty hath nc Fence against superior Cunning: And since it is necessary that there should be a perpetual Intercourse of buying and selling, and dealing upon Credit; where Fraud is permitted or connived at, or hath no Law to punish it, the honest Dealer is always undone, and the Knave gets the Advantage. I remember when I was once interceeding with the King for a Criminal who had wronged his Master of a great Sum of Money, which he had received by Order, and ran away with; and happening to tell his Majesty, by way of Extenuation, that it was only a Breach of Trust; the Emperor thought it monstrous in me to offer, as a Defence, the greatest Aggravation of the Crime: And truly, I had little to say in Return, farther than the common Answer, that different Nations had different Customs; for, I confess, I was heartily ashamed.

Although we usually call Reward and Punishment, the two Hinges upon which all Government turns; yet I could never observe this Maxim to be put in Practice by any Nation, except that of *Lilliput*. Whoever can there bring sufficient Proof that he hath strictly observed the Laws of his Country for Seventy-three Moons, hath a Claim to certain Privileges, according to his Quality and Condition of Life, with a proportionable Sum of Money out of a Fund appropriated for that Use: He likewise acquires the Title of *Snilpall*, or *Legal*, which is added to his Name, but doth not descend to his Posterity. And these People thought it a prodigious Defect of Policy among us, when I told them that our Laws were enforced only by Penalties, without any Mention of Reward. It is upon this account that the Image of Justice, in their Courts of Judicature, is formed with six Eyes, two before, as many behind, and on each Side one, to signify Circumspection; with a Bag of Gold open in her right Hand, and a Sword sheathed in her left, to shew she is more disposed to reward than to punish.

In chusing Persons for all Employments, they have more Regard to good Morals than to great Abilities: For, since Government is necessary to Mankind, they believe that the common Size of human Understandings, is fitted to some Station or other; and that Providence never intended to make the Management of publick Affairs a Mystery, to be comprehended only by a few Persons of sublime Genius, of which there seldom are three born in an Age: But, they suppose Truth, Justice, Temperance, and the like, to be in every Man's Power; the Practice of which Virtues, assisted by Experience and a good Intention, would qualify any Man for the Service of his Country, except where a Course of Study is required. But they thought the Want of Moral Virtues was so far from being supplied by superior Endowments of the Mind, that Employments could never be put into such dangerous Hands as those of Persons so qualified; and at least, that the Mistakes committed by Ignorance in a virtuous Disposition, would never be of such fatal Consequence to the Publick Weal, as the Practices of a Man, whose Inclinations led him to be corrupt, and had great Abilities to manage, to multiply, and defend his Corruptions.

In like Manner, the Disbelief of a Divine Providence renders a Man uncapable of holding any publick Station: For, since Kings avow themselves to be the Deputies of Providence, the *Lilliputians* think nothing can be more absurd than for a Prince to employ such Men as disown the Authority under which he acteth.

In relating these and the following Laws, I would only be understood to mean the original Institutions, and not the most scandalous Corruptions into which these People are fallen by the degenerate Nature of Man. For as to that infamous Practice of acquiring great Employment by dancing on the Ropes, or Badges of Favour and Distinction by leaping over Sticks, and creeping under them; the Reader is to observe, that they were first introduced by the Grandfather of the Emperor now reigning; and grew to the present Height, by the gradual Increase of Party and Faction.

Ingratitude is among them a capital Crime, as we read it to have been in some other Countries: For they reason thus; that whoever makes ill Returns to his Benefactor, must needs be a common Enemy to the rest of Mankind, from whom he hath received no Obligation; and therefore such a Man is not fit to live.

Their Notions relating to the Duties of Parents and Children differ extremely from ours. For, since the Conjunction of Male and Female is founded upon the great Law of Nature, in order to propagate and continue the Species; the *Lilliputians* will needs have it, that Men and Women are joined together like other Animals, by the Motives of Concupiscence; and that their Tenderness towards their Young, proceedeth from the like natural Principle: For which Reason they will never allow, that a Child is under any Obligation to his Father for begetting him, or to his Mother for bringing him into the World; which, considering the Miseries of human Life, was neither a Benefit in itself, nor intended so by his Parents, whose Thoughts in their Love-encounters were otherwise employed. Upon these, and the like Reasonings, their Opinion is, that Parents are the last of all others to be trusted with the Education of their own Children: And therefore they have in every Town publick Nurseries, where all Parents, except Cottagers and Labourers, are obliged to send their Infants of both Sexes to be reared and educated when they come to the Age of twenty Moons; at which Time they are supposed to have some Rudiments of Docility. These Schools are of several Kinds, suited to different Qualities, and to both Sexes. They have certain Professors well skilled in preparing Children for such a Condition of Life as befits the Rank of their Parents, and their own Capacities as well as Inclinations. I shall first say something of the Male Nurseries, and then of the Female.

The Nurseries for Males of Noble or Eminent Birth, are provided with grave and learned Professors, and their several Deputies. The Clothes and Food of the Children are plain and simple. They are bred up in the Principles of Honour, Justice, Courage, Modesty, Clemency, Religion, and Love of their Country: They are always employed in some Business, except in the Times of eating and sleeping, which are very short, and two Hours for Diversions, consisting of bodily Exercises. They are dressed by Men until four Years of Age, and then are obliged to dress themselves, although their Quality be ever so great; and the Women Attendants, who are aged proportionably to ours at fifty, perform only the most menial Offices. They are never suffered to converse with Servants, but go together in small or greater Numbers to take their Diversions, and always in the Presence of a Professor, or one of his Deputies; whereby they avoid those early bad Impressions of Folly and Vice to which our Children are subject. Their Parents are suffered to see them only twice a Year; the Visit is not to last above an Hour; they are allowed to kiss the Child at Meeting and Parting; but a Professor, who always standeth by on those Occasions, will not suffer them to whisper, or use any fondling Expressions, or bring any Presents of Toys, Sweet-meats, and the like.

The Pension from each Family for the Education and Entertainment of a Child, upon Failure of due Payment, is levyed by the Emperor's Officers.

The Nurseries for Children of ordinary Gentlemen, Merchants, Traders, and Handicrafts, are managed proportionably after the same Manner; only those designed for Trades, are put out Apprentices at seven Years old; whereas those of Persons of Quality continue in their Exercises until Fifteen, which answers to One and Twenty with us: But the Confinement is gradually lessened for the last three Years.

In the Female Nurseries, the young Girls of Quality are educated much like the Males, only they are dressed by orderly Servants of their own Sex, but always in the Presence of a Professor or Deputy, until they come to dress themselves, which is at five Years old. And if it be found that these Nurses ever presume to entertain the Girls with frightful or foolish Stories, or the common Follies practised by Chamber-Maids among us; they are publickly whipped thrice about the City, imprisoned for a Year, and banished for Life to the most desolate Parts of the Country. Thus the young Ladies there are as much ashamed of being Cowards and Fools, as the Men; and despise all personal Ornaments beyond Decency and Cleanliness; neither did I perceive any Difference in their Education, made by their Difference of Sex, only that the Exercises of the Females were not altogther so robust; and that some Rules were given them relating to domestick Life, and a smaller Compass of Learning was enjoyned them: For, their Maxim is, that among People of Quality, a Wife should be always a reasonable and agreeable Companion, because she cannot always be young. When the Girls are twelve Years old, which among them is the marriageable Age, their Parents or Guardians take them home, with great Expressions of Gratitude to the Professors, and seldom without Tears of the young Lady and her Companions.

In the Nurseries of Females of the meaner Sort, the Children are instructed in all Kinds of Works proper for their Sex, and their several Degrees: Those intended for Apprentices are dismissed at seven Years old, the rest are kept to eleven.

The meaner Families who have Children at these Nurseries, are obliged, besides their annual Pension, which is as low as possible, to return to the Steward of the Nursery a small Monthly Share of their Gettings, to be a Portion for the Child; and therefore all Parents are limited in their Expences by the Law. For the *Lilliputians* think nothing can be more unjust, than that People, in Subservience to their own Appetites, should bring Children into the World, and leave the Burthen of supporting them on the Publick. As to Persons of Quality, they give Security to appropriate a certain Sum for each Child, suitable to their Condition; and these Funds are always managed with good Husbandry, and the most exact Justice.

The Cottagers and Labourers keep their Children at home, their Business being only to till and cultivate the Earth; and therefore their Education is of little Consequence to the Publick; but the

Old and Diseased among them are supported by Hospitals: For begging is a Trade unknown in this Empire.

And here it may perhaps divert the curious Reader, to give some Account of my Domestick, and my Manner of living in this Country, during a Residence of nine Months and thirteen Days. Having a Head mechanically turned, and being likewise forced by Necessity, I had made for myself a Table and Chair convenient enough, out of the largest Trees in the Royal Park. Two hundred Sempstresses were employed to make me Shirts, and Linnen for my Bed and Table, all of the strongest and coarsest kind they could get; which, however, they were forced to quilt together in several Folds; for the thickest was some Degrees finer than Lawn. Their Linnen is usually three Inches wide, and three Foot make a Piece. The Sempstresses took my Measure as I lay on the Ground, one standing at my Neck, and another at my Mid-Leg, with a strong Cord extended, that each held by the End, while the third measured the Length of the Cord with a Rule of an Inch long. Then they measured my right Thumb, and desired no more; for by a mathematical Computation, that twice round the Thumb is once round the Wrist, and so on to the Neck and the Waist; and by the Help of my old Shirt, which I displayed on the Ground before them for a Pattern, they fitted me exactly. Three hundred Taylors were employed in the same Manner to make me Clothes; but they had another Contrivance for taking my Measure. I kneeled down, and they raised a Ladder from the Ground to my Neck; upon this Ladder one of them mounted, and let fall a Plum-Line from my Collar to the Floor, which just answered the Length of my Coat; but my Waist and Arms I measured myself. When my Cloaths were finished, which was done in my House, (for the largest of theirs would not have been able to hold them) they looked like the Patch-work made by the Ladies in *England*, only that mine were all of a Colour.

I had three hundred Cooks to dress my Victuals, in little convenient Huts built about my House, where they and their Families lived, and prepared me two Dishes a-piece. I took up twenty Waiters in my Hand, and placed them on the Table; an hundred more attended below on the Ground, some with Dishes of Meat, and some with Barrels of Wine, and other Liquors, slung on their Shoulders; all which the Waiters above drew up as I wanted, in a very ingenious Manner, by certain Cords, as we draw the Bucket up a Well in *Europe*. A Dish of their Meat was a good Mouthful, and a Barrel of their Liquor a reasonable Draught. Their Mutton yields to ours, but their Beef is excellent. I have had a Sirloin so large, that I have been forced to make three Bites of it; but this is rare. My Servants were astonished to see me eat it Bones and all, as in our Country we do the Leg of a Lark. Their Geese and Turkeys I usually eat at a Mouthful, and I must confess they far exceed ours. Of their smaller Fowl I could take up twenty or thirty at the End of my Knife.

One day his Imperial Majesty being informed of my Way of living, desired that himself, and his Royal Consort, with the young Princes of the Blood of both Sexes, might have the Happiness (as he was pleased to call it) of dining with me. They came accordingly, and I placed them upon Chairs of State on my Table, just over against me, with their Guards about them. *Flimnap* the Lord High Treasurer attended there likewise, with his white Staff; and I observed he often looked on me with a sour Countenance, which I would not seem to regard, but eat more than usual, in Honour to my dear Country, as well as to fill the Court with Admiration. I have some private Reasons to believe, that this Visit from his Majesty gave *Flimnap* an Opportunity of doing me ill Offices to his Master. That Minister had always been my secret Enemy, although he outwardly caressed me more than was usual to the Moroseness of his Nature. He represented to the Emperor the low Condition of his Treasury; that he was forced to take up Money at great Discount; that Exchequer Bills would not circulate under nine *per Cent.* below Par; that I had cost his Majesty above a Million and a half of *Sprugs*, (their greatest Gold Coin, about the Bigness of a Spangle;) and upon the whole, that it would be advisable in the Emperor to take the first fair Occasion of dismissing me.

I am here obliged to vindicate the Reputation of an excellent Lady, who was an innocent Sufferer upon my Account. The Treasurer took a Fancy to be jealous of his Wife, from the Malice of some evil Tongues, who informed him that her Grace had taken a violent Affection for my Person; and the Court-Scandal ran for some Time that she once came privately to my Lodging. This I solemnly declare to be a most infamous Falshood, without any Grounds, farther than that her Grace was pleased to treat me with all innocent Marks of Freedom and Friendship.[1] I own she came

[1] This affair is another slash at Walpole, who, unlike the over-sensitive Flimnap, was little bothered by his wife's infidelities.

often to my House, but always publickly, nor ever without three more in the Coach, who were usually her Sister, and young Daughter, and some particular Acquaintance; but this was common to many other Ladies of the Court. And I still appeal to my Servants round, whether they at any Time saw a Coach at my Door without knowing what Persons were in it. On those occasions, when a Servant had given me Notice, my Custom was to go immediately to the Door; and after paying my Respects, to take up the Coach and two Horses very carefully in my Hands, (for if there were six Horses, the Postillion always unharnessed four) and place them on a Table, where I had fixed a moveable Rim quite round, of five Inches high, to prevent Accidents. And I have often had four Coaches and Horses at once on my Table full of Company, while I sat in my Chair leaning my Face towards them; and when I was engaged with one Sett, the Coachmen would gently drive the others round my Table. I have passed many an Afternoon very agreeably in these Conversations: But I defy the Treasurer, or his two Informers, (I will name them, and let them make their best of it) *Clustril* and *Drunlo*, to prove that any Person ever came to me *incognito*, except the Secretary *Reldresal*, who was sent by express Command of his Imperial Majesty, as I have before related. I should not have dwelt so long upon this Particular, if it had not been a Point wherein the Reputation of a great Lady is so nearly concerned, to say nothing of my own; although I had the Honour to be a *Nardac*, which the Treasurer himself is not; for all the World knows he is only a *Clumglum*, a Title inferior by one Degree, as that of a Marquess is to a Duke in *England*; yet I allow he preceded me in right of his Post. These false Informations, which I afterwards came to the Knowledge of, by an Accident not proper to mention, made the Treasurer shew his Lady for some Time an ill Countenance, and me a worse: For although he were at last undeceived and reconciled to her, yet I lost all Credit with him; and found my Interest decline very fast with the Emperor himself, who was indeed too much governed by that Favourite.

CHAPTER VII

The Author being informed of a Design to accuse him of High Treason, makes his Escape to Blefuscu. His Reception there.

Before I proceed to give an Account of my leaving this Kingdom, it may be proper to inform the Reader of a private Intrigue which had been for two Months forming against me.

I had been hitherto all my Life a Stranger to Courts, for which I was unqualified by the Meanness of my Condition. I had indeed heard and read enough of the Dispositions of great Princes and Ministers; but never expected to have found such terrible Effects of them in so remote a Country, governed, as I thought, by very different Maxims from those in *Europe*.

When I was just preparing to pay my Attendance on the Emperor of *Blefuscu*; a considerable Person at Court (to whom I had been very serviceable at a time when he lay under the highest Displeasure of his Imperial Majesty) came to my House very privately at Night in a close Chair, and without sending his Name, desired Admittance: The Chair-men were dismissed; I put the Chair, with his Lordship in it, into my Coat-Pocket; and giving Orders to a trusty Servant to say I was indisposed and gone to sleep, I fastened the Door of my House, placed the Chair on the Table, according to my usual Custom, and sat down by it. After the common Salutations were over, observing his Lordship's Countenance full of Concern; and enquiring into the Reason, he desired I would hear him with Patience, in a Matter that highly concerned my Honour and my Life. His Speech was to the following Effect, for I took Notes of it as soon as he left me.

You are to know, said he, that several Committees of Council have been lately called in the most private Manner on your Account: And it is but two Days since his Majesty came to a full Resolution.

You are very sensible that *Skyris Bolgolam* (*Galbet*, or High Admiral) hath been your mortal Enemy almost ever since your Arrival. His original Reasons I know not; but his Hatred is much increased since your great Success against *Blefuscu*, by which his Glory, as Admiral, is obscured. This Lord, in Conjunction with *Flimnap* the High Treasurer, whose Enmity against you is notorious on Account of his Lady; *Limtoc* the General, *Lalcon* the Chamberlain, and *Balmuff* the grand Justiciary, have prepared Articles of Impeachment against you, for Treason, and other capital Crimes.

This Preface made me so impatient, being conscious of my own Merits and Innocence, that I was going to interrupt; when he intreated me to be silent; and thus proceeded.

Out of Gratitude for the Favours you have done me, I procured Information of the whole Proceedings, and a Copy of the Articles, wherein I venture my Head for your Service.

Articles of Impeachment against Quinbus Flestrin,

(the Man-Mountain).[1]

ARTICLE 1

Whereas, by a Statute made in the Reign of his Imperial Majesty *Calin Deffar Plune*, it is enacted, That whoever shall make water within the Precincts of the Royal Palace, shall be liable to the Pains and Penalties of High Treason: Notwithstanding, the said *Quinbus Flestrin*, in open Breach of the said Law, under Colour of extinguishing the Fire kindled in the Apartment of his Majesty's most dear Imperial Consort, did maliciously, traitorously, and devilishly, by discharge of his Urine, put out the said Fire kindled in the said Apartment, lying and being within the Precincts of the said Royal Palace; against the Statute in that Case provided, &c. against the Duty, &c.

ARTICLE 2

That the said *Quinbus Flestrin* having brought the Imperial Fleet of *Blefuscu* into the Royal Port, and being afterwards commanded by his Imperial Majesty to seize all the other Ships of the said Empire of *Blefuscu*, and reduce that Empire to a

---

[1] The investigation of Oxford and Bolingbroke in 1715 (see p. 19, n. 3) led to their impeachment for treason; the charges against them Swift satirizes in the articles that follow.

Province, to be governed by a Vice-Roy from hence; and to destroy and put to death not only all the *Big-Endian Exiles*, but likewise all the People of that Empire, who would not immediately forsake the *Big-Endian* Heresy: He the said *Flestrin*, like a false Traitor against his most Auspicious, Serene, Imperial Majesty, did petition to be excused from the said Service, upon Pretence of Unwillingness to force the Consciences, or destroy the Liberties and Lives of an innocent People.

ARTICLE 3

That, whereas certain Embassadors arrived from the Court of *Blefuscu* to sue for Peace in his Majesty's Court:

He the said *Flestrin* did, like a false Traitor, aid, abet, comfort, and divert the said Embassadors; although he knew them to be Servants to a Prince who was lately an open Enemy to his Imperial Majesty, and in open War against his said Majesty.

ARTICLE 4

That the said *Quinbus Flestrin*, contrary to the Duty of a faithful Subject, is now preparing to make a Voyage to the Court and Empire of *Blefuscu*, for which he hath received only verbal Licence from his Imperial Majesty; and under Colour of the said Licence, doth falsely and traitorously intend to take the said Voyage, and thereby to aid, comfort, and abet the Emperor of *Blefuscu*, so late an Enemy, and in open War with his Imperial Majesty aforesaid.

There are some other Articles, but these are the most important, of which I have read you an Abstract.

In the several Debates upon this Impeachment, it must be confessed that his Majesty gave many Marks of his great *Lenity*; often urging the Services you had done him, and endeavouring to extenuate your Crimes. The Treasurer and Admiral insisted that you should be put to the most painful and ignominious Death, by setting Fire on your House at Night; and the General was to attend with Twenty Thousand Men armed with poisoned Arrows, to shoot you on the Face and Hands. Some of your Servants were to have private Orders to strew a poisonous Juice on your Shirts and Sheets, which would soon make you tear your own Flesh, and die in the utmost Torture. The General came into the same Opinion; so that for a long time there was a Majority against you. But his Majesty resolving, if possible, to spare your Life, at last brought off the Chamberlain.

Upon this Incident, *Reldresal*, principal Secretary for private Affairs, who always approved himself your true Friend, was commanded by the Emperor to deliver his Opinion, which he accordingly did; and therein justified the good Thoughts you have of him. He allowed your Crimes to be great; but that still there was room for Mercy, the most commendable Virtue in a Prince, and for which his Majesty was so justly celebrated. He said, the Friendship between you and him was so well known to the World, that perhaps the most honourable Board might think him partial: However, in Obedience to the Command he had received, he would freely offer his Sentiments. That if his Majesty, in Consideration of your Services, and pursuant to his own merciful Disposition, would please to spare your Life, and only give order to put out both your Eyes; he humbly conceived, that by this Expedient, Justice might in some measure be satisfied, and all the World would applaud the *Lenity* of the Emperor, as well as the fair and generous Proceedings of those who have the Honour to be his Counsellors. That the Loss of your Eyes would be no Impediment to your bodily Strength, by which you might still be useful to his Majesty. That Blindness is an Addition to Courage, by concealing Dangers from us; that the Fear you had for your Eyes, was the greatest Difficulty in bringing over the Enemy's Fleet; and it would be sufficient for you to see by the Eyes of the Ministers, since the greatest Princes do no more.

This Proposal was received with the utmost Disapprobation by the whole Board. *Bolgolam*, the Admiral, could not preserve his Temper; but rising up in Fury, said, he wondered how the Secretary durst presume to give his Opinion for preserving the Life of a Traytor: That the Services you had performed, were, by all true Reasons of State, the great Aggravation of your Crimes; that you, who were able to extinguish the Fire, by discharge of Urine in her Majesty's Apartment (which he mentioned with Horror) might, at another time, raise an Inundation by the same Means, to drown the whole Palace; and the same Strength which enabled you to bring over the Enemy's Fleet, might serve, upon the first Discontent, to carry it back; that he had good Reasons to think you were a *Big-Endian* in your Heart; and as Treason begins in the Heart before it appears in Overt-Acts; so he accused you as a Traytor on that Account, and therefore insisted you should be put to death. The Treasurer was of the same Opinion; he shewed to what Streights his Majesty's Revenue was reduced by the Charge of maintaining you, which would soon grow insupportable: That the Secretary's Expedient of putting out your Eyes, was so far from being a Remedy against this Evil, that it would probably increase it; as it is manifest from the common Practice of blinding some Kind of Fowl, after which they fed the faster, and grew sooner fat: That his sacred Majesty, and the Council, who are your Judges, were in their own Consciences fully convinced of your Guilt; which was a sufficient Argument to condemn you to death, without the *formal Proofs required by the strict Letter of the Law*.

But his Imperial Majesty fully determined against capital Punishment, was graciously pleased to say, that since the Council thought the Loss of your Eyes too easy a Censure, some other may be inflicted hereafter. And your Friend the Secretary humbly desiring to be heard again, in Answer to what the Treasurer had objected concerning the great Charge his Majesty was at in maintaining you; said, that his Excellency, who had the sole Disposal of the Emperor's Revenue, might easily provide against this Evil, by gradually lessening your Establishment; by which, for want of sufficient Food, you would grow weak and faint, and lose your Appetite, and consequently decay and consume in a few Months; neither would the Stench of your Carcass be then so dangerous, when it should become more than half diminished; and immediately upon your Death, five or six Thousand of his Majesty's Subjects might, in two or three Days, cut your Flesh from your Bones, take it away by Cart-loads, and bury it in distant Parts to prevent Infection; leaving the Skeleton as a Monument of Admiration to Posterity.

Thus by the great Friendship of the Secretary, the whole Affair was compromised. It was strictly enjoined, that the Project of starving you by Degrees should be kept a Secret; but the Sentence of putting out your Eyes was entered on the Books; none dissenting except *Bolgolam* the Admiral, who being a Creature of the Empress, was perpetually instigated by her Majesty to insist upon your Death; she having born perpetual Malice against you, on Account of that infamous and illegal Method you took to extinguish the Fire in her Apartment.

In three Days your Friend the Secretary will be directed to come to your House, and read before you the Articles of Impeachment; and then to signify the great *Lenity* and Favour of his Majesty and Council; whereby you are only condemned to the Loss of your Eyes, which his Majesty doth not question you will gratefully and humbly submit to; and Twenty of his Majesty's Surgeons will attend, in order to see the Operation well performed, by discharging very sharp pointed Arrows into the Balls of your Eyes, as you lie on the Ground

I leave to your Prudence what Measures you will take; and to avoid Suspicion, I must immediately return in as private a Manner as I came.

His Lordship did so, and I remained alone, under many Doubts and Perplexities of Mind.

It was a Custom introduced by this Prince and his Ministry, (very different, as I have been assured, from the Practices of former Times) that after the Court had decreed any cruel Execution, either to gratify the Monarch's Resentment, or the Malice of a Favourite; the Emperor always made a Speech to his whole Council, expressing his *great Lenity and Tenderness, as Qualities known and confessed by all the World.* This Speech was immediately published through the Kingdom; nor did any thing terrify the People so much as those Encomiums on his Majesty's Mercy; because it was observed, that the more these Praises were enlarged and insisted on, the more *inhuman* was the Punishment, and the *Sufferer more innocent.* Yet, as to myself, I must confess, having never been designed for a Courtier, either by my Birth or Education, I was so ill a Judge of Things, that I could not discover the *Lenity* and Favour of this Sentence; but conceived it (perhaps erroneously) rather to be rigorous than gentle. I sometimes thought of standing my Tryal; for although I could not deny the Facts alledged in the several Articles, yet I hoped they would admit of some Extenuations. But having in my Life perused many State-Tryals, which I ever observed to terminate as the Judges thought fit to direct; I durst not rely on so dangerous a Decision, in so critical a Juncture, and against such powerful Enemies. Once I was strongly bent upon Resistance: For while I had Liberty, the whole Strength of that Empire could hardly subdue me, and I might easily with Stones pelt the Metropolis to Pieces: But I soon rejected that Project with Horror, by remembering the Oath I had made to the Emperor, the Favours I received from him, and the high Title of *Nardac* he conferred upon me. Neither had I so soon learned the Gratitude of Courtiers, to persuade myself that his Majesty's *present Severities acquitted me of all past Obligations.*

At last I fixed upon a Resolution, for which it is probable I may incur some Censure, and not unjustly; for I confess I owe the preserving my Eyes, and consequently my Liberty, to my own great Rashness and Want of Experience: Because if I had then known the Nature of Princes and Ministers, which I have since observed in many other Courts, and their Methods of treating Criminals less obnoxious than myself; I should with great Alacrity and Readiness have submitted to so *easy* a Punishment. But hurried on by the Precipitancy of Youth; and having his Imperial Majesty's Licence to pay my Attendance upon the Emperor of *Blefuscu*; I took this Opportunity, before the three Days were elapsed, to send a Letter to my Friend the Secretary, signifying my Resolution of setting out that Morning for *Blefuscu*, pursuant to the Leave I had got; and without waiting for an Answer, I went to that Side of the Island where our Fleet lay. I seized a large Man of War, tied a Cable to the Prow, and lifting up the Anchors, I stript myself, put my Cloaths (together with my Coverlet, which I carryed under my Arm) into the Vessel; and drawing it after me, between wading and swimming, arrived at the Royal Port of *Blefuscu*, where the People had long expected me[2]: They lent me two Guides to direct me to the Capital City, which is of the same Name; I held them in my Hands until I came within two Hundred Yards of the Gate; and desired them to signify my Arrival to one of the Secretaries, and let him know, I there waited his Majesty's Commands. I had an Answer in about an Hour, that his Majesty, attended by the Royal Family, and great Officers of the Court, was coming out to receive me. I advanced a Hundred Yards; the Emperor, and his Train, alighted from their Horses, the Empress and Ladies from their Coaches; and I did not perceive they were in any Fright or Concern. I lay on the Ground to kiss his Majesty's and the Empress's Hand. I told his Majesty, that I was come according to my Promise, and with the Licence of the Emperor my Master, to have the Honour of seeing so mighty a Monarch, and to offer him any Service in my Power, consistent with my Duty to my own Prince;

---

[2] Gulliver's departure corresponds to Bolingbroke's escape to France just prior to the trial. Oxford remained in England, and the charges against him were dropped two years later.

not mentioning a Word of my Disgrace, because I had hitherto
no regular Information of it, and might suppose myself wholly
ignorant of any such Design; neither could I reasonably conceive
that the Emperor would discover the Secret while I was out of his
Power: Wherein, however, it soon appeared I was deceived.

I shall not trouble the Reader with the particular Account of
my Reception at this Court, which was suitable to the Generosity
of so great a Prince; nor of the Difficulties I was in for want of a
House and Bed, being forced to lie on the Ground, wrapt up in
my Coverlet.

CHAPTER VIII

*The Author, by a lucky Accident, finds Means to leave
Blefuscu; and, after some Difficulties, returns safe to his
Native Country.*

Three Days after my Arrival, walking out of Curiosity to
the North-East Coast of the Island; I observed, about half a League
off, in the Sea, somewhat that looked like a Boat overturned: I
pulled off my Shoes and Stockings, and wading two or three
Hundred Yards, I found the Object to approach nearer by Force
of the Tide; and then plainly saw it to be a real Boat, which I supposed might, by some Tempest, have been driven from a Ship.
Whereupon I returned immediately towards the City, and desired
his Imperial Majesty to lend me Twenty of the tallest Vessels he
had left after the Loss of his Fleet, and three Thousand Seamen
under the Command of his Vice Admiral. This Fleet sailed round,
while I went back the shortest Way to the Coast where I first
discovered the Boat; I found the Tide had driven it still nearer; the
Seamen were all provided with Cordage, which I had beforehand
twisted to a sufficient Strength. When the Ships came up, I stript
myself, and waded till I came within an Hundred Yards of the
Boat; after which I was forced to swim till I got up to it. The
Seamen threw me the End of the Cord, which I fastened to a Hole

in the fore-part of the Boat, and the other End to a Man of War: But I found all my Labour to little Purpose; for being out of my Depth, I was not able to work. In this Necessity, I was forced to swim behind, and push the Boat forwards as often as I could, with one of my Hands; and the Tide favouring me, I advanced so far, that I could just hold up my Chin and feel the Ground. I rested two or three Minutes, and then gave the Boat another Shove, and so on till the Sea was no higher than my Arm-pits. And now the most laborious Part being over, I took out my other Cables which were stowed in one of the Ships, and fastening them first to the Boat, and then to nine of the Vessels which attended me; the Wind being favourable, the Seamen towed, and I shoved till we arrived within forty Yards of the Shore; and waiting till the Tide was out, I got dry to the Boat, and by the Assistance of two Thousand Men, with Ropes and Engines, I made a shift to turn it on its Bottom, and found it was but little damaged.

I shall not trouble the Reader with the Difficulties I was under by the Help of certain Paddles, which cost me ten Days making, to get my Boat to the Royal Port of *Blefuscu*; where a mighty Concourse of People appeared upon my Arrival, full of Wonder at the Sight of so prodigious a Vessel. I told the Emperor, that my good Fortune had thrown this Boat in my Way, to carry me to some Place from whence I might return into my native Country; and begged his Majesty's Orders for getting Materials to fit it up; together with his Licence to depart; which, after some kind Expostulations, he was pleased to grant.

I did very much wonder, in all this Time, not to have heard of any Express relating to me from our Emperor to the Court of *Blefuscu*. But I was afterwards given privately to understand, that his Imperial Majesty, never imagining I had the least Notice of his Designs, believed I was only gone to *Blefuscu* in Performance of my Promise, according to the Licence he had given me, which was well known at our Court; and would return in a few Days when that Ceremony was ended. But he was at last in pain at my long absence; and, after consulting with the Treasurer, and the rest of that Cabal; a Person of Quality was dispatched with the Copy of the Articles against me. This Envoy had Instructions to represent to the Monarch of *Blefuscu*, the great *Lenity* of his Master, who was content to punish me no further than with the Loss of my Eyes: That I had fled from Justice, and if I did not return in two Hours, I should be deprived of my Title of *Nardac*, and declared a Traitor. The Envoy further added; that in order to maintain the Peace and Amity between both Empires, his Master expected, that his Brother of *Blefuscu* would give Orders to have me sent back to *Lilliput*, bound Hand and Foot, to be punished as a Traitor.

The Emperor of *Blefuscu* having taken three Days to consult, returned an Answer consisting of many Civilities and Excuses. He said, that as for sending me bound, his Brother knew it was impossible; that although I had deprived him of his Fleet, yet he owed great Obligations to me for many good Offices I had done him in making the Peace. That however, both their Majesties would soon be made easy; for I had found a prodigious Vessel on the Shore, able to carry me on the Sea, which he had given order to fit up with my own Assistance and Direction; and he hoped in a few Weeks both Empires would be freed from so insupportable an Incumbrance.

With this Answer the Envoy returned to *Lilliput*, and the Monarch of *Blefuscu* related to me all that had past; offering me at the same time (but under the strictest Confidence) his gracious Protection, if I would continue in his Service; wherein although I believed him sincere, yet I resolved never more to put any Confidence in Princes or Ministers, where I could possibly avoid it; and therefore, with all due Acknowledgments for his favourable Intentions, I humbly begged to be excused. I told him, that since Fortune, whether good or evil, had thrown a Vessel in my Way; I was resolved to venture myself in the Ocean, rather than be an Occasion of Difference between two such mighty Monarchs. Neither did I find the Emperor at all displeased; and I discovered by a certain Accident, that he was very glad of my Resolution, and so were most of his Ministers.

These Considerations moved me to hasten my Departure somewhat sooner than I intended; to which the Court, impatient to have me gone, very readily contributed. Five hundred Workmen were employed to make two Sails to my Boat, according to my Directions, by quilting thirteen fold of their strongest Linnen together. I was at the Pains of making Ropes and Cables, by twisting ten, twenty or thirty of the thickest and strongest of theirs. A great Stone that I happened to find, after a long Search by the Seashore, served me for an Anchor. I had the Tallow of three hundred Cows for greasing my Boat, and other Uses. I was at incredible Pains in cutting down some of the largest Timber Trees for Oars and Masts, wherein I was, however, much assisted by his Majesty's Ship-Carpenters, who helped me in smoothing them, after I had done the rough Work.

In about a Month, when all was prepared, I sent to receive his Majesty's Commands, and to take my leave. The Emperor and Royal Family came out of the Palace; I lay down on my Face to kiss his Hand, which he very graciously gave me; so did the Empress, and young Princes of the Blood. His Majesty presented me with fifty Purses of two hundred *Sprugs* a-piece, together with his Picture at full length, which I put immediately into one of my Gloves, to keep it from being hurt. The Ceremonies at my Departure were too many to trouble the Reader with at this time.

I stored the Boat with the Carcasses of an hundred Oxen, and three hundred Sheep, with Bread and Drink proportionable, and as much Meat ready dressed as four hundred Cooks could provide. I took with me six Cows and two Bulls alive, with as many Yews and Rams, intending to carry them into my own Country and propagate the Breed. And to feed them on board, I had a good Bundle of Hay, and a Bag of Corn. I would gladly have taken a Dozen of the Natives; but this was a thing the Emperor would by no Means permit; and besides a diligent Search into my Pockets, his Majesty engaged my Honour not to carry away any of his Subjects, although with their own Consent and Desire.

Having thus prepared all things as well as I was able; I set sail on the Twenty-fourth Day of *September* 1701, at six in the Morning; and when I had gone about four Leagues to the Northward, the Wind being at South-East; at six in the Evening, I descryed a small Island about half a League to the North-West. I advanced forward, and cast Anchor on the Lee-side of the Island, which seemed to be uninhabited. I then took some Refreshment, and went to my Rest. I slept well, and as I conjecture at least six Hours; for I found the Day broke in two Hours after I awaked. It was a clear Night; I eat my Breakfast before the Sun was up; and heaving Anchor, the Wind being favourable, I steered the same Course that I had done the Day before, wherein I was directed by my Pocket-Compass. My Intention was to reach, if possible, one of those Islands, which I had reason to believe lay to the North-East of *Van Diemen's* Land. I discovered nothing all that Day; but upon the next, about three in the Afternoon, when I had by my Computation made Twenty-four Leagues from *Blefuscu*, I descryed a Sail steering to the South-East; my Course was due East. I hailed her, but could get no Answer; yet I found I gained upon her, for the Wind slackened. I made all the Sail I could, and in half an Hour she spyed me, then hung out her Antient,[1] and discharged a Gun. It is not easy to express the Joy I was in upon the unexpected Hope of once more seeing my beloved Country, and the dear Pledges I had left in it. The Ship slackned her Sails, and I came up with her between five and six in the Evening, *September* 26; but my Heart leapt within me to see her *English* Colours. I put my Cows and Sheep into my Coat-Pockets, and got on board with all my Cargo of Provisions. The Vessel was an *English* Merchant-man, returning from *Japan* by the *North* and *South Seas*; the Captain, Mr. *John Biddel* of *Deptford*, a very civil Man, and an excellent Sailor. We were now in the Latitude of 30 Degrees South; there were about fifty Men in the Ship; and here I met an old Comrade of mine, one *Peter Williams*, who gave me a good Character to the Captain. This Gentleman treated me with Kindness, and desired I would let him know what Place I came from last, and whither I was bound; which I did in few Words; but he thought I was raving, and that the Dangers I underwent had disturbed my Head; whereupon I took my black Cattle and Sheep out of my Pocket, which, after great Astonishment, clearly convinced him of my Veracity. I then shewed him the Gold given me by the Emperor of *Blefuscu*, together with his Majesty's Picture at full Length, and some other Rarities of that Country. I gave him two Purses of two Hundred *Sprugs* each, and promised, when we arrived in *England*, to make him a Present of a Cow and a Sheep big with Young.

I shall not trouble the Reader with a particular Account of this Voyage; which was very prosperous for the most Part. We arrived in the *Downs*[2] on the 13th of *April* 1702. I had only one Misfortune, that the Rats on board carried away one of my Sheep; I found her Bones in a Hole, picked clean from the Flesh. The rest of my Cattle I got safe on Shore, and set them a grazing in a Bowling-Green at *Greenwich*, where the Fineness of the Grass made them feed very heartily, although I had always feared the

[1] Hung out her flag.
[2] A roadstead on the coast of southeastern England.

contrary: Neither could I possibly have preserved them in so long a Voyage, if the Captain had not allowed me some of his best Bisket, which rubbed to Powder, and mingled with Water, was their constant Food. The short Time I continued in *England*, I made a considerable Profit by shewing my Cattle to many Persons of Quality, and others: And before I began my second Voyage, I sold them for six Hundred Pounds. Since my last Return, I find the Breed is considerably increased, especially the Sheep; which I hope will prove much to the Advantage of the Woollen Manufacture, by the Fineness of the Fleeces.

I stayed but two Months with my Wife and Family; for my insatiable Desire of seeing foreign Countries would suffer me to continue no longer. I left fifteen Hundred Pounds with my Wife, and fixed her in a good House at *Redriff*. My remaining Stock I carried with me, Part in Money, and Part in Goods, in Hopes to improve my Fortunes. My eldest Uncle, *John*, had left me an Estate in Land, near *Epping*, of about Thirty Pounds a Year; and I had a long Lease of the *Black-Bull* in *Fetter-Lane*, which yielded me as much more: So that I was not in any Danger of leaving my Family upon the Parish. My Son *Johnny*, named so after his Uncle, was at the Grammar School, and a towardly Child. My Daughter *Betty* (who is now well married, and has Children) was then at her Needle-Work. I took Leave of my Wife, and Boy and Girl, with Tears on both Sides; and went on board the *Adventure*, a Merchant-Ship of Three Hundred Tons, bound for *Surat*, Captain *John Nicholas* of *Liverpool*, Commander. But my Account of this Voyage must be referred to the second Part of my Travels.

The End of the First Part

PART II

A VOYAGE TO BROBDINGNAG

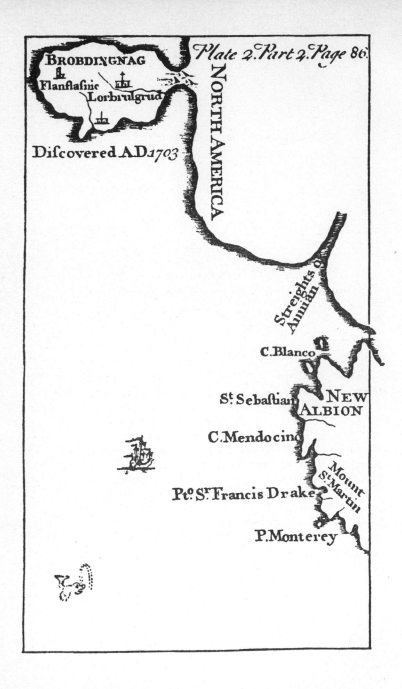

CHAPTER I

A great Storm described. The long Boat sent to fetch Water, the Author goes with it to discover the Country. He is left on Shoar, is seized by one of the Natives, and carried to a Farmer's House. His Reception there, with several Accidents that happened there. A Description of the Inhabitants.

Having been condemned by Nature and Fortune to an active and restless Life; in two Months after my Return, I again left my native Country, and took Shipping in the *Downs* on the 20th Day of *June* 1702, in the *Adventure*, Capt. *John Nicholas*, a *Cornish* Man, Commander, bound for *Surat*. We had a very prosperous Gale till we arrived at the *Cape* of *Good-hope*, where we landed for fresh Water; but discovering a Leak we unshipped our Goods, and wintered there; for the Captain falling sick of an Ague, we could not leave the *Cape* till the End of *March*. We then set sail, and had a good Voyage till we passed the *Streights* of *Madagascar*; but having got Northward of that Island, and to about five Degrees South Latitude, the Winds, which in those Seas are observed to blow a constant equal Gale between the North and West, from the Beginning of *December* to the Beginning of *May*, on the 19th of *April* began to blow with much greater Violence, and more Westerly than usual; continuing so for twenty Days together, during which time we were driven a little to the East of the *Molucca* Islands, and about three Degrees Northward of the Line, as our Captain found by an Observation he took the 2d of *May*, at which time the Wind ceased, and it was a perfect Calm, whereat I was not a little rejoyced. But he being a Man well experienced in the Navigation of those Seas, bid us all prepare against a Storm, which accordingly happened the Day following: For a Southern Wind, called the Southern *Monsoon*, began to set in.

Finding it was like to overblow, we took in our Spritsail, and

stood by to hand the Fore-sail; but making foul Weather, we
looked the Guns were all fast, and handed the Missen. The Ship
lay very broad off, so we thought it better spooning before the
Sea, than trying or hulling. We reeft the Foresail and set him, we
hawled aft the Foresheet; the Helm was hard a Weather. The
Ship wore bravely. We belay'd the Foredown-hall; but the Sail
was split, and we hawl'd down the Yard, and got the Sail into
the Ship, and unbound all the things clear of it. It was a very
fierce Storm; the Sea broke strange and dangerous. We hawl'd off
upon the Lanniard of the Wipstaff, and helped the Man at Helm.
We would not get down our Top-Mast, but let all stand, because
she scudded before the Sea very well, and we knew that the Top-
Mast being aloft, the Ship was the wholesomer, and made better
way through the Sea, seeing we had Sea room. When the Storm
was over, we set Fore-sail and Main-sail, and brought the Ship to.
Then we set the Missen, Maintop-Sail and the Foretop-Sail. Our
Course was East North-east, the Wind was at South-west. We got
the Star-board tacks aboard, we cast off our Weather-braces and
Lifts; we set in the Lee-braces, and hawl'd forward by the Weather-
bowlings, and hawl'd them tight, and belayed them, and hawl'd
over the Missen Tack to Windward, and kept her full and by
as near as she would lye.[1]

During this Storm, which was followed by a strong Wind West
South-west, we were carried by my Computation about five hundred
Leagues to the East, so that the oldest Sailor on Board could not
tell in what part of the World we were. Our Provisions held out
well, our Ship was staunch, and our Crew all in good Health; but
we lay in the utmost Distress for Water. We thought it best to
hold on the same Course rather than turn more Northerly, which
might have brought us to the North-west Parts of great *Tartary*,
and into the frozen Sea.

On the 16*th* Day of *June* 1703, a Boy on the Top-mast discovered Land. On the 17*th* we came in full View of a great Island or
Continent, (for we knew not whether) on the South-side whereof
was a small Neck of Land jutting out into the Sea, and a Creek too
shallow to hold a Ship of above one hundred Tuns. We cast Anchor

---

[1] Gulliver, the "experienced" sailor, has fallen into the worst nautical
jargon. The paragraph, taken almost verbatim from Samuel Sturmy's
Mariners Magazine (1669), is, of course, Swift's hit at specialist language.
See p. 142 for another such parody.

within a League of this Creek, and our Captain sent a dozen of his Men well armed in the Long Boat, with Vessels for Water if any could be found. I desired his leave to go with them, that I might see the Country, and make what Discoveries I could. When we came to Land we saw no River or Spring, nor any Sign of Inhabitants. Our Men therefore wandered on the Shore to find out some fresh Water near the Sea, and I walked alone about a Mile on the other Side, where I observed the Country all barren and rocky. I now began to be weary, and seeing nothing to entertain my Curiosity, I returned gently down towards the Creek; and the Sea being full in my View, I saw our Men already got into the Boat, and rowing for Life to the Ship. I was going to hollow after them, although it had been to little purpose, when I observed a huge Creature walking after them in the Sea, as fast as he could: He walked not much deeper than his Knees, and took prodigious strides: But our Men had the start of him half a League, and the Sea thereabouts being full of sharp pointed Rocks, the Monster was not able to overtake the Boat. This I was afterwards told, for I durst not stay to see the Issue of that Adventure; but run as fast as I could the Way I first went; and then climbed up a steep Hill, which gave me some Prospect of the Country. I found it fully cultivated; but that which first surprized me was the Length of the Grass, which in those Grounds that seemed to be kept for Hay, was above twenty Foot high.

I fell into a high Road, for so I took it to be, although it served to the Inhabitants only as a foot Path through a Field of Barley. Here I walked on for sometime, but could see little on either Side, it being now near Harvest, and the Corn rising at least forty Foot. I was an Hour walking to the end of this Field; which was fenced in with a Hedge of at least one hundred and twenty Foot high, and the Trees so lofty that I could make no Computation of their Altitude. There was a Stile to pass from this Field into the next: It had four Steps, and a Stone to cross over when you came to the uppermost. It was impossible for me to climb this Stile, because every Step was six Foot high, and the upper Stone above twenty. I was endeavouring to find some Gap in the Hedge; when I discovered one of the Inhabitants in the next Field advancing towards the Stile, of the same Size with him whom I saw in the Sea pursuing our Boat. He appeared as Tall as an ordinary Spire-steeple; and took about ten Yards at every Stride, as near as I could guess. I was struck with the utmost Fear and Astonishment, and ran to hide my self in the Corn, from whence I saw him at the Top of the Stile, looking back into the next Field on the right Hand; and heard him call in a Voice many Degrees louder than a speaking Trumpet; but the Noise was so High in the Air, that at first I certainly thought it was Thunder. Whereupon seven Monsters like himself came towards him with Reaping-Hooks in their Hands, each Hook about the largeness of six Scythes. These People were not so well clad as the first, whose Servants or Labourers they seemed to be. For, upon some Words he spoke, they went to reap the Corn in the Field where I lay. I kept from them at as great a Distance as I could, but was forced to move with extream Difficulty; for the Stalks of the Corn were sometimes not above a Foot distant, so that I could hardly squeeze my Body betwixt them. However, I made a shift to go forward till I came to a part of the Field where the Corn had been laid by the Rain and Wind: Here it was impossible for me to advance a step; for the Stalks were so interwoven that I could not creep through, and the Beards of the fallen Ears so strong and pointed, that they pierced through my Cloaths into my Flesh. At the same time I heard the Reapers not above an hundred Yards behind me. Being quite dispirited with Toil, and wholly overcome by Grief and Despair, I lay down between two Ridges, and heartily wished I might there end my Days. I bemoaned my desolate Widow, and Fatherless Children: I lamented my own Folly and Wilfulness in attempting a second Voyage against the Advice of all my Friends and Relations. In this terrible Agitation of Mind I could not forbear thinking of *Lilliput*, whose Inhabitants looked upon me as the greatest Prodigy that ever appeared in the World; where I was able to draw an Imperial Fleet in my Hand, and perform those other Actions which will be recorded for ever in the Chronicles of that Empire, while Posterity shall hardly believe them, although attested by Millions. I reflected what a Mortification it must prove to me to appear as inconsiderable in this Nation, as one single *Lilliputian* would be among us. But, this I conceived was to be the least of my Misfortunes: For, as human Creatures are observed to be more Savage and cruel in Proportion to their Bulk; what could I expect but to be a Morsel in the Mouth of the first among these enormous Barbarians who should happen to seize me? Undoubtedly Philosophers are in the Right when they tell us, that nothing is great or little otherwise than by Comparison: It might have pleased Fortune to let the *Lilliputians* find some Nation, where the People were as diminutive with respect to them, as they were to me. And who knows but that even this prodigious Race of Mortals might be equally overmatched in some distant Part of the World, whereof we have yet no Discovery?

Scared and confounded as I was, I could not forbear going on with these Reflections; when one of the Reapers approaching within ten Yards of the Ridge where I lay, made me apprehend that with the next Step I should be squashed to Death under his Foot, or cut in two with his Reaping Hook. And therefore when he was again about to move, I screamed as loud as Fear could make me. Whereupon the huge Creature trod short, and looking round about under him for some time, at last espied me as I lay on the Ground. He considered a while with the Caution of one who endeavours to lay hold on a small dangerous Animal in such a Manner that it shall not be able either to scratch or to bite him; as I my self have sometimes done with a *Weasel* in *England*. At length he ventured to take me up behind by the middle between his Fore-finger and Thumb, and brought me within three Yards of his Eyes, that he might behold my Shape more perfectly. I guessed his Meaning; and my good Fortune gave me so much Presence of Mind, that I resolved not to struggle in the least as he held me in the Air above sixty Foot from the Ground; although he grievously pinched my Sides, for fear I should slip through his Fingers. All I ventured was to raise my Eyes towards the Sun, and place my Hands together in a supplicating Posture, and to speak some Words in an humble melancholy Tone, suitable to the Condition I then was in. For, I apprehended every Moment that he would dash me against the Ground, as we usually do any little hateful Animal which we have a Mind to destroy. But my good Star would have it, that he appeared pleased with my Voice and Gestures, and began to look upon me as a Curiosity; much wondering to hear me pronounce articulate Words, although he could not understand them. In the mean time I was not able to forbear Groaning and shedding Tears, and turning my Head towards my Sides; letting him know, as well as I could, how cruelly I was hurt by the Pressure of his Thumb and Finger. He seemed to apprehend my Meaning; for, lifting up the Lappet of his Coat, he put me gently into it, and immediately ran along with me to his Master, who was a substantial Farmer, and the same Person I had first seen in the Field.

The Farmer having (as I supposed by their Talk) received such an Account of me as his Servant could give him, took a piece of a small Straw, about the Size of a walking Staff, and therewith lifted up the Lappets of my Coat; which it seems he thought to be some kind of Covering that Nature had given me. He blew my Hairs aside to take a better View of my Face. He called his Hinds about him, and asked them (as I afterwards learned) whether they had ever seen in the Fields any little Creature that resembled me. He then placed me softly on the Ground upon all four; but I got immediately up, and walked slowly backwards and forwards, to let those People see I had no Intent to run away. They all sate down in a Circle about me, the better to observe my Motions. I pulled off my Hat, and made a low Bow towards the Farmer: I fell on my Knees, and lifted up my Hands and Eyes, and spoke several Words as loud as I could: I took a Purse of Gold out of my Pocket, and humbly presented it to him. He received it on the Palm of his Hand, then applied it close to his Eye, to see what it was, and afterwards turned it several times with the Point of a Pin, (which he took out of his Sleeve,) but could make nothing of it. Whereupon I made a Sign that he should place his Hand on the Ground: I then took the Purse, and opening it, poured all the Gold into his Palm. There were six *Spanish*-Pieces of four Pistoles each, besides twenty or thirty smaller Coins. I saw him wet the Tip of his little Finger upon his Tongue, and take up one of my largest Pieces, and then another; but he seemed to be wholly ignorant what they were. He made me a Sign to put them again into my Purse, and the Purse again into my Pocket; which after offering to him several times, I thought it best to do.

The Farmer by this time was convinced I must be a rational Creature. He spoke often to me, but the Sound of his Voice pierced my Ears like that of a Water-Mill; yet his Words were articulate enough. I answered as loud as I could in several Languages; and he often laid his Ear within two Yards of me, but all in vain, for we were wholly unintelligible to each other. He then sent his Servants to their Work, and taking his Handkerchief out of his Pocket, he doubled and spread it on his Hand, which he placed flat on the Ground with the Palm upwards, making me a Sign to step into it, as I could easily do, for it was not above a Foot in thickness. I thought it my part to obey; and for fear of falling, laid my self at full Length upon the Handkerchief, with the Remainder of which he lapped me up to the Head for further Security; and in this Manner carried me home to his House. There he called his Wife, and shewed me to her; but she screamed and ran back as Women in *England* do at the Sight of a Toad or a Spider. However, when she had a while seen my Behaviour, and how well I observed the Signs her Husband made, she was soon reconciled, and by Degrees grew extreamly tender of me.

It was about twelve at Noon, and a Servant brought in Dinner. It was only one substantial Dish of Meat (fit for the plain Condition of an Husband-Man) in a Dish of about four and twenty Foot Diameter. The Company were the Farmer and Wife, three Children, and an old Grandmother: When they were sat down, the Farmer placed me at some Distance from him on the Table, which was thirty Foot high from the Floor. I was in a terrible Fright, and kept as far as I could from the Edge, for fear of falling. The Wife minced a bit of Meat, then crumbled some Bread on a Trencher, and placed it before me. I made her a low Bow, took out my Knife and Fork, and fell to eat; which gave them exceeding Delight. The Mistress sent her Maid for a small Dram-cup, which held about two Gallons; and filled it with Drink: I took up the Vessel with much difficulty in both Hands, and in a most respectful Manner drank to her Lady-ship's Health, expressing the Words as loud as I could in *English*; which made the Company laugh so heartily, that I was almost deafened with the Noise. This Liquour tasted like a small Cyder, and was not unpleasant. Then the Master made me a Sign to come to his Trencher side; but as I walked on the Table, being in great surprize all the time, as the indulgent Reader will easily conceive and excuse, I happened to stumble against a Crust, and fell flat on my Face, but received no hurt. I got up immediately, and observing the good People to be in much Concern, I took my Hat (which I held under my Arm out of good Manners) and waving it over my Head, made three Huzza's, to shew I had got no Mischief by the Fall. But advancing forwards toward my Master (as I shall henceforth call him) his youngest Son who sate next him, an arch Boy of about ten Years old, took me up by the Legs, and held me so high in the Air, that I trembled every Limb; but his Father snatched me from him; and at the same time gave him such a Box on the left Ear, as would have felled an *European* Troop of Horse to the Earth; ordering him to be taken from the Table. But, being afraid the Boy might owe me a Spight; and well remembring how mischievous all Children among us naturally are to Sparrows, Rabbits, young Kittens, and Puppy-Dogs; I fell on my Knees, and pointing to the Boy, made my Master understand, as well as I could, that I desired his Son might be pardoned. The Father complied, and the Lad took his Seat again; whereupon I went to him and kissed his Hand, which my Master took, and made him stroak me gently with it.

In the Midst of Dinner my Mistress's favourite Cat leapt into her Lap. I heard a Noise behind me like that of a Dozen Stocking-Weavers at work; and turning my Head, I found it proceeded from the Purring of this Animal, who seemed to be three Times larger than an Ox, as I computed by the View of her Head, and one of her Paws, while her Mistress was feeding and stroaking her. The Fierceness of this Creature's Countenance altogether discomposed me; although I stood at the further End of the Table, above fifty Foot off; and although my Mistress held her fast for fear she might give a Spring, and seize me in her Talons. But it happened there was no Danger; for the Cat took not the least Notice of me when my Master placed me within three Yards of her. And as I have been always told, and found true by Experience in my Travels, that flying, or discovering Fear before a fierce Animal, is a certain Way to make it pursue or attack you; so I resolved in this dangerous Juncture to shew no Manner of Concern. I walked with Intrepidity five or six Times before the very Head of the Cat, and came within half a Yard of her; whereupon she drew her self back, as if she were more afraid of me: I had less Apprehension concerning the Dogs, whereof three or four came into the Room, as it is usual in Farmers Houses; one of which was a Mastiff equal in Bulk to four Elephants, and a Grey-hound somewhat taller than the Mastiff, but not so large.

When Dinner was almost done, the Nurse came in with a Child of a Year old in her Arms; who immediately spyed me, and began a Squall that you might have heard from *London-Bridge* to *Chelsea*; after the usual Oratory of Infants, to get me for a Play-thing. The Mother out of pure Indulgence took me up, and put me towards the Child, who presently seized me by the Middle, and got my Head in his Mouth, where I roared so loud that the Urchin was frighted, and let me drop; and I should infallibly have broke my

Neck, if the Mother had not held her Apron under me. The Nurse to quiet her Babe made use of a Rattle, which was a Kind of hollow Vessel filled with great Stones, and fastned by a Cable to the Child's Waist: But all in vain, so that she was forced to apply the last Remedy by giving it suck. I must confess no Object ever disgusted me so much as the Sight of her monstrous Breast, which I cannot tell what to compare with, so as to give the curious Reader an Idea of its Bulk, Shape and Colour. It stood prominent six Foot, and could not be less than sixteen in Circumference. The Nipple was about half the Bigness of my Head, and the Hue both of that and the Dug so varified with Spots, Pimples and Freckles, that nothing could appear more nauseous: For I had a near Sight of her, she sitting down the more conveniently to give Suck, and I standing on the Table. This made me reflect upon the fair Skins of our *English* Ladies, who appear so beautiful to us, only because they are of our own Size, and their Defects not to be seen but through a magnifying Glass, where we find by Experiment that the smoothest and whitest Skins look rough and coarse, and ill coloured.

I remember when I was at *Lilliput*, the Complexions of those diminutive People appeared to me the fairest in the World: And talking upon this Subject with a Person of Learning there, who was an intimate Friend of mine; he said, that my Face appeared much fairer and smoother when he looked on me from the Ground, than it did upon a nearer View when I took him up in my Hand, and brought him close; which he confessed was at first a very shocking Sight. He said, he could discover great Holes in my Skin; that the Stumps of my Beard were ten Times stronger than the Bristles of a Boar; and my Complexion made up of several Colours altogether disagreeable: Although I must beg Leave to say for my self, that I am as fair as most of my Sex and Country, and very little Sunburnt by all my Travels. On the other Side, discoursing of the Ladies in that Emperor's Court, he used to tell me, one had Freckles, another too wide a Mouth, a third too large a Nose; nothing of which I was able to distinguish. I confess this Reflection was obvious enough; which, however, I could not forbear, lest the Reader might think those vast Creatures were actually deformed: For I must do them Justice to say they are a comely Race of People; and particularly the Features of my Master's Countenance, although he were but a Farmer, when I beheld him from the Height of sixty Foot, appeared very well proportioned.

When Dinner was done, my Master went out to his Labourers; and as I could discover by his Voice and Gesture, gave his Wife a strict Charge to take Care of me. I was very much tired and disposed to sleep, which my Mistress perceiving, she put me on her own Bed, and covered me with a clean white Handkerchief, but larger and coarser than the Main Sail of a Man of War.

I slept about two Hours, and dreamed I was at home with my Wife and Children, which aggravated my Sorrows when I awaked and found my self alone in a vast Room, between two and three Hundred Foot wide, and above two Hundred high; lying in a Bed twenty Yards wide. My Mistress was gone about her houshold Affairs, and had locked me in. The Bed was eight Yards from the Floor. Some natural Necessities required me to get down: I durst not presume to call, and if I had, it would have been in vain with such a Voice as mine at so great a Distance from the Room where I lay, to the Kitchen where the Family kept. While I was under these Circumstances, two Rats crept up the Curtains, and ran smelling backwards and forwards on the Bed: One of them came up almost to my Face; whereupon I rose in a Fright, and drew out my Hanger[2] to defend my self. These horrible Animals had the Boldness to attack me on both Sides, and one of them held his Fore-feet at my Collar; but I had the good Fortune to rip up his Belly before he could do me any Mischief. He fell down at my Feet; and the other seeing the Fate of his Comrade, made his Escape, but not without one good Wound on the Back, which I gave him as he fled, and made the Blood run trickling from him. After this Exploit I walked gently to and fro on the Bed, to recover my Breath and Loss of Spirits. These Creatures were of the Size of a large Mastiff, but infinitely more nimble and fierce; so that if I had taken off my Belt before I went to sleep, I must have infallibly been torn to Pieces and devoured. I measured the Tail of the dead Rat, and found it to be two Yards long, wanting an Inch; but it went against my Stomach to drag the Carcass off the Bed, where it lay still bleeding; I observed it had yet some Life, but with a strong Slash cross the Neck, I thoroughly dispatched it.

Soon after, my Mistress came into the Room, who seeing me all bloody, ran and took me up in her Hand. I pointed to the dead *Rat*, smiling and making other Signs to shew I was not hurt; whereat she was extremely rejoyced, calling the Maid to take up

---

[2] A short sword attached to his belt.

the dead *Rat* with a Pair of Tongs, and throw it out of the Window. Then she set me on a Table, where I shewed her my Hanger all bloody, and wiping it on the Lappet of my Coat, returned it to the Scabbard. I was pressed to do more than one Thing, which another could not do for me; and therefore endeavoured to make my Mistress understand that I desired to be set down on the Floor; which after she had done, my Bashfulness would not suffer me to express my self farther than by pointing to the Door, and bowing several Times. The good Woman with much Difficulty at last perceived what I would be at; and taking me up again in her Hand, walked into the Garden where she set me down. I went on one Side about two Hundred Yards; and beckoning to her not to look or follow me, I hid my self between two Leaves of Sorrel, and there discharged the Necessities of Nature.

I hope, the gentle Reader will excuse me for dwelling on these and the like Particulars; which however insignificant they may appear to grovelling vulgar Minds, yet will certainly help a Philosopher to enlarge his Thoughts and Imagination, and apply them to the Benefit of publick as well as private Life; which was my sole Design in presenting this and other Accounts of my Travels to the World; wherein I have been chiefly studious of Truth, without affecting any Ornaments of Learning, or of Style. But the whole Scene of this Voyage made so strong an Impression on my Mind, and is so deeply fixed in my Memory, that in committing it to Paper, I did not omit one material Circumstance: However, upon a strict Review, I blotted out several Passages of less Moment which were in my first Copy, for fear of being censured as tedious and trifling, whereof Travellers are often, perhaps not without Justice, accused.

CHAPTER II

A Description of the Farmer's Daughter. The Author carried to a Market-Town, and then to the Metropolis. The Particulars of his Journey.

My Mistress had a Daughter of nine Years old, a Child of towardly Parts for her Age, very dextrous at her Needle, and skilful in dressing her Baby.[1] Her Mother and she contrived to fit up the Baby's Cradle for me against Night: The Cradle was put into a small Drawer of a Cabinet, and the Drawer placed upon a hanging Shelf for fear of the *Rats*. This was my Bed all the Time I stayed with those People, although made more convenient by Degrees, as I began to learn their Language, and make my Wants known. This young Girl was so handy, that after I had once or twice pulled off my Cloaths before her, she was able to dress and undress me, although I never gave her that Trouble when she would let me do either my self. She made me seven Shirts, and some other Linnen of as fine Cloth as could be got, which indeed was coarser than Sackcloth; and these she constantly washed for me with her own Hands. She was likewise my School-Mistress to teach me the Language: When I pointed to any thing, she told me the Name of it in her own Tongue, so that in a few Days I was able to call for whatever I had a mind to. She was very good natured, and not above forty Foot high, being little for her Age. She gave me the Name of *Grildrig*, which the Family took up, and afterwards the whole Kingdom. The Word imports what the *Latins* call *Nanunculus*, the *Italians* *Homunceletino*,[2] and the *English* *Mannikin*. To her I chiefly owe my Preservation in that Country: We never parted

---

[1] Her doll.

[2] No such Latin or Italian words exist. Swift may be undercutting his hero's pretenses as a linguist (see p. 135, n. 5 for a more elaborate instance of this).

74

while I was there; I called her my *Glumdalclitch*, or little Nurse: And I should be guilty of great Ingratitude if I omitted this honourable Mention of her Care and Affection towards me, which I heartily wish it lay in my Power to requite as she deserves, instead of being the innocent but unhappy Instrument of her Disgrace, as I have too much Reason to fear.

It now began to be known and talked of in the Neighbourhood, that my Master had found a strange Animal in the Fields, about the Bigness of a *Splacknuck*, but exactly shaped in every Part like a human Creature; which it likewise imitated in all its Actions; seemed to speak in a little Language of its own, had already learned several Words of theirs, went erect upon two Legs, was tame and gentle, would come when it was called, do whatever it was bid, had the finest Limbs in the World, and a Complexion fairer than a Nobleman's Daughter of three Years old. Another Farmer who lived hard by, and was a particular Friend of my Master, came on a Visit on Purpose to enquire into the Truth of this Story. I was immediately produced, and placed upon a Table; where I walked as I was commanded, drew my Hanger, put it up again, made my Reverence to my Master's Guest, asked him in his own Language how he did, and told him he was welcome; just as my little Nurse had instructed me. This Man, who was old and dimsighted, put on his Spectacles to behold me better, at which I could not forbear laughing very heartily; for his Eyes appeared like the Full-Moon shining into a Chamber at two Windows. Our People, who discovered the Cause of my Mirth, bore me Company in Laughing; at which the old Fellow was Fool enough to be angry and out of Countenance. He had the Character of a great Miser; and to my Misfortune he well deserved it by the cursed Advice he gave my Master, to shew me as a Sight upon a Market-Day in the next Town, which was half an Hour's Riding, about two and twenty Miles from our House. I guessed there was some Mischief contriving, when I observed my Master and his Friend whispering long together, sometimes pointing at me; and my Fears made me fancy that I overheard and understood some of their Words. But, the next Morning *Glumdalclitch* my little Nurse told me the whole Matter, which she had cunningly picked out from her Mother. The poor Girl laid me on her Bosom, and fell a weeping with Shame and Grief. She apprehended some Mischief would happen to me from rude vulgar Folks, who might squeeze me to Death, or break one of my Limbs by taking me in their Hands. She had also observed how modest I was in my Nature, how nicely I regarded my Honour; and what an Indignity I should conceive it to be exposed for Money as a publick Spectacle to the meanest of the People.[3] She said, her *Papa* and *Mamma* had promised that *Grildrig* should be hers; but now she found they meant to serve her as they did last Year, when they pretended to give her a Lamb; and yet, as soon as it was fat, sold it to a Butcher. For my own Part, I may truly affirm that I was less concerned than my Nurse. I had a strong Hope which never left me, that I should one Day recover my Liberty; and as to the Ignominy of being carried about for a Monster, I considered my self to be a perfect Stranger in the Country; and that such a Misfortune could never be charged upon me as a Reproach if ever I should return to *England*; since the King of *Great Britain* himself, in my Condition, must have undergone the same Distress.

My Master, pursuant to the Advice of his Friend, carried me in a Box the next Market-Day to the neighbouring Town; and took along with him his little Daughter my Nurse upon a Pillion behind me. The Box was close on every Side, with a little Door for me to go in and out, and a few Gimlet-holes to let in Air. The Girl had been so careful to put the Quilt of her Baby's Bed into it, for me to lye down on. However, I was terribly shaken and discomposed in this Journey, although it were but of half an Hour. For the Horse went about forty Foot at every Step; and trotted so high, that the Agitation was equal to the rising and falling of a Ship in a great Storm, but much more frequent: Our Journey was somewhat further than from *London* to St. *Albans*. My Master alighted at an Inn which he used to frequent; and after consulting a while with the Inn-keeper, and making some necessary Preparations, he hired the *Grultrud*, or Cryer, to give Notice through the Town, of a strange Creature to be seen at the Sign of the Green *Eagle*, not so big as a *Splacknuck*, (an Animal in that Country very finely shaped, about six Foot long) and in every Part of the Body resembling an human Creature; could speak several Words, and perform an Hundred diverting Tricks.

I was placed upon a Table in the largest Room of the Inn,

[3] In Swift's time, it was quite common to display abnormal creatures, both human and animal, "for Money as a publick Spectacle." Gulliver's hardships are thus firmly rooted in an eighteenth-century diversion.

which might be near three Hundred Foot square. My little Nurse
stood on a low Stool close to the Table, to take care of me, and
direct what I should do. My Master, to avoid a Croud, would suffer
only Thirty People at a Time to see me. I walked about on the
Table as the Girl commanded; she asked me Questions as far as
she knew my Understanding of the Language reached, and I answered them as loud as I could. I turned about several Times to
the Company, paid my humble Respects, said they were welcome;
and used some other Speeches I had been taught. I took up a
Thimble filled with Liquor, which *Glumdalclitch* had given me for
a Cup, and drank their Health. I drew out my Hanger, and
flourished with it after the Manner of Fencers in *England*. My
Nurse gave me Part of a Straw, which I exercised as a Pike, having
learned the Art in my Youth. I was that Day shewn to twelve Sets
of Company; and as often forced to go over again with the same
Fopperies, till I was half dead with Weariness and Vexation. For,
those who had seen me, made such wonderful Reports, that the
People were ready to break down the Doors to come in. My Master
for his own Interest would not suffer any one to touch me, except
my Nurse; and, to prevent Danger, Benches were set round the
Table at such a Distance, as put me out of every Body's Reach.
However, an unlucky School-Boy aimed a Hazel-Nut directly at my
Head, which very narrowly missed me; otherwise, it came with so
much Violence, that it would have infallibly knocked out my Brains;
for it was almost as large as a small Pumpion[4]: But I had the Satisfaction to see the young Rogue well beaten, and turned out of the
Room.

My Master gave publick Notice, that he would shew me again
the next Market-Day: And in the mean time, he prepared a more
convenient Vehicle for me, which he had Reason enough to do;
for I was so tired with my first Journey, and with entertaining Company eight Hours together, that I could hardly stand upon my
Legs, or speak a Word. It was at least three Days before I recovered
my Strength; and that I might have no rest at home, all the neighbouring Gentlemen from an Hundred Miles round, hearing of my
Fame, came to see me at my Master's own House. There could not
be fewer than thirty Persons with their Wives and Children; (for
the Country is very populous;) and my Master demanded the Rate

4 Pumpkin.

of a full Room whenever he shewed me at Home although it were
only to a single Family. So that for some time I had but little
Ease every Day of the Week, (except *Wednesday*, which is their
Sabbath) although I were not carried to the Town.

My Master finding how profitable I was like to be, resolved to
carry me to the most considerable Cities of the Kingdom. Having
therefore provided himself with all things necessary for a long
Journey, and settled his Affairs at Home; he took Leave of his Wife;
and upon the 17*th* of *August* 1703, about two Months after my
Arrival, we set out for the Metropolis, situated near the Middle of
that Empire, and about three Thousand Miles distance from our
House: My Master made his Daughter *Glumdalclitch* ride behind
him. She carried me on her Lap in a Box tied about her Waist.
The Girl had lined it on all Sides with the softest Cloth she could
get, well quilted underneath; furnished it with her Baby's Bed,
provided me with Linnen and other Necessaries; and made every
thing as convenient as she could. We had no other Company but
a Boy of the House, who rode after us with the Luggage.

My Master's Design was to shew me in all the Towns by the
Way, and to step out of the Road for Fifty or an Hundred Miles,
to any Village or Person of Quality's House where he might expect
Custom. We made easy Journies of not above seven or eight Score
Miles a Day: For *Glumdalclitch*, on Purpose to spare me, complained she was tired with the trotting of the Horse. She often
took me out of my Box at my own Desire, to give me Air, and
shew me the Country; but always held me fast by Leading-strings.
We passed over five or six Rivers many Degrees broader and deeper
than the *Nile* or the *Ganges*; and there was hardly a Rivulet so
small as the *Thames* at *London-Bridge*. We were ten Weeks in
our Journey; and I was shewn in Eighteen large Towns, besides
many Villages and private Families.

On the 26th Day of *October*, we arrived at the Metropolis, called
in their Language *Lorbrulgrud*, or *Pride of the Universe*. My Master
took a Lodging in the principal Street of the City, not far from the
Royal Palace; and put out Bills in the usual Form, containing an
exact Description of my Person and Parts. He hired a large Room
between three and four Hundred Foot wide. He provided a Table
sixty Foot in Diameter, upon which I was to act my Part; and pal-
lisadoed it round three Foot from the Edge, and as many high, to
prevent my falling over. I was shewn ten Times a Day to the Won-

der and Satisfaction of all People. I could now speak the Language tolerably well; and perfectly understood every Word that was spoken to me. Besides, I had learned their Alphabet, and could make a shift to explain a Sentence here and there; for *Glumdalclitch* had been my Instructer while we were at home, and at leisure Hours during our Journey. She carried a little Book in her Pocket, not much larger than a *Sanson's Atlas*; it was a common Treatise for the use of young Girls, giving a short Account of their Religion; out of this she taught me my Letters, and interpreted the Words.

CHAPTER III

The Author sent for to Court. The Queen buys him of his Master the Farmer, and presents him to the King. He disputes with his Majesty's great Scholars. An Apartment at Court provided for the Author. He is in high Favour with the Queen. He stands up for the Honour of his own Country. His Quarrels with the Queen's Dwarf.

The frequent Labours I underwent every Day, made in a few Weeks a very considerable Change in my Health: The more my Master got by me, the more unsatiable he grew. I had quite lost my Stomach, and was almost reduced to a Skeleton. The Farmer observed it; and concluding I soon must die, resolved to make as good a Hand of me as he could. While he was thus reasoning and resolving with himself; a *Slardral*, or Gentleman Usher, came from Court, commanding my Master to bring me immediately thither for the Diversion of the Queen and her Ladies. Some of the latter had already been to see me; and reported strange Things of my Beauty, Behaviour, and good Sense. Her Majesty and those who attended her, were beyond Measure delighted with my Demeanor. I fell on my Knees, and begged the Honour of kissing her Imperial Foot; but this Gracious Princess held out her little Finger towards me (after I was set on a table) which I embraced in both my Arms, and put the Tip of it, with the utmost Respect, to my Lip. She made me some general Questions about my Country and my Travels, which I answered as distinctly and in as few Words as I could. She asked, whether I would be content to live at Court. I bowed down to the Board of the Table, and humbly answered, that I was my Master's Slave; but if I were at my own Disposal, I should be proud to devote my Life to her Majesty's Service. She then asked my Master whether he were willing to sell me at a good Price. He, who apprehended I could not live a Month, was ready enough to part with me; and demanded a Thousand Pieces of Gold; which were ordered him on the Spot, each Piece being about the Bigness of eight Hundred Moydores: But, allowing for the Proportion of all Things between that Country and *Europe*, and the high Price of Gold among them; was hardly so great a Sum as a Thousand Guineas would be in *England*. I then said to the Queen; since I was now her Majesty's most humble Creature and Vassal, I must beg the Favour, that *Glumdalclitch*, who had always tended me with so much Care and Kindness, and understood to do it so well, might be admitted into her Service, and continue to be my Nurse and Instructor. Her Majesty agreed to my Petition; and easily got the Farmer's Consent, who was glad enough to have his Daughter preferred at Court: And the poor Girl herself was not able to hide her Joy. My late Master withdrew, bidding me farewell, and saying he had left me in a good Service; to which I replyed not a Word, only making him a slight Bow.

The Queen observed my Coldness; and when the Farmer was gone out of the Apartment, asked me the Reason. I made bold to tell her Majesty, that I owed no other Obligation to my late Master, than his not dashing out the Brains of a poor harmless Creature found by Chance in his Field; which Obligation was amply recompenced by the Gain he had made in shewing me through half the Kingdom, and the Price he had now sold me for. That the Life I had since led, was laborious enough to kill an Animal of ten Times my Strength. That my Health was much impaired by the continual Drudgery of entertaining the Rabble every Hour of the Day; and that if my Master had not thought my Life in Danger, her Majesty perhaps would not have got so cheap a Bargain. But as I was out of all fear of being ill treated under the Protection of so great and good an Empress, the Ornament of Nature, the Darling of the World, the Delight of her Subjects, the Phoenix of the Creation; so, I hoped my late Master's Apprehensions would appear to be groundless; for I already found my Spirits to revive by the Influence of her most August Presence.

This was the Sum of my Speech, delivered with great Improprieties and Hesitation; the latter Part was altogether framed in the Style peculiar to that People, whereof I learned some Phrases from *Glumdalclitch*, while she was carrying me to Court.

The Queen giving great Allowance for my Defectiveness in speaking, was however surprised at so much Wit and good Sense in so diminutive an Animal. She took me in her own Hand, and carried me to the King, who was then retired to his Cabinet. His Majesty, a Prince of much Gravity, and austere Countenance, not well observing my Shape at first View, asked the Queen after a cold Manner, how long it was since she grew fond of a *Splacknuck*; for such it seems he took me to be, as I lay upon my Breast in her Majesty's right Hand. But this Princess, who hath an infinite deal of Wit and Humour, set me gently on my Feet upon the Scrutore; and commanded me to give His Majesty an Account of my self, which I did in a very few Words; and *Glumdalclitch*, who attended at the Cabinet Door, and could not endure I should be out of her Sight, being admitted; confirmed all that had passed from my Arrival at her Father's House.

The King, although he be as learned a Person as any in his Dominions; and had been educated in the Study of Philosophy, and particularly Mathematicks; yet when he observed my Shape exactly, and saw me walk erect, before I began to speak, conceived I might be a piece of Clockwork, (which is in that Country arrived to a very great Perfection) contrived by some ingenious Artist. But, when he heard my Voice, and found what I delivered to be regular and rational, he could not conceal his Astonishment. He was by no means satisfied with the Relation I gave him of the Manner I came into his Kingdom; but thought it a Story concerted between *Glumdalclitch* and her Father, who had taught me a Sett of Words to make me sell at a higher Price. Upon this Imagination he put several other Questions to me, and still received rational Answers, no otherwise defective than by a Foreign Accent, and an imperfect Knowledge in the Language; with some rustick Phrases which I had learned at the Farmer's House, and did not suit the polite Style of a Court.

His Majesty sent for three great Scholars who were then in their weekly waiting (according to the Custom in that Country.) These Gentlemen, after they had a while examined my Shape with much Nicety, were of different Opinion concerning me. They all agreed that I could not be produced according to the regular Laws of Nature; because I was not framed with a Capacity of preserving my Life, either by Swiftness, or climbing of Trees, or digging Holes in the Earth. They observed by my Teeth, which they viewed with great Exactness, that I was a carnivorous Animal; yet most Quadrupeds being an Overmatch for me; and Field-Mice, with some others, too nimble, they could not imagine how I should be able to support my self, unless I fed upon Snails and other Insects; which they offered by many learned Arguments to evince that I could not possibly do. One of them seemed to think that I might be an Embrio, or abortive Birth. But this Opinion was rejected by the other two, who observed my Limbs to be perfect and finished; and that I had lived several Years, as it was manifested from my Beard; the Stumps whereof they plainly discovered through a Magnifying-Glass. They would not allow me to be a Dwarf, because my Littleness was beyond all Degrees of Comparison; for the Queen's favourite Dwarf, the smallest ever known in that Kingdom, was near thirty Foot high. After much Debate, they concluded unanimously that I was only *Relplum Scalcath*, which is interpreted literally *Lusus Naturae*,[1] a Determination exactly agreeable to the Modern Philosophy of *Europe*: whose Professors, disdaining the old Evasion of *occult Causes*, whereby the Followers of *Aristotle* endeavour in vain to disguise their Ignorance; have invented this wonderful Solution of all Difficulties, to the unspeakable Advancement of human Knowledge.

After this decisive Conclusion, I entreated to be heard a Word or two. I applied my self to the King, and assured His Majesty, that I came from a Country which abounded with several Millions of both Sexes, and of my own Stature; where the Animals, Trees, and Houses were all in Proportion; and where by Consequence I might be as able to defend my self, and to find Sustenance, as any of his Majesty's Subjects could do here; which I took for a full Answer to those Gentlemen's Arguments. To this they only replied with a Smile of Contempt; saying, that the Farmer had instructed me very well in my Lesson. The King, who had a much better

[1] A freak of nature.

Understanding, dismissing his learned Men, sent for the Farmer, who by good Fortune was not yet gone out of Town: Having therefore first examined him privately, and then confronted him with me and the young Girl; his Majesty began to think that what we told him might possibly be true. He desired the Queen to order, that a particular Care should be taken of me; and was of Opinion, that *Glumdalclitch* should still continue in her Office of tending me, because he observed we had a great Affection for each other. A convenient Apartment was provided for her at Court; she had a sort of Governess appointed to take care of her Education, a Maid to dress her, and two other Servants for menial Offices; but, the Care of me was wholly appropriated to her self. The Queen commanded her own Cabinet-maker to contrive a Box that might serve me for a Bed-chamber, after the Model that *Glumdalclitch* and I should agree upon. This Man was a most ingenious Artist; and according to my Directions, in three Weeks finished for me a wooden Chamber of sixteen Foot square, and twelve High; with Sash Windows, a Door, and two Closets, like a *London* Bedchamber. The Board that made the Cieling was to be lifted up and down by two Hinges, to put in a Bed ready furnished by her Majesty's Upholsterer; which *Glumdalclitch* took out every Day to air, made it with her own Hands, and letting it down at Night, locked up the Roof over me. A Nice Workman, who was famous for little Curiosities, undertook to make me two Chairs, with Backs and Frames, of a Substance not unlike Ivory; and two Tables, with a Cabinet to put my Things in. The Room was quilted on all Sides, as well as the Floor and the Cieling, to prevent any Accident from the Carelessness of those who carried me; and to break the Force of a Jolt when I went in a Coach. I desired a Lock for my Door to prevent Rats and Mice from coming in: The Smith after several Attempts made the smallest that was ever seen among them; for I have known a larger at the Gate of a Gentleman's House in *England*. I made a shift to keep the Key in a Pocket of my own, fearing *Glumdalclitch* might lose it. The Queen likewise ordered the thinnest Silks that could be gotten, to make me Cloaths; not much thicker than an *English* Blanket, very cumbersome till I was accustomed to them. They were after the Fashion of the Kingdom, partly resembling the *Persian*, and partly the *Chinese*; and are a very grave decent Habit.

The Queen became so fond of my Company, that she could not

dine without me. I had a Table placed upon the same at which her
Majesty eat, just at her left Elbow; and a Chair to sit on. *Glumdalclitch* stood upon a Stool on the Floor, near my Table, to assist
and take Care of me. I had an entire set of Silver Dishes and Plates,
and other Necessaries, which in Proportion to those of the Queen,
were not much bigger than what I have seen in a *London* Toy-shop,
for the Furniture of a Baby-house: These my little Nurse kept in
her Pocket, in a Silver Box, and gave me at Meals as I wanted
them; always cleaning them her self. No Person dined with the
Queen but the two Princesses Royal; the elder sixteen Years old,
and the younger at that time thirteen and a Month. Her Majesty
used to put a Bit of Meat upon one of my Dishes, out of which
I carved for my self; and her Diversion was to see me eat in Miniature. For the Queen (who had indeed but a weak Stomach) took
up at one Mouthful, as much as a dozen *English* Farmers could
eat at a Meal, which to me was for some time a very nauseous
Sight. She would craunch the Wing of a Lark, Bones and all,
between her Teeth, although it were nine Times as large as that
of a full grown Turkey; and put a Bit of Bread in her Mouth, as
big as two twelve-penny Loaves. She drank out of a Golden Cup,
above a Hogshead at a Draught. Her Knives were twice as long as
a Scythe set strait upon the Handle. The Spoons, Forks, and other
Instruments were all in the same Proportion. I remember when
Glumdalclitch carried me out of Curiosity to see some of the Tables
at Court, where ten or a dozen of these enormous Knives and
Forks were lifted up together; I thought I had never till then beheld
so terrible a Sight.

It is the Custom, that every *Wednesday*, (which as I have
before observed, was their Sabbath) the King and Queen, with the
Royal Issue of both Sexes, dine together in the Apartment of his
Majesty; to whom I was now become a Favourite; and at these
Times my little Chair and Table were placed at his left Hand
before one of the Salt-sellers. This Prince took a Pleasure in conversing with me; enquiring into the Manners, Religion, Laws, Government, and Learning of *Europe*, wherein I gave him the best
Account I was able. His Apprehension was so clear, and his Judgment so exact, that he made very wise Reflexions and Observations
upon all I said. But, I confess, that after I had been a little too
copious in talking of my own beloved Country; of our Trade, and
Wars by Sea and Land, of our Schisms in Religion, and Parties in

the State; the Prejudices of his Education prevailed so far, that he could not forbear taking me up in his right Hand, and stroaking me gently with the other; after an hearty Fit of laughing, asked me whether I were a *Whig* or a *Tory*. Then turning to his first Minister, who waited behind him with a white Staff, near as tall as the Main-mast of the Royal *Sovereign*; he observed, how contemptible a Thing was human Grandeur, which could be mimicked by such diminutive Insects as I: And yet, said he, I dare engage, those Creatures have their Titles and Distinctions of Honour; they contrive little Nests and Burrows, that they call Houses and Cities; they make a Figure in Dress and Equipage; they love, they fight, they dispute, they cheat, they betray. And thus he continued on, while my Colour came and went several Times, with Indignation to hear our noble Country, the Mistress of Arts and Arms, the Scourge of *France*, the Arbitress of *Europe*, the Seat of Virtue, Piety, Honour and Truth, the Pride and Envy of the World, so contemptously treated.

But, as I was not in a Condition to resent Injuries, so, upon mature Thoughts, I began to doubt whether I were injured or no. For, after having been accustomed several Months to the Sight and Converse of this People, and observed every Object upon which I cast my Eyes, to be of proportionable Magnitude; the Horror I had first conceived from their Bulk and Aspect was so far worn off, that if I then beheld a Company of *English* Lords and Ladies in their Finery and Birth-day Cloaths, acting their several Parts in the most courtly Manner of Strutting, and Bowing and Prating; to say the Truth, I should have been strongly tempted to laugh as much at them as this King and his Grandees did at me. Neither indeed could I forbear smiling at my self, when the Queen used to place me upon her Hand towards a Looking-Glass, by which both our Persons appeared before me in full View together; and there could nothing be more ridiculous than the Comparison: So that I really began to imagine my self dwindled many Degrees below my usual Size.

Nothing angred and mortified me so much as the Queen's Dwarf, who being of the lowest Stature that was ever in that Country, (for I verily think he was not full Thirty Foot high) became so insolent at seeing a Creature so much beneath him, that he would always affect to swagger and look big as he passed by me in the Queen's Antichamber, while I was standing on some Table

talking with the Lords or Ladies of the Court; and he seldom
failed of a smart Word or two upon my Littleness; against which
I could only revenge my self by calling him *Brother*, challenging
him to wrestle; and such Repartees as are usual in the Mouths of
Court Pages. One Day at Dinner, this malicious little Cubb was
so nettled with something I had said to him, that raising himself
upon the Frame of her Majesty's Chair, he took me up by the
Middle, as I was sitting down, not thinking any Harm, and let me
drop into a large Silver Bowl of Cream; and then ran away as fast
as he could. I fell over Head and Ears, and if I had not been a
good Swimmer, it might have gone very hard with me; for *Glumdalclitch* in that Instant happened to be at the other End of the
Room; and the Queen was in such a Fright, that she wanted Presence of Mind to assist me. But my little Nurse ran to my Relief;
and took me out, after I had swallowed above a Quart of Cream.
I was put to Bed; however I received no other Damage than the
Loss of a Suit of Cloaths, which was utterly spoiled. The Dwarf
was soundly whipped, and as a further Punishment, forced to
drink up the Bowl of Cream, into which he had thrown me; neither
was he ever restored to Favour: For, soon after the Queen bestowed
him to a Lady of high Quality; so that I saw him no more, to my
very great Satisfaction; for I could not tell to what Extremitys such
a malicious Urchin might have carried his Resentment.

He had before served me a scurvy Trick, which set the Queen
a laughing, although at the same time she were heartily vexed,
and would have immediately cashiered him, if I had not been so
generous as to intercede. Her Majesty had taken a Marrow-bone
upon her Plate; and after knocking out the Marrow, placed the
Bone again in the Dish erect as it stood before; the Dwarf watching
his Opportunity, while *Glumdalclitch* was gone to the Side-board,
mounted the Stool that she stood on to take care of me at Meals;
took me up in both Hands, and squeezing my Legs together,
wedged them into the Marrow-bone above my Waist; where I
stuck for some time, and made a very ridiculous Figure. I believe it
was near a Minute before any one knew what was become of me;
for I thought it below me to cry out. But, as Princes seldom get
their Meat hot, my Legs were not scalded, only my Stockings and
Breeches in a sad Condition. The Dwarf at my Entreaty had no
other Punishment than a sound whipping.

I was frequently raillied by the Queen upon Account of my Fearfulness; and she used to ask me whether the People of my Country were as great Cowards as my self. The Occasion was this. The Kingdom is much pestered with Flies in Summer; and these odious Insects, each of them as big as a *Dunstable* Lark, hardly gave me any Rest while I sat at Dinner, with their continual Humming and Buzzing about my Ears. They would sometimes alight upon my Victuals, and leave their loathsome Excrement or Spawn behind, which to me was very visible, although not to the Natives of that Country, whose large Opticks were not so acute as mine in viewing smaller Objects. Sometimes they would fix upon my Nose or Forehead, where they stung me to the Quick, smelling very offensively; and I could easily trace that viscous Matter, which our Naturalists tell us enables those Creatures to walk with their Feet upwards upon a Cieling. I had much ado to defend my self against these detestable Animals, and could not forbear starting when they came on my Face. It was the common Practice of the Dwarf to catch a Number of these Insects in his Hand, as School-boys do among us, and let them out suddenly under my Nose, on Purpose to frighten me, and divert the Queen. My Remedy was to cut them in Pieces with my Knife as they flew in the Air; wherein my Dexterity was much admired.

I remember one Morning when *Glumdalclitch* had set me in my Box upon a Window, as she usually did in fair Days to give me Air, (for I durst not venture to let the Box be hung on a Nail out of the Window, as we do with Cages in *England*) after I had lifted up one of my Sashes, and sat down at my Table to eat a Piece of Sweet-Cake for my Breakfast; above twenty Wasps, allured by the Smell, came flying into the Room, humming louder than the Drones of as many Bagpipes. Some of them seized my Cake, and carried it piecemeal away; others flew about my Head and Face, confounding me with the Noise, and putting me in the utmost Terror of their Stings. However I had the Courage to rise and draw my Hanger, and attack them in the Air. I dispatched four of them, but the rest got away; and I presently shut my Window. These Insects were as large as Partridges; I took out their Stings, found them an Inch and a half long, and as sharp as Needles. I carefully preserved them all, and having since shewn them with some other Curiosities in several Parts of *Europe*;

upon my Return to *England* I gave three of them to *Gresham College*,[2] and kept the fourth for my self.

CHAPTER IV

The Country described. A Proposal for correcting modern Maps. The King's Palace, and some Account of the Metropolis. The Author's Way of travelling. The chief Temple described.

I now intend to give the Reader a short Description of this Country, as far as I travelled in it, which was not above two thousand Miles round *Lorbrulgrud* the Metropolis. For, the Queen, whom I always attended, never went further when she accompanied the King in his Progresses; and there staid till his Majesty returned from viewing his Frontiers. The whole Extent of this Prince's Dominions reacheth about six thousand Miles in Length, and from three to five in Breadth. From whence I cannot but conclude, that our Geographers of *Europe* are in a great Error, by supposing nothing but Sea between *Japan* and *California*: For it was ever my Opinion, that there must be a Balance of Earth to counterpoise the great Continent of *Tartary*; and therefore they ought to correct their Maps and Charts, by joining this vast Tract of Land to the North-west Parts of *America*; wherein I shall be ready to lend them my Assistance.

The Kingdom is a Peninsula, terminated to the North-east by a Ridge of Mountains thirty Miles high which are altogether impassable by Reason of the Volcanoes upon the Tops. Neither do the most Learned know what sort of Mortals inhabit beyond those Mountains, or whether they be inhabited at all. On the three other Sides it is bounded by the Ocean. There is not one Sea-port in the whole Kingdom; and those Parts of the Coasts into which the

[2] The official quarters of the Royal Society of London for Improving Natural Knowledge, that is, of scientific investigation in England.

Rivers issue, are so full of pointed Rocks, and the Sea generally so rough, that there is no venturing with the smallest of their Boats; so that these People are wholly excluded from any Commerce with the rest of the World. But the large Rivers are full of Vessels, and abound with excellent Fish; for they seldom get any from the Sea, because the Sea-fish are of the same Size with those in *Europe*, and consequently not worth catching; whereby it is manifest, that Nature in the Production of Plants and Animals of so extraordinary a Bulk, is wholly confined to this Continent; of which I leave the Reasons to be determined by Philosophers. However, now and then they take a Whale that happens to be dashed against the Rocks, which the common People feed on heartily. These Whales I have known so large that a Man could hardly carry one upon his Shoulders; and sometimes for Curiosity they are brought in Hampers to *Lobrulgrud*: I saw one of them in a Dish at the King's Table, which passed for a Rarity; but I did not observe he was fond of it; for I think indeed the Bigness disgusted him, although I have seen one somewhat larger in *Greenland*.

The Country is well inhabited, for it contains fifty one Cities, near an hundred walled Towns, and a great Number of Villages. To satisfy my curious Reader, it may be sufficient to describe *Lobrulgrud*. This City stands upon almost two equal Parts on each Side the River that passes through. It contains above eighty thousand Houses. It is in Length three *Glonglungs* (which make about fifty four English Miles) and two and a half in Breadth, as I measured it myself in the Royal Map made by the King's Order, which was laid on the Ground on purpose for me, and extended an hundred Feet; I paced the Diameter and Circumference several times Bare-foot, and computing by the Scale, measured it pretty exactly.

The King's Palace is no regular Edifice, but an Heap of Buildings about seven Miles round: The chief Rooms are generally two hundred and forty Foot high, and broad and long in Proportion. A Coach was allowed to *Glumdalclitch* and me, wherein her Governess frequently took her out to see the Town, or go among the Shops; and I was always of the Party, carried in my Box; although the Girl at my own Desire would often take me out, and hold me in her Hand, that I might more conveniently view the Houses and the People as we passed along the Streets. I reckoned our Coach to be about a Square of *Westminster-Hall*, but not

altogether so high, however, I cannot be very exact. One Day the
Governess ordered our Coachman to stop at several Shops; where
the Beggars watching their Opportunity, crouded to the Sides of
the Coach, and gave me the most horrible Spectacles that ever an
European Eye beheld. There was a Woman with a Cancer in her
Breast, swelled to a monstrous Size, full of Holes, in two or three
of which I could have easily crept, and covered my whole Body.
There was a Fellow with a Wen in his Neck, larger than five Wool-
packs; and another with a couple of wooden Legs, each about
twenty Foot high. But, the most hateful Sight of all was the Lice
crawling on their Cloaths: I could see distinctly the Limbs of
these Vermin with my naked Eye, much better than those of an
European Louse through a Microscope; and their Snouts with
which they rooted like Swine. They were the first I ever beheld;
and I should have been curious enough to dissect one of them,
if I had proper Instruments (which I unluckily left behind me in
the Ship) although indeed the Sight was so nauseous, that it
perfectly turned my Stomach.

Beside the large Box in which I was usually carried, the Queen
ordered a smaller one to be made for me, of about twelve Foot
Square, and ten high, for the Convenience of Travelling; because
the other was somewhat too large for *Glumdalclitch's* Lap, and
cumbersom in the Coach; it was made by the same Artist, whom
I directed in the whole Contrivance. This travelling Closet was an
exact Square with a Window in the Middle of three of the Squares,
and each Window was latticed with Iron Wire on the outside, to
prevent Accidents in long Journeys. On the fourth Side, which
had no Window, two strong Staples were fixed, through which the
Person that carried me, when I had a Mind to be on Horseback,
put in a Leathern Belt, and buckled it about his Waist. This was
always the Office of some grave trusty Servant in whom I could
confide, whether I attended the King and Queen in their Progresses,
or were disposed to see the Gardens, or pay a Visit to some great
Lady or Minister of State in the Court, when *Glumdalclitch* happened to be out of Order: For I soon began to be known and
esteemed among the greatest Officers, I suppose more upon Account
of their Majesty's Favour, than any Merit of my own. In Journeys,
when I was weary of the Coach, a Servant on Horseback would
buckle my Box, and place it on a Cushion before him; and there
I had a full Prospect of the Country on three Sides from my three

Windows. I had in this Closet a Field-Bed and a Hammock hung from the Cieling, two Chairs and a Table, neatly screwed to the Floor, to prevent being tossed about by the Agitation of the Horse or the Coach. And having been long used to Sea-Voyages, those Motions, although sometimes very violent, did not much discompose me.

Whenever I had a Mind to see the Town, it was always in my Travelling-Closet; which *Glumdalclitch* held in her Lap in a kind of open Sedan, after the Fashion of the Country, borne by four Men, and attended by two others in the Queen's Livery. The People who had often heard of me, were very curious to croud about the Sedan; and the Girl was complaisant enough to make the Bearers stop, and to take me in her Hand that I might be more conveniently seen.

I was very desirious to see the chief Temple, and particularly the Tower belonging to it, which is reckoned the highest in the Kingdom. Accordingly one Day my Nurse carried me thither, but I may truly say I came back disappointed; for, the Height is not above three thousand Foot, reckoning from the Ground to the highest Pinnacle top; which allowing for the Difference between the Size of those People, and us in *Europe,* is no great matter for Admiration, nor at all equal in Proportion, (if I rightly remember) to *Salisbury* Steeple. But, not to detract from a Nation to which during my Life I shall acknowledge myself extremely obliged; it must be allowed, that whatever this famous Tower wants in Height, is amply made up in Beauty and Strength. For the Walls are near an hundred Foot thick, built of hewn Stone, whereof each is about forty Foot square, and adorned on all Sides with Statues of Gods and Emperors cut in Marble larger than the Life, placed in their several Niches. I measured a little Finger which had fallen down from one of these Statues, and lay unperceived among some Rubbish; and found it exactly four Foot and an Inch in Length. *Glumdalclitch* wrapped it up in a Handkerchief, and carried it home in her Pocket to keep among other Trinkets, of which the Girl was very fond, as Children at her Age usually are.

The King's Kitchen is indeed a noble Building, vaulted at Top, and about six hundred Foot high. The great Oven is not so wide by ten Paces as the Cupola at St. *Paul's:* For I measured the latter on purpose after my Return. But if I should describe the Kitchen-grate, the prodigious Pots and Kettles, the Joints of Meat turning on the Spits, with many other Particulars; perhaps I should be hardly believed; at least a severe Critick would be apt to think I enlarged a little, as Travellers are often suspected to do. To avoid which Censure, I fear I have run too much into the other Extream; and that if this Treatise should happen to be translated into the Language of *Brobdingnag*, (which is the general Name of that Kingdom) and transmitted thither; the King and his People would have Reason to complain; that I had done them an Injury by a false and diminutive Representation.

His Majesty seldom keeps above six hundred Horses in his Stables: They are generally from fifty four to sixty Foot high. But, when he goes abroad on solemn Days, he is attended for State by a Militia Guard of five hundred Horse, which indeed I thought was the most splendid Sight that could be ever beheld, till I saw part of his Army in Battalia; whereof I shall find another Occasion to speak.

CHAPTER V

Several Adventures that happened to the Author. The Execution of a Criminal. The Author shews his Skill in Navigation.

I should have lived happy enough in that Country, if my Littleness had not exposed me to several ridiculous and troublesome Accidents; some of which I shall venture to relate. *Glumdalclitch* often carried me into the Gardens of the Court in my smaller Box, and would sometimes take me out of it and hold me in her Hand, or set me down to walk. I remember, before the Dwarf left the Queen, he followed us one Day into those Gardens; and my Nurse having set me down, he and I being close together, near some Dwarf Apple-trees, I must need shew my Wit by a silly Allusion between him and the Trees, which happens to hold in their Language as it doth in ours. Whereupon, the malicious Rogue watching his Opportunity, when I was walking under one of them, shook it directly over my Head, by which a dozen Apples, each of them near as large as a *Bristol* Barrel, came tumbling about my Ears; one of them hit me on the Back as I chanced to stoop, and knocked me down flat on my Face, but I received no other Hurt; and the Dwarf was pardoned at my Desire, because I had given the Provocation.

Another Day, *Glumdalclitch* left me on a smooth Grassplot to divert my self while she walked at some Distance with her Governess. In the mean time, there suddenly fell such a violent Shower of Hail, that I was immediately by the Force of it struck to the Ground: And when I was down, the Hail-stones gave me such cruel Bangs all over the Body, as if I had been pelted with Tennis-Balls; however I made a Shift to creep on all four, and shelter my self by lying flat on my Face on the Lee-side of a Border of Lemmon Thyme; but so bruised from Head to Foot, that I could not go abroad in ten Days. Neither is this at all to be wondered at; because Nature in that Country observing the same Proportion through all her Operations, a Hail-stone is near Eighteen Hundred Times as large as one in *Europe*; which I can assert upon Experience, having been so curious to weigh and measure them.

But, a more dangerous Accident happened to me in the same Garden, when my little Nurse, believing she had put me in a secure Place, which I often entreated her to do, that I might enjoy my own Thoughts; and having left my Box at home to avoid the Trouble of carrying it, went to another Part of the Gardens with her Governess and some Ladies of her Acquaintance. While she was absent and out of hearing, a small white Spaniel belonging to one of the chief Gardiners, having got by Accident into the Garden, happened to range near the Place where I lay. The Dog following the Scent, came directly up, and taking me in his Mouth, ran strait to his Master, wagging his Tail, and set me gently on the Ground. By good Fortune he had been so well taught, that I was carried between his Teeth without the least Hurt, or even tearing my Cloaths. But, the poor Gardiner, who knew me well, and had a great Kindness for me, was in a terrible Fright. He gently took me up in both his Hands, and asked me how I did; but I was so amazed and out of Breath, that I could not speak a Word. In a few Minutes I came to my self, and he carried me safe to my little Nurse, who by this time had returned to the Place where she left me, and was in cruel Agonies when I did not appear, nor answer when she called; she severely reprimanded the Gardiner on Account of his Dog. But, the Thing was hushed up, and never known at Court; for the Girl was afraid of the Queen's Anger; and truly as to my self, I thought it would not be for my Reputation that such a Story should go about.

This Accident absolutely determined *Glumdalclitch* never to trust me abroad for the future out of her Sight. I had been long afraid of this Resolution; and therefore concealed from her some little unlucky Adventures that happened in those Times when I was left by my self. Once a Kite hovering over the Garden, made a Stoop at me, and if I had not resolutely drawn my Hanger, and run under a thick Espalier, he would have certainly carried me away in his Talons. Another time, walking to the Top of a fresh Molehill, I fell to my Neck, in the Hole through which that Animal had cast up the Earth; and coined some Lye not worth remembring, to excuse my self for spoiling my Cloaths. I likewise broke my right Shin against the Shell of a Snail, which I happened to stumble over, as I was walking alone, and thinking on poor *England*.

I cannot tell whether I were more pleased or mortified to observe in those solitary Walks, that the smaller Birds did not appear to be at all afraid of me; but would hop about within a Yard Distance, looking for Worms, and other Food, with as much Indifference and Security as if no Creature at all were near them. I remember, a Thrush had the Confidence to snatch out of my Hand with his Bill, a Piece of Cake that *Glumdalclitch* had just given me for my Breakfast. When I attempted to catch any of these Birds, they would boldly turn against me, endeavouring to pick my Fingers, which I durst not venture within their Reach; and then they would hop back unconcerned to hunt for Worms or Snails, as they did before. But, one Day I tool a thick Cudgel, and threw it with all my Strength so luckily at a Linnet, that I knocked him down, and seizing him by the Neck with both my Hands, ran with him in Triumph to my Nurse. However, the Bird who had only been stunned, recovering himself, gave me so many Boxes with his Wings on both Sides of my Head and Body, although I held him at Arms Length, and was out of the Reach of his Claws, that I was twenty Times thinking to let him go. But I was soon relieved by one of our Servants, who wrung off the Bird's Neck; and I had him next Day for Dinner by the Queen's Command. This

Linnet, as near as I can remember, seemed to be somewhat larger than an English Swan.

The Maids of Honor often invited *Glumdalclitch* to their Apartments, and desired she would bring me along with her, on Purpose to have the Pleasure of seeing and touching me. They would often strip me naked from Top to Toe, and lay me at full Length in their Bosoms; wherewith I was much disgusted; because, to say the Truth, a very offensive Smell came from their Skins; which I do not mention or intend to the Disadvantage of those excellent Ladies, for whom I have all Manner of Respect: But, I conceive, that my Sense was more acute in Proportion to my Littleness; and that those illustrious Persons were no more disagreeable to their Lovers, or to each other, than People of the same Quality are with us in *England*. And, after all, I found their natural Smell was much more supportable than when they used Perfumes, under which I immediately swooned away. I cannot forget, that an intimate Friend of mine in *Lilliput* took the Freedom in a warm Day, when I had used a good deal of Exercise, to complain of a strong Smell about me; although I am as little faulty that way as most of my Sex: But I suppose, his Faculty of Smelling was as nice with regard to me, as mine was to that of this People. Upon this Point, I cannot forbear doing Justice to the Queen my Mistress, and *Glumdalclitch* my Nurse; whose Persons were as sweet as those of any Lady in *England*.

That which gave me most Uneasiness among these Maids of Honour, when my Nurse carried me to visit them, was to see them use me without any Manner of Ceremony, like a Creature who had no Sort of Consequence. For, they would strip themselves to the Skin, and put on their Smocks in my Presence, while I was placed on their Toylet directly before their naked Bodies; which, I am sure, to me was very far from being a tempting Sight, or from giving me any other Motions than those of Horror and Disgust. Their Skins appeared so coarse and uneven, so variously coloured when I saw them near, with a Mole here and there as broad as a Trencher, and Hairs hanging from it thicker than Pack-threads; to say nothing further concerning the rest of their Persons. Neither did they at all scruple while I was by, to discharge what they had drunk, to the Quantity of at least two Hogsheads, in a Vessel that held above three Tuns. The handsomest among these Maids of

Honour, a pleasant frolicksome Girl of sixteen, would sometimes set me astride upon one of her Nipples; with many other Tricks, wherein the Reader will excuse me for not being over particular. But, I was so much displeased, that I entreated *Glumdalclitch* to contrive some Excuse for not seeing that young Lady any more.

One Day, a young Gentleman who was Nephew to my Nurse's Governess, came and pressed them both to see an Execution. It was of a Man who had murdered one of that Gentleman's intimate Acquaintance. *Glumdalclitch* was prevailed on to be of the Company, very much against her Inclination, for she was naturally tender hearted: And, as for my self, although I abhorred such Kind of Spectacles; yet my Curiosity tempted me to see something that I thought must be extraordinary. The Malefactor was fixed in a Chair upon a Scaffold erected for the Purpose; and his Head cut off at one Blow with a Sword of about forty Foot long. The Veins and Arteries spouted up such a prodigious Quantity of Blood, and so high in the Air, that the great *Jet d'Eau* at *Versailles* was not equal for the Time it lasted; and the Head when it fell on the Scaffold Floor, gave such a Bounce, as made me start, although I were at least an *English* Mile distant.

The Queen, who often used to hear me talk of my Sea-Voyages, and took all Occasions to divert me when I was melancholy, asked me whether I understood how to handle a Sail or an Oar; and whether a little Exercise of Rowing might not be convenient for my Health. I answered, that I understood both very well. For although my proper Employment had been to be Surgeon or Doctor to the Ship; yet often upon a Pinch, I was forced to work like a common Mariner. But, I could not see how this could be done in their Country, where the smallest Wherry was equal to a first Rate Man of War among us; and such a Boat as I could manage, would never live in any of their Rivers: Her Majesty said, if I would contrive a Boat, her own Joyner should make it, and she would provide a Place for me to sail in. The Fellow was an ingenious Workman, and by my Instructions in ten Days finished a Pleasure-Boat with all its Tackling, able conveniently to hold eight *Europeans*. When it was finished, the Queen was so delighted, that she ran with it in her Lap to the King, who ordered it to be put in a Cistern full of Water, with me in it, by way of Tryal; where I could not manage my two Sculls or little Oars for want of Room. But, the Queen had before contrived another Project. She ordered the Joyner to make a wooden Trough of three Hundred Foot long, fifty broad, and eight deep; which being well pitched to prevent leaking, was placed on the Floor along the Wall, in an outer Room of the Palace. It had a Cock near the Bottom, to let out the Water when it began to grow stale; and two Servants could easily fill it in half an Hour. Here I often used to row for my Diversion, as well as that of the Queen and her Ladies, who thought themselves agreeably entertained with my Skill and Agility. Sometimes I would put up my Sail, and then my Business was only to steer, while the Ladies gave me a Gale with their Fans; and when they were weary, some of the Pages would blow my Sail forward with their Breath, while I shewed my Art by steering Starboard or Larboard as I pleased. When I had done, *Glumdalclitch* always carried back my Boat into her Closet, and hung it on a Nail to dry.

In this Exercise I once met an Accident which had like to have cost me my Life. For, one of the Pages having put my Boat into the Trough; the Governess who attended *Glumdalclitch*, very officiously lifted me up to place me in the Boat; but I happened to slip through her Fingers, and should have infallibly fallen down forty Foot upon the Floor, if by the luckiest Chance in the World, I had not been stop'd by a Corking-pin that stuck in the good Gentlewoman's Stomacher; the Head of the Pin passed between my Shirt and the Waistband of my Breeches; and thus I was held by the Middle in the Air, till *Glumdalclitch* ran to my Relief.

Another time, one of the Servants, whose Office it was to fill my Trough every third Day with fresh Water; was so careless to let a huge Frog (not perceiving it) slip out of his Pail. The Frog lay concealed till I was put into my Boat, but then seeing a resting Place, climbed up, and made it lean so much on one Side, that I was forced to balance it with all my Weight on the other, to prevent overturning. When the Frog was got in, it hopped at once half the Length of the Boat, and then over my Head, backwards and forwards, dawbing my Face and Cloaths with its odious Slime. The Largeness of its Features made it appear the most deformed Animal that can be conceived. However, I desired *Glumdalclitch* to let me deal with it alone. I banged it a good while with one of my Sculls, and at last forced it to leap out of the Boat.

But, the greatest Danger I ever underwent in that Kingdom, was from a Monkey, who belonged to one of the Clerks of the Kitchen. *Glumdalclitch* had locked me up in her Closet,[1] while she went somewhere upon Business, or a Visit. The Weather being very warm, the Closet Window was left open, as well as the Windows and the Door of my bigger Box, in which I usually lived, because of its Largeness and Conveniency. As I sat quietly meditating at my Table, I heard something bounce in at the Closet Window, and skip about from one Side to the other; whereat, although I were much alarmed, yet I ventured to look out, but not stirring from my Seat; and then I saw this frolicksome Animal, frisking and leaping up and down, till at last he came to my Box, which he seemed to view with great Pleasure and Curiosity, peeping in at the Door and every Window. I retreated to the farther Corner of my Room, or Box; but the Monkey looking in at every Side, put me into such a Fright, that I wanted Presence of Mind to conceal my self under the Bed, as I might easily have done. After some time spent in peeping, grinning, and chattering, he at last espyed me; and reaching one of his Paws in at the Door, as a Cat does when she plays with a Mouse, although I often shifted Place to avoid him; he at length seized the Lappet of my Coat (which being made of that Country Silk, was very thick and strong) and dragged me out. He took me up in his right Fore-foot, and held me as a Nurse doth a Child she is going to suckle; just as I have seen the same Sort of Creature do with a Kitten in *Europe*: And when I offered to struggle, he squeezed me so hard, that I thought it more prudent to submit. I have good Reason to believe that he took me for a young one of his own Species, by his often stroaking my Face very gently with his other Paw. In these Diversions he was interrupted by a Noise at the Closet Door, as if some Body were opening it; whereupon he suddenly leaped up to the Window at which he had come in, and thence upon the Leads and Gutters, walking upon three Legs, and holding me in the fourth, till he clambered up to a Roof that was next to ours. I heard *Glumdalclitch* give a Shriek at the Moment he was carrying me out. The poor Girl was almost distracted: That Quarter of the Palace was all in an Uproar; the Servants ran for Ladders; the Monkey was seen by Hundreds in the Court, sitting upon the Ridge of a Building, holding me like a Baby in one of his Fore-Paws, and feeding me with the other, by cramming into my Mouth some Victuals he had squeezed out of

---

[1] A small private room.

the Bag on one Side of his Chaps, and patting me when I would not eat; whereat many of the Rabble below could not forbear laughing; neither do I think they justly ought to be blamed; for without Question, the Sight was ridiculous enough to every Body but my self. Some of the People threw up Stones, hoping to drive the Monkey down; but this was strictly forbidden, or else very probably my Brains had been dashed out.

The Ladders were now applied, and mounted by several Men; which the Monkey observing, and finding himself almost encompassed; not being able to make Speed enough with his three Legs, let me drop on a Ridge-Tyle, and made his Escape. Here I sat for some time five Hundred Yards from the Ground, expecting every Moment to be blown down by the Wind, or to fall by my own Giddiness, and come tumbling over and over from the Ridge to the Eves. But an honest Lad, one of my Nurse's Footmen, climbed up, and putting me into his Breeches Pocket, brought me down safe.

I was almost choaked with the filthy Stuff the Monkey had crammed down my Throat; but, my dear little Nurse picked it out of my Mouth with a small Needle; and then I fell a vomiting, which gave me great Relief. Yet I was so weak and bruised in the Sides with the Squeezes given me by this odious Animal, that I was forced to keep my Bed a Fortnight. The King, Queen, and all the Court, sent every Day to enquire after my Health; and her Majesty made me several Visits during my Sickness. The Monkey was killed, and an Order made that no such Animal should be kept about the Palace.

When I attended the King after my Recovery, to return him Thanks for his Favours, he was pleased to railly me a good deal upon this Adventure. He asked me what my Thoughts and Speculations were while I lay in the Monkey's Paw; how I liked the Victuals he gave me, his Manner of Feeding; and whether the fresh Air on the Roof had sharpened my Stomach. He desired to know what I would have done upon such an Occasion in my own Country. I told his Majesty, that in *Europe* we had no Monkies, except such as were brought for Curiosities from other Places, and so small, that I could deal with a Dozen of them together, if they presumed to attack me. And as for that monstrous Animal with whom I was so lately engaged, (it was indeed as large as an Elephant) if my Fears had suffered me to think so far as to make

Use of my Hanger (looking fiercely, and clapping my Hand upon the Hilt as I spoke) when he poked his Paw into my Chamber, perhaps I should have given him such a Wound, as would have made him glad to withdraw it with more Haste than he put it in. This I delivered in a firm Tone, like a Person who was jealous lest his Courage should be called in Question. However, my Speech produced nothing else besides a loud Laughter; which all the Respect due to his Majesty from those about him, could not make them contain. This made me reflect, how vain an Attempt it is for a Man to endeavour doing himself Honour among those who are out of all Degree of Equality or Comparison with him. And yet I have seen the Moral of my own Behaviour very frequent in *England* since my Return; where a little contemptible Varlet, without the least Title to Birth, Person, Wit, or common Sense, shall presume to look with Importance, and put himself upon a Foot with the greatest Persons of the Kingdom.

I was every Day furnishing the Court with some ridiculous Story; and *Glumdalclitch*, although she loved me to Excess, yet was arch enough to inform the Queen, whenever I committed any Folly that she thought would be diverting to her Majesty. The Girl who had been out of Order, was carried by her Governess to take the Air about an Hour's Distance, or thirty Miles from Town. They alighted out of the Coach near a small Foot-path in a Field; and *Glumdalclitch* setting down my travelling Box, I went out of it to walk. There was a Cow-dung in the Path, and I must needs try my Activity by attempting to leap over it. I took a Run, but unfortunately jumped short, and found my self just in the Middle up to my Knees. I waded through with some Difficulty, and one of the Footmen wiped me as clean as he could with his Handkerchief; for I was filthily bemired, and my Nurse confined me to my Box until we returned home; where the Queen was soon informed of what had passed, and the Footmen spread it about the Court; so that all the Mirth, for some Days, was at my Expence.

CHAPTER VI

Several Contrivances of the Author to please the King and Queen. He shews his Skill in Musick. The King enquires into the State of Europe, *which the Author relates to him. The King's Observations thereon.*

I used to attend the King's Levee once or twice a Week, and had often seen him under the Barber's Hand, which indeed was at first very terrible to behold. For, the Razor was almost twice as long as an ordinary Scythe. His Majesty, according to the Custom of the Country, was only shaved twice a Week. I once prevailed on the Barber to give me some of the Suds or Lather, out of which I picked Forty or Fifty of the strongest Stumps of Hair, I then took a Piece of fine Wood, and cut it like the Back of a Comb, making several Holes in it at equal Distance, with as small a Needle as I could get from *Glumdalclitch.* I fixed in the Stumps so artificially, scraping and sloping them with my Knife towards the Points, that I made a very tolerable Comb; which was a seasonable Supply, my own being so much broken in the Teeth, that it was almost useless: Neither did I know any Artist in that Country so nice and exact, as would undertake to make me another.

And this puts me in mind of an Amusement wherein I spent many of my leisure Hours. I desired the Queen's Woman to save for me the Combings of her Majesty's Hair, whereof in time I got a good Quantity; and consulting with my Friend the Cabinet-maker, who had received general Orders to do little Jobbs for me; I directed him to make two Chair-frames, no larger than those I had in my Box, and then to bore little Holes with a fine Awl round those Parts where I designed the Backs and Seats; through these Holes I wove the strongest Hairs I could pick out, just after the Manner of Cane-chairs in *England.* When they were finished, I made a Present of them to her Majesty, who kept them in her Cabinet, and used to shew them for Curiosities; as indeed they

were the Wonder of every one who beheld them. The Queen would
have had me sit upon one of these Chairs, but I absolutely refused
to obey her; protesting I would rather dye a Thousand Deaths
than place a dishonourable Part of my Body on those precious
Hairs that once adorned her Majesty's Head. Of these Hairs (as I
had always a Mechanical Genius) I likewise made a neat little
Purse about five Foot long, with her Majesty's Name decyphered
in Gold Letters; which I gave to *Glumdalclitch*, by the Queen's
Consent. To say the Truth, it was more for Shew than Use, being
not of Strength to bear the Weight of the larger Coins; and therefore she kept nothing in it, but some little Toys that Girls are
fond of.

The King, who delighted in Musick, had frequent Consorts[1] at
Court, to which I was sometimes carried, and set in my Box on a
Table to hear them: But, the Noise was so great, that I could
hardly distinguish the Tunes. I am confident, that all the Drums
and Trumpets of a Royal Army, beating and sounding together
just at your Ears, could not equal it. My Practice was to have my
Box removed from the Places where the Performers sat, as far as
I could; then to shut the Doors and Windows of it, and draw the
Window-Curtains; after which I found their Musick not disagreeable.

I had learned in my Youth to play a little upon the Spinet;
Glumdalclitch kept one in her Chamber, and a Master attended
twice a Week to teach her: I call it a Spinet, because it somewhat
resembled that Instrument, and was play'd upon in the same
Manner. A Fancy came into my Head, that I would entertain the
King and Queen with an *English* Tune upon this Instrument.
But this appeared extremely difficult: For, the Spinet was near
sixty Foot long, each Key being almost a Foot wide; so that,
with my Arms extended, I could not reach to above five Keys;
and to press them down required a good smart stroak with my
Fist, which would be too great a Labour, and to no purpose. The
Method I contrived was this. I prepared two round Sticks about
the Bigness of common Cudgels; they were thicker at one End
than the other; and I covered the thicker End with a Piece of a
Mouse's Skin, that by rapping on them, I might neither Damage
the Tops of the Keys, nor interrupt the Sound. Before the Spinet,

[1] Concerts.

a Bench was placed about four Foot below the Keys, and I was put upon the Bench. I ran sideling upon it that way and this, as fast as I could, banging the proper Keys with my two Sticks; and made a shift to play a Jigg to the great Satisfaction of both their Majesties: But, it was the most violent Exercise I ever underwent, and yet I could not strike above sixteen Keys, nor, consequently, play the Bass and Treble together, as other Artists do; which was a great Disadvantage to my Performance.

The King, who as I before observed, was a Prince of excellent Understanding, would frequently order that I should be brought in my Box, and set upon the Table in his Closet. He would then command me to bring one of my Chairs out of the Box, and sit down within three Yards Distance upon the Top of the Cabinet; which brought me almost to a Level with his Face. In this Manner I had several Conversations with him. I one Day took the Freedom to tell his Majesty, that the Contempt he discovered towards Europe, and the rest of the World, did not seem answerable to those excellent Qualities of Mind, that he was Master of. That, Reason did not extend itself with the Bulk of the Body: On the contrary, we observed in our Country, that the tallest Persons were usually least provided with it. That among other Animals, Bees and Ants had the Reputation of more Industry, Art, and Sagacity than many of the larger Kinds. And that, as inconsiderable as he took me to be, I hoped I might live to do his Majesty some signal Service. The King heard me with Attention; and began to conceive a much better Opinion of me than he had ever before. He desired I would give him as exact an Account of the Government of England as I possibly could; because, as fond as Princes commonly are of their own Customs (for so he conjectured of other Monarchs by my former Discourses) he should be glad to hear of any thing that might deserve Imitation.

Imagine with thy self, courteous Reader, how often I then wished for the Tongue of Demosthenes or Cicero, that might have enabled me to celebrate the Praise of my own dear native Country in a Style equal to its Merits and Felicity.

I began my Discourse by informing his Majesty, that our Dominions consisted of two Islands, which composed three mighty Kingdoms under one Sovereign, besides our Plantations[2] in America. I dwelt long upon the Fertility of our Soil, and the Temperature

² Colonies.

of our Climate. I then spoke at large upon the Constitution of an
English Parliament, partly made up of an illustrious Body called
the House of Peers, Persons of the noblest Blood, and of the most
ancient and ample Patrimonies. I described that extraordinary Care
always taken of their Education in Arts and Arms, to qualify them
for being Counsellors born to the King and Kingdom; to have a
Share in the Legislature, to be Members of the highest Court of
Judicature from whence there could be no Appeal; and to be
Champions always ready for the Defence of their Prince and
Country by their Valour, Conduct and Fidelity. That these were
the Ornament and Bulwark of the Kingdom; worthy Followers of
their most renowned Ancestors, whose Honour had been the
Reward of their Virtue; from which their Posterity were never once
known to degenerate. To these were joined several holy Persons, as
part of that Assembly, under the Title of Bishops; whose peculiar
Business it is, to take care of Religion, and of those who instruct
the People therein. These were searched and sought out through
the whole Nation, by the Prince and wisest Counsellors, among
such of the Priesthood, as were most deservedly distinguished by
the Sanctity of their Lives, and the Depth of their Erudition; who
were indeed the spiritual Fathers of the Clergy and the People.

That, the other Part of the Parliament consisted of an Assembly
called the House of Commons; who were all principal Gentlemen,
freely picked and culled out by the People themselves, for their
great Abilities, and Love of their Country, to represent the Wisdom
of the whole Nation. And, these two Bodies make up the most
august Assembly in *Europe*; to whom, in Conjunction with the
Prince, the whole Legislature is committed.

I then descended to the Courts of Justice, over which the Judges,
those venerable Sages and Interpreters of the Law, presided, for
determining the disputed Rights and Properties of Men, as well as
for the Punishment of Vice, and Protection of Innocence. I mentioned the prudent Management of our Treasury; the Valour and
Atchievements of our Forces by Sea and Land. I computed the
Number of our People, by reckoning how many Millions there
might be of each Religious Sect, or Political Party among us. I did
not omit even our Sports and Pastimes, or any other Particular
which I thought might redound to the Honour of my Country.
And, I finished all with a brief historical Account of Affairs and
Events in *England* for about an hundred Years past.

This Conversation was not ended under five Audiences, each of several Hours; and the King heard the whole with great Attention; frequently taking Notes of what I spoke, as well as Memorandums of what Questions he intended to ask me.

When I had put an End to these long Discourses, his Majesty in a sixth Audience consulting his Notes, proposed many Doubts, Queries, and Objections, upon every Article. He asked, what Methods were used to cultivate the Minds and Bodies of our young Nobility; and in what kind of Business they commonly spent the first and teachable Part of their Lives. What Course was taken to supply that Assembly, when any noble Family became extinct. What Qualifications were necessary in those who are to be created new Lords: Whether the Humour of the Prince, a Sum of Money to a Court-Lady, or a Prime Minister; or a Design of strengthening a Party opposite to the publick Interest, ever happened to be Motives in those Advancements. What Share of Knowledge these Lords had in the Laws of their Country, and how they came by it, so as to enable them to decide the Properties of their Fellow-Subjects in the last Resort. Whether they were always so free from Avarice, Partialities, or Want, that a Bribe, or some other sinister View, could have no Place among them. Whether those holy Lords I spoke of, were constantly promoted to that Rank upon Account of their Knowledge in religious Matters, and the Sanctity of their Lives; had never been compliers with the Times, while they were common Priests; or slavish prostitute Chaplains to some Nobleman, whose Opinions they continued servilely to follow after they were admitted into that Assembly.

He then desired to know, what Arts were practised in electing those whom I called Commoners. Whether, a Stranger with a strong Purse might not influence the vulgar Voters to chuse him before their own Landlords, or the most considerable Gentleman in the Neighbourhood. How it came to pass, that People were so violently bent upon getting into this Assembly, which I allowed to be a great Trouble and Expence, often to the Ruin of their Families, without any Salary or Pension: Because this appeared such an exalted Strain of Virtue and publick Spirit, that his Majesty seemed to doubt it might possibly not be always sincere: And he desired to know, whether such zealous Gentlemen could have any Views of refunding themselves for the Charges and Trouble they were at, by sacrificing the publick Good to the Designs of a weak and vicious Prince, in Conjunction with a corrupted Ministry. He multiplied his Questions, and sifted me thoroughly upon every Part of this Head; proposing numberless Enquiries and Objections, which I think it not prudent or convenient to repeat.

Upon what I said in relation to our Courts of Justice, his Majesty desired to be satisfied in several Points: And, this I was the better able to do, having been formerly almost ruined by a long Suit in Chancery, which was decreed for me with Costs. He asked, what Time was usually spent in determining between Right and Wrong; and what Degree of Expence. Whether Advocates and Orators had Liberty to plead in Causes manifestly known to be unjust, vexatious, or oppressive. Whether Party in Religion or Politicks were observed to be of any Weight in the Scale of Justice. Whether those pleading Orators were Persons educated in the general Knowledge of Equity; or only in provincial, national, and other local Customs. Whether they or their Judges had any Part in penning those Laws, which they assumed the Liberty of interpreting and glossing upon at their Pleasure. Whether they had ever at different Times pleaded for and against the same Cause, and cited Precedents to prove contrary Opinions. Whether they were a rich or a poor Corporation. Whether they received any pecuniary Reward for pleading or delivering their Opinions. And particularly whether they were ever admitted as Members in the lower Senate.

He fell next upon the Management of our Treasury; and said, he thought my Memory had failed me, because I computed our Taxes at about five or six Millions a Year; and when I came to mention the Issues, he found they sometimes amounted to more than double; for, the Notes he had taken were very particular in this Point; because he hoped, as he told me, that the Knowledge of our Conduct might be useful to him; and he could not be deceived in his Calculations. But, if what I told him were true, he was still at a Loss how a Kingdom could run out of its Estate like a private Person. He asked me, who were our Creditors? and, where we found Money to pay them? He wondered to hear me talk of such chargeable and extensive Wars; that, certainly we must be a quarrelsome People, or live among very bad Neighbours; and that our Generals must needs be richer than our Kings. He asked, what Business we had out of our own Islands, unless upon the Score of Trade or Treaty, or to defend the Coasts with our Fleet. Above all, he was amazed to hear me talk of a mercenary standing

Army in the Midst of Peace, and among a free People. He said, if we were governed by our own Consent in the Persons of our Representatives, he could not imagine of whom we were afraid, or against whom we were to fight; and would hear my Opinion, whether a private Man's House might not better be defended by himself, his Children, and Family; than by half a Dozen Rascals picked up at a Venture in the Streets, for small Wages, who might get an Hundred Times more by cutting their Throats.

He laughed at my odd Kind of Arithmetick (as he was pleased to call it) in reckoning the Numbers of our People by a Computation drawn from the several Sects among us in Religion and Politicks. He said, he knew no Reason, why those who entertain Opinions prejudicial to the Publick, should be obliged to change, or should not be obliged to conceal them. And, as it was Tyranny in any Government to require the first, so it was Weakness not to enforce the second: For, a Man may be allowed to keep Poisons in his Closet, but not to vend them about as Cordials.

He observed, that among the Diversions of our Nobility and Gentry, I had mentioned Gaming. He desired to know at what Age this Entertainment was usually taken up, and when it was laid down. How much of their Time it employed; whether it ever went so high as to affect their Fortunes. Whether mean vicious People, by their Dexterity in that Art, might not arrive at great Riches, and sometimes keep our very Nobles in Dependance, as well as habituate them to vile Companions; wholly take them from the Improvement of their Minds, and force them by the Losses they received, to learn and practice that infamous Dexterity upon others.

He was perfectly astonished with the historical Account I gave him of our Affairs during the last Century; protesting it was only an Heap of Conspiracies, Rebellions, Murders, Massacres, Revolutions, Banishments; the very worst Effects that Avarice, Faction, Hypocrisy, Perfidiousness, Cruelty, Rage, Madness, Hatred, Envy, Lust, Malice, and Ambition could produce.

His Majesty in another Audience, was at the Pains to recapitulate the Sum of all I had spoken; compared the Questions he made, with the Answers I had given; then taking me into his Hands, and stroaking me gently, delivered himself in these Words, which I shall never forget, nor the Manner he spoke them in. My little Friend *Grildrig*; you have made a most admirable Panegyrick upon

your Country. You have clearly proved that Ignorance, Idleness,
and Vice are the proper Ingredients for qualifying a Legislator.
That Laws are best explained, interpreted, and applied by those
whose Interest and Abilities lie in perverting, confounding, and
eluding them. I observe among you some Lines of an Institution,
which in its Original might have been tolerable; but these half
erased, and the rest wholly blurred and blotted by Corruptions.
It doth not appear from all you have said, how any one Perfection
is required towards the Procurement of any one Station among
you; much less that Men are ennobled on Account of their Virtue,
that Priests are advanced for their Piety or Learning, Soldiers for
their Conduct or Valour, Judges for their Integrity, Senators for
the Love of their Country, or Counsellors for their Wisdom. As
for yourself (continued the King) who have spent the greatest
Part of your Life in travelling; I am well disposed to hope you
may hitherto have escaped many Vices of your Country. But, by
what I have gathered from your own Relation, and the Answers
I have with much Pains wringed and extorted from you; I cannot
but conclude the Bulk of your Natives, to be the most pernicious
Race of little odious Vermin that Nature ever suffered to crawl
upon the Surface of the Earth.

CHAPTER VII

The Author's Love of his Country. He makes a Proposal
of much Advantage to the King; which is rejected. The
King's great Ignorance in Politicks. The Learning of
that Country very imperfect and confined. Their Laws,
and military Affairs, and parties in the state.

Nothing but an extreme Love of Truth could have hindered
me from concealing this Part of my Story. It was in vain to discover
my Resentments, which were always turned into Ridicule: And
I was forced to rest with Patience, while my noble and most

beloved Country was so injuriously treated. I am heartily sorry as any of my Readers can possibly be, that such an Occasion was given: But this Prince happened to be so curious and inquisitive upon every Particular, that it could not consist either with Gratitude or good Manners to refuse giving him what Satisfaction I was able. Yet thus much I may be allowed to say in my own Vindication; that I artfully eluded many of his Questions; and gave to every Point a more favourable turn by many Degrees than the strictness of Truth would allow. For, I have always born that laudable Partiality to my own Country, which *Dionysius Halicarnassensis* with so much Justice recommends to an Historian.[1] I would hide the Frailties and Deformities of my Political Mother, and place her Virtues and Beauties in the most advantageous Light. This was my sincere Endeavour in those many Discourses I had with that mighty Monarch, although it unfortunately failed of success.

But, great Allowances should be given to a King who lives wholly secluded from the rest of the World, and must therefore be altogether unacquainted with the Manners and Customs that most prevail in other Nations: The want of which Knowledge will ever produce many *Prejudices*, and a certain *Narrowness of Thinking*; from which we and the politer Countries of *Europe* are wholly exempted. And it would be hard indeed, if so remote a Prince's Notions of Virtue and Vice were to be offered as a Standard for all Mankind.

To confirm what I have now said, and further to shew the miserable Effects of a *confined Education*; I shall here insert a Passage which will hardly obtain Belief. In hopes to ingratiate my self farther into his Majesty's Favour, I told him of an Invention discovered between three and four hundred Years ago, to make a certain Powder; into an heap of which the smallest Spark of Fire falling, would kindle the whole in a Moment, although it were as big as a Mountain; and make it all fly up in the Air together, with a Noise and Agitation greater than Thunder. That, a proper Quantity of this Powder rammed into an hollow Tube of Brass or Iron, according to its Bigness, would drive a Ball of Iron or Lead with such Violence and Speed, as nothing was able

---

[1] Swift is here ironic at Gulliver's expense. Dionysius, a Greek writer who lived in Rome under Augustus, celebrated the Romans in order to persuade the conquered Greeks to submit to this superior people.

to sustain its Force. That, the largest Balls thus discharged, would
not only Destroy whole Ranks of an Army at once; but batter the
strongest Walls to the Ground; sink down Ships with a thousand
Men in each, to the Bottom of the Sea; and when linked together
by a Chain, would cut through Masts and Rigging; divide Hundreds
of Bodies in the Middle, and lay all Waste before them. That we
often put this Powder into large hollow Balls of Iron, and discharged them by an Engine into some City we were besieging;
which would rip up the Pavement, tear the Houses to Pieces, burst
and throw Splinters on every Side, dashing out the Brains of all
who came near. That I knew the Ingredients very well, which were
Cheap, and common; I understood the Manner of compounding
them, and could direct his Workmen how to make those Tubes of a
Size proportionable to all other Things in his Majesty's Kingdom;
and the largest need not be above two hundred Foot long; twenty
or thirty of which Tubes, charged with the proper Quantity of
Powder and Balls, would batter down the Walls of the strongest
Town in his Dominions in a few Hours; or destroy the whole
Metropolis, if ever it should pretend to dispute his absolute Commands. This I humbly offered to his Majesty, as a small Tribute of
Acknowledgment in return of so many Marks that I had received
of his Royal Favour and Protection.

The King was struck with Horror at the Description I had given
of those terrible Engines, and the Proposal I had made. He was
amazed how so impotent and groveling an Insect as I (these were
his Expressions) could entertain such inhuman Ideas, and in so
familiar a Manner as to appear wholly unmoved at all the Scenes
of Blood and Desolation, which I had painted as the common
Effects of those destructive Machines; whereof he said, some evil
Genius, Enemy to Mankind, must have been the first Contriver.
As for himself, he protested, that although few Things delighted
him so much as new Discoveries in Art or in Nature; yet he would
rather lose Half his Kingdom than be privy to such a Secret; which
he commanded me, as I valued my Life, never to mention any more.

A strange Effect of *narrow Principles* and *short Views!* that a
Prince possessed of every Quality which procures Veneration, Love
and Esteem; of strong Parts, great Wisdom and profound Learning;
endued with admirable Talents for Government, and almost adored
by his Subjects; should from a *nice unnecessary Scruple*, whereof in
Europe we can have no Conception, let slip an Opportunity put

into his Hands, that would have made him absolute Master of the Lives, the Liberties, and the Fortunes of his People. Neither do I say this with the least Intention to detract from the many Virtues of that excellent King; whose Character I am sensible will on this Account be very much lessened in the Opinion of an *English* Reader: But, I take this Defect among them to have risen from their Ignorance; by not having hitherto reduced *Politicks* into a *Science*, as the more acute Wits of *Europe* have done. For, I remember very well, in a Discourse one Day with the King; when I happened to say, there were several thousand Books among us written upon the *Art of Government*; it gave him (directly contrary to my Intention) a very mean Opinion of our Understandings. He professed both to abominate and despise all *Mystery, Refinement*, and *Intrigue*, either in a Prince or a Minister. He could not tell what I meant by *Secrets of State*, where an Enemy or some Rival Nation were not in the Case. He confined the Knowledge of governing within very *narrow Bounds*; to common Sense and Reason, to Justice and Lenity, to the Speedy Determination of Civil and criminal Causes; with some other obvious Topicks which are not worth considering. And, he gave it for his Opinion; that whoever could make two Ears of Corn, or two Blades of Grass to grow upon a Spot of Ground where only one grew before; would deserve better of Mankind, and do more essential Service to his Country, than the whole Race of Politicians put together.

The Learning of this People is very defective; consisting only in Morality, History, Poetry and Mathematicks; wherein they must be allowed to excel. But, the last of these is wholly applied to what may be useful in Life; to the Improvement of Agriculture and all mechanical Arts; so that among us it would be little esteemed. And as to Ideas, Entities, Abstractions and Transcendentals, I could never drive the least Conception into their Heads.

No Law of that Country must exceed in Words the Number of Letters in their Alphabet; which consists only of two and twenty. But indeed, few of them extend even to that Length. They are expressed in the most plain and simple Terms, wherein those People are not Mercurial enough to discover above one Interpretation. And, to write a Comment upon any Law, is a capital Crime. As to the Decision of civil Causes, or Proceedings against Criminals, their Precedents are so few, that they have little Reason to boast of any extraordinary Skill in either.

They have had the Art of Printing, as well as the *Chinese*, Time out of Mind. But their Libraries are not very large; for that of the King's, which is reckoned the largest, doth not amount to above a thousand Volumes; placed in a Gallery of twelve hundred Foot long; from whence I had Liberty to borrow what Books I pleased. The Queen's Joyner had contrived in one of *Glumdalclitch's* Rooms a Kind of wooden Machine five and twenty Foot high, formed like a standing Ladder; the Steps were each fifty Foot long: it was indeed a movable Pair of Stairs, the lowest End placed at ten Foot Distance from the Wall of the Chamber. The Book I had a Mind to read was put up leaning against the Wall. I first mounted to the upper Step of the Ladder, and turning my Face towards the Book, began at the Top of the Page, and so walking to the Right and Left about eight or ten Paces according to the Length of the Lines, till I had gotten a little below the Level of my Eyes; and then descending gradually till I came to the Bottom: After which I mounted again, and began the other Page in the same Manner, and so turned over the Leaf, which I could easily do with both my Hands, for it was as thick and stiff as a Paste-board, and in the largest Folios not above eighteen or twenty Foot long.

Their Stile is clear, masculine, and smooth, but not Florid; for they avoid nothing more than multiplying unnecessary Words, or using various Expressions. I have perused many of their Books, especially those in History and Morality. Among the latter I was much diverted with a little old Treatise, which always lay in *Glumdalclitch's* Bed-chamber, and belonged to her Governess, a grave elderly Gentlewoman, who dealt in Writings of Morality and Devotion. The Book treats of the Weakness of Human kind; and is in little Esteem except among Women and the Vulgar. However, I was curious to see what an Author of that Country could say upon such a Subject. This Writer went through all the usual Topicks of *European* Moralists; shewing how diminutive, contemptible, and helpless an Animal was Man in his own Nature; how unable to defend himself from the Inclemencies of the Air, or the Fury of wild Beasts: How much he was excelled by one Creature in Strength, by another in Speed, by a third in Foresight, by a fourth in Industry. He added, that Nature was degenerated in these latter declining Ages of the World, and could now produce only small abortive Births in Comparison of those in ancient Times. He said, it was very reasonable to think, not only that the Species of Men were originally much larger, but also that there must have been Giants in former Ages; which, as it is asserted by History and Tradition, so it hath been confirmed by huge Bones and Sculls casually dug up in several Parts of the Kingdom, far exceeding the common dwindled Race of Man in our Days. He argued, that the very Laws of Nature absolutely required we should have been made in the Beginning, of a Size more large and robust, not so liable to Destruction from every little Accident of a Tile falling from an House, or a Stone cast from the Hand of a Boy, or of being drowned in a little Brook. From this Way of Reasoning the Author drew several moral Applications useful in the Conduct of Life, but needless here to repeat. For my own Part, I could not avoid reflecting, how universally this Talent was spread of drawing Lectures in Morality, or indeed rather Matter of Discontent and repining, from the Quarrels we raise with Nature. And, I believe upon a strict Enquiry, those Quarrels might be shewn as ill-grounded among us, as they are among that People.

As to their military Affairs; they boast that the King's Army consists of an hundred and seventy six thousand Foot, and thirty two thousand Horse: If that may be called an Army, which is made up of Tradesmen in the several Cities, and Farmers in the Country, whose Commanders are only the Nobility and Gentry, without Pay or Reward. They are indeed perfect enough in their Exercises; and under very good Discipline, wherein I saw no great Merit: For, how should it be otherwise, where every Farmer is under the Command of his own Landlord, and every Citizen under that of the principal Men in his own City, chosen after the Manner of *Venice* by *Ballot?*

I have often seen the Militia of *Lorbrulgrud* drawn out to Exercise in a great Field near the City, of twenty Miles Square. They were in all not above twenty five thousand Foot, and six thousand Horse; but it was impossible for me to compute their Number, considering the Space of Ground they took up. A *Cavalier* mounted on a large Steed might be about Ninety Foot high. I have seen this Whole Body of Horse upon the Word of Command draw their Swords at once, and brandish them in the Air. Imagination can Figure nothing so Grand, so surprising and so astonishing. It looked as if ten thousand Flashes of Lightning were darting at the same time from every Quarter of the Sky.

I was curious to know how this Prince, to whose Dominions there

is no Access from any other Country, came to think of Armies, or
to teach his People the Practice of military Discipline. But I was
soon informed, both by Conversation, and Reading their Histories.
For, in the Course of many Ages they have been troubled with the
same Disease, to which the whole Race of Mankind is Subject;
the Nobility often contending for Power, the People for Liberty,
and the King for absolute Dominion. All which, however happily
tempered by the Laws of that Kingdom, have been sometimes
violated by each of the three Parties; and have more than once occasioned Civil Wars, the last whereof was happily put an End to
by this Prince's Grandfather in a general Composition; and the
Militia then settled with common Consent hath been ever since
kept in the strictest Duty.

CHAPTER VIII

*The King and Queen make a Progress to the Frontiers.
The Author attends them. The Manner in which he
leaves the Country very particularly related. He returns
to England.*

I had always a strong Impulse that I should some time
recover my Liberty, although it were impossible to conjecture by
what Means, or to form any Project with the least Hope of succeeding. The Ship in which I sailed was the first known to be
driven within Sight of that Coast; and the King had given strict
Orders, that if at any Time another appeared, it should be taken
ashore, and with all its Crew and Passengers brought in a Tum-
bril [1] to *Lorbrulgrud.* He was strongly bent to get me a Woman of
my own Size, by whom I might propagate the Breed: But I think
I should rather have died than undergone the Disgrace of leaving
a Posterity to be kept in Cages like tame Canary Birds; and perhaps
in time sold about the Kingdom to Persons of Quality for Curiosi-

[1] A cart.

ties. I was indeed treated with much Kindness; I was the Favourite of a great King and Queen, and the Delight of the whole Court; but it was upon such a Foot as ill became the Dignity of human Kind. I could never forget those domestick Pledges I had left behind me. I wanted to be among People with whom I could converse upon even Terms; and walk about the Streets and Fields without Fear of being trod to Death like a Frog or young Puppy. But, my Deliverance came sooner than I expected, and in a Manner not very common: The whole Story and Circumstances of which I shall faithfully relate.

I had now been two Years in this Country; and, about the Beginning of the third, *Glumdalclitch* and I attended the King and Queen in Progress to the South Coast of the Kingdom. I was carried as usual in my Travelling-Box, which, as I have already described, was a very convenient Closet of twelve Foot wide. I had ordered a Hammock to be fixed by silken Ropes from the four Corners at the Top; to break the Jolts, when a Servant carried me before him on Horseback, as I sometimes desired; and would often sleep in my Hammock while we were upon the Road. On the Roof of my Closet, set not directly over the Middle of the Hammock, I ordered the Joyner to cut out a Hole of a Foot square to give me Air in hot Weather as I slept; which Hole I shut at pleasure with a Board that drew backwards and forwards through a Groove.

When we came to our Journey's End, the King thought proper to pass a few Days at a Palace he hath near *Flanflasnic*, a City within eighteen *English* Miles of the Sea-side. *Glumdalclitch* and I were much fatigued: I had gotten a small Cold; but the poor Girl was so ill as to be confined to her Chamber. I longed to see the Ocean, which must be the only Scene of my Escape, if ever it should happen. I pretended to be worse than I really was; and desired leave to take the fresh Air of the Sea, with a Page whom I was very fond of, and who had sometimes been trusted with me. I shall never forget with what Unwillingness *Glumdalclitch* consented; nor the strict Charge she gave the Page to be careful of me; bursting at the same time into a Flood of Tears, as if she had some Foreboding of what was to happen. The Boy took me out in my Box about Half an Hour's walk from the Palace, towards the Rocks on the Sea-shore. I ordered him to set me down; and lifting up one of my Sashes, cast many a wistful melancholy Look towards the Sea. I found myself not very well; and told the Page that I had a Mind to take a Nap in my Hammock, which I hoped would do me good. I got in, and the Boy shut the Window close down, to keep out the Cold. I soon fell asleep: And all I can conjecture is, that while I slept, the Page, thinking no Danger could happen, went among the Rocks to look for Birds Eggs; having before observed him from my Window searching about, and picking up one or two in the Clefts. Be that as it will; I found my self suddenly awaked with a violent Pull upon the Ring which was fastned at the Top of my Box for the Conveniency of Carriage. I felt the Box raised very high in the Air, and then born forward with prodigious Speed. The first Jolt had like to have shaken me out of my Hammock; but afterwards the Motion was easy enough. I called out several times as loud as I could raise my Voice, but all to no purpose. I looked towards my Windows, and could see nothing but the Clouds and Sky. I heard a Noise just over my Head like the clapping of Wings; and then began to perceive the woful Condition I was in; that some Eagle had got the Ring of my Box in his Beak, with an Intent to let it fall on a Rock, like a Tortoise in a Shell, and then pick out my Body and devour it. For the Sagacity and Smell of this Bird enable him to discover his Quarry at a great Distance, although better concealed than I could be within a two Inch Board.

In a little time I observed the Noise and flutter of Wings to encrease very fast; and my Box was tossed up and down like a Sign-post in a windy Day. I heard several Bangs or Buffets, as I thought, given to the Eagle (for such I am certain it must have been that held the Ring of my Box in his Beak) and then all on a sudden felt my self falling perpendicularly down for above a Minute; but with such incredible Swiftness that I almost lost my Breath. My Fall was stopped by a terrible Squash, that sounded louder to my Ears than the Cataract of *Niagara*; after which I was quite in the Dark for another Minute, and then my Box began to rise so high that I could see Light from the Tops of my Windows. I now perceived that I was fallen into the Sea. My Box, by the Weight of my Body, the Goods that were in, and the broad Plates of Iron fixed for Strength at the four Corners of the Top and Bottom, floated about five Foot deep in Water. I did then, and do now suppose, that the Eagle which flew away with my Box was pursued by two or three others, and forced to let me drop while he was defending himself against the Rest, who hoped to share in the Prey. The Plates of Iron fastned at the Bottom of the Box, (for those were the strongest) preserved the Balance while it fell; and hindred it from being broken on the Surface of the Water. Every Joint of it was well grooved, and the Door did not move on Hinges, but up and down like a Sash; which kept my Closet so tight that very little Water came in. I got with much Difficulty out of my Hammock, having first ventured to draw back the Slip board on the Roof already mentioned, contrived on purpose to let in Air; for want of which I found my self almost stifled.

How often did I then wish my self with my dear *Glumdalclitch*, from whom one single Hour had so far divided me! And I may say with Truth, that in the midst of my own Misfortune, I could not forbear lamenting my poor Nurse, the Grief she would suffer for my Loss, the Displeasure of the Queen, and the Ruin of her Fortune. Perhaps many Travellers have not been under greater Difficulties and Distress than I was at this Juncture; expecting every Moment to see my Box dashed in Pieces, or at least overset by the first violent Blast, or a rising Wave. A Breach in one single Pane of Glass would have been immediate Death: Nor could any thing have preserved the Windows but the strong Lattice Wires placed on the outside against Accidents in Travelling. I saw the Water ooze in at several Crannies, although the Leaks were not considerable; and I endeavoured to stop them as well as I could. I was not able to lift up the Roof of my Closet, which otherwise I certainly should have done, and sat on the Top of it, where I might at least preserve myself from being shut up, as I may call it, in the Hold. Or, if I escaped these Dangers for a Day or two, what could I expect but a miserable Death of Cold and Hunger! I was four Hours under these Circumstances, expecting and indeed wishing every Moment to be my last.

I have already told the Reader, that there were two strong Staples fixed upon the Side of my Box which had no Window, and into which the Servant, who used to carry me on Horseback, would put a Leathern Belt, and buckle it about his Waist. Being in this disconsolate State, I heard, or at least thought I heard some kind of grating Noise on that Side of my Box where the Staples were fixed; and soon after I began to fancy that the Box was pulled, or towed along in the Sea; for I now and then felt a sort of tugging, which made the Waves rise near the Tops of my Windows, leaving me almost in the Dark. This gave me some faint Hopes of Relief, although I were not able to imagine how it could be brought about.

I ventured to unscrew one of my Chairs, which were always fastned
to the Floor; and having made a hard shift to screw it down again
directly under the Slipping-board that I had lately opened; I
mounted on the Chair, and putting my Mouth as near as I could to
the Hole, I called for Help in a loud Voice, and in all the Languages
I understood. I then fastned my Handkerchief to a Stick I usually
carried, and thrusting it up the Hole, waved it several times in the
Air; that if any Boat or Ship were near, the Seamen might conjecture some unhappy Mortal to be shut up in the Box.

I found no Effect from all I could do, but plainly perceived my
Closet to be moved along; and in the Space of an Hour, or better,
that Side of the Box where the Staples were, and had no Window,
struck against something that was hard. I apprehended it to be a
Rock, and found my self tossed more than ever. I plainly heard a
Noise upon the Cover of my Closet, like that of a Cable, and the
grating of it as it passed through the Ring. I then found my self
hoisted up by Degrees at least three Foot higher than I was before.
Whereupon, I again thrust up my Stick and Handkerchief, calling
for Help till I was almost hoarse. In return to which, I heard a great
Shout repeated three times, giving me such Transports of Joy as are
not to be conceived but by those who feel them. I now heard a
trampling over my Head; and somebody calling through the Hole
with a loud Voice in the *English* Tongue: *If there be any Body
below, let them speak.* I answered, I was an *Englishman*, drawn by
ill Fortune into the greatest Calamity that ever any Creature underwent; and begged, by all that was moving, to be delivered out of the
Dungeon I was in. The Voice replied, I was safe, for my Box was
fastned to their Ship; and the Carpenter should immediately come,
and saw an Hole in the Cover, large enough to pull me out. I answered, that was needless, and would take up too much Time; for
there was no more to be done, but let one of the Crew put his
Finger into the Ring, and take the Box out of the Sea into the Ship,
and so into the Captain's Cabbin. Some of them upon hearing me
talk so wildly, thought I was mad; others laughed; for indeed it
never came into my Head, that I was now got among People of my
own Stature and Strength. The Carpenter came, and in a few Minutes sawed a Passage about four Foot square; then let down a small
Ladder, upon which I mounted, and from thence was taken into
the Ship in a very weak Condition.

The Sailors were all in Amazement, and asked me a thousand

Questions, which I had no Inclination to answer. I was equally confounded at the Sight of so many Pigmies; for such I took them to
be, after having so long accustomed my Eyes to the monstrous
Objects I had left. But the Captain, Mr. *Thomas Wilcocks*, an
honest worthy *Shropshire* Man, observing I was ready to faint, took
me into his Cabbin, gave me a Cordial to comfort me, and made
me *turn in* upon his own Bed; advising me to take a little Rest,
of which I had great need. Before I went to sleep I gave him to
understand, that I had some valuable Furniture in my Box too good
to be lost; a fine Hammock, an handsome Field-Bed, two Chairs, a
Table and a Cabinet: That my Closet was hung on all Sides, or
rather quilted with Silk and Cotton: That if he would let one of the
Crew bring my Closet into his Cabbin, I would open it before
him, and shew him my Goods. The Captain hearing me utter these
Absurdities, concluded I was raving: However, (I suppose to pacify
me) he promised to give Order as I desired; and going upon Deck,
sent some of his Men down into my Closet, from whence (as I
afterwards found) they drew up all my Goods, and stripped off the
Quilting; but the Chairs, Cabinet and Bed-sted being screwed to
the Floor, were much damaged by the Ignorance of the Seamen,
who tore them up by Force. Then they knocked off some of the
Boards for the Use of the Ship; and when they had got all they had
a Mind for, let the Hulk drop into the Sea, which by Reason of
many Breaches made in the Bottom and Sides, sunk *to rights*.
And indeed I was glad not to have been a Spectator of the Havock
they made; because I am confident it would have sensibly touched
me, by bringing former Passages into my Mind, which I had rather
forget.

I slept some Hours, but perpetually disturbed with Dreams of the
Place I had left, and the Dangers I had escaped. However, upon
waking I found my self much recovered. It was now about eight a
Clock at Night, and the Captain ordered Supper immediately,
thinking I had already fasted too long. He entertained me with great
Kindness, observing me not to look wildly, or talk inconsistently;
and when we were left alone, desired I would give him a Relation of
my Travels, and by what Accident I came to be set adrift in that
monstrous wooden Chest. He said, that about twelve a Clock at
Noon, as he was looking through his Glass, he spied it at a Distance,
and thought it was a Sail, which he had a Mind to make; being not
much out of his Course, in hopes of buying some Biscuit, his own

beginning to fall short. That, upon coming nearer, and finding his
Error, he sent out his Long-boat to discover what I was; that his
Men came back in a Fright, swearing they had seen a swimming
House. That he laughed at their Folly, and went himself in the
Boat, ordering his Men to take a strong Cable along with them.
That the Weather being calm, he rowed round me several times,
observed my Windows, and the Wire Lattices that defended them.
That he discovered two Staples upon one Side, which was all of
Boards, without any Passage for Light. He then commanded his
Men to row up to that Side; and fastning a Cable to one of the
Staples, ordered his Men to tow my Chest (as he called it) towards
the Ship. When it was there, he gave Directions to fasten another
Cable to the Ring fixed in the Cover, and to raise up my Chest
with Pullies, which all the Sailors were not able to do above two
or three Foot. He said, they saw my Stick and Handkerchief thrust
out of the Hole, and concluded, that some unhappy Man must be
shut up in the Cavity. I asked whether he or the Crew had seen
any prodigious Birds in the Air about the Time he first discovered
me: To which he answered, that discoursing this Matter with the
Sailors while I was asleep, one of them said he had *observed* three
Eagles flying towards the North; but remarked nothing of their
being larger than the usual Size; which I suppose must be imputed
to the great Height they were at: And he could not guess the Reason of my Question. I then asked the Captain how far he reckoned
we might be from Land; he said, by the best Computation he could
make, we were at least an hundred Leagues. I assured him, that he
must be mistaken by almost half; for I had not left the Country
from whence I came, above two Hours before I dropt into the Sea.
Whereupon he began again to think that my Brain was disturbed, of
which he gave me a Hint, and advised me to go to Bed in a Cabin
he had provided. I assured him I was well refreshed with his good
Entertainment and Company, and as much in my Senses as ever I
was in my Life. He then grew serious, and desired to ask me freely
whether I were not troubled in Mind by the Consciousness of some
enormous Crime, for which I was punished at the Command of
some Prince, by exposing me in that Chest; as great Criminals in
other Countries have been forced to Sea in a leaky Vessel without
Provisions: For, although he should be sorry to have taken so ill a
Man into his Ship, yet he would engage his Word to set me safe
on Shore in the first Port where we arrived. He added, that his

Suspicions were much increased by some very absurd Speeches I had delivered at first to the Sailors, and afterwards to himself, in relation to my Closet or Chest, as well as by my odd Looks and Behaviour while I was at Supper.

I begged his Patience to hear me tell my Story; which I faithfully did from the last Time I left *England*, to the Moment he first discovered me. And, as Truth always forceth its Way into rational Minds; so, this honest worthy Gentleman, who had some Tincture of Learning, and very good Sense, was immediately convinced of my Candor and Veracity. But, further to confirm all I had said, I entreated him to give Order that my Cabinet should be brought, of which I kept the Key in my Pocket, (for he had already informed me how the Seamen disposed of my Closet) I opened it in his Presence, and shewed him the small Collection of Rarities I made in the Country from whence I had been so strangely delivered. There was the Comb I had contrived out of the Stumps of the King's Beard; and another of the same Materials, but fixed into a paring of her Majesty's Thumb-nail, which served for the Back. There was a Collection of Needles and Pins from a Foot to half a Yard long. Four Wasp-Stings, like Joyners Tacks: Some Combings of the Queen's Hair: A Gold Ring which one Day she made me a Present of in a most obliging Manner, taking it from her little Finger, and throwing it over my Head like a Collar. I desired the Captain would please to accept this Ring in Return of his Civilities; which he absolutely refused. I shewed him a Corn that I had cut off with my own Hand from a Maid of Honour's Toe; it was about the Bigness of a *Kentish* Pippin, and grown so hard, that when I returned to *England*, I got it hollowed into a Cup and set in Silver. Lastly, I desired him to see the Breeches I had then on, which were made of a Mouse's Skin.

I could force nothing on him but a Footman's Tooth, which I observed him to examine with great Curiosity, and found he had a Fancy for it. He received it with abundance of Thanks, more than such a Trifle could deserve. It was drawn by an unskilful Surgeon in a Mistake from one of *Glumdalclitch's* Men, who was afflicted with the Tooth-ach; but it was as sound as any in his Head. I got it cleaned, and put it into my Cabinet. It was about a Foot long, and four Inches in Diameter.

The Captain was very well satisfied with this plain Relation I had given him; and said, he hoped when we returned to *England*, I

would oblige the World by putting it in Paper, and making it publick. My Answer was, that I thought we were already over-stocked
with Books of Travels: That nothing could now pass which was not
extraordinary; wherein I doubted, some Authors less consulted
Truth than their own Vanity or Interest, or the Diversion of ignorant Readers. That my Story could contain little besides common Events, without those ornamental Descriptions of strange
Plants, Trees, Birds, and other Animals; or the barbarous Customs
and Idolatry of savage People, with which most Writers abound.
However, I thanked him for his good Opinion, and promised to
take the Matter into my Thoughts.

He said, he wondered at one Thing very much; which was, to
hear me speak so loud; asking me whether the King or Queen of
that Country were thick of Hearing. I told him it was what I had
been used to for above two Years past; and that I admired as much
at the Voices of him and his Men, who seemed to me only to
whisper, and yet I could hear them well enough. But, when I spoke
in that Country, it was like a Man talking in the Street to another
looking out from the Top of a Steeple, unless when I was placed
on a Table, or held in any Person's Hand. I told him, I had likewise observed another Thing; that when I first got into the Ship,
and the Sailors stood all about me, I thought they were the most
little contemptible Creatures I had ever beheld. For, indeed, while
I was in that Prince's Country, I could never endure to look in a
Glass after my Eyes had been accustomed to such prodigious Objects; because the Comparison gave me so despicable a Conceit of
my self. The Captain said, that while we were at Supper, he observed me to look at every thing with a Sort of Wonder; and that I
often seemed hardly able to contain my Laughter; which he knew
not well how to take, but imputed it to some Disorder in my Brain.
I answered, it was very true; and I wondered how I could forbear,
when I saw his Dishes of the Size of a Silver Three-pence, a Leg
of Pork hardly a Mouthful, a Cup not so big as a Nutshell: And
so I went on, describing the rest of his Houshold stuff and Provisions after the same Manner. For although the Queen had ordered
a little Equipage of all Things necessary for me while I was in her
Service; yet my Ideas were wholly taken up with what I saw on
every Side of me; and I winked at my own Littleness, as People do
at their own Faults. The Captain understood my Raillery very well,
and merrily replied with the old *English* Proverb, that he doubted,

my Eyes were bigger than my Belly; for he did not observe my Stomach so good, although I had fasted all Day: And continuing in his Mirth, protested he would have gladly given an Hundred Pounds to have seen my Closet in the Eagle's Bill, and afterwards in its Fall from so great an Height into the Sea; which would certainly have been a most astonishing Object, worthy to have the Description of it transmitted to future Ages: And the Comparison of *Phaeton* was so obvious, that he could not forbear applying it, although I did not much admire the Conceit.[2]

The Captain having been at *Tonquin*, was in his Return to *England* driven North Eastward to the Latitude of 44 Degrees, and of Longitude 143. But meeting a Trade Wind two Days after I came on board him, we sailed Southward a long Time, and coasting *New-Holland*,[3] kept our Course West-south-west, and then South-south-west till we doubled the *Cape of Good-hope*. Our Voyage was very prosperous, but I shall not trouble the Reader with a Journal of it. The Captain called in at one or two Ports, and sent in his Longboat for Provisions and fresh Water; but I never went out of the Ship till we came into the *Downs*, which was on the 3d Day of *June* 1706, about nine Months after my Escape. I offered to leave my Goods in Security for Payment of my Freight; but the Captain protested he would not receive one Farthing. We took kind Leave of each other; and I made him promise he would come to see me at my House in *Redriff*. I hired a Horse and Guide for five Shillings, which I borrowed of the Captain.

As I was on the Road; observing the Littleness of the Houses, the Trees, the Cattle and the People, I began to think my self in *Lilliput*. I was afraid of trampling on every Traveller I met; and often called aloud to have them stand out of the Way; so that I had like to have gotten one or two broken Heads for my Impertinence.

When I came to my own House, for which I was forced to enquire, one of the Servants opening the Door, I bent down to go in (like a Goose under a Gate) for fear of striking my Head. My Wife ran out to embrace me, but I stooped lower than her Knees, thinking she could otherwise never be able to reach my Mouth. My Daughter kneeled to ask me Blessing, but I could not see her till she

---

[2] A witty turn of thought.
[3] "Tonquin": Tongking, a port in French Indo-China; "coasting New Holland": following the coast line of Australia.

arose; having been so long used to stand with my Head and Eyes erect to above Sixty Foot; and then I went to take her up with one Hand, by the Waist. I looked down upon the Servants, and one or two Friends who were in the House, as if they had been Pigmies, and I a Giant. I told my Wife, she had been too thrifty; for I found she had starved herself and her Daughter to nothing. In short, I behaved my self so unaccountably, that they were all of the Captain's Opinion when he first saw me; and concluded I had lost my Wits. This I mention as an Instance of the great Power of Habit and Prejudice.

In a little Time I and my Family and Friends came to a right Understanding: But my Wife protested I should never go to Sea any more; although my evil Destiny so ordered, that she had not Power to hinder me; as the Reader may know hereafter. In the mean Time, I here conclude the second Part of my unfortunate Voyages.

The End of the Second Part

PART III

A VOYAGE TO LAPUTA, BALNIBARBI, GLUBBDUBDRIB, LUGGNAGG, AND JAPAN

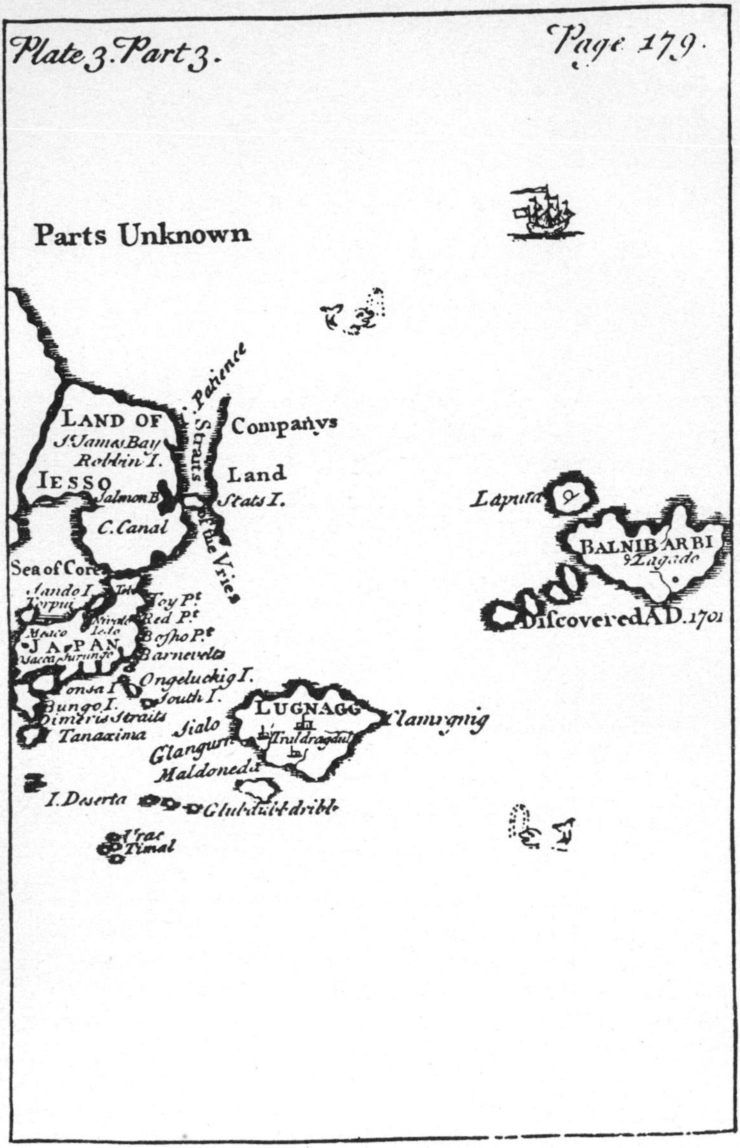

Plate 3. Part 3.

Parts Unknown

LAND OF
S.t James Bay
Robbin I.

IESSO
Salmon B.

C. Canal

Straits of the Vries

Patience

Companys

Land

Stats I.

Lapüta

BALNIBARBI
Lagado

Discovered AD. 1701

Sea of Corea
Mando I.
Torpie
Tsu
Meaco   Iedo
Yacu churinge

Toy P.t
Mindt   Red P.t
Bosho P.t
Barnevelt

Ongeluckig I.
Youth I.

LUGNAGG
Inuldrusdul
Flanwgnig

Onsa I.
Bungo I.
Dimeris Straits
Tanaxina

Sialo
Glanguri
Maldonedi

I. Deserta
Glubdubdribb

Trac
Tinal

CHAPTER I

The Author sets out on his Third Voyage. Is taken by Pyrates. The Malice of a Dutchman. His Arrival at an Island. He is received into Laputa.

I had not been at home above ten Days, when Captain William Robinson, a Cornish Man, Commander of the *Hopewell*, a stout Ship of three Hundred Tuns, came to my House. I had formerly been Surgeon of another Ship where he was Master, and a fourth Part Owner, in a Voyage to the *Levant*. He had always treated me more like a Brother than an inferior Officer; and hearing of my Arrival made me a Visit, as I apprehended only out of Friendship, for nothing passed more than what is usual after long Absence. But repeating his Visits often, expressing his Joy to find me in good Health, asking whether I were now settled for Life, adding that he intended a Voyage to the *East-Indies*, in two Months, at last he plainly invited me, although with some Apologies, to be Surgeon of the Ship. That I should have another Surgeon under me, besides our two Mates; that my Sallary should be double to the usual Pay; and that having experienced my Knowledge in Sea-Affairs to be at least equal to his, he would enter into any Engagement to follow my Advice, as much as if I had Share in the Command.

He said so many other obliging things, and I knew him to be so honest a Man, that I could not reject his Proposal; the Thirst I had of seeing the World, notwithstanding my past Misfortunes, continuing as violent as ever. The only Difficulty that remained, was to persuade my Wife, whose Consent however I at last obtained, by the Prospect of Advantage she proposed to her Children.

We set out the 5th Day of *August*, 1706, and arrived at Fort St. George,[1] the 11th of *April* 1707. We stayed there three Weeks to refresh our Crew, many of whom were sick. From thence we went to *Tonquin*, where the Captain resolved to continue some time;

---

[1] Madras, in southeastern India.

because many of the Goods he intended to buy were not ready, nor could he expect to be dispatched in several Months. Therefore in hopes to defray some of the Charges he must be at, he bought a Sloop, loaded it with several Sorts of Goods, wherewith the *Tonquinese* usually trade to the neighbouring Islands; and putting Fourteen Men on Board, whereof three were of the Country, he appointed me Master of the Sloop, and gave me Power to traffick, while he transacted his Affairs at *Tonquin*.

We had not sailed above three Days, when a great Storm arising, we were driven five Days to the North-North-East, and then to the East; after which we had fair Weather, but still with a pretty strong Gale from the West. Upon the tenth Day we were chased by two Pyrates, who soon overtook us; for my Sloop was so deep loaden, that she sailed very slow; neither were we in a Condition to defend our selves.

We were boarded about the same Time by both the Pyrates, who entered furiously at the Head of their Men; but finding us all prostrate upon our Faces, (for so I gave Order), they pinioned us with strong Ropes, and setting a Guard upon us, went to search the Sloop.

I observed among them a *Dutchman*, who seemed to be of some Authority, although he were not Commander of either Ship. He knew us by our Countenances to be *Englishmen*, and jabbering to us in his own Language, swore we should be tyed Back to Back, and thrown into the Sea. I spoke *Dutch* tolerably well; I told him who we were, and begged him in Consideration of our being Christians and Protestants, of neighbouring Countries, in strict Alliance, that he would move the Captains to take some Pity on us. This inflamed his Rage; he repeated his Threatnings, and turning to his Companions, spoke with great Vehemence, in the *Japanese* Language, as I suppose; often using the Word *Christianos*.[2]

The largest of the two Pyrate Ships was commanded by a *Japanese* Captain, who spoke a little *Dutch*, but very imperfectly. He came up to me, and after several Questions, which I answered in

---

[2] Though allied militarily against France in 1707 (the year of Gulliver's voyage), Holland and England remained vigorous commercial rivals. Moreover, Swift detested the Dutch policy of religious tolerance, which undermined the concept of a national church. Hence, Swift's attitude to the Dutch, and the combination here of Dutch–pirate–antiChristian (see also pp. 185-187).

great Humility, he said we should not die. I made the Captain a very low Bow, and then turning to the *Dutchman*, said, I was sorry to find more Mercy in a Heathen, than in a Brother Christian. But I had soon Reason to repent those foolish Words; for that malicious Reprobate, having often endeavoured in vain to persuade both the Captains that I might be thrown into the Sea, (which they would not yield to after the Promise made me, that I should not die) however prevailed so far as to have a Punishment inflicted on me, worse in all human Appearance than Death it self. My Men were sent by an equal Division into both the Pyrate-Ships, and my Sloop new manned. As to my self, it was determined that I should be set a-drift, in a small Canoe, with Paddles and a Sail, and four Days Provisions; which last the *Japanese* Captain was so kind to double out of his own Stores, and would permit no Man to search me. I got down into the Canoe, while the *Dutchman* standing upon the Deck, loaded me with all the Curses and injurious Terms his Language could afford.

About an Hour before we saw the Pyrates, I had taken an Observation, and found we were in the Latitude of 46 N. and of Longitude 183. When I was at some Distance from the Pyrates, I discovered by my Pocket-Glass several Islands to the South-East. I set up my Sail, the Wind being fair, with a Design to reach the nearest of those Islands, which I made a Shift to do in about three Hours. It was all rocky; however I got many Birds Eggs; and striking Fire, I kindled some Heath and dry Sea Weed, by which I roasted my Eggs. I eat no other Supper, being resolved to spare my Provisions as much as I could. I passed the Night under the Shelter of a Rock, strowing some Heath under me, and slept pretty well.

The next Day I sailed to another Island, and thence to a third and fourth, sometimes using my Sail, and sometimes my Paddles. But not to trouble the Reader with a particular Account of my Distresses; let it suffice, that on the 5th Day, I arrived at the last Island in my Sight, which lay South-South-East to the former. This Island was at a greater Distance than I expected, and I did not reach it in less than five Hours. I encompassed it almost round before I could find a convenient Place to land in, which was a small Creek, about three Times the Wideness of my Canoe. I found the Island to be all rocky, only a little intermingled with Tufts of Grass, and sweet smelling Herbs. I took out my small Provisions, and after having refreshed myself, I secured the Remainder in a Cave, whereof there were great Numbers. I gathered Plenty of Eggs upon the Rocks, and got a Quantity of dry Sea-weed, and parched Grass, which I designed to kindle the next Day, and roast my Eggs as well as I could. (For I had about me my Flint, Steel, Match, and Burning-glass.) I lay all Night in the Cave where I had lodged my Provisions. My Bed was the same dry Grass and Sea-weed which I intended for Fewel. I slept very little; for the Disquiets of my Mind prevailed over my Wearyness, and kept me awake. I considered how impossible it was to preserve my Life, in so desolate a Place; and how miserable my End must be. Yet I found my self so listless and desponding, that I had not the Heart to rise; and before I could get Spirits enough to creep out of my Cave, the Day was far advanced. I walked a while among the Rocks, the Sky was perfectly clear, and the Sun so hot, that I was forced to turn my Face from it: When all on a Sudden it became obscured, as I thought, in a Manner very different from what happens by the Interposition of a Cloud. I turned back, and perceived a vast Opake Body between me and the Sun, moving forwards towards the Island: It seemed to be about two Miles high, and hid the Sun six or seven Minutes, but I did not observe the Air to be much colder, or the Sky more darkned, than if I had stood under the Shade of a Mountain. As it approached nearer over the Place where I was, it appeared to be a firm Substance, the Bottom flat, smooth, and shining very bright from the Reflexion of the Sea below. I stood upon a Height about two Hundred Yards from the Shoar, and saw this vast Body descending almost to a Parallel with me, at less than an *English* Mile Distance. I took out my Pocket-Perspective, and could plainly discover Numbers of People moving up and down the Sides of it, which appeared to be sloping, but what those People were doing, I was not able to distinguish.

The natural Love of Life gave me some inward Motions of Joy; and I was ready to entertain a Hope, that this Adventure might some Way or other help to deliver me from the desolate Place and Condition I was in. But, at the same Time, the Reader can hardly conceive my Astonishment, to behold an Island in the Air, inhabited by Men, who were able (as it should seem) to raise, or sink, or put it into a progressive Motion, as they pleased.[3] But not being,

---

[3] The conception of a flying island was not original with Swift; for some of his sources, see the Bibliography, below: Eddy, *Gulliver's Travels*, and Nicolson and Mohler, "Swift's Flying Island . . ."

at that Time, in a Disposition to philosophise upon this Phaeno-
menon, I rather chose to observe what Course the Island would
take; because it seemed for a while to stand still. Yet soon after it
advanced nearer; and I could see the Sides of it, encompassed with
several Gradations of Galleries and Stairs, at certain Intervals, to
descend from one to the other. In the lowest Gallery, I beheld some
People fishing with long Angling Rods, and others looking on. I
waved my Cap, (for my Hat was long since worn out), and my
Handkerchief towards the Island; and upon its nearer Approach, I
called and shouted with the utmost Strength of my Voice; and then
looking circumspectly, I beheld a Crowd gathered to that Side which
was most in my View. I found by their pointing towards me and
to each other, that they plainly discovered me, although they made
no Return to my Shouting: But I could see four or five Men running in great Haste up the Stairs to the Top of the Island, who
then disappeared. I happened rightly to conjecture, that these were
sent for Orders to some Person in Authority upon this Occasion.

The Number of People increased; and in less than Half an Hour,
the Island was moved and raised in such a Manner, that the lowest
Gallery appeared in a Parallel of less than an Hundred Yards Distance from the Height where I stood. I then put my self into the
most supplicating Postures, and spoke in the humblest Accent, but
received no Answer. Those who stood nearest over-against me,
seemed to be Persons of Distinction, as I supposed by their Habit.
They conferred earnestly with each other, looking often upon me.
At length one of them called out in a clear, polite, smooth Dialect,
not unlike in Sound to the *Italian*; and therefore I returned an
Answer in that Language, hoping at least that the Cadence might
be more agreeable to his Ears. Although neither of us understood
the other, yet my Meaning was easily known, for the People saw
the Distress I was in.

They made Signs for me to come down from the Rock, and go
towards the Shoar, which I accordingly did; and the flying Island
being raised to a convenient Height, the Verge directly over me, a
Chain was let down from the lowest Gallery, with a Seat fastned to
the Bottom, to which I fixed my self, and was drawn up by Pullies.

CHAPTER II

The Humours and Dispositions of the Laputians *described. An Account of their Learning. Of the King and his Court. The Author's Reception there. The Inhabitants subject to Fears and Disquietudes. An Account of the Women.*

At my alighting I was surrounded by a Crowd of People, but those who stood nearest seemed to be of better Quality. They beheld me with all the Marks and Circumstances of Wonder; neither indeed was I much in their Debt; having never till then seen a Race of Mortals so singular in their Shapes, Habits, and Countenances. Their Heads were all reclined to the Right, or the Left; one of their Eyes turned inward, and the other directly up to the Zenith.[1] Their outward Garments were adorned with the Figures of Suns, Moons, and Stars, interwoven with those of Fiddles, Flutes, Harps, Trumpets, Harpsicords, and many more Instruments of Musick, unknown to us in *Europe.* I observed here and there many in the Habit of Servants, with a blown Bladder fastned like a Flail to the End of a short Stick, which they carried in their Hands. In each Bladder was a small Quantity of dried Pease, or little Pebbles, (as I was afterwards informed.) With these Bladders they now and then flapped the Mouths and Ears of those who stood near them, of which Practice I could not then conceive the Meaning. It seems, the Minds of these People are so taken up with intense Speculations, that they neither can speak, or attend to the Discourses of others, without being rouzed by some external Taction upon the Organs of Speech and Hearing; for which Reason, those Persons

[1] Swift intended the Laputians to represent those of his contemporaries who had given themselves to abstract science, mathematics, and musical theory, disciplines he considered wildly impractical and irrelevant to man's proper concern, ethics.

who are able to afford it, always keep a *Flapper*, (the Original is *Climenole*) in their Family, as one of their Domesticks; nor ever walk abroad or make Visits without him. And the Business of this Officer is, when two or more Persons are in Company, gently to strike with his Bladder the Mouth of him who is to speak, and the Right Ear of him or them to whom the Speaker addresseth himself. This *Flapper* is likewise employed diligently to attend his Master in his Walks, and upon Occasion to give him a soft Flap on his Eyes; because he is always so wrapped up in Cogitation, that he is in manifest Danger of falling down every Precipice, and bouncing his Head against every Post; and in the Streets, of jostling others, or being jostled himself into the Kennel.[2]

It was necessary to give the Reader this Information, without which he would be at the same Loss with me, to understand the Proceedings of these People, as they conducted me up the Stairs to the Top of the Island, and from thence to the Royal Palace. While we were ascending, they forgot several Times what they were about, and left me to my self, till their Memories were again rouzed by their *Flappers*; for they appeared altogether unmoved by the Sight of my foreign Habit and Countenance, and by the Shouts of the Vulgar, whose Thoughts and Minds were more disengaged.

At last we entered the Palace, and proceeded into the Chamber of Presence; where I saw the King[3] seated on his Throne, attended on each Side by Persons of prime Quality. Before the Throne, was a large Table filled with Globes and Spheres, and Mathematical Instruments of all Kinds. His Majesty took not the least Notice of us, although our Entrance were not without sufficient Noise, by the Concourse of all Persons belonging to the Court. But, he was then deep in a Problem, and we attended at least an Hour, before he could solve it. There stood by him on each Side, a young Page, with Flaps in their Hands; and when they saw he was at Leisure, one of them gently struck his Mouth, and the other his Right Ear; at which he started like one awaked on the sudden, and looking towards me, and the Company I was in, recollected the Occasion of our coming, whereof he had been informed before. He spoke some Words; whereupon immediately a young Man with a Flap came up to my Side, and flapt me gently on the Right Ear; but I

---

[2] The gutter.
[3] Swift's target is again George I, who, though a patron of music and science, had no real knowledge of either.

made Signs as well as I could, that I had no Occasion for such an Instrument; which as I afterwards found, gave his Majesty and the whole Court a very mean Opinion of my Understanding. The King, as far as I could conjecture, asked me several Questions, and I addressed my self to him in all the Languages I had. When it was found, that I could neither understand nor be understood, I was conducted by his Order to an Apartment in his Palace, (this Prince being distinguished above all his Predecessors for his Hospitality to Strangers,) where two Servants were appointed to attend me. My Dinner was brought, and four Persons of Quality, whom I remembered to have seen very near the King's Person, did me the Honour to dine with me. We had two Courses, of three Dishes each. In the first Course, there was a Shoulder of Mutton, cut into an Æquilateral Triangle; a Piece of Beef into a Rhomboides; and a Pudding into a Cycloid. The second Course was two Ducks, trussed up into the Form of Fiddles; Sausages and Puddings resembling Flutes and Haut-boys,⁴ and a Breast of Veal in the Shape of a Harp. The Servants cut our Bread into Cones, Cylinders, Parallelograms, and several other Mathematical Figures.

While we were at Dinner, I made bold to ask the Names of several Things in their Language; and those noble Persons, by the Assistance of their *Flappers*, delighted to give me Answers, hoping to raise my Admiration of their great Abilities, if I could be brought to converse with them. I was soon able to call for Bread, and Drink, or whatever else I wanted.

After Dinner my Company withdrew, and a Person was sent to me by the King's Order, attended by a *Flapper*. He brought with him Pen, Ink, and Paper, and three or four Books; giving me to understand by Signs, that he was sent to teach me the Language. We sat together four Hours, in which Time I wrote down a great Number of Words in Columns, with the Translations over against them. I likewise made a Shift to learn several short Sentences. For my Tutor would order one of my Servants to fetch something, to turn about, to make a Bow, to sit, or stand, or walk, and the like. Then I took down the Sentence in Writing. He shewed me also in one of his Books, the Figures of the Sun, Moon, and Stars, the Zodiack, the Tropics and Polar Circles, together with the Denominations of many Figures of Planes and Solids. He gave me the

---

⁴ Oboes.

Names and Descriptions of all the Musical Instruments, and the general Terms of Art in playing on each of them. After he had left me, I placed all my Words with their Interpretations in alphabetical Order. And thus in a few Days, by the Help of a very faithful Memory, I got some Insight into their Language.

The Word, which I interpret the *Flying* or *Floating Island*, is in the Original *Laputa*; whereof I could never learn the true Etymology. *Lap* in the old obsolete Language signifieth *High*, and *Untuh* a *Governor*; from which they say by Corruption was derived *Laputa* from *Lapuntuh*. But I do not approve of this Derivation, which seems to be a little strained. I ventured to offer to the Learned among them a Conjecture of my own, that *Laputa* was *quasi Lap outed*; *Lap* signifying properly the dancing of the Sun Beams in the Sea; and *outed* a Wing, which however I shall not obtrude, but submit to the judicious Reader.[5]

Those to whom the King had entrusted me, observing how ill I was clad, ordered a Taylor to come next Morning, and take my Measure for a Suit of Cloths. This Operator did his Office after a different Manner from those of his Trade in *Europe*. He first took my Altitude by a Quadrant, and then with Rule and Compasses, described the Dimensions and Out-Lines of my whole Body; all which he entred upon Paper, and in six Days brought my Cloths very ill made, and quite out of Shape, by happening to mistake a Figure in the Calculation. But my Comfort was, that I observed such Accidents very frequent, and little regarded.

During my Confinement for want of Cloaths, and by an Indisposition that held me some Days longer, I much enlarged my Dictionary; and when I went next to Court, was able to understand many Things the King spoke, and to return him some Kind of Answers. His Majesty had given Orders, that the Island should move North-East and by East, to the vertical Point over *Lagado*, the Metropolis of the whole Kingdom, below upon the firm Earth. It was about Ninety Leagues distant, and our Voyage lasted four Days and an Half. I was not in the least sensible of the progressive Motion made in the Air by the Island. On the second Morning, about Eleven o'Clock, the King himself in Person, attended by his Nobil-

[5] Another Swift parody, this time of the philology of his day. Gulliver misses the likely derivation, the Spanish *la puta*, "the whore," an apt, if ironic, name for a people that has dealt so unnaturally with its physical nature.

ity, Courtiers, and Officers, having prepared all their Musical Instruments, played on them for three Hours without Intermission; so that I was quite stunned with the Noise; neither could I possibly guess the Meaning, till my Tutor informed me. He said, that the People of their Island had their Ears adapted to hear the Musick of the Spheres, which always played at certain Periods; and the Court was now prepared to bear their Part in whatever Instrument they most excelled.

In our Journey towards *Lagado* the Capital City, his Majesty ordered that the Island should stop over certain Towns and Villages, from whence he might receive the Petitions of his Subjects. And to this Purpose, several Packthreads were let down with small Weights at the Bottom. On these Packthreads the People strung their Petitions, which mounted up directly like the Scraps of Paper fastned by School-boys at the End of the String that holds their Kite. Sometimes we received Wine and Victuals from below, which were drawn up by Pullies.

The Knowledge I had in Mathematicks gave me great Assistance in acquiring their Phraseology, which depended much upon that Science and Musick; and in the latter I was not unskilled. Their Ideas are perpetually conversant in Lines and Figures. If they would, for Example, praise the Beauty of a Woman, or any other Animal, they describe it by Rhombs, Circles, Parallelograms, Ellipses, and other Geometrical Terms; or else by Words of Art drawn from Musick, needless here to repeat. I observed in the King's Kitchen all Sorts of Mathematical and Musical Instruments, after the Figures of which they cut up the Joynts that were served to his Majesty's Table.

Their Houses are very ill built, the Walls bevil, without one right Angle in any Apartment; and this Defect ariseth from the Contempt they bear for practical Geometry; which they despise as vulgar and mechanick, those Instructions they give being too refined for the Intellectuals of their Workmen; which occasions perpetual Mistakes. And although they are dextrous enough upon a Piece of Paper, in the Management of the Rule, the Pencil, and the Divider, yet in the common Actions and Behaviour of Life, I have not seen a more clumsy, awkward, and unhandy People, nor so slow and perplexed in their Conceptions upon all other Subjects, except those of Mathematicks and Musick. They are very bad Reasoners, and vehemently given to Opposition, unless when they happen to be of the right Opinion, which is seldom their Case. Imagination, Fancy, and Invention, they are wholly Strangers to, nor have any Words in their Language by which those Ideas can be expressed; the whole Compass of their Thoughts and Mind, being shut up within the two forementioned Sciences.

Most of them, and especially those who deal in the Astronomical Part, have great Faith in judicial Astrology, although they are ashamed to own it publickly. But, what I chiefly admired, and thought altogether unaccountable, was the strong Disposition I observed in them towards News and Politicks; perpetually enquiring into publick Affairs, giving their Judgments in Matters of State; and passionately disputing every Inch of a Party Opinion. I have indeed observed the same Disposition among most of the Mathematicians I have known in *Europe*; although I could never discover the least Analogy between the two Sciences; unless those People suppose, that because the smallest Circle hath as many Degrees as the largest, therefore the Regulation and Management of the World require no more Abilities than the handling and turning of a Globe. But, I rather take this Quality to spring from a very common Infirmity of human Nature, inclining us to be more curious and conceited in Matters where we have least Concern, and for which we are least adapted either by Study or Nature.

These People are under continual Disquietudes, never enjoying a Minute's Peace of Mind; and their Disturbances proceed from Causes which very little affect the rest of Mortals. Their Apprehensions[6] arise from several Changes they dread in the Celestial Bodies. For instance; that the Earth by the continual Approaches of the Sun towards it, must in Course of Time be absorbed or swallowed up. That the Face of the Sun will by Degrees be encrusted with its own Effluvia, and give no more Light to the World. That, the Earth very narrowly escaped a Brush from the Tail of the last Comet, which would have infallibly reduced it to Ashes; and that the next, which they have calculated for One and Thirty Years hence, will probably destroy us. For, if in its Perihelion it should approach within a certain Degree of the Sun, (as by their Calculations they have Reason to dread) it will conceive a Degree of Heat ten Thousand Times more intense than that of red hot glowing

* The catalogue of fears that follows is based on actual speculations by the scientists of Swift's time (see in the Bibliography, Nicolson and Mohler, "The Scientific Background of Swift's *Voyage to Laputa*").

Iron; and in its Absence from the Sun, carry a blazing Tail Ten
Hundred Thousand and Fourteen Miles long; through which if the
Earth should pass at the Distance of one Hundred Thousand Miles
from the *Nucleus*, or main Body of the Comet, it must in its Passage be set on Fire, and reduced to Ashes. That the Sun daily
spending its Rays without any Nutriment to supply them, will at
last be wholly consumed and annihilated; which must be attended
with the Destruction of this Earth, and of all the Planets that receive their Light from it.

They are so perpetually alarmed with the Apprehensions of these
and the like impending Dangers, that they can neither sleep quietly
in their Beds, nor have any Relish for the common Pleasures or
Amusements of Life. When they meet an Acquaintance in the
Morning, the first Question is about the Sun's Health; how he
looked at his Setting and Rising, and what Hopes they have to
avoid the Stroak of the approaching Comet. This Conversation
they are apt to run into with the same Temper that Boys discover,
in delighting to hear terrible Stories of Sprites and Hobgoblins,
which they greedily listen to, and dare not go to Bed for fear.

The Women of the Island have Abundance of Vivacity; they
contemn their Husbands, and are exceedingly fond of Strangers,
whereof there is always a considerable Number from the Continent below, attending at Court, either upon Affairs of the several
Towns and Corporations, or their own particular Occasions; but are
much despised, because they want the same Endowments. Among
these the Ladies chuse their Gallants: But the Vexation is, that
they act with too much Ease and Security; for the Husband is always so rapt in Speculation, that the Mistress and Lover may proceed to the greatest Familiarities before his Face, if he be but
provided with Paper and Implements, and without his *Flapper* at
his Side.

The Wives and Daughters lament their Confinement to the
Island, although I think it the most delicious Spot of Ground in
the World; and although they live here in the greatest Plenty and
Magnificence, and are allowed to do whatever they please: They
long to see the World, and take the Diversions of the Metropolis,
which they are not allowed to do without a particular Licence from
the King; and this is not easy to be obtained, because the People of
Quality have found by frequent Experience, how hard it is to persuade their Women to return from below. I was told, that a great

Court Lady, who had several Children, is married to the prime Minister, the richest Subject in the Kingdom, a very graceful Person, extremely fond of her, and lives in the finest Palace of the Island; went down to *Lagado*, on the Pretence of Health, there hid her self for several Months, till the King sent a Warrant to search for her; and she was found in an obscure Eating-House all in Rags, having pawned her Cloths to maintain an old deformed Footman, who beat her every Day, and in whose Company she was taken much against her Will. And although her Husband received her with all possible Kindness, and without the least Reproach; she soon after contrived to steal down again with all her Jewels, to the same Gallant, and hath not been heard of since.

This may perhaps pass with the Reader rather for an *European* or *English Story*, than for one of a Country so remote. But he may please to consider, that the Caprices of Womankind are not limited by any Climate or Nation; and that they are much more uniform than can be easily imagined.

In about a Month's Time I had made a tolerable Proficiency in their Language, and was able to answer most of the King's Questions, when I had the Honour to attend him. His Majesty discovered not the least Curiosity to enquire into the Laws, Government, History, Religion, or Manners of the Countries where I had been; but confined his Questions to the State of Mathematicks, and received the Account I gave him, with great Contempt and Indifference, though often rouzed by his *Flapper* on each Side.

CHAPTER III

A Phænomenon solved by modern Philosophy and Astronomy. The Laputians *great Improvements in the latter. The King's Method of suppressing Insurrections.*

I desired Leave of this Prince to see the Curiosities of the Island; which he was graciously pleased to grant, and ordered my

Tutor to attend me. I chiefly wanted to know to what Cause in
Art or in Nature, it owed its several Motions; whereof I will now
give a philosophical Account to the Reader.[1]

The flying or floating Island is exactly circular; its Diameter 7837
Yards, or about four Miles and an Half, and consequently contains
ten Thousand Acres. It is three Hundred Yards thick. The Bottom,
or under Surface, which appears to those who view it from below, is
one even regular Plate of Adamant, shooting up to the Height of
about two Hundred Yards. Above it lye the several Minerals in their
usual Order; and over all is a Coat of rich Mould ten or twelve
Foot deep. The Declivity of the upper Surface, from the Circumference to the Center, is the natural Cause why all the Dews and
Rains which fall upon the Island, are conveyed in small Rivulets
towards the Middle, where they are emptied into four large Basons,
each of about Half a Mile in Circuit, and two Hundred Yards distant from the Center. From these Basons the Water is continually
exhaled by the Sun in the Day-time, which effectually prevents their
overflowing. Besides, as it is in the Power of the Monarch to raise
the Island above the Region of Clouds and Vapours, he can prevent
the falling of Dews and Rains whenever he pleases. For the highest
Clouds cannot rise above two Miles, as Naturalists agree, at least
they were never known to do so in that Country.

At the Center of the *Island* there is a Chasm about fifty Yards in
Diameter, from whence the Astronomers descend into a large
Dome, which is therefore called *Flandona Gagnole*, or the *Astronomers Cave*; situated at the Depth of an Hundred Yards beneath
the upper Surface of the Adamant. In this Cave are Twenty Lamps
continually burning, which from the Reflection of the Adamant
cast a strong Light into every Part. The Place is stored with great
Variety of Sextants, Quadrants, Telescopes, Astrolabes, and other
Astronomical Instruments. But the greatest Curiosity, upon which
the Fate of the Island depends, is a Load-stone of a prodigious Size,
in Shape resembling a Weaver's Shuttle. It is in Length six Yards,
and in the thickest Part at least three Yards over. This Magnet is
sustained by a very strong Axle of Adamant, passing through its
Middle, upon which it plays, and is poized so exactly that the
weakest Hand can turn it. It is hooped round with an hollow

---

[1] The "philosophical account" in the next several paragraphs is Swift's
parody of the typical scientific paper published in the *Transactions* of the
Royal Society.

Plate 4. Part 3.

Page 205

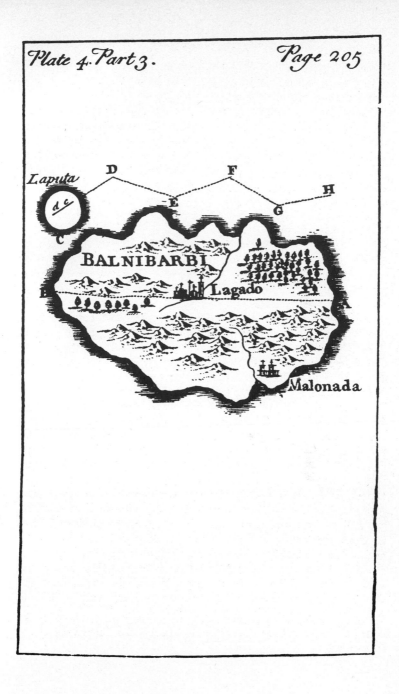

Cylinder of Adamant, four Foot deep, as many thick, and twelve Yards in Diameter, placed horizontally, and supported by Eight Adamantine Feet, each Six Yards high. In the Middle of the Concave Side there is a Groove Twelve Inches deep, in which the Extremities of the Axle are lodged, and turned round as there is Occasion.

This Stone cannot be moved from its Place by any Force, because the Hoop and its Feet are one continued Piece with that Body of Adamant which constitutes the Bottom of the Island.

By Means of his Load-stone, the Island is made to rise and fall, and move from one Place to another. For, with respect to that Part of the Earth over which the Monarch presides, the Stone is endued at one of its Sides with an attractive Power, and at the other with a repulsive. Upon placing the Magnet erect with its attracting End towards the Earth, the Island descends; but when the repelling Extremity points downwards, the Island mounts directly upwards. When the Position of the Stone is oblique, the Motion of the Island is so too. For in this Magnet the Forces always act in Lines parallel to its Direction.

By this oblique Motion the Island is conveyed to different Parts of the Monarch's Dominions. To explain the Manner of its Progress, let A B represent a Line drawn cross the Dominions of *Balnibarbi*; let the Line *c d* represent the Load-stone, of which let *d* be the repelling End, and *c* the attracting End, the Island being over *C*; let the Stone be placed in the Position *c d* with its repelling End downwards; then the Island will be driven upwards obliquely towards D. When it is arrived at D, let the Stone be turned upon its Axle till its attracting End points towards E, and then the Island will be carried obliquely towards E; where if the Stone be again turned upon its Axle till it stands in the Position E F, with its repelling Point downwards, the Island will rise obliquely towards F, where by directing the attracting End towards G, the Island may be carried to G, and from G to H, by turning the Stone, so as to make its repelling Extremity point directly downwards. And thus by changing the Situation of the Stone as often as there is Occasion, the Island is made to rise and fall by Turns in an oblique Direction; and by those alternate Risings and Fallings (the Obliquity being not considerable) is conveyed from one Part of the Dominions to the other.

But it must be observed, that this Island cannot move beyond the Extent of the Dominions below; nor can it rise above the Height of four Miles. For which the Astronomers (who have written large Systems concerning the Stone) assign the following Reason: That the Magnetick Virtue does not extend beyond the Distance of four Miles, and that the Mineral which acts upon the Stone in the Bowels of the Earth, and in the Sea about six Leagues distant from the Shoar, is not diffused through the whole Globe, but terminated with the Limits of the King's Dominions: And it was easy from the great Advantage of such a superior Situation, for a Prince to bring under his Obedience whatever Country lay within the Attraction of that Magnet.

When the Stone is put parallel to the Plane of the Horizon, the Island standeth still; for in that Case, the Extremities of it being at equal Distance from the Earth, act with equal Force, the one in drawing downwards, the other in pushing upwards; and consequently no Motion can ensue.

This Load-stone is under the Care of certain Astronomers, who from Time to Time give it such Positions as the Monarch directs. They spend the greatest Part of their Lives in observing the celestial Bodies, which they do by the Assistance of Glasses, far excelling ours in Goodness. For, although their largest Telescopes do not exceed three Feet, they magnify much more than those of a Hundred with us, and shew the Stars with greater Clearness. This Advantage hath enabled them to extend their Discoveries much farther than our Astronomers in *Europe*. They have made a Catalogue of ten Thousand fixed Stars, whereas the largest of ours do not contain above one third Part of that Number. They have likewise discovered two lesser Stars, or *Satellites*, which revolve about *Mars*; whereof the innermost is distant from the Center of the primary Planet exactly three of his Diameters, and the outermost five; the former revolves in the Space of ten Hours, and the latter in Twenty-one and an Half; so that the Squares of their periodical Times, are very near in the same Proportion with the Cubes of their Distance from the Center of *Mars*; which evidently shews them to be governed by the same Law of Gravitation, that influences the other heavenly Bodies.

They have observed Ninety-three different Comets, and settled their Periods with great Exactness. If this be true, (and they affirm it with great Confidence) it is much to be wished that their Observations were made publick; whereby the Theory of Comets, which at present is very lame and defective, might be brought to the same Perfection with other Parts of Astronomy.

The King would be the most absolute Prince in the Universe, if he could but prevail on a Ministry to join with him; but these having their Estates below on the Continent, and considering that the Office of a Favourite hath a very uncertain Tenure, would never consent to the enslaving their Country.

If any Town should engage in Rebellion or Mutiny, fall into violent Factions, or refuse to pay the usual Tribute; the King hath two Methods of reducing them to Obedience. The first and the mildest Course is by keeping the Island hovering over such a Town, and the Lands about it; whereby he can deprive them of the Benefit of the Sun and the Rain, and consequently afflict the Inhabitants with Dearth and Diseases. And if the Crime deserve it, they are at the same time pelted from above with great Stones, against which they have no Defence, but by creeping into Cellars or Caves, while the Roofs of their Houses are beaten to Pieces. But if they still continue obstinate, or offer to raise Insurrections; he proceeds to the last Remedy, by letting the Island drop directly upon their Heads, which makes a universal Destruction both of Houses and Men. However, this is an Extremity to which the Prince is seldom driven, neither indeed is he willing to put it in Execution; nor dare his Ministers advise him to an Action, which as it would render them odious to the People, so it would be a great Damage to their own Estates that lie all below; for the Island is the King's Demesn.

But there is still indeed a more weighty Reason, why the Kings of this Country have been always averse from executing so terrible an Action, unless upon the utmost Necessity. For if the Town intended to be destroyed should have in it any tall Rocks, as it generally falls out in the larger Cities; a Situation probably chosen at first with a View to prevent such a Catastrophe: Or if it abound in high Spires or Pillars of Stone, a sudden Fall might endanger the Bottom or under Surface of the Island, which although it consist as I have said, of one entire Adamant two hundred Yards thick, might happen to crack by too great a Choque, or burst by approaching too near the Fires from the Houses below; as the Backs both of Iron and Stone will often do in our Chimneys. Of all this the People are well apprized, and understand how far to carry their Obstinacy, where their Liberty or Property is concerned.

And the King, when he is highest provoked, and most determined to press a City to Rubbish, orders the Island to descend with great Gentleness, out of a Pretence of Tenderness to his People, but indeed for fear of breaking the Adamantine Bottom; in which Case it is the Opinion of all their Philosophers, that the Load-stone could no longer hold it up, and the whole Mass would fall to the Ground.

About three Years before my Arrival among them,[2] while the King was in his Progress over his Dominions there happened an extraordinary Accident which had like to have put a Period to the Fate of that Monarchy, at least as it is now instituted. Lindalino the second City in the Kingdom was the first his Majesty visited in his Progress. Three Days after his Departure, the Inhabitants who had often complained of great Oppressions, shut the Town Gates, seized on the Governor, and with incredible Speed and Labour erected four large Towers, one at every Corner of the City (which is an exact Square) equal in Height to a strong pointed Rock that stands directly in the Center of the City. Upon the Top of each Tower, as well as upon the Rock, they fixed a great Loadstone, and in case their Design should fail, they had provided a vast Quantity of the most combustible Fewel, hoping to burst therewith the adamantine Bottom of the Island, if the Loadstone Project should miscarry.

It was eight Months before the King had perfect Notice that the Lindalinians were in Rebellion. He then commanded that the Island should be wafted over the City. The People were unanimous, and had laid in Store of Provisions, and a great River runs through the middle of the Town. The King hovered over them several Days to deprive them of the Sun and the Rain. He ordered many Packthreads to be let down, yet not a Person offered to send up a

---

[2] This paragraph, and the next four, were omitted from all editions (including the first) until introduced in 1899. The first publishers of *Gulliver*, fearing government reprisals, found them too dangerous to include; others omitted them most likely through ignorance of their existence. Allegorically, they tell of Ireland's campaign against the introduction of a debased currency manufactured by an ironmonger named Wood who had purchased the privilege from a mistress of George I. Swift sided with the Irish, pressing the cause in a series of letters (1724) under the name of M. B., Drapier. These letters (alluded to in the allegory as a "most combustible Fewel") were influential in forcing England to cancel the project. Dublin is here disguised as Lindalino.

Petition, but instead thereof, very bold Demands, the Redress of
all their Grievances, great Immunitys, the Choice of their own
Governor, and other the like Exorbitances. Upon which his Majesty
commanded all the Inhabitants of the Island to cast great Stones
from the lower gallery into the Town; but the Citizens had provided
against this Mischief by conveying their Persons and Effects into
the four Towers, and other strong Buildings, and Vaults under
Ground.

The King being now determined to reduce this proud People,
ordered that the Island should descend gently within fourty Yards
of the Top of the Towers and Rock. This was accordingly done;
but the Officers employed in that Work found the Descent much
speedier than usual, and by turning the Loadstone could not without great Difficulty keep it in a firm position, but found the
Island inclining to fall. They sent the King immediate Intelligence
of this astonishing Event and begged his Majesty's Permission to
raise the Island higher; the King consented, a general Council
was called, and the Officers of the Loadstone ordered to attend.
One of the oldest and expertest among them obtained leave to try
an Experiment. He took a strong Line of an Hundred Yards, and
the Island being raised over the Town above the attracting Power
they had felt, He fastened a Piece of Adamant to the End of his
Line which had in it a Mixture of Iron mineral, of the same
Nature with that whereof the Bottom or lower Surface of the
Island is composed, and from the lower Gallery let it down slowly
towards the Top of the Towers. The Adamant was not descended
four Yards, before the Officer felt it drawn so strongly downwards,
that he could hardly pull it back. He then threw down several
small Pieces of Adamant, and observed that they were all violently
attracted by the Top of the Tower. The same Experiment was
made on the other three Towers, and on the Rock with the same
Effect.

This Incident broke entirely the King's Measures and (to dwell
no longer on other Circumstances) he was forced to give the Town
their own Conditions.

I was assured by a great Minister, that if the Island had descended
so near the Town, as not to be able to raise it self, the Citizens
were determined to fix it for ever, to kill the King and all his
Servants, and entirely change the Government.

By a fundamental Law of this Realm, neither the King nor either of his two elder Sons, are permitted to leave the Island; nor the Queen till she is past Child-bearing.

CHAPTER IV

The Author leaves Laputa, is conveyed to Balnibarbi, arrives at the Metropolis. A Description of the Metropolis, and the Country adjoining. The Author hospitably received by a great Lord. His Conversation with that Lord.

Although I cannot say that I was ill treated in this Island, yet I must confess I thought my self too much neglected, not without some Degree of Contempt. For neither Prince nor People appeared to be curious in any Part of Knowledge, except Mathematicks and Musick, wherein I was far their inferior, and upon that Account very little regarded.

On the other Side, after having seen all the Curiosities of the Island, I was very desirous to leave it, being heartily weary of those People. They were indeed excellent in two Sciences for which I have great Esteem, and wherein I am not unversed; but at the same time so abstracted and involved in Speculation, that I never met with such disagreeable Companions. I conversed only with Women, Tradesmen, *Flappers*, and Court-Pages, during two Months of my Abode there; by which at last I rendered my self extremely contemptible; yet these were the only People from whom I could ever receive a reasonable Answer.

I had obtained by hard Study a good Degree of Knowledge in their Language: I was weary of being confined to an Island where I received so little Countenance; and resolved to leave it with the first Opportunity.

There was a great Lord at Court, nearly related to the King, and for that Reason alone used with Respect. He was universally reckoned the most ignorant and stupid Person among them. He had performed many eminent Services for the Crown, had great natural and acquired Parts, adorned with Integrity and Honour; but so ill an Ear for Musick, that his Detractors reported he had been often known to beat Time in the wrong Place; neither could his Tutors without extreme Difficulty teach him to demonstrate the most easy Proposition in the Mathematicks. He was pleased to shew me many Marks of Favour, often did me the Honour of a Visit, desired to be informed in the Affairs of *Europe*, the Laws and Customs, the Manners and Learning of the several Countries where I had travelled. He listened to me with great Attention, and made very wise Observations on all I spoke. He had two *Flappers* attending him for State, but never made use of them except at Court, and in Visits of Ceremony; and would always command them to withdraw when we were alone together.

I intreated this illustrious Person to intercede in my Behalf with his Majesty for Leave to depart; which he accordingly did, as he was pleased to tell me, with Regret: For, indeed he had made me several Offers very advantageous, which however I refused with Expressions of the highest Acknowledgment.

On the 16th Day of *February*, I took Leave of his Majesty and the Court. The King made me a Present to the Value of about two Hundred Pounds *English*; and my Protector his Kinsman as much more, together with a Letter of Recommendation to a Friend of his in *Lagado*, the Metropolis: The Island being then hovering over a Mountain about two Miles from it, I was let down from the lowest Gallery, in the same Manner as I had been taken up.

The Continent, as far as it is subject to the Monarch of the *Flying Island*, passeth under the general Name of *Balnibarbi*; and the Metropolis, as I said before, is called *Lagado*. I felt some little Satisfaction in finding my self on firm Ground. I walked to the City without any Concern, being clad like one of the Natives, and sufficiently instructed to converse with them. I soon found out the Person's House to whom I was recommended; presented my Letter from his Friend the Grandee in the Island, and was received with much Kindness. This great Lord, whose Name was *Munodi*,[1] ordered me an Apartment in his own House, where I continued during my Stay, and was entertained in a most hospitable Manner.

---

[1] One scholar has suggested that "Munodi" may be derived from *mundum odi* ("I hate the world"). Lord Munodi may be either Bolingbroke or Oxford, perhaps a composite of both.

The next Morning after my Arrival he took me in his Chariot to see the Town, which is about half the Bigness of *London*; but the Houses very strangely built, and most of them out of Repair. The People in the Streets walked fast, looked wild, their Eyes fixed, and were generally in Rags. We passed through one of the Town Gates, and went about three Miles into the Country, where I saw many Labourers working with several Sorts of Tools in the Ground, but was not able to conjecture what they were about; neither did I observe any Expectation either of Corn or Grass, although the Soil appeared to be excellent. I could not forbear admiring at these odd Appearances both in Town and Country; and I made bold to desire my Conductor, that he would be pleased to explain to me what could be meant by so many busy Heads, Hands and Faces, both in the Streets and the Fields, because I did not discover any good Effects they produced; but on the contrary, I never knew a Soil so unhappily cultivated, Houses so ill contrived and so ruinous, or a People whose Countenances and Habit expressed so much Misery and Want.

This Lord *Munodi* was a Person of the first Rank, and had been some Years Governor of *Lagado*; but by a Cabal of Ministers was discharged for Insufficiency. However the King treated him with Tenderness, as a well-meaning Man, but of a low contemptible Understanding.

When I gave that free Censure of the Country and its Inhabitants, he made no further Answer than by telling me, that I had not been long enough among them to form a Judgment; and that the different Nations of the World had different Customs; with other common Topicks to the same Purpose. But when we returned to his Palace, he asked me how I liked the Building, what Absurdities I observed, and what Quarrel I had with the Dress or Looks of his Domesticks. This he might safely do; because every Thing about him was magnificent, regular and polite. I answered, that his Excellency's Prudence, Quality, and Fortune, had exempted him from those Defects which Folly and Beggary had produced in others. He said, if I would go with him to his Country House about Twenty Miles distant, where his Estate lay, there would be more Leisure for this Kind of Conversation. I told his Excellency, that I was entirely at his Disposal; and accordingly we set out next Morning.

During our Journey, he made me observe the several Methods

used by Farmers in managing their Lands; which to me were wholly
unaccountable: For except in some very few Places, I could not
discover one Ear of Corn, or Blade of Grass. But, in three Hours
travelling, the Scene was wholly altered; we came into a most
beautiful Country; Farmers Houses at small Distances, neatly
built, the Fields enclosed, containing Vineyards, Corn-grounds and
Meadows. Neither do I remember to have seen a more delightful
Prospect. His Excellency observed my Countenance to clear up;
he told me with a Sigh, that there his Estate began, and would
continue the same till we should come to his House. That his
Countrymen ridiculed and despised him for managing his Affairs
no better, and for setting so ill an Example to the Kingdom; which
however was followed by very few, such as were old and wilful,
and weak like himself.

We came at length to the House, which was indeed a noble
Structure, built according to the best Rules of ancient Architecture.
The Fountains, Gardens, Walks, Avenues, and Groves were all
disposed with exact Judgment and Taste. I gave due Praises to
every Thing I saw, whereof his Excellency took not the least Notice
till after Supper; when, there being no third Companion, he told
me with a very melancholy Air, that he doubted he must throw
down his Houses in Town and Country, to rebuild them after the
present Mode; destroy all his Plantations, and cast others into such
a Form as modern Usage required; and give the same Directions
to all his Tenants, unless he would submit to incur the Censure of
Pride, Singularity, Affectation, Ignorance, Caprice; and perhaps
encrease his Majesty's Displeasure.

That the Admiration I appeared to be under, would cease or
diminish when he had informed me of some Particulars, which
probably I never heard of at Court, the People there being too
much taken up in their own Speculations, to have Regard to what
passed here below.

The Sum of his Discourse was to this Effect. That about Forty
Years ago, certain Persons went up to *Laputa*, either upon Business
or Diversion; and after five Months Continuance, came back with
a very little Smattering in Mathematicks, but full of Volatile Spirits
acquired in that Airy Region. That these Persons upon their
Return, began to dislike the Management of every Thing below;
and fell into Schemes of putting all Arts, Sciences, Languages, and
Mechanics upon a new Foot. To this End they procured a Royal

Patent for erecting an Academy of PROJECTORS in *Lagado*:[2] And
the Humour prevailed so strongly among the People, that there is
not a Town of any Consequence in the Kingdom without such an
Academy. In these Colleges, the Professors contrive new Rules and
Methods of Agriculture and Building, and new Instruments and
Tools for all Trades and Manufactures, whereby, as they undertake,
one Man shall do the Work of Ten; a Palace may be built in a
Week, of Materials so durable as to last for ever without repairing.
All the Fruits of the Earth shall come to Maturity at whatever
Season we think fit to chuse, and increase an Hundred Fold more
than they do at present; with innumerable other happy Proposals.
The only Inconvenience is, that none of these Projects are yet
brought to Perfection; and in the mean time, the whole Country
lies miserably waste, the Houses in Ruins, and the People without
Food or Cloaths. By all which, instead of being discouraged, they
are Fifty Times more violently bent upon prosecuting their Schemes,
driven equally on by Hope and Despair: That, as for himself, being
not of an enterprizing Spirit, he was content to go on in the old
Forms; to live in the Houses his Ancestors had built, and act as
they did in every Part of Life without Innovation. That, some few
other Persons of Quality and Gentry had done the same; but were
looked on with an Eye of Contempt and ill Will, as Enemies to
Art, ignorant, and ill Commonwealthsmen, preferring their own
Ease and Sloth before the general Improvement of their Country.

His Lordship added, that he would not by any further Particulars prevent the Pleasure I should certainly take in viewing the
grand Academy, whither he was resolved I should go. He only
desired me to observe a ruined Building upon the Side of a Mountain about three Miles distant, of which he gave me this Account.
That he had a very convenient Mill within Half a Mile of his
House, turned by a Current from a large River, and sufficient for
his own Family as well as a great Number of his Tenants. That,
about seven Years ago, a Club of those Projectors came to him
with Proposals to destroy this Mill, and build another on the Side
of that Mountain, on the long Ridge whereof a long Canal must
be cut for a Repository of Water, to be conveyed up by Pipes and
Engines to supply the Mill: Because the Wind and Air upon a

[2] Swift intended the Academy of Lagado to correspond to the Royal
Society, while by a "Projector" he meant anyone given to impractical or
visionary schemes and activities.

Height agitated the Water, and thereby made it fitter for Motion: And because the Water descending down a Declivity would turn the Mill with half the Current of a River whose Course is more upon a Level. He said, that being then not very well with the Court, and pressed by many of his Friends, he complyed with the Proposal; and after employing an Hundred Men for two Years, the Work miscarryed, the Projectors went off, laying the Blame intirely upon him; railing at him ever since, and putting others upon the same Experiment, with equal Assurance of Success, as well as equal Disappointment.

In a few Days we came back to Town; and his Excellency, considering the bad Character he had in the Academy, would not go with me himself, but recommended me to a Friend of his to bear me Company thither. My Lord was pleased to represent me as a great Admirer of Projects, and a Person of much Curiosity and easy Belief; which indeed was not without Truth; for I had my self been a Sort of Projector in my younger Days.

CHAPTER V

The Author permitted to see the grand Academy of Lagado. The Academy largely described. The Arts wherein the Professors employ themselves.

This Academy is not an entire single Building, but a Continuation of several Houses on both Sides of a Street; which growing waste, was purchased and applyed to that Use.

I was received very kindly by the Warden, and went for many Days to the Academy. Every Room hath in it one or more Projectors; and I believe I could not be in fewer than five Hundred Rooms.

The first Man I saw was of a meagre Aspect, with sooty Hands and Face, his Hair and Beard long, ragged and singed in several Places. His Clothes, Shirt, and Skin were all of the same Colour. He had been Eight Years upon a Project for extracting Sun-Beams out of Cucumbers, which were to be put into Vials hermetically sealed, and let out to warm the Air in raw inclement Summers.[1] He told me, he did not doubt in Eight Years more, that he should be able to supply Governors Gardens with Sun-shine at a reasonable Rate; but he complained that his Stock was low, and intreated me to give him something as an Encouragement to Ingenuity, especially since this had been a very dear Season for Cucumbers. I made him a small Present, for my Lord had furnished me with Money on purpose, because he knew their Practice of begging from all who go to see them.

I went into another Chamber, but was ready to hasten back, being almost overcome with a horrible Stink. My Conductor pressed me forward, conjuring me in a Whisper to give no Offence, which would be highly resented; and therefore I durst not so much as stop my Nose. The Projector of this Cell was the most ancient Student of the Academy. His Face and Beard were of a pale Yellow; his Hands and Clothes dawbed over with Filth. When I was presented to him, he gave me a very close Embrace, (a Compliment I could well have excused). His Employment from his first coming into the Academy, was an Operation to reduce human Excrement to its original Food, by separating the several Parts, removing the Tincture which it receives from the Gall, making the Odour exhale, and scumming off the Saliva. He had a weekly Allowance from the Society, of a Vessel filled with human Ordure, about the Bigness of a *Bristol* Barrel.

I saw another at work to calcine Ice into Gunpowder; who likewise shewed me a Treatise he had written concerning the Malleability of Fire, which he intended to publish.

There was a most ingenious Architect who had contrived a new Method for building Houses, by beginning at the Roof, and working downwards to the Foundation; which he justified to me by the like Practice of those two prudent Insects the Bee and the Spider.

There was a Man born blind, who had several Apprentices in his own Condition: Their Employment was to mix Colours for Painters, which their Master taught them to distinguish by feeling and smelling. It was indeed my Misfortune to find them at that Time not very perfect in their Lessons; and the Professor himself

---

[1] The experiments described in this chapter are based on actual experiments undertaken or proposed by Swift's contemporaries.

happened to be generally mistaken: This Artist is much encouraged and esteemed by the whole Fraternity.

In another Apartment I was highly pleased with a Projector, who had found a Device of plowing the Ground with Hogs, to save the Charges of Plows, Cattle, and Labour. The Method is this: In an Acre of Ground you bury at six Inches Distance, and eight deep, a Quantity of Acorns, Dates, Chestnuts, and other Maste or Vegetables whereof these Animals are fondest; then you drive six Hundred or more of them into the Field, where in a few Days they will root up the whole Ground in search of their Food, and make it fit for sowing, at the same time manuring it with their Dung. It is true, upon Experiment they found the Charge and Trouble very great, and they had little or no Crop. However, it is not doubted that this Invention may be capable of great Improvement.

I went into another Room, where the Walls and Ceiling were all hung round with Cobwebs, except a narrow Passage for the Artist to go in and out. At my Entrance he called aloud to me not to disturb his Webs. He lamented the fatal Mistake the World had been so long in of using Silk-Worms, while we had such plenty of domestick Insects, who infinitely excelled the former, because they understood how to weave as well as spin. And he proposed farther, that by employing Spiders, the Charge of dying Silks would be wholly saved; whereof I was fully convinced when he shewed me a vast Number of Flies most beautifully coloured, wherewith he fed his Spiders; assuring us, that the Webs would take a Tincture from them; and as he had them of all Hues, he hoped to fit every Body's Fancy, as soon as he could find proper Food for the Flies, of certain Gums, Oyls, and other glutinous Matter, to give a Strength and Consistence to the Threads.

There was an Astronomer who had undertaken to place a Sun-Dial upon the great Weather-Cock on the Town-House, by adjusting the annual and diurnal Motions of the Earth and Sun, so as to answer and coincide with all accidental Turnings of the Wind.

I was complaining of a small Fit of the Cholick; upon which my Conductor led me into a Room, where a great Physician resided, who was famous for curing that Disease by contrary Operations from the same Instrument. He had a large Pair of Bellows, with a long slender Muzzle of Ivory. This he conveyed eight Inches up the Anus, and drawing in the Wind, he affirmed he could make the Guts as lank as a dried Bladder. But when the Disease was more stubborn and violent, he let in the Muzzle while the Bellows was full of Wind, which he discharged into the Body of the Patient; then withdrew the Instrument to replenish it, clapping his Thumb strongly against the Orifice of the Fundament; and this being repeated three or four Times, the adventitious Wind would rush out, bringing the noxious along with it (like Water put into a Pump) and the Patient recovers. I saw him try both Experiments upon a Dog, but could not discern any Effect from the former. After the latter, the Animal was ready to burst, and made so violent a Discharge, as was very offensive to me and my Companions. The Dog died on the Spot, and we left the Doctor endeavouring to recover him by the same Operation.

I visited many other Apartments, but shall not trouble my Reader with all the Curiosities I observed, being studious of Brevity.

I had hitherto seen only one Side of the Academy, the other being appropriated to the Advancers of speculative Learning; of whom I shall say something when I have mentioned one illustrious Person more, who is called among them *the universal Artist.* He told us, he had been Thirty Years employing his Thoughts for the Improvement of human Life. He had two large Rooms full of wonderful Curiosities, and Fifty Men at work. Some were condensing Air into a dry tangible Substance, by extracting the Nitre, and letting the aqueous or fluid Particles percolate: Others softening Marble for Pillows and Pin-cushions; others petrifying the Hoofs of a living Horse to preserve them from foundring. The Artist himself was at that Time busy upon two great Designs: The first, to sow Land with Chaff, wherein he affirmed the true seminal Virtue to be contained, as he demonstrated by several Experiments which I was not skilful enough to comprehend. The other was, by a certain Composition of Gums, Minerals, and Vegetables outwardly applied, to prevent the Growth of Wool upon two young Lambs; and he hoped in a reasonable Time to propagate the Breed of naked Sheep all over the Kingdom.

We crossed a Walk to the other Part of the Academy, where, as I have already said, the Projectors in speculative Learning resided.

The first Professor I saw was in a very large Room, with Forty Pupils about him. After Salutation, observing me to look earnestly upon a Frame, which took up the greatest Part of both the Length and Breadth of the Room; he said, perhaps I might wonder to see him employed in a Project for improving speculative Knowledge by practical and mechanical Operations. But the World would soon be sensible of its Usefulness; and he flattered himself, that a more noble exalted Thought never sprang in any other Man's Head. Every one knew how laborious the usual Method is of attaining to Arts and Sciences; whereas by his Contrivance, the most ignorant Person at a reasonable Charge, and with a little bodily Labour, may write Books in Philosophy, Poetry, Politicks, Law, Mathematicks and Theology, without the least Assistance from Genius or Study. He then led me to the Frame, about the Sides whereof all his Pupils stood in Ranks. It was Twenty Foot square, placed in the Middle of the Room. The Superficies was composed of several Bits of Wood, about the Bigness of a Dye, but some larger than others. They were all linked together by slender Wires. These Bits of Wood were covered on every Square with Papers pasted on them; and on these Papers were written all the Words of their Language in their several Moods, Tenses, and Declensions, but without any Order. The Professor then desired me to observe, for he was going to set his Engine at work. The Pupils at his Command took each of them hold of an Iron Handle, whereof there were Forty fixed round the Edges of the Frame; and giving them a sudden Turn, the whole Disposition of the Words was entirely changed. He then commanded Six and Thirty of the Lads to read the several Lines softly as they appeared upon the Frame; and where they found three or four Words together that might make Part of a Sentence, they dictated to the four remaining Boys who were Scribes. This Work was repeated three or four Times, and at every Turn the Engine was so contrived, that the Words shifted into new Places, as the square Bits of Wood moved upside down.

Six Hours a-Day the young Students were employed in this Labour; and the Professor shewed me several Volumes in large Folio already collected, of broken Sentences, which he intended to piece together; and out of those rich Materials to give the World a compleat Body of all Arts and Sciences; which however might be still improved, and much expedited, if the Publick would raise a Fund for making and employing five Hundred such Frames in *Lagado*, and oblige the Managers to contribute in common their several Collections.

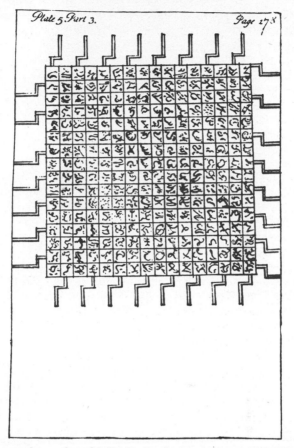

He assured me, that this Invention had employed all his Thoughts from his Youth; that he had emptyed the whole Vocabulary into his Frame, and made the strictest Computation of the general Proportion there is in Books between the Numbers of Particles, Nouns, and Verbs, and other Parts of Speech.

I made my humblest Acknowledgments to this illustrious Person for his great Communicativeness; and promised if ever I had the good Fortune to return to my native Country, that I would do him Justice, as the sole Inventor of this wonderful Machine; the Form and Contrivance of which I desired Leave to delineate upon Paper as in the Figure here annexed. I told him, although it were the Custom of our Learned in *Europe* to steal Inventions from each other, who had thereby at least this Advantage, that it became a Controversy which was the right Owner; yet I would take such Caution, that he should have the Honour entire without a Rival.

We next went to the School of Languages, where three Professors sat in Consultation upon improving that of their own Country.

The first Project was to shorten Discourse by cutting Polysyllables into one, and leaving out Verbs and Participles; because in Reality all things imaginable are but Nouns.

The other, was a Scheme for entirely abolishing all Words whatsoever: And this was urged as a great Advantage in Point of Health as well as Brevity. For, it is plain, that every Word we speak is in some Degree a Diminution of our Lungs by Corrosion; and consequently contributes to the shortening of our Lives. An Expedient was therefore offered, that since Words are only Names for *Things*, it would be more convenient for all Men to carry about them, such *Things* as were necessary to express the particular Business they are to discourse on. And this Invention would certainly have taken Place, to the great Ease as well as Health of the Subject, if the Women in Conjunction with the Vulgar and Illiterate had not threatned to raise a Rebellion, unless they might be allowed the Liberty to speak with their Tongues, after the Manner of their Forefathers: Such constant irreconcileable Enemies to Science are the common People. However, many of the most Learned and Wise adhere to the new Scheme of expressing themselves by *Things*; which hath only this Inconvenience attending it; that if a Man's Business be very great, and of various Kinds, he must be obliged in Proportion to carry a greater Bundle of *Things* upon his Back, unless he can afford one or two strong Servants to attend him. I have often beheld two of those Sages almost sinking under the Weight of their Packs, like Pedlars among us, who when they met in the Streets, would lay down their Loads, open their Sacks, and hold Conversation for an Hour together; then put up their Implements, help each other to resume their Burthens, and take their Leave.

But, for short Conversations a Man may carry Implements in his Pockets and under his Arms, enough to supply him, and in his House he cannot be at a Loss; therefore the Room where Company meet who practice this Art, is full of all *Things* ready at Hand, requisite to furnish Matter for this Kind of artificial Converse.

Another great Advantage proposed by this Invention, was, that it would serve as an universal Language to be understood in all civilized Nations, whose Goods and Utensils are generally of the same Kind, or nearly resembling, so that their Uses might easily be comprehended. And thus, Embassadors would be qualified to treat with foreign Princes or Ministers of State, to whose Tongues they were utter Strangers.

I was at the Mathematical School, where the Master taught his Pupils after a Method scarce imaginable to us in *Europe*. The Proposition and Demonstration were fairly written on a thin Wafer, with Ink composed of a Cephalick Tincture. This the Student was to swallow upon a fasting Stomach, and for three Days following eat nothing but Bread and Water. As the Wafer digested, the Tincture mounted to his Brain, bearing the Proposition along with it. But the Success hath not hitherto been answerable, partly by some Error in the *Quantum* or Composition, and partly by the Perverseness of Lads; to whom this Bolus is so nauseous, that they generally steal aside, and discharge it upwards before it can operate: neither have they been yet persuaded to use so long an Abstinence as the Prescription requires.

CHAPTER VI

A further Account of the Academy. The Author proposeth some Improvements, which are honourably received.

In the School of political Projectors I was but ill entertained; the Professors appearing in my Judgment wholly out of their Senses; which is a Scene that never fails to make me melancholy. These unhappy People were proposing Schemes for persuading Monarchs to chuse Favourites upon the Score of their Wisdom,

Capacity and Virtue; of teaching Ministers to consult the publick
Good; of rewarding Merit, great Abilities, and eminent Services;
of instructing Princes to know their true Interest, by placing it on
the same Foundation with that of their People: Of chusing for
Employments Persons qualified to exercise them; with many other
wild impossible Chimæras, that never entered before into the
Heart of Man to conceive; and confirmed in me the old Observation, that there is nothing so extravagant and irrational which some
Philosophers have not maintained for Truth.

But, however I shall so far do Justice to this Part of the Academy,
as to acknowledge that all of them were not so visionary. There
was a most ingenious Doctor who seemed to be perfectly versed in
the whole Nature and System of Government. This illustrious
Person had very usefully employed his Studies in finding out effectual Remedies for all Diseases and Corruptions, to which the several
Kinds of publick Administration are subject by the Vices or Infirmities of those who govern, as well as by the Licentiousness of those
who are to obey. For Instance: Whereas all Writers and Reasoners
have agreed, that there is a strict universal Resemblance between
the natural and the political Body; can there be any thing more
evident, than that the Health of both must be preserved, and the
Diseases cured by the same Prescriptions? It is allowed, that Senates
and great Councils are often troubled with redundant, ebullient,
and other peccant Humours; with many Diseases of the Head, and
more of the Heart; with strong Convulsions, with grievous Con-
tractions of the Nerves and Sinews in both Hands, but especially
the Right: With Spleen, Flatus, Vertigoes and Deliriums; with
scrophulous Tumours full of fœtid purulent Matter; with sower
frothy Ructations; with Canine Appetites and Crudeness of Digestion; besides many others needless to mention. This Doctor therefore proposed, that upon the meeting of a Senate, certain Physicians
should attend at the three first Days of their sitting, and at the
Close of each Day's Debate, feel the Pulses of every Senator; after
which having maturely considered, and consulted upon the Nature
of the several Maladies, and the Methods of Cure; they should on
the fourth Day return to the Senate-House, attended by their
Apothecaries stored with proper Medicines; and before the Members sat, administer to each of them Lenitives, Aperitives, Abster-
sives, Corrosives, Restringents, Palliatives, Laxatives, Cephalalgicks,
Ictericks, Apophlegmaticks, Acousticks, as their several Cases re-

quired; and according as these Medicines should operate, repeat, alter, or omit them at the next Meeting.

This Project could not be of any great Expence to the Publick; and might in my poor Opinion, be of much Use for the Dispatch of Business in those Countries where Senates have any Share in the legislative Power; beget Unanimity, shorten Debates, open a few Mouths which are now closed, and close many more which are now open; curb the Petulancy of the Young, and correct the positiveness of the Old; rouze the Stupid, and damp the Pert.

Again; Because it is a general Complaint that the Favourites of Princes are troubled with short and weak Memories; the same Doctor proposed, that whoever attended a first Minister, after having told his Business with the utmost Brevity, and in the plainest Words; should at his Departure give the said Minister a Tweak by the Nose, or a Kick in the Belly, or tread on his Corns, or lug him thrice by both Ears, or run a Pin into his Breech, or pinch his Arm black and blue; to prevent Forgetfulness: And at every Levee Day repeat the same Operation, till the Business were done or absolutely refused.

He likewise directed, that every Senator in the great Council of a Nation, after he had delivered his Opinion, and argued in the Defence of it, should be obliged to give his Vote directly contrary; because if that were done, the Result would infallibly terminate in the Good of the Publick.

When Parties in a State are violent, he offered a wonderful Contrivance to reconcile them. The Method is this. You take an Hundred Leaders of each Party; you dispose them into Couples of such whose Heads are nearest of a Size; then let two nice Operators saw off the *Occiput* of each Couple at the same Time, in such a Manner that the Brain may be equally divided. Let the *Occiputs* thus cut off be interchanged, applying each to the Head of his opposite Party-man. It seems indeed to be a Work that requireth some Exactness; but the Professor assured us, that if it were dextrously performed, the Cure would be infallible. For he argued thus; that the two half Brains being left to debate the Matter between themselves within the Space of one Scull, would soon come to a good Understanding, and produce that Moderation as well as Regularity of Thinking, so much to be wished for in the Heads of those, who imagine they came into the World only to watch and govern its Motion: And as to the Difference of Brains in Quantity or Quality, among those who are Directors in Faction; the Doctor assured us from his own Knowledge, that it was a perfect Trifle.

I heard a very warm Debate between two Professors, about the most commodious and effectual Ways and Means of raising Money without grieving the Subject. The first affirmed, the justest Method would be to lay a certain Tax upon Vices and Folly; and the Sum fixed upon every Man, to be rated after the fairest Manner by a Jury of his Neighbours. The second was of an Opinion directly contrary; to tax those Qualities of Body and Mind for which Men chiefly value themselves; the Rate to be more or less according to the Degrees of excelling; the Decision whereof should be left entirely to their own Breast. The highest Tax was upon Men, who are the greatest Favourites of the other Sex; and the Assessments according to the Number and Natures of the Favours they have received; for which they are allowed to be their own Vouchers. Wit, Valour, and Politeness were likewise proposed to be largely taxed, and collected in the same Manner, by every Person giving his own Word for the Quantum of what he possessed. But, as to Honour, Justice, Wisdom and Learning, they should not be taxed at all; because, they are Qualifications of so singular a Kind, that no Man will either allow them in his Neighbour, or value them in himself.

The Women were proposed to be taxed according to their Beauty and Skill in Dressing; wherein they had the same Privilege with the Men, to be determined by their own Judgment. But Constancy, Chastity, good Sense, and good Nature were not rated, because they would not bear the Charge of Collecting.

To keep Senators in the Interest of the Crown, it was proposed that the Members should raffle for Employments; every Man first taking an Oath, and giving Security that he would vote for the Court, whether he won or no; after which the Losers had in their Turn the Liberty of raffling upon the next Vacancy. Thus, Hope and Expectation would be kept alive; none would complain of broken Promises, but impute their Disappointments wholly to Fortune, whose Shoulders are broader and stronger than those of a Ministry.

Another Professor shewed me a large Paper of Instructions for discovering Plots and Conspiracies against the Government. He advised great Statesmen to examine into the Dyet of all suspected Persons; their Times of eating; upon which Side they lay in Bed; with which Hand they wiped their Posteriors; to take a strict View of their Excrements, and from the Colour, the Odour, the Taste, the Consistence, the Crudeness, or Maturity of Digestion, form a Judgment of their Thoughts and Designs: Because Men are never so serious, thoughtful, and intent, as when they are at Stool; which he found by frequent Experiment: For in such Conjunctures, when he used merely as a Trial to consider which was the best Way of murdering the King, his Ordure would have a Tincture of Green; but quite different when he thought only of raising an Insurrection, or burning the Metropolis.

The whole Discourse was written with great Acuteness, containing many Observations both curious and useful for Politicians, but as I conceived not altogether compleat. This I ventured to tell the Author, and offered if he pleased to supply him with some Additions. He received my Proposition with more Compliance than is usual among Writers, especially those of the Projecting Species; professing he would be glad to receive farther Information.

I told him, that in the Kingdom of *Tribnia*, by the Natives called *Langden*,[1] where I had long sojourned, the Bulk of the People consisted wholly of Discoverers, Witnesses, Informers, Accusers, Prosecutors, Evidences, Swearers; together with their several subservient and subaltern Instruments; all under the Colours, the Conduct, and pay of Ministers and their Deputies. The Plots in that Kingdom are usually the Workmanship of those Persons who desire to raise their own Characters of profound Politicians; to restore new Vigour to a crazy Administration; to stifle or divert general Discontents; to fill their Coffers with Forfeitures; and raise or sink the Opinion of publick Credit, as either shall best answer their private Advantage. It is first agreed and settled among them, what suspected Persons shall be accused of a Plot: Then, effectual Care is taken to secure all their Letters and other Papers, and put the Owners in Chains. These Papers are delivered to a Set of Artists very dextrous in finding out the mysterious Meanings of Words, Syllables and Letters. For Instance, they can decypher a Close-stool to signify a Privy-Council; a Flock of Geese, a Senate; a lame Dog, an Invader; the Plague, a standing Army; a Buzard, a Minister; the Gout, a High Priest; a Gibbet, a Secretary of State; a Chamber pot, a Committee of Grandees; a Sieve, a Court Lady; a Broom, a Revolution; a Mouse-trap, an Employment; a bottomless Pit, the Treasury; a Sink, a C[our]t; a Cap and Bells, a Favourite; a broken

---

[1] Anagrams of "Britain" and "England."

Reed, a Court of Justice; an empty Tun, a General; a running Sore, the Administration.

When this Method fails, they have two others more effectual; which the Learned among them call Acrosticks, and Anagrams. *First*, they can decypher all initial Letters into political Meanings: Thus, *N*, shall signify a Plot; *B*, a Regiment of Horse; *L*, a Fleet at Sea. Or, *secondly*, by transposing the Letters of the Alphabet, in any suspected Paper, they can lay open the deepest Designs of a discontented Party. So for Example, if I should say in a Letter to a Friend, *Our Brother* Tom *hath just got the Piles*; a Man of Skill in this Art would discover how the same Letters which compose that Sentence, may be analysed into the following Words; *Resist,* ——a *Plot is brought home*——*The Tour*. And this is the Anagrammatick Method.[2]

The Professor made me great Acknowledgments for communicating these Observations, and promised to make honourable mention of me in his Treatise.

I saw nothing in this Country that could invite me to a longer Continuance; and began to thir̄ of returning home to *England*.

CHAPTER VII

The Author leaves Lagado, *arrives at* Maldonada. *No Ship ready. He takes a short Voyage to* Glubbdubdrib. *His Reception by the Governor.*

The Continent of which this Kingdom is a part, extends itself, as I have Reason to believe, Eastward to that unknown Tract of *America*, Westward of *California*, and North to the Pacifick Ocean, which is not above an hundred and fifty Miles from *Lagado*; where there is a good Port and much Commerce with the great Island of *Luggnagg*; situated to the North-West about 29 Degrees

---

[2] Swift seems doubly allusive in these paragraphs: to the kind of evidence he thought fabricated by the government in the trial (1723) of his friend Bishop Atterbury; to the earlier proceedings against another friend, Bolingbroke, who had used the pseudonym "La Tour" (see p. 19, n.3; p. 53, n. 2).

North Latitude, and 140 Longitude. This Island of *Luggnagg* stands South Eastwards of *Japan*, about an hundred Leagues distant. There is a strict Alliance between the *Japanese* Emperor and the King of *Luggnagg*, which affords frequent Opportunities of sailing from one Island to the other. I determined therefore to direct my Course this Way, in order to my Return to *Europe*. I hired two Mules with a Guide to shew me the Way, and carry my small Baggage. I took leave of my noble Protector, who had shewn me so much Favour, and made me a generous Present at my Departure.

My Journey was without any Accident or Adventure worth relating. When I arrived at the Port of *Maldonada*, (for so it is called) there was no Ship in the Harbour bound for *Luggnagg*, nor like to be in some Time. The Town is about as large as *Portsmouth*. I soon fell into some Acquaintance, and was very hospitably received. A Gentleman of Distinction said to me, that since the Ships bound for *Luggnagg* could not be ready in less than a Month, it might be no disagreeable Amusement for me to take a Trip to the little Island of *Glubbdubdrib*, about five Leagues off to the South-West. He offered himself and a Friend to accompany me, and that I should be provided with a small convenient Barque for the Voyage.

GLUBBDUBDRIB, as nearly as I can interpret the Word, signifies the Island of *Sorcerers or Magicians*. It is about one third as large as the Isle of *Wight*, and extreamly fruitful: It is governed by the Head of a certain Tribe, who are all Magicians. This Tribe marries only among each other; and the eldest in Succession is Prince or Governor. He hath a noble Palace, and a Park of about three thousand Acres, surrounded by a Wall of hewn Stone twenty Foot high. In this Park are several small Inclosures for Cattle, Corn and Gardening.

The Governor and his Family are served and attended by Domesticks of a Kind somewhat unusual. By his Skill in Necromancy, he hath Power of calling whom he pleaseth from the Dead, and commanding their Service for twenty four Hours, but no longer; nor can he call the same Persons up again in less than three Months, except upon very extraordinary Occasions.

When we arrived at the Island, which was about Eleven in the Morning, one of the Gentlemen who accompanied me, went to the Governor, and desired Admittance for a Stranger, who came on purpose to have the Honour of attending on his Highness. This was immediately granted, and we all three entered the Gate of the

Palace between two Rows of Guards, armed and dressed after a
very antick Manner. and something in their Countenances that
made my Flesh creep with a Horror I cannot express. We passed
through several Apartments between Servants of the same Sort,
ranked on each Side as before, till we came to the Chamber of
Presence, where after three profound Obeysances, and a few general
Questions, we were permitted to sit on three Stools near the lowest
Step of his Highness's Throne. He understood the Language of
Balnibarbi, although it were different from that of his Island. He
desired me to give him some Account of my Travels; and to let
me see that I should be treated without Ceremony, he dismissed
all his Attendants with a Turn of his Finger, at which to my great
Astonishment they vanished in an Instant, like Visions in a Dream,
when we awake on a sudden. I could not recover myself in some
Time, till the Governor assured me that I should receive no Hurt;
and observing my two Companions to be under no Concern, who
had been often entertained in the same Manner, I began to take
Courage; and related to his Highness a short History of my several
Adventures, yet not without some Hesitation, and frequently looking behind me to the Place where I had seen those domestick
Spectres. I had the Honour to dine with the Governor, where a
new Set of Ghosts served up the Meat, and waited at Table. I now
observed myself to be less terrified than I had been in the Morning.
I stayed till Sun-set, but humbly desired his Highness to excuse
me for not accepting his Invitation of lodging in the Palace. My
two Friends and I lay at a private House in the Town adjoining,
which is the Capital of this little Island; and the next Morning
we returned to pay our Duty to the Governor, as he was pleased to
command us.

After this Manner we continued in the Island for ten Days,
most Part of every Day with the Governor, and at Night in our
Lodging. I soon grew so familiarized to the Sight of Spirits, that
after the third or fourth Time they gave me no Emotion at all;
or if I had any Apprehensions left, my Curiosity prevailed over
them. For his Highness the Governor ordered me to call up whatever Persons I would chuse to name, and in whatever Numbers
among all the Dead from the Beginning of the World to the
present Time, and command them to answer any Questions I
should think fit to ask; with this Condition, that my Questions
must be confined within the Compass of the Times they lived in.

And one Thing I might depend upon, that they would certainly tell me Truth; for Lying was a Talent of no Use in the lower World.

I made my humble Acknowledgments to his Highness for so great a Favour. We were in a Chamber, from whence there was a fair Prospect into the Park. And because my first Inclination was to be entertained with Scenes of Pomp and Magnificence, I desired to see *Alexander* the Great, at the Head of his Army just after the Battle of *Arbela*; which upon a Motion of the Governor's Finger immediately appeared in a large Field under the Window, where we stood. *Alexander* was called up into the Room: It was with great Difficulty that I understood his *Greek*, and had but little of my own. He assured me upon his Honour that he was not poisoned, but dyed of a Fever by excessive Drinking.

Next I saw *Hannibal* passing the *Alps*, who told me he had not a Drop of Vinegar in his Camp.[1]

I saw *Cæsar* and *Pompey* at the Head of their Troops just ready to engage. I saw the former in his last great Triumph. I desired that the Senate of *Rome* might appear before me in one large Chamber, and a modern Representative, in Counterview, in another. The first seemed to be an Assembly of Heroes and Demy-Gods; the other a Knot of Pedlars, Pick-pockets, Highwaymen and Bullies. The Governor at my Request gave the Sign for *Cæsar* and *Brutus* to advance towards us. I was struck with a profound Veneration at the Sight of *Brutus*; and could easily discover the most consummate Virtue, the greatest Intrepidity, and Firmness of Mind, the truest Love of his Country, and general Benevolence for Mankind in every Lineament of his Countenance. I observed with much Pleasure, that these two Persons were in good Intelligence with each other; and *Cæsar* freely confessed to me, that the greatest Actions of his own Life were not equal by many Degrees to the Glory of taking it away. I had the Honour to have much Conversation with *Brutus*; and was told that his Ancestor *Junius, Socrates, Epaminondas, Cato* the Younger, Sir *Thomas More* and himself, were perpetually together: A *Sextumvirate* to which all the Ages of the World cannot add a Seventh.

It would be tedious to trouble the Reader with relating what

---

[1] A large rock supposedly prevented Hannibal's army from crossing the Alps; his solution was to heat it and then wet it with vinegar, whereupon it cut easily.

vast Numbers of illustrious Persons were called up, to gratify that
insatiable Desire I had to see the World in every Period of Antiquity placed before me. I chiefly fed my Eyes with beholding
the Destroyers of Tyrants and Usurpers, and the Restorers of Liberty to oppressed and injured Nations. But it is impossible to
express the Satisfaction I received in my own Mind, after such a
Manner as to make it a suitable Entertainment to the Reader.

CHAPTER VIII

A further Account of Glubbdubdrib. *Antient and Modern History corrected.*

Having a Desire to see those Antients, who were most
renowned for Wit and Learning, I set apart one Day on purpose.
I proposed that *Homer* and *Aristotle* might appear at the Head
of all their Commentators; but these were so numerous, that some
Hundreds were forced to attend in the Court and outward Rooms
of the Palace. I knew and could distinguish those two Heroes at
first Sight, not only from the Croud, but from each other. *Homer*
was the taller and comelier Person of the two, walked very erect
for one of his Age, and his Eyes were the most quick and piercing
I ever beheld.[1] *Aristotle* stooped much, and made use of a Staff.
His Visage was meager, his Hair lank and thin, and his Voice
hollow. I soon discovered, that both of them were perfect Strangers
to the rest of the Company, and had never seen or heard of them
before. And I had a Whisper from a Ghost, who shall be nameless,
that these Commentators always kept in the most distant Quarters
from their Principals in the lower World, through a Consciousness
of Shame and Guilt, because they had so horribly misrepresented
the Meaning of those Authors to Posterity. I introduced *Didymus*
and *Eustathius* to *Homer*, and prevailed on him to treat them

---

[1] Swift has Gulliver correct the traditionally accepted view that Homer
was blind.

better than perhaps they deserved; for he soon found they wanted
a Genius to enter into the Spirit of a Poet. But *Aristotle* was out
of all Patience with the Account I gave him of *Scotus* and *Ramus*,
as I presented them to him; and he asked them whether the rest
of the Tribe were as great Dunces as themselves.[2]

I then desired the Governor to call up *Descartes* and *Gassendi*,
with whom I prevailed to explain their Systems to *Aristotle*. This
great Philosopher freely acknowledged his own Mistakes in Natural
Philosophy, because he proceeded in many things upon Conjecture,
as all Men must do; and he found, that *Gassendi*, who had made
the Doctrine of *Epicurus* as palatable as he could, and the *Vortices*
of *Descartes*, were equally exploded.[3] He predicted the same Fate to
Attraction,[4] whereof the present Learned are such zealous Assertcrs.
He said, that ncw Systems of Nature were but new Fashions, which
would vary in every Age; and even those who pretend to demonstrate them from Mathematical Principles, would flourish but a
short Period of Time, and be out of Vogue when that was determined.

I spent five Days in conversing with many others of the antient
Learned. I saw most of the first *Roman* Emperors. I prevailed on
the Governor to call up *Eliogabalus's* Cooks[5] to dress us a Dinner;
but they could not shew us much of their Skill, for want of Materials. A *Helot* of *Agesilaus* made us a Dish of *Spartan* Broth, but
I was not able to get down a second Spoonful.

The two Gentlemen who conducted me to the Island were
pressed by their private Affairs to return in three Days, which I
employed in seeing some of the modern Dead, who had made the
greatest Figure for two or three Hundred Years past in our own
and other Countries of *Europe*; and having been always a great
Admirer of old illustrious Families, I desired the Governor would
call up a Dozen or two of Kings with their Ancestors in order, for

[2] Didymus and Eustathius: commentators on Homer. Duns Scotus: a
thirteenth-century proponent of Aristotle; Pierre de la Ramée: a sixteenth-
century humanist, critical of Aristotle.

[3] René Descartes: seventeenth-century philosopher and mathematician
whose theory that all motions are circular Swift thought preposterous.
Pierre Gassendi: a contemporary of Descartes and proponent of the
Epicurean system of physics—hence an opponent of both Aristotle and
Descartes.

[4] Newton's theory of gravitation.

[5] Heliogabalus, a Roman Emperor noted for over-eating.

eight or nine Generations. But my Disappointment was grievous
and unexpected. For, instead of a long Train with Royal Diadems,
I saw in one Family two Fidlers, three spruce Courtiers, and an
Italian Prelate. In another, a Barber, an Abbot, and two Cardinals.
I have too great a Veneration for crowned Heads to dwell any
longer on so nice a Subject: But as to Counts, Marquesses, Dukes,
Earls, and the like, I was not so scrupulous. And I confess it was
not without some Pleasure that I found my self able to trace the
particular Features, by which certain Families are distinguished up
to their Originals. I could plainly discover from whence one Family
derives a long Chin; why a second hath abounded with Knaves for
two Generations, and Fools for two more; why a third happened
to be crack-brained, and a fourth to be Sharpers. Whence it came,
what *Polydore Virgil* says of a certain great House, *Nec Vir fortis,
nec Fæmina Casta.*[6] How Cruelty, Falshood, and Cowardice grew
to be Characteristicks by which certain Families are distinguished as
much as by their Coat of Arms. Who first brought the Pox into
a noble House, which hath lineally descended in scrophulous
Tumours to their Posterity. Neither could I wonder at all this, when
I saw such an Interruption of Lineages by Pages, Lacqueys, Valets,
Coachmen, Gamesters, Fidlers, Players, Captains, and Pickpockets.

I was chiefly disgusted with modern History. For having strictly
examined all the Persons of greatest Name in the Courts of Princes
for an Hundred Years past, I found how the World had been
misled by prostitute Writers, to ascribe the greatest Exploits in
War to Cowards, the wisest Counsel to Fools, Sincerity to Flat-
terers, *Roman* Virtue to Betrayers of their Country, Piety to
Atheists, Chastity to Sodomites, Truth to Informers. How many
innocent and excellent Persons had been condemned to Death or
Banishment, by the practising of great Ministers upon the Corruption of Judges, and the Malice of Factions. How many Villains
had been exalted to the highest Places of Trust, Power, Dignity,
and Profit: How great a Share in the Motions and Events of
Courts, Councils, and Senates might be challenged by Bawds,
Whores, Pimps, Parasites, and Buffoons: How low an Opinion I
had of human Wisdom and Integrity, when I was truly informed
of the Springs and Motives of great Enterprizes and Revolutions

"Not a man of them brave, not a woman pure." Polydore Virgil was
a sixteenth-century Italian clergyman who composed a history of England
in Latin.

in the World, and of the contemptible Accidents to which they owed their Success.

Here I discovered the Roguery and Ignorance of those who pretend to write *Anecdotes*, or secret History; who send so many Kings to their Graves with a Cup of Poison; will repeat the Discourse between a Prince and chief Minister, where no Witness was by; unlock the Thoughts and Cabinets of Embassadors and Secretaries of State; and have the perpetual Misfortune to be mistaken. Here I discovered the true Causes of many great events that have surprized the World: How a Whore can govern the Backstairs, the Back-stairs a Council, and the Council a Senate. A General confessed in my Presence that he got a Victory purely by the Force of Cowardice and ill Conduct: And an Admiral, that for want of proper Intelligence, he beat the Enemy to whom he intended to betray the Fleet. Three Kings protested to me, that in their whole Reigns they did never once prefer any Person of Merit, unless by Mistake or Treachery of some Minister in whom they confided: Neither would they do it if they were to live again; and they shewed with great Strength of Reason, that the Royal Throne could not be supported without Corruption; because, that positive, confident, restive Temper, which Virtue infused into Man, was a perpetual Clog to publick Business.

I had the Curiosity to enquire in a particular Manner, by what Method great Numbers had procured to themselves high Titles of Honour, and prodigious Estates; and I confined my Enquiry to a very modern Period: However, without grating upon present Times, because I would be sure to give no Offence even to Foreigners (for I hope the Reader need not be told that I do not in the least intend my own Country in what I say upon this Occasion) a great Number of Persons concerned were called up, and upon a very slight Examination, discovered such a Scene of Infamy, that I cannot reflect upon it without some Seriousness. Perjury, Oppression, Subornation, Fraud, Pandarism, and the like *Infirmities* were amongst the most excusable Arts they had to mention; and for these I gave, as it was reasonable, due Allowance. But when some confessed, they owed their Greatness and Wealth to Sodomy or Incest; others to the prostituting of their own Wives and Daughters; others to the betraying their Country or their Prince; some to poisoning, more to the perverting of Justice in order to destroy the Innocent: I hope I may be pardoned if these Discoveries inclined me a little to abate of that profound Veneration which I am naturally apt to pay to Persons of high Rank, who ought to be treated with the utmost Respect due to their sublime Dignity, by us their Inferiors.

I had often read of some great Services done to Princes and States, and desired to see the Persons by whom those Services were performed. Upon Enquiry I was told, that their Names were to be found on no Record, except a few of them whom History hath represented as the vilest Rogues and Traitors. As to the rest, I had never once heard of them. They all appeared with dejected Looks, and in the meanest Habit; most of them telling me they died in Poverty and Disgrace, and the rest on a Scaffold or a Gibbet.

Among others there was one Person whose Case appeared a little singular. He had a Youth about Eighteen Years old standing by his Side. He told me, he had for many Years been Commander of a Ship; and in the Sea Fight at *Actium*, had the good Fortune to break through the Enemy's great Line of Battle, sink three of their Capital Ships, and take a fourth, which was the sole Cause of *Antony's* Flight, and of the Victory that ensued: That the Youth standing by him, his only Son, was killed in the Action. He added, that upon the Confidence of some Merit, the War being at an End, he went to *Rome*, and solicited at the Court of *Augustus* to be preferred to a greater Ship, whose Commander had been killed; but without any regard to his Pretensions, it was given to a Boy who had never seen the Sea, the Son of a *Libertina*, who waited on one of the Emperor's Mistresses. Returning back to his own Vessel, he was charged with Neglect of Duty, and the Ship given to a favourite Page of *Publicola* the Vice-Admiral; whereupon he retired to a poor Farm, at a great Distance from *Rome*, and there ended his Life. I was so curious to know the Truth of this Story, that I desired *Agrippa* might be called, who was Admiral in that Fight. He appeared, and confirmed the whole Account, but with much more Advantage to the Captain; whose Modesty had extenuated or concealed a great Part of his Merit.

I was surprized to find Corruption grown so high and so quick in that Empire, by the Force of Luxury so lately introduced; which made me less wonder at many parallel Cases in other Countries, where Vices of all Kinds have reigned so much longer, and where the whole Praise as well as Pillage hath been engrossed by the chief Commander, who perhaps had the least Title to either.

As every Person called up made exactly the same Appearance he had done in the World, it gave me melancholy Reflections to observe how much the Race of human Kind was degenerate among us, within these Hundred Years past. How the Pox under all its Consequences and Denominations had altered every Lineament of an *English* Countenance; shortened the Size of Bodies, unbraced the Nerves, relaxed the Sinews and Muscles, introduced a sallow Complexion, and rendered the Flesh loose and *rancid*.

I descended so low as to desire that some *English* Yeomen of the old Stamp, might be summoned to appear; once so famous for the Simplicity of their Manners, Dyet and Dress; for Justice in their Dealings; for their true Spirit of Liberty; for their Valour and Love of their Country. Neither could I be wholly unmoved after comparing the Living with the Dead, when I considered how all these pure native Virtues were prostituted for a Piece of Money by their Grand-children; who in selling their Votes, and managing at Elections have acquired every Vice and Corruption that can possibly be learned in a Court.

CHAPTER IX

The Author's return to Maldonada. *Sails to the Kingdom of* Luggnagg. *The Author confined. He is sent for to Court. The Manner of his Admittance. The King's great Lenity to his Subjects.*

The Day of our Departure being come, I took leave of his Highness the Governor of *Glubbdubdrib*, and returned with my two Companions to *Maldonada*, where after a Fortnight's waiting, a Ship was ready to sail for *Luggnagg*. The two Gentlemen and some others were so generous and kind as to furnish me with Provisions, and see me on Board. I was a Month in Voyage. We had one violent Storm, and were under a Necessity of steering Westward to get into the Trade-Wind, which holds for above sixty Leagues. On the 21st of *April*, 1708, we sailed in the River of *Clumegnig*, which is a Sea-port Town, at the South-East Point of *Luggnagg*. We cast Anchor within a League of the Town, and made a Signal for a Pilot. Two of them came on Board in less than half an Hour, by whom we were guided between certain Shoals and Rocks, which are very dangerous in the Passage, to a large Basin, where a Fleet may ride in Safety within a Cable's Length of the Town-Wall.

Some of our Sailors, whether out of Treachery or Inadvertence, had informed the Pilots that I was a Stranger and a great Traveller, whereof these gave Notice to a Custom-House Officer, by whom I was examined very strictly upon my landing. This Officer spoke to me in the Language of *Balnibarbi*, which by the Force of much Commerce is generally understood in that Town, especially by Seamen, and those employed in the Customs. I gave him a short Account of some Particulars, and made my Story as plausible and consistent as I could; but I thought it necessary to disguise my Country, and call my self a *Hollander*; because my Intentions were for *Japan*, and I knew the *Dutch* were the only *Europeans* permitted to enter into that Kingdom.[1] I therefore told the Officer, that having been shipwrecked on the Coast of *Balnibarbi*, and cast on a Rock, I was received up into *Laputa*, or the flying Island (of which he had often heard) and was now endeavouring to get to *Japan*, from whence I might find a Convenience of returning to my own Country. The Officer said, I must be confined till he could receive Orders from Court, for which he would write immediately, and hoped to receive an Answer in a Fortnight. I was carried to a convenient Lodging, with a Centry placed at the Door; however I had the Liberty of a large Garden, and was treated with Humanity enough, being maintained all the Time at the King's Charge. I was visited by several Persons, chiefly out of Curiosity, because it was reported I came from Countries very remote, of which they had never heard.

I hired a young Man who came in the same Ship to be an Interpreter; he was a Native of *Luggnagg*, but had lived some Years at *Maldonada*, and was a perfect Master of both Languages. By his Assistance I was able to hold a Conversation with those that came to visit me; but this consisted only of their Questions and my Answers.

[1] Japan was closed to all, except the Dutch and Chinese, after the anti-Christian rebellions of 1637.

The Dispatch came from Court about the Time we expected. It contained a Warrant for conducting me and my Retinue to *Traldragdubh* or *Trildrogdrib*, (for it is pronounced both Ways as near as I can remember) by a Party of Ten Horse. All my Retinue was that poor Lad for an Interpreter, whom I persuaded into my Service. At my humble Request we had each of us a Mule to ride on. A Messenger was dispatched half a Day's Journey before us, to give the King Notice of my Approach, and to desire that his Majesty would please to appoint a Day and Hour, when it would be his gracious Pleasure that I might have the Honour to *lick the Dust before his Footstool*. This is the Court Style, and I found it to be more than Matter of Form: For upon my Admittance two Days after my Arrival, I was commanded to crawl upon my Belly, and lick the Floor as I advanced; but on account of my being a Stranger, Care was taken to have it so clean that the Dust was not offensive. However, this was a peculiar Grace, not allowed to any but Persons of the highest Rank, when they desire an Admittance: Nay, sometimes the Floor is strewed with Dust on purpose, when the Person to be admitted happens to have powerful Enemies at Court: And I have seen a great Lord with his Mouth so crammed, that when he had crept to the proper Distance from the Throne, he was not able to speak a Word. Neither is there any Remedy, because it is capital for those who receive an Audience to spit or wipe their Mouths in his Majesty's Presence. There is indeed another Custom, which I cannot altogether approve of. When the King hath a Mind to put any of his Nobles to Death in a gentle indulgent Manner; he commands to have the Floor strowed with a certain brown Powder, of a deadly Composition, which being licked up infallibly kills him in twenty-four Hours. But in Justice to this Prince's great Clemency, and the Care he hath of his Subjects Lives (wherein it were much to be wished that the Monarchs of *Europe* would imitate him) it must be mentioned for his Honour, that strict Orders are given to have the infected Parts of the Floor well washed after every such Execution; which if his Domesticks neglect, they are in Danger of incurring his Royal Displeasure. I my self heard him give Directions, that one of his Pages should be whipt, whose Turn it was to give Notice about washing the Floor after an Execution, but maliciously had omitted it; by which Neglect a young Lord of great Hopes coming to an Audience, was unfortunately poisoned, although the

King at that Time had no Design against his Life. But this good Prince was so gracious, as to forgive the Page his Whipping, upon Promise that he would do so no more, without special Orders.

To return from this Digression; when I had crept within four Yards of the Throne, I raised my self gently upon my Knees, and then striking my Forehead seven Times against the Ground, I pronounced the following Words, as they had been taught me the Night before, *Ickpling Gloffthrobb Squutserumm blhiop Mlashnalt Zwin tnodbalkguffh Slhiophad Gurdlubh Asht*. This is the Compliment established by the Laws of the Land for all Persons admitted to the King's Presence. It may be rendered into *English* thus: *May your cœlestial Majesty out-live the Sun, eleven Moons and an half.* To this the King returned some Answer, which although I could not understand, yet I replied as I had been directed; *Fluft drin Yalerick Dwuldum prastrad mirplush*, which properly signifies, *My Tongue is in the Mouth of my Friend*; and by this Expression was meant that I desired leave to bring my Interpreter; whereupon the young Man already mentioned was accordingly introduced; by whose Intervention I answered as many Questions as his Majesty could put in above an Hour. I spoke in the *Balnibarbian* Tongue, and my Interpreter delivered my Meaning in that of *Luggnagg*.

The King was much delighted with my Company, and ordered his *Bliffmarklub* or High Chamberlain to appoint a Lodging in the Court for me and my Interpreter, with a daily Allowance for my Table, and a large Purse of Gold for my common Expences.

I stayed three Months in this Country out of perfect Obedience to his Majesty, who was pleased highly to favour me, and made me very honourable Offers. But I thought it more consistent with Prudence and Justice to pass the Remainder of my Days with my Wife and Family.

CHAPTER X

The Luggnuggians *commended. A particular Description of the* Struldbruggs, *with many Conversations between the Author and some eminent Persons upon that Subject.*

The *Luggnuggians* are a polite and generous People, and although they are not without some Share of that Pride which is peculiar to all *Eastern* Countries, yet they shew themselves courteous to Strangers, especially such who are countenanced by the Court. I had many Acquaintance among Persons of the best Fashion, and being always attended by my Interpreter, the Conversation we had was not disagreeable.

One Day in much good Company, I was asked by a Person of Quality, whether I had seen any of their *Struldbruggs* or *Immortals.* I said I had not; and desired he would explain to me what he meant by such an Appellation, applyed to a mortal Creature. He told me, that sometimes, although very rarely, a Child happened to be born in a Family with a red circular Spot in the Forehead, directly over the left Eye-brow, which was an infallible Mark that it should never dye. The Spot, as he described it, was about the Compass of a Silver Threepence, but in the Course of Time grew larger, and changed its Colour; for at Twelve Years old it became green, so continued till Five and Twenty, then turned to a deep blue; at Five and Forty it grew coal black, and as large as an *English* Shilling; but never admitted any farther Alteration. He said these Births were so rare, that he did not believe there could be above Eleven Hundred *Struldbruggs* of both Sexes in the whole Kingdom, of which he computed about Fifty in the Metropolis, and among the rest a young Girl born about three Years ago. That, these Productions were not peculiar to any Family, but a meer Effect of Chance; and the Children of the *Struldbruggs* themselves, were equally mortal with the rest of the People.

I freely own myself to have been struck with inexpressible Delight upon hearing this Account: And the Person who gave it me
happening to understand the *Balnibarbian* Language, which I spoke
very well, I could not forbear breaking out into Expressions perhaps
a little too extravagant. I cryed out as in a Rapture; Happy Nation,
where every Child hath at least a Chance for being immortal!
Happy People who enjoy so many living Examples of antient Virtue, and have Masters ready to instruct them in the Wisdom of all
former Ages! But, happiest beyond all Comparison are those excellent *Struldbruggs*, who being born exempt from that universal
Calamity of human Nature, have their Minds free and disingaged,
without the Weight and Depression of Spirits caused by the continual Apprehension of Death. I discovered my Admiration that I
had not observed any of these illustrious Persons at Court; the
black Spot on the Fore-head, being so remarkable a Distinction,
that I could not have easily overlooked it: And it was impossible
that his Majesty, a most judicious Prince, should not provide himself with a good Number of such wise and able Counsellors. Yet
perhaps the Virtue of those Reverend Sages was too strict for the
corrupt and libertine Manners of a Court. And we often find by
Experience, that young Men are too opinionative and volatile to
be guided by the sober Dictates of their Seniors. However, since the
King was pleased to allow me Access to his Royal Person, I was resolved upon the very first Occasion to deliver my Opinion to him
on this Matter freely, and at large by the Help of my Interpreter;
and whether he would please to take my Advice or no, yet in one
Thing I was determined, that his Majesty having frequently offered me an Establishment in this Country, I would with great
Thankfulness accept the Favour, and pass my Life here in the
Conversation of those superiour Beings the *Struldbruggs*, if they
would please to admit me.

The Gentleman to whom I addressed my Discourse, because (as
I have already observed) he spoke the Language of *Balnibarbi*, said
to me with a Sort of a Smile, which usually ariseth from Pity to the
Ignorant, that he was glad of any Occasion to keep me among them,
and desired my Permission to explain to the Company what I had
spoke. He did so; and they talked together for some time in their
own Language, whereof I understood not a Syllable, neither could
I observe by their Countenances what Impression my Discourse had
made on them. After a short Silence, the same Person told me, that

his Friends and mine (so he thought fit to express himself) were very much pleased with the judicious Remarks I had made on the great Happiness and Advantages of immortal Life; and they were desirous to know in a particular Manner, what Scheme of Living I should have formed to myself, if it had fallen to my Lot to have been born a *Struldbrugg*.

I answered, it was easy to be eloquent on so copious and delightful a Subject, especially to me who have been often apt to amuse myself with Visions of what I should do if I were a King, a General, or a great Lord: And upon this very Case I had frequently run over the whole System how I should employ myself, and pass the Time if I were sure to live for ever.

That, if it had been my good Fortune to come into the World a *Struldbrugg*; as soon as I could discover my own Happiness by understanding the Difference between Life and Death, I would first resolve by all Arts and Methods whatsoever to procure myself Riches: In the Pursuit of which, by Thrift and Management, I might reasonably expect in about two Hundred Years, to be the wealthiest Man in the Kingdom. In the second Place, I would from my earliest Youth apply myself to the Study of Arts and Sciences, by which I should arrive in time to excel all others in Learning. Lastly, I would carefully record every Action and Event of Consequence that happened in the Publick, impartially draw the Characters of the several Successions of Princes, and great Ministers of State; with my own Observations on every Point. I would exactly set down the several Changes in Customs, Languages, Fashions of Dress, Dyet and Diversions. By all which Acquirements, I should be a living Treasury of Knowledge and Wisdom, and certainly become the Oracle of the Nation.

I would never marry after Threescore, but live in an hospitable Manner, yet still on the saving Side. I would entertain myself in forming and directing the Minds of hopeful young Men, by convincing them from my own Remembrance, Experience and Observation, fortified by numerous Examples, of the Usefulness of Virtue in publick and private Life. But, my choise and constant Companions should be a Sett of my own immortal Brotherhood, among whom I would elect a Dozen from the most ancient down to my own Contemporaries. Where any of these wanted Fortunes, I would provide them with convenient Lodges round my own Estate, and have some of them always at my Table, only mingling

a few of the most valuable among you Mortals, whom Length of
Time would harden me to lose with little or no Reluctance, and
treat your Posterity after the same Manner; just as a Man diverts
himself with the annual Succession of Pinks and Tulips in his
Garden, without regretting the Loss of those which withered the
preceding Year.

These *Struldbruggs* and I would mutually communicate our Observations and Memorials through the Course of Time; remark
the several Gradations by which Corruption steals into the World,
and oppose it in every Step, by giving perpetual Warning and Instruction to Mankind; which, added to the strong Influence of our
own Example, would probably prevent that continual Degeneracy of
human Nature, so justly complained of in all Ages.

Add to all this, the Pleasure of seeing the various Revolutions of
States and Empires; the Changes in the lower and upper World;
antient Cities in Ruins, and obscure Villages become the Seats of
Kings. Famous Rivers lessening into shallow Brooks; the Ocean
leaving one Coast dry, and overwhelming another: The Discovery
of many Countries yet unknown. Barbarity over-running the politest
Nations, and the most barbarous becoming civilized. I should then
see the Discovery of the *Longitude*, the *perpetual Motion*, the *universal Medicine*, and many other great Inventions brought to the
utmost Perfection.

What wonderful Discoveries should we make in Astronomy, by
outliving and confirming our own Predictions, by observing the
Progress and Returns of Comets, with the Changes of Motion in
the Sun, Moon and Stars.

I enlarged upon many other Topicks, which the natural Desire
of endless Life and sublunary Happiness could easily furnish me
with. When I had ended, and the Sum of my Discourse had been
interpreted as before, to the rest of the Company, there was a good
Deal of Talk among them in the Language of the Country, not
without some Laughter at my Expence. At last the same Gentleman who had been my Interpreter, said, he was desired by the rest
to set me right in a few Mistakes, which I had fallen into through
the common Imbecility of human Nature, and upon that Allowance was less answerable for them. That, this Breed of *Struldbruggs*
was peculiar to their Country, for there were no such People either
in *Balnibarbi* or *Japan*, where he had the Honour to be Embassador
from his Majesty, and found the Natives in both those Kingdoms

very hard to believe that the Fact was possible; and it appeared from my Astonishment when he first mentioned the Matter to me, that I received it as a Thing wholly new, and scarcely to be credited. That in the two Kingdoms above-mentioned, where during his Residence he had conversed very much, he observed long Life to be the universal Desire and Wish of Mankind. That, whoever had one Foot in the Grave, was sure to hold back the other as strongly as he could. That the oldest had still Hopes of living one Day longer, and looked on Death as the greatest Evil, from which Nature always prompted him to retreat; only in this Island of *Luggnagg*, the Appetite for living was not so eager, from the continual Example of the *Struldbruggs* before their Eyes.

That the System of Living contrived by me was unreasonable and unjust, because it supposed a Perpetuity of Youth, Health, and Vigour, which no Man could be so foolish to hope, however extravagant he might be in his Wishes. That, the Question therefore was not whether a Man would chuse to be always in the Prime of Youth, attended with Prosperity and Health; but how he would pass a perpetual Life under all the usual Disadvantages which old Age brings along with it. For although few Men will avow their Desires of being immortal upon such hard Conditions, yet in the two Kingdoms before mentioned of *Balnibarbi* and *Japan*, he observed that every Man desired to put off Death for sometime longer, let it approach ever so late; and he rarely heard of any Man who died willingly, except he were incited by the Extremity of Grief or Torture. And he appealed to me whether in those Countries I had travelled as well as my own, I had not observed the same general Disposition.

After this Preface, he gave me a particular account of the *Struldbruggs* among them. He said they commonly acted like Mortals, till about Thirty Years old, after which by Degrees they grew melancholy and dejected, increasing in both till they came to Fourscore. This he learned from their own Confession; for otherwise there not being above two or three of that Species born in an Age, they were too few to form a general Observation by. When they came to Fourscore Years, which is reckoned the Extremity of living in this Country, they had not only all the Follies and Infirmities of other old Men, but many more which arose from the dreadful Prospect of never dying. They were not only opinionative, peevish, covetous, morose, vain, talkative; but uncapable of Friendship, and dead to all natural Affection, which never descended below their Grand-children. Envy and impotent Desires, are their prevailing Passions. But those Objects against which their Envy seems principally directed, are the Vices of the younger Sort, and the Deaths of the old. By reflecting on the former, they find themselves cut off from all Possibility of Pleasure; and whenever they see a Funeral, they lament and repine that others are gone to an Harbour of Rest, to which they themselves never can hope to arrive. They have no Remembrance of any thing but what they learned and observed in their Youth and middle Age, and even that is very imperfect: And for the Truth or Particulars of any Fact, it is safer to depend on common Traditions than upon their best Recollections. The least miserable among them, appear to be those who turn to Dotage, and entirely lose their Memories; these meet with more Pity and Assistance, because they want many bad Qualities which abound in others.

If a *Struldbrugg* happen to marry one of his own Kind, the Marriage is dissolved of Course by the Courtesy of the Kingdom, as soon as the younger of the two comes to be Fourscore. For the Law thinks it a reasonable Indulgence, that those who are condemned without any Fault of their own to a perpetual Continuance in the World, should not have their Misery doubled by the Load of a Wife.

As soon as they have compleated the Term of Eighty Years, they are looked on as dead in Law; their Heirs immediately succeed to their Estates, only a small Pittance is reserved for their Support; and the poor ones are maintained at the publick Charge. After that Period they are held incapable of any Employement of Trust or Profit; they cannot purchase Lands, or take Leases, neither are they allowed to be Witnesses in any Cause, either Civil or Criminal, not even for the Decision of Meers and Bounds.

At Ninety they lose their Teeth and Hair; they have at that Age no Distinction of Taste, but eat and drink whatever they can get, without Relish or Appetite. The Diseases they were subject to, still continue without encreasing or diminishing. In talking they forget the common Appellation of Things, and the Names of Persons, even of those who are their nearest Friends and Relations. For the same Reason they never can amuse themselves with reading, because their Memory will not serve to carry them from the Beginning of a Sentence to the End; and by this Defect they are deprived of the only Entertainment whereof they might otherwise be capable.

The Language of this Country being always upon the Flux, the *Struldbruggs* of one Age do not understand those of another; neither are they able after two Hundred Years to hold any Conversation (farther than by a few general Words) with their Neighbours the Mortals; and thus they lye under the Disadvantage of living like Foreigners in their own Country.

This was the Account given me of the *Struldbruggs*, as near as I can remember. I afterwards saw five or six of different Ages, the youngest not above two Hundred Years old, who were brought to me at several Times by some of my Friends; but although they were told that I was a great Traveller, and had seen all the World, they had not the least Curiosity to ask me a Question; only desired I would give them *Slumskudask*, or a Token of Remembrance; which is a modest Way of begging, to avoid the Law that strictly forbids it, because they are provided for by the Publick, although indeed with a very scanty Allowance.

They are despised and hated by all Sorts of People: When one of them is born, it is reckoned ominous, and their Birth is recorded very particularly; so that you may know their Age by consulting the Registry, which however hath not been kept above a Thousand Years past, or at least hath been destroyed by Time or publick Disturbances. But the usual Way of computing how old they are, is, by asking them what Kings or great Persons they can remember, and then consulting History; for infallibly the last Prince in their Mind did not begin his Reign after they were Fourscore Years old.

They were the most mortifying Sight I ever beheld; and the Women more horrible than the Men. Besides the usual Deformities in extreme old Age, they acquired an additional Ghastliness in Proportion to their Number of Years, which is not to be described; and among half a Dozen I soon distinguished which was the oldest, although there were not above a Century or two between them.

The Reader will easily believe, that from what I had heard and seen, my keen Appetite for Perpetuity of Life was much abated. I grew heartily ashamed of the pleasing Visions I had formed; and thought no Tyrant could invent a Death into which I would not run with Pleasure from such a Life. The King heard of all that had passed between me and my Friends upon this Occasion, and raillied me very pleasantly; wishing I would send a Couple of *Struldbruggs* to my own Country, to arm our People against the Fear of Death; but this it seems is forbidden by the fundamental Laws of the Kingdom; or else I should have been well content with the Trouble and Expence of transporting them.

I could not but agree, that the Laws of this Kingdom relating to the *Struldbruggs*, were founded upon the strongest Reasons, and such as any other Country would be under the Necessity of enacting in the like Circumstances. Otherwise, as Avarice is the necessary Consequent of old Age, those Immortals would in time become Proprietors of the whole Nation, and engross the Civil Power; which, for want of Abilities to manage, must end in the Ruin of the Publick.

CHAPTER XI

The Author leaves Luggnagg *and sails to* Japan. *From thence he returns in a* Dutch *Ship to* Amsterdam, *and from* Amsterdam *to* England.

I thought this Account of the *Struldbruggs* might be some Entertainment to the Reader, because it seems to be a little out of the common Way; at least, I do not remember to have met the like in any Book of Travels that hath come to my Hands: And if I am deceived, my Excuse must be, that it is necessary for Travellers, who describe the same Country, very often to agree in dwelling on the same Particulars, without deserving the Censure of having borrowed or transcribed from those who wrote before them.

There is indeed a perpetual Commerce between this Kingdom and the great Empire of *Japan*; and it is very probable that the *Japanese* Authors may have given some Account of the *Struldbruggs*; but my Stay in *Japan* was so short, and I was so entirely a Stranger to the Language, that I was not qualified to make any Enquiries. But I hope the *Dutch* upon this Notice will be curious and able enough to supply my Defects.

His Majesty having often pressed me to accept some Employment in his Court, and finding me absolutely determined to return
to my Native Country; was pleased to give me his Licence to depart; and honoured me with a Letter of Recommendation under
his own Hand to the Emperor of *Japan*. He likewise presented me
with four Hundred forty-four large Pieces of Gold (this Nation delighting in even Numbers) and a red Diamond which I sold in
England for Eleven Hundred Pounds.

On the 6th Day of *May*, 1709, I took a solemn Leave of his
Majesty, and all my Friends. This Prince was so gracious as to
order a Guard to conduct me to *Glanguenstald*, which is a Royal
Port to the *South-West* Part of the Island. In six Days I found a
Vessel ready to carry me to *Japan*; and spent fifteen Days in the
Voyage. We landed at a small Port-Town called *Xamoschi*, situated
on the *South-East* Part of *Japan*. The Town lies on the *Western*
Part, where there is a narrow Streight, leading *Northward* into a
long Arm of the Sea, upon the *North-West* Part of which *Yedo*
the Metropolis stands. At landing I shewed the Custom-House
Officers my Letter from the King of *Luggnagg* to his Imperial
Majesty: They knew the Seal perfectly well; it was as broad as the
Palm of my Hand. The Impression was, *A King lifting up a lame
Beggar from the Earth*. The Magistrates of the Town hearing of my
Letter, received me as a publick Minister; they provided me with
Carriages and Servants, and bore my Charges to *Yedo*, where I was
admitted to an Audience, and delivered my Letter; which was
opened with great Ceremony, and explained to the Emperor by an
Interpreter, who gave me Notice of his Majesty's Order, that I
should signify my Request; and whatever it were, it should be
granted for the sake of his Royal Brother of *Luggnagg*. This Interpreter was a Person employed to transact Affairs with the *Hol-
landers*: He soon conjectured by my Countenance that I was an
European, and therefore repeated his Majesty's Commands in
Low-Dutch, which he spoke perfectly well. I answered, (as I had
before determined) that I was a *Dutch* Merchant, shipwrecked in
a very remote Country, from whence I travelled by Sea and Land to
Luggnagg, and then took Shipping for *Japan*, where I knew my
Countrymen often traded, and with some of these I hoped to get
an Opportunity of returning into *Europe*: I therefore most humbly
entreated his Royal Favour to give Order, that I should be conducted in Safety to *Nangasac*. To this I added another Petition,

that for the sake of my Patron the King of *Luggnagg*, his Majesty
would condescend to excuse my performing the Ceremony imposed
on my Countrymen, of *trampling upon the Crucifix*; because I had
been thrown into his Kingdom by my Misfortunes, without any
Intention of trading. When this latter Petition was interpreted to
the Emperor, he seemed a little surprised; and said, he believed I
was the first of my Countrymen who ever made any Scruple in this
Point; and that he began to doubt whether I were a real *Hollander*
or no; but rather suspected I must be a Christian. However, for
the Reasons I had offered, but chiefly to gratify the King of *Luggnagg*, by an uncommon Mark of his Favour, he would comply
with the *singularity* of my Humour; but the Affair must be managed with Dexterity, and his Officers should be commanded to
let me pass as it were by Forgetfulness. For he assured me, that if
the Secret should be discovered by my Countrymen, the *Dutch*,
they would cut my Throat in the Voyage. I returned my Thanks by
the Interpreter for so unusual a Favour; and some Troops being at
that Time on their March to *Nangasac*, the Commanding Officer
had Orders to convey me safe thither, with particular Instructions
about the Business of the *Crucifix*.

On the 9th Day of *June*, 1709, I arrived at *Nangasac*, after a very
long and troublesome Journey. I soon fell into Company of some
Dutch Sailors belonging to the *Amboyna* of *Amsterdam*, a stout
Ship of 450 Tuns. I have lived long in *Holland*, pursuing my Studies
at *Leyden*, and I spoke *Dutch* well: The Seamen soon knew from
whence I came last; they were curious to enquire into my Voyages
and Course of Life. I made up a Story as short and probable as I
could, but concealed the greatest Part. I knew many Persons in
Holland; I was able to invent Names for my Parents, whom I pretended to be obscure People in the Province of *Guelderland*. I
would have given the Captain (one *Theodorus Vangrult*) what he
pleased to ask for my Voyage to *Holland*; but, understanding I was
a Surgeon, he was contented to take half the usual Rate, on Condition that I would serve him in the Way of my Calling. Before
we took Shipping, I was often asked by some of the Crew, whether
I had performed the Ceremony above-mentioned? I evaded the
Question by general Answers, that I had satisfied the Emperor and
Court in all Particulars. However, a malicious Rogue of a Skipper[1]

---

[1] A common seaman.

went to an Officer, and pointing to me, told him, I had not yet *trampled on the Crucifix*: But the other, who had received Instructions to let me pass, gave the Rascal twenty Strokes on the Shoulders with a Bamboo; after which I was no more troubled with such Questions.

Nothing happened worth mentioning in this Voyage. We sailed with a fair Wind to the *Cape of Good Hope*, where we staid only to take in fresh Water. On the 6th of *April* we arrived safe at *Amsterdam*, having lost only three Men by Sickness in the Voyage, and a fourth who fell from the Fore-mast into the Sea, not far from the Coast of *Guinea*. From *Amsterdam* I soon after set sail for *England* in a small Vessel belonging to that City.

On the 10th of *April*, 1710, we put in at the *Downs*. I landed the next Morning, and saw once more my Native Country after an Absence of five Years and six Months compleat. I went strait to *Redriff*, whither I arrived the same Day at two in the Afternoon, and found my Wife and Family in good Health.

The End of the Third Part

PART IV

A VOYAGE TO THE COUNTRY
OF THE HOUYHNHNMS

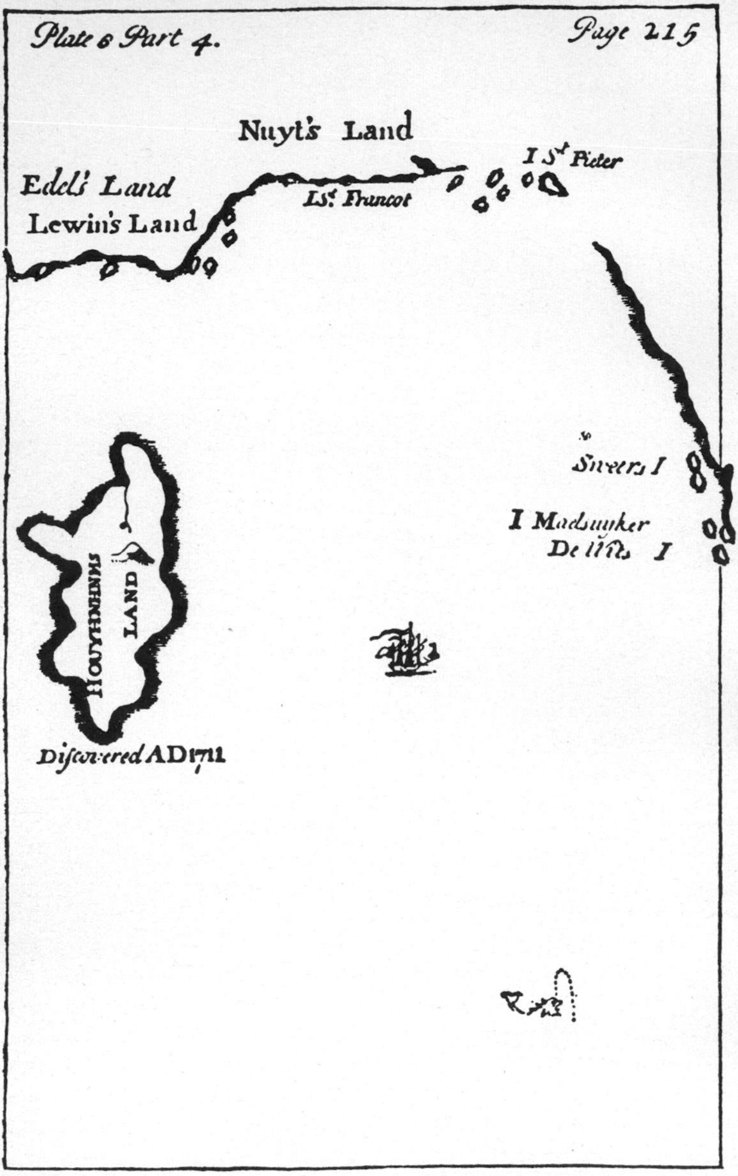
Plate 6 Part 4.
Page 215
Nuyt's Land
Edels Land
Lewin's Land
I St Pieter
Is. St Francot
Sweers I
I Madbuyker
De Wits I
HOUYHNHNMS LAND
Discovered AD 1711

CHAPTER I

The Author sets out as Captain of a Ship. His Men conspire against him, confine him a long Time to his Cabbin, set him on Shore in an unknown Land. He travels up into the Country. The Yahoos, a strange Sort of Animal, described. The Author meets two Houyhnhnms.

I continued at home with my Wife and Children about five Months in a very happy Condition, if I could have learned the Lesson of knowing when I was well. I left my poor Wife big with Child, and accepted an advantageous Offer made me to be Captain of the *Adventure,* a stout Merchant-man of 350 Tuns: For I understood Navigation well, and being grown weary of a Surgeon's Employment at Sea, which however I could exercise upon Occasion, I took a skilful young Man of that Calling, one *Robert Purefoy,* into my Ship. We set sail from *Portsmouth* upon the 7th Day of *September,* 1710; on the 14th we met with Captain *Pocock* of *Bristol,* at *Tenariff,* who was going to the Bay of *Campeachy,* to cut Logwood. On the 16th he was parted from us by a Storm: I heard since my Return, that his Ship foundered, and none escaped, but one Cabbin-Boy. He was an honest Man, and a good Sailor, but a little too positive in his own Opinions, which was the Cause of his Destruction, as it hath been of several others. For if he had followed my Advice, he might at this Time have been safe at home with his Family as well as my self.

I had several Men died in my Ship of Calentures,[1] so that I was forced to get Recruits out of *Barbadoes,* and the *Leeward Islands,* where I touched by the Direction of the Merchants who employed me; which I had soon too much Cause to repent; for I found afterwards that most of them had been Buccaneers. I had fifty Hands on Board; and my Orders were, that I should trade with the *Indians* in the *South-Sea,* and make what Discoveries I could. These

[1] Tropical fever, accompanied by delirium: a foretelling (perhaps) of Gulliver's future enraptures.

Rogues whom I had picked up, debauched my other Men, and they all formed a Conspiracy to seize the Ship and secure me; which they did one Morning, rushing into my Cabbin, and binding me Hand and Foot, threatening to throw me overboard, if I offered to stir. I told them, I was their Prisoner, and would submit. This they made me swear to do, and then unbound me, only fastening one of my Legs with a Chain near my Bed; and placed a Centry at my Door with his Piece charged, who was commanded to shoot me dead if I attempted my Liberty. They sent me down Victuals and Drink, and took the Government of the Ship to themselves. Their Design was to turn Pirates, and plunder the *Spaniards*, which they could not do, till they got more Men. But first they resolved to sell the Goods in the Ship, and then go to *Madagascar* for Recruits, several among them having died since my Confinement. They sailed many Weeks, and traded with the *Indians*; but I knew not what Course they took, being kept close Prisoner in my Cabbin, and expecting nothing less than to be murdered, as they often threatened me.

Upon the 9th Day of *May*, 1711, one *James Welch* came down to my Cabbin; and said he had Orders from the Captain to set me ashore. I expostulated with him, but in vain; neither would he so much as tell me who their new Captain was. They forced me into the Long-boat, letting me put on my best Suit of Cloaths, which were as good as new, and a small Bundle of Linnen, but no Arms except my Hanger; and they were so civil as not to search my Pockets, into which I conveyed what Money I had, with some other little Necessaries. They rowed about a League; and then set me down on a Strand. I desired them to tell me what Country it was: They all swore, they knew no more than my self, but said, that the Captain (as they called him) was resolved, after they had sold the Lading, to get rid of me in the first Place where they discovered Land. They pushed off immediately, advising me to make haste, for fear of being overtaken by the Tide; and bade me farewell.

In this desolate Condition I advanced forward, and soon got upon firm Ground, where I sat down on a Bank to rest my self, and consider what I had best to do. When I was a little refreshed, I went up into the Country, resolving to deliver my self to the first Savages I should meet; and purchase my Life from them by some Bracelets, Glass Rings, and other Toys, which Sailors usually provide themselves with in those Voyages, and whereof I had some about me:

The Land was divided by long Rows of Trees, not regularly planted, but naturally growing; there was great Plenty of Grass, and several Fields of Oats. I walked very circumspectly for fear of being surprised, or suddenly shot with an Arrow from behind, or on either Side. I fell into a beaten Road, where I saw many Tracks of human Feet, and some of Cows, but most of Horses. At last I beheld several Animals in a Field, and one or two of the same Kind sitting in Trees. Their Shape was very singular, and deformed, which a little discomposed me, so that I lay down behind a Thicket to observe them better. Some of them coming forward near the Place where I lay, gave me an Opportunity of distinctly marking their Form. Their Heads and Breasts were covered with a thick Hair, some frizzled and others lank; they had Beards like Goats, and a long Ridge of Hair down their Backs, and the fore Parts of their Legs and Feet; but the rest of their Bodies were bare, so that I might see their Skins, which were of a brown Buff Colour. They had no Tails, nor any Hair at all on their Buttocks, except about the *Anus*; which, I presume Nature had placed there to defend them as they sat on the Ground; for this Posture they used, as well as lying down, and often stood on their hind Feet. They climbed high Trees, as nimbly as a Squirrel, for they had strong extended Claws before and behind, terminating in sharp Points, and hooked. They would often spring, and bound, and leap with prodigious Agility. The Females were not so large as the Males; they had long lank Hair on their Heads, and only a Sort of Down on the rest of their Bodies, except about the *Anus*, and *Pudenda*. Their Dugs hung between their fore Feet, and often reached almost to the Ground as they walked. The Hair of both Sexes was of several Colours, brown, red, black and yellow. Upon the whole, I never beheld in all my Travels so disagreeable an Animal, or one against which I naturally conceived so strong an Antipathy. So that thinking I had seen enough, full of Contempt and Aversion, I got up and pursued the beaten Road, hoping it might direct me to the Cabbin of some *Indian*. I had not gone far when I met one of these Creatures full in my Way, and coming up directly to me. The ugly Monster, when he saw me, distorted several Ways every Feature of his Visage, and stared as at an Object he had never seen before; then approaching nearer, lifted up his fore Paw, whether out of Curiosity or Mischief, I could not tell: But I drew my Hanger, and gave him a good Blow with the flat Side of it; for I durst not strike him with the Edge, fearing the Inhabitants might be provoked against me, if they should come to know, that I had killed or maimed any of their Cattle. When the Beast felt the Smart, he drew back, and roared so loud, that a Herd of at least forty came flocking about me from the next Field, howling and making odious Faces; but I ran to the Body of a Tree, and leaning my Back against it, kept them off, by waving my Hanger. Several of this cursed Brood getting hold of the Branches behind, leaped up into the Tree, from whence they began to discharge their Excrements on my Head: However, I escaped pretty well, by sticking close to the Stem of the Tree, but was almost stifled with the Filth, which fell about me on every Side.

In the Midst of this Distress, I observed them all to run away on a sudden as fast as they could; at which I ventured to leave the Tree, and pursue the Road, wondering what it was that could put them into this Fright. But looking on my Left-Hand, I saw a Horse walking softly in the Field; which my Persecutors having sooner discovered, was the Cause of their Flight. The Horse started a little when he came near me, but soon recovering himself, looked full in my Face with manifest Tokens of Wonder: He viewed my Hands and Feet, walking round me several times. I would have pursued my Journey, but he placed himself directly in the Way, yet looking with a very mild Aspect, never offering the least Violence. We stood gazing at each other for some time; at last I took the Boldness, to reach my Hand towards his Neck, with a Design to stroak it; using the common Style and Whistle of Jockies when they are going to handle a strange Horse. But, this Animal seeming to receive my Civilities with Disdain, shook his Head, and bent his Brows, softly raising up his Left Fore-Foot to remove my Hand. Then he neighed three or four times, but in so different a Cadence, that I almost began to think he was speaking to himself in some Language of his own.

While He and I were thus employed, another Horse came up; who applying himself to the first in a very formal Manner, they gently struck each others Right Hoof before, neighing several times by Turns, and varying the Sound, which seemed to be almost articulate. They went some Paces off, as if it were to confer together, walking Side by Side, backward and forward, like Persons deliberating upon some Affair of Weight; but often turning their Eyes towards me, as it were to watch that I might not escape. I was amazed to see such Actions and Behaviour in Brute Beasts; and concluded with myself, that if the Inhabitants of this Country were endued with a proportionable Degree of Reason, they must needs be the wisest People upon Earth. This Thought gave me so much Comfort, that I resolved to go forward untill I could discover some House or Village, or meet with any of the Natives; leaving the two Horses to discourse together as they pleased. But the first, who was a Dapple-Grey, observing me to steal off, neighed after me in so expressive a Tone, that I fancied myself to understand what he meant; whereupon I turned back, and came near him, to expect his farther Commands; but concealing my Fear as much as I could; for I began to be in some Pain, how this Adventure might terminate; and the Reader will easily believe I did not much like my present Situation.

The two Horses came up close to me, looking with great Earnestness upon my Face and Hands. The grey Steed rubbed my Hat all round with his Right Fore-hoof, and discomposed it so much, that I was forced to adjust it better, by taking it off, and settling it again; whereat both he and his Companion (who was a brown Bay) appeared to be much surprized; the latter felt the Lappet of my Coat, and finding it to hang loose about me, they both looked with new Signs of Wonder. He stroaked my Right Hand, seeming to admire the Softness, and Colour; but he squeezed it so hard between his Hoof and his Pastern, that I was forced to roar; after which they both touched me with all possible Tenderness. They were under great Perplexity about my Shoes and Stockings, which they felt very often, neighing to each other, and using various Gestures, not unlike those of a Philosopher, when he would attempt to solve some new and difficult Phænomenon.

Upon the whole, the Behaviour of these Animals was so orderly and rational, so acute and judicious, that I at last concluded, they must needs be Magicians, who had thus metamorphosed themselves upon some Design; and seeing a Stranger in the Way, were resolved to divert themselves with him; or perhaps were really amazed at the Sight of a Man so very different in Habit, Feature and Complexion from those who might probably live in so remote a Climate. Upon the Strength of this Reasoning, I ventured to address them in the following Manner: Gentlemen, if you be Conjurers, as I have good Cause to believe, you can understand any Language; therefore I make bold to let your Worships know, that

I am a poor distressed *Englishman*, driven by his Misfortunes upon your Coast; and I entreat one of you, to let me ride upon his Back, as if he were a real Horse, to some House or Village, where I can be relieved. In return of which Favour, I will make you a Present of this Knife and Bracelet, (taking them out of my Pocket.) The two Creatures stood silent while I spoke, seeming to listen with great Attention; and when I had ended, they neighed frequently towards each other, as if they were engaged in serious Conversation. I plainly observed, that their Language expressed the Passions very well, and the Words might with little Pains be resolved into an Alphabet more easily than the *Chinese*.

I could frequently distinguish the Word *Yahoo*, which was repeated by each of them several times; and although it were impossible for me to conjecture what it meant, yet while the two Horses were busy in Conversation, I endeavoured to practice this word upon my Tongue; and as soon as they were silent, I boldly pronounced *Yahoo* in a loud Voice, imitating, at the same time, as near as I could, the Neighing of a Horse; at which they were both visibly surprized, and the Grey repeated the same Word twice, as if he meant to teach me the right Accent, wherein I spoke after him as well as I could, and found myself perceivably to improve every time, although very far from any Degree of Perfection. Then the Bay tried me with a second Word, much harder to be pronounced; but reducing it to the *English Orthography*, may be spelt thus, *Houyhnhnm*.[2] I did not succeed in this so well as the former, but after two or three farther Trials, I had better Fortune; and they both appeared amazed at my Capacity.

After some farther Discourse, which I then conjectured might relate to me, the two Friends took their Leaves, with the same Compliment of striking each other's Hoof; and the Grey made me Signs that I should walk before him; wherein I thought it prudent to comply, till I could find a better Director. When I offered to slacken my Pace, he would cry *Hhuun, Hhuun*; I guessed his Meaning, and gave him to understand, as well as I could, that I was weary, and not able to walk faster; upon which, he would stand a while to let me rest.

---

[2] The whinny of a horse; perhaps best pronounced, *Whin-num*.

CHAPTER II

The Author conducted by a Houyhnhnm *to his house.
The House described. The Author's Reception. The
Food of the* Houyhnhnms. *The Author in Distress for
Want of Meat, is at last relieved. His Manner of feeding
in that Country.*

Having travelled about three Miles, we came to a long
Kind of Building, made of Timber, stuck in the Ground, and wat-
tled a-cross; the Roof was low, and covered with Straw. I now began
to be a little comforted; and took out some Toys, which Travellers
usually carry for Presents to the Savage *Indians* of *America* and
other Parts, in hopes the People of the House would be thereby
encouraged to receive me kindly. The Horse made me a Sign to go
in first; it was a large Room with a smooth Clay Floor, and a Rack
and Manger extending the whole Length on one Side. There were
three Nags, and two Mares, not eating, but some of them sitting
down upon their Hams, which I very much wondered at; but wondered more to see the rest employed in domestick Business: The last
seemed but ordinary Cattle; however this confirmed my first Opinion, that a People who could so far civilize brute Animals, must
needs excel in Wisdom all the Nations of the World The Grey
came in just after, and thereby prevented any ill Treatment, which
the others might have given me. He neighed to them several times
in a Style of Authority, and received Answers.

Beyond this Room there were three others, reaching the Length
of the House, to which you passed through three Doors, opposite
to each other, in the Manner of a Vista: We went through the
second Room towards the third; here the Grey walked in first,
beckoning me to attend: I waited in the second Room, and got
ready my Presents, for the Master and Mistress of the House: They
were two Knives, three Bracelets of false Pearl, a small Looking

Glass and a Bead Necklace. The Horse neighed three or four Times, and I waited to hear some answers in a human Voice, but I heard no other Returns than in the same Dialect, only one or two a little shriller than his. I began to think that this House must belong to some Person of great Note among them, because there appeared so much Ceremony before I could gain Admittance. But, that a Man of Quality should be served all by Horses, was Beyond my Comprehension. I feared my Brain was disturbed by my Sufferings and Misfortunes: I roused my self, and looked about me in the Room where I was left alone; this was furnished as the first, only after a more elegant Manner. I rubbed my Eyes often, but the same Objects still occurred. I pinched my Arms and Sides, to awake my self, hoping I might be in a Dream. I then absolutely concluded, that all these Appearances could be nothing else but Necromancy and Magick. But I had no Time to pursue these Reflections; for the Grey Horse came to the Door, and made me a Sign to follow him into the third Room; where I saw a very comely Mare, together with a Colt and Fole, sitting on their Haunches, upon Mats of Straw, not unartfully made, and perfectly neat and clean.

The Mare soon after my Entrance, rose from her Mat, and coming up close, after having nicely observed my Hands and Face, gave me a most contemptuous Look; then turning to the Horse, I heard the Word *Yahoo* often repeated betwixt them; the meaning of which Word I could not then comprehend, although it were the first I had learned to pronounce; but I was soon better informed, to my everlasting Mortification: For the Horse beckoning to me with his Head, and repeating the Word *Hhuun, Hhuun,* as he did upon the Road, which I understood was to attend him, led me out into a kind of Court, where was another Building at some Distance from the House. Here we entered, and I saw three of those detestable Creatures, which I first met after my landing, feeding upon Roots, and the Flesh of some Animals, which I afterwards found to be that of Asses and Dogs, and now and then a Cow dead by Accident or Disease. They were all tied by the Neck with strong Wyths, fastened to a Beam; they held their Food between the Claws of their fore Feet, and tore it with their Teeth.

The Master Horse ordered a Sorrel Nag, one of his Servants, to untie the largest of these Animals, and take him into a Yard. The Beast and I were brought close together; and our Countenances diligently compared, both by Master and Servant, who thereupon repeated several Times the Word *Yahoo*. My Horror and Astonishment are not to be described, when I observed, in this abominable Animal, a perfect human Figure; the Face of it indeed was flat and broad, the Nose depressed, the Lips large, and the Mouth wide: But these Differences are common to all savage Nations, where the Lineaments of the Countenance are distorted by the Natives suffering their Infants to lie grovelling on the Earth, or by carrying them on their Backs, nuzzling with their Face against the Mother's Shoulders. The Fore-feet of the *Yahoo* differed from my Hands in nothing else, but the Length of the Nails, the Coarseness and Brownness of the Palms, and the Hairiness on the Backs. There was the same Resemblance between our Feet, with the same Differences, which I knew very well, although the Horses did not, because of my Shoes and Stockings; the same in every Part of our Bodies, except as to Hairiness and Colour, which I have already described.

The great Difficulty that seemed to stick with the two Horses, was, to see the rest of my Body so very different from that of a *Yahoo*, for which I was obliged to my Cloaths, whereof they had no Conception: The Sorrel Nag offered me a Root, which he held (after their Manner, as we shall describe in its proper Place) between his Hoof and Pastern; I took it in my Hand, and having smelt it, returned it to him again as civilly as I could. He brought out of the *Yahoo's* Kennel a Piece of Ass's Flesh, but it smelt so offensively that I turned from it with loathing; he then threw it to the *Yahoo*, by whom it was greedily devoured. He afterwards shewed me a Wisp of Hay, and a Fettlock full of Oats; but I shook my Head, to signify that neither of these were Food for me. And indeed, I now apprehended, that I must absolutely starve, if I did not get to some of my own Species: For as to those filthy *Yahoos*, although there were few greater Lovers of Mankind, at that time, than myself; yet I confess I never saw any sensitive Being so detestable on all Accounts; and the more I came near them, the more hateful they grew, while I stayed in that Country. This the Master Horse observed by my Behaviour, and therefore sent the *Yahoo* back to his Kennel. He then put his Fore-hoof to his Mouth, at which I was much surprized, although he did it with Ease, and with a Motion that appear'd perfectly natural; and made other Signs to know what I would eat; but I could not return him such an Answer as he was able to apprehend; and if he had understood me, I did not see how it was possible to contrive any way for finding myself Nourishment. While we were thus engaged, I observed a Cow passing by; whereupon I pointed to her, and expressed a Desire to let me go and milk her. This had its Effect; for he led me back into the House, and ordered a Mare-servant to open a Room, where a good Store of Milk lay in Earthen and Wooden Vessels, after a very orderly and cleanly Manner. She gave me a large Bowl full, of which I drank very heartily, and found myself well refreshed.

About Noon I saw coming towards the House a Kind of Vehicle, drawn like a Sledge by four *Yahoos.* There was in it an old Steed, who seemed to be of Quality; he alighted with his Hind-feet forward, having by Accident got a Hurt in his Left Fore-foot. He came to dine with our Horse, who received him with great Civility. They dined in the best Room, and had Oats boiled in Milk for the second Course, which the old Horse eat warm, but the rest cold. Their Mangers were placed circular in the Middle of the Room, and divided into several Partitions, round which they sat on their Haunches upon Bosses of Straw. In the Middle was a large Rack with Angles answering to every Partition of the Manger. So that each Horse and Mare eat their own Hay, and their own Mash of Oats and Milk, with much Decency and Regularity. The Behaviour of the young Colt and Fole appeared very modest; and that of the Master and Mistress extremely chearful and complaisant to their Guest. The Grey ordered me to stand by him; and much Discourse passed between him and his Friend concerning me, as I found by the Stranger's often looking on me, and the frequent Repetition of the Word *Yahoo.*

I happened to wear my Gloves; which the Master Grey observing, seemed perplexed; discovering Signs of Wonder what I had done to my Fore-feet; he put his Hoof three or four times to them, as if he would signify, that I should reduce them to their former Shape, which I presently did, pulling off both my Gloves, and putting them into my Pocket. This occasioned farther Talk, and I saw the Company was pleased with my Behaviour, whereof I soon found the good Effects. I was ordered to speak the few Words I understood; and while they were at Dinner, the Master taught me the Names for Oats, Milk, Fire, Water, and some others; which I could readily pronounce after him; having from my Youth a great Facility in learning Languages.

When Dinner was done, the Master Horse took me aside, and by Signs and Words made me understand the Concern he was in, that

I had nothing to eat. Oats in their Tongue are called *Hlunnh.* This Word I pronounced two or three times; for although I had refused them at first, yet upon second Thoughts, I considered that I could contrive to make a Kind of Bread, which might be sufficient with Milk to keep me alive, till I could make my Escape to some other Country, and to Creatures of my own Species. The Horse immediately ordered a white Mare-servant of his Family to bring me a good Quantity of Oats in a Sort of wooden Tray. These I heated before the Fire as well as I could, and rubbed them till the Husks came off, which I made a shift to winnow from the Grain; I ground and beat them between two Stones, then took Water, and made them into a Paste or Cake, which I toasted at the Fire, and eat warm with Milk. It was at first a very insipid Diet, although common enough in many Parts of *Europe,* but grew tolerable by Time; and having been often reduced to hard Fare in my Life, this was not the first Experiment I had made how easily Nature is satisfied. And I cannot but observe, that I never had one Hour's Sickness, while I staid in this Island. It is true, I sometimes made a shift to catch a Rabbet, or Bird, by Springes made of *Yahoos* Hairs; and I often gathered wholesome Herbs, which I boiled, or eat as Salades with my Bread; and now and then, for a Rarity, I made a little Butter, and drank the Whey. I was at first at a great Loss for Salt; but Custom soon reconciled the Want of it; and I am confident that the frequent Use of Salt among us is an Effect of Luxury, and was first introduced only as a Provocative to Drink; except where it is necessary for preserving of Flesh in long Voyages, or in Places remote from great Markets. For we observe no Animal to be fond of it but Man:[1] And as to myself, when I left this Country, it was a great while before I could endure the Taste of it in any thing that I eat.

This is enough to say upon the Subject of my Dyet, wherewith other Travellers fill their Books, as if the Readers were personally concerned, whether we fare well or ill. However, it was necessary to mention this Matter, lest the World should think it impossible that I could find Sustenance for three Years in such a Country, and among such Inhabitants.

When it grew towards Evening, the Master Horse ordered a Place for me to lodge in; it was but Six Yards from the House, and

[1] Gulliver's (not necessarily Swift's) error: many animals are very fond of salt.

separated from the Stable of the *Yahoos*. Here I got some Straw, and covering myself with my own Cloaths, slept very sound. But I was in a short time better accommodated, as the Reader shall know hereafter, when I come to treat more particularly about my Way of living.

CHAPTER III

The Author studious to learn the Language, the Houy- *hnhnm his Master assists in teaching him. The Language described. Several* Houyhnhnms *of Quality come out of Curiosity to see the Author. He gives his Master a short Account of his Voyage.*

My principal Endeavour was to learn the Language, which my Master (for so I shall henceforth call him) and his Children, and every Servant of his House were desirous to teach me. For they looked upon it as a Prodigy, that a brute Animal should discover such Marks of a rational Creature. I pointed to every thing, and enquired the Name of it, which I wrote down in my *Journal Book* when I was alone, and corrected my bad Accent, by desiring those of the Family to pronounce it often. In this Employment, a Sorrel Nag, one of the under Servants, was very ready to assist me.

In speaking, they pronounce through the Nose and Throat, and their Language approaches nearest to the *High Dutch* or *German*, of any I know in *Europe*; but is much more graceful and significant. The Emperor *Charles* V. made almost the same Observation, when he said, That if he were to speak to his Horse, it should be in *High Dutch*.[1]

The Curiosity and Impatience of my Master were so great, that he spent many Hours of his Leisure to instruct me. He was convinced (as he afterwards told me) that I must be a *Yahoo*, but my

---

[1] Charles was reputed to have said he would address his God in Spanish, his mistress in Italian, and his horse in German.

Teachableness, Civility and Cleanliness astonished him; which were Qualities altogether so opposite to those Animals. He was most perplexed about my Cloaths, reasoning sometimes with himself, whether they were a Part of my Body; for I never pulled them off till the Family were asleep, and got them on before they waked in the Morning. My Master was eager to learn from whence I came; how I acquired those Appearances of Reason, which I discovered in all my Actions; and to know my Story from my own Mouth, which he hoped he should soon do by the great Proficiency I made in learning and pronouncing their Words and Sentences. To help my Memory, I formed all I learned into the *English* Alphabet, and writ the Words down with the Translations. This last, after some time, I ventured to do in my Master's Presence. It cost me much Trouble to explain to him what I was doing; for the Inhabitants have not the least Idea of Books or Literature.

In about ten Weeks time I was able to understand most of his Questions; and in three Months could give him some tolerable Answers. He was extremely curious to know from what Part of the Country I came, and how I was taught to imitate a rational Creature; because the *Yahoos*, (whom he saw I exactly resembled in my Head, Hands and Face, that were only visible,) with some Appearance of Cunning, and the strongest Disposition to Mischief, were observed to be the most unteachable of all Brutes. I answered; that I came over the Sea, from a far Place, with many others of my own Kind, in a great hollow Vessel made of the Bodies of Trees: That, my Companions forced me to land on this Coast, and then left me to shift for myself. It was with some Difficulty, and by the Help of many Signs, that I brought him to understand me. He replied, That I must needs be mistaken, or that I *said the thing which was not.* (For they have no Word in their Language to express Lying or Falshood.) He knew it was impossible that there could be a Country beyond the Sea, or that a Parcel of Brutes could move a wooden Vessel whither they pleased upon Water. He was sure no *Houyhnhnm* alive could make such a Vessel, or would trust *Yahoos* to manage it.

The Word *Houyhnhnm*, in their Tongue, signifies a *Horse*; and in its Etymology, *the Perfection of Nature*. I told my Master, that I was at a Loss for Expression, but would improve as fast as I could; and hoped in a short time I should be able to tell him Wonders: He was pleased to direct his own Mare, his Colt and Fole, and the

Servants of the Family to take all Opportunities of instructing me;
and every Day for two or three Hours, he was at the same Pains
himself: Several Horses and Mares of Quality in the Neighbourhood
came often to our House, upon the Report spread of a wonderful
Yahoo, that could speak like a *Houyhnhnm*, and seemed in his
Words and Actions to discover some Glimmerings of Reason. These
delighted to converse with me; they put many Questions, and
received such Answers, as I was able to return. By all which Advantages, I made so great a Progress, that in five Months from my
Arrival, I understood whatever was spoke, and could express myself
tolerably well.

The *Houyhnhnms* who came to visit my Master, out of a Design
of seeing and talking with me, could hardly believe me to be a
right *Yahoo*, because my Body had a different Covering from others
of my Kind. They were astonished to observe me without the
usual Hair or Skin, except on my Head, Face and Hands: but I discovered that Secret to my Master, upon an Accident, which happened about a Fortnight before.

I have already told the Reader, that every Night when the Family
were gone to Bed, it was my Custom to strip and cover myself with
my Cloaths: It happened one Morning early, that my Master sent
for me, by the Sorrel Nag, who was his Valet; when he came, I was
fast asleep, my Cloaths fallen off on one Side, and my Shirt above
my Waste. I awaked at the Noise he made, and observed him to
deliver his Message in some Disorder; after which he went to my
Master, and in a great Fright gave him a very confused Account
of what he had seen: This I presently discovered; for going as soon
as I was dressed, to pay my Attendance upon his Honour, he asked
me the Meaning of what his Servant had reported; that I was not
the same Thing when I slept as I appeared to be at other times; that
his Valet assured him, some Part of me was white, some yellow, at
least not so white, and some brown.

I had hitherto concealed the Secret of my Dress, in order to
distinguish myself as much as possible, from that cursed Race of
Yahoos; but now I found it in vain to do so any longer. Besides,
I considered that my Cloaths and Shoes would soon wear out, which
already were in a declining Condition, and must be supplied by
some Contrivance from the Hides of *Yahoos*, or other Brutes;
whereby the whole Secret would be known. I therefore told my
Master, that in the Country from whence I came, those of my

Kind always covered their Bodies with the Hairs of certain Animals prepared by Art, as well for Decency, as to avoid Inclemencies of Air both hot and cold; of which, as to my own Person I would give him immediate Conviction, if he pleased to command me; only desiring his Excuse, if I did not expose those Parts that Nature taught us to conceal. He said, my Discourse was all very strange, but especially the last Part; for he could not understand why Nature should teach us to conceal what Nature had given. That neither himself nor Family were ashamed of any Parts of their Bodies; but however I might do as I pleased. Whereupon, I first unbuttoned my Coat, and pulled it off. I did the same with my Waste-coat; I drew off my Shoes, Stockings and Breeches. I let my Shirt down to my Waste, and drew up the Bottom, fastening it like a Girdle about my Middle to hide my Nakedness.

My Master observed the whole Performance with great Signs of Curiosity and Admiration. He took up all my Cloaths in his Pastern, one Piece after another, and examined them diligently; he then stroaked my Body very gently, and looked round me several Times: after which he said, it was plain I must be a perfect *Yahoo*; but that I differed very much from the rest of my Species, in the Whiteness, and Smoothness of my Skin, my want of Hair in several Parts of my Body, the Shape and Shortness of my Claws behind and before, and my Affectation of walking continually on my two hinder Feet. He desired to see no more; and gave me leave to put on my Cloaths again, for I was shuddering with Cold.

I expressed my Uneasiness at his giving me so often the Appellation of *Yahoo*, an odious Animal, for which I had so utter an Hatred and Contempt. I begged he would forbear applying that Word to me, and take the same Order in his Family, and among his Friends whom he suffered to see me. I requested likewise, that the Secret of my having a false Covering to my Body might be known to none but himself, at least as long as my present Cloathing should last: For as to what the Sorrel Nag his Valet had observed, his Honour might command him to conceal it.

All this my Master very graciously consented to; and thus the Secret was kept till my Cloaths began to wear out, which I was forced to supply by several Contrivances, that shall hereafter be mentioned. In the mean Time, he desired I would go on with my utmost Diligence to learn their Language, because he was more astonished at my Capacity for Speech and Reason, than at the

Figure of my Body, whether it were covered or no; adding, that he waited with some Impatience to hear the Wonders which I promised to tell him.

From thenceforward he doubled the Pains he had been at to instruct me; he brought me into all Company, and made them treat me with Civility, because, as he told them privately, this would put me into good Humour, and make me more diverting.

Every Day when I waited on him, beside the Trouble he was at in teaching, he would ask me several Questions concerning my self, which I answered as well as I could; and by those Means he had already received some general Ideas, although very imperfect. It would be tedious to relate the several Steps, by which I advanced to a more regular Conversation: But the first Account I gave of my self in any Order and Length, was to this Purpose:

That, I came from a very far Country, as I already had attempted to tell him, with about fifty more of my own Species; that we travelled upon the Seas, in a great hollow Vessel made of Wood, and larger than his Honour's House. I described the Ship to him in the best Terms I could; and explained by the Help of my Handkerchief displayed, how it was driven forward by the Wind. That, upon a Quarrel among us, I was set on Shoar on this Coast, where I walked forward without knowing whither, till he delivered me from the Persecution of those execrable *Yahoos*. He asked me, Who made the Ship, and how it was possible that the *Houyhnhnms* of my Country would leave it to the Management of Brutes? My Answer was, that I durst proceed no farther in my Relation, unless he would give me his Word and Honour that he would not be offended; and then I would tell him the Wonders I had so often promised. He agreed; and I went on by assuring him, that the Ship was made by Creatures like myself, who in all the Countries I had travelled, as well as in my own, were the only governing, rational Animals; and that upon my Arrival hither, I was as much astonished to see the *Houyhnhnms* act like rational Beings, as he or his Friends could be in finding some Marks of Reason in a Creature he was pleased to call a *Yahoo*; to which I owned my Resemblance in every Part, but could not account for their degenerate and brutal Nature. I said farther, That if good Fortune ever restored me to my native Country, to relate my Travels hither, as I resolved to do; every Body would believe that I *said the Thing which was not*: that I invented the Story out of my own Head:

And with all possible Respect to Himself, his Family, and Friends, and under his Promise of not being offended, our Countrymen would hardly think it probable, that a *Houyhnhnm* should be the presiding Creature of a Nation, and a *Yahoo* the Brute.

CHAPTER IV

The Houyhnhnms *Notion of Truth and Falsehood. The Author's Discourse disapproved by his Master. The Author gives a more particular Account of himself, and the Accidents of his Voyage.*

My Master heard me with great Appearances of Uneasiness in his Countenance; because *Doubting* or *not believing*, are so little known in this Country, that the Inhabitants cannot tell how to behave themselves under such Circumstances. And I remember in frequent Discourses with my Master concerning the Nature of Manhood, in other Parts of the World; having Occasion to talk of *Lying*, and *false Representation*, it was with much Difficulty that he comprehended what I meant; although he had otherwise a most acute Judgment. For he argued thus; That the Use of Speech was to make us understand one another, and to receive Information of Facts; now if any one *said the Thing which was not*, these Ends were defeated; because I cannot properly be said to understand him; and I am so far from receiving Information, that he leaves me worse than in Ignorance; for I am led to believe a Thing *Black* when it is *White*, and *Short* when it is *Long*. And these were all the Notions he had concerning that Faculty of *Lying*, so perfectly well understood, and so universally practised among human Creatures.

To return from this Digression; when I asserted that the *Yahoos* were the only governing Animals in my Country, which my Master said was altogether past his Conception, he desired to know, whether we had *Houyhnhnms* among us, and what was their Employment: I told him, we had great Numbers; that in Summer they grazed in the Fields, and in Winter were kept in Houses, with Hay and Oats, where *Yahoo* Servants were employed to rub their Skins smooth, comb their Manes, pick their Feet, serve them with Food, and make their Beds. I understand you well, said my Master; it is now very plain from all you have spoken, that whatever Share of Reason the *Yahoos* pretend to, the *Houyhnhnms* are your Masters; I heartily wish our *Yahoos* would be so tractable. I begged his Honour would please to excuse me from proceeding any farther, because I was very certain that the Account he expected from me would be highly displeasing. But he insisted in commanding me to let him know the best and the worst: I told him he should be obeyed. I owned, that the *Houyhnhnms* among us, whom we called *Horses*, were the most generous and comely Animal we had; that they excelled in Strength and Swiftness; and when they belonged to Persons of Quality, employed in Travelling, Racing, and drawing Chariots, they were treated with much Kindness and Care, till they fell into Diseases, or became foundered in the Feet; but then they were sold, and used to all kind of Drudgery till they died; after which their Skins were stripped and sold for what they were worth, and their Bodies left to be devoured by Dogs and Birds of Prey. But the common Race of Horses had not so good Fortune, being kept by Farmers and Carriers, and other mean People, who put them to greater Labour, and feed them worse. I described as well as I could, our Way of Riding; the Shape and Use of a Bridle, a Saddle, a Spur, and a Whip; of Harness and Wheels. I added, that we fastened Plates of a certain hard Substance called *Iron* at the Bottom of their Feet, to preserve their Hoofs from being broken by the Stony Ways on which we often travelled.

My Master, after some Expressions of great Indignation, wondered how we dared to venture upon a *Houyhnhnm's* Back; for he was sure, that the weakest Servant in his House would be able to shake off the strongest *Yahoo*; or by lying down, and rouling upon his Back, squeeze the Brute to Death. I answered, That our Horses were trained up from three or four Years old to the several Uses we intended them for; That if any of them proved intolerably vicious, they were employed for Carriages; that they were severely beaten while they were young for any mischievous Tricks: That the Males, designed for the common Use of Riding or Draught, were generally *castrated* about two Years after their Birth, to take down

their Spirits, and make them more tame and gentle: That they
were indeed sensible of Rewards and Punishments; but his Honour
would please to consider, that they had not the least Tincture of
Reason any more than the *Yahoos* in this Country.

It put me to the Pains of many Circumlocutions to give my
Master a right Idea of what I spoke; for their Language doth not
abound in Variety of Words, because their Wants and Passions
are fewer than among us. But it is impossible to express his noble
Resentment at our savage Treatment of the *Houyhnhnm* Race;
particularly after I had explained the Manner and Use of *Castrating*
Horses among us, to hinder them from propagating their Kind, and
to render them more servile. He said, if it were possible there could
be any Country where *Yahoos* alone were endued with Reason,
they certainly must be the governing Animal, because Reason will
in Time always prevail against Brutal Strength. But, considering
the Frame of our Bodies, and especially of mine, he thought no
Creature of equal Bulk was so ill-contrived, for employing that
Reason in the common Offices of Life; whereupon he desired to
know whether those among whom I lived, resembled me or the
Yahoos of his Country. I assured him, that I was as well shaped as
most of my Age; but the younger and the Females were much
more soft and tender, and the Skins of the latter generally as white
as Milk. He said, I differed indeed from other *Yahoos*, being much
more cleanly, and not altogether so deformed; but in point of real
Advantage, he thought I differed for the worse. That my Nails
were of no Use either to my fore or hinder Feet: As to my fore
Feet, he could not properly call them by that Name, for he never
observed me to walk upon them; that they were too soft to bear
the Ground; that I generally went with them uncovered, neither
was the Covering I sometimes wore on them, of the same Shape,
or so strong as that on my Feet behind. That I could not walk with
any Security; for if either of my hinder Feet slipped, I must
inevitably fall. He then began to find fault with other Parts of
my Body; the Flatness of my Face, the Prominence of my Nose,
my Eyes placed directly in Front, so that I could not look on either
Side without turning my Head: That I was not able to feed my
self, without lifting one of my fore Feet to my Mouth: And therefore Nature had placed those Joints to answer that Necessity. He
knew not what could be the Use of those several Clefts and
Divisions in my Feet behind; that these were too soft to bear the

Hardness and Sharpness of Stones without a Covering made from
the Skin of some other Brute; that my whole Body wanted a
Fence against Heat and Cold, which I was forced to put on and
off every Day with Tediousness and Trouble. And lastly, that he
observed every Animal in this Country naturally to abhor the
Yahoos, whom the Weaker avoided, and the Stronger drove from
them. So that supposing us to have the Gift of Reason, he could
not see how it were possible to cure that natural Antipathy which
every Creature discovered against us; nor consequently, how we
could tame and render them serviceable. However, he would (as
he said) debate the Matter no farther, because he was more
desirous to know my own Story, the Country where I was born,
and the several Actions and Events of my Life before I came
hither.

I assured him, how extreamly desirous I was that he should be
satisfied in every Point; but I doubted much, whether it would
be possible for me to explain my self on several Subjects whereof
his Honour could have no Conception, because I saw nothing in
his Country to which I could resemble them. That however, I
would do my best, and strive to express my self by Similitudes,
humbly desiring his Assistance when I wanted proper Words;
which he was pleased to promise me.

I said, my Birth was of honest Parents, in an Island called
England, which was remote from this Country, as many Days
Journey as the strongest of his Honour's Servants could travel in
the Annual Course of the Sun. That I was bred a Surgeon, whose
Trade it is to cure Wounds and Hurts in the body, got by Accident
or Violence. That my Country was governed by a Female Man,
whom we called a *Queen*. That I left it to get Riches, whereby
I might maintain my self and Family when I should return. That
in my last Voyage, I was Commander of the Ship and had about
fifty *Yahoos* under me, many of which died at Sea, and I was
forced to supply them by others picked out from several Nations.
That our Ship was twice in Danger of being sunk; the first Time
by a great Storm, and the second, by striking against a Rock. Here
my Master interposed, by asking me, How I could persuade Strangers out of different Countries to venture with me, after the Losses
I had sustained, and the Hazards I had run. I said, they were
Fellows of desperate Fortunes, forced to fly from the Places of their
Birth, on Account of their Poverty or their Crimes. Some were

undone by Law-suits; others spent all they had in Drinking, Whoring and Gaming; others fled for Treason; many for Murder, Theft, Poysoning, Robbery, Perjury, Forgery, Coining false Money; for committing Rapes or Sodomy; for flying from their Colours, or deserting to the enemy; and most of them had broken Prison. None of these durst return to their native Countries for fear of being hanged, or of starving in a Jail; and therefore were under a Necessity of seeking a Livelihood in other Places.

During this Discourse, my Master was pleased often to interrupt me. I had made Use of many Circumlocutions in describing to him the Nature of the several Crimes, for which most of our Crew had been forced to fly their Country. This Labour took up several Days Conversation before he was able to comprehend me. He was wholly at a Loss to know what could be the Use or Necessity of practising those Vices. To clear up which I endeavoured to give him some Ideas of the Desire of Power and Riches; of the terrible Effects of Lust, Intemperance, Malice, and Envy. All this I was forced to define and describe by putting of Cases, and making Suppositions. After which, like one whose Imagination was struck with something never seen or heard of before, he would lift up his Eyes with Amazement and Indignation. Power, Government, War, Law, Punishment, and a Thousand other Things had no Terms, wherein that Language could express them; which made the Difficulty almost insuperable to give my Master any Conception of what I meant: But being of an excellent Understanding, much improved by Contemplation and Converse, he at last arrived at a competent Knowledge of what human Nature in our Parts of the World is capable to perform; and desired I would give him some particular Account of that Land, which we call *Europe*, especially, of my own Country.

CHAPTER V

The Author, at his Master's Commands informs him of the State of England. The Causes of War among the Princes of Europe. The Author begins to explain the English Constitution.

The Reader may please to observe, that the following Extract of many Conversations I had with my Master, contains a Summary of the most material Points, which were discoursed at several times for above two Years; his Honour often desiring fuller Satisfaction as I farther improved in the *Houyhnhnm* Tongue. I laid before him, as well as I could, the whole State of *Europe*; I discoursed of Trade and Manufactures, of Arts and Sciences; and the Answers I gave to all the Questions he made, as they arose upon several Subjects, were a Fund of Conversation not to be exhausted. But I shall here only set down the Substance of what passed between us concerning my own Country, reducing it into Order as well as I can, without any Regard to Time or other Circumstances, while I strictly adhere to Truth. My only Concern is, that I shall hardly be able to do Justice to my Master's Arguments and Expressions; which must needs suffer by my Want of Capacity, as well as by a Translation into our barbarous *English*.

In Obedience therefore to his Honour's Commands, I related to him the *Revolution* under the Prince of *Orange*; the long War with *France* entered into by the said Prince, and renewed by his Successor the present Queen; wherein the greatest Powers of *Christendom* were engaged, and which still continued:[1] I computed at his Request, that about a Million of *Yahoos* might have been killed in the whole Progress of it; and perhaps a Hundred or more Cities taken, and five times as many Ships burnt or sunk.

[1] Gulliver refers to the revolution that put William and Mary on the throne in 1689, and to the War of the Spanish Succession.

He asked me what were the usual Causes or Motives that made one Country go to War with another. I answered, they were innumerable; but I should only mention a few of the chief. Sometimes the Ambition of Princes, who never think they have Land or People enough to govern: Sometimes the Corruption of Ministers, who engage their Master in a War in order to stifle or divert the Clamour of the Subjects against their evil Administration. Difference in Opinions hath cost many Millions of Lives: For Instance, whether *Flesh* be *Bread*, or *Bread* be *Flesh*: Whether the Juice of a certain *Berry* be *Blood* or *Wine*: Whether *Whistling* be a Vice or a Virtue: Whether it be better to *kiss a Post*, or throw it into the Fire: What is the best Colour for a *Coat*, whether *Black, White, Red* or *Grey*; and whether it should be *long* or *short, narrow* or *wide, dirty* or *clean*;[2] with many more. Neither are any Wars so furious and bloody, or of so long Continuance, as those occasioned by Difference in Opinion, especially if it be in things indifferent.

Sometimes the Quarrel between two Princes is to decide which of them shall dispossess a Third of his Dominions, where neither of them pretend to any Right. Sometimes one Prince quarrelleth with another, for fear the other should quarrel with him. Sometimes a War is entered upon, because the Enemy is too *strong*, and sometimes because he is too *weak*. Sometimes our Neighbours *want* the *Things* which we *have*, or *have* the *Things* which we want; and we both fight, till they take ours or give us theirs. It is a very justifiable Cause of War to invade a Country after the People have been wasted by Famine, destroyed by Pestilence, or embroiled by Factions amongst themselves. It is justifiable to enter into a War against our nearest Ally, when one of his Towns lies convenient for us, or a Territory of Land, that would render our Dominions round and compact. If a Prince send Forces into a Nation, where the People are poor and ignorant, he may lawfully put half of them to Death, and make Slaves of the rest, in order to civilize and reduce them from their barbarous Way of Living. It is a very kingly, honourable, and frequent Practice, when one Prince desires the Assistance of another to secure him against an Invasion, that the Assistant, when he hath driven out the

---

[2] Religious differences relating to the reality of transubstantiation, the use of music in church services, the importance of the crucifix as symbol, and the color, cut, and propriety of ecclesiastical vestments.

Invader, should seize on the Dominions himself, and kill, imprison or banish the Prince he came to relieve. Allyance by Blood or Marriage, is a sufficient Cause of War between Princes; and the nearer the Kindred is, the greater is their Disposition to quarrel: *Poor* Nations are *hungry*, and *rich* Nations are *proud*; and Pride and Hunger will ever be at Variance. For these Reasons, the Trade of a *Soldier* is held the most honourable of all others: Because a *Soldier* is a *Yahoo* hired to kill in cold Blood as many of his own Species, who have never offended him, as possibly he can.

There is likewise a Kind of beggarly Princes in *Europe*, not able to make War by themselves, who hire out their Troops to richer Nations for so much a Day to each Man; of which they keep three Fourths to themselves, and it is the best Part of their Maintenance; such are those in many *Northern* Parts of *Europe*.

What you have told me, (said my Master) upon the Subject of War, doth indeed discover most admirably the Effects of that Reason you pretend to: However, it is happy that the *Shame* is greater than the *Danger*; and that Nature hath left you utterly uncapable of doing much Mischief: For your Mouths lying flat with your Faces, you can hardly bite each other to any Purpose, unless by Consent. Then, as to the Claws upon your Feet before and behind, they are so short and tender, that one of our *Yahoos* would drive a Dozen of yours before him. And therefore in recounting the Numbers of those who have been killed in Battle, I cannot but think that you have *said the Thing which is not.*

I could not forbear shaking my Head and smiling a little at his Ignorance. And, being no Stranger to the Art of War, I gave him a Description of Cannons, Culverins, Muskets, Carabines, Pistols, Bullets, Powder, Swords, Bayonets, Battles, Sieges, Retreats, Attacks, Undermines, Countermines, Bombardments, Sea-fights; Ships sunk with a Thousand Men; twenty Thousand killed on each Side; dying Groans, Limbs flying in the Air: Smoak, Noise, Confusion, trampling to Death under Horses Feet: Flight, Pursuit, Victory; Fields strewed with Carcases left for Food to Dogs, and Wolves, and Birds of Prey; Plundering, Stripping, Ravishing, Burning and Destroying. And, to set forth the Valour of my own dear Countrymen, I assured him, that I had seen them blow up a Hundred Enemies at once in a Siege, and as many in a Ship; and beheld the dead Bodies drop down in Pieces from the Clouds, to the great Diversion of all the Spectators.

I was going on to more Particulars, when my Master commanded me Silence. He said, whoever understood the Nature of *Yahoos* might easily believe it possible for so vile an Animal, to be capable of every Action I had named, if their Strength and Cunning equalled their Malice. But, as my Discourse had increased his Abhorrence of the whole Species, so he found it gave him a Disturbance in his Mind, to which he was wholly a Stranger before. He thought his Ears being used to such abominable Words, might by Degrees admit them with less Detestation. That, although he hated the *Yahoos* of this Country, yet he no more blamed them for their odious Qualities, than he did a *Gnnayh* (a Bird of Prey) for its Cruelty, or a sharp Stone for cutting his Hoof. But, when a Creature pretending to Reason, could be capable of such Enormities, he dreaded lest the Corruption of that Faculty might be worse than Brutality itself. He seemed therefore confident, that instead of Reason, we were only possessed of some Quality fitted to increase our natural Vices; as the Reflection from a troubled Stream returns the Image of an ill-shapen Body, not only *larger*, but more *distorted*.

He added, That he had heard too much upon the Subject of War, both in this, and some former Discourses. There was another Point which a little perplexed him at present. I had said, that some of our Crew left their Country on Account of being ruined by *Law*: That I had already explained the Meaning of the Word; but he was at a Loss how it should come to pass, that the *Law* which was intended for *every* Man's Preservation, should be any Man's Ruin. Therefore he desired to be farther satisfied what I meant by *Law*, and the Dispensers thereof, according to the present Practice in my own Country: Because he thought, Nature and Reason were sufficient Guides for a reasonable Animal, as we pretended to be, in shewing us what we ought to do, and what to avoid.

I assured his Honour, that *Law* was a Science wherein I had not much conversed, further than by employing Advocates, in vain, upon some Injustices that had been done me. However. I would give him all the Satisfaction I was able.

I said there was a Society of Men among us, bred up from their Youth in the Art of proving by Words multiplied for the Purpose, that *White* is *Black*, and *Black* is *White*, according as they are paid. To this Society all the rest of the People are Slaves.

For Example. If my Neighbour hath a mind to my *Cow*. he

hires a Lawyer to prove that he ought to have my *Cow* from me.
I must then hire another to defend my Right; it being against
all Rules of *Law* that any Man should be allowed to speak for
himself. Now in this Case, I who am the true Owner lie under
two great Disadvantages. First, my Lawyer being practiced almost
from his Cradle in defending Falshood; is quite out of his Element
when he would be an Advocate for Justice, which as an Office
unnatural, he always attempts with great Awkwardness, if not with
Ill-will. The second Disadvantage is, that my Lawyer must proceed
with great Caution: Or else he will be reprimanded by the Judges,
and abhorred by his Brethren, as one who would lessen the Practice
of the Law. And therefore I have but two Methods to preserve my
Cow. The first is, to gain over my Adversary's Lawyer with a double
Fee; who will then betray his Client, by insinuating that he hath
Justice on his Side. The second Way is for my Lawyer to make
my Cause appear as unjust as he can; by allowing the *Cow* to
belong to my Adversary; and this if it be skilfully done, will certainly bespeak the Favour of the Bench.

Now, your Honour is to know, that these Judges are Persons
appointed to decide all Controversies of Property, as well as for
the Tryal of Criminals; and picked out from the most dextrous
Lawyers who are grown old or lazy: And having been byassed
all their Lives against Truth and Equity, lie under such a fatal
Necessity of favouring Fraud, Perjury and Oppression; that I have
known some of them to have refused a large Bribe from the Side
where Justice lay, rather than injure the *Faculty*,[3] by doing any
thing unbecoming their Nature or their Office.

It is a Maxim among these Lawyers, that whatever hath been
done before, may legally be done again: And therefore they take
special Care to record all the Decisions formerly made against
common Justice and the general Reason of Mankind. These, under
the Name of *Precedents*, they produce as Authorities to justify
the most iniquitous Opinions; and the Judges never fail of directing
accordingly.

In pleading, they studiously avoid entering into the *Merits* of the
Cause; but are loud, violent and tedious in dwelling upon all
Circumstances which are not to the Purpose. For Instance, in the
Case already mentioned: They never desire to know what Claim or

---

* The profession.

Title my Adversary hath to my *Cow*; but whether the said *Cow* were Red or Black; her Horns long or short; whether the Field I graze her in be round or square; whether she were milked at home or abroad; what Diseases she is subject to, and the like. After which they consult *Precedents*, adjourn the Cause, from Time to Time, and in Ten, Twenty, or Thirty Years come to an Issue.

It is likewise to be observed, that this Society hath a peculiar Cant and Jargon of their own, that no other Mortal can understand, and wherein all their Laws are written, which they take special Care to multiply; whereby they have wholly confounded the very Essence of Truth and Falshood, of Right and Wrong; so that it will take Thirty Years to decide whether the Field, left me by my Ancestors for six Generations, belong to me, or to a Stranger three Hundred Miles off.

In the Tryal of Persons accused for Crimes against the State, the Method is much more short and commendable: The Judge first sends to sound the Disposition of those in Power; after which he can easily hang or save the Criminal, strictly preserving all the Forms of Law.

Here my Master interposing, said it was a Pity, that Creatures endowed with such prodigious Abilities of Mind as these Lawyers, by the Description I gave of them must certainly be, were not rather encouraged to be Instructors of others in Wisdom and Knowledge. In Answer to which, I assured his Honour, that in all Points out of their own Trade, they were usually the most ignorant and stupid Generation among us, the most despicable in common Conversation, avowed Enemies to all Knowledge and Learning; and equally disposed to pervert the general Reason of Mankind, in every other Subject of Discourse as in that of their own Profession.

CHAPTER VI

A Continuation of the State of England, *under* Queen
Anne. *The Character of a first Minister in the Courts of*
Europe.

My Master was yet wholly at a Loss to understand what
Motives could incite this Race of Lawyers to perplex, disquiet, and
weary themselves by engaging in a Confederacy of Injustice, merely
for the Sake of injuring their Fellow-Animals; neither could he
comprehend what I meant in saying they did it for *Hire.* Whereupon I was at much Pains to describe to him the Use of *Money,*
the Materials it was made of, and the Value of the Metals: That
when a *Yahoo* had got a great Store of this precious Substance, he
was able to purchase whatever he had a mind to; the finest Cloathing, the noblest Houses, great Tracts of Land, the most costly
Meats and Drinks; and have his Choice of the most beautiful
Females. Therefore since *Money* alone, was able to perform all
these Feats, our *Yahoos* thought, they could never have enough
of it to spend or to save, as they found themselves inclined from
their natural Bent either to Profusion or Avarice. That, the rich
Man enjoyed the Fruit of the poor Man's Labour, and the latter
were a Thousand to One in Proportion to the former. That the
Bulk of our People was forced to live miserably, by labouring every
Day for small Wages to make a few live plentifully. I enlarged
myself much on these and many other Particulars to the same
Purpose: But his Honour was still to seek: For he went upon a
Supposition that all Animals had a Title to their Share in the
Productions of the Earth; and especially those who presided over
the rest. Therefore he desired I would let him know, what these
costly Meats were, and how any of us happened to want them.
Whereupon I enumerated as many Sorts as came into my Head,
with the various Methods of dressing them, which could not be
done without sending Vessels by Sea to every Part of the World,

as well for Liquors to drink, as for Sauces, and innumerable other Conveniencies. I assured him, that this whole Globe of Earth must be at least three Times gone round, before one of our better Female *Yahoos* could get her Breakfast, or a Cup to put it in. He said, That must needs be a miserable Country which cannot furnish Food for its own Inhabitants. But what he chiefly wondered at, was how such vast Tracts of Ground as I described, should be wholly without *Fresh-water*, and the People put to the Necessity of sending over the Sea for Drink. I replied, that *England* (the dear Place of my Nativity) was computed to produce three Times the Quantity of Food, more than its Inhabitants are able to consume, as well as Liquors extracted from Grain, or pressed out of the Fruit of certain Trees, which made excellent Drink; and the same Proportion in every other Convenience of Life. But, in order to feed the Luxury and Intemperance of the Males, and the Vanity of the Females, we sent away the greatest Part of our necessary Things to other Countries, from whence in Return we brought the Materials of Diseases, Folly, and Vice, to spend among ourselves. Hence it follows of Necessity, that vast Numbers of our People are compelled to seek their Livelihood by Begging, Robbing, Stealing, Cheating, Pimping, Forswearing, Flattering, Suborning, Forging, Gaming, Lying, Fawning, Hectoring, Voting, Scribling, Stargazing, Poysoning, Whoring, Canting, Libelling, Free-thinking, and the like Occupations: Every one of which Terms, I was at much Pains to make him understand.

That, *Wine* was not imported among us from foreign Countries, to supply the Want of Water or other Drinks, but because it was a Sort of Liquid which made us merry, by putting us out of our Senses; diverted all melancholy Thoughts, begat wild extravagant Imaginations in the Brain, raised our Hopes, and banished our Fears; suspended every Office of Reason for a Time, and deprived us of the Use of our Limbs, until we fell into a profound Sleep; although it must be confessed, that we always awaked sick and dispirited; and that the Use of this Liquor filled us with Diseases, which made our Lives uncomfortable and short.

But beside all this, the Bulk of our People supported themselves by furnishing the Necessities or Conveniencies of Life to the Rich, and to each other. For Instance, when I am at home and dressed as I ought to be, I carry on my Body the Workmanship of an Hundred Tradesmen; the Building and Furniture of my House employ as many more; and Five Times the Number to adorn my Wife.

I was going on to tell him of another Sort of People, who get their Livelihood by attending the Sick; having upon some Occasions informed his Honour that many of my Crew had died of Diseases. But here it was with the utmost Difficulty, that I brought him to apprehend what I meant. He could easily conceive, that a *Houyhnhnm* grew weak and heavy a few Days before his Death; or by some Accident might hurt a Limb. But that Nature, who worketh all things to Perfection, should suffer any Pains to breed in our Bodies, he thought impossible; and desired to know the Reason of so unaccountable an Evil. I told him, we fed on a Thousand Things which operated contrary to each other; that we eat when we were not hungry, and drank without the Provocation of Thirst: That we sat whole Nights drinking strong Liquors without eating a Bit; which disposed us to Sloth, enflamed our Bodies, and precipitated or prevented Digestion. That, prostitute Female *Yahoos* acquired a certain Malady, which bred Rottenness in the Bones of those, who fell into their Embraces: That this and many other Diseases, were propagated from Father to Son; so that great Numbers come into the World with complicated Maladies upon them: That, it would be endless to give him a Catalogue of all Diseases incident to human Bodies; for they could not be fewer than five or six Hundred, spread over every Limb, and Joynt: In short, every Part, external and intestine, having Diseases appropriated to each. To remedy which, there was a Sort of People bred up among us, in the Profession or Pretence of curing the Sick. And because I had some Skill in the Faculty, I would in Gratitude to his Honour, let him know the whole Mystery and Method by which they proceed.

Their Fundamental is, that all Diseases arise from *Repletion*; from whence they conclude, that a great *Evacuation* of the Body is necessary, either through the natural Passage, or upwards at the Mouth. Their next Business is, from Herbs, Minerals, Gums, Oyls, Shells, Salts, Juices, Seaweed, Excrements, Barks of Trees, Serpents, Toads, Frogs, Spiders, dead Mens Flesh and Bones, Birds, Beasts and Fishes, to form a Composition for Smell and Taste the most abominable, nauseous and detestable, that they can possibly contrive, which the Stomach immediately rejects with Loathing: And this they call a *Vomit*. Or else from the same Store-house, with some other poysonous Additions, they command us to take in at

the Orifice *above* or *below*, (just as the Physician then happens to
be disposed) a Medicine equally annoying and disgustful to the
Bowels; which relaxing the Belly, drives down all before it: And
this they call a *Purge*, or a *Clyster*. For Nature (as the Physicians
alledge) having intended the superior anterior Orifice only for the
Intromission of Solids and Liquids, and the inferior Posterior for
Ejection; these Artists ingeniously considering that in all Diseases
Nature is forced out of her Seat; therefore to replace her in it, the
Body must be treated in a Manner directly contrary, by inter-
changing the Use of each Orifice; forcing Solids and Liquids in
at the *Anus*, and making Evacuations at the Mouth.

But, besides real Diseases, we are subject to many that are only
imaginary, for which the Physicians have invented imaginary Cures;
these have their several Names, and so have the Drugs that are
proper for them; and with these our Female *Yahoos* are always
infested.

One great Excellency in this Tribe is their Skill at *Prognosticks*,
wherein they seldom fail; their Predictions in real Diseases, when
they rise to any Degree of Malignity, generally portending *Death*,
which is always in their Power, when Recovery is not: And therefore, upon any unexpected Signs of Amendment, after they have
pronounced their Sentence, rather than be accused as false Prophets,
they know how to approve their Sagacity to the World by a seasonable Dose.

They are likewise of special Use to Husbands and Wives, who
are grown weary of their Mates; to eldest Sons, to great Ministers
of State, and often to Princes.

I had formerly upon Occasion discoursed with my Master upon
the Nature of *Government* in general, and particularly of our own
excellent Constitution, deservedly the Wonder and Envy of the
whole World. But having here accidentally mentioned a *Minister
of State*; he commanded me some Time after to inform him, what
Species of *Yahoo* I particularly meant by that Appellation.

I told him, that a *First* or *Chief Minister of State*, whom I
intended to describe, was a Creature wholly exempt from Joy and
Grief, Love and Hatred, Pity and Anger; at least makes use of no
other Passions but a violent Desire of Wealth, Power, and Titles:
That he applies his Words to all Uses, except to the Indication of
his Mind; That he never tells a *Truth*, but with an Intent that
you should take it for a *Lye*; nor a *Lye*, but with a Design that

you should take it for a *Truth*; That those he speaks worst of behind their Backs, are in the surest way to Preferment; and whenever he begins to praise you to others or to your self, you are from that Day forlorn. The worst Mark you can receive is a Promise, especially when it is confirmed with an Oath; after which every wise Man retires, and gives over all Hopes.

There are three Methods by which a Man may rise to be Chief Minister: The first is, by knowing how with Prudence to dispose of a Wife, a Daughter, or a Sister: The second, by betraying or undermining his Predecessor: And the third is, by a *furious Zeal* in publick Assemblies against the Corruptions of the Court. But a wise Prince would rather chuse to employ those who practise the last of these Methods; because such Zealots prove always the most obsequious and subservient to the Will and Passions of their Master. That, these *Ministers* having all Employments at their Disposal, preserve themselves in Power by bribing the Majority of a Senate or great Council; and at last by an Expedient called an *Act of Indemnity* (whereof I described the Nature to him) they secure themselves from After-reckonings, and retire from the Publick, laden with the Spoils of the Nation.

The Palace of a *Chief Minister*, is a Seminary to breed up others in his own Trade: The Pages, Lacquies, and Porter, by imitating their Master, become *Ministers of State* in their several Districts, and learn to excel in the three principal *Ingredients*, of *Insolence, Lying*, and *Bribery*. Accordingly, they have a *Subaltern* Court paid to them by Persons of the best Rank and sometimes by the Force of Dexterity and Impudence, arrive through several Gradations to be Successors to their Lord.

He is usually governed by a decayed Wench, or favourite Footman, who are the Tunnels through which all Graces are conveyed, and may properly be called, *in the last Resort*, the Governors of the Kingdom.

One Day, my Master, having heard me mention the *Nobility* of my Country, was pleased to make me a Compliment which I could not pretend to deserve: That, he was sure, I must have been born of some Noble Family, because I far exceeded in Shape, Colour, and Cleanliness, all the *Yahoos* of his Nation, although I seemed to fail in Strength, and Agility, which must be imputed to my different Way of Living from those other Brutes; and besides, I was not only endowed with the Faculty of Speech, but likewise with some Rudiments of Reason, to a Degree, that with all his Acquaintance I passed for a Prodigy.

He made me observe, that among the *Houyhnhnms*, the *White*, the *Sorrel*, and the *Iron-grey*, were not so exactly shaped as the *Bay*, the *Dapple-grey*, and the *Black*; nor born with equal Talents of Mind, or a Capacity to improve them; and therefore continued always in the Condition of Servants, without ever aspiring to match out of their own Race, which in that Country would be reckoned monstrous and unnatural.

I made his Honour my most humble Acknowledgements for the good Opinion he was pleased to conceive of me; but assured him at the same Time, that my Birth was of the lower Sort, having been born of plain, honest Parents, who were just able to give me a tolerable Education: That, *Nobility* among us was altogether a different Thing from the Idea he had of it; That, our young *Noblemen* are bred from their Childhood in Idleness and Luxury; that, as soon as Years will permit, they consume their Vigour, and contract odious Diseases among lewd Females; and when their Fortunes are almost ruined, they marry some Woman of mean Birth, disagreeable Person, and unsound Constitution, merely for the sake of Money, whom they hate and despise. That, the Productions of such Marriages are generally scrophulous, rickety or deformed Children; by which Means the Family seldom continues above three Generations, unless the Wife take Care to provide a healthy Father among her Neighbours, or Domesticks, in order to improve and continue the Breed. That, a weak diseased Body, a meager Countenance, and sallow Complexion, are the true Marks of *noble Blood*; and a healthy robust Appearance is so disgraceful in a Man of Quality, that the World concludes his real Father to have been a Groom or a Coachman. The Imperfections of his Mind run parallel with those of his Body; being a Composition of Spleen, Dulness, Ignorance, Caprice, Sensuality and Pride.

Without the Consent of this illustrious Body, no Law can be enacted, repealed, or altered: And these Nobles have likewise the Decision of all our Possessions without Appeal.

CHAPTER VII

The Author's great Love of his Native Country. His Master's Observations upon the Constitution and Administration of England, as described by the Author, with parallel Cases and Comparisons. His Master's Observations upon human Nature.

The Reader may be disposed to wonder how I could prevail on my self to give so free a Representation of my own Species, among a Race of Mortals who were already too apt to conceive the vilest Opinion of Human Kind, from that entire Congruity betwixt me and their *Yahoos.* But I must freely confess, that the many Virtues of those excellent *Quadrupeds* placed in opposite View to human Corruptions, had so far opened my Eyes, and enlarged my Understanding, that I began to view the Actions and Passions of Man in a very different Light; and to think the Honour of my own kind not worth managing; which, besides, it was impossible for me to do before a Person of so acute a Judgment as my Master, who daily convinced me of a thousand Faults in my self, whereof I had not the least Perception before, and which with us would never be numbered even among human Infirmities. I had likewise learned from his Example an utter Detestation of all Falsehood or Disguise; and *Truth* appeared so amiable to me, that I determined upon sacrificing every thing to it.

Let me deal so candidly with the Reader, as to confess, that there was yet a much stronger Motive for the Freedom I took in my Representation of Things. I had not been a Year in this Country, before I contracted such a Love and Veneration for the Inhabitants, that I entered on a firm Resolution never to return to human Kind, but to pass the rest of my Life among these admirable *Houyhnhnms* in the Contemplation and Practice of every Virtue; where I could have no Example or Incitement to Vice. But it was decreed by Fortune, my perpetual Enemy, that so great a Felicity should not fall to my Share. However, it is now some Comfort to reflect, that in what I said of my Country-men, I *extenuated* their Faults as much as I durst before so strict an Examiner; and upon every Article, gave as *favourable* a Turn as the Matter would bear. For, indeed, who is there alive that will not be swayed by his Byass and Partiality to the Place of his Birth?

I have related the Substance of several Coñversations I had with my Master, during the greatest Part of the Time I had the Honour to be in his Service; but have indeed for Brevity sake omitted much more than is here set down.

When I had answered all his Questions, and his Curiosity seemed to be fully satisfied; he sent for me one Morning early, and commanding me to sit down at some Distance, (an Honour which he had never before conferred upon me) He said, he had been very seriously considering my whole Story, as far as it related both to my self and my Country: That, he looked upon us as a Sort of Animals to whose Share, by what Accident he could not conjecture, some small Pittance of *Reason* had fallen, whereof we made no other Use than by its Assistance to aggravate our *natural* Corruptions, and to acquire new ones which Nature had not given us. That, we disarmed our selves of the few Abilities she had bestowed; had been very successful in multiplying our original Wants, and seemed to spend our whole Lives in vain Endeavours to supply them by our own Inventions. That, as to my self, it was manifest I had neither the Strength or Agility of a common *Yahoo*; that I walked infirmly on my hinder Feet; had found out a Contrivance to make my Claws of no Use or Defence, and to remove the Hair from my Chin, which was intended as a Shelter from the Sun and the Weather. Lastly, That I could neither run with Speed, nor climb Trees like my *Brethren* (as he called them) the *Yahoos* in this Country.

That, our Institutions of *Government* and *Law* were plainly owing to our gross Defects in *Reason*, and by consequence, in *Virtue*; because *Reason* alone is sufficient to govern a *Rational* Creature; which was therefore a Character we had no Pretence to challenge, even from the Account I had given of my own People; although he manifestly perceived, that in order to favour them, I had concealed many Particulars, and often *said the Thing which was not.*

He was the more confirmed in this Opinion, because he observed, that as I agreed in every Feature of my Body with other *Yahoos,* except where it was to my real Disadvantage in point of Strength, Speed and Activity, the Shortness of my Claws, and some other Particulars where Nature had no Part; so, from the Representation I had given him of our Lives, our Manners, and our Actions, he found as near a Resemblance in the Disposition of our Minds. He said, the *Yahoos* were known to hate one another more than they did any different Species of Animals; and the Reason usually assigned, was, the Odiousness of their own Shapes, which all could see in the rest, but not in themselves. He had therefore begun to think it not unwise in us to *cover* our Bodies, and by that Invention, conceal many of our Deformities from each other, which would else be hardly supportable. But, he now found he had been mistaken; and that the Dissentions of those Brutes in his Country were owing to the same Cause with ours, as I had described them. For, if (said he) you throw among five *Yahoos* as much Food as would be sufficient for fifty, they will, instead of eating peaceably, fall together by the Ears, each single one impatient to *have all to it self*; and therefore a Servant was usually employed to stand by while they were feeding abroad, and those kept at home were tied at a Distance from each other. That, if a Cow died of Age or Accident, before a *Houyhnhnm* could secure it for his own *Yahoos*, those in the Neighbourhood would come in Herds to seize it, and then would ensue such a Battle as I had described, with terrible Wounds made by their Claws on both Sides, although they seldom were able to kill one another, for want of such convenient Instruments of Death as we had invented. At other Times the like Battles have been fought between the *Yahoos* of several Neighbourhoods without any visible Cause: Those of one District watching all Opportunities to surprise the next before they are prepared. But if they find their Project hath miscarried, they return home, and for want of Enemies, engage in what I call a *Civil War* among themselves.

That, in some Fields of his Country, there are certain *shining Stones* of several Colours, whereof the *Yahoos* are violently fond; and when Part of these *Stones* are fixed in the Earth, as it sometimes happeneth, they will dig with their Claws for whole Days to get

them out, and carry them away, and hide them by Heaps in their
Kennels; but still looking round with great Caution, for fear their
Comrades should find out their Treasure. My Master said, he
could never discover the Reason of this unnatural Appetite, or how
these *Stones* could be of any Use to a *Yahoo*; but now he believed
it might proceed from the same Principle of *Avarice*, which I had
ascribed to Mankind. That he had once, by way of Experiment,
privately removed a Heap of these *Stones* from the Place where
one of his *Yahoos* had buried it: Whereupon, the sordid Animal
missing his Treasure, by his loud lamenting brought the whole
Herd to the Place, there miserably howled, then fell to biting and
tearing the rest; began to pine away, would neither eat nor sleep,
nor work, till he ordered a Servant privately to convey the *Stones*
into the same Hole, and hide them as before; which when his
Yahoo had found, he presently recovered his Spirits and good
Humour; but took Care to remove them to a better hiding Place;
and hath ever since been a very serviceable Brute.

My Master farther assured me, which I also observed my self;
That in the Fields where these *shining Stones* abound, the fiercest
and most frequent Battles are fought, occasioned by perpetual
Inroads of the neighbouring *Yahoos*.

He said, it was common when two *Yahoos* discovered such a
Stone in a Field, and were contending which of them should be
the Proprietor, a third would take the Advantage, and carry it
away from them both; which my Master would needs contend to
have some Resemblance with our *Suits at Law*; wherein I thought
it for our Credit not to undeceive him; since the Decision he
mentioned was much more equitable than many Decrees among
us: Because the Plaintiff and Defendant there lost nothing beside
the *Stone* they contended for; whereas our *Courts of Equity*,
would never have dismissed the Cause while either of them had
any thing left.

My Master continuing his Discourse, said, There was nothing that
rendered the *Yahoos* more odious, than their undistinguished
Appetite to devour every thing that came in their Way, whether
Herbs, Roots, Berries, corrupted Flesh of Animals, or all mingled
together: And it was peculiar in their Temper, that they were
fonder of what they could get by Rapine or Stealth at a greater
Distance, than much better Food provided for them at home. If
their Prey held out, they would eat till they were ready to burst,

after which Nature had pointed out to them a certain *Root* that gave them a general Evacuation.

There was also another Kind of *Root* very *juicy*, but something rare and difficult to be found, which the *Yahoos* fought for with much Eagerness, and would suck it with great Delight: It produced the same Effects that Wine hath upon us. It would make them sometimes hug, and sometimes tear one another; they would howl and grin, and chatter, and reel, and tumble, and then fall asleep in the Mud.

I did indeed observe, that the *Yahoos* were the only Animals in this Country subject to any Diseases; which however, were much fewer than Horses have among us, and contracted not by any ill Treatment they meet with, but by the Nastiness and Greediness of that sordid Brute. Neither has their Language any more than a general Appellation for those Maladies; which is borrowed from the Name of the Beast, and called *Hnea Yahoo*, or the *Yahoo's-Evil*; and the Cure prescribed is a Mixture of *their own Dung* and *Urine*, forcibly put down the *Yahoo's* Throat. This I have since often known to have been taken with Success: And do here freely recommend it to my Countrymen, for the publick Good, as an admirable Specifick against all Diseases produced by Repletion.

As to Learning, Government, Arts, Manufactures, and the like; my Master confessed he could find little or no Resemblance between the *Yahoos* of that Country and those in ours. For, he only meant to observe what Parity there was in our Natures. He had heard indeed some curious *Houyhnhnms* observe, that in most Herds there was a Sort of ruling *Yahoo*, (as among us there is generally some leading or principal Stag in a Park) who was always more *deformed* in Body, and *mischievous in Disposition*, than any of the rest. That, this *Leader* had usually a Favourite as *like himself* as he could get, whose Employment was to *lick his Master's Feet and Posteriors, and drive the Female* Yahoos to *his Kennel*; for which he was now and then rewarded with a Piece of Ass's Flesh. This *Favourite* is hated by the whole Herd; and therefore to protect himself, keeps always *near the Person of his Leader*. He usually continues in Office till a worse can be found; but the very Moment he is discarded, his Successor, at the Head of all the *Yahoos* in that District, Young and Old, Male and Female, come in a Body, and discharge their excrements upon him from Head to Foot. But how far this might be applicable to our *Courts* and *Favourites*, and *Ministers of State*, my Master said I could best determine.

I durst make no Return to this malicious Insinuation, which debased human Understanding below the Sagacity of a common *Hound*, who hath Judgment enough to distinguish and follow the Cry of the *ablest Dog in the Pack*, without being ever mistaken.

My Master told me, there were some Qualities remarkable in the *Yahoos*, which he had not observed me to mention, or at least very slightly, in the Accounts I had given him of human Kind. He said, those Animals, like other Brutes, had their Females in common; but in this they differed, that the She-*Yahoo* would admit the Male, while she was pregnant; and that the Hees would quarrel and fight with the Females as fiercely as with each other. Both which Practices were such Degrees of infamous Brutality, that no other sensitive Creature ever arrived at.

Another Thing he wondered at in the *Yahoos*, was their strange Disposition to Nastiness and Dirt; whereas there appears to be a natural Love of Cleanliness in all other Animals. As to the two former Accusations, I was glad to let them pass without any Reply, because I had not a Word to offer upon them in Defence of my Species, which otherwise I certainly had done from my own Inclinations. But I could have easily vindicated human Kind from the Imputation of Singularity upon the last Article, if there had been any *Swine* in that Country, (as unluckily for me there were not) which although it may be a *sweeter Quadruped* than a *Yahoo*, cannot I humbly conceive in Justice pretend to more Cleanliness; and so his Honour himself must have owned, if he had seen their filthy Way of feeding, and their Custom of wallowing and sleeping in the Mud.

My Master likewise mentioned another Quality, which his Servants had discovered in several *Yahoos*, and to him was wholly unaccountable. He said, a Fancy would sometimes take a *Yahoo*, to retire into a Corner, to lie down and howl, and groan, and spurn away all that came near him, although he were young and fat, and wanted neither Food nor Water; nor did the Servants imagine what could possibly ail him. And the only Remedy they found was to set him to hard Work, after which he would infallibly come to himself. To this I was silent out of Partiality to my own Kind;

yet here I could plainly discover the true Seeds of *Spleen*,[1] which only seizeth on the *Lazy*, the *Luxurious*, and the *Rich*; who, if they were forced to undergo the *same Regimen*, I would undertake for the Cure.

His Honour had farther observed, that a Female-*Yahoo* would often stand behind a Bank or a Bush, to gaze on the young Males passing by, and then appear, and hide, using many antick Gestures and Grimaces; at which time it was observed, that she had a most *offensive Smell*; and when any of the Males advanced, would slowly retire, looking often back, and with a counterfeit Shew of Fear, run off into some convenient Place where she knew the Male would follow her.

At other times, if a Female Stranger came among them, three or four of her own Sex would get about her, and stare and chatter, and grin, and smell her all over; and then turn off with Gestures that seemed to express Contempt and Disdain.

Perhaps my Master might refine a little in these Speculations, which he had drawn from what he observed himself, or had been told by others; However, I could not reflect without some Amazement, and much Sorrow, that the Rudiments of *Lewdness*, *Coquetry*, *Censure*, and *Scandal*, should have Place by Instinct in Womankind.

I expected every Moment, that my Master would accuse the *Yahoos* of those unnatural Appetites in both Sexes, so common among us. But Nature it seems hath not been so expert a Schoolmistress; and these politer Pleasures are entirely the Productions of Art and Reason, on our Side of the Globe.

[1] Hypochondria, languor—a fashionable illness, much affected in Swift's day.

CHAPTER VIII

The Author relateth several Particulars of the Yahoos. *The great Virtues of the* Houyhnhnms. *The Education and Exercises of their Youth. Their general Assembly.*

As I ought to have understood human Nature much better than I supposed it possible for my Master to do, so it was easy to apply the Character he gave of the *Yahoos* to myself and my Countrymen; and I believed I could yet make farther Discoveries from my own Observation. I therefore often begged his Honour to let me go among the Herds of *Yahoos* in the Neighbourhood; to which he always very graciously consented, being perfectly convinced that the Hatred I bore those Brutes would never suffer me to be corrupted by them; and his Honour ordered one of his Servants, a strong Sorrel Nag, very honest and good-natured, to be my Guard; without whose Protection I durst not undertake such Adventures. For I have already told the Reader how much I was pestered by those odious Animals upon my first Arrival. I afterwards failed very narrowly three or four times of falling into their Clutches, when I happened to stray at any Distance without my Hanger. And I have Reason to believe, they had some Imagination that I was of their own Species, which I often assisted myself, by stripping up my Sleeves, and shewing my naked Arms and Breast in their Sight, when my Protector was with me; At which times they would approach as near as they durst, and imitate my Actions after the Manner of Monkeys, but ever with great Signs of Hatred; as a tame *Jack Daw* with Cap and Stockings, is always persecuted by the wild ones, when he happens to be got among them.

They are prodigiously nimble from their Infancy; however, I once caught a young Male of three Years old, and endeavoured by all Marks of Tenderness to make it quiet; but the little Imp fell a squalling, and scratching, and biting with such Violence, that I was forced to let it go; and it was high time, for a whole Troop of old ones came about us at the Noise; but finding the Cub was safe, (for away it ran) and my Sorrel Nag being by, they durst not venture near us. I observed the young Animal's Flesh to smell very rank, and the Stink was somewhat between a *Weasel* and a *Fox*, but much more disagreeable. I forgot another Circumstance, (and perhaps I might have the Reader's Pardon, if it were wholly omitted) that while I held the odious Vermin in my Hands, it voided its filthy Excrements of a yellow liquid Substance, all over my Cloaths; but by good Fortune there was a small Brook hard by, where I washed myself as clean as I could; although I durst not come into my Master's Presence, until I were sufficiently aired.

By what I could discover, the *Yahoos* appear to be the most unteachable of all Animals, their Capacities never reaching higher than to draw or carry Burthens. Yet I am of Opinion, this Defect ariseth chiefly from a perverse, restive Disposition. For they are cunning, malicious, treacherous and revengeful. They are strong and hardy, but of a cowardly Spirit, and by Consequence insolent, abject, and cruel. It is observed, that the *Red-haired* of both Sexes are more libidinous and mischievous than the rest, whom yet they much exceed in Strength and Activity.

The *Houyhnhnms* keep the *Yahoos* for present Use in Huts not far from the House; but the rest are sent abroad to certain Fields, where they dig up Roots, eat several Kinds of Herbs, and search about for Carrion, or sometimes catch *Weasels* and *Luhimuhs* (a Sort of *wild Rat*) which they greedily devour. Nature hath taught them to dig deep Holes with their Nails on the Side of a rising Ground, wherein they lie by themselves; only the Kennels of the Females are larger, sufficient to hold two or three Cubs.

They swim from their Infancy like Frogs, and are able to continue long under Water, where they often take Fish, which the Females carry home to their Young. And upon this Occasion, I hope the Reader will pardon my relating an odd Adventure.

Being one Day abroad with my Protector the Sorrel Nag, and the Weather exceeding hot, I entreated him to let me bathe in a River that was near. He consented, and I immediately stripped myself stark naked, and went down softly into the Stream. It happened that a young Female *Yahoo* standing behind a Bank, saw the whole Proceeding; and inflamed by Desire, as the Nag and I conjectured, came running with all Speed, and leaped into the Water within five Yards of the Place where I bathed. I was never in my Life so terribly frighted; the Nag was grazing at some Distance, not suspecting any Harm: She embraced me after a most fulsome Manner; I roared as loud as I could, and the Nag came galloping towards me, whereupon she quitted her Grasp, with the utmost Reluctancy, and leaped upon the opposite Bank, where she stood gazing and howling all the time I was putting on my Cloaths.

This was Matter of Diversion to my Master and his Family, as well as of Mortification to my self. For now I could no longer deny, that I was a real *Yahoo*, in every Limb and Feature, since the Females had a natural Propensity to me as one of their own Species: Neither was the Hair of this Brute of a Red Colour, (which might have been some Excuse for an Appetite a little irregular) but black as a Sloe, and her Countenance did not make an Appearance altogether so hideous as the rest of the Kind; for, I think, she could not be above Eleven Years old.

Having already lived three Years in this Country, the Reader I suppose will expect, that I should, like other Travellers, give him some Account of the Manners and Customs of its Inhabitants, which it was indeed my principal Study to learn.

As these noble *Houyhnhnms* are endowed by Nature with a general Disposition to all Virtues, and have no Conceptions or Ideas of what is evil in a rational Creature; so their grand Maxim is, to cultivate *Reason*, and to be wholly governed by it. Neither is *Reason* among them a Point problematical as with us, where Men can argue with Plausibility on both Sides of a Question; but strikes you with immediate Conviction; as it must needs do where it is not mingled, obscured, or discoloured by Passion and Interest. I remember it was with extreme Difficulty that I could bring my Master to understand the Meaning of the Word *Opinion*, or how a Point could be disputable; because *Reason* taught us to affirm or deny only where we are certain; and beyond our Knowledge we cannot do either. So that Controversies, Wranglings, Disputes, and Positiveness in false or dubious Propositions, are Evils unknown among the *Houyhnhnms*. In the like Manner when I used to explain to him our several Systems of *Natural Philosophy*, he would laugh that a Creature pretending to *Reason*, should value itself upon the Knowledge of other Peoples Conjectures, and in Things, where that Knowledge, if it were certain, could be of no Use. Wherein he agreed entirely with the

Sentiments of *Socrates*, as *Plato* delivers them; which I mention as the highest Honour I can do that Prince of Philosophers. I have often since reflected what Destruction such a Doctrine would make in the Libraries of *Europe*; and how many Paths to Fame would be then shut up in the Learned World.

Friendship and *Benevolence* are the two principal Virtues among the *Houyhnhnms*; and these not confined to particular Objects, but universal to the whole Race. For, a Stranger from the remotest Part, is equally treated with the nearest Neighbour, and where-ever he goes, looks upon himself as at home. They preserve *Decency* and *Civility* in the highest Degrees, but are altogether ignorant of *Ceremony*. They have no Fondness[1] for their Colts or Foles; but the Care they take in educating them proceedeth entirely from the Dictates of *Reason*. And, I observed my Master to shew the same Affection to his Neighbour's Issue that he had for his own. They will have it that *Nature* teaches them to love the whole Species, and it is *Reason* only that maketh a Distinction of Persons, where there is a superior Degree of Virtue.

When the Matron *Houyhnhnms* have produced one of each Sex, they no longer accompany with their Consorts, except they lose one of their Issue by some Casualty, which very seldom happens: But in such a Case they meet again; or when the like Accident befalls a Person, whose Wife is past bearing, some other Couple bestows on him one of their own Colts, and then go together a second Time, until the Mother be pregnant. This Caution is necessary to prevent the Country from being overburthened with Numbers. But the Race of inferior *Houyhnhnms* bred up to be Servants is not so strictly limited upon this Article; these are allowed to produce three of each Sex, to be Domesticks in the Noble Families.

In their Marriages they are exactly careful to chuse such Colours as will not make any disagreeable Mixture in the Breed. *Strength* is chiefly valued in the Male, and *Comeliness* in the Female; not upon the Account of *Love*, but to preserve the Race from degenerating: For, where a Female happens to excel in *Strength*, a Consort is chosen with regard to *Comeliness*. Courtship, Love, Presents, Joyntures, Settlements, have no Place in their Thoughts; or Terms whereby to express them in their Language. The young Couple meet and are joined, merely because it is the Determination of their Parents and Friends: It is what they see done every

[1] Excessive doting.

Day; and they look upon it as one of the necessary Actions in a reasonable Being. But the Violation of Marriage, or any other Unchastity, was never heard of: And the married Pair pass their Lives with the same Friendship, and mutual Benevolence that they bear to all others of the same Species, who come in their Way; without Jealousy, Fondness, Quarrelling, or Discontent.

In educating the Youth of both Sexes, their Method is admirable, and highly deserveth our Imitation. These are not suffered to taste a Grain of *Oats*, except upon certain Days, till Eighteen Years old; nor *Milk*, but very rarely; and in Summer they graze two Hours in the Morning, and as many in the Evening, which their Parents likewise observe; but the Servants are not allowed above half that Time; and a great Part of the Grass is brought home, which they eat at the most convenient Hours, when they can be best spared from Work.

Temperance, Industry, Exercise and *Cleanliness,* are the Lessons equally enjoyned to the young ones of both Sexes: And my Master thought it monstrous in us to give the Females a different Kind of Education from the Males, except in some Articles of Domestick Management; whereby, as he truly observed, one Half of our Natives were good for nothing but bringing Children into the World: And to trust the Care of their Children to such useless Animals, he said was yet a greater Instance of Brutality.

But the *Houyhnhnms* train up their Youth to Strength, Speed, and Hardiness, by exercising them in running Races up and down steep Hills, or over hard stony Grounds; and when they are all in a Sweat, they are ordered to leap over Head and Ears into a Pond or a River. Four times a Year the Youth of certain Districts meet to shew their Proficiency in Running, and Leaping, and other Feats of Strength or Agility; where the Victor is rewarded with a Song made in his or her Praise. On this Festival the Servants drive a Herd of *Yahoos* into the Field, laden with Hay, and Oats, and Milk for a Repast to the *Houyhnhnms*; after which, these Brutes are immediately driven back again, for fear of being noisome to the Assembly.

Every fourth Year, at the *Vernal Equinox,* there is a Representative Council of the whole Nation, which meets in a Plain about twenty Miles from our House, and continueth about five or six Days. Here they inquire into the State and Condition of the several Districts; whether they abound or be deficient in Hay or Oats, or Cows or *Yahoos*? And where-ever there is any Want (which is but seldom) it is immediately supplied by unanimous Consent and Contribution. Here likewise the Regulation of Children is settled: As for instance, if a *Houyhnhnm* hath two Males, he changeth one of them with another who hath two Females: And when a Child hath been lost by any Casualty, where the Mother is past Breeding, it is determined what Family in the District shall breed another to supply the Loss.

CHAPTER IX

A grand Debate at the General Assembly of the Houyhnhnms, *and how it was determined. The Learning of the* Houyhnhnms. *Their Buildings. Their Manner of Burials. The Defectiveness of their Language.*

One of these Grand Assemblies was held in my time, about three Months before my Departure, whither my Master went as the Representative of our District. In this Council was resumed their old Debate, and indeed, the only Debate that ever happened in their Country; whereof my Master after his Return gave me a very particular Account.

The Question to be debated, was, Whether the *Yahoos* should be exterminated from the Face of the Earth. One of the *Members* for the Affirmative offered several Arguments of great Strength and Weight; alledging, That, as the *Yahoos* were the most filthy, noisome, and deformed Animal which Nature ever produced, so they were the most restive and indocible, mischievous and malicious: They would privately suck the Teats of the *Houyhnhnms* Cows; kill and devour their Cats, trample down their Oats and Grass, if they were not continually watched; and commit a Thousand other Extravagancies. He took Notice of a general Tradition, that *Yahoos* had not been always in their Country: But, that many Ages ago, two of these Brutes appeared together upon a Mountain;

whether produced by the Heat of the Sun upon corrupted Mud and Slime, or from the Ooze and Froth of the Sea, was never known. That these *Yahoos* engendered, and their Brood in a short time grew so numerous as to over-run and infest the whole Nation. That the *Houyhnhnms* to get rid of this Evil, made a general Hunting, and at last inclosed the whole Herd; and destroying the Older, every *Houyhnhnm* kept two young Ones in a Kennel, and brought them to such a Degree of Tameness, as an Animal so savage by Nature can be capable of acquiring; using them for Draught and Carriage. That, there seemed to be much Truth in this Tradition, and that those Creatures could not be *Ylnhniamshy* (or *Aborigines* of the Land) because of the violent Hatred the *Houyhnhnms* as well as all other Animals, bore them; which although their evil Disposition sufficiently deserved, could never have arrived at so high a Degree, if they had been *Aborigines*, or else they would have long since been rooted out. That, the Inhabitants taking a Fancy to use the Service of the *Yahoos*, had very imprudently neglected to cultivate the Breed of *Asses*, which were a comely Animal, easily kept, more tame and orderly, without any offensive Smell, strong enough for Labour, although they yield to the other in Agility of Body; and if their Braying be no agreeable Sound, it is far preferable to the horrible Howlings of the *Yahoos*.

Several others declared their Sentiments to the same Purpose; when my Master proposed an Expedient to the Assembly, whereof he had indeed borrowed the Hint from me. He approved of the Tradition, mentioned by the *Honourable Member*, who spoke before; and affirmed, that the two *Yahoos* said to be first seen among them, had been driven thither over the Sea; that coming to Land, and being forsaken by their Companions, they retired to the Mountains, and degenerating by Degrees, became in Process of Time, much more savage than those of their own Species in the Country from whence these two Originals came. The Reason of his Assertion was, that he had now in his Possession, a certain wonderful *Yahoo*, (meaning myself) which most of them had heard of, and many of them had seen. He then related to them, how he first found me; that, my Body was all covered with an artificial Composure of the Skins and Hairs of other Animals: That, I spoke in a Language of my own; and had thoroughly learned theirs: That, I had related to him the Accidents which brought me thither: That, when he saw me without my Covering, I was an exact *Yahoo* in

every Part, only of a whiter Colour, less hairy, and with shorter
Claws. He added, how I had endeavoured to persuade him, that
in my own and other Countries the *Yahoos* acted as the governing,
rational Animal, and held the *Houyhnhnms* in Servitude: That, he
observed in me all the Qualities of a *Yahoo*, only a little more
civilized by some Tincture of Reason; which however was in a
Degree as far inferior to the *Houyhnhnm* Race, as the *Yahoos* of
their Country were to me: That, among other things, I mentioned a
Custom we had of *castrating Houyhnhnms* when they were young,
in order to render them tame; that the Operation was easy and safe;
that it was no Shame to learn Wisdom from Brutes, as Industry is
taught by the Ant, and Building by the Swallow. (For so I translate
the Word *Lyhannh*, although it be a much larger Fowl.) That, this
Invention might be practiced upon the younger *Yahoos* here,
which, besides rendering them tractable and fitter for Use, would
in an Age put an End to the whole Species without destroying
Life. That, in the mean time the *Houyhnhnms* should be *exhorted*
to cultivate the Breed of Asses, which, as they are in all respects
more valuable Brutes; so they have this Advantage, to be fit for Service at five Years old, which the others are not till Twelve.

This was all my Master thought fit to tell me at that Time, of
what passed in the Grand Council. But he was pleased to conceal
one Particular, which related personally to myself, whereof I soon
felt the unhappy Effect, as the Reader will know in its proper
Place, and from whence I date all the succeeding Misfortunes of
my Life.

The *Houyhnhnms* have no Letters, and consequently, their
Knowledge is all traditional. But there happening few Events of
any Moment among a People so well united, naturally disposed to
every Virtue, wholly governed by Reason, and cut off from all
Commerce with other Nations; the historical Part is easily preserved
without burthening their Memories. I have already observed, that
they are subject to no Diseases, and therefore can have no Need of
Physicians. However, they have excellent Medicines composed of
Herbs, to cure accidental Bruises and Cuts in the Pastern or Frog
of the Foot by sharp Stones, as well as other Maims and Hurts in
the several Parts of the Body.

They calculate the Year by the Revolution of the Sun and the
Moon, but use no Subdivisions into Weeks. They are well enough
acquainted with the Motions of those two Luminaries, and under-

stand the Nature of *Eclipses*; and this is the utmost Progress of their *Astronomy*.

In *Poetry* they must be allowed to excel all other Mortals; wherein the Justness of their Similes, and the Minuteness, as well as Exactness of their Descriptions, are indeed inimitable. Their Verses abound very much in both of these; and usually contain either some exalted Notions of Friendship and Benevolence, or the Praises of those who were Victors in Races, and other bodily Exercises. Their Buildings, although very rude and simple, are not inconvenient, but well contrived to defend them from all Injuries of Cold and Heat. They have a Kind of Tree, which at Forty Years old loosens in the Root, and falls with the first Storm; it grows very strait, and being pointed like Stakes with a sharp Stone, (for the *Houyhnhnms* know not the Use of Iron) they stick them erect in the Ground about ten Inches asunder, and then weave in Oat-straw, or sometimes Wattles betwixt them. The Roof is made after the same Manner, and so are the Doors.

The *Houyhnhnms* use the hollow Part between the Pastern and the Hoof of their Fore-feet, as we do our Hands, and this with greater Dexterity, than I could at first imagine. I have seen a white Mare of our Family thread a Needle (which I lent her on Purpose) with that Joynt. They milk their Cows, reap their Oats, and do all the Work which requires Hands, in the same Manner. They have a Kind of hard Flints, which by grinding against other Stones, they form into Instruments, that serve instead of Wedges, Axes, and Hammers. With Tools made of these Flints, they likewise cut their Hay, and reap their Oats, which there groweth naturally in several Fields: The *Yahoos* draw home the Sheaves in Carriages, and the Servants tread them in certain covered Hutts, to get out the Grain, which is kept in Stores. They make a rude Kind of earthen and wooden Vessels, and bake the former in the Sun.

If they can avoid Casualties, they die only of old Age, and are buried in the obscurest Places that can be found, their Friends and Relations expressing neither Joy nor Grief at their Departure; nor does the dying Person discover the least Regret that he is leaving the World, any more than if he were upon returning home from a Visit to one of his Neighbours: I remember, my Master having once made an Appointment with a Friend and his Family to come to his House upon some Affair of Importance; on the Day fixed, the Mistress and her two Children came very late; she made two Ex-

cuses, first for her Husband, who, as she said, happened that very
Morning to *Lhnuwnh*. The Word is strongly expressive in their
Language, but not easily rendered into *English*; it signifies, *to retire
to his first Mother*. Her Excuse for not coming sooner, was, that her
Husband dying late in the Morning, she was a good while consulting
her Servants about a convenient Place where his Body should be
laid; and I observed she behaved herself at our House, as chearfully
as the rest: She died about three Months after.

They live generally to Seventy or Seventy-five Years, very seldom
to Fourscore: Some Weeks before their Death they feel a gradual
Decay, but without Pain. During this time they are much visited
by their Friends, because they cannot go abroad with their usual
Ease and Satisfaction. However, about ten Days before their Death,
which they seldom fail in computing, they return the Visits that
have been made by those who are nearest in the Neighbourhood,
being carried in a convenient Sledge drawn by *Yahoos*; which
Vehicle they use, not only upon this Occasion, but when they grow
old, upon long Journeys, or when they are lamed by any Accident.
And therefore when the dying *Houyhnhnms* return those Visits,
they take a solemn Leave of their Friends, as if they were going to
some remote Part of the Country, where they designed to pass the
rest of their Lives.

I know not whether it may be worth observing, that the *Houyhnhnms* have no Word in their Language to express any thing that
is *evil*, except what they borrow from the Deformities or ill Qualities of the *Yahoos*. Thus they denote the Folly of a Servant, an
Omission of a Child, a Stone that cuts their Feet, a Continuance
of foul or unseasonable Weather, and the like, by adding to each
the Epithet of *Yahoo*. For Instance, *Hhnm Yahoo*, *Whnaholm
Yahoo*, *Ynlhmndwihlma Yahoo*, and an ill contrived House, *Yn-
holmhnmrohlnw Yahoo*.

I could with great Pleasure enlarge farther upon the Manners
and Virtues of this excellent People; but intending in a short time
to publish a Volume by itself expressly upon that Subject, I refer the
Reader thither. And in the mean time, proceed to relate my own
sad Catastrophe.

CHAPTER X

The Author's Oeconomy, and happy Life among the
Houyhnhnms. His great Improvement in Virtue, by
conversing with them. Their Conversations. The Author
hath Notice given him by his Master that he must de-
part from the Country. He falls into a Swoon for Grief,
but submits. He contrives and finishes a Canoo, by the
Help of a Fellow-Servant, and puts to Sea at a Venture.

I had settled my little Oeconomy to my own Heart's Content. My Master had ordered a Room to be made for me after their
Manner, about six Yards from the House; the Sides and Floors of
which I plaistered with Clay, and covered with Rush-mats of my
own contriving; I had beaten Hemp, which there grows wild, and
made of it a Sort of Ticking: This I filled with the Feathers of
several Birds I had taken with Springes made of *Yahoos* Hairs;
and were excellent Food. I had worked two Chairs with my Knife,
the Sorrel Nag helping me in the grosser and more laborious Part.
When my Cloaths were worn to Rags, I made my self others with
the Skins of Rabbits, and of a certain beautiful Animal about the
same Size, called *Nnuhnoh*, the Skin of which is covered with a
fine Down. Of these I likewise made very tolerable Stockings. I
soaled my Shoes with Wood which I cut from a Tree, and fitted
to the upper Leather, and when this was worn out, I supplied it
with the Skins of *Yahoos*, dried in the Sun. I often got Honey out
of hollow Trees, which I mingled with Water, or eat it with my
Bread. No Man could more verify the Truth of these two Maxims,
That, Nature is very easily satisfied; and, *That, Necessity is the*
Mother of Invention. I enjoyed perfect Health of Body, and Tranquility of Mind; I did not feel the Treachery or Inconstancy of a
Friend, nor the Injuries of a secret or open Enemy. I had no Occasion of bribing, flattering or pimping, to procure the Favour of

any great Man, or of his Minion. I wanted no Fence against Fraud or Oppression: Here was neither Physician to destroy my Body, nor Lawyer to ruin my Fortune: No Informer to watch my Words and Actions, or forge Accusations against me for Hire: Here were no Gibers, Censurers, Backbiters, Pick-pockets, Highwaymen, House-breakers, Attorneys, Bawds, Buffoons, Gamesters, Politicians, Wits, Spleneticks, tedious Talkers, Controvertists, Ravishers, Murderers, Robbers, Virtuosos; no Leaders or Followers of Party and Faction; no Encouragers to Vice, by Seducement or Examples: No Dungeon, Axes, Gibbets, Whipping posts, or Pillories; no cheating Shop-keepers or Mechanicks: No Pride, Vanity or Affectation: No Fops, Bullies, Drunkards, strolling Whores, or Poxes: No ranting, lewd, expensive Wives: No stupid, proud Pedants: No importunate, over-bearing, quarrelsome, noisy, roaring, empty, conceited, swearing Companions: No Scoundrels raised from the Dust upon the Merit of their Vices; or Nobility thrown into it on account of their Virtues: No Lords, Fidlers, Judges or Dancing-Masters.

I had the Favour of being admitted to several *Houyhnhnms*, who came to visit or dine with my Master; where his Honour graciously suffered me to wait in the Room, and listen to their Discourse. Both he and his Company would often descend to ask me Questions, and receive my Answers. I had also sometimes the Honour of attending my Master in his Visits to others. I never presumed to speak, except in answer to a Question; and then I did it with inward Regret, because it was a Loss of so much Time for improving my self: But I was infinitely delighted with the Station of an humble Auditor in such Conversations, where nothing passed but what was useful, expressed in the fewest and most significant Words: Where (as I have already said) the greatest *Decency* was observed, without the least Degree of Ceremony; where no Person spoke without being pleased himself, and pleasing his Companions: Where there was no Interruption, Tediousness, Heat, or Difference of Sentiments. They have a Notion, That when People are met together, a short Silence doth much improve Conversation: This I found to be true; for during those little Intermissions of Talk, new Ideas would arise in their Minds, which very much enlivened the Discourse. Their Subjects are generally on Friendship and Benevolence; on Order and Oeconomy; sometimes upon the visible Operations of Nature, or ancient Traditions; upon the Bounds and Limits of Virtue; upon the unerring Rules of Reason; or upon some

Determinations, to be taken at the next great Assembly; and often upon the various Excellencies of *Poetry.* I may add, without Vanity, that my Presence often gave them sufficient Matter for Discourse, because it afforded my Master an Occasion of letting his Friends into the History of me and my Country, upon which they were all pleased to discant in a Manner not very advantageous to human Kind; and for that Reason I shall not repeat what they said: Only I may be allowed to observe, That his Honour, to my great Admiration, appeared to understand the Nature of *Yahoos* much better than my self. He went through all our Vices and Follies, and discovered many which I had never mentioned to him; by only supposing what Qualities a *Yahoo* of their Country, with a small Proportion of Reason, might be capable of exerting: And concluded, with too much Probability, how vile as well as miserable such a Creature must be.

I freely confess, that all the little Knowledge I have of any Value, was acquired by the Lectures I received from my Master, and from hearing the Discourses of him and his Friends; to which I should be prouder to listen, than to dictate to the greatest and wisest Assembly in *Europe.* I admired the Strength, Comeliness and Speed of the Inhabitants; and such a Constellation of Virtues in such amiable Persons produced in me the highest Veneration. At first, indeed, I did not feel that natural Awe which the *Yahoos* and all other Animals bear towards them; but it grew upon me by Degress, much sooner than I imagined, and was mingled with a respectful Love and Gratitude, that they would condescend to distinguish me from the rest of my Species.

When I thought of my Family, my Friends, my Countrymen, or human Race in general, I considered them as they really were, *Yahoos* in Shape and Disposition, perhaps a little more civilized, and qualified with the Gift of Speech; but making no other Use of Reason, than to improve and multiply those Vices, whereof their Brethren in this Country had only the Share that Nature allotted them. When I happened to behold the Reflection of my own Form in a Lake or Fountain, I turned away my Face in Horror and detestation of my self; and could better endure the Sight of a common *Yahoo,* than of my own Person. By conversing with the *Houyhnhnms,* and looking upon them with Delight, I fell to imitate their Gait and Gesture, which is now grown into a Habit; and my Friends often tell me in a blunt Way, that *I trot like a*

Horse; which, however, I take for a great Compliment: Neither shall I disown, that in speaking I am apt to fall into the Voice and manner of the *Houyhnhnms*, and hear my self ridiculed on that Account without the least Mortification.

In the Midst of this Happiness, when I looked upon my self to be fully settled for Life, my Master sent for me one Morning a little earlier than his usual Hour. I observed by his Countenance that he was in some Perplexity, and at a Loss how to begin what he had to speak. After a short Silence, he told me, he did not know how I would take what he was going to say: That, in the last general Assembly, when the Affair of the *Yahoos* was entered upon, the Representatives had taken Offence at his keeping a *Yahoo* (meaning my self) in his Family more like a *Houyhnhnm* than a Brute Animal. That, he was known frequently to converse with me, as if he could receive some Advantage or Pleasure in my Company: That, such a Practice was not agreeable to Reason or Nature, or a thing ever heard of before among them. The Assembly did therefore *exhort* him, either to employ me like the rest of my Species, or command me to swim back to the Place from whence I came. That, the first of these Expedients was utterly rejected by all the *Houyhnhnms*, who had ever seen me at his House or their own: For, they alledged, That because I had some Rudiments of Reason, added to the natural Pravity of those Animals, it was to be feared, I might be able to seduce them into the woody and mountainous Parts of the Country, and bring them in Troops by Night to destroy the *Houyhnhnms* Cattle, as being naturally of the ravenous Kind, and averse from Labour.

My Master added, That he was daily pressed by the *Houyhnhnms* of the Neighbourhood to have the Assembly's *Exhortation* executed, which he could not put off much longer. He doubted, it would be impossible for me to swim to another Country; and therefore wished I would contrive some Sort of Vehicle resembling those I had described to him, that might carry me on the Sea; in which Work I should have the Assistance of his own Servants, as well as those of his Neighbours. He concluded, that for his own Part he could have been content to keep me in his Service as long as I lived; because he found I had cured myself of some bad Habits and Dispositions, by endeavouring, as far as my inferior Nature was capable, to imitate the *Houyhnhnms*.

I should here observe to the Reader, that a Decree of the general

Assembly in this Country, is expressed by the Word *Hnhloayn*, which signifies an *Exhortation*; as near as I can render it: For they have no Conception how a rational Creature can be *compelled*, but only advised, or *exhorted*; because no Person can disobey Reason, without giving up his Claim to be a rational Creature.

I was struck with the utmost Grief and Despair at my Master's Discourse; and being unable to support the Agonies I was under, I fell into a Swoon at his Feet: When I came to myself, he told me, that he concluded I had been dead. (For these People are subject to no such Imbecillities of Nature) I answered, in a faint Voice, that Death would have been too great an Happiness; that although I could not blame the Assembly's *Exhortation*, or the Urgency of his Friends; yet in my weak and corrupt Judgment, I thought it might consist with Reason to have been less rigorous. That, I could not swim a League, and probably the nearest Land to theirs might be distant above an Hundred: That, many Materials, necessary for making a small Vessel to carry me off, were wholly wanting in this Country, which however, I would attempt in Obedience and Gratitude to his Honour, although I concluded the thing to be impossible, and therefore looked on myself as already devoted to Destruction. That, the certain Prospect of an unnatural Death, was the least of my Evils: For, supposing I should escape with Life by some strange Adventure, how could I think with Temper,[1] of passing my Days among *Yahoos*, and relapsing into my old Corruptions, for want of Examples to lead and keep me within the Paths of Virtue. That, I knew too well upon what solid Reasons all the Determinations of the wise *Houyhnhnms* were founded, not to be shaken by Arguments of mine, a miserable *Yahoo*; and therefore after presenting him with my humble Thanks for the Offer of his Servants Assistance in making a Vessel, and desiring a reasonable Time for so difficult a Work, I told him, I would endeavour to preserve a wretched Being; and, if ever I returned to *England*, was not without Hopes of being useful to my own Species, by celebrating the Praises of the renowned *Houyhnhnms*, and proposing their Virtues to the Imitation of Mankind.

My Master in a few Words made me a very gracious Reply, allowed me the Space of two *Months* to finish my Boat; and ordered the Sorrel Nag, my Fellow-Servant, (for so at this Distance I may presume to call him) to follow my Instructions, because I told my

[1] Temperateness, tranquility.

Master, that his Help would be sufficient, and I knew he had a Tenderness for me.

In his Company my first Business was to go to that Part of the Coast, where my rebellious Crew had ordered me to be set on Shore. I got upon a Height, and looking on every Side into the Sea, fancied I saw a small Island, towards the *North-East*: I took out my Pocket-glass, and could then clearly distinguish it about five Leagues off, as I computed; but it appeared to the Sorrel Nag to be only a blue Cloud: For, as he had no Conception of any Country beside his own, so he could not be as expert in distinguishing remote Objects at Sea, as we who so much converse in that Element.

After I had discovered this Island, I considered no farther; but resolved, it should, if possible, be the first Place of my Banishment, leaving the Consequence to Fortune.

I returned home, and consulting with the Sorrel Nag, we went into a Copse at some Distance, where I with my Knife, and he with a sharp Flint fastened very artificially,[2] after their Manner, to a wooden Handle, cut down several Oak Wattles about the Thickness of a Walking-staff, and some larger Pieces. But I shall not trouble the Reader with a particular Description of my own Mechanicks: Let it suffice to say, that in six Weeks time, with the Help of the Sorrel Nag, who performed the Parts that required most Labour, I finished a Sort of *Indian* Canoo; but much larger, covering it with the Skins of *Yahoos*, well stitched together, with hempen Threads of my own making. My Sail was likewise composed of the Skins of the same Animal; but I made use of the youngest I could get; the older being too tough and thick; and I likewise provided myself with four Paddles. I laid in a Stock of boiled Flesh, of Rabbets and Fowls; and took with me two Vessels, one filled with Milk, and the other with Water.

I tried my Canoo in a large Pond near my Master's House, and then corrected in it what was amiss; stopping all the Chinks with *Yahoos* Tallow, till I found it stanch, and able to bear me, and my Freight. And when it was as compleat as I could possibly make it, I had it drawn on a Carriage very gently by *Yahoos*, to the Sea-side, under the Conduct of the Sorrel Nag, and another Servant.

When all was ready, and the Day came for my Departure, I took Leave of my Master and Lady, and the whole Family, my Eyes flowing with Tears, and my Heart quite sunk with Grief. But his

[2] Adroitly.

Honour, out of Curiosity, and perhaps (if I may speak it without Vanity) partly out of Kindness, was determined to see me in my Canoo; and got several of his neighbouring Friends to accompany him. I was forced to wait above an Hour for the Tide, and then observing the Wind very fortunately bearing towards the Island, to which I intended to steer my Course, I took a second Leave of my Master: But as I was going to prostrate myself to kiss his Hoof, he did me the Honour to raise it gently to my Mouth. I am not ignorant how much I have been censured for mentioning this last Particular. Detractors are pleased to think it improbable, that so illustrious a Person should descend to give so great a Mark of Distinction to a Creature so inferior as I. Neither have I forgot, how apt some Travellers are to boast of extraordinary Favours they have received. But, if these Censurers were better acquainted with the noble and courteous Disposition of the *Houyhnhnms*, they would soon change their Opinion. I paid my Respects to the rest of the *Houyhnhnms* in his Honour's Company; then getting into my Canoo, I pushed off from Shore.

CHAPTER XI

The Author's dangerous Voyage. He arrives at New-Holland, hoping to settle there. Is wounded with an Arrow by one of the Natives. Is seized and carried by Force into a Portugueze *Ship. The great Civilities of the Captain. The Author arrives at* England.

I began this desperate Voyage on *February* 15, 1714/5,[1] at 9 o'Clock in the Morning. The Wind was very favourable; however, I made use at first only of my Paddles; but considering I should soon be weary, and that the Wind might probably chop about, I ventured to set up my little Sail; and thus, with the Help

[1] 1715, according to our calendar. In Swift's time, the new year dated from March 25.

of the Tide, I went at the Rate of a League and a Half an Hour, as near as I could guess. My Master and his Friends continued on the Shoar, till I was almost out of Sight; and I often heard the Sorrel Nag (who always loved me) crying out, *Hnuy illa nyha maiah Yahoo*, Take Care of thy self, gentle *Yahoo*.

My Design was, if possible, to discover some small Island un-inhabited, yet sufficient by my Labour to furnish me with Neces-saries of Life, which I would have thought a greater Happiness than to be first Minister in the politest Court of *Europe*; so hor-rible was the Idea I conceived of returning to live in the Society and under the Government of *Yahoos*. For in such a Solitude as I desired, I could at least enjoy my own Thoughts, and reflect with Delight on the Virtues of those inimitable *Houyhnhnms*, without any Opportunity of degenerating into the Vices and Corruptions of my own Species.

The Reader may remember what I related when my Crew con-spired against me, and confined me to my Cabbin. How I con-tinued there several Weeks, without knowing what Course we took; and when I was put ashore in the Longboat, how the Sailors told me with Oaths, whether true or false, that they knew not in what Part of the World we were. However, I did then believe us to be about ten Degrees *Southward* of the *Cape of Good Hope*, or about 45 Degrees *Southern* Latitude, as I gathered from some general Words I overheard among them, being I supposed to the *South-East* in their intended Voyage to *Madagascar*. And al-though this were but little better than Conjecture, yet I resolved to steer my Course *Eastward*, hoping to reach the *South-West* Coast of *New-Holland*, and perhaps some such Island as I desired, lying *Westward* of it. The Wind was full West, and by six in the Eve-ning I computed I had gone *Eastward* at least eighteen Leagues; when I spied a very small Island about half a League off, which I soon reached. It was nothing but a Rock with one Creek, nat-urally arched by the Force of Tempests. Here I put in my Canoo, and climbing a Part of the Rock, I could plainly discover Land to the *East*, extending from *South* to *North*. I lay all Night in my Canoo; and repeating my Voyage early in the Morning, I arrived in seven Hours to the *South-East* Point of *New-Holland*. This con-firmed me in the Opinion I have long entertained, that the *Maps* and *Charts* place this Country at least three Degrees more to the *East* than it really is; which Thought I communicated many Years ago to my worthy Friend Mr. *Herman Moll*,[2] and gave him my Reasons for it, although he hath rather chosen to follow other Authors.

I saw no Inhabitants in the Place where I landed; and being unarmed, I was afraid of venturing far into the Country. I found some Shell-Fish on the Shore, and eat them raw, not daring to kindle a Fire, for fear of being discovered by the Natives. I continued three Days feeding on Oysters and Limpits, to save my own Provisions; and I fortunately found a Brook of excellent Water, which gave me great Relief.

On the fourth Day, venturing out early a little too far, I saw twenty or thirty Natives upon a Height, not above five hundred Yards from me. They were stark naked, Men, Women and Children round a Fire, as I could discover by the Smoke. One of them spied me, and gave Notice to the rest; five of them advanced towards me, leaving the Women and Children at the Fire. I made what haste I could to the Shore, and getting into my Canoo, shoved off: The Savages observing me retreat, ran after me; and before I could get far enough into the Sea, discharged an Arrow, which wounded me deeply on the Inside of my left Knee (I shall carry the Mark to my Grave.) I apprehended the Arrow might be poisoned; and paddling out of the Reach of their Darts (being a calm Day) I made a shift to suck the Wound, and dress it as well as I could.

I was at a Loss what to do, for I durst not return to the same Landing-place, but stood to the *North*, and was forced to paddle; for the Wind, although very gentle, was against me, blowing *North-West*. As I was looking about for a secure Landing-place, I saw a Sail to the *North North-East*, which appearing every Minute more visible, I was in some Doubt, whether I should wait for them or no; but at last my Detestation of the *Yahoo* Race prevailed; and turning my Canoo, I sailed and paddled together to the *South*, and got into the same Creek from whence I set out in the Morning; choosing rather to trust my self among these *Barbarians* than live with *European Yahoos*. I drew up my Canoo as close as I could to the Shore, and hid my self behind a Stone by the little Brook, which, as I have already said, was excellent Water.

The Ship came within half a League of this Creek, and sent out

[2] Of Dutch origins, Moll was a noted map-maker who had settled in London.

her Long-Boat with Vessels to take in fresh Water (for the Place it seems was very well known) but I did not observe it until the Boat was almost on Shore; and it was too late to seek another Hiding-Place. The Seamen at their landing observed my Canoo, and rummaging it all over, easily conjectured that the Owner could not be far off. Four of them well armed searched every Cranny and Lurking-hole, till at last they found me flat on my Face behind the Stone. They gazed a while in Admiration at my strange uncouth Dress; my Coat made of Skins, my wooden-soaled Shoes, and my furred Stockings; from whence, however, they concluded I was not a Native of the Place, who all go naked. One of the Seamen in *Portugueze* bid me rise, and asked who I was. I understood that Language very well, and getting upon my Feet, said, I was a poor *Yahoo*, banished from the *Houyhnhnms*, and desired they would please to let me depart. They admired to hear me answer them in their own Tongue, and saw by my Complection I must be an *European*; but were at a Loss to know what I meant by *Yahoos* and *Houyhnhnms*, and at the same Time fell a laughing at my strange Tone in speaking, which resembled the Neighing of a Horse. I trembled all the while betwixt Fear and Hatred: I again desired Leave to depart, and was gently moving to my Canoo; but they laid hold on me, desiring to know what Country I was of? whence I came? with many other Questions. I told them, I was born in *England*, from whence I came about five Years ago, and then their Country and ours was at Peace. I therefore hoped they would not treat me as an Enemy, since I meant them no Harm, but was a poor *Yahoo*, seeking some desolate Place where to pass the Remainder of his unfortunate Life.

When they began to talk, I thought I never heard or saw any thing so unnatural; for it appeared to me as monstrous as if a Dog or a Cow should speak in *England*, or a *Yahoo* in *Houyhnhnm-Land*. The honest *Portugueze* were equally amazed at my strange Dress, and the odd Manner of delivering my Words, which however they understood very well. They spoke to me with great Humanity, and said they were sure their Captain would carry me *gratis* to *Lisbon*, from whence I might return to my own Country; that two of the Seamen would go back to the Ship, to inform the Captain of what they had seen, and receive his Orders; in the mean Time, unless I would give my solemn Oath not to fly, they would secure me by Force. I thought it best to comply with their Proposal.

They were very curious to know my Story, but I gave them very little Satisfaction; and they all conjectured, that my Misfortunes had impaired my Reason. In two Hours the Boat, which went loaden with Vessels of Water, returned with the Captain's Commands to fetch me on Board. I fell on my Knees to preserve my Liberty; but all was in vain, and the Men having tied me with Cords, heaved me into the Boat, from whence I was taken into the Ship, and from thence into the Captain's Cabbin.

His Name was *Pedro de Mendez*; he was a very courteous and generous Person; he entreated me to give some Account of my self, and desired to know what I would eat or drink; said, I should be used as well as himself, and spoke so many obliging Things, that I wondered to find such Civilities from a *Yahoo*. However, I remained silent and sullen; I was ready to faint at the very Smell of him and his Men. At last I desired something to eat out of my own Canoo; but he ordered me a Chicken and some excellent Wine, and then directed that I should be put to Bed in a very clean Cabbin. I would not undress my self, but lay on the Bed-cloaths; and in half an Hour stole out, when I thought the Crew was at Dinner; and getting to the Side of the Ship, was going to leap into the Sea, and swim for my Life, rather than continue among *Yahoos*. But one of the Seamen prevented me, and having informed the Captain, I was chained to my Cabbin.

After Dinner *Don Pedro* came to me, and desired to know my Reason for so desperate an Attempt; assured me he only meant to do me all the Service he was able; and spoke so very movingly, that at last I descended to treat him like an Animal which had some little Portion of Reason. I gave him a very short Relation of my Voyage; of the Conspiracy against me by my own Men; of the Country where they set me on Shore, and of my five Years Residence there. All which he looked upon as if it were a Dream or a Vision; whereat I took great Offence: For I had quite forget the Faculty of Lying, so peculiar to *Yahoos* in all Countries where they preside, and consequently the Disposition of suspecting Truth in others of their own Species. I asked him, Whether it were the Custom of his Country to *say the Thing that was not?* I assured him I had almost forgot what he meant by Falshood; and if I had lived a thousand Years in *Houyhnhnmland*, I should never have heard a Lie from the meanest Servant. That I was altogether indifferent whether he believed me or no; but however, in return for his Favours, I would give so much Allowance to the Corruption of his Nature, as to answer any Objection he would please to make; and he might easily discover the Truth.

The Captain, a wise Man, after many Endeavours to catch me tripping in some Part of my Story, at last began to have a better Opinion of my Veracity. But he added, that since I professed so inviolable an Attachment to Truth, I must give him my Word of Honour to bear him Company in this Voyage without attempting any thing against my Life; or else he would continue me a Prisoner till we arrived at *Lisbon.* I gave him the Promise he required; but at the same time protested that I would suffer the greatest Hardships rather than return to live among *Yahoos.*

Our Voyage passed without any considerable Accident. In Gratitude to the Captain I sometimes sate with him at his earnest Request, and strove to conceal my Antipathy against human Kind, although it often broke out; which he suffered to pass without Observation. But the greatest Part of the Day, I confined myself to my Cabbin, to avoid seeing any of the Crew. The Captain had often intreated me to strip myself of my savage Dress, and offered to lend me the best Suit of Cloaths he had. This I would not be prevailed on to accept, abhorring to cover myself with any thing that had been on the Back of a *Yahoo.* I only desired he would lend me two clean Shirts, which having been washed since he wore them, I believed would not so much defile me. These I changed every second Day, and washed them myself.

We arrived at *Lisbon, Nov.* 5, 1715. At our landing, the Captain forced me to cover myself with his Cloak, to prevent the Rabble from crouding about me. I was conveyed to his own House; and at my earnest Request, he led me up to the highest Room backwards.[3] I conjured him to conceal from all Persons what I had told him of the *Houyhnhnms;* because the least Hint of such a Story would not only draw Numbers of People to see me, but probably put me in Danger of being imprisoned, or burnt by the *Inquisition.* The Captain persuaded me to accept a Suit of Cloaths newly made; but I would not suffer the Taylor to take my Measure; however, Don *Pedro* being almost of my Size, they fitted me well enough. He accoutred me with other Necessaries all new, which I aired for Twenty-four Hours before I would use them.

The Captain had no Wife, nor above three Servants, none of

[3] At the rear.

which were suffered to attend at Meals; and his whole Deportment was so obliging, added to very good *human* Understanding, that I really began to tolerate his Company. He gained so far upon me, that I ventured to look out of the back Window. By Degrees I was brought into another Room, from whence I peeped into the Street, but drew my Head back in a Fright. In a Week's Time he seduced me down to the Door. I found my Terror gradually lessened, but my Hatred and Contempt seemed to increase. I was at last bold enough to walk the Street in his Company, but kept my Nose well stopped with Rue, or sometimes with Tobacco.

In ten Days, Don *Pedro*, to whom I had given some Account of my domestick Affairs, put it upon me as a Point of Honour and Conscience, that I ought to return to my native Country, and live at home with my Wife and Children. He told me, there was an *English* Ship in the Port just ready to sail, and he would furnish me with all things necessary. It would be tedious to repeat his Arguments, and my Contradictions. He said, it was altogether impossible to find such a solitary Island as I had desired to live in; but I might command in my own House, and pass my time in a Manner as recluse as I pleased.

I complied at last, finding I could not do better. I left *Lisbon* the 24th Day of *November*, in an *English* Merchant-man, but who was the Master I never inquired. Don *Pedro* accompanied me to the Ship, and lent me Twenty Pounds. He took kind Leave of me, and embraced me at parting; which I bore as well as I could. During this last Voyage I had no Commerce with the Master, or any of his Men; but pretending I was sick kept close in my Cabbin. On the Fifth of *December*, 1715, we cast Anchor in the *Downs* about Nine in the Morning, and at Three in the Afternoon I got safe to my House at *Redriff*.

My Wife and Family received me with great Surprize and Joy, because they concluded me certainly dead; but I must freely confess, the Sight of them filled me only with Hatred, Disgust and Contempt; and the more, by reflecting on the near Alliance I had to them. For, although since my unfortunate Exile from the *Houyhnhnm* Country, I had compelled myself to tolerate the Sight of *Yahoos*, and to converse with Don *Pedro de Mendez*; yet my Memory and Imaginations were perpetually filled with the Virtues and Ideas of those exalted *Houyhnhnms*. And when I began to consider, that by copulating with one of the *Yahoo*-Species, I had become a Parent of more; it struck me with the utmost Shame, Confusion and Horror.

As soon as I entered the House, my Wife took me in her Arms, and kissed me; at which, having not been used to the Touch of that odious Animal for so many Years, I fell in a Swoon for almost an Hour. At the Time I am writing, it is five Years since my last Return to *England*: During the first Year I could not endure my Wife or Children in my Presence, the very Smell of them was intolerable; much less could I suffer them to eat in the same Room. To this Hour they dare not presume to touch my Bread, or drink out of the same Cup; neither was I ever able to let one of them take me by the Hand. The first Money I laid out was to buy two young Stone-Horses,[4] which I keep in a good Stable, and next to them the Groom is my greatest Favourite; for I feel my Spirits revived by the Smell he contracts in the Stable. My Horses understand me tolerably well; I converse with them at least four Hours every Day. They are Strangers to Bridle or Saddle; they live in great Amity with me, and Friendship to each other.

[4] Stallions.

CHAPTER XII

The Author's Veracity. His Design in publishing this Work. His Censure of those Travellers who swerve from the Truth. The Author clears himself from any sinister Ends in writing. An Objection answered. The Method of planting Colonies. His Native Country commended. The Right of the Crown to those Countries described by the Author, is justified. The Difficulty of conquering them. The Author takes his last Leave of the Reader; proposeth his Manner of Living for the future; gives good Advice, and concludeth.

Thus, gentle Reader, I have given thee a faithful History of my Travels for Sixteen Years, and above Seven Months; wherein I have not been so studious of Ornament as of Truth. I could perhaps like others have astonished thee with strange improbable Tales; but I rather chose to relate plain Matter of Fact in the simplest Manner and Style; because my principal Design was to inform, and not to amuse thee.

It is easy for us who travel into remote Countries, which are seldom visited by *Englishmen* or other *Europeans*, to form Descriptions of wonderful Animals both at Sea and Land. Whereas, a Traveller's chief Aim should be to make Men wiser and better, and to improve their Minds by the bad, as well as good Example of what they deliver concerning foreign Places.

I could heartily wish a Law were enacted, that every Traveller, before he were permitted to publish his Voyages, should be obliged to make Oath before the *Lord High Chancellor*, that all he intended to print was absolutely true to the best of his Knowledge; for then the World would no longer be deceived as it usually is, while some Writers, to make their Works pass the better upon the Publick, impose the grossest Falsities on the unwary Reader. I have

perused several Books of Travels with great Delight in my younger
Days; but, having since gone over most Parts of the Globe, and
been able to contradict many fabulous Accounts from my own
Observation; it hath given me a great Disgust against this Part of
Reading, and some Indignation to see the Credulity of Mankind so
impudently abused. Therefore, since my Acquaintance were pleased
to think my poor Endeavours might not be unacceptable to my
Country; I imposed on myself as a Maxim, never to be swerved
from, that I would *strictly adhere to Truth*; neither indeed can I
be ever under the least Temptation to vary from it, while I retain
in my Mind the Lectures and Example of my noble Master, and
the other illustrious *Houyhnhnms*, of whom I had so long the
Honour to be an humble Hearer.

———Nec si miserum Fortuna Sinonem
Finxit, vanum etiam, mendacemque improba finget.[1]

I know very well, how little Reputation is to be got by Writings
which require neither Genius nor Learning, nor indeed any other
Talent, except a good Memory, or an exact *Journal*. I know likewise, that Writers of Travels, like *Dictionary*-Makers, are sunk into
Oblivion by the Weight and Bulk of those who come last, and
therefore lie uppermost. And it is highly probable, that such Travellers who shall hereafter visit the Countries described in this Work
of mine, may by detecting my Errors, (if there be any) and adding
many new Discoveries of their own, jostle me out of Vogue, and
stand in my Place; making the World forget that ever I was an
Author. This indeed would be too great a Mortification if I wrote
for Fame: But, as my sole Intention was the PUBLICK GOOD, I cannot be altogether disappointed. For, who can read the Virtues I
have mentioned in the glorious *Houyhnhnms*, without being
ashamed of his own Vices, when he considers himself as the reasoning, governing Animal of his Country? I shall say nothing of
those remote Nations where *Yahoos* preside; amongst which the
least corrupted are the *Brobdingnagians*, whose wise Maxims in

---

[1] "Though Fortune has made Sinon wretched, she has not made him
untrue and a liar" (*Aeneid*, II, 79-80). Gulliver's quotation is accurate,
but he has mistaken the context. These are Sinon's words, belied by the
very speech in which they occur.

Morality and Government, it would be our Happiness to observe. But I forbear descanting further, and rather leave the judicious Reader to his own Remarks and Applications.

I am not a little pleased that this Work of mine can possibly meet with no Censurers: For what Objections can be made against a Writer who relates only plain Facts that happened in such distant Countries, where we have not the least Interest with respect either to Trade or Negotiations? I have carefully avoided every Fault with which common Writers of Travels are often too justly charged. Besides, I meddle not the least with any *Party*, but write without Passion, Prejudice, or Ill-will against any Man or Number of Men whatsoever. I write for the noblest End, to inform and instruct Mankind, over whom I may, without Breach of Modesty, pretend to some Superiority, from the Advantages I received by conversing so long among the most accomplished *Houyhnhnms*. I write without any View towards Profit or Praise. I never suffer a Word to pass that may look like Reflection, or possibly give the least Offence even to those who are most ready to take it. So that, I hope, I may with Justice pronounce myself an Author perfectly blameless; against whom the Tribes of Answerers, Considerers, Observers, Reflectors, Detecters, Remarkers, will never be able to find Matter for exercising their Talents.

I confess, it was whispered to me, that I was bound in Duty as a Subject of *England*, to have given in a Memorial to a Secretary of State, at my first coming over; because, whatever Lands are discovered by a Subject, belong to the Crown. But I doubt, whether our Conquests in the Countries I treat of, would be as easy as those of *Ferdinando Cortez* over the naked *Americans*. The *Lilliputians* I think, are hardly worth the Charge of a Fleet and Army to reduce them; and I question whether it might be prudent or safe to attempt the *Brobdingnagians*: Or, whether an *English* Army would be much at their Ease with the Flying Island over their Heads. The *Houyhnhnms*, indeed, appear not to be so well prepared for War, a Science to which they are perfect Strangers, and especially against missive Weapons. However, supposing myself to be a Minister of State, I could never give my Advice for invading them. Their Prudence, Unanimity, Unacquaintedness with Fear, and their Love of their Country would amply supply all Defects in the military Art. Imagine twenty Thousand of them breaking into the Midst

of an *European* Army, confounding the Ranks, overturning the
Carriages, battering the Warriors Faces into Mummy,[2] by terrible
Yerks from their hinder Hoofs: For they would well deserve the
Character given to *Augustus*; *Recalcitrat undique tutus.*[3] But instead of Proposals for conquering that magnanimous Nation, I
rather wish they were in a Capacity or Disposition to send a sufficient Number of their Inhabitants for civilizing *Europe*; by teaching us the first Principles of Honour, Justice, Truth, Temperance,
publick Spirit, Fortitude, Chastity, Friendship, Benevolence, and
Fidelity. The *Names* of all which Virtues are still retained among
us in most Languages, and are to be met with in modern as well as
ancient Authors; which I am able to assert from my own small
Reading.

But, I had another Reason which made me less forward to en-
large his Majesty's Dominions by my Discoveries: To say the Truth,
I had conceived a few Scruples with relation to the distributive
Justice of Princes upon those Occasions. For Instance, A Crew of
Pyrates are driven by a Storm they know not whither; at length a
Boy discovers Land from the Top-mast; they go on Shore to rob
and plunder; they see an harmless People, are entertained with
Kindness, they give the Country a new Name, they take formal
Possession of it for the King, they set up a rotton Plank or a Stone
for a Memorial, they murder two or three Dozen of the Natives,
bring away a Couple more by Force for a Sample, return home, and
get their Pardon. Here commences a new Dominion acquired with
a Title by *Divine Right*. Ships are sent with the first Opportunity;
the Natives driven out or destroyed, their Princes tortured to discover their Gold; a free Licence given to all Acts of Inhumanity and
Lust; the Earth reeking with the Blood of its Inhabitants: And
this execrable Crew of Butchers employed in so pious an Expedition, is a *modern Colony* sent to convert and civilize an idolatrous
and barbarous People.

But this Description, I confess, doth by no means affect the
British Nation, who may be an Example to the whole World for
their Wisdom, Care, and Justice in planting Colonies; their liberal
Endowments for the Advancement of Religion and Learning; their
Choice of devout and able Pastors to propagate *Christianity*; their

[2] Pulp.
[3] "He kicks backwards, protected on each side" (Horace, *Satires*, II, i,
20)

Caution in stocking their Provinces with People of sober Lives and Conversations from this the Mother Kingdom; their strict Regard to the Distribution of Justice, in supplying the Civil Administration through all their Colonies with Officers of the greatest Abilities, utter Strangers to Corruption: And to crown all, by sending the most vigilant and virtuous Governors, who have no other Views than the Happiness of the People over whom they preside, and the Honour of the King their Master.

But, as those Countries which I have described do not appear to have any Desire of being conquered, and enslaved, murdered or driven out by Colonies; nor abound either in Gold, Silver, Sugar or Tobacco; I did humbly conceive they were by no Means proper Objects of our Zeal, our Valour, or our Interest. However, if those whom it may concern, think fit to be of another Opinion, I am ready to depose, when I shall be lawfully called, That no *European* did ever visit these Countries before me. I mean, if the Inhabitants ought to be believed.

But, as to the Formality of taking Possession in my Sovereign's Name, it never came once into my Thoughts; and if it had, yet as my Affairs then stood, I should perhaps in point of Prudence and Self-Preservation, have put it off to a better Opportunity.

Having thus answered the *only* Objection that can be raised against me as a Traveller; I here take a final Leave of my Courteous Readers, and return to enjoy my own Speculations in my little Garden at *Redriff*; to apply those excellent Lessons of Virtue which I learned among the *Houyhnhnms*; to instruct the *Yahoos* of my own Family as far as I shall find them docible Animals; to behold my Figure often in a Glass, and thus if possible habituate my self by Time to tolerate the Sight of a human Creature: To lament the Brutality of *Houyhnhnms* in my own Country, but always treat their Persons with Respect, for the Sake of my noble Master, his Family, his Friends, and the whole *Houyhnhnm* Race, whom these of ours have the Honour to resemble in all their Lineaments, however their Intellectuals came to degenerate.

I began last Week to permit my Wife to sit at Dinner with me, at the farthest End of a long Table; and to answer (but with the utmost Brevity) the few Questions I ask her. Yet the Smell of a *Yahoo* continuing very offensive, I always keep my Nose well stopt with Rue, Lavender, or Tobacco-Leaves. And although it be hard for a Man late in Life to remove old Habits; I am not altogether out of Hopes in some Time to suffer a Neighbour *Yahoo* in my Company, without the Apprehensions I am yet under of his Teeth or his Claws.

My Reconcilement to the *Yahoo*-kind in general might not be so difficult, if they would be content with those Vices and Follies only which Nature hath entitled them to. I am not in the least provoked at the Sight of a Lawyer, a Pick-pocket, a Colonel, a Fool, a Lord, a Gamster, a Politician, a Whoremunger, a Physician, an Evidence, a Suborner, an Attorney, a Traytor, or the like: This is all according to the due Course of Things: But, when I behold a Lump of Deformity, and Diseases both in Body and Mind, smitten with *Pride*, it immediately breaks all the Measures of my Patience; neither shall I be ever able to comprehend how such an Animal and such a Vice could tally together. The wise and virtuous *Houyhnhnms*, who abound in all Excellencies that can adorn a rational Creature, have no Name for this Vice in their Language, which hath no Terms to express any thing that is evil, except those whereby they describe the detestable Qualities of their *Yahoos*; among which they were not able to distinguish this of Pride, for want of thoroughly understanding Human Nature, as it sheweth it self in other Countries, where that Animal presides. But I, who had more Experience, could plainly observe some Rudiments of it among the wild *Yahoos*.

But the *Houyhnhnms*, who live under the Government of Reason, are no more proud of the good Qualities they possess, than I should be for not wanting a Leg or an Arm, which no Man in his Wits would boast of, although he must be miserable without them. I dwell the longer upon this Subject from the Desire I have to make the Society of an *English Yahoo* by any Means not insupportable; and therefore I here intreat those who have any Tincture of this absurd Vice, that they will not presume to appear in my Sight.

FINIS

The Texts of
A Tale of a Tub
and Other Prose

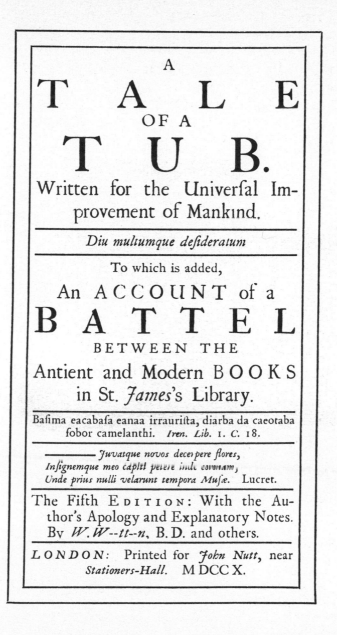

A
T A L E
OF A
T U B.
Written for the Univerſal Im-
provement of Mankind.

Diu multumque deſideratum

To which is added,

An ACCOUNT of a
B A T T E L
BETWEEN THE
Antient and Modern B O O K S
in St. *James*'s Library.

Baſima eacabaſa eanaa irrauriſta, diarba da caeotaba
fobor camelanthi. *Iren. Lib.* 1. *C.* 18.

——— *Juvatque novos decerpere flores,*
Inſignemque meo capiti petere inde coronam,
Unde prius nulli velarunt tempora Muſæ. Lucret.

The Fifth E D I T I O N: With the Author's Apology and Explanatory Notes.
By *W. W--tt--n*, B. D. and others.

L O N D O N: Printed for *John Nutt*, near
Stationers-Hall. M DCC X.

Editorial notes to the title page and to the texts of *A Tale of a Tub, The Battel of the Books,* and *A Fragment* appear on pp. 415–420.

Treatises wrote by the same Author, most of them mentioned in the following Discourses; which will be speedily published.

A *Character of the present Set of* Wits *in this Island.*
A *Panegyrical Essay upon the Number* T H R E E.
A *Dissertation upon the principal Productions of* Grub-street.[1]
Lectures upon a Dissection of Human Nature.
A *Panegyrick upon the World.*
An *Analytical Discourse upon Zeal,* Histori-theo-physi-logically *considered.*
A *general History of* Ears.
A *modest Defence of the Proceedings of the* Rabble *in all Ages.*
A *Description of the Kingdom of* Absurdities.
A *Voyage into* England, *by a Person of Quality in* Terra Australis incognita, *translated from the Original.*
A *Critical Essay upon the Art of* Canting, *Philosophically, Physically, and Musically considered.*

An Apology For the, &c.[2]

IF good and ill Nature equally operated upon Mankind, I might have saved my self the Trouble of this Apology; for it is manifest by the Reception the following Discourse hath met with, that those who approve it, are a great Majority among the Men of Tast; yet there have been two or three Treatises[3] written expresly against it, besides many others that have flirted at it occasionally, without one Syllable having been ever published in its Defence, or even Quotation to its Advantage, that I can remember, except by the Polite Author of a late Discourse between a Deist and a Socinian.

Therefore, since the Book seems calculated to live at least as long as our Language, and our Tast admit no great Alterations, I am content to convey some Apology along with it.

The greatest Part of that Book was finished above thirteen Years since, 1696, which is eight Years before it was published. The Author was then young, his Invention at the Height, and his Reading fresh in his Head. By the Assistance of some Thinking, and much Conversation, he had endeavour'd to Strip himself of as many real Prejudices as he could; I say real ones, because under the Notion of Prejudices, he knew to what dangerous Heights some Men have proceeded. Thus prepared, he thought the numerous and gross Corruptions in Religion and Learning[4] might furnish Matter for a Satyr, that would be useful and diverting: He resolved to proceed in a manner, that should be altogether new, the World having been already too long nauseated with endless Repetitions upon every Subject. The Abuses in Religion he proposed to set forth in the Allegory of the Coats, and the three Brothers, which was to make up the Body of the Discourse. Those in Learning he chose to introduce by way of Digressions. He was then a young Gentleman much in the World, and wrote to the Tast of those who were like himself; therefore in order to allure them, he gave a Liberty to his Pen, which might not suit with maturer Years, or graver Characters, and which he could have easily corrected with a very few Blots, had he been Master of his Papers for a Year or two before their Publication.

Not that he would have governed his Judgment by the ill-placed Cavils of the Sour, the Envious, the Stupid, and the Tastless, which he mentions with disdain. He acknowledges there are several youthful Sallies, which from the Grave and the Wise may deserve a Rebuke. But he desires to be answerable no farther than he is guilty, and that his Faults may not be multiply'd by the ignorant,

the unnatural, and uncharitable Applications of those who have nei-
ther Candor to suppose good Meanings, nor Palate to distinguish
true Ones. After which, he will forfeit his Life, if any one Opinion
can be fairly deduced from that Book, which is contrary to Religion
or Morality.

Why should any Clergyman of our Church be angry to see the
Follies of Fanaticism and Superstition exposed, tho' in the most
ridiculous Manner? since that is perhaps the most probable way to
cure them, or at least to hinder them from farther spreading.
Besides, tho' it was not intended for their Perusal; it raillies nothing
but what they preach against. It contains nothing to provoke them
by the least Scurillity upon their Persons or their Functions. It Cel-
ebrates the Church of England as the most perfect of all others in
Discipline and Doctrine, it advances no Opinion they reject, nor
condemns any they receive. If the Clergy's Resentments lay upon
their Hands, in my humble Opinion, they might have found more
proper Objects to employ them on: Nondum tibi defuit Hostis;[5] I
mean those heavy, illiterate Scriblers, prostitute in their Reputa-
tions, vicious in their Lives, and ruin'd in their Fortunes, who to
the shame of good Sense as well as Piety, are greedily read, meerly
upon the Strength of bold, false, impious Assertions, mixt with
unmannerly Reflections upon the Priesthood, and openly intended
against all Religion; in short, full of such Principles as are kindly
received, because they are levell'd to remove those Terrors that Religion tells Men will be the Consequence of immoral Lives. Nothing
like which is to be met with in this Discourse, tho' some of them
are pleased so freely to censure it. And I wish, there were no other
Instance of what I have too frequently observed, that many of that
Reverend Body are not always very nice in distinguishing between
their Enemies and their Friends.

Had the Author's Intentions met with a more candid Interpretation from some whom out of Respect he forbears to name, he
might have been encouraged to an Examination of Books written
by some of those Authors above-described, whose Errors, Ignorance,
Dullness and Villany, he thinks he could have detected and exposed
in such a Manner, that the Persons who are most conceived to be
infected by them, would soon lay them aside and be ashamed: But
he has now given over those Thoughts, since the weightiest Men in
the weightiest Stations are pleased to think it a more dangerous
Point to laugh at those Corruptions in Religion, which they themselves must disapprove, than to endeavour pulling up those very
Foundations, wherein all Christians have agreed.

He thinks it no fair Proceeding, that any Person should offer
determinately to fix a name upon the Author of this Discourse,

who hath all along concealed himself from most of his nearest Friends: Yet several have gone a farther Step, and pronounced* another Book to have been the Work of the same Hand with this; which the Author di- * Letter of Enthusiasm.

rectly affirms to be a thorough mistake; he having yet never so much as read that Discourse, a plain Instance how little Truth, there often is in general Surmises, or in Conjectures drawn from a Similitude of Style, or way of thinking.

Had the Author writ a Book to expose the Abuses in Law, or in Physick, he believes the Learned Professors in either Faculty, would have been so far from resenting it, as to have given him Thanks for his Pains, especially if he had made an honourable Reservation for the true Practice of either Science: But Religion they tell us ought not to be ridiculed, and they tell us Truth, yet surely the Corruptions in it may; for we are taught by the tritest Maxim in the World, that Religion being the best of Things, its Corruptions are likely to be the worst.

There is one Thing which the judicious Reader cannot but have observed, that some of those Passages in this Discourse, which appear most liable to Objection are what they call Parodies, where the Author personates the Style and Manner of other Writers,[6] *whom he has a mind to expose. I shall produce one Instance, it is in the 51st Page.*[7] *Dryden, L'Estrange, and some others I shall not name, are here levelled at, who having spent their Lives in Faction, and Apostacies, and all manner of Vice, pretended to be Sufferers for Loyalty and Religion. So Dryden tells us in one of his Prefaces of his Merits and Suffering, thanks God that he possesses his Soul in Patience: In other Places he talks at the same Rate, and L'Estrange often uses the like Style, and I believe the Reader may find more Persons to give that Passage an Application: But this is enough to direct those who may have over-look'd the Authors Intention.*

There are three or four other Passages which prejudiced or ignorant Readers have drawn by great Force to hint at ill Meanings; as if they glanced at some Tenets in Religion, in answer to all which, the Author solemnly protests he is entirely Innocent, and never had it once in his Thoughts that any thing he said would in the least be capable of such Interpretations,[8] *which he will engage to deduce full as fairly from the most innocent Book in the World. And it will be obvious to every Reader,*[9] *that this was not any part of his Scheme or Design, the Abuses he notes being such as all Church of England Men agree in, nor was it proper for his Subject to meddle with other Points, than such as have been perpetually controverted since the Reformation.*

To instance only in that Passage about the three wooden Ma-

chines[10] mentioned in the Introduction: In the Original Manuscript
there was a description of a Fourth, which those who had the
Papers in their Power, blotted out, as having something in it of
Satyr, that I suppose they thought was too particular, and therefore
they were forced to change it to the Number Three, from whence
some have endeavour'd to squeeze out a dangerous Meaning that
was never thought on. And indeed the Conceit was half spoiled by
changing the Numbers; that of Four being much more Cabalistick,
and therefore better exposing the pretended Virtue of Numbers, a
Superstition there intended to be ridicul'd.

Another Thing to be observed is, that there generally runs an
Irony through the Thread of the whole Book,[11] which the Men of
Tast will observe and distinguish, and which will render some
Objections that have been made, very weak and insignificant.

This Apology being chiefly intended for the Satisfaction of future
Readers, it may be thought unnecessary to take any notice of such
Treatises as have been writ against this ensuing Discourse, which
are already sunk into waste Paper and Oblivion; after the usual Fate
of common Answerers to Books, which are allowed to have any Merit:
They are indeed like Annuals that grow about a young Tree, and
seem to vye with it for a Summer, but fall and die with the Leaves
in Autumn, and are never heard of any more. When Dr. Eachard
writ his Book about the Contempt of the Clergy, numbers of those
Answerers immediately started up, whose Memory if he had not
kept alive by his Replies, it would now be utterly unknown that he
were ever answered at all. There is indeed an Exception, when any
great Genius thinks it worth his while to expose a foolish Piece; so
we still read Marvel's Answer to Parker with Pleasure, tho' the Book
it answers be sunk long ago; so the Earl of Orrery's Remarks will be
read with Delight, when the Dissertation he exposes will neither be
sought nor found; but these are no Enterprises for common Hands,
nor to be hoped for above once or twice in an Age. Men would be
more cautious of losing their Time in such an Undertaking, if they
did but consider, that to answer a Book effectually, requires more
Pains and Skill, more Wit, Learning, and Judgment than were
employ'd in the Writing it. And the Author assures those Gentlemen who have given themselves that Trouble with him, that his
Discourse is the Product of the Study, the Observation, and the
Invention of several Years, that he often blotted out much more
than he left, and if his Papers had not been a long time out of his
Possession, they must have still undergone more severe Corrections;
and do they think such a Building is to be battered with Dirt-Pel-
lets however envenom'd the Mouths may be that discharge them.
He hath seen the Productions but of two Answerers, One of

which[12] *first appear'd as from an unknown hand, but since avowed by a Person, who upon some Occasions hath discover'd no ill Vein of Humor. 'Tis a Pity any Occasions should put him under a necessity of being so hasty in his Productions, which otherwise might often be entertaining. But there were other Reasons obvious enough for his Miscarriage in this; he writ against the Conviction of his Talent, and enter'd upon one of the wrongest Attempts in Nature, to turn into ridicule by a Weeks Labour, a Work which had cost so much time, and met with so much Success in ridiculing others, the manner how he has handled his* Subject, *I have now forgot, having just look'd it over when it first came out, as others did, meerly for the sake of the Title.*

The other[13] *Answer is from a Person of a graver Character, and is made up of half Invective, and half Annotation. In the latter of which he hath generally succeeded well enough. And the Project at that time was not amiss, to draw in Readers to his Pamphlet, several having appear'd desirous that there might be some Explication of the more difficult Passages. Neither can he be altogether blamed for offering at the Invective Part, because it is agreed on all hands that the Author had given him sufficient Provocation. The great Objection is against his manner of treating it, very unsuitable to one of his Function. It was determined by a fair Majority, that this Answerer had in a way not to be pardon'd, drawn his Pen against a certain great Man then alive, and universally reverenced for every good Quality that could possibly enter into the Composition of the most accomplish'd Person; it was observed, how he was pleased and affected to have that noble Writer call'd his Adversary, and it was a Point of Satyr well directed, for I have been told,* Sir W. T.[14] *was sufficiently mortify'd at the Term. All the Men of Wit and Politeness were immediately up in Arms, through Indignation, which prevailed over their Contempt, by the Consequences they apprehended from such an Example, and it grew to be Porsenna's Case;* Idem trecenti juravimus.[15] *In short, things were ripe for a general Insurrection, till my Lord Orrery had a little laid the Spirit, and settled the Ferment. But his Lordship being principally engaged with another Antagonist,*[16] *it was thought necessary in order to quiet the Minds of Men, that this Opposer should receive a Reprimand, which partly occasioned that Discourse of the Battle of the Books, and the Author was farther at the Pains to insert one or two Remarks on him in the Body of the Book.*

This Answerer has been pleased to find Fault with about a dozen Passages, which the Author will not be at the Trouble of defending, farther than by assuring the Reader, that for the greater Part the Reflecter is entirely mistaken, and forces Interpretations which never once entered into the Writer's Head, nor will he is sure into that of any Reader of Tast and Candor; he allows two or three at most there produced to have been deliver'd unwarily, for which he desires to plead the Excuse offered already, of his Youth, and Franckness of Speech, and his Papers being out of his Power at the Time they were published.

But this Answerer insists, and says, what he chiefly dislikes, is the Design; what that was I have already told, and I believe there is not a Person in England who can understand that Book, that ever imagined it to have been any thing else, but to expose the Abuses and Corruptions in Learning and Religion.

But it would be good to know what Design this Reflecter was serving, when he concludes his Pamphlet with a Caution to Readers, to beware of thinking the Authors Wit was entirely his own, surely this must have had some Allay of Personal Animosity, at least mixt with the Design of serving the Publick by so useful a Discovery; and it indeed touches the Author in a very tender Point, who insists upon it, that through the whole Book he has not borrowed one single Hint from any Writer in the World; and he thought, of all Criticisms, that would never have been one, He conceived it was never disputed to be an Original, whatever Faults it might have. However this Answerer produces three Instances to prove this Author's Wit is not his own in many Places. The first is, that the Names of Peter, Martin and Jack are borrowed from a Letter of the late Duke of Buckingham. Whatever Wit is contained in those three Names, the Author is content to give it up, and desires his Readers will substract as much as they placed upon that Account; at the same time protesting solemnly that he never once heard of that Letter, except in this Passage of the Answerer: So that the Names were not borrowed as he affirms, tho' they should happen to be the same which however is odd enough, and what he hardly believes; that of Jack, being not quite so obvious as the other two. The second Instance to shew the Author's Wit is not his own, is Peter's Banter (as he calls it in his Alsatia[17] Phrase) upon Transubstantiation, which is taken from the same Duke's Conference with an Irish Priest, where a Cork is turned into a Horse. This the Author confesses to have seen, about ten Years after his Book was writ, and a Year or two after it was published. Nay, the Answerer overthrows this himself; for he allows the Tale was writ in 1697; and I think that Pamphlet was not printed in many Years after. It was necessary, that Corruption should have some Allegory as well as the rest; and the Author invented the properest he could, without enquiring what other People had writ, and the commonest Reader will find, there is not the least Resemblance between the two Stories. The third Instance is in these Words: I have been assured, that the Battle in St. *James's* Library, is *mutatis mutandis,* taken out of a *French* Book, entituled, *Combat des livres,* if I misremember not. *In which Passage there are two Clauses observable:* I have been assured; *and, if* I misremember not. *I desire first to know, whether if that Conjecture proves an utter falshood, those two Clauses will be a sufficient Excuse for this worthy Critick. The Matter is a Trifle; but, would he venture to pronounce at this Rate upon one of greater Moment? I know nothing more contemptible in a Writer than the Character of a Plagiary; which he here fixes at a venture, and this, not for a Passage, but a whole Discourse, taken out from another Book only* mutatis mutandis.[18] *The Author is as much in the dark about this as the Answerer; and will imitate him by an Affirmation at Random; that if there be a word of Truth in this Reflection, he is a paultry, imitating Pedant, and the Answerer is a Person of Wit, Manners and Truth. He takes his Boldness, from never having seen any such Treatise in his Life nor heard of it before; and he is sure it is impossible for two Writers of different Times and Countries to agree in their Thoughts after such a Manner, that two continued Discourses shall be the same only* mutatis mutandis. *Neither will he insist upon the mistake of the Title, but let the Answerer and his Friend produce any Book they please, he defies them to shew one single Particular, where the judicious Reader will affirm he has been obliged for the smallest Hint; giving only Allowance for the accidental encountring of a single Thought, which he knows may sometimes happen; tho he has never yet found it in that Discourse, nor has heard it objected by any body else.*

So that if ever any design was unfortunately executed, it must be that of this Answerer; who when he would have it observed that the Author's Wit is not his own, is able to produce but three Instances, two of them meer Trifles, and all three manifestly false. If this be the way these Gentlemen deal with the World in those Criticisms, where we have not Leisure to defeat them, their Readers had need be cautious how they rely upon their Credit; and whether this Proceeding can be reconciled to Humanity or Truth, let those who think it worth their while, determine.

It is agreed, this Answerer would have succeeded much better, if he had stuck wholly to his Business as a Commentator upon the Tale of a Tub, *wherein it cannot be deny'd that he hath been of some Service to the Publick, and has given very fair Conjectures towards clearing up some difficult Passages; but, it is the frequent Error of those Men (otherwise very commendable for their Labors) to make Excursions beyond their Talent and their Office, by pre-*

tending to point out the Beauties and the Faults; which is no part of their Trade, which they always fail in, which the World never expected from them, nor gave them any thanks for endeavouring at. The Part of Min-ellius,[19] *or Farnaby would have fallen in with his Genius, and might have been serviceable to many Readers who cannot enter into the abstruser Parts of that Discourse; but* Optat ephippia bos piger. *The dull, unwieldy, ill-shaped Ox would needs put on the Furniture of a Horse, not considering he was born to Labour, to plow the Ground for the Sake of superior Beings, and that he has neither the Shape, Mettle nor Speed of that nobler Animal he would affect to personate.*

It is another Pattern of this Answerer's fair dealing, to give us Hints that the Author is dead, and yet to lay the Suspicion upon somebody, I know not who, in the Country; to which can be only returned, that he is absolutely mistaken in all his Conjectures; and surely Conjectures are at best too light a Pretence to allow a Man to assign a Name in Publick. He condemns a Book, and consequently the Author, of whom he is utterly ignorant, yet at the same time fixes in Print, what he thinks a disadvantageous Character upon those who never deserved it. A Man who receives a Buffet in the Dark may be allowed to be vexed; but it is an odd kind of Revenge to go to Cuffs in broad day with the first he meets with, and lay the last Nights Injury at his Door. And thus much for this discreet, candid, pious, *and* ingenious *Answerer.*

How the Author came to be without his Papers, is a Story not proper to be told, and of very little use, being a private Fact of which the Reader would believe as little or as much as he thought good. He had however a blotted Copy by him, which he intended to have writ over, with many Alterations, and this the Publishers were well aware of, having put it into the Booksellers Preface, that they apprehended a surreptitious Copy, which was to be altered, &c. This though not regarded by Readers, was a real Truth, only the surreptitious Copy was rather that which was printed, and they made all hast they could, which indeed was needless; the Author not being at all prepared; but he has been told, the Bookseller was in much Pain, having given a good Sum of Money for the Copy.

In the Authors Original Copy there were not so many Chasms as appear in the Book; and why some of them were left he knows not; had the Publication been trusted to him, he should have made several Corrections of Passages against which nothing hath been ever objected. He should likewise have altered a few of those that seem with any Reason to be excepted against, but to deal freely, the greatest Number he should have left untouch'd, as never suspecting it possible any wrong Interpretations could be made of them.

The Author observes, at the End of the Book there is a Discourse called A Fragment; *which he more wondered to see in Print than all the rest. Having been a most imperfect Sketch with the Addition of a few loose Hints, which he once lent a Gentleman who had designed a Discourse of somewhat the same Subject; he never thought of it afterwards, and it was a sufficient Surprize to see it pieced up together, wholly out of the Method and Scheme he had intended, for it was the Ground-work of a much larger Discourse, and he was sorry to observe the Materials so foolishly employ'd.*

There is one farther Objection made by those who have answered this Book, as well as by some others, that Peter *is frequently made to repeat Oaths and Curses. Every Reader observes it was necessary to know that* Peter *did Swear and Curse. The Oaths are not printed out, but only supposed, and the Idea of an Oath is not immoral, like the Idea of a Prophane or Immodest Speech. A Man may laugh at the Popish Folly of cursing People to Hell, and imagine them swearing, without any crime; but lewd Words, or dangerous Opinions though printed by halves, fill the Readers Mind with ill Idea's; and of these the Author cannot be accused. For the judicious Reader will find that the severest Stroaks of Satyr in his Book are levelled against the modern Custom of Employing Wit upon those Topicks, of which there is a remarkable Instance in the* 153d,[20] *Page, as well as in several others, tho' perhaps once or twice exprest in too free a manner, excusable only for the Reasons already alledged. Some Overtures have been made by a third Hand to the Bookseller for the Author's altering those Passages which he thought might require it. But it seems the Bookseller will not hear of any such Thing, being apprehensive it might spoil the Sale of the Book.*

The Author cannot conclude this Apology, without making this one Reflection; that, as Wit is the noblest and most useful Gift of humane Nature, so Humor is the most agreeable, and where these two enter far into the Composition of any Work, they will render it always acceptable to the World. Now, the great Part of those who have no Share or Tast of either, but by their Pride, Pedantry and Ill Manners, lay themselves bare to the Lashes of Both, think the Blow is weak, because they are insensible, and where Wit hath any mixture of Raillery; 'Tis but calling it Banter, *and the work is done. This Polite Word of theirs was first borrowed from the Bullies in* White-Fryars,[21] *then fell among the Footmen, and at last retired to the Pedants, by whom it is applied as properly to the Productions of Wit, as if I should apply it to Sir* Isaac Newton's *Mathematicks, but, if this* Bantring *as they call it, be so despisable a Thing, whence comes it to pass they have such a perpetual Itch* towards it themselves? *To instance only in the Answerer already mentioned; it is grievous to see him in some of his Writings at every turn going out of his way to be waggish, to tell us of a Cow that prickt up her Tail, and in his answer to this Discourse, he says it is all a Farce and a Ladle: With other Passages equally shining. One may say of these Impedimenta Literarum, that Wit ows them a Shame; and they cannot take wiser Counsel than to keep out of harms way, or at least not to come till they are sure they are called.*

To conclude; with those Allowances above-required, this Book should be read, after which the Author conceives, few things will remain which may not be excused in a young Writer. He wrote only to the Men of Wit and Tast, and he thinks he is not mistaken in his Accounts, when he says they have been all of his side, enough to give him the vanity of telling his Name, wherein the World with all its wise Conjectures, is yet very much in the dark, which Circumstance is no disagreeable Amusement either to the Publick or himself.

The Author is informed, that the Bookseller has prevailed on several Gentlemen, to write some explanatory Notes, for the goodness of which he is not to answer, having never seen any of them, nor intends it, till they appear in Print, when it is not unlikely he may have the Pleasure to find twenty Meanings, which never enter'd into his Imagination.

June 3, 1709.

POSTSCRIPT

SINCE the writing of this which was about a Year ago; a Prostitute Bookseller[22] *hath publish'd a foolish Paper, under the Name of Notes on the* Tale of a Tub, *with some Account of the Author, and with an Insolence which I suppose is punishable by Law, hath presumed to assign certain Names. It will be enough for the Author to assure the World, that the Writer of that Paper is utterly wrong in all his Conjectures upon that Affair. The Author farther asserts that the whole Work is entirely of one Hand, which every Reader of Judgment will easily discover. The Gentleman who gave the Copy to the Bookseller, being a Friend of the Author, and using no other Liberties besides that of expunging certain Passages where now the Chasms appear under the Name of* Desiderata. *But if any Person will prove his Claim to three Lines in the whole Book, let him step forth and tell his Name and Titles, upon which the Bookseller shall have Orders to prefix them to the next Edition, and the Claimant shall from henceforward be acknowledged the undisputed Author.*

To the Right Honourable,
John Lord Sommers[23]

My L O R D,

THO' the Author has written a large Dedication, yet That being address'd to a Prince, whom I am never likely to have the Honor of being known to; A Person, besides, as far as I can observe, not at all regarded, or thought on by any of our present Writers; And, being wholly free from that Slavery, which Booksellers usually lie under, to the Caprices of Authors; I think it a wise Piece of Presumption, to inscribe these Papers to your Lordship, and to implore your Lordship's Protection of them. God and your Lordship know their Faults, and their Merits; for as to my own Particular, I am altogether a Stranger to the Matter; And, tho' every Body else should be equally ignorant, I do not fear the Sale of the Book, at all the worse, upon that Score. Your Lordship's Name on the Front, in Capital Letters, will at any time get off one Edition: Neither would I desire any other Help, to grow an Alderman, than a Patent for the sole Priviledge of Dedicating to your Lordship.

I should now, in right of a Dedicator, give your Lordship a List of your own Virtues, and at the same time, be very unwilling to offend your Modesty; But, chiefly, I should celebrate your Liberality towards Men of great Parts and small Fortunes, and give you broad Hints, that I mean my self. And, I was just going on in the usual Method, to peruse a hundred or two of Dedications, and transcribe an Abstract, to be applied to your Lordship; But, I was diverted by a certain Accident. For, upon the Covers of these Papers, I casually observed written in large Letters, the two following Words, *D E T U R   D I G N I S S I M O*; which, for ought I knew, might contain some important Meaning. But, it unluckily fell out, that none of the Authors I employ, understood *Latin* (tho' I have them often in pay, to translate out of that Language) I was therefore compelled to have recourse to the Curate of our Parish, who Englished it thus, *Let it be given to the Worthiest*; And his Comment was, that the Author meant, his Work should be dedicated to the sublimest Genius of the Age, for Wit, Learning, Judgment, Eloquence and Wisdom. I call'd at a Poet's Chamber (who works for my Shop) in an Alley hard by, shewed him the Translation, and desired his Opinion, who it was that the Author could mean; He told me, after some Consideration, that Vanity was a Thing he abhorr'd; but by the Description, he thought Himself to be the Person aimed at; And, at the same time, he very kindly offer'd his own Assistance *gratis*, towards penning a Dedication to Himself. I desired him, however, to give a second Guess; Why then, said he, It must be I, or my Lord *Sommers*. From thence I went to several other Wits of my Acquaintance, with no small Hazard and Weariness to my Person, from a prodigious Number of dark, winding Stairs; But found them all in the same Story, both of your Lordship and themselves. Now, your Lordship is to understand, that this Proceeding was not of my own Invention; For, I have somewhere heard, it is a Maxim, that those, to whom every Body allows the second Place, have an undoubted Title to the First.

T H I S infallibly convinced me, that your Lordship was the Person intended by the Author. But, being very unacquainted in the Style and Form of Dedications, I employ'd those Wits aforesaid, to furnish me with Hints and Materials, towards a Panegyrick upon your Lordship's Virtues.

I N two Days, they bought me ten Sheets of Paper, fill'd up on every Side. They swore to me, that they had ransack'd whatever could be found in the Characters of *Socrates*, *Aristides*, *Epaminondas*, *Cato*, *Tully*, *Atticus*, and other hard Names, which I cannot now recollect. However, I have Reason to believe, they imposed upon my Ignorance, because, when I came to read over their Collections, there was not a Syllable there, but what I and every body else knew as well as themselves: Therefore, I grievously suspect a Cheat; and, that these Authors of mine, stole and transcribed every Word, from the universal Report of Mankind. So that I look upon my self, as fifty Shillings out of Pocket, to no manner of Purpose.

I F, by altering the Title, I could make the same Materials serve for another Dedication (as my Betters have done) it would help to make up my Loss: But, I have made several Persons, dip here and there in those Papers, and before they read three Lines, they have all assured me, plainly, that they cannot possibly be applied to any Person besides your Lordship.

I expected, indeed, to have heard of your Lordship's Bravery, at the Head of an Army; Of your undaunted Courage, in mounting a Breach, or scaling a Wall; Or, to have had your Pedigree trac'd in a Lineal Descent from the House of *Austria*; Or, of your wonderful Talent at Dress and Dancing; Or, your Profound Knowledge in *Algebra*, *Metaphysicks*, and the Oriental Tongues. But to ply the World with an old beaten Story of your Wit, and Eloquence, and Learning, and Wisdom, and Justice, and Politeness, and Candor, and Evenness of Temper in all Scenes of Life; Of that great Discernment in Discovering, and Readiness in Favouring deserving

Men; with forty other common Topicks: I confess, I have neither Conscience, nor Countenance to do it. Because, there is no Virtue, either of a Publick or Private Life, which some Circumstances of your own, have not often produced upon the Stage of the World; And those few, which for want of Occasions to exert them, might otherwise have pass'd unseen or unobserved by your *Friends*, your *Enemies* have at length brought to Light.

'T I S true, I should be very loth, the Bright Example of your Lordship's Virtues should be lost to After-Ages, both for their sake and your own; but chiefly, because they will be so very necessary to adorn the History of a *late Reign*; And That is another Reason, why I would forbear to make a Recital or them here; Because, I have been told by Wise Men, that as Dedications have run for some Years past, a good Historian will not be apt to have Recourse thither, in search of Characters.

T H E R E is one Point, wherein I think we Dedicators would do well to change our Measures; I mean, instead of running on so far, upon the Praise of our Patron's *Liberality*, to spend a Word or two, in admiring their *Patience*. I can put no greater Compliment on your Lordship's, than by giving you so ample an Occasion to exercise it at present. Tho', perhaps, I shall not be apt to reckon much Merit to your Lordship upon that Score, who having been formerly used to tedious Harangues, and sometimes to as little Purpose, will be the readier to pardon this, especially, when it is offered by one, who is with all Respect and Veneration,

My Lo r d,

Your Lordship's most Obedient,
and most Faithful Servant,
The Bookseller.

The Bookseller to the Reader

IT is now Six Years since these Papers came first to my Hand, which seems to have been about a Twelvemonth after they were writ: For, the Author tells us in his Preface to the first Treatise, that he hath calculated it for the Year 1697, and in several Passages of that Discourse, as well as the second, it appears, they were written about that Time.

As to the Author, I can give no manner of Satisfaction; However, I am credibly informed that this Publication is without his Knowledge; for he concludes the Copy is lost, having lent it to a Person, since dead, and being never in Possession of it after: So that, whether the Work received his last Hand, or, whether he intended to fill up the defective Places, is like to remain a Secret.

If I should go about to tell the Reader, by what Accident, I became Master of these Papers, it would, in this unbelieving Age, pass for little more than the Cant, or Jargon of the Trade. I, therefore, gladly spare both him and my self so unnecessary a Trouble. There yet remains a difficult Question, why I publish'd them no sooner. I forbore upon two Accounts: First, because I thought I had better Work upon my Hands; and Secondly, because, I was not without some Hope of hearing from the Author, and receiving his Directions. But, I have been lately alarm'd with Intelligence of a surreptitious Copy, which a certain great Wit had new polish'd and refin'd, or as our present Writers express themselves, fitted to the Humor of the Age; as they have already done, with great Felicity, to Don Quixot, Boccalini, la Bruyere and other Authors. However, I thought it fairer Dealing, to offer the whole Work in its Naturals. If any Gentleman will please to furnish me with a Key, in order to explain the more difficult Parts, I shall very gratefully acknowledge the Favour, and print it by it self.

The Epistle Dedicatory, to
His Royal Highness Prince Posterity

SIR,

I HERE present *Your Highness* with the Fruits of a very few leisure Hours, stollen from the short Intervals of a World of Business, and of an Employment quite alien from such Amusements as this: The poor Production of that Refuse of Time which has lain heavy upon my Hands, during a long Prorogation of Parliament, a great Dearth of Forein News, and a tedious Fit of rainy Weather: For which, and other Reasons, it cannot chuse extreamly to deserve such a Patronage as that of *Your Highness*, whose numberless Virtues in so few Years, make the World look upon You as the future Example to all Princes: For altho' *Your Highness* is hardly got clear of Infancy, yet has the universal learned World already resolv'd upon appealing to Your future Dictates with the lowest and most resigned Submission: Fate having decreed You sole Arbiter of the Productions of human Wit, in this polite and most accomplish'd Age. Methinks, the Number of Appellants were enough to shock and startle any Judge of a Genius less unlimited than Yours: But in order to prevent such glorious Tryals, the *Person* (it seems) to whose Care the Education of *Your Highness* is committed, has resolved (as I am told) to keep you in almost an universal Ignorance of our Studies, which it is Your inherent Birth-right to inspect.

IT is amazing to me, that this *Person* should have Assurance in the face of the Sun, to go about persuading *Your Highness*, that our Age is almost wholly illiterate, and has hardly produc'd one Writer upon any Subject. I know very well, that when *Your Highness* shall come to riper Years, and have gone through the Learning of Antiquity, you will be too curious to neglect inquiring into the Authors of the very age before You: And to think that this *Inso-*

The Citation out of Irenæus in the Title-Page, *which seems to be all* Gibberish, *is a Form of Initiation used antiently by the* Marcosian *Hereticks.* W. Wotton.

It is the usual Style of decry'd Writers to appeal to Posterity, *who is here represented as a Prince in his Nonage, and* Time *as his Governor, and the Author begins in a way very frequent with him, by personating other Writers, who sometimes offer such Reasons and Excuses for publishing their Works as they ought chiefly to conceal and be asham'd of.* [All notes in the margins and at the bottoms of the pages of the *Tale, Battel,* and *Fragment* were affixed or approved by Swift for the 1710 edition of these works. All notes to these works by the present editors (indicated in the text by arabic numbers) can be found in a unit immediately following the *Fragment* (pp. 415–420).—*Editors*]

lent, in the Account he is preparing for Your View, designs to
reduce them to a Number so insignificant as I am asham'd to mention; it moves my Zeal and my Spleen for the Honor and Interest
of our vast flourishing Body, as well as of myself, for whom I know
by long Experience, he has profess'd, and still continues a peculiar
Malice.

'T I S not unlikely, that when *Your Highness* will one day peruse
what I am now writing, You may be ready to expostulate with Your
Governour upon the Credit of what I here affirm, and command
Him to shew You some of our Productions. To which he will
answer, (for I am well informed of his Designs) by asking *Your
Highness,* where they are? and what is become of them? and pretend it a Demonstration that there never were any, because they are
not then to be found: Not to be found! Who has mislaid them?
Are they sunk in the Abyss of Things? 'Tis certain, that in their
own Nature they were *light* enough to swim upon the Surface for
all Eternity. Therefore the Fault is in Him, who tied Weights so
heavy to their Heels, as to depress them to the Center. Is their very
Essence destroyed? Who has annihilated them? Were they
drowned by *Purges* or martyred by *Pipes?* Who administred them
to the Posteriors of ———? But that it may no longer be a Doubt
with *Your Highness,* who is to be the Author of this universal Ruin;
I beseech You to observe that large and terrible *Scythe* which your
Governour affects to bear continually about him. Be pleased to
remark the Length and Strength, the Sharpness and Hardness of his
Nails and *Teeth:* Consider his baneful abominable *Breath,* Enemy
to Life and Matter, infectious and corrupting: And then reflect
whether it be possible for any mortal Ink and Paper of this Generation to make a suitable Resistance. Oh, that *Your Highness* would
one day resolve to disarm this Usurping * *Maitre du Palais,* of his
furious Engins, and bring Your Empire † *hors de Page.*

I T were endless to recount the several Methods of Tyranny and
Destruction, which Your *Governour* is pleased to practise upon this
Occasion. His inveterate Malice is such to the Writings of our Age,
that of several Thousands produced yearly from this renowned City,
before the next Revolution of the Sun, there is not one to be heard
of: Unhappy Infants, many of them barbarously destroyed, before
they have so much as learnt their *Mother-Tongue* to beg for Pity.
Some he stifles in their Cradles, others he frights into Convulsions,
whereof they suddenly die; Some he flays alive, others he tears Limb
from Limb. Great Numbers are offered to *Moloch,* and the rest
tainted by his Breath, die of a languishing Consumption.

* *Comptroller.*
† *Out of Guardianship.*

B U T the Concern I have most at Heart, is for our Corporation of *Poets*, from whom I am preparing a Petition to *Your Highness*, to be subscribed with the Names of one hundred thirty six of the first Rate, but whose immortal Productions are never likely to reach your Eyes, tho' each of them is now an humble and an earnest Appellant for the Laurel, and has large comely Volumes ready to shew for a Support to his Pretensions. The *never-dying* Works of these illustrious Persons, Your *Governour*, Sir, has devoted to unavoidable Death, and *Your Highness* is to be made believe, that our Age has never arrived at the Honor to produce one single Poet.

W E confess *Immortality* to be a great and powerful Goddess, but in vain we offer up to her our Devotions and our Sacrifices, if *Your Highness's Governour,* who has usurped the *Priesthood,* must by an unparallel'd Ambition and Avarice, wholly intercept and devour them.

T O affirm that our Age is altogether Unlearned, and devoid of Writers in any kind, seems to be an Assertion so bold and so false, that I have been sometime thinking, the contrary may almost be proved by uncontroulable Demonstration. 'Tis true indeed, that altho' their Numbers be vast, and their Productions numerous in proportion, yet are they hurryed so hastily off the Scene, that they escape our Memory, and delude our Sight. When I first thought of this Address, I had prepared a copious List of *Titles* to present *Your Highness* as an undisputed Argument for what I affirm. The Originals were posted fresh upon all Gates and Corners of Streets; but returning in a very few Hours to take a Review, they were all torn down, and fresh ones in their Places: I enquired after them among Readers and Booksellers, but I enquired in vain, the *Memorial of them was lost among Men, their Place was no more to be found;* and I was laughed to scorn, for a *Clown* and a *Pedant,* without all Taste and Refinement, little versed in the Course of present Affairs, and that knew nothing of what had pass'd in the best Companies of Court and Town. So that I can only avow in general to *Your Highness,* that we do abound in Learning and Wit; but to fix upon Particulars, is a Task too slippery for my slender Abilities. If I should venture in a windy Day, to affirm to *Your Highness,* that there is a large Cloud near the *Horizon* in the Form of a *Bear,* another in the *Zenith* with the Head of an *Ass,* a third to the Westward with Claws like a *Dragon;* and *Your Highness* should in a few Minutes think fit to examine the Truth, 'tis certain, they would all be changed in Figure and Position, new ones would arise, and all we could agree upon would be, that Clouds there were, but that I was grosly mistaken in the *Zoography* and *Topography* of them.

B U T Your *Governour,* perhaps, may still insist, and put the

Question: What is then become of those immense Bales of Paper, which must needs have been employ'd in such Numbers of Books? Can these also be wholly annihilate, and so of a sudden as I pretend? What shall I say in return of so invidious an Objection? It ill befits the Distance between *Your Highness* and Me, to send You for ocular Conviction to a *Jakes*, or an *Oven*; to the Windows of a *Bawdy-house*, or to a sordid *Lanthorn*. Books, like Men their Authors, have no more than one Way of coming into the World, but there are ten Thousand to go out of it, and return no more.

I profess to *Your Highness*, in the Integrity of my Heart, that what I am going to say is literally true this Minute I am writing: What Revolutions may happen before it shall be ready for your Perusal, I can by no means warrant: However I beg You to accept it as a Specimen of our Learning, our Politeness and our Wit. I do therefore affirm upon the Word of a sincere Man, that there is now actually in being, a certain Poet called *John Dryden*, whose Translation of *Virgil* was lately printed in a large Folio, well bound, and if diligent search were made, for ought I know, is yet to be seen. There is another call'd *Nahum Tate*, who is ready to make Oath that he has caused many Rheams of Verse to be published, whereof both himself and his Bookseller (if lawfully required) can still produce authentick Copies, and therefore wonders why the World is pleased to make such a Secret of it. There is a Third, known by the Name of *Tom Durfey*, a Poet of a vast Comprehension, an universal Genius, and most profound Learning. There are also one Mr. *Rymer*, and one Mr. *Dennis*, most profound Criticks. There is a Person styl'd Dr. B——tl—y, who has written near a thousand Pages of immense Erudition, *giving a full and true Account* of a certain *Squable* of wonderful Importance between himself and a Bookseller: He is a Writer of infinite Wit and Humour; no Man raillyes with a better Grace, and in more sprightly Turns. Farther, I avow to *Your Highness*, that with these Eyes I have beheld the Person of *William W——tt—n*, B. D. who has written a good sizeable Volume against a *Friend of Your Governor* (from whom, alas! he must therefore look for little Favour) in a most gentlemanly Style, adorned with utmost Politeness and Civility; replete with Discoveries equally valuable for their Novelty and Use: and embellish'd with *Traits* of Wit so poignant and so apposite, that he is a worthy Yokemate to his fore-mention'd *Friend*.

W H Y should I go upon farther Particulars, which might fill a Volume with the just Elogies of my cotemporary Brethren? I shall bequeath this Piece of Justice to a larger Work: wherein I intend to write a Character of the present Set of *Wits* in our Nation: Their

Persons I shall describe particularly, and at Length, their Genius and Understandings in *Mignature*.

I N the mean time, I do here make bold to present *Your Highness* with a faithful Abstract drawn from the Universal Body of all Arts and Sciences, intended wholly for your Service and Instruction: Nor do I doubt in the least, but *Your Highness* will peruse it as carefully, and make as considerable Improvements, as *other* young *Princes* have already done by the many Volumes of late Years written for a Help to their Studies.

THAT *Your Highness* may advance in Wisdom and Virtue, as well as Years, and at last out-shine all Your Royal Ancestors, shall be the daily Prayer of,

S I R,

Decemb.
1697.

Your Highness's

Most devoted, &c.

The Preface

THE Wits of the present Age being so very numerous and penetrating, it seems, the Grandees of *Church* and *State* begin to fall under horrible Apprehensions, lest these Gentlemen, during the intervals of a long Peace, should find leisure to pick Holes in the weak sides of Religion and Government. To prevent which, there has been much Thought employ'd of late upon certain Projects for taking off the Force, and Edge of those formidable Enquirers, from canvasing and reasoning upon such delicate Points. They have at length fixed upon one, which will require some Time as well as Cost, to perfect. Mean while the Danger hourly increasing, by new Levies of Wits all appointed (as there is Reason to fear) with Pen, Ink, and Paper which may at an hours Warning be drawn out into Pamphlets, and other Offensive Weapons, ready for immediate Execution: It was judged of absolute necessity, that some present Expedient be thought on, till the main Design can be brought to Maturity. To this End, at a Grand Committee, some Days ago, this important Discovery was made by a certain curious and refined Observer; That Sea-men have a Custom when they meet a *Whale*, to fling him out an empty *Tub*, by way of Amusement, to divert him from laying violent Hands upon the Ship. This Parable was immediately mythologiz'd: The *Whale* was interpreted to be *Hobbes's Leviathan*, which tosses and plays with all other Schemes of Religion and Government, whereof a great many are hollow, and dry, and empty, and noisy, and wooden, and given to Rotation, This is the *Leviathan* from whence the terrible Wits of our Age are said to borrow their Weapons. The *Ship* in danger, is easily understood to be its old Antitype the *Commonwealth*. But, how to analyze the *Tub*, was a Matter of difficulty; when after long Enquiry and Debate, the literal Meaning was preserved: And it was decreed, that in order to prevent these *Leviathans* from tossing and sporting with the *Commonwealth*, (which of it self is too apt to *fluctuate*) they should be diverted from that Game by a *Tale of a Tub*. And my Genius being conceived to lye not unhappily that way, I had the Honor done me to be engaged in the Performance.

THIS is the sole Design in publishing the following Treatise, which I hope will serve for an *Interim* of some Months to employ those unquiet Spirits, till the perfecting of that great Work: into the Secret of which, it is reasonable the courteous Reader should have some little Light.

IT is intended that a large Academy be erected, capable of containing nine thousand seven hundred forty and three Persons; which by modest Computation is reckoned to be pretty near the current Number of *Wits* in this Island. These are to be disposed into the several Schools of this Academy, and there pursue those Studies to which their Genius most inclines them. The Undertaker himself will publish his Proposals with all convenient speed, to which I shall refer the curious Reader for a more particular Account, mentioning at present only a few of the Principal Schools. There is first, a large *Pederastick* School, with *French* and *Italian* Masters. There is also, the *Spelling* School, *a very spacious Building*: the School of *Looking Glasses*: The School of *Swearing*: the School of *Criticks*: the School of *Salivation*: The School of *Hobby-Horses*: The School of *Poetry*:* The School of *Tops*: The School of *Spleen*: The School of *Gaming*: with many others too tedious to recount. No Person to be admitted Member into any of these Schools, without an Attestation under two sufficient Persons Hands, certifying him to be a *Wit*.

B U T, to return. I am sufficiently instructed in the Principal Duty of a Preface, if my Genius were capable of arriving at it. Thrice have I forced my Imagination to make the *Tour* of my Invention, and thrice it has returned empty; the latter having been wholly drained by the following Treatise. Not so, my more successful Brethren the *Moderns*, who will by no means let slip a Preface or Dedication, without some notable distinguishing Stroke, to surprize the Reader at the Entry, and kindle a Wonderful Expectation of what is to ensue. Such was that of a most ingenious Poet, who solliciting his Brain for something new, compared himself to the *Hangman*, and his Patron to the *Patient*: This was † *Insigne, recono, indictum ore alio,*   † *Hor.*
When I went thro' That necessary and noble || Course of Study, I had the happiness to observe many such egregious Touches, || *Reading Prefaces*, &c.
which I shall not injure the Authors by transplanting: Because I have remarked, that nothing is so very tender as a *Modern* Piece of Wit, and which is apt to suffer so much in the Carriage. Some things are extreamly witty *to day*, or *fasting*, or *in this place*, or *at eight a clock*, or *over a Bottle*, or *spoke by Mr.* What d'y'call'm, or *in a Summer's Morning*: Any of which, by the smallest Transposal or Misapplication, is utterly annihilate. Thus, *Wit* has its Walks and Purlieus, out of which it may not stray the breadth

---

* *This I think the Author should have omitted, it being of the very same Nature with the School of Hobby-Horses, if one may venture to censure one who is so severe a Censurer of others, perhaps with too little Distinction.*
† *Something extraordinary, new and never hit upon before.*

of an Hair, upon peril of being lost. The *Moderns* have artfully
fixed this *Mercury*, and reduced it to the Circumstances of Time,
Place and Person. Such a Jest there is, that will not pass out of
Covent-Garden; and such a one, that is no where intelligible but
at *Hide-Park* Corner. Now, tho' it sometimes tenderly affects me to
consider, that all the towardly Passages I shall deliver in the following Treatise, will grow quite out of date and relish with the first
shifting of the present Scene: yet I must need subscribe to the
Justice of this Proceeding: because, I cannot imagine why we
should be at Expence to furnish Wit for succeeding Ages, when the
former have made no sort of Provision for ours; wherein I speak the
Sentiment of the very newest, and consequently the most Orthodox
Refiners, as well as my own. However, being extreamly sollicitous,
that every accomplished Person who has got into the Taste of Wit,
calculated for this present Month of *August,* 1697, should descend
to the very *bottom* of all the *Sublime* throughout this Treatise; I
hold fit to lay down this general Maxim. Whatever Reader desires
to have a thorow Comprehension of an Author's Thoughts, cannot
take a better Method, than by putting himself into the Circumstances and Postures of Life, that the Writer was in, upon every
important Passage as it flow'd from his Pen; For this will introduce
a Parity and strict Correspondence of Idea's between the Reader
and the Author. Now, to assist the diligent Reader in so delicate an
Affair, as far as brevity will permit, I have recollected, that the
shrewdest Pieces of this Treatise, were conceived in Bed, in a Garret: At other times (for a Reason best known to my self) I thought
fit to sharpen my Invention with Hunger; and in general, the whole
Work was begun, continued, and ended, under a long Course of
Physick, and a great want of Money. Now, I do affirm, it will be
absolutely impossible for the candid Peruser to go along with me in
a great many bright Passages, unless upon the several Difficulties
emergent, he will please to capacitate and prepare himself by these
Directions. And this I lay down as my principal *Postulatum.*

B E C A U S E I have profess'd to be a most devoted Servant of all
Modern Forms: I apprehend some curious *Wit* may object against
me, for proceeding thus far in a Preface, without declaiming,
according to the Custom, against the Multitude of Writers whereof
the whole Multitude of Writers most reasonably complains. I am
just come from perusing some hundreds of Prefaces, wherein the
Authors do at the very beginning address the gentle Reader concerning this enormous Grievance. Of these I have preserved a few
Examples, and shall set them down as near as my Memory has been
able to retain them.

One begins thus;

For a Man to set up for a Writer, when the Press swarms with, &c.

Another;

The Tax upon Paper does not lessen the Number of Scriblers, who daily pester, &c.

Another;

When every little Would-be-wit takes Pen in hand, 'tis in vain to enter the Lists, &c.

Another;

To observe what Trash the Press swarms with, &c.

Another;

S I R, It is meerly in Obedience to your Commands that I venture into the Publick; for who upon a less Consideration would be of a Party with such a Rabble of Scriblers, &c.

N O W, I have two Words in my own Defence, against this Objection. First: I am far from granting the Number of Writers, a Nuisance to our Nation, having strenuously maintained the contrary in several Parts of the following Discourse. Secondly: I do not well understand the Justice of this Proceeding, because I observe many of these polite Prefaces, to be not only from the same Hand, but from those who are most voluminous in their several Productions. Upon which I shall tell the Reader a short Tale.

A Mountebank in Leicester-Fields, *had drawn a huge Assembly about him. Among the rest, a fat unweildy Fellow, half stifled in the Press, would be every fit crying out, Lord! what a filthy Crowd is here? Pray, good People, give way a little, Bless me! what a Devil has rak'd this Rabble together: Z——ds, what squeezing is this! Honest Friend, remove your Elbow. At last, a* Weaver *that stood next him could hold no longer: A Plague confound you* (said he) *for an over-grown Sloven; and who* (in the Devil's Name) *I wonder, helps to make up the Crowd half so much as yourself? Don't you consider* (with a Pox) *that you take up more room with that Carkass than any five here? Is not the Place as free for us as for you? Bring your own Guts to a reasonable Compass* (and be d——n'd) *and then I'll engage we shall have room enough for us all.*

T H E R E are certain common Privileges of a Writer, the Benefit whereof, I hope, there will be no Reason to doubt; Particularly, that where I am not understood, it shall be concluded, that something very useful and profound is coucht underneath, And again, that whatever word or Sentence is Printed in a different Character, shall be judged to contain something extraordinary either of *Wit* or *Sublime.*

A S for the Liberty I have thought fit to take of praising my self, upon some Occasions or none; I am sure it will need no Excuse, if a Multitude of great Examples be allowed sufficient Authority: For it is here to be noted, that *Praise* was originally a Pension paid by the World: but the *Moderns* finding the Trouble and Charge too great in collecting it, have lately bought out the *Fee-Simple*; since which time, the Right of Presentation is wholly in our selves. For this Reason it is, that when an Author makes his own Elogy, he uses a certain form to declare and insist upon his Title, which is commonly in these or the like words, *I speak without Vanity*; which I think plainly shews it to be a Matter of Right and Justice. Now, I do here once for all declare, that in every Encounter of this Nature, thro' the following Treatise, the Form aforesaid is imply'd; which I mention, to save the Trouble of repeating it on so many Occasions.

'TIS a great Ease to my Conscience that I have writ so elaborate and useful a Discourse without one grain of Satyr intermixt; which is the sole point wherein I have taken leave to dissent from the famous Originals of our Age and Country. I have observ'd some Satyrists to use the Publick much at the Rate that Pedants do a naughty Boy ready Hors'd for Discipline: First expostulate the Case, then plead the Necessity of the Rod, from great Provocations, and conclude every Period with a Lash. Now, if I know any thing of Mankind, these Gentlemen might very well spare their Reproof and Correction: For there is not, through all Nature, another so callous and insensible a Member as the *World's Posteriors*, whether you apply to it the *Toe* or the *Birch*. Besides, most of our late Satyrists seem to lye under a sort of Mistake, that because Nettles have the Prerogative to Sting, therefore all *other Weeds* must do so too. I make not this Comparison out of the least Design to detract from these worthy Writers: For it is well known among *Mythologists*, that *Weeds* have the Preeminence over all other Vegetables; and therefore the first *Monarch* of this Island,[24] whose Taste and Judgment were so acute and refined, did very wisely root out the *Roses* from the Collar of the *Order*, and plant the *Thistles*[25] in their stead as the nobler Flower of the two. For which Reason it is conjectured by profounder Antiquaries, that the Satyrical Itch, so prevalent in this part of our Island, was first brought among us from beyond the *Tweed*. Here may it long flourish and abound; May it survive and neglect the Scorn of the World, with as much Ease and Contempt as the World is insensible to the Lashes of it. May their own Dullness, or that of their Party, be no Discouragement for the Authors to proceed; but let them remember, it is with *Wits* as with *Razors*, which are never so apt to *cut* those they are employ'd on, as when they have *lost their Edge*. Besides, those whose Teeth are too rotten to bite, are best of all others, qualified to revenge that Defect with their Breath.

I am not like other Men, to envy or undervalue the Talents I cannot reach; for which Reason I must needs bear a true Honour to this large eminent Sect of our *British* Writers. And I hope, this little Panegyrick will not be offensive to their Ears, since it has the Advantage of being only designed for themselves. Indeed, Nature her self has taken order, that Fame and Honour should be purchased at a better Pennyworth by Satyr, than by any other Productions of the Brain; the World being soonest provoked to *Praise* by *Lashes*, as Men are to *Love*. There is a Problem in an ancient Author, why Dedications, and other Bundles of Flattery run all upon stale musty Topicks, without the smallest Tincture of any thing New; not only to the torment and nauseating of the *Christian* Reader, but (if not suddenly prevented) to the universal spreading of that pestilent Disease, the Lethargy, in this Island: whereas, there is very little Satyr which has not something in it untouch'd before, The Defects of the former are usually imputed to the want of Invention among those who are Dealers in that kind: But, I think, with a great deal of Injustice; the Solution being easy and natural. For, the Materials of Panegyrick being very few in Number, have been long since exhausted: For, as Health is but one Thing, and has been always the same, whereas Diseases are by thousands, besides new and daily Additions; So, all the Virtues that have been ever in Mankind, are to be counted upon a few Fingers, but his Follies and Vices are innumerable, and Time adds hourly to the Heap. Now, the utmost a poor Poet can do, is to get by heart a List of the Cardinal Virtues, and deal them with his utmost Liberality to his Hero or his Patron: He may ring the Changes as far as it will go, and vary his Phrase till he has talk'd round; but the Reader quickly finds, it is all * *Pork*, with a little variety of Sawce: For there is no   * *Plutarch.* inventing Terms of Art beyond our Idea's; and when Idea's are exhausted, Terms of Art must be so too.

B U T, tho' the Matter for Panegyrick were as fruitful as the Topicks of Satyr, yet would it not be hard to find out a sufficient Reason, why the latter will be always better received than the first. For, this being bestowed only upon one or a few Persons at a time, is sure to raise Envy, and consequently ill words from the rest, who have no share in the Blessing: But Satyr being levelled at all, is never resented for an offence by any, since every individual Person makes bold to understand it of others, and very wisely removes his particular Part of the Burthen upon the shoulders of the World, which are broad enough, and able to bear it. To this purpose, I have sometimes reflected upon the Difference between *Athens* and *England,* with respect to the Point before us. In the Attick * Commonwealth, it was the Privilege and Birth-right of every Citizen and Poet, to rail aloud and in publick, or to expose upon the Stage by Name, any Person they pleased, tho' of the greatest Figure, whether a *Creon,* an *Hyperbolus,* an *Alcibiades,* or a *Demosthenes*: But on the other side, the least reflecting word let fall against the *People* in general, was immediately caught up, and revenged upon the Authors, however considerable for their Quality or their Merits. Whereas, in *England* it is just the Reverse of all this. Here, you may securely display your utmost *Rhetorick* against Mankind, in the Face of the World; tell them, *"That all are gone astray; That there is none that doth good, no not one; That we live in the very Dregs of Time; That Knavery and Atheism are Epidemick as the Pox; That Honesty is fled with Astræa"*; with any other Common places *equally* new and eloquent, which are furnished by the † *Splendida bilis.*[26] And when you have done, the whole Audience, far from being offended, shall return you thanks as a Deliverer of precious and useful Truths. Nay farther; It is but to venture your Lungs, and you may preach in *Covent-Garden* against Foppery and Fornication, and *something else*: Against Pride, and Dissimulation, and Bribery, at *White Hall*: You may expose Rapine and Injustice in the *Inns* of *Court* Chappel: And in a *City* Pulpit be as fierce as you please, against Avarice, Hypocrisie and Extortion. 'Tis but a *Ball* bandied to and fro, and every Man carries a *Racket* about Him to strike it from himself among the rest of the Company. But on the other side, whoever should mistake the Nature of things so far, as to drop but a single Hint in publick, How *such a one,* starved half the Fleet, and half-poison'd the rest: How *such a one,* from a true Principle of *Love* and *Honour,* pays no Debts but for *Wenches* and *Play*: How *such a one* has got a Clap and runs out of his Estate: || How *Paris* bribed by *Juno* and *Venus,* loath to offend either Party, slept out the whole Cause on the Bench: Or, how *such an Orator* makes long Speeches in the Senate with much Thought, little Sense, and to no Purpose; whoever, I say, should venture to be thus particular, must expect to be imprisoned for *Scandalum Magnatum*: to have *Challenges* sent him; to be sued for *Defamation*; and to be *brought before the Bar of the House.*

BUT I forget that I am expatiating on a Subject, wherein I have

* *Vid. Xenoph.*

† *Hor.*

---

† *Spleen.*
|| *Juno and* Venus *are Money and a Mistress, very powerful Bribes to a Judge, if Scandal says true. I remember such Reflexions were cast about that time, but I cannot fix the Person intended here.*

no concern, having neither a Talent nor an Inclination for Satyr. On the other side, I am so entirely satisfied with the whole present Procedure of human Things, that I have been for some Years preparing Materials towards *A Panegyrick upon the World*; to which I intended to add a Second Part, entituled, *A Modest Defence of the Proceedings of the Rabble in all Ages*. Both these I had Thoughts to publish by way of Appendix to the following Treatise; but finding my Common-Place-Book fill much slower than I had reason to expect, I have chosen to defer them to another Occasion. Besides, I have been unhappily prevented in that Design, by a certain Domestick Misfortune, in the Particulars whereof, tho' it would be very seasonable, and much in the *Modern* way, to inform the *gentle Reader*, and would also be of great Assistance towards extending this Preface into the Size now in Vogue, which by Rule ought to be *large* in proportion as the subsequent Volume is *small*; Yet I shall now dismiss our impatient Reader from any farther Attendance at the *Porch*; and having duly prepared his Mind by a preliminary Discourse, shall gladly introduce him to the sublime Mysteries that ensue.

A Tale of a Tub, &c.

SECT. I. *The Introduction*

WHOEVER hath an Ambition to be heard in a Crowd, must press, and squeeze, and thrust, and climb with indefatigable Pains, till he has exalted himself to a certain Degree of Altitude above them. Now, in all Assemblies, tho' you wedge them ever so close, we may observe this peculiar Property; that, over their Heads there is Room enough; but how to reach it, is the difficult Point; It being as hard to get quit of *Number* as of *Hell*;

> * ———— *Evadere ad auras,*
> *Hoc opus, hic labor est.*[27]

TO this End, the Philosopher's Way in all Ages has been by erecting certain *Edifices in the Air;* But, whatever Practice and Reputation these kind of Structures have formerly possessed, or may still continue in, not excepting even that of *Socrates,* when he was suspended in a Basket to help Contemplation; I think, with due Submission, they seem to labour under two Inconveniences. *First,* That the Foundations being laid too high, they have been often out of *Sight,* and ever out of *Hearing. Secondly,* That the Materials, being very transitory, have suffer'd much from Inclemencies of Air, especially in these North-West Regions.

THEREFORE, towards the just Performance of this great Work, there remain but three Methods that I can think on; Whereof the Wisdom of our Ancestors being highly sensible, has, to encourage all aspiring Adventurers, thought fit to erect three wooden Machines, for the Use of those Orators who desire to talk much without Interruption. These are, the *Pulpit,* the *Ladder,* and the *Stage-Itinerant.* For, as to the *Bar,* tho' it be compounded of the same Matter, and designed for the same Use, it cannot however be well allowed the Honor of a fourth, by reason of its level or inferior Situation, exposing it to perpetual Interruption from Collaterals. Neither can the *Bench* it self, tho raised to a proper Eminency, put in a better Claim, whatever its Advocates insist on. For if they please to look into the original Design of its Erection, and the Circumstances or Adjuncts subservient to that Design, they will soon acknowledge the present Practice exactly correspondent to the Prim-

---

* *But to return, and view the cheerful Skies;*
In this the Task and mighty Labour lies.

itive Institution, and both to answer the Etymology of the Name, which in the *Phœnician* Tongue is a Word of great Signification, importing, if literally interpreted, *The Place of Sleep*; but in common Acceptation, *A Seat well bolster'd and cushion'd, for the Repose of old and gouty Limbs: Senes ut in otia tuta recedant.*[28] Fortune being indebted to them this Part of Retaliation, that, as formerly, they have long *Talkt*, whilst others *Slept*, so now they may *Sleep* as long whilst others *Talk*.

BUT if no other Argument could occur to exclude the *Bench* and the *Bar* from the List of Oratorial Machines, it were sufficient, that the Admission of them would overthrow a Number which I was resolved to establish, whatever Argument it might cost me; in imitation of that prudent Method observed by many other Philosophers and great Clerks, whose chief Art in Division has been, to grow fond of some proper mystical Number, which their Imaginations have rendred Sacred, to a Degree, that they force common Reason to find room for it in every part of Nature; reducing, including, and adjusting every *Genus* and *Species* within that Compass, by coupling some against their Wills, and banishing others at any Rate. Now among all the rest, the profound Number *T H R E E* is that which hath most employ'd my sublimest Speculations, nor ever without wonderful Delight. There is now in the Press, (and will be publish'd next Term) a Panegyrical Essay of mine upon this Number, wherein I have by most convincing Proofs, not only reduced the *Senses* and the *Elements* under its Banner, but brought over several Deserters from its two great Rivals *S E V E N* and *N I N E*.

N O W, the first of these Oratorial Machines[29] in Place as well as Dignity, is the *Pulpit*. Of *Pulpits* there are in this Island several sorts; but I esteem only That made of Timber from the *Sylva Caledonia*,[30] which agrees very well with our Climate. If it be upon its Decay, 'tis the better, both for Conveyance of Sound, and for other Reasons to be mentioned by and by. The Degree of Perfection in Shape and Size, I take to consist, in being extreamly narrow, with little Ornament, and best of all without a Cover; (for by antient Rule, it ought to be the only uncover'd *Vessel* in every Assembly where it is rightfully used) by which means, from its near Resemblance to a Pillory, it will ever have a mighty influence on human Ears.[31]

OF *Ladders* I need say nothing: 'Tis observed by Foreigners themselves, to the Honor of our Country, that we excel all Nations in our Practice and Understanding of this Machine. The ascending Orators do not only oblige their Audience in the agreeable Delivery, but the whole World in their *early* Publication of these Speeches; which I look upon as the choicest Treasury of our *British* Eloquence, and whereof I am informed, that worthy Citizen and Bookseller, Mr. *John Dunton,* hath made a faithful and a painful Collection, which he shortly designs to publish in Twelve Volumes in Folio, illustrated with Copper-Plates. A Work highly useful and curious, and altogether worthy of such a Hand.

T H E last Engine of Orators, is the * *Stage Itinerant,* erected with much Sagacity, † *sub Jove pluvio, in triviis & quadriviis.* It is the great Seminary of the two former, and its Orators are sometimes preferred to the One, and sometimes to the Other, in proportion to their Deservings, there being a strict and perpetual Intercourse between all three.

F R O M this accurate Deduction it is manifest, that for obtaining Attention in Publick, there is of necessity required a *superiour Position of Place.* But, altho' this Point be generally granted, yet the Cause is little agreed in; and it seems to me, that very few Philosophers have fallen into a true, natural Solution of this *Phænomenon.* The deepest Account, and the most fairly digested of any I have yet met with, is this, That Air being a heavy Body, and therefore (according to the System of * *Epicurus*) continually descending, must needs be more so, when loaden and press'd down by Words; which   * *Lucret.* Lib.2, are also Bodies of much Weight and Gravity, as it is manifest from those deep *Impressions* they make and leave upon us; and therefore must be delivered from a due Altitude, or else they will neither carry a good Aim, nor fall down with a sufficient Force.

|| *Corpoream quoque enim vocem constare fatendum est,*
Et sonitum, quoniam possunt impellere Sensus. Lucr. Lib.4.[32]

AND I am the readier to favour this Conjecture, from a common Observation; that in the several Assemblies of these Orators, Nature it self hath instructed the Hearers, to stand with their Mouths open, and erected parallel to the Horizon, so as they may be intersected by a perpendicular Line from the Zenith to the Center of the Earth. In which Position, if the Audience be well compact, every one carries home a Share, and little or nothing is lost.

I confess, there is something yet more refined in the Contrivance and Structure of our Modern Theatres. For, First; the Pit is sunk

---

* *Is the* Mountebank's Stage, *whose Orators the Author determines either to the* Gallows *or a* Conventicle.
† *In the open Air, and in Streets where the greatest Resort is.*
|| *'Tis certain then, that* Voice *that thus can wound*
Is all Material; Body *every* Sound.

below the Stage with due regard to the Institution above-deduced; that whatever *weighty* Matter shall be delivered thence (whether it be *Lead* or *Gold*) may fall plum into the Jaws of certain *Criticks* (as I think they are called) which stand ready open to devour them. Then, the Boxes are built round, and raised to a Level with the Scene, in deference to the Ladies, because, That large Portion of Wit laid out in raising Pruriences and Protuberances, is observ'd to run much upon a Line, and ever in a Circle. The whining Passions and little starved Conceits, are gently wafted up by their own extreme Levity, to the middle Region, and there fix and are frozen by the frigid Understandings of the Inhabitants. Bombast and Buffoonry, by Nature lofty and light, soar highest of all, and would be lost in the Roof, if the prudent Architect had not with much Foresight contrived for them a fourth Place, called *the Twelve-Peny Gallery*, and there planted a suitable Colony, who greedily intercept them in their Passage.

N O W this Physico-logical Scheme of Oratorial Receptacles or Machines, contains a great Mystery, being a Type, a Sign, an Emblem, a Shadow, a Symbol, bearing Analogy to the spacious Commonwealth of Writers,[33] and to those Methods by which they must exalt themselves to a certain Eminency above the inferiour World. By the *Pulpit* are adumbrated the Writings of our *Modern Saints*[34] in *Great Britain*, as they have spiritualized and refined them from the Dross and Grossness of *Sense* and *Human Reason*. The Matter, as we have said, is of rotten Wood, and that upon two Considerations; Because it is the Quality of rotten Wood to give *Light* in the Dark: And secondly, Because its Cavities are full of Worms: which is a * Type with a Pair of Handles, having a Respect to the two principal Qualifications of the Orator, and the two different Fates attending upon his Works.

THE *Ladder* is an adequate Symbol of *Faction* and of *Poetry*, to both of which so noble a Number of Authors are indebted for their Fame. Of *Faction*, because † * * * * * * * *
* * * * * * * * * * * * * *   *Hiatus in MS.*
* * * * * * * * * * * * * * * * * *
* * * * * * * * * * * * * * * * * *
* * * * * * * * * * * * * * * * * *

Of *Poetry*, because its Orators do *perorare*[35] with a Song; and

---

* *The Two Principal Qualifications of a Phanatick Preacher are, his Inward Light, and his Head full of Maggots, and the Two different Fates of his Writings are, to be burnt or Worm eaten.*
† *Here is pretended a Defect in the Manuscript, and this is very frequent with our Author, either when he thinks he cannot say any thing worth Reading, or when he has no mind to enter on the Subject, or when it is a Matter of little Moment, or perhaps to amuse his Reader (whereof he is frequently very fond) or lastly, with some Satyrical Intention.*

because climbing up by slow Degrees, Fate is sure to turn them off before they can reach within many Steps of the Top: And because it is a Preferment attained by transferring of Propriety, and a confounding of *Meum* and *Tuum*.[36]

UNDER the *Stage-Itinerant* are couched those Productions designed for the Pleasure and Delight of Mortal Man; such as, *Sixpeny-worth of Wit*, Westminster *Drolleries, Delightful Tales, Compleat Jesters*, and the like; by which the Writers of and for G R U B-STREET, have in these latter Ages so nobly triumph'd over *Time*; have clipt his Wings, pared his Nails, filed his Teeth, turn'd back his Hour-Glass, blunted his Scythe, and drawn the Hob-Nails out of his Shoes. It is under this Classis, I have presumed to list my present Treatise, being just come from having the Honor conferred upon me, to be adopted a Member of that Illustrious Fraternity.

NOW, I am not unaware, how the Productions of the *Grub-street* Brotherhood, have of late Years fallen under many Prejudices, nor how it has been the perpetual Employment of two *Junior* start-up Societies, to ridicule them and their Authors, as unworthy their established Post in the Commonwealth of Wit and Learning. Their own Consciences will easily inform them, whom I mean; Nor has the World been so negligent a Looker on, as not to observe the continual Efforts made by the Societies of *Gresham*[37] *and of* * *Will's* to edify a Name and Reputation upon the Ruin of O U R S. And this is yet a more feeling Grief to Us upon the Regards of Tenderness as well as of Justice, when we reflect on their Proceedings, not only as unjust, but as ungrateful, undutiful, and unnatural. For, how can it be forgot by the World or themselves, (to say nothing of our Records, which are full and clear in the Point) that they both are Seminaries, not only of our *Planting*, but our *Watering* too? I am informed, Our two *Rivals* have lately made an Offer to enter into the Lists with united Forces, and Challenge us to a Comparison of Books, both as to *Weight* and *Number*. In Return to which, (with Licence from our *President*) I humbly offer two Answers: First, We say, the proposal is like that which *Archimedes* made upon a * *smaller* Affair, including an impossibility in the Practice; For, where can   * Viz. *About* they find Scales of *Capacity* enough for the   *moving the Earth.* first, or an Arithmetician of *Capacity* enough for the Second. Secondly, We are ready to accept the Challenge, but with this Condition, that a third indifferent Person be assigned, to whose impartial Judgment it shall be left to decide, which Society each Book, Trea-

---

* *Will's* Coffee-House, *was formerly the Place where the Poets usually met, which tho it be yet fresh in memory, yet in some Years may be forgot, and want this Explanation.*

tise or Pamphlet do most properly belong to. This Point, God knows, is very far from being fixed at present; For, We are ready to produce a Catalogue of some Thousands, which in all common Justice ought to be entitled to Our Fraternity, but by the revolted and new-fangled Writers, most perfidiously ascribed to the others. Upon all which, we think it very unbecoming our Prudence, that the Determination should be remitted to the Authors themselves; when our Adversaries by Briguing[38] and Caballing, have caused so universal a Defection from us, that the greatest Part of our Society hath already deserted to them, and our nearest Friends begin to stand aloof, as if they were half-ashamed to own Us.

THIS is the utmost I am authorized to say upon so ungrateful and melancholy a Subject; because We are extreme unwilling to inflame a Controversy, whose Continuance may be so fatal to the Interests of Us All, desiring much rather that Things be amicably composed; and We shall so far advance on our Side, as to be ready to receive the two *Prodigals* with open Arms, whenever they shall think fit to return from their *Husks* and their *Harlots*; which I think from the * present Course of their Studies they most properly may be said to be engaged in; and like an indulgent Parent, continue to them our Affection and our Blessing.

* *Virtuoso Experiments, and Modern Comedies.*

BUT the greatest Maim[39] given to that general Reception, which the Writings of our Society have formerly received, (next to the transitory State of all sublunary Things,) hath been a superficial Vein among many Readers of the present Age, who will by no means be persuaded to inspect beyond the Surface and the Rind of Things; whereas, *Wisdom* is a *Fox*, who after long hunting, will at last cost you the Pains to dig out: 'Tis a *Cheese*, which by how much the richer, has the thicker, the homelier, and the courser Coat; and whereof to a judicious Palate, the *Maggots* are the best. 'Tis a *Sack-Posset*, wherein the deeper you go, you will find it the sweeter. *Wisdom* is a *Hen*, whose *Cackling* we must value and consider, because it is attended with an *Egg*; But then, lastly, 'tis a *Nut*, which unless you chuse with Judgment, may cost you a Tooth, and pay you with nothing but a *Worm*. In consequence of these momentous Truths, the *Grubæan* Sages have always chosen to convey their Precepts and their Arts, shut up within the Vehicles of Types and Fables, which having been perhaps more careful and curious in adorning, than was altogether necessary, it has fared with these Vehicles after the usual Fate of Coaches over-finely painted and gilt; that the transitory Gazers have so dazzled their Eyes, and fill'd their Imaginations with the outward Lustre, as neither to regard or consider, the Person or the Parts of the Owner within. A Misfortune we undergo with somewhat less Reluctancy, because it has been common to us with *Pythagoras, Æsop, Socrates,* and other of our Predecessors.

HOWEVER, that neither the World nor our selves may any longer suffer by such misunderstandings, I have been prevailed on, after much importunity from my Friends, to travel in a compleat and laborious Dissertation upon the prime Productions of our Society, which besides their beautiful Externals for the Gratification of superficial Readers, have darkly and deeply couched under them, the most finished and refined Systems of all Sciences and Arts; as I do not doubt to lay open by Untwisting or Unwinding, and either to draw up by Exantlation,[40] or display by Incision.

THIS great Work was entred upon some Years ago, by one of our most eminent Members: He began with the History of † *Reynard* the *Fox,* but neither lived to publish his Essay, nor to proceed farther in so useful an Attempt which is very much to be lamented, because the Discovery he made, and communicated with his Friends, is now universally received; nor, do I think, any of the Learned will dispute, that famous Treatise to be a compleat Body of Civil Knowledge, and the *Revelation,* or rather the *Apocalyps* of all State-*Arcana.* But the Progress I have made is much greater, having already finished my Annotations upon several Dozens; From some of which, I shall impart a few Hints to the candid Reader, as far as will be necessary to the Conclusion at which I aim.

THE first Piece I have handled is that of *Tom Thumb,*[41] whose Author was a *Pythagorean* Philosopher. This dark Treatise contains the whole Scheme of the *Metampsycosis,* deducing the Progress of the Soul thro' all her Stages.

THE next is Dr. *Faustus,* penn'd by *Artephius,* an Author *honæ notæ,* and an *Adeptus;*[42] He published it in the * nine hundred eighty fourth Year of his   * *He lived a thousand.*[43] Age; this Writer proceeds wholly by *Reincrudation,* or in the *via humida*: And the Marriage between *Faustus* and *Helen,* does most conspicuously dilucidate the fermenting of the *Male* and *Female Dragon.*

WHITTINGTON *and his Cat,* is the Work of that Mysterious *Rabbi, Jehuda Hannasi,* containing a Defence of the *Gemara* of the *Jerusalem Misna,* and its just preference to that of *Babylon,* contrary to the vulgar Opinion.

† *The Author seems here to be mistaken, for I have seen a Latin Edition of* Reynard *the* Fox, *above an hundred Years old, which I take to be the Original; for the rest it has been thought by many People to contain some Satyrical Design in it.*

THE *Hind and Panther*. This is the Master-piece of a famous Writer † now living, intended for a compleat Abstract of sixteen thousand School-

† *Viz* **in the Year 1698.**

men from *Scotus* to *Bellarmin*.

TOMMY POTTS. Another Piece supposed by the same Hand, by way of Supplement to the former.

THE *Wise Men of* Goatham,[44] *cum Appendice*. This is a Treatise of immense Erudition, being the great Original and Fountain of those Arguments, bandied about both in *France* and *England*, for a just Defence of the *Modern* Learning and Wit, against the Presumption, the Pride, and the Ignorance of the *Antients*. This unknown Author hath so exhausted the Subject, that a penetrating Reader will easily discover, whatever hath been written since upon that Dispute, to be little more than Repetition. * An Abstract of this Treatise hath been lately published by a *worthy Member* of our Society.

THESE Notices may serve to give the Learned Reader an Idea as well as a Taste of what the whole Work is likely to produce: wherein I have now altogether circumscribed my Thoughts and my Studies; and if I can bring it to a Perfection before I die, shall reckon I have well employ'd the † poor Remains of an unfortunate Life. This indeed is more than I can justly expect from a Quill worn to the Pith in the Service of the State, in *Pro's* and *Con's* upon *Popish Plots*, and || *Meal-Tubs*, and *Exclusion Bills*, and *Passive Obedience*, and *Addresses of Lives and Fortunes*; and *Prerogative*, and *Property*, and *Liberty of Conscience*, and *Letters to a Friend*: From an Understanding and a Conscience, thread-bare and ragged with perpetual turning; From a Head broken in a hundred places, by the Malignants of the opposite Factions, and from a Body spent with Poxes ill cured, by trusting to Bawds and Surgeons, who, (as it afterwards appeared) were profess'd Enemies to Me and the Government, and revenged their Party's Quarrel upon my Nose and Shins. Four-score and eleven Pamphlets have I written under three Reigns, and for the Service of six and thirty Factions. But finding the State has no farther Occasion for Me and my Ink, I retire willingly to draw it out into Speculations more becoming a Philosopher, having, to my unspeakable Comfort, passed a long Life, with a Conscience void of Offence.

BUT to return. I am assured from the Reader's Candor, that the

---

* *This I suppose to be understood of Mr.* W—tt—ns *Discourse of Antient and Modern Learning.*
† *Here the Author seems to personate L'estrange, Dryden, and some others, who after having past their Lives in Vices, Faction and Falshood, have the Impudence to talk of Merit and Innocence and Sufferings.*
|| *In King* Charles *the* II. *Time, there was an Account of a* Presbyterian *Plot, found in a* Tub, *which then made much Noise.*

brief Specimen I have given, will easily clear all the rest of our
Society's Productions from an Aspersion grown, as it is manifest,
out of Envy and Ignorance: That they are of little farther Use or
Value to Mankind, beyond the common Entertainments of their
Wit and their Style: For these I am sure have never yet been disputed by our keenest Adversaries: In both which, as well as the
more profound and mystical Part, I have throughout this Treatise
closely followed the most applauded Originals. And to render all
compleat, I have with much Thought and Application of Mind, so
ordered, that the chief Title prefixed to it, (I mean, That under
which I design it shall pass in the common Conversations of Court
and Town) is modelled exactly after the Manner peculiar to *Our
Society.*

I confess to have been somewhat liberal in the Business
of * Titles, having observed the Humor of
multiplying them, to bear great Vogue
among certain Writers, whom I exceedingly
Reverence. And indeed, it seems not unreasonable, that Books, the Children of the

*The Title Page in the
Original was so torn, that
it was not possible to
recover several Titles
which the Author here
speaks of.*

Brain, should have the Honor to be Christned with variety of
Names, as well as other Infants of Quality. Our famous *Dryden*
has ventured to proceed a Point farther, endeavouring to introduce
also a Multiplicity of * God-fathers;[45]
which is an Improvement of much more

See Virgil translated, &c.

Advantage, upon a very obvious Account. 'Tis a Pity this admirable
Invention has not been better cultivated, so as to grow by this time
into general Imitation, when such an Authority serves it for a
Precedent. Nor have my Endeavours been wanting to second so
useful an Example: But it seems, there is an unhappy Expence
usually annexed to the Calling of a God-Father, which was clearly
out of my Head, as it is very reasonable to believe. Where the
Pinch lay, I cannot certainly affirm; but having employ'd a World
of Thoughts and Pains, to split my Treatise into forty Sections, and
having entreated forty Lords of my Acquaintance, that they would
do me the Honor to stand, they all made it a Matter of Conscience,
and sent me their Excuses.

SECTION II

ONCE upon a Time, there was a Man who had Three * Sons by
one Wife, and all at a Birth, neither could the Mid-Wife tell cer-

* *By these three Sons,* Peter, Martyn *and* Jack; Popery, *the* Church *of* England,
and our Protestant Dissenters *are designed.* W. Wotton.

tainly which was the Eldest. Their Father died while they were young, and upon his Death-Bed, calling the Lads to him, spoke thus,

SONS; *because I have purchased no Estate, nor was born to any, I have long considered of some good Legacies to bequeath You; And at last, with much Care as well as Expence, have provided each of you* (here they are) *a new* † *Coat. Now, you are to understand, that these Coats have two Virtues contained in them: One is, that with good wearing, they will last you fresh and sound as long as you live: The other is, that they will grow in the same proportion with your Bodies, lengthning and widening of themselves, so as to be always fit. Here, let me see them on you before I die. So, very well, Pray Children, wear them clean, and brush them often. You will find in my* || *Will* (here it is) *full Instructions in every particular concerning the Wearing and Management of your Coats; wherein you must be very exact, to avoid the Penalties I have appointed for every Transgression or Neglect, upon which your future Fortunes will entirely depend. I have also commanded in my Will, that you should live together in one House like Brethren and Friends, for then you will be sure to thrive, and not otherwise.*

HERE the Story says, this good Father died, and the three Sons went all together to seek their Fortunes.

I shall not trouble you with recounting what Adventures they met for the first seven Years, any farther than by taking notice, that they carefully observed their Father's Will, and kept their Coats in very good Order; That they travelled thro' several Countries, encountred a reasonable Quantity of Gyants, and slew certain Dragons.

BEING now arrived at the proper Age for producing themselves, they came up to Town, and fell in love with the Ladies, but especially three, who about that time were in chief Reputation: The * Dutchess *d'Argent, Madame de Grands Titres*, and the Countess *d'Orgueil*. On their first Appearance, our three Adventurers met with a very bad Reception; and soon with great Sagacity guessing out the Reason, they quickly began to improve in the good Qualities of the Town: They Writ, and Raillyed, and Rhymed, and Sung, and Said, and said Nothing; They Drank, and Fought, and Whor'd, and Slept, and Swore, and took Snuff: They went to new

---

† *By his Coats which he gave his Sons, the Garments of the* Israelites. W. Wotton.
    An Error (with Submission) of the learned Commentator; for by the Coats are meant the Doctrine and Faith of Christianity, *by the Wisdom of the Divine Founder fitted to all Times, Places and Circumstances*. Lambin.
|| *The New Testament.*
* *Their Mistresses are the* Dutchess d'Argent, Madamoiselle de Grands Titres, *and the* Countess d'Orgueil, *i.e.* Covetousness, Ambition *and* Pride, *which were the three great Vices that the ancient Fathers inveighed against as the first Corruptions of Christianity.* W. Wotton.

Plays on the first Night, haunted the *Chocolate*-Houses, beat the Watch, lay on Bulks, and got Claps: They bilkt Hackney-Coachmen, ran in Debt with Shop-keepers, and lay with their Wives: They kill'd Bayliffs, kick'd Fidlers down Stairs, eat at *Locket's*, loytered at *Will's*: They talk'd of the Drawing-Room and never came there, Dined with Lords they never saw; Whisper'd a Dutchess, and spoke never a Word; exposed the Scrawls of their Laundress for Billetdoux of Quality: came ever just from Court and were never seen in it; attended the Levee *sub dio*;[46] Got a list of Peers by heart in one Company, and with great Familiarity retailed them in another. Above all, they constantly attended those Committees of Senators who are silent in the *House*, and loud in the *Coffee-House*, where they nightly adjourn to chew the Cud of Politicks, and are encompass'd with a Ring of Disciples, who lye in wait to catch up their Droppings. The three Brothers had acquired forty other Qualifications of the like Stamp, too tedious to recount, and by consequence, were justly reckoned the most accomplish'd Persons in the Town: But all would not suffice, and the Ladies aforesaid continued still inflexible: To clear up which Difficulty, I must with the Reader's good Leave and Patience, have recourse to some Points of Weight, which the Authors of that Age have not sufficiently illustrated.

FOR, * about this Time it happened a Sect arose, whose Tenents obtained and spread very far, especially in the *Grand Monde*, and among every Body of good Fashion. They worshipped a sort of † *Idol*, who, as their Doctrine delivered, did daily create Men, by a kind of Manufactory Operation. This *Idol* they placed in the highest Parts of the House, on an Altar erected about three Foot: He was shewn in the Posture of a *Persian* Emperor, sitting on a *Superficies*, with his Legs interwoven under him. This God had a *Goose*[47] for his Ensign; whence it is, that some Learned Men pretend to deduce his Original from *Jupiter Capitolinus*.[48] At his left Hand, beneath the Altar, *Hell*[49] seemed to open, and catch at the Animals the *Idol* was creating; to prevent which, certain of his Priests hourly flung in Pieces of the uninformed Mass, or Substance, and sometimes whole Limbs already enlivened, which that horrid Gulph insatiably swallowed, terrible to behold. The *Goose* was also held a subaltern Divinity, or *Deus minorum Gentium*,[50] before whose Shrine was sacrificed that Creature, whose hourly Food is humane Gore, and who is in so great Renown abroad, for being the Delight and Favourite of the || *Ægyptian Cercopithecus*. Millions of these Animals were cruelly slaughtered every Day, to

* *This is an Occasional Satyr upon Dress and Fashion, in order to introduce what follows.*
† *By this* Idol *is meant a Taylor.*
|| *The Ægyptians worship'd a Monkey, which Animal is very fond of eating Lice, styled here Creatures that feed on Human Gore.*

appease the Hunger of that consuming Deity. The chief *Idol* was also worshipped as the Inventor of the *Yard* and the *Needle*, whether as the God of Seamen, or on Account of certain other mystical Attributes, hath not been sufficiently cleared.

THE Worshippers of this Deity had also a System of their Belief, which seemed to turn upon the following Fundamental. They held the Universe to be a large *Suit of Cloaths*, which *invests* every Thing: That the Earth is *invested* by the Air; The Air is *invested* by the Stars; and the Stars are *invested* by the *Primum Mobile*. Look on this Globe of Earth, you will find it to be a very compleat and fashionable *Dress*. What is that which some call *Land*, but a fine Coat faced with Green? or the Sea, but a Wastcoat of Water-Tabby?[51] Proceed to the particular Works of the Creation, you will find how curious *Journey-man* Nature hath been, to trim up the *vegetable* Beaux: Observe how sparkish a Perewig adorns the Head of a *Beech*, and what a fine Doublet of white Satin is worn by the *Birch*. To conclude from all, what is Man himself but a * *Micro-Coat*, or rather a compleat Suit of Cloaths with all its Trimmings? As to his Body, there can be no dispute; but examine even the Acquirements of his Mind, you will find them all contribute in their Order, towards furnishing out an exact Dress: To instance no more; Is not Religion a *Cloak*, Honesty a *Pair of Shoes*, worn out in the Dirt, Self-Love a *Surtout*, Vanity a *Shirt*, and Conscience a *Pair of Breeches*, which, tho' a Cover for Lewdness as well as Nastiness, is easily slipt down for the Service of both.

THESE *Postulata* being admitted, it will follow in due Course of Reasoning, that those Beings which the World calls improperly *Suits of Cloaths*, are in Reality the most refined Species of Animals, or to proceed higher, that they are Rational Creatures, or Men. For, is it not manifest, that They live, and move, and talk, and perform all other Offices of Human Life? Are not Beauty, and Wit, and Mien, and Breeding, their inseparable Proprieties? In short, we see nothing but them, hear nothing but them. Is it not they who walk the Streets, fill up *Parliament* ——, *Coffee* ——, *Play* ——, *Bawdy-Houses*? 'Tis true indeed, that these Animals, which are vulgarly called *Suits of Cloaths*, or *Dresses*, do according to certain Compositions receive different Appellations. If one of them be trimm'd up with a Gold Chain, and a red Gown, and a white Rod, and a great Horse, it is called a *Lord-Mayor*; If certain Ermins and Furs be placed in a certain Position, we stile them a *Judge*, and so, an apt Conjunction of Lawn and black Sattin, we intitle a *Bishop*.

OTHERS of these Professors though agreeing in the main

* *Alluding to the Word* Microcosm, *or a little World, as Man hath been called by Philosophers.*

System, were yet more refined upon certain Branches of it; and held that Man was an Animal compounded of two *Dresses*, the *Natural* and the *Celestial Suit*, which were the Body and the Soul: That the Soul was the outward, and the Body the inward Cloathing; that the latter was *ex traduce*;[52] but the former of daily Creation and Circumfusion. This last they proved by *Scripture*, because, *in Them we Live, and Move, and have our Being*: As likewise by Philosophy, because they are *All in All, and All in every Part*. Besides, said they, separate these two, and you will find the Body to be only a senseless unsavory Carcass. By all which it is manifest, that the outward Dress must needs be the Soul.

TO this System of Religion were tagged several subaltern Doctrines, which were entertained with great Vogue: as particularly, the Faculties of the Mind were deduced by the Learned among them in this manner: *Embroidery*, was *Sheer wit*; *Gold Fringe* was *agreeable Conversation*, *Gold Lace* was *Repartee*, a huge long *Periwig* was *Humor*, and a *Coat full of Powder* was very good *Raillery*: All which required abundance of *Finesse* and *Delicatesse* to manage with Advantage, as well as a strict Observance after Times and Fashions.

I have with much Pains and Reading, collected out of antient Authors, this short Summary of a Body of Philosophy and Divinity, which seems to have been composed by a Vein and Race of Thinking, very different from any other Systems, either *Antient* or *Modern*. And it was not meerly to entertain or satisfy the Reader's Curiosity, but rather to give him Light into several Circumstances of the following Story: that knowing the State of Dispositions and Opinions in an Age so remote, he may better comprehend those great Events which were the issue of them. I advise therefore the courteous Reader, to peruse with a world of Application, again and again, whatever I have written upon this Matter. And leaving these broken Ends, I carefully gather up the chief Thread of my Story, and proceed.

THESE Opinions therefore were so universal, as well as the Practices of them, among the refined Part of Court and Town, that our three Brother-Adventurers, as their Circumstances then stood, were strangely at a loss. * For, on the one side, the three Ladies they

* *The first part of the* Tale *is the History of* Peter; *thereby* Popery *is exposed, every Body knows the* Papists *have made great Additions to Christianity, that indeed is the great Exception which the* Church of England *makes against them, accordingly* Peter *begins his Pranks, with adding a* Shoulder-knot *to his Coat.* W. Wotton.
His Description of the Cloth of which the Coat was made, has a farther meaning than the Words may seem to import, "The Coats their Father had left them, were of very good Cloth, and besides so neatly Sown, you would swear it had been all of a Piece, but at the same time very plain with little or no Ornament." *This is the distinguishing Character of the Christian Religion.* Christiana Religio absoluta & simplex, *was* Ammianus Marcellinus's *Description of it, who was himself a Heathen.* W. Wotton.

address'd themselves to, (whom we have named already) were ever at the very Top of the Fashion, and abhorred all that were below it, but the breadth of a Hair. On the other side, their Father's Will was very precise, and it was the main Precept in it, with the greatest Penalties annexed, not to add to, or diminish from their Coats, one Thread, without a positive Command in the Will. Now, the Coats their Father had left them were, 'tis true, of very good Cloth, and besides, so neatly sown, you would swear they were all of a Piece, but at the same time, very plain, and with little or no Ornament; And it happened, that before they were a Month in Town, great * Shoulder-knots came up; Strait, all the World was Shoulder-knots; no approaching the Ladies Ruelles without the Quota of Shoulder-knots. That Fellow, cries one, has no Soul; where is his Shoulder-knot? Our three Brethren soon discovered their Want by sad Experience, meeting in their Walks with forty Mortifications and Indignities. If they went to the Play-house, the Door-keeper shewed them into the Twelve-peny Gallery. If they called a Boat, says a Water-man, I am first Sculler: If they stept to the Rose to take a Bottle, the Drawer would cry, Friend, we sell no Ale. If they went to visit a Lady, a Footman met them at the Door with, Pray send up your Message. In this unhappy Case, they went immediately to consult their Father's Will, read it over and over, but not a Word of the Shoulder-knot. What should they do? What Temper should they find? Obedience was absolutely necessary, and yet Shoulder-knots appeared extreamly requisite. After much Thought, one of the brothers who happened to be more Book-learned than the other two, said he had found an Expedient. 'Tis true, said he, there is nothing here in this Will, † totidem verbis, making mention of Shoulder-knots, but I dare conjecture, we may find them inclusivè, or totidem syllabis. This Distinction was immediately approved by all; and so they fell again to examine the Will. But their evil Star had so directed the Matter, that the first Syllable was not to be found in the whole Writing. Upon which Disappointment, he, who found the former Evasion, took heart, and said, Brothers, there is yet Hopes; for tho' we cannot find them totidem verbis, nor totidem syllabis, I dare engage we shall make them out tertio modo, or totidem literis. This Discovery was also highly commended, upon which they fell once more to the Scrutiny, and soon picked out S, H, O, U, L, D, E, R; when the same Planet, Enemy to their

---

* By this is understood the first introducing of Pageantry, and unnecessary Ornaments in the Church, such as were neither for Convenience nor Edification, as a Shoulder-knot, in which there is neither Symmetry nor Use.
† When the Papists cannot find any thing which they want in Scripture, they go to Oral Tradition: Thus Peter is introduced satisfy'd with the Tedious way of looking for all the Letters of any Word, which he has occasion for in the Will, when neither the constituent Syllables, nor much less the whole Word, were there in Terminis. W. Wotton,

Repose, had wonderfully contrived, that a *K* was not to be found.
Here was a weighty Difficulty! But the distinguishing Brother (for
whom we shall hereafter find a Name) now his Hand was in, proved
by a very good Argument, that *K* was a modern illegitimate Letter,
unknown to the Learned Ages, nor any where to be found in antient
Manuscripts. 'Tis true, said he, the Word *Calendæ*[53] hath
in * *Q.V.C.*[54] been sometimes writ with a
K, but erroneously, for in the best Copies it   * *Quibusdam Veteribus*
is ever spelt with a *C*. And by consequence   *Codicibus.*
it was a gross Mistake in our Language to spell *Knot* with a *K*, but
that from henceforward, he would take care it should be writ with a
C. Upon this, all farther Difficulty vanished; *Shoulder-Knots* were
made clearly out, to be *Jure Paterno*,[55] and our three Gentlemen
swaggered with as large and as flanting ones as the best.

BUT, as human Happiness is of a very short Duration, so in
those Days were human Fashions, upon which it entirely depends.
Shoulder-Knots had their Time, and we must now imagine them in
their Decline; for a certain Lord came just from *Paris*, with fifty
Yards of *Gold Lace* upon his Coat, exactly trimm'd after the Court-
Fashion of that *Month*. In two Days, all Mankind appear'd closed
up in Bars of || *Gold Lace*: whoever durst peep abroad without his
Complement of *Gold Lace*, was as scandalous as a ———, and as
ill received among the Women. What should our three Knights do
in this momentous Affair? They had sufficiently strained a Point
already, in the Affair of *Shoulder-Knots*: Upon Recourse to the
Will, nothing appeared there but *altum silentium*.[56] That of the
Shoulder-Knots was a loose, flying, circumstantial Point; but this of
Gold Lace, seemed too considerable an Alteration without better
Warrant; it did *aliquo modo essentiæ adhærere*,[57] and therefore
required a positive Precept. But about this time it fell out, that the
Learned Brother aforesaid, had read *Aristotelis Dialectica*, and especially that wonderful Piece *de Interpretatione*, which has the Fac-
ulty of teaching its Readers to find out a Meaning in every Thing
but it self; like Commentators on the *Revelations*, who proceed
Prophets without understanding a Syllable of the Text. *Brothers*,
said he, * *You are to be informed, that, of Wills*, duo sunt genera,
† *Nuncupatory*[58] *and scriptory: that in the Scriptory Will here
before us, there is no Precept or Mention about Gold Lace*, conced-

---

* *Some antient Manuscripts.*
|| *I cannot tell whether the Author means any new Innovation by this Word, or
whether it be only to introduce the new Methods of forcing and perverting
Scripture.*
* *The next Subject of our Author's Wit, is the Glosses and Interpretations of
Scripture, very many absurd ones of which are allow'd in the most Authentick
Books of the Church of Rome. W. Wotton.*
† *By this is meant Tradition, allowed to have equal Authority with the Scripture,
or rather greater.*

itur: *But,* si idem affirmetur de nuncupatorio, negatur,[59] *For Broth-ers, if you remember, we heard a Fellow say when we were Boys, that he heard my Father's Man say, that he heard my Father say, that he would advise his Sons to get* Gold Lace *on their Coats, as soon as ever they could procure Money to buy it. By G—— that is very true,* cries the other; *I remember it perfectly well,* said the third. And so without more ado they got the largest *Gold Lace* in the Parish, and walk'd about as fine as Lords.

A while after, there came up *all in Fashion,* a pretty sort of * *flame Coloured Sattin* for Linings, and the *Mercer* brought a Pat-tern of it immediately to our three Gentlemen, *An please your* Worships (said he) † *My Lord C——, and Sir J.W. had Linings out of this very Piece last Night; it takes wonderfully, and I shall not have a Remnant left, enough to make my Wife a Pin-cushion by to morrow Morning at ten a Clock.* Upon this, they fell again to romage the Will, because the present Case also required a positive Precept, the Lining being held by Orthodox Writers to be of the Essence of the Coat. After long search, they could fix upon nothing to the Matter in hand, except a short Advice of their Fathers in the Will, || to take care of *Fire,* and put out their *Candles* before they went to Sleep. This tho' a good deal for the Purpose, and helping very far towards Self-Conviction, yet not seeming wholly of Force to establish a Command; and being resolved to avoid farther Scruple, as well as future Occasion for Scandal, says He that was the Scholar; *I remember to have read in Wills, of a Codicil annexed, which is indeed a Part of the Will, and what it contains hath equal authority with the rest. Now, I have been considering of this same Will here before us, and I cannot reckon it to be compleat for want of such a Codicil. I will therefore fasten one in its proper Place very dexterously; I have had it by me some Time, it was written by* a * *Dog-keeper of my Grand-father's, and talks a great deal (as good Luck would have it) of this very flame-colour'd Sattin.* The

---

* *This is Purgatory, whereof he speaks more particularly hereafter, but here only to shew how Scripture was perverted to prove it, which was done by giving equal Authority with the* Canon *to* Apocrypha, *called here a* Codicil *annex'd.*

It is likely the Author, in every one of these Changes in the Brother's Dresses, referrs to some particular Error in the Church of Rome; *tho' it is not easy I think to apply them all, but by this of* Flame Colour'd Satin *is manifestly intended* Purgatory; *by* Gold Lace *may perhaps be understood, the lofty Ornaments and Plate in the Churches, The* Shoulder-Knots *and* Silver Fringe, *are not so obvious, at least to me; but the* Indian *Figures of Men, Women and Children plainly relate to the Pictures in the* Romish *Churches, of God like an old Man, of the Virgin* Mary *and our Saviour as a Child.*

† *This shews the Time the Author writ, it being about fourteen Years since those two Persons were reckoned the fine Gentlemen of the Town.*

|| *That is, to take care of Hell, and, in order to do that, to subdue and extinguish their Lusts.*

* *I believe this refers to that part of the* Apocrypha *where mention is made of* Tobit *and his Dog.*

Project was immediately approved by the other two; an old Parchment Scrowl was tagged on according to Art, in the Form of a *Codicil annext*, and the *Sattin* bought and worn.

NEXT Winter a Player, hired for the Purpose by the Corporation of *Fringe-makers*, acted his Part in a new Comedy, all covered with † *Silver Fringe*, and according to the laudable Custom gave Rise to that Fashion. Upon which, the Brothers consulting their Father's Will, to their great Astonishment found these Words; Item, *I charge and command my said three Sons, to wear no sort of Silver Fringe upon or about their said Coats*, &c. with a Penalty in case of Disobedience, too long here to insert. However, after some Pause the Brother so often mentioned for his Erudition, who was well Skill'd in Criticisms, had found in a certain Author, which he said should be nameless, that the same Word which in the Will is called *Fringe*, does also signifie a *Broom-stick*; and doubtless ought to have the same Interpretation in this Paragraph. This, another of the Brothers disliked, because of that Epithet, *Silver*, which could not, he humbly conceived, in Propriety of Speech be reasonably applied to a *Broom-stick*: but it was replied upon him, that this Epithet was understood in a *Mythological*, and *Allegorical* Sense. However, he objected again, why their Father should forbid them to wear a *Broom-stick* on their Coats, a Caution that seemed unnatural and impertinent; upon which he was taken up short, as one that spoke irreverently of a *Mystery*, which doubtless was very useful and significant, but ought not to be over-curiously pryed into, or nicely reasoned upon. And in short, their Father's Authority being now considerably sunk, this Expedient was allowed to serve as a lawful Dispensation, for wearing their full Proportion of *Silver Fringe*.

A while after, was revived an old Fashion, long antiquated, of *Embroidery* with * *Indian Figures* of Men, Women and Children. Here they had no Occasion to examine the Will. They remembered but too well, how their Father had always abhorred this Fashion; that he made several Paragraphs on purpose, importing his utter Detestation of it, and bestowing his everlasting Curse to his Sons whenever they should wear it. For all this, in a few Days, they appeared higher in the Fashion than any Body else in the Town. But they solved the Matter by saying, that these Figures were not at all the *same* with those that were formerly worn, and were meant in the Will. Besides, they did not wear them in that Sense, as forbid-

---

† *This is certainly the farther introducing the Pomps of Habit and Ornament.*
* *The Images of Saints, the Blessed Virgin, and our Saviour an Infant.*
  Ibid. *Images in the* Church of Rome *give him but too fair a Handle*, The Brothers remembered, &c. *The Allegory here is direct*. W. Wotton.

den by their Father but as they were a commendable Custom, and of great Use to the Publick. That these rigorous Clauses in the Will did therefore require some *Allowance*, and a favourable Interpretation, and ought to be understood *cum grano Salis*.

B U T, Fashions perpetually altering in that Age, the Scholastick Brother grew weary of searching farther Evasions, and solving everlasting Contradictions. Resolved therefore at all Hazards, to comply with the Modes of the World, they concerted Matters together, and agreed unanimously, to * lock up their Father's Will in a *Strong-Box*, brought out of *Greece* or *Italy*, (I have forgot which) and trouble themselves no farther to examine it, but only refer to its Authority whenever they thought fit. In consequence whereof, a while after, it grew a general Mode to wear an infinite Number of *Points*, most of them *tagg'd with Silver*: Upon which the Scholar pronounced † *ex Cathedra*, that *Points* were absolutely *Jure Paterno*, as they might very well remember. 'Tis true indeed, the Fashion prescribed somewhat more than were directly named in the Will; However, that they, as Heirs general of their Father, had power to make and add certain Clauses for publick Emolument, though not deducible, *totidem verbis*, from the Letter of the Will, or else, *Multa absurda sequerentur*.[60] This was understood for *Canonical*, and therefore on the following *Sunday* they came to Church all covered with *Points*.

T H E Learned Brother so often mentioned, was reckon'd the best Scholar in all that or the next Street to it; insomuch, as having run something behind-hand with the World, he obtained the Favour from a || *certain Lord*, to receive him into his House, and to teach his Children. A while after, the *Lord* died, and he by long Practice of his Father's Will, found the way of contriving a *Deed of Conveyance* of that House to Himself and his Heirs: Upon which he took Possession, turned the young Squires out, and received his Brothers in their stead.

---

* *The Papists formerly forbad the People the Use of Scripture in a Vulgar Tongue*, Peter *therefore* locks up his Father's Will in a Strong Box, brought out of *Greece* or *Italy*. *Those Countries are named because the* New Testament *is written in* Greek; *and the* Vulgar Latin, *which is the Authentick Edition of the* Bible *in the Church of* Rome, *is in the Language of old* Italy. W. Wotton.
† *The* Popes *in their Decretals and Bulls, have given their Sanction to very many gainful Doctrines which are now received in the* Church of Rome *that are not mention'd in Scriptures, and are unknown to the Primitive Church*, Peter *accordingly pronounces* ex Cathedra, *That* Points *tagged with Silver were absolutely* Jure Paterno, *and so they wore them in great Numbers*. W. Wotton.
|| *This was* Constantine the Great, *from whom the* Popes *pretend a Donation of* St. Peter's *Patrimony, which they have been never able to produce.*
Ibid *The* Bishops *of* Rome *enjoyed their Priviledges in* Rome *at first by the favour of Emperors, whom at last they shut out of their own Capital City, and then forged a Donation from* Constantine the Great, *the better to justifie what they did. In Imitation of this*, Peter having run something behind hand with the World, obtained Leave of a certain Lord *&c.* W. Wotton.

S E C T. III. *A Digression concerning Criticks*

T H O' I have been hitherto as cautious as I could, upon all Occasions, most nicely to follow the Rules and Methods of Writing, laid down by the Example of our illustrious *Moderns*; yet has the unhappy shortness of my Memory led me into an Error, from which I must immediately extricate my self, before I can decently pursue my Principal Subject. I confess with Shame, it was an unpardonable Omission to proceed so far as I have already done, before I had performed the due Discourses, Expostulatory, Supplicatory, or Deprecatory with my *good Lords* the *Criticks*. Towards some Atonement for this grievous Neglect, I do here make humbly bold to present them with a short Account of themselves and their *Art*, by looking into the Original and Pedigree of the Word as it is generally understood among us, and very briefly considering the antient and present State thereof.

B Y the Word, *Critick*, at this Day so frequent in all Conversations, there have sometimes been distinguished three very different Species of Mortal Men, according as I have read in *Antient Books and Pamphlets*. For first, by this Term were understood such Persons as invented or drew up Rules for themselves and the World, by observing which, a careful Reader might be able to pronounce upon the productions of the *Learned*, form his Taste to a true Relish of the *Sublime* and the *Admirable*, and divide every Beauty of Matter or of Style from the Corruption that Apes it: In their common perusal of Books, singling out the Errors and Defects, the Nauseous, the Fulsome, the Dull, and the Impertinent, with the Caution of a Man that walks thro' *Edenborough* Streets in a Morning, who is indeed as careful as he can, to watch diligently, and spy out the Filth in his Way, not that he is curious to observe the Colour and Complexion of the Ordure, or take its Dimensions, much less to be padling in, or tasting it: but only with a Design to come out as cleanly as he may. These men seem, tho' very erroneously, to have understood the Appellation of *Critick* in a literal Sence; That one principal part of his Office was to Praise and Acquit; and, that a *Critick*, who sets up to Read, only for an Occasion of Censure and Reproof, is a Creature as barbarous as a *Judge*, who should take up a Resolution to hang all Men that came before him upon a Tryal.

A G A I N; by the Word *Critick*, have been meant, the Restorers

of Antient Learning from the Worms, and Graves, and Dust of
Manuscripts.

N O W, the Races of these two have been for some Ages utterly
extinct; and besides, to discourse any farther of them would not be
at all to my purpose.

T H E Third, and Noblest Sort, is that of the *TRUE CRITICK*,
whose Original is the most Antient of all. Every *True Critick* is a
Hero born, descending in a direct Line from a Celestial Stem, by
Momus and *Hybris*, who begat *Zoilus*, who begat *Tigellius*,[61] who
begat *Etcætera* the Elder, who begat B——tl—y, and *Rym*—r, and
W—*tton*, and *Perrault*, and *Dennis*, who begat *Etcætera* the
Younger.

A N D these are the *Criticks* from whom the Commonwealth of
Learning has in all Ages received such immense Benefits, that the
Gratitude of their Admirers placed their Origine in Heaven, among
those of *Hercules, Theseus, Perseus,* and other great Deservers
of Mankind. But Heroick Virtue it self hath not been exempt
from the Obloquy of Evil Tongues. For it hath been objected, that
those Antient Heroes, famous for their Combating so many Giants,
and Dragons, and Robbers, were in their own Persons a greater
Nuisance to Mankind, than any of those Monsters they subdued;
and therefore, to render their Obligations more Compleat, when all
other Vermin were destroy'd, should in Conscience have concluded
with the same Justice upon themselves: *Hercules* most generously
did, and hath upon that Score, procured to himself more Temples
and Votaries than the best of his Fellows. For these Reasons, I suppose, it is why some have conceived, it would be very expedient for
the Publick Good of Learning, that every *True Critick*, as soon as
he had finished his Task assigned, should immediately deliver himself up to Rats-bane, or Hemp, or from some convenient *Altitude*,
and that no Man's Pretensions to so illustrious a Character, should
by any means be received, before That Operation were performed.

N O W, from this Heavenly Descent of *Criticism*, and the close
Analogy it bears to *Heroick Virtue*, 'tis easie to Assign the proper
Employment of a *True Antient Genuine Critick*; which is, to travel
thro' this vast World of Writings: to pursue and hunt those Monstrous Faults bred within them: to drag out the lurking Errors like
Cacus from his Den; to multiply them like *Hydra's* Heads; and
rake them together like *Augea's* Dung. Or else to drive away a sort
of *Dangerous Fowl*, who have a perverse Inclination to plunder the
best Branches of the *Tree of Knowledge*, like those *Stimphalian*
Birds that eat up the Fruit.

T H E S E Reasonings will furnish us with an adequate Definition of a true *Critick*; that, He is *a Discoverer and Collector of*

Writers Faults. Which may be farther put beyond Dispute by the following Demonstration: That whoever will examine the Writings in all kinds, wherewith this antient Sect has honour'd the World, shall immediately find, from the whole Thread and Tenour of them, that the Idea's of the Authors have been altogether conversant, and taken up with the Faults and Blemishes, and Oversights, and Mistakes of other Writers; and let the Subject treated on be whatever it will, their Imaginations are so entirely possess'd and replete with the Defects of other Pens, that the very Quintessence of what is bad, does of necessity distill into their own: by which means the Whole appears to be nothing else but an *Abstract* of the *Criticisms* themselves have made.

H A V I N G thus briefly consider'd the Original and Office of a *Critick*, as the Word is understood in its most noble and universal Acceptation, I proceed to refute the Objections of those who argue from the Silence and Pretermission of Authors; by which they pretend to prove, that the very Art of *Criticism*, as now exercised, and by me explained, is wholly *Modern*; and consequently, that the *Criticks* of *Great Britain* and *France*, have no Title to an Original so Antient and Illustrious as I have deduced. Now, if I can clearly make out on the contrary, that the most Antient Writers have particularly described, both the Person and the Office of a *True Critick*, agreeable to the Definition laid down by me; their Grand Objection, from the Silence of Authors, will fall to the Ground.

I confess to have for a long time born a part in this general Error; from which I should never have acquitted my self, but thro' the Assistance of our Noble *Moderns*; whose most edifying Volumes I turn indefatigably over Night and Day, for the Improvement of my Mind, and the good of my Country: These have with unwearied Pains made many useful Searches into the weak sides of the *Antients*, and given us a comprehensive List of them. Besides, they have proved beyond contradiction, that the very finest Things delivered of old, have been long since invented, and brought to   * *See* Wotton *of Antient and Modern Learning.* Light by much later Pens, and that the noblest Discoveries those *Antients* ever made, of Art or of Nature, have all been produced by the transcending Genius of the present Age. Which clearly shews, how little Merit those *Antients* can justly pretend to; and takes off that blind Admiration paid them by Men in a Corner, who have the Unhappiness of conversing too little with *present Things.* Reflecting maturely upon all this, and taking in the whole Compass of Human Nature, I easily concluded, that these *Antients*, highly sensible of their many Imperfections, must needs have endeavoured from some Passages in their Works, to obviate, soften, or divert the Censorious Reader, by *Satyr*, or *Panegyrick* upon the *True Criticks*, in Imitation of their *Masters* the *Moderns*. Now, in the *Common-Places* of * both these, I was plentifully instructed, by a long Course of useful Study in *Prefaces* and *Prologues*; and therefore immediately resolved to try what I could discover of either, by a diligent Perusal of the most Antient Writers, and especially those who treated of the earliest Times. Here I found to my great Surprize, that although they all entred, upon Occasion, into particular Descriptions of the *True Critick*, according as they were governed by their Fears or their Hopes; yet whatever they touch'd of that kind, was with abundance of Caution, adventuring no farther than *Mythology* and *Hieroglyphick*. This, I suppose, gave ground to superficial Readers, for urging the Silence of Authors, against the Antiquity of the *True Critick*; tho' the *Types* are so apposite, and the Applications so necessary and natural, that it is not easy to conceive, how any Reader of a *Modern Eye* and *Taste* could over-look them. I shall venture from a great Number to produce a few, which I am very confident, will put this Question beyond Dispute.

> * *Satyr, and Panegyrick upon Criticks.*

I T well deserves considering, that these *Antient Writers* in treating Enigmatically upon the Subject, have generally fixed upon the very *same Hieroglyph*, varying only the Story according to their Affections or their Wit. For first; *Pausanias* is of Opinion, that the Perfection of Writing correct was entirely owing to the Institution of *Criticks*; and, that he can possibly mean no other than the *True Critick*, is, I think, manifest enough from the following Description. He says, *They were a Race of Men, who delighted to nibble at the Superfluities, and Excrescencies of Books; which the Learned at length observing, took Warning of their own Accord, to lop the Luxuriant, the Rotten, the Dead, the Sapless, and the Overgrown Branches from their Works*. But now, all this he cunningly shades under the following Allegory; *that the* * *Nauplians in Argia, learned the Art of pruning their Vines, by observing, that when an ASS had browsed upon one of them, it thrived the better, and bore fairer Fruit.* But † *Herodotus* holding the very same *Hieroglyph*, speaks much plainer, and almost *in terminis*. He hath been so bold as to tax the *True Criticks*, of Ignorance and Malice; telling us openly, for I think nothing can be plainer, that *in the Western Part of* Libya, *there were* A S S E S *with* H O R N S: Upon which Relation * *Ctesias* yet refines, mentioning the very same Animal about *India, adding, That whereas all other* ASSES *wanted a* Gall, *these horned*

> * *Lib——*
>
> † *Lib.* 4.
>
> * Vide *excerpta ex eo* apud Photium.

ones were so redundant in that Part, that their Flesh was not to be eaten because of its extream Bitterness.

NOW, the Reason why those Antient Writers treated this Subject only by Types and Figures, was, because they durst not make open Attacks against a Party so Potent and so Terrible, as the *Criticks* of those Ages were: whose very Voice was so Dreadful, that a Legion of Authors would tremble, and drop their Pens at the Sound; For so * *Herodotus* tells us expressly in another Place, how *a vast Army* * *Lib.* 4. of Scythians *was put to flight in a Panick Terror, by the Braying of an* A S S. From hence it is conjectured by certain profound *Philologers*, that the great Awe and Reverence paid to a *True Critick*, by the Writers of *Britain*, have been derived to Us, from those our *Scythian* Ancestors. In short, this Dread was so universal, that in process of Time, those Authors who had a mind to publish their Sentiments more freely, in describing the *True Criticks* of their several Ages, were forced to leave off the use of the former *Hieroglyph*, as too nearly approaching the *Prototype*, and invented other Terms instead thereof that were more cautious and mystical; so † *Diodorus* speaking to the same purpose, ventures no farther than to say, That † *Lib.* *in the Mountains of* Helicon *there grows a certain* Weed, *which bears a Flower of so damned a Scent, as to poison those who offer to smell it.* Lucretius gives exactly the Same Relation.

||*Est etiam in magnis Heliconis montibus arbos,*
Floris odore hominem retro consueta necare. Lib. 6.[62]

BUT *Ctesias*, whom we lately quoted, hath been a great deal bolder; He had been used with much severity by the *True Criticks* of his own Age, and therefore could not forbear to leave behind him, at least one deep Mark of his Vengeance against the whole Tribe. His Meaning is so near the Surface, that I wonder how it possibly came to be overlook'd by those who deny the Antiquity of *True Criticks*. For pretending to make a Description of many strange Animals about *India*, he hath set down these remarkable Words. *Amongst the rest, says he, there is a* Serpent *that wants* Teeth, *and consequently cannot bite, but if its* Vomit *(to which it is much addicted) happens to fall upon any Thing, a certain Rotennness or Corruption ensues: These* Serpents *are generally found among the Mountains where* Jewels *grow, and they frequently emit a* poisonous Juice *whereof, whoever drinks, that Person's Brains* flie out of his Nostrils. THERE was also among the *Antients* a sort of *Critick*, not dis-

|| *Near* Helicon, *and round the Learned Hill,*
Grow Trees, whose Blossoms with their Odour kill.

tinguisht in *Specie* from the Former, but in Growth or Degree, who seem to have been only the *Tyro's* or *junior* Scholars: yet, because of their differing Employments, they are frequently mentioned as a Sect by themselves. The usual exercise of these younger Students, was to attend constantly at Theatres, and learn to Spy out the *worst Parts* of the Play, whereof they were obliged carefully to take Note, and render a rational Account, to their Tutors. Flesht at these smaller Sports, like young Wolves, they grew up in Time, to be nimble and strong enough for hunting down large Game. For it hath been observed both among Antients and Moderns, that a *True Critick* hath one Quality in common with a *Whore* and an *Alderman*, never to change his Title or his Nature; that a *Grey Critick* has been certainly a *Green* one, the Perfections and Acquirements of his Age being only the improved Talents of his Youth; like *Hemp*, which some Naturalists inform us, is bad for *Suffocations*, tho' taken but in the Seed. I esteem the Invention, or at least the Refinement of *Prologues*, to have been owing to these younger Proficients, of whom *Terence* makes frequent and honourable mention, under the Name of *Malevoli*.

NOW, 'tis certain, the Institution of the *True Criticks*, was of absolute Necessity to the Commonwealth of Learning. For all Human Actions seem to be divided like *Themistocles* and his Company; One Man can *Fiddle*, and another can make *a small Town a great City*, and he that cannot do either one or the other, deserves to be kick'd out of the Creation. The avoiding of which Penalty, has doubtless given the first Birth to the Nation of *Criticks* and withal, an Occasion for their secret Detractors to report; that a *True Critick* is a sort of Mechanick, set up with a Stock and Tools for his Trade, at as little Expence as a *Taylor*; and that there is much Analogy between the Utensils and Abilities of both: That the *Taylor's Hell* is the Type of a Critick's *Common-Place-Book*, and his Wit and Learning held forth by the *Goose*: That it requires at least as many of these, to the making up of one Scholar, as of the others to the Composition of a Man: That the Valour of both is equal, and their *Weapons* near of a Size. Much may be said in answer to these invidious Reflections; and I can positively affirm the first to be a Falshood: For, on the contrary, nothing is more certain, than that it requires greater Layings out, to be free of the *Critick's* Company, than of any other you can name. For, as to be a *true Beggar*, it will cost the richest Candidate every Groat he is worth; so, before one can commence a *True Critick*, it will cost a man all the good Qualities of his Mind; which, perhaps, for a less Purchase, would be thought but an indifferent Bargain.

HAVING thus amply proved the Antiquity of *Criticism*, and

described the Primitive State of it; I shall now examine the present Condition of this Empire, and shew how well it agrees with its antient self. * A certain Author, whose Works have many Ages since been entirely lost, does in his fifth Book and eighth Chapter, say of *Criticks*, that *their Writings are the Mirrors of Learning*.

* *A Quotation after the manner of a great Author. Vide* Bentley's *Dissertation, &c.*

This I understand in a literal Sense, and suppose our Author must mean, that whoever designs to be a perfect Writer, must inspect into the Books of *Criticks*, and correct his Invention there as in a Mirror. Now, whoever considers, that the *Mirrors* of the Antients were made of *Brass*, and *sine Mercurio*, may presently apply the two Principal Qualifications of a *True Modern Critick*, and consequently, must needs conclude, that these have always been, and must be for ever the same. For, *Brass* is an Emblem of Duration, and when it is skilfully burnished, will cast *Reflections* from its own *Superficies*, without any Assistance of *Mercury* from behind. All the other Talents of a *Critick* will not require a particular Mention, being included, or easily deducible to these. However, I shall conclude with three Maxims, which may serve both as Characteristicks to distinguish a *True Modern Critick* from a Pretender, and will be also of admirable Use to those worthy Spirits, who engage in so useful and honourable an Art.

THE first is, That *Criticism*, contrary to all other Faculties of the Intellect, is ever held the truest and best, when it is the very *first* Result of the *Critik*'s Mind: As Fowlers reckon the first aim for the surest, and seldom fail of missing the Mark, if they stay for a Second.

SECONDLY; The *True Criticks* are known by their Talent of swarming about the noblest Writers, to which they are carried meerly by Instinct, as a Rat to the best Cheese, or a Wasp to the fairest Fruit. So, when the *King* is a Horse-back, he is sure to be the *dirtiest* Person of the Company, and they that make their Court best, are such as *bespatter* him most.

LASTLY; A *True Critick*, in the Perusal of a Book, is like a *Dog* at a Feast, whose Thoughts and Stomach are wholly set upon what the Guests *fling away*, and consequently, is apt to *Snarl* most, when there are the fewest *Bones*.

THUS much, I think, is sufficient to serve by way of Address to my Patrons, the *True Modern Criticks*, and may very well atone for my past Silence, as well as That which I am like to observe for the future. I hope I have deserved so well of their whole *Body*, as to meet with generous and tender Usage at their *Hands*. Supported by which Expectation, I go on boldly to pursue those Adventures already so happily begun.

SECT. IV. *A Tale of a Tub*

I HAVE now with much Pains and Study, conducted the Reader to a Period, where he must expect to hear of great Revolutions. For no sooner had Our *Learned Brother*, so often mentioned, got a warm House of his own over his Head, than he began to look big, and to take mightily upon him; insomuch, that unless the Gentle Reader out of his great Candour, will please a little to exalt his Idea, I am afraid he will henceforth hardly know the *Hero* of the Play, when he happens to meet Him; his part, his Dress, and his Mien being so much altered.

HE told his Brothers, he would have them to know, that he was their Elder, and consequently his Father's sole Heir; Nay, a while after, he would not allow them to call Him, Brother, but Mr. *PETER*; And then he must be styl'd, *Father PETER*; and sometimes, *My Lord PETER*. To support this Grandeur, which he soon began to consider, could not be maintained without a Better *Fonde* than what he was born to; After much Thought, he cast about at last, to turn *Projector* and *Virtuoso*, wherein he so well succeeded, that many famous Discoveries, Projects and Machines, which bear great Vogue and Practice at present in the World, are owing entirely to *Lord Peter's* Invention. I will deduce the best Account I have been able to collect of the Chief amongst them, without considering much the Order they came out in; because, I think, Authors are not well agreed as to that Point.

I hope, when this Treatise of mine shall be translated into Foreign Languages, (as I may without Vanity affirm, That the Labour of collecting, the Faithfulness in recounting, and the great Usefulness of the Matter to the Publick, will amply deserve that Justice) that the worthy Members of the several *Academies* abroad, especially those of *France* and *Italy*, will favourably accept these humble Offers, for the Advancement of Universal Knowledge. I do also advertise the most Reverend Fathers the *Eastern* Missionaries, that I have purely for their Sakes, made use of such Words and Phrases, as will best admit an easie Turn into any of the *Oriental* Languages, especially the *Chinese*. And so I proceed with great Content of Mind, upon reflecting, how much Emolument this whole Globe of Earth is like to reap by my Labours.

THE first Undertaking of Lord *Peter*, was to purchase a * Large Continent, lately said to have been discovered in *Terra Australis incognita*. This Tract of Land he bought at a very great Penny-

* *That is Purgatory.*

worth from the Discoverers themselves, (tho' some pretended to doubt whether they had ever been there) and then retailed it into several Cantons to certain Dealers, who carried over Colonies, but were all Shipwreckt in the Voyage. Upon which, *Lord Peter* sold the said Continent to other Customers *again*, and *again*, and *again*, and *again*, with the same Success.

THE second Project I shall mention, was his † Sovereign Remedy for the *Worms*, especially those in the *Spleen*. * The Patient was to eat nothing after Supper for three Nights: as soon as he went to Bed, he was carefully to lye on one Side, and when he grew weary, to turn upon the other: He must also duly confine his two Eyes to the same Object; and by no means break Wind at both Ends together, without manifest Occasion. These Prescriptions diligently observed, the *Worms* would void insensibly by Perspiration, ascending thro' the *Brain*.

A third Invention, was the Erecting of a || *Whispering-Office*, for the Publick Good and Ease of all such as are Hypochondriacal, or troubled with the Cholick; as likewise of all Eves-droppers, Physicians, Midwives, small Politicians, Friends fallen out, Repeating Poets, Lovers Happy or in Despair, Bawds, Privy-Counsellours, Pages, Parasites and Buffoons; In short, of all such as are in Danger of bursting with too much *Wind*. An *Asse*'s Head was placed so conveniently, that the Party affected might easily with his Mouth accost either of the Animal's Ears; which he was to apply close for a certain Space, and by a fugitive Faculty, peculiar to the Ears of that Animal, receive immediate Benefit, either by Eructation, or Expiration, or Evomition.

ANOTHER very beneficial Project of *Lord Peter*'s was an † *Office of Ensurance*, for Tobacco-Pipes, Martyrs of the Modern Zeal; Volumes of Poetry, Shadows,————————and Rivers: That these, nor any of these shall receive Damage by *Fire*. From whence our *Friendly Societies*[63] may plainly find themselves, to be only Transcribers from this Original; tho' the one and the other have been of *great* Benefit to the Undertakers, as well as of *equal* to the Publick.

LORD *Peter* was also held the Original Author of * *Puppets* and

---

† *Penance and Absolution are plaid upon under the Notion of a* Sovereign Remedy for the Worms, *especially in the Spleen, which by observing* Peters *Prescription would void sensibly by Perspiration ascending thro' the Brain,* &c. W. Wotton.
* *Here the Author ridicules the Penances of the Church of* Rome, *which may be made as easy to the Sinner as he pleases, provided he will pay for them accordingly.*
|| *By his* Whispering-Office, *for the Relief of Eves-droppers, Physitians, Bawds, and Privy-counsellours, he ridicules Auricular Confession, and the Priest who takes it, is described by the Asses Head.* W. Wotton.
† *This I take to be the Office of* Indulgences, *the gross Abuses whereof first gave Occasion for the Reformation.*
* *I believe are the Monkeries and ridiculous Processions,* &c. *among the Papists.*

Raree-Shows; the great Usefulness whereof being so generally known, I shall not enlarge farther upon this Particular.

BUT, another Discovery for which he was much renowned, was his famous Universal † *Pickle.* For having remark'd how your ‖ Common *Pickle* in use among Huswives, was of no farther Benefit than to preserve dead Flesh, and certain kinds of Vegetables; *Peter,* with great Cost as well as Art, had contrived a *Pickle* proper for Houses, Gardens, Towns, Men, Women, Children, and Cattle; wherein he could preserve them as Sound as Insects in Amber. Now, this *Pickle* to the Taste, the Smell, and the Sight, appeared exactly the same, with what is in common Service for Beef and Butter, and Herrings, (and has been often that way applied with great Success) but for its many Sovereign Virtues was a quite different Thing. For *Peter* would put in a certain Quantity of his * *Powder Pimperlim pimp,* after which it never failed of Success. The Operation was performed by *Spargefaction*⁶⁴ in a proper Time of the Moon. The Patient who was to be *pickled,* if it were a House, would infalliby be preserved from all Spiders, Rats and Weazels; If the Party affected were a Dog he should be exempt from Mange, and Madness, and Hunger. It also infallibly took away all Scabs and Lice, and scall'd Heads from Children, never hindring the Patient from any Duty, either at Bed or Board.

BUT all of Peter's Rarities, he most valued a certain Set of † *Bulls,* whose Race was by great Fortune preserved in a lineal Descent from those that guarded the *Golden Fleece.* Tho' some who pretended to observe them curiously, doubted the Breed had not been kept entirely chast; because they had degenerated from their Ancestors in some Qualities and had acquired others very extraordinary, but a Forein Mixture. The *Bulls* of *Colchos* are recorded to have *brazen Feet;* But whether it happen'd by ill Pasture and Running, by an Allay from intervention of other Parents, from stolen Intrigues; Whether a Weakness in their Progenitors had impaired the seminal Virtue; Or by a Decline necessary thro' a long Course of Time, the Originals of Nature being depraved in these latter sinful Ages of the World; Whatever was the Cause, 'tis cer-

---

† *Holy Water, he calls an* Universal Pickle *to preserve Houses, Gardens, Towns, Men, Women, Children and Cattle, wherein he could preserve them as sound as Insects in Amber.* W. Wotton.
‖ *This is easily understood to be Holy Water, composed of the same Ingredients with many other Pickles.*
* *And because Holy Water differs only in Consecration from common Water, therefore he tells us that his Pickle by the Powder of* Pimperlim pimp *receives new Virtues though it differs not in Sight nor Smell from the common Pickle, which preserves Beef, and Butter, and Herrings.* W. Wotton.
† *The Papal Bulls are ridicul'd by Name, So that here we are at no loss for the Authors Meaning.* W. Wotton.
Ibid. *Here the Author has kept the Name, and means the Popes Bulls, or rather his Fulminations and Excommunications, of Heretical Princes, all sign'd with Lead and the Seal of the Fisherman.*

tain that *Lord Peter's Bulls* were extreamely vitiated by the Rust of
Time in the Mettal of their Feet, which was now sunk into common
Lead. However the terrible *roaring* peculiar to their Lineage, was
preserved; as likewise that Faculty of breathing out *Fire* from their
Nostrils; which notwithstanding many of their Detractors took
to be a Feat of Art, and to be nothing so terrible as it appeared;
proceeding only from their usual Course of Dyet, which was of *
Squibs and *Crackers*. However, they had two peculiar Marks which
extreamly distinguished them from the *Bulls of Jason*, and which I
have not met together in the Description of any other Monster, beside
that in *Horace*;

Varias inducere plumas,
and
Atrum desinit in piscem.[65]

For, these had *Fishes Tails*, yet upon Occasion, could *out-fly* any
Bird in the Air. *Peter* put these *Bulls* upon several Employs. Sometimes he would set them a *roaring* to fright † *Naughty Boys*, and
make them quiet. Sometimes he would send them out upon
Errands of great Importance; where it is wonderful to recount, and
perhaps the cautious Reader may think much to believe it; An
Appetitus Sensibilis, deriving itself thro' the whole Family, from
their Noble Ancestors, Guardians of the *Golden Fleece*; they continued so extremely fond of *Gold*, that if *Peter* sent them abroad,
though it were only upon a Compliment; they would *Roar*, and
Spit, and *Belch*, and *Piss*, and *Fart*, and *Snivel* out *Fire*, and keep a
perpetual Coyl, till you flung them a Bit of *Gold*; but then, *Pul-
veris exigui jactu*,[66] they would grow calm and quiet as Lambs. In
short, whether by secret Connivance, or Encouragement from their
Master, or out of their own Liquorish Affection to Gold, or both; it
is certain they were no better than a sort of sturdy, swaggering Beggars; and where they could not prevail to get an Alms, would make
Women miscarry, and Children fall into Fits: who, to this very
Day, usually call Sprites and Hobgoblins by the Name of *Bull-Beg-
gars*. They grew at last so very troublesome to the Neighbourhood,
that some Gentlemen of the *North-West*, got a Parcel of right *English Bull-Dogs*, and baited them so terribly, that they felt it ever
after.

I must needs mention one more of *Lord Peter's* Projects, which
was very extraordinary, and discovered him to be Master of a high
Reach, and profound Invention. Whenever it happened that any
Rogue of *Newgate* was condemned to be hang'd, *Peter* would offer

---

* *These are the Fulminations of the Pope threatning Hell and Damnation to those
Princes who offend him.*
† *That is Kings who incurr his Displeasure.*

him a Pardon for a certain Sum of Money, which when the poor
Caitiff had made all Shifts to scrape up and send; *His Lordship*
would return a * Piece of Paper in this Form.

*TO all Mayors, Sheriffs, Jaylors, Constables, Bayliffs, Hangmen,
&c. Whereas we are informed that A. B. remains in the Hands of
you, or any of you, under the Sentence of Death. We will and
command you upon Sight hereof, to let the said Prisoner depart to
his own Habitation, whether he stands condemned for Murder,
Sodomy, Rape, Sacrilege, Incest, Treason, Blasphemy, &c. for which
this shall be your sufficient Warrant: And if you fail hereof, G——
d—mn You and Yours to all Eternity. And so we bid you heartily
Farewel.*

Your most Humble

Man's Man,

EMPEROR PETER.

THE Wretches trusting to this, lost their Lives and Money too.

I desire of those whom the *Learned* among Posterity will appoint
for Commentators upon this elaborate Treatise; that they will proceed with great Caution upon certain dark points, wherein all who
are not *Verè adepti*, may be in Danger to form rash and hasty Conclusions, especially in some mysterious Paragraphs, where certain
Arcana are joyned for brevity sake, which in the Operation must be
divided. And, I am certain, that future Sons of Art, will return large
Thanks to my Memory, for so grateful, so useful an *Innuendo*.

IT will be no difficult Part to persuade the Reader, that so many
worthy Discoveries met with great Success in the World; tho' I
may justly assure him that I have related much the smallest Number; My Design having been only to single out such, as will be of
most Benefit for Publick Imitation, or which best served to give
some Idea of the Reach and Wit of the Inventor. And therefore it
need not be wondred, if by this Time, *Lord Peter* was become
exceedingly Rich. But alas, he had kept his Brain so long, and so
violently upon the Rack, that at last it *shook* it self, and began to
turn round for a little Ease. In short, what with Pride, Projects, and
Knavery, poor *Peter* was grown distracted, and conceived the strang-
est Imaginations in the World. In the Height of his Fits (as it is
usual with those who run mad out of Pride) He would call Himself
† *God Almighty*, and sometimes *Monarch of the Universe*. I have

seen him, (says my Author) take three old † *highcrown'd Hats*, and clap them all on his Head, three Story high, with a huge Bunch of || *Keys* at his Girdle, and an *Angling Rod* in his Hand. In which Guise, whoever went to take him by the Hand in the way of Salutation, *Peter* with much Grace like a well educated Spaniel, would present them with his ** *Foot*, and if they refused his Civility, then he would raise it as high as their Chops, and give them a damn'd Kick on the Mouth, which hath ever since been call'd a *Salute*. Whoever walkt by, without paying him their Compliments, having a wonderful strong Breath, he would blow their Hats off into the Dirt. Mean time, his Affairs at home went upside down; and his two Brothers had a wretched Time; Where his first * *Boutade* was, to kick both their † *Wives* one Morning out of Doors, and his own too, and in their stead, gave Orders to pick up the first three Strolers could be met with in the Streets. A while after, he nail'd up the Cellar-Door: and would not allow his Brothers a || Drop of *Drink* to their Victuals. Dining one Day at an Alderman's in the City, *Peter* observed him expatiating after the Manner of his Brethren, in the Praises of his Surloyn of Beef. *Beef*, said the Sage Magistrate, *is the King of Meat; Beef comprehends in it the Quintesscence of Partridge, and Quail, and Venison, and Phesant, and Plum-pudding and Custard.* When *Peter* came home, he would needs take the Fancy of cooking up this Doctrine into Use, and apply the Precept in default of a Surloyn, to his brown Loaf: *Bread*, says he, *Dear Brothers, is the Staff of Life; in which Bread is contained*, inclusive, *the Quintessence of Beef, Mutton, Veal, Venison, Partridge, Plum-pudding, and Custard: And to render all compleat, there is intermingled a due Quantity of Water, whose Crudities are also corrected by Yeast or Barm, thro' which means it becomes a wholesome fermented Liquor, diffused thro' the Mass of the Bread.* Upon the Strength of these Conclusions, next Day at Dinner was the brown Loaf served up in all the Formality of a City Feast. *Come Brothers*, said Peter, *fall to, and spare not; here is excellent good ‡ Mutton; or hold, now my Hand is in, I'll help you.* At which word,

---

† *The Triple Crown.*
|| *The Keys of the Church.*
   Ibid. *The Pope's Universal Monarchy, and his Triple Crown, and Fisher's Ring.* W. Wotton.
** *Neither does his arrogant way of requiring men to kiss his Slipper, escape Reflexion.* Wotton.
* *This Word properly signifies a sudden Jerk, or Lash of an Horse, when you do not expect it.*
† *The* Celibacy of the *Romish* Clergy *is struck at in* Peter's *beating his own and Brothers Wives out of Doors.* W. Wotton.
|| *The Pope's refusing the Cup to the Laity, persuading them that the Blood is contain'd in the Bread, and that the Bread is the real and entire Body of* Christ.
‡ Transubstantiation. Peter *turns his Bread into Mutton, and according to the Popish Doctrine of Concomitants, his Wine too, which in his way he calls, Pauming his damn'd Crusts upon the Brothers for Mutton.* W. Wotton.

in much Ceremony, with Fork and Knife, he carves out two good Slices of the Loaf, and presents each on a Plate to his Brothers. The Elder of the two not suddenly entring into *Lord Peter's* Conceit, began with very civil Language to examine the Mystery. *My Lord,* said he, *I doubt, with great Submission, there may be some Mistake.* *What,* says *Peter, you are pleasant; Come then, let us hear this Jest, your Head is so big with. None in the World, my Lord; but unless I am very much deceived, your Lordship was pleased a while ago, to let fall a Word about Mutton, and I would be glad to see it with all my Heart.* How, said *Peter,* appearing in great Surprise, *I do not comprehend this at all—* Upon which, the younger interposing, to set the Business right; *My Lord,* said he, *My Brother, I suppose is hungry, and longs for the Mutton, your Lordship hath promised us to Dinner. Pray,* said Peter, *take me along with you, either you are both mad, or disposed to be merrier than I approve of; If You there, do not like your Piece, I will carve you another, tho' I should take that to be the choice Bit of the whole Shoulder. What then, my Lord,* replied the first, *it seems this is a shoulder of Mutton all this while. Pray Sir,* says *Peter, eat your Vittles and leave off your Impertinence, if you please, for I am not disposed to relish it at present*: But the other could not forbear, being overprovoked at the affected Seriousness of *Peter's* Countenance. *By G——, My Lord,* said he, *I can only say, that to my Eyes, and Fingers, and Teeth, and Nose, it seems to be nothing but a Crust of Bread.* Upon which, the second put in his Word: *I never saw a Piece of Mutton in my Life, so nearly resembling a Slice from a Twelve-peny Loaf.* Look ye, *Gentlemen,* cries *Peter* in a Rage, *to convince you, what a couple of blind, positive, ignorant, wilful Puppies you are, I will use but this plain Argument; By G——, it is true, good, natural Mutton as any in* Leaden-Hall *Market; and G——, confound you both eternally, if you offer to believe otherwise.* Such a thundring Proof as this, left no farther Room for Objection: The two Unbelievers began to gather and pocket up their Mistake as hastily as they could. *Why, truly,* said the first, *upon more mature Consideration—* Ay, says the other, interrupting him, *now I have thought better on the Thing, your Lordship seems to have a great deal of Reason. Very well,* said Peter, *Here Boy, fill me a Beer-Glass of Claret. Here's to you both with all my Heart.* The two Brethren much delighted to see him so readily appeas'd returned their most humble Thanks, and said, they would be glad to pledge His Lordship. *That you shall,* said Peter, *I am not a Person to refuse you any Thing that is reasonable; Wine moderately taken, is a Cordial; Here is a Glass apiece for you; 'Tis true natural Juice from the Grape; none of your damn'd* Vintners Brewings. Hav-

ing spoke thus, he presented to each of them another large dry
Crust, bidding them drink it off, and not be bashful, for it would
do them no Hurt. The two Brothers, after having performed the
usual Office in such delicate Conjunctures, of staring a sufficient
Period at *Lord Peter,* and each other; and finding how Matters were
like to go, resolved not to enter on a new Dispute, but let him carry
the Point as he pleased; for he was now got into one of his mad Fits,
and to Argue or Expostulate further, would only serve to render
him a hundred times more untractable.

I have chosen to relate this worthy Matter in all its Circumstances, because it gave a principal Occasion to that great and famous
* *Rupture,* which happened about the same time among these
Brethren, and was never afterwards made up. But, of That, I shall
treat at large in another Section.

HOWEVER, it is certain, that *Lord Peter,* even in his lucid
Intervals, was very lewdly given in his common Conversation,
extream wilful and positive, and would at any time rather argue to
the Death, than allow himself to be once in an Error. Besides, he
had an abominable Faculty of telling huge palpable *Lies* upon all
Occasions; and swearing, not only to the Truth, but cursing the
whole Company to Hell, if they pretended to make the least Scruple of believing Him. One time, he swore, he had a † *Cow* at
home, which gave as much Milk at a Meal, as would fill three thousand Churches; and what was yet more extraordinary, would never
turn Sower. Another time, he was telling of an old ‖ *Sign-Post* that
belonged to his *Father,* with Nails and Timber enough on it, to
build sixteen large Men of War. Talking one Day of *Chinese* Waggons, which were made so light as to sail over Mountains: Z——nds,
said *Peter, where's the Wonder of that? By* G——, *I saw a* ‡ *Large
House of Lime and Stone travel over Sea and Land (granting that
it stopt sometimes to bait) above two thousand* German *Leagues.*
And that which was the good of it, he would swear desperately all
the while, that he never told a Lye in his Life; And at every Word;
By G——, *Gentlemen, I tell you nothing but the Truth; And the*
D——*l broil them eternally that will not believe me.*

IN short, *Peter* grew so scandalous, that all the Neighbourhood

* *By this* Rupture *is meant the* Reformation.
† *The ridiculous Multiplying of the Virgin* Mary's *Milk among the Papists, under
the Allegory of a Cow, which gave as much Milk at a Meal, as would fill three
thousand Churches.* W. Wotton.
‖ *By this* Sign-Post *is meant the* Cross *of our Blessed Saviour.*
‡ *The Chappel of* Loretto. *He falls here only upon the ridiculous Inventions of
Popery: The Church of* Rome *intended by these Things, to gull silly, superstitious
People, and rook them of their Money; that the World had been too long in
Slavery, our Ancestors gloriously redeem'd us from that Yoke. The Church of*
Rome *therefore ought to be expos'd, and he deserves well of Mankind that does
expose it.* W. Wotton.
    Ibid. *The Chappel of* Loretto, *which travell'd from the* Holy Land *to* Italy.

began in plain Words to say, he was no better than a Knave. And his two Brothers long weary of his ill Usage, resolved at last to leave him; but first, they humbly desired a Copy of their Father's *Will*, which had now lain by neglected, time out of Mind. Instead of granting this Request, he called them *damn'd Sons of Whores, Rogues, Traytors*, and the rest of the vile Names he could muster up. However, while he was abroad one Day upon his Projects, the two Youngsters watcht their Opportunity, made a Shift to come at the *Will*, || and took a *Copia vera*, by which they presently saw how grosly they had been abused; Their Father having left them equal Heirs, and strictly commanded, that whatever they got, should lye in common among them all. Pursuant to which, their next Enterprise was to break open the Cellar-Door, and get a little good * *Drink* to spirit and comfort their Hearts. In copying the *Will*, they had met another Precept against Whoring, Divorce, and separate Maintenance; Upon which, their next † Work was to discard their Concubines, and send for their Wives. Whilst all this was in agitation, there enters a Sollicitor from *Newgate*, desiring *Lord Peter* would please to procure a *Pardon* for a *Thief* that was to be *hanged* to morrow. But the two Brothers told him, he was a Coxcomb to seek Pardons from a Fellow, who deserv'd to be hang'd much better than his Client; and discovered all the Method of that Imposture, in the same Form I delivered it a while ago, advising the Sollicitor to put his Friend upon obtaining || *a Pardon from the King.* In the midst of all this Clutter and Revolution, in comes *Peter* with a File of * Dragoons at his Heels, and gathering from all Hands what was in the Wind, He and his Gang, after several Millions of Scurrilities and Curses, not very important here to repeat, by main Force, very fairly † kicks them both out of Doors, and would never let them come under his Roof from that Day to this.

S E C T. V.   *A Digression in the Modern Kind*

WE whom the World is pleased to honor with the Title of *Modern Authors*, should never have been able to compass our great Design of an everlasting Remembrance, and never-dying Fame, if

|| *Translated the Scriptures into the vulgar Tongues.*
* *Administered the Cup to the Laity at the Communion.*
† *Allowed the Marriages of Priests.*
|| *Directed Penitents not to trust to Pardons and Absolutions procur'd for Money, but sent them to implore the Mercy of God, from whence alone Remission is to be obtain'd.*
* *By* Peter's *Dragoons, is meant the Civil Power which those Princes, who were bigotted to the Romish Superstition, employ'd against the Reformers.*
† *The Pope shuts all who dissent from him out of the Church.*

our Endeavours had not been so highly serviceable to the general
Good of Mankind. This, O *Universe*, is the Adventurous Attempt
of me thy Secretary;

—————————— *Quemvis perferre laborem*
Suadet, & inducit noctes vigilare serenas.[67]

TO this End, I have some Time since, with a World of Pains
and Art, dissected the Carcass of *Humane Nature*, and read many
useful Lectures upon the several Parts, both *Containing* and *Contained*; till at last it *smelt* so strong, I could preserve it no longer.
Upon which, I have been at a great Expence to fit up all the Bones
with exact Contexture, and in due Symmetry; so that I am ready to
shew a very compleat Anatomy thereof to all curious *Gentlemen
and others*. But not to Digress farther in the midst of a Digression,
as I have known some Authors inclose Digressions in one another,
like a Nest of Boxes; I do affirm, that having carefully cut up
Humane Nature, I have found a very strange, new, and important
Discovery; That the Publick Good of Mankind is performed by two
Ways, *Instruction*, and *Diversion*. And I have farther proved in my
said several Readings, (which, perhaps, the World may one day see,
if I can prevail on any Friend to steal a Copy, or on certain Gentlemen of my Admirers, to be very Importunate) that, as Mankind is
now disposed, he receives much greater Advantage by being
Diverted than *Instructed*; His Epidemical Diseases being *Fastidios-
ity, Amorphy*, and *Oscitation*;[68] whereas in the present universal
Empire of Wit and Learning, there seems but little Matter left for
Instruction. However, in Compliance with a Lesson of Great Age
and Authority, I have attempted carrying the Point in all its Heights;
and accordingly throughout this Divine Treatise, have skilfully
kneaded up both together with a *Layer* of *Utile* and a *Layer* of
Dulce.[69]

WHEN I consider how exceedingly our Illustrious *Moderns* have
eclipsed the weak glimmering Lights of the *Antients*, and turned
them out of the Road of all fashionable Commerce, to a degree,
that our choice * Town-Wits of most refined Accomplishments, are
in grave Dispute, whether there have been ever any *Antients* or no:
In which Point we are like to receive wonderful Satisfaction from
the most useful Labours and Lucubrations of that Worthy *Modern*,
Dr. B——*tly*: I say, when I consider all this, I cannot but bewail,
that no famous *Modern* hath ever yet attempted an universal
System in a small portable Volume, of all Things that are to be
Known, or Believed, or Imagined, or Practised in Life. I am, how-

* *The Learned Person here meant by our Author* [i.e., Bentley—Editors], *hath
been endeavouring to annihilate so many Antient Writers, that until he is pleas'd
to stop his hand it will be dangerous to affirm, whether there have been any
Antients in the World.*

ever, forced to acknowledge, that such an enterprise was thought on some Time ago by a great Philosopher of * O. Brazile. The Method he proposed, was by a certain curious Receipt, a Nostrum, which after his untimely Death, I found among his Papers; and do here out of my great Affection to the Modern Learned, present them with it, not doubting, it may one Day encourage some worthy Undertaker.

YOU take fair correct Copies, well bound in Calfs Skin, and Lettered at the Back, of all Modern Bodies of Arts and Sciences whatsoever, and in what Language you please. These you distil in balneo Mariæ,[70] infusing Quintessence of Poppy Q. S.[71] together with three Pints of Lethe, to be had from the Apothecaries. You cleanse away carefully the Sordes and Caput mortuum,[72] letting all that is volatile evaporate. You preserve only the first Running, which is again to be distilled seventeen times, till what remains will amount to about two Drams. This you keep in a Glass Viol Hermetically sealed, for one and twenty Days. Then you begin your Catholick Treatise, taking every Morning fasting, (first shaking the Viol) three Drops of this Elixir, snuffing it strongly up your Nose. It will dilate it self about the Brain (where there is any) in fourteen Minutes, and you immediately perceive in your Head an infinite Number of Abstracts, Summaries, Compendiums, Extracts, Collections, Medulla's, Excerpta quædam's, Florilegia's[73] and the like, all disposed into great Order, and reducible upon Paper.

I must needs own, it was by the Assistance of this Arcanum, that I, tho' otherwise impar, have adventured upon so daring an Attempt; never atchieved or undertaken before, but by a certain Author called Homer, in whom, tho' otherwise a Person not without some Abilities, and for an Ancient, of a tolerable Genius; I have discovered many gross Errors, which are not to be forgiven his very Ashes, if by chance any of them are left. For whereas, we are assured, he design'd his Work for a * compleat Body of all Knowledge Human, Divine, Political, and Mechanick; it is manifest, he hath wholly neglected some, and been very imperfect in the rest. For, first of all, as eminent a Cabbalist as his Disciples would represent Him, his Account of the Opus magnum[75] is extreamly poor and deficient; he seems to have read but very superficially, either Sendivogus,[76] Behmen,[77] or †

* Homerus omnes res humanas Poematis complexus est. Xenoph. in conviv.[74]

* This is an imaginary Island, of Kin to that which is call'd the Painters Wives Island, placed in some unknown part of the Ocean, meerly at the Fancy of the Map-maker.
† A Treatise written about fifty Years ago, by a Welsh Gentleman of Cambridge, his Name, as I remember, was Vaughan, as appears by the Answer to it, writ by the Learned Dr. Henry Moor, it is a Piece of the most unintelligible Fustian, that, perhaps, was ever publish'd in any Language.

Anthroposophia Theomagica. He is also quite mistaken about the
Sphæra Pyroplastica,[78] a neglect not to be attoned for; and (if the
Reader will admit so severe a Censure) *Vix crederem Autorem
hunc, unquam audivisse ignis vocem.*[79] His Failings are not less
prominent in several Parts of the *Mechanicks.* For, having read his
Writings with the utmost Application usual among *Modern Wits*,
I could never yet discover the least Direction about the Structure
of that useful Instrument a *Save-all.*[80] For want of which, if the
Moderns had not lent their Assistance, we might yet have wandred
in the Dark. But I have still behind, a Fault far more notorious to
tax this Author with; I mean, * his gross Ignorance in the *Common
Laws of this Realm,* and in the Doctrine as well as Discipline of
the Church of *England.* A Defect indeed, for which both he and
all the Ancients stand most justly censured by my worthy and
ingenious Friend Mr. W—tt—on, Batchelor of Divinity, in his
incomparable Treatise of *Ancient and Modern Learning;* A Book
never to be sufficiently valued, whether we consider the happy
Turns and Flowings of the Author's Wit, the great Usefulness of
his sublime Discoveries upon the Subject of *Flies* and *Spittle,* or
the laborious Eloquence of his Stile. And I cannot forbear doing
that Author the Justice of my publick Acknowledgments, for the
great *Helps* and *Liftings* I had out of his incomparable Piece, while
I was penning this Treatise.

BUT, besides these Omissions in *Homer* already mentioned, the
curious Reader will also observe several Defects in that Author's
Writings, for which he is not altogether so accountable. For whereas
every Branch of Knowledge has received such wonderful Acquirements since his Age, especially within these last three Years, or
thereabouts; it is almost impossible, he could be so very perfect in
Modern Discoveries, as his Advocates pretend. We freely acknowledge Him to be the Inventor of the *Compass,* of *Gun-Powder,*
and the *Circulation of the Blood:* But, I challenge any of his
Admirers to shew me in all his Writings, a compleat Account of the
Spleen; Does he not also leave us wholly to seek in the Art of *Political Wagering?* What can be more defective and unsatisfactory than
his long Dissertation upon *Tea?* and as to his Method of *Salivation
without Mercury,* so much celebrated of late, it is to my own
Knowledge and Experience, a Thing very little to be relied on.

I T was to supply such momentous Defects, that I have been prevailed on after long Sollicitation, to take Pen in Hand; and I dare
venture to Promise, the Judicious Reader shall find nothing neglected here, that can be of Use upon any Emergency of Life. I am

---

* *Mr. W—tt—n (to whom our Author never gives any Quarter) in his Comparison of Antient and Modern Learning, Numbers Divinity, Law, &c. among those
Parts of Knowledge wherein we excel the Antients.*

confident to have included and exhausted all that Human Imagination can *Rise* or *Fall* to. Particularly, I recommend to the Perusal of the Learned, certain Discoveries that are wholly untoucht by others; whereof I shall only mention among a great many more; *My New help of Smatterers,* or the *Art of being Deep-learned, and Shallow-read. A curious Invention about Mouse-Traps. An Universal Rule of Reason, or Every Man his own Carver;* Together with a most useful Engine for *catching of Owls.* All which the judicious Reader will find largely treated on, in the several Parts of this Discourse.

I hold my self obliged to give as much Light as is possible, into the Beauties and Excellencies of what I am writing, because it is become the Fashion and Humor most applauded among the first Authors of this Polite and Learned Age, when they would correct the ill Nature of Critical, or inform the Ignorance of Courteous Readers. Besides, there have been several famous Pieces lately published both in Verse and Prose; wherein, if the Writers had not been pleas'd, out of their great Humanity and Affection to the Publick, to give us a nice Detail of the *Sublime,* and the *Admirable* they contain; it is a thousand to one, whether we should ever have discovered one Grain of either. For my own particular, I cannot deny, that whatever I have said upon this Occasion, had been more proper in a Preface, and more agreeable to the Mode, which usually directs it there. But I here think fit to lay hold on that great and honourable Privilege of being the *Last Writer;* I claim an absolute Authority in Right, as the *freshest Modern,* which gives me a Despotick Power over all Authors before me. In the Strength of which Title, I do utterly disapprove and declare against that pernicious Custom, of making the Preface a Bill of Fare to the Book. For I have always lookt upon it as a high Point of Indiscretion in *Monster-mongers* and other *Retailers of strange Sights;* to hang out a fair large Picture over the Door, drawn after the Life, with a most eloquent Description underneath: This hath saved me many a Three-pence, for my Curiosity was fully satisfied, and I never offered to go in, tho' often invited by the urging and attending Orator, with his last *moving* and *standing* Piece of Rhetorick; *Sir, Upon my Word, we are just going to begin.* Such is exactly the Fate, at this Time, of *Prefaces, Epistles, Advertisements, Introductions, Prolegomena's, Apparatus's, To-the-Reader's.* This Expedient was admirable at first; Our Great *Dryden* has long carried it as far as it would go, and with incredible Success. He has often said to me in Confidence, that the World would have never suspected him to be so great a Poet, if he had not assured them so frequently in his Prefaces, that it was impossible they could either doubt or forget it. Perhaps it may be so; However, I much fear, his Instructions have edify'd out of their Place, and taught Men to grow Wiser in certain Points, where he never intended they should; For it is lamentable to behold, with what a lazy Scorn, many of the yawning Readers in our Age, do now a-days twirl over forty or fifty Pages of *Preface* and *Dedication,* (which is the usual *Modern* Stint) as if it were so much *Latin.* Tho' it must be also allowed on the other Hand that a very considerable Number is known to proceed *Criticks* and *Wits,* by reading nothing else. Into which two Factions, I think, all present Readers may justly be divided. Now, for my self, I profess to be of the former Sort; and therefore having the *Modern* Inclination to expatiate upon the Beauty of my own Productions, and display the bright Parts of my Discourse; I thought best to do it in the Body of the Work, where, as it now lies, it makes a very considerable Addition to the Bulk of the Volume, *a Circumstance by no means to be neglected by a skilful Writer.*

HAVING thus paid my due Deference and Acknowledgment to an establish'd Custom of our newest Authors, by *a long Digression unsought for,* and *an universal Censure unprovoked;* By forcing into the Light, with much Pains and Dexterity, my own Excellencies and other Mens Defaults, with great Justice to my self and candor to them; I now happily resume my Subject, to the Infinite Satisfaction both of the Reader and the Author.

SECT. VI. *A Tale of a Tub*

WE left *Lord Peter* in open Rupture with his two Brethren; both for ever discarded from his House, and resigned to the wide World, with little or nothing to trust to. Which are Circumstances that render them proper Subjects for the Charity of a Writer's Pen to work on; Scenes of Misery, ever affording the fairest Harvest for great Adventures. And in this, the World may perceive the Difference between the Integrity of a generous Author, and that of a common Friend. The latter is observed to adhere close in Prosperity, but on the Decline of Fortune, to drop suddenly off. Whereas, the generous Author, just on the contrary, finds his Hero on the Dunghil, from thence by gradual Steps, raises Him to a Throne, and then immediately withdraws, expecting not so much as Thanks for his Pains: In imitation of which Example, I have placed *Lord Peter* in a Noble House, given Him a Title to wear, and Money to spend. There I shall leave Him for some Time; returning where common Charity directs me, to the Assistance of his two Brothers, at their lowest Ebb. However, I shall by no means forget my Character of an Historian, to follow the Truth, step by step, whatever happens, or where-ever it may lead me.

T H E two Exiles so nearly united in Fortune and Interest, took a Lodging together; Where, at their first Leisure, they began to reflect on the numberless Misfortunes and Vexations of their Life past, and could not tell, on the sudden, to what Failure in their Conduct they ought to impute them; When, after some Recollection, they called to Mind the Copy of their Father's *Will*, which they had so happily recovered. This was immediately produced, and a firm Resolution taken between them, to alter whatever was already amiss, and reduce all their future Measures to the strictest Obedience prescribed therein. The main Body of the *Will* (as the Reader cannot easily have forgot) consisted in certain admirable Rules about the wearing of their Coats; in the Perusal whereof, the two Brothers at every Period duly comparing the Doctrine with the Practice, there was never seen a wider Difference between two Things; horrible down-right Transgressions of every Point. Upon which, they both resolved without further Delay, to fall immediately upon reducing the Whole, exactly after their Father's Model.

B U T, here it is good to stop the hasty Reader, ever impatient to see the End of an Adventure, before We Writers can duly prepare him for it. I am to record, that these two Brothers began to be distinguished at this Time, by certain Names. One of them desired to be called * M A R T I N, and the other took the Appellation of † J A C K. These two had lived in much Friendship and Agreement under the Tyranny of their Brother *Peter*, as it is the Talent of Fellow-Sufferers to do; Men in Misfortune, being like Men in the Dark, to whom all Colours are the same: But when they came forward into the World, and began to display themselves to each other, and to the Light, their Complexions appear'd extreamly different; which the present Posture of their Affairs gave them sudden Opportunity to discover.

B U T, here the severe Reader may justly tax me as a Writer of short Memory, a Deficiency to which a true *Modern* cannot but of Necessity be a little subject: Because, *Memory* being an Employment of the Mind upon things past, is a Faculty, for which the Learned, in our Illustrious Age, have no manner of Occasion, who deal entirely with *Invention*, and strike all Things out of themselves, or at least, by Collision, from each other: Upon which Account we think it highly Reasonable to produce our great Forget-

* *Martin Luther.*
† *John Calvin.*

fulness, as an Argument unanswerable for our great Wit. I ought in Method, to have informed the Reader about fifty Pages ago, of a Fancy Lord *Peter* took, and infused into his Brothers, to wear on their Coats what ever Trimmings came up in Fashion: never pulling off any, as they went out of the Mode, but keeping on all together; which amounted in time to a Medley, the most Antick you can possibly conceive; and this to a Degree, that upon the Time of their falling out there was hardly a Thread of the Original Coat to be seen, but an infinite Quantity of *Lace*, and *Ribbands*, and *Fringe*, and *Embroidery*, and *Points*; (I mean, only those * *tagg'd with Silver*, for the rest fell off.) Now, this material Circumstance, having been forgot in due Place; as good Fortune hath ordered, comes in very properly here, when the two Brothers are just going to reform their Vestures into the Primitive State, prescribed by their Father's *Will*.

THEY both unanimously entred upon this great Work, looking sometimes on their Coats, and sometimes on the *Will. Martin* laid the first Hand; at one twitch brought off a large Handful of *Points*, and with a second pull, stript away ten dozen Yards of *Fringe*. But when He had gone thus far, he demurred a while: He knew very well, there yet remained a great deal more to be done; however, the first Heat being over, his Violence began to cool, and he resolved to proceed more moderately in the rest of the Work; having already very narrowly scap'd a swinging Rent in pulling off the *Points*, which being *tagged with Silver* (as we have observed before) the judicious Workman had with much Sagacity, double sown, to preserve them from *falling*. Resolving therefore to rid his Coat of a huge Quantity of *Gold Lace*; he pickt up the Stitches with much Caution, and diligently gleaned out all the loose Threads as he went, which proved to be a Work of Time. Then he fell about the embroidered *Indian* Figures of Men, Women and Children; against which, as you have heard in its due Place, their Father's Testament was extreamly exact and severe: These, with much Dexterity and Application, were after a while, quite eradicated, or utterly defaced. For the rest, where he observed the Embroidery to be workt so close, as not to be got away without damaging the Cloth, or where it served to hide or strengthen any Flaw in the Body of the Coat, contracted by the perpetual tampering of Workmen upon it; he concluded the wisest Course was to let it remain; resolving in no Case whatsoever, that the Substance of the Stuff should suffer Injury; which he thought the best Method for serving the true

* *Points tagg'd with Silver, are those Doctrines that Promote the Greatness and Wealth of the Church, which have been therefore woven deepest in the Body of Popery.*

Intent and Meaning of his Father's *Will*. And this is the nearest Account I have been able to collect, of *Martin's* Proceedings upon this great Revolution.[81]

BUT his Brother *Jack*, whose Adventures will be so extraordinary, as to furnish a great Part in the Remainder of this Discourse; entred upon the matter with other Thoughts, and a quite different Spirit. For, the Memory of *Lord Peter's* injuries, produced a Degree of Hatred and Spight, which had a much greater Share of inciting Him, than any Regards after his Father's Commands, since these appeared at best, only Secondary and Subservient to the other. However, for this Meddly of Humor, he made a Shift to find a very plausible Name, honoring it with the Title of *Zeal*; which is, perhaps, the most significant Word that hath been ever yet produced in any Language; As, I think, I have fully proved in my excellent *Analytical* Discourse upon that Subject; wherein I have deduced a *Histori-theo-physi-logical* Account of *Zeal*, shewing how it first proceeded from a *Notion* into a *Word*, and from thence in a hot Summer, ripned into a *tangible Substance*. This Work containing three large Volumes in Folio, I design very shortly to publish by the *Modern* way of *Subscription*, not doubting but the Nobility and Gentry of the Land will give me all possible Encouragement, having already had such a Taste of what I am able to perform.

I record therefore, that Brother *Jack*, brimful of this miraculous Compound, reflecting with Indignation upon *PETER's* Tyranny, and farther provoked by the Despondency of *Martin*; prefaced his Resolutions to this purpose. *What*; said he; *A Rogue that lock'd up his Drink, turned away our Wives, cheated us of our Fortunes; paumed his damned Crusts upon us for Mutton; and at last kickt us out of Doors; must we be in His Fashions with a Pox? a Rascal, besides, that all the Street cries out against.* Having thus kindled and enflamed himself as high as possible, and by Consequence, in a delicate Temper for beginning a Reformation, he set about the Work immediately, and in three Minutes, made more Dispatch than *Martin* had done in as many Hours. For, (Courteous Reader) you are given to understand, that *Zeal* is never so highly obliged, as when you set it a *Tearing*: and *Jack*, who doated on that Quality in himself, allowed it at this Time its full Swinge. Thus it happened, that stripping down a Parcel of *Gold Lace*, a little too hastily, he rent the *main Body* of his *Coat* from Top to Bottom; and whereas his Talent was not of the happiest in *taking up a Stitch*, he knew no better way, than to dern it again with *Packthred* and a *Scewer*. But the Matter was yet infinitely worse (I record it with Tears) when he proceeded to the *Embroidery*: For, being Clumsy by Nature, and of Temper, Impatient; withal, beholding Millions of

Stitches, that required the nicest Hand, and sedatest Constitution, to extricate; in a great Rage, he tore off the whole Piece, Cloth and all, and flung it into the Kennel, and furiously thus continuing his Career; *Ah, Good Brother* Martin, said he, *do as I do, for the Love of God; Strip, Tear, Pull, Rent, Flay off all, that we may appear as unlike the Rogue* Peter, *as it is possible: I would not for a hundred Pounds carry the least Mark about me, that might give Occasion to the Neighbours, of suspecting I was related to such a Rascal.* But *Martin,* who at this Time happened to be extremely flegmatick and sedate, *begged his Brother of all Love, not to damage his Coat by any Means; for he never would get such another:* Desired him *to consider, that it was not their Business to form their Actions by any Reflection upon* Peter's, *but by observing the Rules prescribed in their Father's* Will. That *he should remember,* Peter *was still their Brother, whatever Faults or Injuries he had committed; and therefore they should by all means avoid such a Thought, as that of taking Measures for Good and Evil, from no other Rule, than of Opposition to him.* That *it was true, the Testament of their good Father was very exact in what related to the wearing of their* Coats; *yet was it no less penal and strict in prescribing Agreement, and Friendship, and Affection between them. And therefore, if straining a Point were at all dispensable, it would certainly be so, rather to the Advance of Unity, than Increase of Contradiction.*

MARTIN had still proceeded as gravely as he began; and doubtless, would have delivered an admirable Lecture of Morality, which might have exceedingly contributed to my Reader's *Repose, both of Body and Mind:* (the true ultimate End of *Ethicks;*) But *Jack* was already gone a Flight-shot beyond his Patience. And as in Scholastick Disputes, nothing serves to rouze the Spleen of him that Opposes, so much as a kind of Pedantick affected Calmness in the *Respondent;* Disputants being for the most part like unequal Scales, where the *Gravity* of one Side advances the *Lightness* of the Other, and causes it to fly up and kick the Beam; So it happened here, that the *Weight* of *Martin's* Arguments exalted *Jack's Levity,* and made him fly out and spurn against his Brother's Moderation. In short, *Martin's Patience* put *Jack* in a *Rage;* but that which most afflicted him was, to observe his Brother's Coat so well reduced into the State of Innocence; while his own was either wholly rent to his Shirt; or those Places which had scaped his cruel Clutches, were still in *Peter's* Livery. So that he looked like a drunken *Beau,* half rifled by *Bullies;* Or like a fresh Tenant of *Newgate,* when he has refused the Payment of *Garnish;* Or like a discovered *Shoplifter,* left to the Mercy of *Exchange-Women;* Or like a *Bawd* in her old Velvet-Petticoat, resign'd into the secular Hands of the *Mobile.*[82] Like any, or like all of these, a Meddley of *Rags*, and *Lace*, and *Rents*, and *Fringes*, unfortunate *Jack* did now appear: He would have been extremely glad to see his Coat in the Condition of *Martin's*, but infinitely gladder to find that of *Martin's* in the same Predicament with his. However, since neither of these was likely to come to pass, he thought fit to lend the whole Business another Turn, and to dress up Necessity into a Virtue. Therefore, after as many of the *Fox's* Arguments, as he could muster up, for bringing *Martin* to *Reason*, as he called it; or, as he meant it, into his own ragged, bob-tail'd Condition; and observing he said all to little purpose; what, alas, was left for the forlorn *Jack* to do, but after a Million of Scur-rilities against his Brother, to run mad with Spleen, and Spight, and Contradiction. To be short, here began a mortal Breach between these two. *Jack* went immediately to *New Lodgings*, and in a few Days it was for certain reported, that he had run out of his Wits. In a short time after, he appeared abroad, and confirmed the Report, by falling into the oddest Whimsies that ever a sick Brain conceived.

AND now the little Boys in the Streets began to salute him with several Names. Sometimes they would call Him, * *Jack the Bald*; sometimes, † *Jack with a Lanthorn*; sometimes, || *Dutch Jack*; some-times, * *French Hugh*; sometimes, † *Tom the Beggar*; and some-times, || *Knocking Jack of the North*. And it was under one or some, or all of these Appellations (which I leave the Learned Reader to determine) that he hath given Rise to the most Illustrious and Epi-demick Sect of *Æolists*, who with honourable Commemoration, do still acknowledge the Renowned *JACK* for their Author and Foun-der. Of whose Original, as well as Principles, I am now advancing to gratify the World with a very particular Account.

——— *Mellœo contingens cuncta Lepore.*[83]

SECT. VII. *A Digression in Praise of Digressions*

I HAVE sometimes *heard* of an *Iliad* in a *Nut-shell*; but it hath been my Fortune to have much oftner *seen* a *Nut-shell* in an *Iliad*.[84] There is no doubt, that Human Life has received most wonderful

---

* *That is* Calvin, *from* Calvus, *Bald*.
† *All those who pretend to Inward Light*.
|| Jack *of* Leyden, *who gave Rise to the* Anabaptists.
* The Hugonots.
† *The Gueuses, by which Name some Protestants in* Flanders *were call'd*.
|| John Knox, *the Reformer of* Scotland.

Advantages from both; but to which of the two the World is chiefly indebted, I shall leave among the Curious, as a Problem worthy of their utmost Enquiry. For the Invention of the latter, I think the Commonwealth of Learning is chiefly obliged to the great *Modern* Improvement of *Digressions:* The late Refinements in Knowledge, running parallel to those of Dyet in our Nation, which among Men of a judicious Taste, are drest up in various Compounds, consisting in *Soups* and *Ollio's, Fricassées* and *Ragousts.*

'TIS true, there is a sort of morose, detracting, ill-bred People, who pretend utterly to disrelish these polite Innovations: And as to the Similitude from Dyet, they allow the Parallel, but are so bold to pronounce the Example it self, a Corruption and Degeneracy of Taste. They tell us, that the Fashion of jumbling fifty Things together in a Dish, was at first introduced in Compliance to a depraved and *debauched Appetite*, as well as to a *crazy Constitution*; And to see a Man hunting thro' an *Ollio*, after the *Head* and *Brains* of a *Goose*, a *Wigeon*, or a *Woodcock*, is a Sign, he wants a Stomach and Digestion for more substantial Victuals. Farther, they affirm, that *Digressions* in a Book, are like *Forein Troops* in a *State*, which argue the Nation to want a *Heart* and *Hands* of its own, and often, either *subdue* the *Natives*, or drive them into the most *unfruitful Corners.*

BUT, after all that can be objected by these supercilious Censors; 'tis manifest, the Society of Writers would quickly be reduced to a very inconsiderable Number, if Men were put upon making Books, with the fatal Confinement of delivering nothing beyond what is to the Purpose. 'Tis acknowledged, that were the Case the same among Us, as with the *Greeks* and *Romans*, when Learning was in its *Cradle*, to be reared and fed, and cloathed by *Invention*; it would be an easy Task to fill up Volumes upon particular Occasions, without farther exspatiating from the Subject, than by moderate Excursions, helping to advance or clear the main Design. But with *Knowledge*, it has fared as with a numerous Army, encamped in a fruitful Country; which for a few Days maintains it self by the Product of the Soyl it is on; Till Provisions being spent, they send to forrage many a Mile, among Friends or Enemies it matters not. Mean while, the neighbouring Fields trampled and beaten down, become barren and dry, affording no Sustenance but Clouds of Dust.

T H E whole Course of Things, being thus entirely changed between Us and the *Antients*; and the *Moderns* wisely sensible of it, we of this Age have discovered a shorter, and more prudent Method, to become *Scholars* and *Wits*, without the Fatigue of *Reading* or of *Thinking*. The most accomplisht Way of using Books at present, is twofold: Either first, to serve them as some Men do *Lords*, learn their *Titles* exactly, and then brag of their Acquaintance. Or Secondly, which is indeed the choicer, the profounder, and politer Method, to get a thorough Insight into the *Index*, by which the whole Book is governed and turned, like *Fishes* by the *Tail*. For, to enter the Palace of Learning at the *great Gate*, requires an Expence of Time and Forms; therefore Men of much Haste and little Ceremony, are content to get in by the *Back-Door*. For, the Arts are all in a *flying* March, and therefore more easily subdued by attacking them in the *Rear*. Thus Physicians discover the State of the whole Body, by consulting only what comes from *Behind*. Thus Men catch Knowledge by throwing their *Wit* on the *Posteriors* of a Book, as Boys do Sparrows with flinging *Salt* upon their *Tails*. Thus Human Life is best understood by the wise man's Rule of *Regarding the End*. Thus are the Sciences found like *Hercules's* Oxen, by *tracing them Backwards*. Thus are *old Sciences* unravelled like *old Stockings*, by beginning at the *Foot*.

B E S I D E S all this, the Army of the Sciences hath been of late with a world of Martial Discipline, drawn into its *close Order*, so that a View, or a Muster may be taken of it with abundance of Expedition. For this great Blessing we are wholly indebted to *Systems* and *Abstracts*, in which the *Modern* Fathers of Learning, like prudent Usurers, spent their Sweat for the Ease of Us their Children. For *Labor* is the Seed of *Idleness*, and it is the peculiar Happiness of our Noble Age to gather the *Fruit*.

N O W the Method of growing Wise, Learned, and *Sublime*, having become so regular an Affair, and so established in all its Forms; the Number of Writers must needs have increased accordingly, and to a Pitch that has made it of absolute Necessity for them to interfere continually with each other. Besides, it is reckoned, that there is not at this present, a sufficient Quantity of new Matter left in Nature, to furnish and adorn any one particular Subject to the Extent of a Volume. This I am told by a very skillful *Computer*, who hath given a full Demonstration of it from Rules of *Arithmetick*.

T H I S, perhaps, may be objected against, by those, who maintain the Infinity of Matter, and therefore, will not allow that any *Species* of it can be exhausted. For Answer to which, let us examine the noblest Branch of *Modern* Wit or Invention, planted and cultivated by the present Age, and, which of all others, hath born the most, and the fairest Fruit. For tho' some Remains of it were left us by the *Antients*, yet have not any of those, as I remember, been translated or compiled into Systems for *Modern* Use. Therefore We may affirm, to our own Honor, that it has in some sort, been both

invented, and brought to a Perfection by the same Hands. What I
mean, is that highly celebrated Talent among the *Modern* Wits, of
deducing Similitudes, Allusions, and Applications, very Surprizing,
Agreeable, and Apposite, from the *Genitals*[85] of either Sex, together
with *their proper Uses*. And truly, having observed how little Invention bears any Vogue, besides what is derived into these *Channels*,
I have sometimes had a Thought, That the happy Genius of our
Age and Country, was prophetically held forth by that
antient * typical Description of the *Indian*
Pygmies; *whose Stature did not exceed*   * *Ctesiae fragm. apud*
above two Foot; Sed quorum pudenda   *Photium.*
crassa, & ad talos usque pertingentia.[86] Now, I have been very
curious to inspect the late Productions, wherein the Beauties of
this kind have most prominently appeared. And altho' this *Vein*
hath bled so freely, and all Endeavours have been used in the
Power of Human Breath, to dilate, extend, and keep it open: Like
the Scythians, † *who had a Custom, and an*
Instrument, to blow up the Privities of   † *Herodot. L. 4.*
their Mares, that they might yield the more Milk; Yet I am under
an Apprehension, it is near growing dry, and past all Recovery; And
that either some new *Fonde* of Wit should, if possible, be provided,
or else that we must e'en be content with Repetition here, as well
as upon all other Occasions.

T H I S will stand as an uncontestable Argument, that our
Modern Wits are not to reckon upon the Infinity of Matter, for a
constant Supply. What remains therefore, but that our last
Recourse must be had to large *Indexes*, and little *Compendiums*;
Quotations must be plentifully gathered, and bookt in Alphabet; To
this End, tho' Authors need be little consulted, yet *Criticks*, and
Commentators, and *Lexicons* carefully must. But above all, those
judicious Collectors of *bright Parts, and Flowers, and Observanda's*,
are to be nicely dwelt on; by some called the *Sieves* and *Boulters* of
Learning; tho' it is left undetermined, whether they dealt in *Pearls*
or Meal; and consequently, whether we are more to value that
which *passed thro'*, or what *staid behind*.

B Y these Methods, in a few Weeks, there starts up many a
Writer, capable of managing the profoundest, and most universal
Subjects. For, what tho' his *Head* be empty, provided his *Com-*
mon-place-Book be full; And if you will bate him but the Circumstances of *Method*, and *Style*, and *Grammar*, and *Invention*; allow
him but the common Priviledges of transcribing from others, and
digressing from himself, as often as he shall see Occasion; He will
desire no more Ingredients towards fitting up a Treatise, that shall
make a very comely Figure on a Bookseller's Shelf, there to be pre-

served neat and clean, for a long Eternity, adorn'd with the Heraldry of its Title, fairly inscribed on a Label; never to be thumb'd or greas'd by Students, nor bound to everlasting Chains of Darkness in a Library: But when the Fulness of time is come, shall happily undergo the Tryal of Purgatory, in order *to ascend the Sky*.

W I T H O U T these Allowances, how is it possible, we *Modern* Wits should ever have an Opportunity to introduce our Collections listed under so many thousand Heads of a different Nature? for want of which, the Learned World would be deprived of infinite Delight, as well as Instruction, and we our selves buried beyond Redress in an inglorious and undistinguisht Oblivion.

F R O M such Elements as these, I am alive to behold the Day, wherein the Corporation of Authors can out-vie all its Brethren in the *Field*. A Happiness derived to us with a great many others, from our *Scythian* Ancestors; among whom, the Number of *Pens* was so infinite, that the * *Grecian* Eloquence had no other way of expressing it, than by saying, *That in the Regions, far to the* North, *it was hardly possible for a Man to travel, the very Air was so replete with* Feathers.

* *Herodot. L. 4.*

T H E Necessity of this Digression, will easily excuse the Length; and I have chosen for it as proper a Place as I could readily find. If the judicious Reader can assign a fitter, I do here empower him to remove it into any other Corner he pleases. And so I return with great Alacrity to pursue a more important Concern.

S E C T. VIII. *A Tale of a Tub*

T H E Learned * *Æolists*, maintain the Original Cause of all Things to be *Wind*, from which Principle this whole Universe was at first produced, and into which it must at last be resolved; that the same Breath which had kindled, and blew *up* the Flame of Nature, should one Day blow it *out*.

Quod procul à nobis flectat Fortuna gubernans.[87]

T H I S is what the *Adepti* understand by their *Anima Mundi*; that is to say, the *Spirit*, or *Breath*, or *Wind* of the World: Or Examine the whole System by the Particulars of Nature, and you will find it not to be disputed. For, whether you please to call the *Forma informans* of Man, by the Name of *Spiritus, Animus, Afflatus*, or *Anima*; What are all these but several Appellations for

* *All Pretenders to Inspiration whatsoever.*

Wind? which is the ruling *Element* in every Compound, and into which they all resolve upon their Corruption. Farther, what is Life itself, but as it is commonly call'd, the *Breath* of our Nostrils? Whence it is very justly observed by Naturalists, that *Wind* still continues of great Emolument in *certain Mysteries* not to be named, giving Occasion for those happy Epithets of *Turgidus*, and *Inflatus*, apply'd either to the *Emittent*, or *Recipient* Organs.

B Y what I have gathered out of antient Records, I find the *Compass* of their Doctrine took in two and thirty Points, wherein it would be tedious to be very particular. However, a few of their most important Precepts, deducible from it, are by no means to be omitted; among which the following Maxim was of much Weight; That since *Wind* had the Master-Share, as well as Operation in every Compound, by Consequence, those Beings must be of chief Excellence, wherein that *Primordium* appears most prominently to abound; and therefore, *Man* is in highest Perfection of all created Things, as having by the great Bounty of Philosophers, been endued with three distinct *Anima's* or *Winds*, to which the Sage *Æolists*, with much Liberality, have added a fourth of equal Necessity, as well as Ornament with the other three; by this *quartum Principium*, taking in our four Corners of the World; which gave Occasion to that Renowned *Cabbalist*, * *Bumbastus*, of placing the Body of Man, in due position to the four *Cardinal* Points.

I N Consequence of this, their next Principle was, that *Man* brings with him into the World a peculiar Portion or Grain of *Wind*, which may be called a *Quinta essentia*, extracted from the other four. This *Quintessence* is of a Catholick Use upon all Emergencies of Life, is improvable into all Arts and Sciences, and may be wonderfully refined, as well as enlarged by certain Methods in Education. This, when *blown* up to its Perfection, ought not to be covetously hoarded up, stifled, or hid under a Bushel, but freely communicated to Mankind. Upon these Reasons, and others of equal Weight, the Wise *Æolists*, affirm the Gift of B E L C H I N G, to be the noblest Act of a Rational Creature. To cultivate which Art, and render it more serviceable to Mankind, they made Use of several Methods. At certain Seasons of the Year, you might behold the Priests amongst them in vast Numbers, with their † *Mouths gaping wide against a Storm*. At other times were to be seen several Hundreds link'd together in a circular Chain, with every Man a Pair of Bellows applied to his Neighbour's Breech, by which they blew up each other to the Shape and Size of a *Tun*; and for that

---

* *This is one of the Names of* Paracelsus; *He was call'd* Christophorus, Theophrastus, Paracelsus, Bumbastus.
† *This is meant of those Seditious Preachers, who blow up the Seeds of Rebellion,* &c.

Reason, with great Propriety of Speech, did usually call their
Bodies, their *Vessels*. When, by these and the like Performances,
they were grown sufficiently replete, they would immediately depart,
and disembogue for the Publick Good, a plentiful Share of their
Acquirements into their Disciples Chaps. For we must here observe,
that all Learning was esteemed among them to be compounded
from the same Principle. Because, First, it is generally affirmed, or
confess'd that Learning *puffeth Men up*: And Secondly, they proved
it by the following Syllogism; *Words are but Wind; and Learning is
nothing but Words*; Ergo, *Learning is nothing but Wind*. For this
Reason, the Philosophers among them, did in their Schools, deliver
to their Pupils, all their Doctrines and Opinions by *Eructation*,
wherein they had acquired a wonderful Eloquence, and of incredible Variety. But the great Characteristick, by which their chief
Sages were best distinguished, was a certain Position of Countenance, which gave undoubted Intelligence to what Degree or Proportion, the Spirit agitated the inward Mass. For, after certain Gripings, the *Wind* and Vapours issuing forth; having first by their
Turbulence and Convulsions within, caused an Earthquake in Man's
little World; distorted the Mouth, bloated the Cheeks, and gave
the Eyes a terrible kind of *Relievo*. At which Junctures, all their
Belches were received for Sacred, the Sourer the better, and swallowed with infinite Consolation by their meager Devotees. And to
render these yet more compleat, because the Breath of Man's Life is
in his Nostrils, therefore, the choicest, most edifying, and most
enlivening *Belches*, were very wisely conveyed thro' that Vehicle, to
give them a Tincture as they passed.

T H E I R Gods were the four *Winds*, whom they worshipped, as
the Spirits that pervade and enliven the Universe, and as those
from whom alone all *Inspiration* can properly be said to proceed.
However, the Chief of these, to whom they performed the Adora-
tion of *Latria*,[88] was the *Almighty-North*. An antient Deity, whom
the Inhabitants of *Megalopolis* in *Greece*, had likewise in highest
Reverence. * *Omnium Deorum Boream*
Pausan. L. 8   *maxime celebrant*.[89] This God, tho'
endued with Ubiquity, was yet supposed by the profounder *Æolists*, to possess one peculiar Habitation, or (to speak in Form) a
Cœlum Empyræum, wherein he was more intimately present. This
was situated in a certain Region, well known to the Antient *Greeks*,
by them called, Σκοτία, or the *Land of Darkness*. And altho' many
Controversies have arisen upon that Matter; yet so much is undisputed, that from a Region of the *like Denomination*, the most
refined *Æolists* have borrowed their Original, from whence, in
every Age, the zealous among their Priesthood, have brought over

their choicest *Inspiration*, fetching it with their own Hands, from the Fountain Head, in certain *Bladders*, and disploding it among the Sectaries in all Nations, who did, and do, and ever will, daily Gasp and Pant after it.

N O W, their Mysteries and Rites were performed in this Manner. 'Tis well known among the Learned, that the Virtuoso's of former Ages, had a Contrivance for carrying and preserving *Winds* in Casks or Barrels, which was of great Assistance upon long Sea Voyages; and the Loss of so useful an Art at present, is very much to be lamented, tho' I know not how, with great Negligence omitted by * *Pancirollus*. It was an Invention ascribed to *Æolus* himself, from whom this Sect is denominated, and who in Honour of their Founder's Memory, have to this Day preserved great Numbers of those *Barrels*, whereof they fix one in each of their Temples, first beating out the Top; into this *Barrel*, upon Solemn Days, the Priest enters; where, having before duly prepared himself by the methods already described, a secret Funnel is also convey'd from his Posteriors, to the Bottom of the Barrel, which admits new Supplies of Inspiration from a *Northern* Chink or Crany. Whereupon, you behold him swell immediately to the Shape and Size of his *Vessel*. In this Posture he disembogues whole Tempests upon his Auditory, as the Spirit from beneath gives him Utterance; which issuing *ex adytis*, and *penetralibus*,[90] is not performed without much Pain and Gripings. And the *Wind* in breaking forth, † deals with his Face, as it does with that of the Sea; first *blackning*, then *wrinkling*, and at last, *bursting it into a Foam*. It is in this Guise, the Sacred *Æolist* delivers his oracular *Belches* to his panting Disciples; Of whom, some are greedily gaping after the sanctified Breath; others are all the while hymning out the Praises of the *Winds*; and gently wafted to and fro by their own Humming, do thus represent the soft Breezes of their Deities appeased.

IT is from this Custom of the Priests, that some Authors maintain these *Æolists*, to have been very antient in the World. Because, the Delivery of their Mysteries, which I have just now mention'd, appears exactly the same with that of other antient Oracles, whose Inspirations were owing to certain subterraneous *Effluviums* of *Wind*, delivered with the same Pain to the Priest, and much about the *same* Influence on the People. It is true indeed, that these were frequently managed and directed by *Female* Officers, whose Organs were understood to be better disposed for the Admission of those Oracular *Gusts*, as entring and passing up thro' a Receptacle of greater Capacity, and causing also a Pruriency

---

* *An Author who writ* De Artibus Perditis, *&c. of Arts lost, and of Arts invented.*
† *This is an exact Description of the Changes made in the Face by Enthusiastick Preachers.*

by the Way, such as with due Management, hath been refined from
a Carnal, into a Spiritual Extasie. And to strengthen this profound
Conjecture, it is farther insisted, that this Custom of * *Female*
Priests is kept up still in certain refined Colleges of our *Modern*
Æolists, who are agreed to receive their Inspiration, derived thro'
the Receptacle aforesaid, like their Ancestors, the *Sibyls*.

AND, whereas the mind of Man, when he gives the Spur and
Bridle to his Thoughts, doth never stop, but naturally sallies out
into both extreams of High and Low, of Good and Evil; His first
Flight of Fancy, commonly transports Him to Idea's of what is
most Perfect, finished, and exalted; till having soared out of his own
Reach and Sight, not well perceiving how near the Frontiers of
Height and Depth, border upon each other; With the same Course
and Wing, he falls down plum into the lowest Bottom of Things;
like one who travels the *East* into the *West*; or like a strait Line
drawn by its own Length into a Circle. Whether a Tincture of
Malice in our Natures, makes us fond of furnishing every bright
Idea with its Reverse; Or, whether Reason reflecting upon the Sum
of Things, can, like the Sun, serve only to enlighten one half of the
Globe, leaving the other half, by Necessity, under Shade and Darkness, Or, whether Fancy, flying up to the imagination of what is
Highest and Best, becomes over-short, and Spent, and weary, and
suddenly falls like a dead Bird of Paradise, to the Ground. Or,
whether after all these *Metaphysical* Conjectures, I have not
entirely missed the true Reason; The Proposition, however, which
hath stood me in so much Circumstance, is altogether true; That,
as the most unciviliz'd Parts of Mankind, have some way or other,
climbed up into the Conception of a *God*, or Supream Power, so
they have seldom forgot to provide their Fears with certain ghastly
Notions, which instead of better, have served them pretty tolerably
for a *Devil*. And this Proceeding seems to be natural enough; For it
is with Men, whose Imaginations are lifted up very high, after the
same Rate, as with those, whose Bodies are so; that, as they are
delighted with the Advantage of a nearer Contemplation upwards,
so they are equally terrified with the dismal Prospect of the Precipice below. Thus, in the Choice of a *Devil*, it hath been the usual
Method of Mankind, to single out some Being, either in Act, or in
Vision, which was in most Antipathy to the God they had framed.
Thus also the Sect of *Æolists*, possessed themselves with a Dread,
and Horror, and Hatred of two Malignant Natures, betwixt whom,
and the Deities they adored, perpetual Enmity was established. The
first of these, was the † *Camelion*[91] sworn Foe to *Inspiration*, who

* *Quakers who suffer their Women to preach and pray.*
† *I do not well understand what the Author aims at here, any more than by the*
terrible Monster, mention'd in the following Lines, called Moulinavent, *which is*
the French *Word for a Windmill.*

in Scorn, devoured large Influences of their God; without refunding the smallest Blast by *Eructation*. The other was a huge terrible Monster, called *Moulinavent*, who with four strong Arms, waged eternal Battel with all their Divinities, dextrously turning to avoid their Blows, and repay them with Interest.

T H U S furnisht, and set out with *Gods*, as well as *Devils*, was the renowned Sect of *Æolists*; which makes at this Day so illustrious a Figure in the World, and whereof, that Polite Nation of *Laplanders*, are beyond all Doubt, a most Authentick Branch; Of whom, I therefore cannot, without Injustice, here omit to make honourable Mention; since they appear to be so closely allied in Point of Interest, as well as Inclinations, with their Brother *Æolists* among Us, as not only to buy their *Winds* by wholesale from the *same* Merchants, but also to retail them after the *same* Rate and Method, and to Customers much alike.

N O W, whether the System here delivered, was wholly compiled by *Jack*, or, as some Writers believe, rather copied from the Original at *Delphos*, with certain Additions and Emendations suited to Times and Circumstances, I shall not absolutely determine. This I may affirm, that *Jack* gave it at least a new Turn, and formed it into the same Dress and Model, as it lies deduced by me.

I have long sought after this Opportunity, of doing Justice to a Society of Men, for whom I have a peculiar Honour, and whose Opinions, as well as Practices, have been extreamly misrepresented, and traduced by the Malice or Ignorance of their Adversaries. For, I think it one of the greatest, and best of humane Actions, to remove Prejudices, and place Things in their truest and fairest Light; which I therefore boldly undertake without any Regards of my own, beside the Conscience, the Honour, and the Thanks.

S E C T. IX. *A Digression concerning the Original, the Use and Improvement of Madness in a Commonwealth*

NOR shall it any ways detract from the just Reputation of this famous Sect, that its Rise and Institution are owing to such an Author as I have described *Jack* to be; A Person whose Intellectuals were overturned, and his Brain shaken out of its Natural Position; which we commonly suppose to be a Distemper, and call by the Name of *Madness* or *Phrenzy*. For, if we take a Survey of the greatest Actions that have been performed in the World, under the Influence of Single Men; which are, *The Establishment of New Empires by Conquest: The Advance and Progress of New Schemes in Philosophy; and the contriving, as well as the propagating of New Religions:*[92] We shall find the Authors of them all, to have been Persons, whose natural Reason hath admitted great Revolutions from their Dyet, their Education, the Prevalency of some certain Temper, together with the particular Influence of Air and Climate. Besides, there is something Individual in human Minds, that easily kindles at the accidental Approach and Collision of certain Circumstances, which tho' of paltry and mean Appearance, do often flame out into the greatest Emergencies of Life. For great Turns are not always given by strong Hands, but by lucky Adaption, and at proper Seasons; and it is of no import, where the Fire was kindled, if the Vapor has once got up into the Brain. For the *upper Region* of Man, is furnished like the *middle Region* of the Air; The Materials are formed from Causes of the widest Difference, yet produce at last the same Substance and Effect. Mists arise from the Earth, Steams from Dunghils, Exhalations from the Sea, and Smoak from Fire; yet all Clouds are the same in Composition, as well as Consequences: and the Fumes issuing from a Jakes, will furnish as comely and useful a Vapor, as Incense from an Altar. Thus far, I suppose, will easily be granted me; and then it will follow, that as the Face of Nature never produces Rain, but when it is overcast and disturbed, so Human Understanding, seated in the Brain, must be troubled and overspread by Vapours, ascending from the lower Faculties, to water the Invention, and render it fruitful. Now, altho' these Vapours (as it hath been already said) are of as various Original, as those of the Skies, yet the Crop they produce, differs both in Kind and Degree, meerly according to the Soil. I will produce two Instances to prove and Explain what I am now advancing.

* A certain Great Prince raised a mighty Army, filled his Coffers with infinite Treasures, provided an invincible Fleet, and all this, without giving the least Part of his Design to his greatest Ministers, or his nearest Favourites. Immediately the whole World was alarmed; the neighbouring Crowns, in trembling Expectation, towards what Point the Storm would burst; the small Politicians, every where forming profound Conjectures. Some believed he had laid a Scheme for Universal Monarchy: Others, after much Insight, determined the Matter to be a Project for pulling down the *Pope,* and setting up the *Reformed* Religion, which had once been his own. Some, again, of a deeper Sagacity, sent him into *Asia* to subdue the *Turk,* and recover *Palestine.* In the midst of all these Projects and Preparations; a certain † *State-Surgeon,* gathering the Nature of the Disease by these Symptoms, attempted the Cure, at

* *This was* Harry *the Great of* France.
† Ravillac, *who stabb'd* Henry *the Great in his Coach.*

one Blow performed the Operation, broke the Bag, and out flew the
Vapour; nor did any thing want to render it a compleat Remedy,
only, that the Prince unfortunately happened to Die in the Performance. Now, is the Reader exceeding curious to learn, from
whence this *Vapour* took its Rise, which had so long set the Nations
at a Gaze? What secret Wheel, what hidden Spring could put into
Motion so wonderful an Engine? It was afterwards discovered,
that the Movement of this whole Machine had been directed by an
absent *Female*, whose Eyes had raised a Protuberancy, and before
Emission, she was removed into an Enemy's Country. What should
an unhappy Prince do in such ticklish Circumstances as these?
He tried in vain the Poet's never-failing Receipt of *Corpora
quæque*;[93] For,

> *Idque petit corpus mens unde est saucia amore;*[94]
> *Unde feritur, eo tendit, gestitq; coire.* Lucr.[95]

H A V I N G to no purpose used all peaceable Endeavours, the
collected part of the *Semen*, raised and enflamed, became adust,
converted to Choler, turned head upon the spinal Duct, and
ascended to the Brain. The very same Principle that influences a
Bully to break the Windows of a Whore, who has jilted him, naturally stirs up a Great Prince to raise mighty Armies, and dream of
nothing but Sieges, Battles, and Victories.

> *Cunnus teterrima belli*
> *Causa* ————————————[96]

T H E other * Instance is, what I have read somewhere, in a very
antient Author, of a mighty King, who for the space of above thirty
Years, amused himself to take and lose Towns; beat Armies, and be
beaten; drive Princes out of their Dominions; fright Children from
their Bread and Butter; burn, lay waste, plunder, dragoon, massacre
Subject and Stranger, Friend and Foe, Male and Female. 'Tis
recorded, that the Philosophers of each Country were in grave Dispute, upon Causes Natural, Moral, and Political, to find out where
they should assign an original Solution of this *Phœnomenon*. At last
the *Vapour* or *Spirit*, which animated the Hero's Brain, being in
perpetual Circulation, seized upon that Region of Human Body, so
renown'd for furnishing the † *Zibeta Occidentalis*, and gathering
there into a Tumor, left the rest of the World for that Time in
Peace. Of such mighty Consequence it is, where those Exhalations

---

* *This is meant of the Present* French *King.*

† Paracelsus, *who was so famous for Chymistry, try'd an Experiment upon human
Excrement, to make a Perfume of it, which when he had brought to Perfection, he
called* Zibeta Occidentalis, *or* Western-Civet, *the back Parts of Man (according to
his Division mention'd by the Author, page 341.) being the* West.

fix; and of so little, from whence they proceed. The same Spirits
which in their superior Progress would conquer a Kingdom,
descending upon the *Anus*, conclude in a *Fistula*.

L E T us next examine the great Introducers of new Schemes in
Philosophy, and search till we can find, from what Faculty of the
Soul the Disposition arises in mortal Man, of taking it into his
Head, to advance new Systems with such an eager Zeal, in things
agreed on all hands impossible to be known: from what Seeds this
Disposition springs, and to what Quality of human Nature these
Grand Innovators have been indebted for their Number of Disciples. Because, it is plain, that several of the chief among them,
both *Antient* and *Modern*, were usually mistaken by their Adversaries, and indeed, by all, except their own Followers, to have been
Persons Crazed, or out of their Wits, having generally proceeded in
the common Course of their Words and Actions, by a Method very
different from the vulgar Dictates of *unrefined* Reason: agreeing
for the most Part in their several Models, with their present
undoubted Successors in the *Academy* of *Modern Bedlam* (whose
Merits and Principles I shall farther examine in due Place.) Of this
Kind were *Epicurus, Diogenes, Apollonius, Lucretius, Paracelsus,
Des Cartes*, and others; who, if they were now in the World, tied
fast, and separate from their Followers, would in this our undistinguishing Age, incur manifest Danger of *Phlebotomy*, and *Whips*,
and *Chains*, and *dark Chambers*, and *Straw*. For, what Man in the
natural State, or Course of Thinking, did ever conceive it in his
Power, to reduce the Notions of all Mankind, exactly to the same
Length, and Breadth, and Heighth of his own? Yet this is the first
humble and civil Design of all Innovators in the Empire of Reason.
Epicurus, modestly hoped, that one Time or other, a certain Fortuitous Concourse of all Mens Opinions, after perpetual Justlings,
the Sharp with the Smooth, the Light and the Heavy, the Round
and the Square, would by certain *Clinamina*,[97] unite in the
Notions of *Atoms* and *Void*, as these did in the Originals of all
Things. *Cartesius* reckoned to see before he died, the Sentiments
of all Philosophers, like so many lesser Stars in his *Romantick*
System, rapt and drawn within his own *Vortex*. Now, I would
gladly be informed, how it is possible to account for such Imaginations as these in particular Men, without Recourse to my
Phœnomenon of *Vapours*, ascending from the lower Faculties to
over-shadow the Brain, and there distilling into Conceptions, for
which the Narrowness of our Mother-Tongue has not yet assigned
any other Name, besides that of *Madness* or *Phrenzy*. Let us therefore now conjecture how it comes to pass, that none of these great
Prescribers, do ever fail providing themselves and their Notions,

with a Number of implicite Disciples. And, I think, the Reason is easie to be assigned: For, there is a peculiar *String* in the Harmony of Human Understanding, which in several individuals is exactly of the same Tuning. This, if you can dexterously screw up to its right Key, and then strike gently upon it; Whenever you have the Good Fortune to light among those of the same Pitch, they will by a secret necessary Sympathy, strike exactly at the same time. And in this one Circumstance, lies all the Skill or Luck of the Matter; for if you chance to jar the String among those who are either above or below your own Height, instead of subscribing to your Doctrine, they will tie you fast, call you Mad, and feed you with Bread and Water. It is therefore a Point of the nicest Conduct to distinguish and adapt this noble Talent, with respect to the Differences of Persons and of Times. *Cicero* understood this very well, when writing to a Friend in *England*, with a Caution, among other Matters, to beware of being cheated by our *Hackney-Coachmen*[98] (who, it seems, in those days, were as arrant Rascals as they are now) has these remarkable Words. * *Est quod gaudeas te in ista loca venisse, ubi aliquid sapere viderere.*[99] For, to speak a bold Truth, it is a fatal Miscarriage, so ill to order Affairs, as to pass for a *Fool* in one Company, when in another you might be treated as a *Philosopher.* Which I desire *some certain Gentlemen of my Acquaintance,* to lay up in their Hearts, as a very seasonable *Innuendo.*

* Epist. ad Fam. Trebatio.

T H I S, indeed, was the Fatal Mistake of that worthy Gentleman, my most ingenious Friend, Mr. W—*tt*—*n*: A Person, in appearance ordain'd for great Designs, as well as Performances; whether you will consider his *Notions* or his *Looks.* Surely, no Man ever advanced into the Publick, with fitter Qualifications of Body and Mind, for the Propagation of a new Religion. Oh, had those happy Talents misapplied to vain Philosophy, been turned into their proper Channels of *Dreams* and *Visions,* where *Distortion* of Mind and Countenance, are of such Sovereign Use; the base detracting World would not then have dared to report, that something is amiss, that his Brain hath undergone an unlucky Shake; which even his Brother *Modernists* themselves, like Ungrates, do whisper so loud, that it reaches up to the very Garret I am now writing in.

L A S T L Y, Whosoever pleases to look into the Fountains of *Enthusiasm,* from whence, in all Ages, have eternally proceeded such fatning Streams, will find the Spring Head to have been as *troubled* and *muddy* as the Current; Of such great Emolument, is a Tincture of this *Vapour,* which the World calls *Madness,* that without its Help, the World would not only be deprived of those two great Blessings, *Conquests* and *Systems*, but even all Mankind would unhappily be reduced to the same Belief in Things Invisible. Now, the former *Postulatum* being held, that it is of no Import from what Originals this *Vapour* proceeds, but either in what *Angles* it strikes and spreads over the Understanding, or upon what *Species* of Brain it ascends; It will be a very delicate Point, to cut the Feather, and divide the several Reasons to a Nice and Curious Reader, how this numerical Difference in the Brain, can produce Effects of so vast a Difference from the same *Vapour*, as to be the sole Point of Individuation between *Alexander the Great, Jack of Leyden*,[100] and Monsieur *Des Cartes*. The present Argument is the most abstracted that ever I engaged in, it strains my Faculties to their highest Stretch; and I desire the Reader to attend with utmost Perpensity; For, I now proceed to unravel this knotty Point.

* There is in Mankind a certain * * * * * *

* * * * * * * * * * * *

* * * * * * * *
Hic multa desiderantur.

* * * * * * * * * * * *

* * * * * * * And this I take to be a clear Solution of the Matter.

HAVING therefore so narrowly past thro' this intricate Difficulty, the Reader will, I am sure, agree with me in the Conclusion; that if the *Moderns* mean by *Madness*, only a Disturbance or Transposition of the Brain, by Force of certain *Vapours* issuing up from the lower Faculties; Then has this *Madness* been the parent of all those mighty Revolutions, that have happened in *Empire*, in *Philosophy*, and in *Religion*. For, the Brain, in its natural Position and State of Serenity, disposeth its Owner to pass his Life in the common Forms, without any Thought of subduing Multitudes to his own *Power*, his *Reasons* or his *Visions*; and the more he shapes his Understanding by the Pattern of Human Learning, the less he is inclined to form Parties after his particular Notions; because that instructs him in his private Infirmities, as well as in the stubborn Ignorance of the People. But when a Man's Fancy gets *astride* on his Reason, when Imagination is at Cuffs with the Senses, and common Understanding, as well as common Sense, is Kickt out of Doors; the first Proselyte he makes, is Himself, and when that is once compass'd, the Difficulty is not so great in bringing over others; A strong Delusion always operating from *without*, as vigorously as from *within*. For, Cant and Vision are to the Ear and the

---

* *Here is another Defect in the Manuscript, but I think the Author did wisely, and that the Matter which thus strained his Faculties, was not worth a Solution; and it were well if all Metaphysical Cobweb Problems were no otherwise answered.*

Eye, the same that Tickling is to the Touch. Those Entertainments and Pleasures we most value in Life, are such as *Dupe* and play the Wag with the Senses. For, if we take an Examination of what is generally understood by *Happiness*, as it has Respect, either to the Understanding or the Senses, we shall find all its Properties and Adjuncts will herd under this short Definition: That, *it is a perpetual Possession of being well Deceived*. And first, with Relation to the Mind or Understanding; 'tis manifest, what mighty Advantages Fiction has over Truth; and the Reason is just at our Elbow; because Imagination can build nobler Scenes, and produce more wonderful Revolutions than Fortune or Nature will be at Expence to furnish. Nor is Mankind so much to blame in his Choice, thus determining him, if we consider that the Debate meerly lies between *Things past*, and *Things conceived*;[101] and so the Question is only this; Whether Things that have Place in the *Imagination*, may not as properly be said to *Exist*, as those that are seated in the *Memory*; which may be justly held in the Affirmative, and very much to the Advantage of the former, since This is acknowledged to be the *Womb* of Things, and the other allowed to be no more than the *Grave*. Again, if we take this Definition of Happiness, and examine it with Reference to the Senses, it will be acknowledged wonderfully adapt. How fading and insipid do all Objects accost us that are not convey'd in the Vehicle of *Delusion?* How shrunk is every Thing, as it appears in the Glass of Nature? So, that if it were not for the Assistance of Artificial *Mediums*, false Lights, refracted Angles, Varnish, and Tinsel; there would be a mighty Level in the Felicity and Enjoyments of Mortal Men. If this were seriously considered by the World, as I have a certain Reason to suspect it hardly will; Men would no longer reckon among their high Points of Wisdom, the Art of exposing weak Sides, and publishing Infirmities; an Employment in my Opinion, neither better nor worse than that of *Unmasking*, which I think, has never been allowed fair Usage, either in the *World* or the *Play-House*.

I N the Proportion that Credulity is a more peaceful Possession of the Mind, than Curiosity, so far preferable is that Wisdom, which converses about the Surface, to that pretended Philosophy which enters into the Depth of Things, and then comes gravely back with Informations and Discoveries, that in the inside they are good for nothing. The two Senses, to which all Objects first address themselves, are the Sight and the Touch; These never examine farther than the Colour, the Shape, the Size, and whatever other Qualities dwell, or are drawn by Art upon the Outward of Bodies;[102] and then comes Reason officiously, with Tools for cutting, and opening, and mangling, and piercing, offering to demon-

strate, that they are not of the same consistence quite thro'. Now, I
take all this to be the last Degree of perverting Nature; one of
whose Eternal Laws it is, to put her best Furniture forward. And
therefore, in order to save the Charges of all such expensive Anatomy for the Time to come; I do here think fit to inform the
Reader, that in such Conclusions as these, Reason is certainly in the
Right; and that in most Corporeal Beings, which have fallen under
my Cognizance, the *Outside* hath been infinitely preferable to the
In: Whereof I have been farther convinced from some late Experiments. Last Week I saw a Woman *flay'd,* and you will hardly
believe, how much it altered her Person for the worse. Yesterday I
ordered the Carcass of a *Beau* to be stript in my Presence; when we
were all amazed to find so many unsuspected Faults under one Suit
of Cloaths: Then I laid open his *Brain,* his *Heart,* and his *Spleen;*
But, I plainly perceived at every Operation, that the farther we proceeded, we found the Defects encrease upon us in Number and
Bulk: from all which, I justly formed this Conclusion to my self;
That whatever Philosopher or Projector can find out an Art to
sodder and patch up the Flaws and Imperfections of Nature, will
deserve much better of Mankind, and teach us a more useful Science, than that so much in present Esteem, of widening and exposing them (like him who held *Anatomy* to be the ultimate End of
Physick.) And he, whose Fortunes and Dispositions have placed
him in a convenient Station to enjoy the Fruits of this noble Art;
He that can with *Epicurus* content his Ideas with the *Films* and
Images that fly off upon his Senses from the *Superficies* of Things;
Such a Man truly wise, creams off Nature, leaving the Sower and
the Dregs, for Philosophy and Reason to lap up. This is the sublime
and refined Point of Felicity, called, *the Possession of being well
deceived;* The Serene Peaceful State of being a Fool among Knaves.

   B U T to return to *Madness.* It is certain, that according to the
System I have above deduced; every *Species* thereof proceeds from a
Redundancy of *Vapour;* therefore, as some Kinds of *Phrenzy* give
double Strength to the Sinews, so there are of other *Species,* which
add Vigor, and Life, and Spirit to the Brain: Now, it usually happens, that these active Spirits, getting Possession of the Brain,
resemble those that haunt other waste and empty Dwellings, which
for want of Business, either vanish, and carry away a Piece of the
House, or else stay at home and fling it all out of the Windows. By
which are mystically display'd the two principal Branches of *Madness,* and which some Philosophers not considering so well as I,
have mistook to be different in their Causes, over-hastily assigning
the first to Deficiency, and the other to Redundance.

   I think it therefore manifest, from what I have here advanced, that the main Point of Skill and Address, is to furnish Employment for this Redundancy of *Vapour*, and prudently to adjust the Seasons of it; by which means it may certainly become of Cardinal and Catholick Emolument in a Commonwealth. Thus one Man chusing a proper Juncture, leaps into a Gulph, from thence proceeds a Hero, and is called the Saver of his Country; Another atchieves the same Enterprise, but unluckily timing it, has left the Brand of *Madness*, fixt as a Reproach upon his Memory; Upon so nice a Distinction are we taught to repeat the Name of *Curtius* with Reverence and Love; that of *Empedocles*, with Hatred and Contempt. Thus, also it is usually conceived, that the Elder *Brutus* only personated the *Fool* and *Madman*, for the Good of the Publick: but this was nothing else, than a Redundancy of the same *Vapor*, long misapplied, called by the Latins, * *Ingenium par negotiis*:[103] Or, (to translate it as nearly as I can) a sort of   * *Tacit.* *Phrenzy*, never in its right Element, till you take it up in Business of the State.

UPON all which, and many other Reasons of equal Weight, though not equally curious; I do here gladly embrace an Opportunity I have long sought for, of Recommending it as a very noble Undertaking, to Sir E——d S——r, Sir C——r M——ve, Sir J——n B——ls, J——n H——w, Esq; and other Patriots concerned, that they would move for Leave to bring in a Bill, for appointing Commissioners to Inspect into *Bedlam*, and the Parts adjacent;[104] who shall be empowered to *send for Persons, Papers, and Records*: to examine into the Merits and Qualifications of every Student and Professor; to observe with utmost Exactness their several Dispositions and Behaviour; by which means, duly distinguishing and adapting their Talents, they might produce admirable Instruments for the several Offices in a state,   *   *   *   *   * *Civil* and *Military*; proceeding in such Methods as I shall here humbly propose. And, I hope the Gentle Reader will give some Allowance to my great Solicitudes in this important Affair, upon Account of that high Esteem I have ever born that honourable Society, whereof I had some Time the Happiness to be an unworthy Member.

I S any Student tearing his Straw in piece-meal, Swearing and Blaspheming, biting his Grate, foaming at the Mouth, and emptying his Pispot in the Spectator's Faces? Let the Right Worshipful, the *Commissioners of Inspection*, give him a Regiment of Dragoons, and send him into *Flanders* among the *Rest*. Is another eternally talking, sputtering, gaping, bawling, in a Sound without Period or Article? What wonderful Talents are here mislaid!

Let him be furnished immediately with a green Bag and Papers, and * *three Pence* in his Pocket, and away with Him to *Westminster-Hall*. You will find a Third, gravely taking the Dimensions of his Kennel; A Person of Foresight and Insight, tho' kept quite in the Dark; for why, like *Moses, Ecce * cornuta erat ejus facies*. He walks duly in one Pace, intreats your Penny with due Gravity and Ceremony; talks much of hard Times, and Taxes, and the *Whore of Babylon*; Bars up the woodden Window of his Cell constantly at eight a Clock: Dreams of *Fire*, and *Shop-lifters*, and *Court-Customers*, and *Priviledg'd Places*. Now, what a Figure would all these Acquirements amount to, if the Owner were sent into the *City* among his Brethren! Behold a Fourth, in much and deep Conversations with himself, biting his Thumbs at proper Junctures; His Countenance chequered with Business and Design; sometimes walking very fast; with his Eyes nailed to a Paper that he holds in His Hands: A great Saver of Time, somewhat thick of Hearing, very short of Sight, but more of Memory. A Man ever in Haste, a great Hatcher and Breeder of Business, and excellent at the Famous Art of *whispering Nothing*. A huge Idolater of Monosyllables and Procrastination; so ready to *Give* his Word to every Body, that he never *keeps* it. One that has forgot the common *Meaning* of Words, but an admirable Retainer of the *Sound*. Extreamly subject to the *Looseness*, for his *Occasions* are perpetually *calling him away*. If you approach his Grate in his familiar Intervals; *Sir*, says he, *Give me a Penny, and I'll sing you a Song: But give me the Penny first*. (Hence comes the common Saying, and commoner Practice of parting with Money for a *Song*.) What a compleat System of *Court-Skill* is here described in every Branch of it, and all utterly lost with wrong Application? Accost the Hole of another Kennel, first stopping your Nose, you will behold a surley, gloomy, nasty, slovenly Mortal, raking in his own Dung, and dabling in his Urine. The best Part of his Diet, is the Reversion of his own Ordure, which exspiring into Steams, whirls perpetually about, and at last reinfunds. His Complexion is of a dirty Yellow, with a thin scattered Beard, exactly agreeable to that of his Dyet upon its first Declination; like other Insects, who having their Birth and Education in an Excrement, from thence borrow their Colour and their Smell. The Student of this Apartment is very sparing of his Words, but somewhat over-liberal of his Breath; He holds his Hand out ready to receive your Penny, and immediately upon Receipt, withdraws to his former Occupations. Now, is it not amazing to think, the Society of *Warwick-Lane*,[105] should have no more Concern,

* *A Lawyer's Coach-hire.*

* Cornutus, *is either Horned or Shining, and by this Term,* Moses *is described in the vulgar* Latin *of the Bible.*

for the Recovery of so useful a Member, who, if one may judge
from these Appearances, would become the greatest Ornament to
that Illustrious Body? Another Student struts up fiercely to your
Teeth, puffing with his Lips, half squeezing out his Eyes, and very
graciously holds you out his Hand to kiss. The *Keeper*
desires you not to be afraid of this Professor, for he will do you no
Hurt: To him alone is allowed the Liberty of the Anti-Chamber,
and the *Orator* of the Place gives you to understand, that this
solemn Person is a *Taylor* run mad with Pride. This considerable
Student is adorned with many other Qualities, upon which, at
present, I shall not farther enlarge. - - - - - - - - - - - - - - - - -
* *Heark in your Ear* -
I am strangely mistaken, if all his Address, his Motions, and his
Airs, would not then be very natural, and in their proper Element.

I shall not descend so minutely, as to insist upon the vast Number of *Beaux, Fidlers, Poets*, and *Politicians*, that the World
might recover by such a Reformation; But what is more material,
besides the clear Gain redounding to the Commonwealth, by so
large an Acquisition of Persons to employ, whose Talents and
Acquirements, if I may be so bold to affirm it, are now buried, or at
least misapplied: It would be a mighty Advantage accruing to the
Publick from this Enquiry, that all these would very much excel,
and arrive at great Perfection in their several Kinds; which, I think,
is manifest from what I have already shewn; and shall inforce by
this one plain Instance; That even, I my self, the Author of these
momentous Truths, am a Person, whose Imaginations are hard-
mouth'd, and exceedingly disposed to run away with his *Reason*,
which I have observed from long Experience, to be a very light
Rider, and easily shook off; upon which Account, my Friends will
never trust me alone, without a solemn Promise, to vent my Speculations in this, or the like manner, for the universal Benefit of
Human kind; which, perhaps, the gentle, courteous, and candid
Reader, brimful of that *Modern* Charity and Tenderness, usually
annexed to his *Office*, will be very hardly persuaded to believe.

S E C T. X. *A Tale of a Tub*

IT is an unanswerable Argument of a very refined Age, the wonderful Civilities that have passed of late Years, between the Nation
of *Authors*, and that of *Readers*. There can hardly † pop out a *Play*,

---

* *I cannot conjecture what the Author means here, or how this Chasm could be
fill'd, tho' it is capable of more than one Interpretation.*
† *This is literally true, as we may observe in the Prefaces to most Plays, Poems,*
&c.

a *Pamphlet*, or a *Poem*, without a Preface full of Acknowledgements to the World, for the general Reception and Applause
they have given it, which the Lord knows where, or when, or how,
or from whom it received. In due Deference to so laudable a
Custom, I do here return my humble Thanks to *His Majesty*, and
both Houses of *Parliament*; To the *Lords* of the King's most honourable Privy-Council, to the Reverend the *Judges*: To the *Clergy*,
and *Gentry*, and *Yeomantry* of this Land: But in a more especial
manner, to my worthy Brethren and Friends at *Will's Coffee-
House*, and *Gresham-College*, and *Warwick-Lane*, and *Moor-
Fields*,[106] *and Scotland-Yard*, and *Westminster-Hall*, and *Guild-
Hall*; In short, to all Inhabitants and Retainers whatsoever, either in
Court, or Church, or Camp, or City, or Country; for their generous
and universal Acceptance of this Divine Treatise. I accept their
Approbation and good Opinion with extream Gratitude, and to the
utmost of my poor Capacity, shall take hold of all Opportunities to
return the Obligation.

I am also happy, that Fate has flung me into so blessed an Age
for the mutual Felicity of *Booksellers* and *Authors*, whom I may
safely affirm to be at this Day the two only satisfied Parties in *England*. Ask an *Author* how his last Piece hath succeeded; *Why, truly
he thanks his Stars, the World has been very favorable, and he has
not the least Reason to complain: And yet, By G——, He writ it in
a Week at Bits and Starts, when he could steal an Hour from his
urgent Affairs*; as it is a hundred to one, you may see farther in the
Preface, to which he refers you; and for the rest, to the Bookseller.
There you go as a Customer, and make the same Question: *He
blesses his God, the* Thing *takes wonderfully, he is just Printing a
Second Edition, and has but three left in his Shop. You beat down
the* Price: *Sir, we shall not differ*; and in hopes of your Custom
another Time, lets you have it as reasonable as you please; *And,
pray send as many of your Acquaintance as you will, I shall upon
your Account furnish them all at the same Rate.*

N O W, it is not well enough consider'd, to what Accidents and
Occasions the World is indebted for the greatest Part of those
noble Writings, which hourly start up to entertain it. If it were not
for a *rainy Day, a drunken Vigil, a Fit of the Spleen, a Course of
Physick, a sleepy Sunday, an ill Run at Dice, a long Taylor's Bill, a
Beggar's Purse, a factious Head, a hot Sun, costive Dyet, Want of
Books, and a just Contempt of Learning*. But for these Events I
say, and some Others too long to recite, (especially *a prudent Neglect of taking Brimstone inwardly,*) I doubt, the Number of
Authors, and of *Writings* would dwindle away to a Degree most
woful to behold. To confirm this Opinion, hear the Words of the

famous *Troglodyte*[107] Philosopher: *'Tis certain* (said he) *some Grains of Folly are of course annexed, as Part of the Composition of Human Nature, only the Choice is left us, whether we please to wear them* Inlaid *or* Embossed; *And we need not go very far to seek how that is usually determined, when we remember, it is with Human Faculties as with Liquors, the lightest will be ever at the Top.*

T H E R E is in this famous Island of *Britain* a certain paultry *Scribbler*, very voluminous, whose Character the Reader cannot wholly be a Stranger to. He deals in a pernicious Kind of Writings, called *Second Parts*, and usually passes under the Name of *The Author of the First*. I easily foresee, that as soon as I lay down my Pen, this nimble *Operator* will have stole it, and treat me as inhumanly as he hath already done Dr. *Bl——re*, *L——ge*, and many others who shall here be nameless. I therefore fly for Justice and Relief, into the Hands of that great *Rectifier of Saddles*, and *Lover of Mankind*, Dr. *B——tley*, begging he will take this enormous Grievance into his most *Modern* Consideration: And if it should so happen, that the *Furniture of an Ass*, in the Shape of a *Second Part*, must for my Sins be clapt, by a Mistake upon my Back, that he will immediately please, in the Presence of the World, to lighten me of the Burthen, and take it home to *his own House*, till the *true Beast* thinks fit to call for it.

I N the mean time I do here give this publick Notice, that my Resolutions are, to circumscribe within this Discourse the whole Stock of Matter I have been so many Years providing. Since my *Vein* is once opened, I am content to exhaust it all at a Running, for the peculiar Advantage of my dear Country, and for the universal Benefit of Mankind. Therefore hospitably considering the Number of my Guests, they shall have my whole Entertainment at a Meal; And I scorn to set up the *Leavings* in the Cupboard. What the *Guests* cannot eat may be given to the *Poor*, and the * *Dogs* under the Table may gnaw the *Bones*; This I understand for a more generous Proceeding, than to turn the Company's Stomachs, by inviting them again to morrow to a scurvy Meal of *Scraps*.

I F the Reader fairly considers the Strength of what I have advanced in the foregoing Section, I am convinced it will produce a wonderful Revolution in his Notions and Opinions; And he will be abundantly better prepared to receive and to relish the concluding Part of this miraculous Treatise. Readers may be divided into three Classes, the *Superficial*, the *Ignorant*, and the *Learned*: And I have with much Felicity fitted my Pen to the Genius and Advantage of

---

* *By Dogs, the Author means common injudicious Criticks, as he explains it himself before in his* Digression upon Criticks, *(Page 317.)*.

each. The *Superficial* Reader will be strangely provoked to *Laughter*; which clears the Breast and the Lungs, is Soverain against the *Spleen*, and the most innocent of all *Diureticks*. The *Ignorant* Reader (between whom and the former, the Distinction is extreamly nice) will find himself disposed to *Stare*; which is an admirable Remedy for ill Eyes, serves to raise and enliven the Spirits, and wonderfully helps *Perspiration*. But the Reader truly *Learned*, chiefly for whose Benefit I wake, when others sleep, and sleep when others wake,[108] will here find sufficient Matter to employ his Speculations for the rest of his Life. It were much to be wisht, and I do here humbly propose for an Experiment, that every Prince in *Christendom* will take seven of the *deepest Scholars* in his Dominions, and shut them up close for *seven* Years, in *seven* Chambers, with a Command to write *seven* ample Commentaries on this comprehensive Discourse. I shall venture to affirm, that whatever Difference may be found in their several Conjectures, they will be all, without the least Distortion, manifestly deduceable from the Text. Mean time, it is my earnest Request, that so useful an Undertaking may be entered upon (if their Majesties please) with all convenient speed: because I have a strong Inclination, before I leave the World, to taste a Blessing, which we *mysterious* Writers can seldom reach, till we have got into our Graves. Whether it is, that *Fame* being a Fruit grafted on the Body, can hardly grow, and much less ripen, till the *Stock* is in the Earth: Or, whether she be a Bird of Prey, and is lured among the rest, to pursue after the Scent of a *Carcass*: Or, whether she conceives, her Trumpet sounds best and farthest, when she stands on a *Tomb*, by the Advantage of a rising Ground, and the Echo of a hollow Vault.

'T I S true, indeed, the Republick of *dark* Authors, after they once found out this excellent Expedient of *Dying*, have been peculiarly happy in the Variety, as well as Extent of their Reputation. For, *Night* being the universal Mother of Things, wise Philosophers hold all Writings to be *fruitful* in the Proportion they are *dark*; And therefore, the * *true illuminated* (that is to say, the *Darkest* of all) have met with such numberless Commentators, whose *Scholiastick* Midwifry hath deliver'd them of Meanings, that the Authors themselves, perhaps, never conceived, and yet may very justly be allowed the Lawful Parents of them: * The Words of such Writers being like Seed, which, however scattered at random, when they light upon a fruitful Ground, will multiply far beyond either the Hopes or Imagination of the Sower.

A N D therefore in order to promote so useful a Work, I will

* *A Name of the Rosycrucians.*

* *Nothing is more frequent than for Commentators to force Interpretation, which the Author never meant.*

here take Leave to glance a few *Innuendo's*, that may be of great Assistance to those sublime Spirits, who shall be appointed to labor in a universal Comment upon this wonderful Discourse. And First, || I have couched a very profound Mystery in the Number of O's multiply'd by *Seven*, and divided by *Nine*. Also, if a devout Brother of the *Rosy Cross* will pray fervently for sixty three Mornings, with a lively Faith, and then transpose certain Letters and Syllables according to Prescription, in the second and fifth Section; they will certainly reveal into a full Receit of the *Opus Magnum*. Lastly, Whoever will be at the Pains to calculate the whole Number of each Letter in this Treatise, and sum up the Difference exactly between the several Numbers, assigning the true natural Cause for every such Difference; the Discoveries in the Product, will plentifully reward his Labour. But then he must be aware of † *Bythus* and *Sigè*, and to be sure not to forget the Qualities of *Acamoth*; *A cujus lacrymis humecta prodit Substantia, à risu lucida, à tristitiâ solida, & à timore mobilis*,[109] wherein * *Eugenius Philalethes* hath committed an unpardonable Mistake.

* *Vid. Anima magica abscondita.*

SECT. XI.   A *Tale of a Tub*

AFTER so wide a Compass as I have wandred, I do now gladly overtake, and close in with my Subject, and shall henceforth hold on with it an even Pace to the End of my Journey, except some beautiful Prospect appears within sight of my Way; whereof, tho' at present I have neither Warning nor Expectation, yet upon such an Accident, come when it will, I shall beg my Readers Favour and Company, allowing me to conduct him thro' it along with my

|| *This is what the* Cabbalists *among the* Jews *have done with the* Bible, *and pretend to find wonderful Mysteries by it.*
† *I was told by an Eminent Divine, whom I consulted on this Point, that these two Barbarous Words, with that of* Acamoth *and its Qualities, as here set down, are quoted from* Irenæus. *This he discover'd by searching that Antient Writer for another Quotation of our Author, which he has placed in the Title Page, and refers to the Book and Chapter; the Curious were very Inquisitive, whether those Barbarous Words,* Basima Eacabasa, &c. *are really in* Irenæus, *and upon enquiry 'twas found they were a sort of Cant or Jargon of certain Hereticks, and therefore very properly prefix'd to such a Book as this of our Author.*
* *To the abovementioned Treatise, called* Anthroposophia Theomagica, *there is another annexed, called* Anima Magica Abscondita, *written by the same Author* Vaughan, *under the Name of* Eugenius Philalethes, *but in neither of those Treatises is there any mention of* Acamoth *or its Qualities, so that this is nothing but Amusement, and a Ridicule of dark, unintelligible Writers; only the Words,* A cujus lacrymis, &c. *are as we have said, transcribed from* Irenæus, *tho' I know not from what part. I believe one of the Authors Designs was to set curious Men a hunting thro' Indexes, and enquiring for Books out of the common Road.*

self. For in *Writing*, it is as in *Travelling*: If a Man is in haste to
be at home, (which I acknowledge to be none of my Case, having
never so little Business, as when I am there) if his *Horse* be tired
with long Riding, and ill Ways, or be naturally a Jade, I advise him
clearly to make the straitest and the commonest Road, be it ever
so dirty; But, then surely, we must own such a Man to be a scurvy
Companion at best; He *spatters* himself and his Fellow-Travellers at
every Step: All their Thoughts, and Wishes, and Conversation turn
entirely upon the Subject of their Journey's End; and at every
Splash, and Plunge, and Stumble, they heartily wish one another at
the Devil.

O N the other side, when a Traveller and his *Horse* are in Heart
and Plight, when his Purse is full, and the Day before him; he takes
the Road only where it is clean or convenient; entertains his Company there as agreeably as he can; but upon the first Occasion, carries them along with him to every delightful Scene in View,
whether of Art, of Nature, or of both; and if they chance to refuse
out of Stupidity or Weariness; let them jog on by themselves, and
be d——n'd; He'll overtake them at the next Town; at which arriving, he Rides furiously thro', the Men, Women, and Children run
out to gaze, a hundred * noisy *Curs* run *barking* after him, of
which, if he honors the boldest with a *Lash of his Whip*, it is rather
out of Sport than Revenge: But should some *sourer Mungrel* dare
too near an Approach, he receives a *Salute* on the Chaps by an accidental Stroak from the Courser's Heels, (nor is any Ground lost by
the Blow) which sends him yelping and limping home.

I now proceed to sum up the singular Adventures of my
renowned *Jack*; the State of whose Dispositions and Fortunes, the
careful Reader does, no doubt, most exactly remember, as I last
parted with them in the Conclusion of a former Section. Therefore,
his next Care must be from two of the foregoing, to extract a
Scheme of Notions, that may best fit his Understanding for a true
Relish of what is to ensue.

J A C K had not only calculated the first Revolution of his Brain
so prudently, as to give Rise to that Epidemick Sect of *Æolists*, but
succeeding also into a new and strange Variety of Conceptions, the
Fruitfulness of his Imagination led him into certain Notions,
which, altho' in Appearance very unaccountable, were not without
their Mysteries and their Meanings, nor wanted Followers to countenance and improve them. I shall therefore be extreamly careful
and exact in recounting such material Passages of this Nature, as I
have been able to collect, either from undoubted Tradition, or inde-

* *By these are meant what the Author calls The* True Criticks, *Page 312.*

fatigable Reading; and shall describe them as graphically as it is possible, and as far as Notions of that Height and Latitude can be brought within the Compass of a Pen. Nor do I at all question, but they will furnish Plenty of noble Matter for such, whose converting Imaginations dispose them to reduce all Things into *Types*; who can make *Shadows*, no thanks to the Sun; and then mold them into Substances, no thanks to Philosophy; whose peculiar Talent lies in fixing Tropes and Allegories to the *Letter*, and refining what is Literal into Figure and Mystery.

J A C K had provided a fair Copy of his Father's *Will*, engrossed in Form upon a large Skin of Parchment; and resolving to act the Part of a most dutiful Son, he became the fondest Creature of it imaginable. For, altho', as I have often told the Reader, it consisted wholly in certain plain, easy Directions about the management and wearing of their Coats, with Legacies and Penalties, in case of Obedience or Neglect; yet he began to entertain a Fancy, that the Matter was *deeper* and *darker*, and therefore must needs have a great deal more of Mystery at the Bottom. *Gentlemen*, said he, *I will prove this very Skin of Parchment to be Meat, Drink, and Cloth, to be the Philosopher's Stone, and the Universal Medicine.* * In consequence of which Raptures, he resolved to make use of it in the most necessary, as well as the most paltry Occasions of Life. He had a Way of working it into any Shape he pleased; so that it served him for a Night-cap when he went to Bed, and for an Umbrello in rainy Weather. He would lap a Piece of it about a sore Toe, or when he had Fits, burn two Inches under his Nose; or if any Thing lay heavy on his Stomach, scrape off, and swallow as much of the Powder as would lie on a silver Penny, they were all infallible Remedies. With Analogy to these Refinements, his common Talk and Conversation, † ran wholly in the Phrase of his Will, and he circumscribed the utmost of his Eloquence within that Compass, not daring to let slip a Syllable without Authority from thence. Once at a strange House, he was suddenly taken short, upon an urgent Juncture, whereon it may not be allowed too particularly to dilate; and being not able to call to mind, with that Suddenness, the Occasion required, an Authentick Phrase for demanding the Way to the Backside; he chose rather as the more prudent Course, to incur the Penalty in such Cases usually annexed. Neither was it possible for the united Rhetorick of Mankind to prevail with

---

* *The Author here lashes those Pretenders to Purity, who place so much Merit in using Scripture Phrase on all Occasions.*
† *The* Protestant Dissenters *use* Scripture Phrases *in their serious Discourses, and Composures more than the* Church of England-Men, *accordingly* Jack *is introduced making his common Talk and Conversation to run wholly in the Phrase of his* WILL. W. Wotton.

him to make himself clean again: Because having consulted the Will upon this Emergency, he met a with a * Passage near the Bottom (whether foisted in by the Transcriber, is not known) which seemed to forbid it.

H E made it a Part of his Religion, never to say † Grace to his Meat, nor could all the World persuade him, as the common Phrase is, to || eat his Victuals *like a Christian.*

H E bore a strange kind of Appetite to ** *Snap Dragon,* and to the livid Snuffs of a burning Candle, which he would catch and swallow with an Agility, wonderful to conceive; and by this Procedure, maintained a perpetual Flame in his Belly, which issuing in a glowing Steam from both his Eyes, as well as his Nostrils, and his Mouth; made his Head appear in a dark Night, like the Scull of an Ass, wherein a roguish Boy hath conveyed a Farthing Candle, *to the Terror of His Majesty's Liege Subjects.* Therefore, he made use of no other Expedient to light himself home, but was wont to say, That *a Wise Man was his own Lanthorn.*

H E would shut his Eyes as he walked along the Streets, and if he happened to bounce his Head against a Post, or fall into the Kennel (as he seldom missed either to do one or both) he would tell the gibing Prentices, who looked on, that *he submitted with entire Resignation, as to a Trip, or a Blow of Fate, with whom he found, by long Experience, how vain it was either to wrestle or to cuff; and whoever durst undertake to do either, would be sure to come off with a swinging Fall, or a bloody Nose. It was ordained,* said he, *some few Days before the Creation, that my Nose and this very Post should have a Rencounter; and therefore, Providence*[110] *thought fit to send us both into the World in the same Age, and to make us Country-men and Fellow-Citizens. Now, had my Eyes been open, it is very likely, the Business might have been a great deal worse; For, how many a confounded Slip is daily got by Man, with all his Foresight about him? Besides, the Eyes of the Understanding see best, when those of the Senses are out of the way; and therefore, blind Men are observed to tread their Steps with much more Caution, and Conduct, and Judgment, than those who rely with too much Confidence, upon the Virtue of the visual Nerve, which every little Accident shakes out of Order, and a Drop, or a Film, can wholly disconcert; like a Lanthorn among a Pack of roaring Bullies, when they scower the Streets; exposing its Owner, and*

---

* *I cannot guess the Author's meaning here, which I would be very glad to know, because it seems to be of Importance.*
† *The slovenly way of Receiving the Sacrament among the Fanaticks.*
|| *This is a common Phrase to express Eating cleanlily, and is meant for an Invective against that undecent Manner among some People in Receiving the Sacrament, so in the Lines before, which is to be understood of the Dissenters refusing to kneel at the Sacrament.*
** *I cannot well find the Author's meaning here, unless it be the hot, untimely, blind Zeal of Enthusiasts.*

it self, to outward Kicks and Buffets, which both might have escaped, if the Vanity of Appearing would have suffered them to walk in the Dark. But, farther; if we examine the Conduct of these boasted *Lights,* it will prove yet a great deal worse than their Fortune: *'Tis true, I have broke my Nose against this Post, because* Providence[111] *either forgot, or did not think it convenient to twitch me by the Elbow, and give me notice to avoid it.* But, let not this encourage either the present Age or Posterity, to trust their Noses into the keeping of their Eyes, which may prove the fairest Way of losing them for good and all. For, O ye Eyes, Ye blind Guides; miserable Guardians are Ye of our frail Noses; Ye, I say, who fasten upon the first Precipice in view, and then tow our wretched willing Bodies after You, to the very Brink of Destruction: But, alas, that Brink is rotten, our Feet slip, and we tumble down prone into a Gulph, without one hospitable Shrub in the Way to break the Fall; a Fall, to which not any Nose of mortal Make is equal, except that of the Giant * Laurcalco, who was Lord of the Silver   * *Vide* Don Quixot. Bridge. Most properly, therefore, O Eyes, and with great Justice, may You be compared to those foolish Lights, which conduct Men thro' Dirt and Darkness, till they fall into a deep Pit, or a noisom Bog.

T H I S I have produced, as a Scantling of *Jack's* great Eloquence, and the Force of his Reasoning upon such abstruse Matters.

H E was besides, a Person of great Design and Improvement in Affairs of *Devotion,* having introduced a new Deity, who hath since met with a vast Number of Worshippers; by some called *Babel,* by other, *Chaos;* who had an antient Temple of *Gothick* Structure upon *Salisbury-*Plain; famous for its Shrine, and Celebration by Pilgrims.

* W H E N he had some Roguish Trick to play, he would down with his Knees, up with his Eyes, and fall to Prayers, tho' in the midst of the Kennel. Then it was that those who understood his Pranks, would be sure to get far enough out of his Way; And whenever Curiosity attracted Strangers to Laugh, or to Listen; he would of a sudden, with one Hand out with his *Gear,* and piss full in their Eyes, and with the other, all to-bespatter them with Mud.

† I N Winter he went always loose and unbuttoned, and clad as thin as possible, to let *in* the ambient Heat; and in Summer, lapt himself close and thick to keep it *out.*

‖ I N all Revolutions of Government, he would make his Court for the Office of *Hangman* General; and in the Exercise of that

---

* *The Villanies and Cruelties committed by Enthusiasts and Phanaticks among us, were all performed under the Disguise of Religion and long Prayers.*
† *They affect Differences in Habit and Behaviour.*
‖ *They are severe Persecutors, and all in a Form of Cant and Devotion.*

Dignity, wherein he was very dextrous, would make use of † no other *Vizard* than a long *Prayer*.

H E had a Tongue so Musculous and Subtil, that he could twist it up into his Nose, and deliver a strange Kind of Speech from thence. He was also the first in these Kingdoms, who began to improve the *Spanish* Accomplishment of *Braying*; and having large Ears, perpetually exposed and arrected, he carried his Art to such a Perfection, that it was a Point of great Difficulty to distinguish either by the View or the Sound, between the *Original* and the *Copy*.

HE was troubled with a Disease, reverse to that called the Stinging of the *Tarantula*; and would * run Dog-mad, at the Noise of *Musick*, especially a *Pair of Bag-Pipes*. But he would cure himself again, by taking two or three Turns in *Westminster-Hall*, or *Billingsgate*, or in a *Boarding-School* or the *Royal-Exchange*, or a *State Coffee-House*.

H E was a Person that || *feared* no *Colours*, but mortally *hated* all, and upon that Account, bore a cruel Aversion to *Painters*, insomuch, that in his Paroxysms, as he walked the Streets, he would have his Pockets loaden with Stones, to pelt at the *Signs*.

HAVING from this manner of Living, frequent Occasions to *wash* himself, he would often leap over Head and Ears into the Water, tho' it were in the midst of the Winter, but was always observed to come out again much *dirtier*, if possible, than he went in.

HE was the first that ever found out the Secret of contriving a ** *Soporiferous* Medicine to be convey'd in at the *Ears*; It was a Compound of *Sulphur* and *Balm of Gilead*, with a little *Pilgrim's Salve*.

HE wore a large Plaister of artificial *Causticks* on his Stomach, with the Fervor of which, he could set himself a *groaning*, like the famous *Board* upon Application of a red-hot Iron.

† HE would stand in the Turning of a Street, and calling to those who passed by, would cry to One; *Worthy Sir, do me the Honour of a good Slap in the Chaps*: To another, *Honest Friend, pray, favour me with a handsom Kick on the Arse: Madam, shall I entreat a small Box on the Ear, from your Ladyship's fair Hands? Noble Captain, Lend a reasonable Thwack, for the Love of God*

---

† Cromwell *and his Confederates went, as they called it,* to seek God, *when they resolved to murther the King.*
* *This is to expose our Dissenters Aversion to Instrumental Musick in Churches.* W. Wotton.
|| *They quarrel at the most Innocent Decency and Ornament, and defaced the Statues and Paintings on all the Churches in* England.
** *Fanatick Preaching, composed either of Hell and Damnation, or a fulsome Description of the Joys of Heaven, both in such a dirty, nauseous Style, as to be well resembled to Pilgrims Salve.*
† *The Fanaticks have always had a way of affecting to run into Persecution, and count vast Merit upon every little Hardship they suffer.*

with that Cane of yours, over these poor Shoulders. And when he had by such earnest Sollicitations, made a shift to procure a Basting sufficient to swell up his Fancy and his Sides, He would return home extremely comforted, and full of terrible Accounts of what he had undergone for the *Publick Good. Observe this Stroak,* (said he, shewing his bare Shoulders) *a plaguy* Janisary *gave it me this very Morning at seven a Clock, as, with much ado, I was driving off the* Great Turk. *Neighbours mine, this broken Head deserves a Plaister; had poor* Jack *been tender of his Noodle, you would have seen the* Pope, *and the* French King, *long before this time of Day, among your Wives and your Ware-houses.* Dear Christians, *the* Great Mogul *was come as far as* White-Chappel, *and you may thank these poor Sides that he hath not* (God bless us) *already swallowed up Man, Woman, and Child.*

* I T was highly worth observing, the singular Effects of that Aversion, or Antipathy, which *Jack* and his Brother *Peter* seemed, even to an Affectation, to bear toward each other. *Peter* had lately done *some Rogueries,* that forced him to abscond; and he seldom ventured to stir out before Night, for fear of Bayliffs. Their Lodgings were at the two most distant Parts of the Town, from each other; and whenever their Occasions, or Humors called them abroad, they would make Choice of the oddest unlikely Times, and most uncouth Rounds they could invent; that they might be sure to avoid one another: Yet after all this, it was their perpetual Fortune to meet. The Reason of which, is easy enough to apprehend: For, the Phrenzy and the Spleen of both, having the same Foundation, we may look upon them as two Pair of Compasses, equally extended, and the fixed Foot of each, remaining in the same Center; which, tho' moving contrary Ways at first, will be sure to encounter somewhere or other in the Circumference. Besides, it was among the great Misfortunes of *Jack,* to bear a huge Personal Resemblance with his Brother *Peter.* Their Humours and Dispositions were not only the same, but there was a close Analogy in their Shape, their Size and their Mien. Insomuch, as nothing was more frequent than for a Bayliff to seize *Jack* by the Shoulders, and cry, *Mr.* Peter, You *are the King's Prisoner.* Or, at other Times, for one of *Peter's* nearest Friends, to accost *Jack* with open Arms, *Dear* Peter, *I am glad to see thee, pray send me one of your best Medicines for the Worms.* This we may suppose, was a mortifying Return of those Pains and Proceedings, *Jack* had laboured in so long; And finding,

---

* *The Papists and Fanaticks, tho' they appear the most Averse to each other, yet bear a near Resemblance in many things, as has been observed by Learned Men.*
Ibid. *The Agreement of our Dissenters and the Papists in that which Bishop* Stillingfleet *called,* The Fanaticism of the Church of *Rome, is ludicrously described for several Pages together by* Jack's *Likeness to* Peter, *and their being often mistaken for each other, and their frequent Meeting, when they least intended it.* W. Wotton.

how directly opposite all his Endeavours had answered to the sole
End and Intention, which he had proposed to himself; How could
it avoid having terrible Effects upon a Head and Heart so furnished
as his? However, the poor Remainders of his *Coat* bore all the
Punishment; The orient Sun never entred upon his diurnal Progress, without missing a Piece of it. He hired a Taylor to stitch up
the Collar so close, that it was ready to choak him, and squeezed
out his Eyes at such a Rate, as one could see nothing but the
White. What little was left of the main Substance of the Coat, he
rubbed every day for two hours, against a rough-cast Wall, in order
to grind away the Remnants of *Lace* and *Embroidery*; but at the
same time went on with so much Violence, that he proceeded a
Heathen Philosopher. Yet after all he could do of this kind, the
Success continued still to disappoint his Expectation. For, as it is
the Nature of Rags, to bear a kind of mock Resemblance to Finery;
there being a sort of fluttering Appearance in both, which is not
to be distinguished at a Distance, in the Dark, or by short-sighted
Eyes: So, in those Junctures, it fared with *Jack* and his Tatters,
that they offered to the first View a ridiculous Flanting, which
assisting the Resemblance in Person and Air, thwarted all his
Projects of Separation, and left so near a Similitude
between them, as frequently deceived the very Disciples
and Followers of both.   *   *   *   *   *   *   *   *
*   *   *   *   *   *   *   *   *   *   *   *
                         *   *   *   *   *   *   *   *
Desunt nonnulla.   *   *   *   *   *   *   *   *
                         *   *   *   *   *   *   *   *
*   *   *   *   *   *   *   *   *   *   *   *

T H E old *Sclavonian* Proverb said well, That *it is with* Men, *as
with* Asses; *whoever would keep them fast, may find a very good
Hold at their Ears.* Yet, I think, we may affirm, and it hath been
verified by repeated Experience, that,

Effugiet tamen hæc sceleratus vincula Proteus.[112]

I T is good therefore, to read the Maxims of our Ancestors, with
great Allowances to Times and Persons: For, if we look into Primitive Records, we shall find, that no Revolutions have been so great,
or so frequent, as those of human *Ears.* In former Days, there was a
curious Invention to catch and keep them; which, I think, we may
justly reckon among the *Artes perditæ*: And how can it be otherwise, when in these latter Centuries, the very Species is not only
diminished to a very lamentable Degree, but the poor Remainder is
also degenerated so far, as to mock our skilfullest *Tenure?* For, if
the only slitting of one *Ear* in a Stag, hath been found sufficient to

propagate the Defect thro' a whole Forest; Why should we wonder at the greatest Consequences, from so many Loppings and Mutilations, to which the *Ears* of our Fathers and our own, have been of late so much exposed: 'Tis true, indeed, that while this *Island* of ours, was under the *Dominion of Grace*, many Endeavours were made to improve the Growth of *Ears* once more among us. The Proportion of Largeness, was not only lookt upon as an Ornament of the *Outward* Man, but as a Type of Grace in the *Inward*. Besides, it is held by Naturalists, that if there be a Protuberancy of Parts in the *Superiour* Region of the Body, as in the *Ears* and *Nose*, there must be a Parity also in the *Inferior*: And therefore in that truly pious Age, the *Males* in every Assembly, according as they were gifted, appeared very forward in exposing their *Ears* to view, and the Regions about them; because * *Hippocrates* tells us, that *when the Vein behind the Ear happens to be cut,*   * *Lib. de aëre locis & aquis.* *a Man becomes a Eunuch:* And the *Females* were nothing backwarder in beholding and edifying by them: Whereof those who had already *used the Means*, lookt about them with great Concern, in hopes of conceiving a suitable Offspring by such a Prospect: Others, who stood Candidates for *Benevolence*, found there a plentiful Choice, and were sure to fix upon such as discovered the largest *Ears*, that the Breed might not dwindle between them. Lastly, the devouter Sisters, who lookt upon all extraordinary Dilatations of that Member, as Protrusions of Zeal, or spiritual Excrescencies, were sure to honor every Head they sat upon, as if they had been *cloven Tongues*;[113] but, especially, that of the Preacher, whose *Ears* were usually of the prime Magnitude; which upon that Account, he was very frequent and exact in exposing with all Advantages to the People: in his Rhetorical *Paroxysms*, turning sometimes to *hold forth* the one, and sometimes to *hold forth* the other. From which Custom, the whole Operation of Preaching is to this very Day among their Professors, styled by the Phrase of *Holding forth*.

S U C H was the Progress of the *Saints*, for advancing the Size of that Member; And it is thought, the Success would have been every way answerable, if in Process of time, a * cruel King had not arose, who raised a bloody Persecution against all *Ears*,[114] above a certain Standard: Upon which, some were glad to hide their flourishing Sprouts in a black Border, others crept wholly under a Perewig: some were slit, others cropt, and a great Number sliced off to the Stumps. But of this, more hereafter, in my *general History of Ears*; which I design very speedily to bestow upon the Publick.

---

* *This was King* Charles *the Second, who at his Restoration, turned out all the Dissenting Teachers that would not conform.*

F R O M this brief Survey of the falling State of *Ears*, in the last
Age, and the small Care had to advance their antient Growth in the
present, it is manifest, how little Reason we can have to rely upon
a Hold so short, so weak, and so slippery; and that, whoever desires
to catch Mankind fast, must have Recourse to some other Methods. Now, he that will examine Human Nature with Circumspection enough, may discover several *Handles*, whereof the
* *Six* Senses afford one apiece, beside a
great Number that are screw'd to the Passions, and some few riveted to the Intellect. Among these last,
Curiosity is one, and of all others, affords the firmest Grasp: *Curiosity*, that Spur in the side, that Bridle in the Mouth, that Ring in
the Nose, of a lazy, an impatient, and a grunting Reader. By this
Handle it is, that an Author should seize upon his Readers; which
as soon as he hath once compast, all Resistance and struggling are
in vain; and they become his Prisoners as close as he pleases, till
Weariness or Dullness force him to let go his Gripe.

* Including Scaliger's.

AND therefore, I the Author of this miraculous Treatise, having
hitherto, beyond Expectation, maintained by the aforesaid *Handle*,
a firm Hold upon my gentle Readers; It is with great Reluctance,
that I am at length compelled to remit my Grasp; leaving them in
the Perusal of what remains, to that natural *Oscitancy* inherent in
the Tribe. I can only assure thee, Courteous Reader, for both our
Comforts, that my Concern is altogether equal to thine, for my
Unhappiness in losing, or mislaying among my Papers the remaining Part of these Memoirs; which consisted of Accidents, Turns,
and Adventures, both New, Agreeable, and Surprizing; and therefore, calculated in all due Points, to the delicate Taste of this our
noble Age. But, alas, with my utmost Endeavours, I have been able
only to retain a few of the Heads. Under which, there was a full
Account, how *Peter* got a *Protection* out of the *King's-Bench*; And
of a * *Reconcilement* between *Jack* and Him, upon a Design they
had in a certain *rainy Night*, to trepan Brother *Martin* into a
Spunging-house, and there strip him to the Skin. How *Martin*, with
much ado, shew'd them both a fair pair of Heels. How a *new Warrant* came out against *Peter*: upon which, how *Jack* left him in the
lurch, *stole his Protection, and made use of it himself*. How *Jack's*
Tatters came into Fashion in *Court* and *City*; How *he* † *got upon a*

---

* *In the Reign of King* James *the Second, the Presbyterians by the King's
Invitation, joined with the Papists, against the Church of* England, *and Address
him for Repeal of the Penal-Laws and Test. The King by his Dispensing Power,
gave Liberty of Conscience, which both Papists and Presbyterians made use of, but
upon the Revolution, the Papists being down of Course, the Presbyterians freely
continued their Assemblies, by Virtue of King* James's *Indulgence, before they had
a Toleration by Law; this I believe the Author means by* Jack's *stealing* Peter's
Protection, and making use of it himself.
† *Sir* Humphry Edwyn, *a Presbyterian, was some Years ago Lord-Mayor of*
London, *and had the Insolence to go in his Formalities to a Conventicle, with the
Ensigns of his Office.*

great Horse, and eat * *Custard.* But the Particulars of all these, with several others, which have now slid out of my Memory, are lost beyond all Hopes of Recovery. For which Misfortune, leaving my Readers to condole with each other, as far as they shall find it to agree with their several Constitutions; but conjuring them by all the Friendship that hath passed between Us, from the Title-Page to this, not to proceed so far as to injure their Healths, for an Accident past Remedy; I now go on to the Ceremonial Part of an accomplish'd Writer, and therefore, by a Courtly *Modern*, least of all others to be omitted.

THE CONCLUSION

GOING *too long* is a Cause of Abortion as effectual, tho' not so frequent, as *Going too short*; and holds true especially in the *Labors* of the Brain. Well fare the Heart of that Noble * *Jesuit*, who first adventur'd to confess in Print, that Books must be suited to   * *Pere d'Orleans.* their several Seasons, like Dress, and Dyet, and Diversions: And better fare our noble Nation, for refining upon this, among other *French* Modes. I am living fast, to see the Time, when a *Book* that misses its Tide, shall be neglected, as the *Moon* by Day, or like *Mackarel* a Week after the Season. No Man hath more nicely observed our Climate, than the Bookseller who bought the Copy of this Work; He knows to a Tittle what Subjects will best go off in a *dry Year*, and which it is proper to expose foremost, when the Weather-glass is fallen to *much Rain.* When he had seen this Treatise, and consulted his *Almanack* upon it; he gave me to understand, that he had maturely considered the two Principal Things, which were the *Bulk,* and the *Subject;* and found, it would never *take,* but after a long Vacation, and then only, in case it should happen to be a hard Year for Turnips. Upon which I desired to know, *considering my urgent Necessities,* what he thought might be acceptable this Month. He lookt *Westward,* and said, *I doubt we shall have a Fit of bad Weather; However, if you could prepare some pretty little* Banter *(but not in Verse) or a small Treatise upon the ——— it would run like Wild-Fire. But, if it hold up, I have already hired an Author to write something against* Dr. B——tl—y, *which, I am sure, will turn to Account.*

AT length we agreed upon this Expedient; That when a Customer comes for one of these, and desires in Confidence to know

* *Custard is a famous Dish at a Lord-Mayors Feast.*

the Author; he will tell him very privately, as a Friend, naming which ever of the Wits shall happen to be that Week in the Vogue; and if *Durfy's* last Play should be in Course, I had as lieve he may be the Person as *Congreve*. This I mention, because I am wonderfully well acquainted with the present Relish of Courteous Readers; and have often observed, with singular Pleasure, that a *Fly* driven from a *Honey-pot*, will immediately, with very good Appetite alight, and finish his Meal on an *Excrement*.

I have one Word to say upon the Subject of *Profound Writers*, who are grown very numerous of late; And, I know very well, the judicious World is resolved to list me in that Number. I conceive therefore, as to the Business of being *Profound*, that it is with *Writers*, as with *Wells*; A Person with good Eyes may see to the Bottom of the deepest, provided any *Water* be there; and, that often, when there is nothing in the World at the Bottom, besides *Dryness* and *Dirt*, tho' it be but a Yard and half under Ground, it shall pass, however, for wondrous *Deep*, upon no wiser a Reason than because it is wondrous *Dark*.

I am now trying an Experiment very frequent among Modern Authors; which is, to *write upon Nothing*; When the Subject is utterly exhausted, to let the Pen still move on; by some called, the Ghost of Wit, delighting to walk after the Death of its Body. And to say the Truth, there seems to be no Part of Knowledge in fewer Hands, than That of Discerning *when to have Done*. By the Time that an Author has writ out a Book, he and his Readers are become old Acquaintance, and grow very loth to part: So that I have sometimes known it to be in Writing, as in Visiting, where the Ceremony of taking Leave, has employ'd more Time than the whole Conversation before. The Conclusion of a Treatise, resembles the Conclusion of Human Life, which hath sometimes been compared to the End of a Feast; where few are satisfied to depart, *ut plenus vita conviva*:[115] For Men will sit down after the fullest Meal, tho' it be only to *doze*, or to *sleep* out the rest of the Day. But, in this latter, I differ extreamly from other Writers; and shall be too proud, if by all my Labors, I can have any ways contributed to the *Repose* of Mankind in * Times so turbulent and unquiet as these. Neither, do I think such an Employment so very alien from the Office of a *Wit*, as some would suppose. For among a very Polite Nation in * *Greece*, there were the *same* Temples built and consecrated to *Sleep* and the *Muses*, between which two Deities, they believed the strictest Friendship was established.

* *Trezenii Pausan.* 1.2.

I have one concluding Favour, to request of my Reader; that he

* *This was writ before the Peace of* Riswick.

will not expect to be equally diverted and informed by every Line, or every Page of this Discourse; but give some Allowance to the Author's Spleen, and short Fits or Intervals of Dullness, as well as his own; And lay it seriously to his Conscience, whether, if he were walking the Streets, in dirty Weather, or a rainy Day; he would allow it fair Dealing in Folks at their Ease from a Window, to Critick his Gate, and ridicule his Dress at such a Juncture.

IN my Disposure of Employments of the Brain, I have thought fit to make *Invention* the *Master*, and give *Method* and *Reason*, the Office of its *Lacquays*. The Cause of this Distribution was, from observing it my peculiar Case, to be often under a Temptation of being *Witty*, upon Occasion, where I could be neither *Wise* nor *Sound*, nor any thing to the Matter in hand. And, I am too much a Servant of the *Modern* Way, to neglect any such Opportunities, whatever Pains or Improprieties I may be at, to introduce them. For, I have observed, that from a laborious Collection of Seven Hundred Thirty Eight *Flowers*, and *shining Hints* of the best *Modern* Authors, digested with great Reading, into my Book of *Common-places*; I have not been able after five Years to draw, hook, or force into common Conversation, any more than a Dozen. Of which Dozen, the one Moiety failed of Success, by being dropt among unsuitable Company; and the other cost me so many Strains, and Traps, and *Ambages* to introduce, that I at length resolved to give it over. Now, this Disappointment, (to discover a Secret) I must own, gave me the first Hint of setting up for an *Author*; and, I have since found among some particular Friends, that it is become a very general Complaint, and has produced the same Effects upon many others. For, I have remarked many a *towardly Word*, to be wholly neglected or despised in *Discourse*, which hath passed very smoothly, with some Consideration and Esteem, after its Preferment and Sanction in *Print*. But now, since by the Liberty and Encouragement of the Press, I am grown absolute Master of the Occasions and Opportunities, to expose the Talents I have acquired; I already discover, that the *Issues* of my *Observanda* begin to grow too large for the *Receipts*. Therefore, I shall here pause awhile, till I find, by feeling the World's Pulse, and my own, that it will be of absolute Necessity for us both, to resume my Pen.

FINIS

A

Full and True Account
OF THE

BATTEL

Fought laſt *FRIDAY*,

Between the

Antient and the *Modern*

BOOKS

IN

St. *JAMES*'s

LIBRARY.

LONDON:
Printed in the Year, MDCCX.

The Bookseller to the Reader

The following Discourse, as it is unquestionably of the same Author,[1] so it seems to have been written about the same time with the former, I mean, the Year 1697, when the famous Dispute was on Foot, about *Antient and Modern Learning*. The Controversy took its Rise from an Essay of Sir *William Temple's*, upon that Subject; which was answer'd by W. *Wotton*, B.D. with an Appendix by Dr. *Bentley*, endeavouring to destroy the Credit of *Æsop* and *Phalaris*, for Authors, whom Sir *William Temple* had in the Essay before-mentioned, highly commended. In that Appendix, the Doctor falls hard upon a new Edition of *Phalaris*, put out by the Honourable *Charles Boyle* (now *Earl* of *Orrery*) to which, Mr. *Boyle* replyed at large, with great Learning and Wit; and the Doctor, voluminously, rejoyned. In this Dispute,[2] the Town highly resented to see a Person of Sir *William Temple's* Character and Merits, roughly used by the two Reverend Gentlemen aforesaid, and without any manner of Provocation. At length, there appearing no End of the Quarrel, our Author tells us, that the B O O K S in St. *James's* Library, looking upon themselves as Parties principally concerned, took up the Controversie, and came to a decisive Battel; But, the Manuscript, by the Injury of Fortune, or Weather, being in several Places imperfect, we cannot learn to which side the Victory fell.

I must warn the Reader, to beware of applying to Persons what is here meant, only of Books in the most literal Sense. So, when *Virgil* is mentioned, we are not to understand the Person of a famous Poet, call'd by that Name, but only certain Sheets of Paper, bound up in Leather, containing in Print, the Works of the said Poet, and so of the rest.

The Preface of the Author

SATYR is a sort of Glass, wherein Beholders do generally dis-cover every body's Face but their Own; which is the chief Reason for that kind Reception it meets in the World, and that so very few are offended with it. But if it should happen otherwise, the Danger is not great; and, I have learned from long Experience, never to apprehend Mischief from those Understandings, I have been able to provoke; For, Anger and Fury, though they add Strength to the Sinews of the Body, yet are found to relax those of the Mind, and to render all its Efforts feeble and impotent.

THERE is a Brain that will endure but one Scumming: Let the Owner gather it with Discretion, and manage his little Stock with Husbandry; but of all things, let him beware of bringing it under the Lash of his Betters; because, That will make it all bubble up into Impertinence, and he will find no new Supply: Wit, with-out knowledge, being a Sort of Cream, which gathers in a Night to the Top, and by a skilful Hand, may be soon whipt into Froth; but once scumm'd away, what appears underneath will be fit for nothing, but to be thrown to the Hogs.

A Full and True Account of the Battel
Fought last Friday, &c.

WHOEVER examines with due Circumspection into the * *Annual Records* of *Time*, will find it remarked, that *War is the Child of Pride*, and *Pride the Daughter of Riches*; The for-mer of which Assertions may be soon granted; but one cannot so easily subscribe to the latter: For *Pride* is nearly related to Beggary and *Want*, either by Father or Mother, and sometimes by both; And, to speak naturally, it very seldom happens among Men to fall out, when all have enough: Invasions usually travelling from *North* to *South*, that is to say, from Poverty upon Plenty. The most antient and natural Grounds of Quarrels, are *Lust* and *Avarice*; which, tho' we may allow to be Brethren or collateral Branches of *Pride*, are certainly the Issues of *Want*. For, to speak in the Phrase of Writers upon the Politicks, we may observe in the Republick of *Dogs*, (which in its Original seems to be an Institution of the *Many*) that the whole State is ever in the profoundest Peace, after a full Meal; and, that Civil Broils arise among them, when it happens for one great *Bone* to be seized on by some *leading Dog*, who either divides it among the *Few*, and then it falls to an *Oligarchy*, or keeps it to Himself, and then it runs up to a *Tyranny*. The same Reasoning also, holds Place among them, in those Dissensions we behold upon a Turgescency in any of their Females. For, the Right of Possession lying in common (it being impossible to establish a Property in so delicate a Case) Jealousies and Suspicions do so abound, that the whole Common-wealth of that Street, is reduced to a manifest *State of War*, of every *Citizen* against every *Citizen*; till some One of more Courage, Conduct, or Fortune than the rest, seizes and enjoys the Prize; Upon which, naturally arises Plenty of Heart-burning, and Envy, and Snarling against the *Happy Dog*. Again, if we look upon any of these Republicks engaged in a Forein War, either of Invasion or Defence, we shall find, the same Reasoning will serve, as to the Grounds and Occasions of each; and that *Poverty*, or *Want*, in some Degree or other, (whether Real, or in Opinion, which makes no Alteration in the Case) has a great Share, as well as *Pride*, on the Part of the Aggressor.

> * *Riches produceth Pride; Pride is War's Ground, &c. Vid. Ephem. de Mary Clarke; opt. Edit.*

N O W, whoever will please to take this Scheme, and either reduce or adapt it to an Intellectual State, or Commonwealth of Learning, will soon discover the first Ground of Disagreement between the two great Parties at this Time in Arms; and may form just Conclusions upon the Merits of either Cause. But the Issue or Events of this War are not so easie to conjecture at: For, the present Quarrel is so enflamed by the warm Heads of either Faction, and the Pretensions *somewhere or other* so exorbitant, as not to admit the least Overtures of Accommodation: This Quarrel first began (as I have heard it affirmed by an old Dweller in the Neighbourhood) about a small Spot of Ground, *lying* and *being* upon one of the two Tops of the Hill *Parnassus*; the highest and largest of which, had it seems, been time out of Mind, in quiet Possession of certain Tenants, call'd the *Antients*; And the other was held by the *Moderns*. But, these disliking their present Station, sent certain Ambassadors to the *Antients*, complaining of a great Nuisance, how the Height of that Part of *Parnassus*, quite spoiled the Prospect of theirs, especially towards the *East*; and therefore, to avoid a War, offered them the Choice of this Alternative; either that the *Antients* would please to remove themselves and their Effects down to the lower Summity, which the *Moderns* would graciously surrender to them, and advance in their Place; or else, that the said *Antients* will give leave to the *Moderns* to come with Shovels and Mattocks, and level the said Hill, as low as they shall think it convenient. To which, the *Antients* made Answer: How little they expected such a Message as this, from a Colony, whom they had admitted out of their own Free Grace, to so near a Neighbourhood. That, as to their own Seat, they were *Aborigines* of it, and therefore, to talk with them of a Removal or Surrender, was a Language they did not understand. That, if the Height of the Hill, on their side, shortned the Prospect of the *Moderns*, it was a Disadvantage they could not help, but desired them to consider, whether that Injury (if it be any) were not largely recompenced by the *Shade* and *Shelter* it afforded them. That, as to levelling or digging down, it was either Folly or Ignorance to propose it, if they did, or did not know, how that side of the Hill was an entire Rock, which would break their Tools and Hearts; without any Damage to itself. That they would therefore advise the *Moderns*, rather to raise their own side of the Hill, than dream of pulling down that of the *Antients*, to the former of which, they would not only give Licence, but also largely contribute. All this was rejected by the *Moderns*, with much Indignation, who still insisted upon one of the two Expedients; And so this Difference broke out into a long and obstinate War, maintain'd on the one Part, by Resolution, and by the Courage of certain

Leaders and Allies; but, on the other, by the greatness of their Number, upon all Defeats, affording continual Recruits. In this Quarrel, whole Rivulets of *Ink* have been exhausted, and the Virulence of both Parties enormously augmented. Now, it must here be understood, that *Ink* is the great missive Weapon, in all Battels of the *Learned*, which, convey'd thro' a sort of Engine, call'd a *Quill*, infinite Numbers of these are darted at the Enemy, by the Valiant on each side, with equal Skill and Violence, as if it were an Engagement of *Porcupines*. This malignant Liquor was compounded by the Engineer, who invented it, of two Ingredients, which are *Gall* and *Copperas*, by its Bitterness and Venom, to *Suit* in some Degree, as well as to *Foment* the Genius of the Combatants. And as the *Grecians*, after an Engagement, when they could not *agree* about the Victory, were wont to set up Trophies on both sides, the beaten Party being content to be at the same Expence, to keep it self in Countenance (A laudable and antient Custom, happily reviv'd of late, in the Art of War) so the *Learned*, after a sharp and bloody Dispute, do on both sides hang out their Trophies too, which-ever comes by the worst. These Trophies have largely inscribed on them the Merits of the Cause; a full impartial Account of such a Battel, and how the Victory fell clearly to the Party that set them up. They are known to the World under several Names; As, *Disputes, Arguments, Rejoynders, Brief Considerations, Answers, Replies, Remarks, Reflexions, Objections, Confutations.* For a very few Days they are fixed up in all Publick Places, either by themselves or their * Representatives,

* *Their Title-Pages.*   for Passengers to gaze at: From whence the chiefest and largest are removed to certain Magazines, they call, *Libraries*, there to remain in a Quarter purposely assign'd them, and from thenceforth, begin to be called, *Books of Controversie*.

IN these Books, is wonderfully instilled and preserved, the Spirit of each Warrier, while he is alive; and after his Death, his Soul transmigrates there, to inform them. This, at least, is the more common Opinion; But, I believe, it is with Libraries, as with other Cemeteries, where some Philosophers affirm, that a certain Spirit, which they call *Brutum hominis*, hovers over the Monument, till the Body is corrupted, and turns to *Dust*, or to *Worms*, but then vanishes or dissolves: So, we may say, a restless Spirit haunts over every *Book*, till *Dust* or *Worms* have seized upon it; which to some, may happen in a few Days, but to others, later; And therefore, *Books* of Controversy, being of all others, haunted by the most disorderly Spirits, have always been confined in a separate Lodge from the rest; and for fear of mutual violence against each other, it was thought Prudent by our Ancestors, to bind them to the Peace with strong Iron Chains. Of which Invention, the original Occasion was this: When the Works of *Scotus* first came out, they were carried to a certain great Library, and had Lodgings appointed them; But this Author was no sooner settled, than he went to visit his Master *Aristotle*, and there both concerted together to seize *Plato* by main Force, and turn him out from his antient Station among the *Divines*, where he had peaceably dwelt near Eight Hundred Years. The Attempt succeeded, and the two Usurpers have reigned ever since in his stead: But to maintain Quiet for the future, it was decreed, that all *Polemicks* of the larger Size, should be held fast with a Chain.

B Y this Expedient, the publick Peace of Libraries, might certainly have been preserved, if a new Species of controversial Books had not arose of late Years, instinct with a most malignant Spirit, from the War above-mentioned, between the *Learned*, about the higher Summity of *Parnassus*.

W H E N these Books were first admitted into the Publick Libraries, I remember to have said upon Occasion, to several Persons concerned, how I was sure, they would create Broyls wherever they came, unless a World of Care were taken: And therefore, I advised, that the Champions of each side should be coupled together, or otherwise mixt, that like the blending of contrary Poysons, their Malignity might be employ'd among themselves. And it seems, I was neither an ill Prophet, nor an ill Counsellor; for it was nothing else but the Neglect of this Caution, which gave Occasion to the terrible Fight that happened on *Friday* last between the *Antient* and *Modern Books* in the *King's Library*. Now, because the Talk of this Battel is so fresh in every body's Mouth, and the Expectation of the Town so great to be informed in the Particulars; I, being possessed of all Qualifications requisite in an *Historian*, and retained by neither Party; have resolved to comply with the urgent *Importunity of my Friends*, by writing down a full impartial Account thereof.

T H E *Guardian* of the *Regal Library*,[3] a Person of great Valor, but chiefly renowned for his * *Humanity*, had been a fierce Champion for the *Moderns*, and in an Engagement upon *Parnassus*, had vowed, with his own Hands, to knock down two of the *Antient* Chiefs, who guarded a small Pass on the superior Rock; but endeavouring to climb up, was cruelly obstructed by his own unhappy Weight, and tendency towards his Center; a Quality, to which,

---

* *The Honourable Mr.* Boyle, *in the Preface to his Edition of* Phalaris, *says, he was refus'd a Manuscript by the Library-Keeper*, pro solita Humanitate suâ.

those of the *Modern* Party, are extreme subject; For, being light-headed, they have in Speculation, a wonderful Agility, and conceive nothing too high for them to mount; but in reducing to Practice, discover a mighty Pressure about their Posteriors and their Heels. Having thus failed in his Design, the disappointed Champion bore a cruel Rancour to the *Antients*, which he resolved to gratifie, by shewing all Marks of his Favour to the *Books* of their Adversaries, and lodging them in the fairest Apartments; when at the same time, whatever *Book* had the boldness to own it self for an Advocate of the *Antients*, was buried alive in some obscure Corner, and threatned upon the least Displeasure, to be turned out of Doors. Besides, it so happened, that about this time, there was a strange Confusion of Place among all the *Books* in the Library; for which several Reasons were assigned. Some imputed it to a great heap of *learned Dust*, which a perverse Wind blew off from a Shelf of *Moderns* into the *Keeper's* Eyes. Others affirmed, He had a Humour to pick the *Worms* out of the *Schoolmen*, and swallow them fresh and fasting; whereof some fell upon his *Spleen*, and some climbed up into his Head, to the great Perturbation of both. And lastly, others maintained, that by walking much in the dark about the Library, he had quite lost the Situation of it out of his Head; And therefore, in replacing his *Books*, he was apt to mistake, and clap *Des-Cartes* next to *Aristotle*; Poor *Plato* had got between *Hobbes* and the *Seven Wise Masters*, and *Virgil* was hemm'd in with *Dryden* on one side, and *Withers* on the other.

M E A N while, those *Books* that were Advocates for the *Moderns*, chose out one from among them, to make a Progress thro' the whole Library, examine the Number and Strength of their Party, and concert their Affairs. This Messenger performed all things very industriously, and brought back with him a List of their Forces, in all Fifty Thousand, consisting chiefly of *light Horse*, *heavy-armed Foot*, and *Mercenaries*; Whereof the *Foot* were in general but sorrily armed, and worse clad; Their *Horses* large, but extremely out of Case and Heart; However, some few by trading among the *Antients*, had furnisht themselves tolerably enough.

W H I L E Things were in this Ferment; *Discord* grew extremely high, hot Words passed on both sides, and ill blood was plentifully bred. Here a solitary *Antient*, squeezed up among a whole Shelf of *Moderns*, offered fairly to dispute the Case, and to prove by manifest Reasons, that the Priority was due to them, from long Possession, and in regard of their Prudence, Antiquity, and above all, their great Merits towards the *Moderns*. But these denied the Premises, and seemed very much to wonder, how the *Antients* could pretend to insist upon their Antiquity, when it was so plain (if they went to that) that the *Moderns* were much the more * *Antient* of the two. As for any Obligations they owed to the *Antients*, they renounced them all. *'Tis true,* said they, *we*

are informed, some few of our Party have been so mean to borrow their Subsistence from You; But the rest, infinitely the greater Number (and especially, we French *and* English) *were so far from stooping to so base an Example, that there never passed, till this very hour, six Words between us.* For, our Horses are of our own breeding, our Arms of our own forging, and our Cloaths of our own cutting out and sowing. Plato was by chance upon the next Shelf, and observing those that spoke to be in the ragged Plight, mentioned a while ago; their *Jades* lean and foundred, their *Weapons* of rotten Wood, their *Armour* rusty, and nothing but Raggs underneath; he laugh'd loud, and in his pleasant way, swore, *By G——*, *he believ'd them.*

NOW, the *Moderns* had not proceeded in their late Negotiation, with Secrecy enough to escape the Notice of the Enemy. For, those Advocates, who had begun the Quarrel, by setting first on Foot the Dispute of Precedency, talkt so loud of coming to a Battel, that *Temple* happened to over-hear them, and gave immediate Intelligence to the *Antients*; who thereupon drew up their scattered Troops together, resolving to act upon the defensive; Upon which, several of the *Moderns* fled over to their Party, and among the rest, *Temple* himself. This *Temple* having been educated and long conversed among the *Antients*, was, of all the *Moderns*, their greatest Favorite, and became their greatest Champion.

T H I N G S were at this Crisis, when a material Accident fell out. For, upon the highest Corner of a large Window, there dwelt a certain *Spider*,⁵ swollen up to the first Magnitude, by the Destruction of infinite Numbers of *Flies*, whose Spoils lay scattered before the Gates of his Palace, like human Bones before the Cave of some Giant. The Avenues to his Castle were guarded with Turn-pikes, and Palissadoes, all after the *Modern* way of Fortification. After you had passed several Courts, you came to the Center, wherein you might behold the *Constable* himself in his own Lodgings, which had Windows fronting to each Avenue, and Ports to sally out upon all Occasions of Prey or Defence. In this Mansion he had for some Time dwelt in Peace and Plenty, without Danger to his *Person* by *Swallows* from above, or to his *Palace* by *Brooms* from below: When it was the Pleasure of Fortune to conduct thither a wandring *Bee*, to whose Curiosity a broken Pane in the Glass had discovered it self; and in he went, where expatiating a while, he at last happened to alight upon one of the outward Walls of the *Spider's* Cit-

tadel; which yielding to the unequal Weight, sunk down to the very
Foundation. Thrice he endeavoured to force his Passage, and Thrice
the Center shook. The *Spider* within, feeling the terrible Convul-
sion, supposed at first, that *Nature* was approaching to her final Dis-
solution; or else, that *Beelzebub* with all his Legions, was come to
revenge the Death of many thousands of his Subjects, whom his
Enemy had slain and devoured. However, he at length valiantly
resolved to issue forth, and meet his Fate. Mean while, the *Bee* had
acquitted himself of his Toils, and posted securely at some Distance, was employed in cleansing his Wings, and disengaging them
from the ragged Remnants of the Cobweb. By this Time the *Spider*
was adventured out, when beholding the Chasms, and Ruins, and
Dilapidations of his Fortress, he was very near at his Wit's end, he
stormed and swore like a Mad-man, and swelled till he was ready to
burst. At length, casting his Eye upon the *Bee*, and wisely gathering
Causes from Events, (for they knew each other by Sight) A *Plague
split you*, said he, *for a giddy Son of a Whore; Is it you, with a
Vengeance, that have made this Litter here? Could you not look
before you, and be d——n'd? Do you think I have nothing else to
do (in the Devil's Name) but to Mend and Repair after your Arse?*
Good Words, Friend, said the *Bee*, (having now pruned himself,
and being disposed to drole) *I'll give you my Hand and Word to
come near your Kennel no more; I was never in such a confounded
Pickle since I was born.* Sirrah, replied the *Spider*, *if it were not for
breaking an old Custom in our Family, never to stir abroad against
an Enemy, I should come and teach you better Manners. I pray,
have Patience*, said the *Bee*, *or you will spend your Substance, and
for ought I see, you may stand in need of it all, towards the Repair
of your House.* Rogue, Rogue, replied the *Spider*, *yet, methinks,
you should have more Respect to a Person, whom all the World
allows to be so much your Betters.* By my Troth, said the *Bee*, *the
Comparison will amount to a very good Jest, and you will do me a
Favour, to let me know the Reasons, that all the World is pleased
to use in so hopeful a Dispute.* At this, the *Spider* having swelled
himself into the Size and Posture of a Disputant, began his Argument in the true Spirit of Controversy, with a Resolution to be
heartily scurrilous and angry, to urge *on* his own Reasons, without
the least Regard to the Answers or Objections of his Opposite; and
fully predetermined in his Mind against all Conviction.

N O T *to disparage myself*, said he, *by the Comparison with such
a Rascal; What art thou but a Vagabond without House or Home,
without Stock or Inheritance? Born to no Possession of your own,
but a Pair of Wings, and a Drone-Pipe. Your Livelihood is an universal Plunder upon Nature; a Freebooter over Fields and Gardens;*

and for the sake of Stealing, will rob a Nettle as readily as a Violet. Whereas I am a domestick Animal, furnisht with a Native Stock within my self. This large Castle (to shew my Improvements in the Mathematicks) is all built with my own Hands, and the Materials extracted altogether out of my own Person.

I am glad, answered the *Bee, to hear you grant at least, that I am come honestly by my Wings and my Voice, for then, it seems, I am obliged to Heaven alone for my Flights and my Musick; and Providence would never have bestowed two such Gifts, without designing them for the noblest Ends. I visit, indeed, all the Flowers and Blossoms of the Field and the Garden, but whatever I collect from thence, enriches my self, without the least Injury to their Beauty, their Smell, or their Taste. Now, for you and your Skill in Architecture, and other Mathematicks, I have little to say: In that Building of yours, there might, for ought I know, have been Labor and Method enough, but by woful Experience for us both, 'tis too plain, the Materials are nought, and I hope, you will henceforth take Warning, and consider Duration and matter, as well as method and Art. You, boast, indeed, of being obliged to no other Creature, but of drawing, and spinning out all from your self; That is to say, if we may judge of the Liquor in the Vessel by what issues out, You possess a good plentiful Store of Dirt and Poison in your Breast; And, tho' I would by no means, lessen or disparage your genuine Stock of either, yet, I doubt you are somewhat obliged for an Encrease of both, to a little foreign Assistance. Your inherent Portion of Dirt, does not fail of Acquisitions, by Sweepings exhaled from below: and one Insect furnishes you with a share of Poison to destroy another. So that in short, the Question comes all to this; Whether is the nobler Being of the two, That which by a lazy Contemplation of four Inches round; by an over-weening Pride, which feeding and engendering on it self, turns all into Excrement and Venom; producing nothing at last, but Fly-bane and a Cobweb: Or That, which, by an universal Range, with long Search, much Study, true Judgment, and Distinction of Things, brings home Honey and Wax.*

T H I S Dispute was managed with such Eagerness, Clamor, and Warmth, that the two Parties of *Books* in Arms below, stood Silent a while, waiting in Suspense what would be the Issue; which was not long undetermined: For the *Bee* grown impatient at so much loss of Time, fled strait away to a bed of Roses, without looking for a Reply; and left the *Spider* like an Orator, *collected* in himself, and just prepared to burst out.

I T happened upon this Emergency, that *Æsop* broke silence first. He had been of late most barbarously treated by a strange Effect of the *Regent's Humanity*, who had tore off his Title-page, sorely defaced one half of his Leaves, and chained him fast among a Shelf of *Moderns*. Where soon discovering how high the Quarrel was like to proceed, He tried all his Arts, and turned himself to a thousand Forms: At length in the borrowed Shape of an *Ass*, the *Regent* mistook Him for a *Modern*; by which means, he had Time and Opportunity to escape to the *Antients*, just when the *Spider* and the *Bee* were entring into their Contest; to which He gave His Attention with a world of Pleasure; and when it was ended, swore in the loudest Key, that in all his Life, he had never known two Cases so parallel and adapt to each other, as That in the Window, and this upon the Shelves. The *Disputants*, said he, *have admirably managed the Dispute between them, have taken in the full Strength of all that is to be said on both sides, and exhausted the Substance of every Argument* pro *and* con. *It is but to adjust the Reasonings of both to the present Quarrel, then to compare and apply the Labors and Fruits of each, as the* Bee *has learnedly deduced them; and we shall find the Conclusions fall plain and close upon the* Moderns *and* Us. *For, pray Gentlemen, was ever any thing so* Modern *as the* Spider *in his Air, his Turns, and his Paradoxes? He argues in the Behalf of* You *his Brethren, and Himself, with many Boastings of his native Stock, and great Genius; that he Spins and Spits wholly from himself, and scorns to own any Obligation or Assistance from without. Then he displays to you his great Skill in Architecture, and Improvement in the Mathematicks. To all this, the* Bee, *as an Advocate, retained by us the* Antients, *thinks fit to Answer; That if one may judge of the great Genius or Inventions of the* Moderns, *by what they have produced, you will hardly have Countenance to bear you out in boasting of either. Erect your Schemes with as much Method and Skill as you please; yet, if the materials be nothing but Dirt, spun out of your own Entrails (the Guts of Modern Brains) the Edifice will conclude at last in a* Cobweb: *The Duration of which, like that of other Spiders Webs, may be imputed to their being forgotten, or neglected, or hid in a Corner. For any Thing else of Genuine, that the* Moderns *may pretend to, I cannot recollect; unless it be a large Vein of Wrangling and Satyr, much of a Nature and Substance with the* Spider's *Poison; which, however, they pretend to spit wholly out of themselves, is improved by the same Arts, by feeding upon the* Insects *and Vermin of the Age. As for Us, the Antients, We are content with the* Bee, *to pretend to Nothing of our own, beyond our Wings and our Voice: that is to say, our Flights and our Language; For the rest, whatever we have got, has been by infinite Labor, and search, and ranging thro' every Corner of Nature: The Difference is, that instead of Dirt and*

Poison, *we have rather chose to fill our Hives with* Honey *and* Wax, *thus furnishing Mankind with the two Noblest of Things, which are* Sweetness *and* Light.

'T I S wonderful to conceive the Tumult arisen among the *Books,* upon the Close of this long Descant of *Æsop;* Both Parties took the Hint, and heightened their Animosities so on a sudden, that they resolved it should come to a Battel. Immediately, the two main Bodies withdrew under their several Ensigns, to the farther Parts of the Library, and there entred into Cabals, and Consults upon the present Emergency. The *Moderns* were in very warm Debates upon the Choice of their *Leaders,* and nothing less than the Fear impending from their Enemies, could have kept them from Mutinies upon this Occasion. The Difference was greatest among the *Horse,* where every private *Trooper* pretended to the chief Command, from *Tasso* and *Milton,* to *Dryden* and *Withers.* The *Light-Horse*⁶ were Commanded by *Cowly,* and *Despreaux.* There, came the *Bowmen* under their valiant Leaders, *Des-Cartes, Gassendi,* and *Hobbes,* whose Strength was such, that they could shoot their Arrows beyond the *Atmosphere,* never to fall down again, but turn like that of *Evander,* into *Meteors,* or like the *Canonball* into *Stars. Paracelsus* brought a *Squadron* of *Stink-Pot-Flingers* from the snowy Mountains of *Rhœtia.* There, came a vast Body of *Dragoons,* of different Nations, under the leading of *Harvey,* their great *Aga:* Part armed with *Scythes,* the Weapons of Death; Part with *Launces* and long *Knives,* all steept in *Poison;* Part shot *Bullets* of a most malignant Nature, and used *white Powder* which infallibly killed without *Report.* There, came several Bodies of *heavy-armed Foot,* all *Mercenaries,* under the Ensigns of *Guiccardine, Davila, Polydore Virgil, Buchanan, Mariana, Cambden,* and others. The *Engineers* were commanded by *Regiomontanus* and *Wilkins.* The rest were a confused Multitude, led by *Scotus, Aquinas,* and *Bellarmine;* of mighty Bulk and Stature, but without either Arms, Courage, or Discipline. In the last Place, came infinite Swarms of * *Calones,* a disorderly Rout led by *Lestrange;* Rogues and Raggamuffins, that follow the Camp for nothing but the Plunder; All without *Coats* to cover them.

T H E Army of the *Antients* was much fewer in Number; *Homer* led the *Horse,* and *Pindar* the *Light-Horse; Euclid* was chief *Engineer: Plato* and *Aristotle* commanded the *Bow men, Herodotus* and *Livy* the *Foot, Hippocrates* the *Dragoons.* The *Allies,* led by *Vossius* and *Temple,* brought up the Rear.

A L L things violently tending to a decisive Battel; *Fame,* who much frequented, and had a large Apartment formerly assigned her

* *These are Pamphlets, which are not bound or cover'd.*

in the *Regal Library*, fled up strait to *Jupiter*, to whom she delivered a faithful account of all that passed between the two Parties below. (For, among the Gods, she always tells Truth.) *Jove* in great concern, convokes a Council in the *Milky-Way*. The Senate assembled, he declares the Occasion of convening them; a bloody Battel just impendent between two mighty Armies of *Antient* and *Modern* Creatures, call'd *Books*, wherein the Celestial Interest was but too deeply concerned. *Momus*, the Patron of the *Moderns*, made an Excellent Speech in their Favor, which was answered by *Pallas* the Protectress of the *Antients*. The Assembly was divided in their affections; when *Jupiter* commanded the Book of Fate to be laid before Him. Immediately were brought by *Mercury*, three large Volumes in Folio, containing Memoirs of all Things past, present, and to come. The Clasps were of Silver, double Gilt; the Covers, of Celestial Turky-leather, and the Paper such as here on Earth might almost pass for Vellum. *Jupiter* having silently read the Decree, would communicate the Import to none, but presently shut up the Book.

W I T H O U T the Doors of this Assembly, there attended a vast Number of light, nimble Gods, menial Servants to *Jupiter*: These are his ministring Instruments in all Affairs below. They travel in a Caravan, more or less together, and are fastened to each other like a Link of Gally-slaves, by a light Chain, which passes from them to *Jupiter*'s great Toe: And yet in receiving or delivering a Message, they may never approach above the lowest Step of his Throne, where he and they whisper to each other thro' a long hollow Trunk. These Deities are call'd by mortal Men, *Accidents*, or *Events*; but the Gods call them, *Second Causes*. *Jupiter* having delivered his Message to a certain Number of these Divinities, they flew immediately down to the Pinnacle of the Regal Library, and consulting a few Minutes, entered unseen, and disposed the Parties according to their Orders.

M E A N while, *Momus* fearing the worst, and calling to mind an antient Prophecy, which bore no very good Face to his Children the *Moderns*; bent his Flight to the Region of a malignant Deity, call'd *Criticism*. She dwelt on the Top of a snowy Mountain in *Nova Zembla*; there *Momus* found her extended in her Den, upon the Spoils of numberless Volumes half devoured. At her right Hand sat *Ignorance*, her Father and Husband, blind with Age; at her left, *Pride* her Mother, dressing her up in the Scraps of Paper herself had torn. There, was *Opinion* her Sister, light of Foot, hoodwinkt, and headstrong, yet giddy and perpetually turning. About her play'd her Children, *Noise* and *Impudence*, *Dullness* and *Vanity*, *Positiveness*, *Pedantry*, and *Ill-Manners*. The Goddess herself had Claws like a Cat: Her Head, and Ears, and Voice, resembled those of an

Ass; Her Teeth fallen out before; Her Eyes turned inward, as if she lookt only upon herself: Her *Diet* was the overflowing of her own *Gall:* Her *Spleen* was so large, as to stand prominent like a Dug of the first Rate, nor wanted Excrescencies in form of Teats, at which a Crew of ugly Monsters were greedily sucking; and, what is wonderful to conceive, the bulk of Spleen encreased faster than the Sucking could diminish it. *Goddess, said Momus, can you sit idly here, while our devout Worshippers, the* Moderns, *are this Minute entring into a cruel Battel, and, perhaps, now lying under the Swords of their Enemies; Who then hereafter, will ever sacrifice, or build Altars to our Divinities? Haste therefore to the* British Isle, *and, if possible, prevent their Destruction, while I make Factions among the Gods, and gain them over to our Party.*

M O M U S having thus delivered himself, staid not for an answer, but left the Goddess to her own Resentments; Up she rose in a Rage, and as it is the Form upon such Occasions, began a Soliloquy. 'Tis I (said she) *who give Wisdom to Infants and Idiots; By Me, Children grow wiser than their Parents. By Me,* Beaux *become Politicians; and* School boys, *Judges of Philosophy. By Me,* Sophisters *debate, and conclude upon the Depths of Knowledge; and* Coffee-house Wits *instinct by Me, can correct an* Author's *Style, and display his minutest Errors, without understanding a Syllable of his Matter or his Language. By Me,* Striplings *spend their Judgment, as they do their Estate, before it comes into their Hands. 'Tis I, who have deposed Wit and Knowledge from their Empire over* Poetry, *and advanced my self in their stead. And shall a few upstart* Antients *dare to oppose me?* —— *But, come, my aged Parents, and you, my Children dear, and thou my beauteous Sister; let us ascend my Chariot, and hast to assist our devout* Moderns, *who are now sacrificing to us a* Hecatomb, *as I perceive by that grateful Smell, which from thence reaches my Nostrils.*

T H E Goddess and her Train having mounted the Chariot, which was drawn by *tame Geese,* flew over infinite Regions, shedding her Influence in due Places, till at length, she arrived at her beloved island of *Britain;* but in hovering over its *Metropolis,* what Blessings did she not let fall upon her Seminaries of *Gresham* and *Covent-Garden?* And now she reach'd the fatal Plain of St. *James's* Library, at what time the two Armies were upon the Point to engage; where entring with all her Caravan, unseen, and landing upon a Case of Shelves, now desart, but once inhabited by a Colony of *Virtuoso's,* she staid a while to observe the Posture of both Armies.

B U T here, the tender Cares of a Mother began to fill her Thoughts, and move in her Breast. For, at the Head of a Troop of *Modern Bow-men,* she cast her Eyes upon her Son W—tt—n; to whom the Fates had assigned a very short Thread. W—tt—n, a young Hero, whom an unknown Father of mortal Race, begot by stollen Embraces with this Goddess. He was the Darling of his Mother, above all her Children, and she resolved to go and comfort Him. But first, according to the good old Custom of Deities, she cast about to change her Shape; for fear the Divinity of her Countenance might dazzle his Mortal Sight, and over-charge the rest of his Senses. She therefore gathered up her Person into an *Octavo* Compass: Her Body grew white and arid, and split in pieces with Driness; the thick turned into Pastboard, and the thin into Paper, upon which, her Parents and Children, artfully strowed a Black Juice, or Decoction of Gall and Soot, in Form of Letters; her Head, and Voice, and Spleen, kept their primitive Form, and that which before, was a Cover of Skin, did still continue so. In which Guise, she march'd on towards the *Moderns*, undistinguishable in Shape and Dress from the *Divine B—ntl—y*, *W—tt—n's* dearest Friend. *Brave W—tt—n*, said the Goddess, *Why do our Troops stand idle here, to spend their present Vigour and Opportunity of the Day? Away, let us haste to the Generals, and advise to give the Onset immediately.* Having spoke thus, she took the ugliest of her Monsters, full glutted from her Spleen, and flung it invisibly into his Mouth; which flying strait up into his Head, squeez'd out his Eye-Balls, gave him a distorted Look, and half over-turned his Brain. Then she privately ordered two of her beloved Children, *Dulness* and *Ill-Manners*, closely to attend his Person in all Encounters. Having thus accoutred him, she vanished in a Mist, and the *Hero* perceived it was the Goddess, his Mother.

T H E destined Hour of Fate, being now arrived, the Fight began; whereof, before I dare adventure to make a particular Description, I must, after the Example of other Authors, petition for a hundred Tongues, and Mouths, and Hands, and Pens; which would all be too little to perform so immense a Work. Say, Goddess, that presidest over History; who it was that first advanced in the Field of Battel. *Paracelsus*, at the Head of his *Dragoons*, observing *Galen* in the adverse Wing, darted his Javelin with a mighty Force, which the brave *Antient* received upon his Shield, the Point breaking in the second fold.

          *   *   *   *   *   *   *   *

Hic pauca desunt.   *   *   *   *   *   *   *   *

          *   *   *   *   *   *   *   *

They bore the wounded *Aga*, on their Shields to his Chariot *

          *   *   *   *   *   *   *   *

Desunt nonnulla.   *   *   *   *   *   *   *   *

          *   *   *   *   *   *   *   *

T H E N *Aristotle* observing Bacon advance with a furious Mien, drew his Bow to the Head, and let fly his Arrow, which mist the valiant *Modern,* and went hizzing over his Head; but *Des-Cartes* it hit; The Steel Point quickly found a *Defect* in his *Head-piece;* it pierced the Leather and the Past-board, and went in at his Right Eye. The Torture of the Pain, whirled the valiant *Bow-man* round, till Death, like a Star of superior Influence, drew him into his own *Vortex.*   *   *   *   *   *   *   *   *   *   *

*   *   *   *   *   *   *   *

*   *   *   *   *   *   *   *   *Ingens hiatus hic in MS.*

*   *   *   *   *   *   *   *

when *Homer* appeared at the Head of the Cavalry, mounted on a furious Horse, with Difficulty managed by the Rider himself, but which no other Mortal durst approach; He rode among the Enemies Ranks, and bore down all before him. Say, Goddess, whom he slew first, and whom he slew last. First, *Gondibert* advanced against Him, clad in heavy Armour, and mounted on a staid sober Gelding, not so famed for his Speed as his Docility in kneeling, whenever his Rider would mount or alight. He had made a Vow to *Pallas,* that he would never leave the Field, till he had spoiled * *Homer* of his Armour; Madman, who had never once *seen* the Wearer, nor under-   * *Vid. Homer.* stood his Strength. Him *Homer* overthrew, Horse and Man to the Ground, there to be trampled and choak'd in the Dirt. Then, with a long Spear, he slew *Denham,* a stout *Modern,* who from his † Father's side, derived his Lineage from *Apollo,* but his Mother was of Mortal Race. He fell, and bit the Earth. The Celestial Part *Apollo* took, and made it a Star, but the Terrestrial lay wallowing upon the Ground. Then *Homer* slew W——*sl*—*y* with a kick of his Horse's heel; He took *Perrault* by mighty Force out of his Saddle, then hurl'd him at *Fontenelle,* with the same Blow dashing out both their Brains.

O N the left Wing of the Horse, *Virgil* appeared in shining Armor, compleatly fitted to his Body; He was mounted on a dapple grey Steed, the slowness of whose Pace, was an effect of the highest Mettle and Vigour. He cast his Eye on the adverse Wing, with a desire to find an Object worthy of his valour, when behold, upon a sorrel Gelding of a monstrous Size, appear'd a Foe, issuing from among the thickest of the Enemy's Squadrons; But his Speed was less than his Noise; for his Horse, old and lean, spent the Dregs of his Strength in a high Trot, which tho' it made slow advances, yet caused a loud Clashing of his Armor, terrible to hear. The two

† *Sir* John Denham's *Poems are very Unequal, extremely Good, and very Indifferent, so that his Detractors said, he was not the real Author of* Coopers-Hill.

Cavaliers had now approached within the Throw of a Lance, when the Stranger desired a Parley, and lifting up the Vizard of his Helmet, a Face hardly appeared from within, which after a pause, was known for that of the renowned *Dryden*. The brave *Antient* suddenly started, as one possess'd with Surprize and Disappointment together: For, the Helmet was nine times too large for the Head, which appeared Situate far in the hinder Part, even like the Lady[7] in a Lobster, or like a Mouse under a Canopy of State, or like a shrivled Beau from within the Pent-house of a modern Perewig: And the voice was suited to the Visage, sounding weak and remote. *Dryden* in a long Harangue soothed up the good *Antient*, called him *Father*, and by a large deduction of Genealogies, made it plainly appear, that they were nearly related. Then he humbly proposed an Exchange of Armor, as a lasting Mark of Hospitality between them. * *Virgil* consented (for the

* *Vid. Homer.*

Goddess *Diffidence* came unseen, and cast a Mist before his Eyes) tho' his was of Gold, and cost a hundred Beeves, the others but of rusty Iron. However, this glittering Armor became the *Modern* yet worse than his Own. Then, they agreed to exchange Horses; but when it came to the Trial, *Dryden* was afraid, and utterly unable to mount.   *   *   *   *   *   *   *

*   *   *   *   *   *   *   *

Alter hiatus in MS.   *   *   *   *   *   *   *   *

*   *   *   *   *   *   *   *

Lucan appeared upon a fiery Horse, of admirable Shape, but headstrong, bearing the Rider where he list, over the Field; he made a mighty Slaughter among the Enemy's Horse; which Destruction to stop, *Bl—ckm—re*, a famous *Modern* (but one of the *Mercenaries*) strenuously opposed himself; and darted a Javelin, with a strong Hand, which falling short of its Mark, struck deep in the Earth. Then *Lucan* threw a Lance; but *Æsculapius* came unseen, and turn'd off the Point. *Brave* Modern, *said* Lucan, *I perceive some God protects you, for never did my Arm so deceive me before; But, what Mortal can contend with a God? Therefore, let us Fight no longer, but present Gifts to each other.* Lucan then bestowed the *Modern* a Pair of Spurs, and *Bl—ckm—re* gave *Lucan* a Bridle.   *   *   *   *   *   *   *   *   *

Pauca desunt.   *   *   *   *   *   *   *   *

*   *   *   *   *   *   *   *

Creech;[8] But, the Goddess *Dulness* took a Cloud, formed into the Shape of *Horace*, armed and mounted, and placed it in a flying Posture before Him. Glad was the Cavalier, to begin a Combat with a flying Foe, and pursued the Image, threatning loud; till at last it led him to the peaceful Bower of his Father *Ogleby*,[9] by whom he was disarmed, and assigned to his Repose.

THEN *Pindar* slew ———, and ———, and *Oldham*, and
——— and *Afra* the *Amazon* light of foot; Never advancing in a
direct Line, but wheeling with incredible Agility and Force, he
made a terrible Slaughter among the Enemies *Light-Horse*. Him,
when *Cowley*[10] observed, his generous Heart burnt within him,
and he advanced against the fierce *Antient*, imitating his Address,
and Pace, and Career, as well as the Vigour of his Horse, and his
own Skill would allow. When the two Cavaliers had approach'd
within the Length of three Javelins; first *Cowley* threw a Lance,
which miss'd *Pindar*, and passing into the Enemy's Ranks, fell
ineffectual to the Ground. Then *Pindar* darted a Javelin, so large
and weighty, that scarce a dozen *Cavaliers*, as *Cavaliers* are in our
degenerate Days, could raise it from the Ground: yet he threw it
with Ease, and it went by an unerring Hand, singing through the
Air; Nor could the *Modern* have avoided present Death, if he had
not luckily opposed the Shield that had been given Him by *Venus*.
And now both Hero's drew their Swords, but the *Modern* was so
aghast and disordered, that he knew not where he was; his Shield
dropt from his Hands; thrice he fled, and thrice he could not
escape; at last he turned, and lifting up his Hands, in the Posture
of a Suppliant, *God-like* Pindar, said he, *spare my Life, and possess
my Horse with these Arms; besides the Ransom which my Friends
will give, when they hear I am alive, and your Prisoner*. Dog, said
Pindar, *Let your Ransom stay with your Friends; But your Carcass
shall be left for the* Fowls of the Air, *and the* Beasts of the Field.
With that, he raised his Sword, and with a mighty Stroak, cleft the
wretched *Modern* in twain, the Sword pursuing the Blow; and one
half lay panting on the Ground, to be trod in pieces by the Horses
Feet, the other half was born by the frighted Steed thro' the Field.
This * *Venus* took, and wash'd it seven times in *Ambrosia*, then
struck it thrice with a Sprig of *Amarant*; upon which, the Leather
grew round and soft, and the Leaves turned into Feathers, and
being gilded before, continued gilded still; so it became a *Dove*,
and She harness'd it to her Chariot.   *   *   *   *   *   *

*   *   *   *   *   *   *   *   *   *   *

*   *   *   *   *   *   *   *   *Hiatus valdè deflendus*
                                        in MS.
*   *   *   *   *   *   *   *

*   *   *   *   *   *   *   *   *   *   *

DAY being far spent, and the numerous Forces of the *Moderns*
half inclining to a Retreat, there issued forth from a Squadron of
their *heavy armed Foot*, * a Captain, whose
Name was *B—ntl—y*; in Person, the most   * *The Episode of*
deformed of all the *Moderns*; Tall, but   *B—ntl—y and W—tt—n.*

* *I do not approve the Author's Judgment in this, for I think* Cowley's Pindaricks
are much preferable to his Mistress.

without Shape or Comeliness; Large, but without Strength or Proportion. His Armour was patch'd up of a thousand incoherent Pieces; and the Sound of it, as he march'd, was loud and dry, like that made by the Fall of a Sheet of Lead, which an *Etesian* Wind blows suddenly down from the Roof of some Steeple. His Helmet was of old rusty Iron, but the Vizard was Brass, which tainted by his Breath, corrupted into Copperas, nor wanted Gall from the same Fountain; so, that whenever provoked by Anger or Labour, an atramentous[11] Quality, of most malignant Nature, was seen to distil from his Lips. In his * right Hand he grasp'd a Flail, and (that he might never be unprovided of an *offensive* Weapon) a Vessel full of *Ordure* in his Left: Thus, compleatly arm'd, he advanc'd with a slow and heavy Pace, where the *Modern* Chiefs were holding a Consult upon the Sum of Things; who, as he came onwards, laugh'd to behold his crooked Leg, and hump Shoulder, which his Boot and Armour vainly endeavouring to hide were forced to comply with, and expose. The Generals made use of him for his Talent of Railing; which kept within Government, proved frequently of great Service to their Cause, but at other times did more Mischief than Good; For at the least Touch of Offence, and often without any at all, he would, like a wounded Elephant, convert it against his Leaders. Such, at this Juncture, was the Disposition of B—ntl—y, grieved to see the Enemy prevail, and dissatisfied with every Body's Conduct but his own. * He

* *Vid. Homer. de Thersite.*

humbly gave the *Modern* Generals to understand, that he conceived, with great Submission, they were all a Pack of *Rogues*, and *Fools*, and *Sons of Whores*, and *d——mn'd Cowards*, and *confounded Logger-heads*, and *illiterate Whelps*, and *nonsensical Scoundrels*; That if Himself had been constituted General, those *presumptuous Dogs*, the *Antients*, would long before this, have been beaten out of the Field. *You*, said he, *sit here idle, but, when I, or any other valiant* Modern, *kill an Enemy, you are sure to seize the Spoil. But, I will not march one Foot against the Foe, till you all swear to me, that, whomever I take or kill, his Arms I shall quietly possess.* B—ntl—y having spoke thus, *Scaliger* bestowing him a sower Look; *Miscreant* Prater, said he, *Eloquent only in thine own Eyes, Thou railest without Wit, or Truth, or Discretion. The Malignity of thy Temper perverteth Nature, Thy* Learning *makes thee more* Barbarous, *thy Study of* Humanity, *more* Inhuman; *Thy* Converse *amongst Poets more* groveling, miry, *and* dull. *All Arts of* civilizing *others, render thee* rude *and* untractable; *Courts have taught thee* ill Manners, *and* polite

* *The Person here spoken of, is famous for letting fly at every Body without Distinction, and using mean and foul Scurrilities.*

Conversation *has finish'd thee a* Pedant. *Besides, a greater Coward burtheneth not the Army. But never despond, I pass my Word, whatever Spoil thou takest, shall certainly be thy own; though, I hope, that vile Carcass will first become a prey to Kites and Worms.*

B—N T L—Y durst not reply; but half choaked with Spleen and Rage, withdrew, in full Resolution of performing some great Achievement. With him, for his Aid and Companion, he took his beloved W—*tt*—*n*; resolving by Policy or Surprize, to attempt some neglected Quarter of the *Antients* Army. They began their March over Carcasses of their slaughtered Friends; then to the Right of their own Forces: then wheeled Northward, till they came to *Aldrovandus's* Tomb, which they pass'd on the side of the declining Sun. And now they arrived with Fear towards the Enemy's Out-guards; looking about, if haply, they might spy the Quarters of the Wounded, or some straggling Sleepers, unarm'd and remote from the rest. As when two *Mungrel-Curs*, whom *native Greediness*, and *domestick Want*, provoke, and join in Partnership, though fearful, nightly to invade the Folds of some rich Grazier; They, with Tails depress'd, and lolling Tongues, creep soft and slow; mean while, the conscious *Moon*, now in her *Zenith*, on their guilty Heads, darts perpendicular Rays; Nor dare they bark, though much provok'd at her refulgent Visage, whether seen in Puddle by Reflexion, or in Sphear direct; but one surveys the Region round, while t'other scouts the Plain, if haply, to discover at distance from the Flock, some *Carcass* half devoured, the Refuse of gorged Wolves, or ominous Ravens. So march'd this lovely, loving Pair of Friends, nor with less Fear and Circumspection; when, at distance, they might perceive two shining Suits of Armor, hanging upon an Oak, and the Owners not far off in a profound Sleep. The two Friends drew Lots, and the pursuing of this Adventure, fell to B—*ntl*—*y*; On he went, and in his Van *Confusion and Amaze*; while *Horror* and *Affright* brought up the Rear. As he came near; Behold two Hero's of the *Antients* Army, *Phalaris* and *Æsop*, lay fast asleep: B—*ntl*—*y* would fain have dispatch'd them both, and stealing close, aimed his Flail at *Phalaris's* Breast. But, then, the Goddess *Affright* interposing, caught the *Modern* in her icy Arms, and dragg'd him from the Danger she foresaw; For both the dormant Hero's happened to turn at the same Instant, tho' soundly Sleeping, and busy in a Dream. * For *Phalaris* was just that Minute dreaming, how a most vile *Poetaster* had lampoon'd him, and how he had got him roaring in his *Bull*.[12] And *Æsop* dream'd, that as he and the *Antient Chiefs* were lying on the Ground, a *Wild Ass* broke loose, ran about trampling

---

* *This is according to* Homer, *who tells the Dreams of those who were kill'd in their Sleep.*

and kicking, and dunging in their Faces, *B—ntl—y* leaving the two Hero's asleep, seized on both their Armors, and withdrew in quest of his darling *W—tt—n.*

H E, in the mean time, had wandred long in search of some Enterprize, till at length, he arrived at a small *Rivulet*, that issued from a Fountain hard by, call'd in the Language of mortal Men, *Helicon.* Here he stopt, and, parch'd with thirst, resolved to allay it in this limpid Stream. Thrice, with profane Hands, he essay'd to raise the Water to his Lips, and thrice it slipt all thro' his Fingers. Then he stoop'd prone on his Breast, but e'er his Mouth had kiss'd the liquid Crystal, *Apollo* came, and, in the Channel, held his *Shield* betwixt the *Modern* and the Fountain, so that he drew up nothing but *Mud.* For, altho' no Fountain on Earth can compare with the Clearness of *Helicon,* yet there lies at Bottom, a thick sediment of *Slime* and *Mud;* For, so *Apollo* begg'd of *Jupiter,* as a Punishment to those who durst attempt to taste it with unhallowed Lips, and for a Lesson to all, not to *draw too deep,* or *far from the Spring.*

A T the Fountain Head, *W—tt—n* discerned two Hero's; The one he could not distinguish, but the other was soon known for *Temple,* General of the *Allies* to the *Antients.* His Back was turned, and he was employ'd in Drinking large Draughts in his Helmet, from the Fountain, where he had withdrawn himself to rest from the Toils of the War. *W—tt—n,* observing him, with quaking Knees, and trembling Hands, spoke thus to Himself: * *Oh, that I could kill this Destroyer of our Army, what Renown should I pur-* * Vid. Homer. *chase among the Chiefs! But to issue out against Him, Man for Man, Shield against Shield, and Launce against Launce; what Modern of us dare? For, he fights like a God, and Pallas or Apollo are ever at his Elbow. But, Oh, Mother! if what Fame reports, be true, that I am the Son of so great a Goddess, grant me to Hit* Temple *with this Launce, that the Stroak may send Him to Hell, and that I may return in Safety and Triumph, laden with his Spoils.* The first Part of his Prayer, the Gods granted, at the Intercession of His *Mother* and of *Momus;* but the rest, by a perverse Wind sent from *Fate,* was scattered in the Air. Then *W—tt—n* grasp'd his Launce, and brandishing it thrice over his head, darted it with all his Might, the *Goddess,* his *Mother,* at the same time, adding Strength to his Arm. Away the Launce went hizzing, and reach'd even to the Belt of the averted *Antient,* upon which, lightly grazing, it fell to the Ground. *Temple* neither felt the Weapon touch him, nor heard it fall; And *W—tt—n,* might have escaped to his Army, with the Honor of having remitted his Launce against so great a

Leader, unrevenged; But, *Apollo* enraged, that a Javelin, flung by
the Assistance of so foul a *Goddess*, should pollute his Fountain,
put on the shape of ————,[13] and softly came to young *Boyle*, who
then accompanied *Temple:* He pointed, first to the Launce, then to
the distant *Modern* that flung it, and commanded the young Hero
to take immediate Revenge. *Boyle*, clad in a suit of Armor which
had been *given him by all the Gods*, immediately advanced against
the trembling Foe, who now fled before him. As a young Lion, in
the *Libyan Plains*, or *Araby Desart*, sent by his aged Sire to hunt
for Prey, or Health, or Exercise; He scours along, wishing to meet
some Tiger from the Mountains, or a furious Boar; If Chance, a
Wild Ass, with Brayings importune, affronts his Ear, the generous
Beast, though loathing to distain his Claws with Blood so vile, yet
much provok'd at the offensive Noise; which *Echo*, foolish Nymph,
like her *ill judging Sex*, repeats much louder, and with more
Delight than *Philomela*'s Song: He vindicates the Honor of the
Forest, and hunts the noisy, long-ear'd Animal. So W—*tt*—*n* fled,
so *Boyle* pursued. But W—*tt*—*n* heavy-arm'd, and slow of foot,
began to slack his Course; when his Lover B—*ntl*—*y* appeared,
returning laden with the Spoils of the two sleeping *Antients*. *Boyle*
observed him well, and soon discovering the Helmet and Shield of
Phalaris, his Friend, both which he had lately with his own Hands,
new polish'd and gilded; Rage sparkled in His Eyes, and leaving his
Pursuit after W—*tt*—*n*, he furiously rush'd on against this new
Approacher. Fain would he be revenged on both; but both now fled
different Ways: * And as a Woman in a lit-
tle House, that gets a painful Livelihood by   *Vid. Homer.*
Spinning; if chance her *Geese* be scattered o'er the Common, she
courses round the Plain from side to side, compelling here and there,
the Stragglers to the Flock; They cackle loud, and flutter o'er the
Champain. So *Boyle* pursued, so fled this Pair of Friends: finding
at length, their Flight was vain, they bravely joyn'd, and drew themselves in *Phalanx*. First, B—*ntl*—*y* threw a Spear with all his Force,
hoping to pierce the Enemy's Breast; But *Pallas* came unseen, and
in the Air took off the Point, and clap'd on one of *Lead*, which
after a dead Bang against the Enemy's Shield, fell blunted to the
Ground. Then *Boyle* observing well his Time, took a Launce of
wondrous Length and sharpness; and as this Pair of Friends com-
pacted stood close Side to Side, he wheel'd him to the right, and
with unusual Force, darted the Weapon. B—*ntl*—*y* saw his Fate
approach, and flanking down his Arms, close to his Ribs, hoping to
save his Body; in went the Point, passing through Arm and Side,

---

* *This is also, after the manner of* Homer; *the Woman's getting a painful
Livelihood by Spinning, has nothing to do with the Similitude, nor would be
excusable without such an Authority.*

nor stopt, or spent its Force, till it had also pierc'd the valiant
W—tt—n, who going to sustain his dying Friend, shared his Fate.
As, when a skilful Cook has truss'd a Brace of *Woodcocks*, He, with
Iron Skewer, pierces the tender Sides of both, their Legs and Wings
close pinion'd to their Ribs; So was this pair of Friends transfix'd,
till down they fell, joyn'd in their Lives, joyn'd in their Deaths; so
closely joyn'd, that *Charon* would mistake them both for one, and
waft them over *Styx* for half his Fare. Farewel, beloved, loving Pair;
Few Equals have you left behind: And happy and immortal shall
you be, if all my Wit and Eloquence can make you.

A N D, now   *   *   *   *   *   *   *   *   *
*   *   *   *   *   *   *   *   *   *   *   *
*   *   *   *   *   *   *   *   *   *   *   *
*   *   *   *   *Desunt cætera.*

FINIS

A

DISCOURSE

Concerning the

Mechanical Operation

OF THE

SPIRIT.

IN A

LETTER

To a FRIEND.

A

FRAGMENT.

LONDON:
Printed in the Year, MDCCX.

The Bookseller's Advertisement

T H E *following Discourse came into my Hands perfect and entire. But there being several Things in it, which the present Age would not very well bear, I kept it by me some Years, resolving it should never see the Light. At length, by the Advice and Assistance of a judicious Friend, I retrench'd those Parts that might give most Offence, and have now ventured to publish the Remainder; Concerning the Author, I am wholly ignorant; neither can I conjecture, whether it be the same with That of the two foregoing Pieces, the Original having been sent me at a different Time, and in a different Hand. The Learned Reader will better determine; to whose Judgment I entirely submit it.*

A Discourse Concerning the Mechanical Operation of the Spirit, &c.

For T. H. Esquire, at his Chambers in the Academy of the Beaux Esprits in New-Holland[1]

SIR,

IT is now a good while since I have had in my Head something, not only very material, but absolutely necessary to my Health, that the World should be informed in. For, to tell you a Secret, I am able to *contain* it no longer. However, I have been perplexed for some time, to resolve what would be the most proper Form to send it abroad in. To which End, I have three Days been coursing thro' *Westminster-Hall*, and St. *Paul's Church yard*, and *Fleet-street*, to peruse *Titles*; and, I do not find any which holds so general a Vogue, as that of A *Letter to a Friend*: Nothing is more common than to meet with long Epistles address'd to Persons and Places, where, at first thinking, one would be apt to imagine it not altogether so necessary or Convenient; Such as, *a Neighbour at next Door, a mortal Enemy, a perfect Stranger,* or *a Person of Quality in the Clouds*; and these upon Subjects, in appearance, the least proper for Conveyance by the Post; as, *long Schemes in Philosophy; dark and wonderful Mysteries of State; Laborious Dissertations in Criticism and Philosophy, Advice to Parliaments,* and the like.

NOW, Sir, to proceed after the Method in present Wear. (For, let me say what I will to the contrary, I am afraid you will publish this *Letter*, as soon as ever it comes to your Hands;) I desire you will be my Witness to the World, how careless and sudden a Scribble it has been; That it was but Yesterday, when You and I began accidentally to fall into Discourse on this Matter: That I was not very well, when we parted; That the Post is in such haste, I have had no manner of Time to digest it into Order, or correct the Style; And if any other Modern Excuses, for Haste and Negligence, shall occur to you in Reading, I beg you to insert them, faithfully promising they shall be thankfully acknowledged.

This Discourse is not altogether equal to the two Former, the best Parts of it being omitted; whether the Bookseller's Account be true, that he durst not print the rest, I know not, nor indeed is it easie to determine whether he may be rely'd on, in any thing he says of this, or the former Treatises, only as to the Time they were writ in, which, however, appears more from the Discourses themselves than his Relation.

P R A Y, Sir, in your next Letter to the *Iroquois Virtuosi*, do me the Favour to present my humble Service to that illustrious Body, and assure them, I shall send an Account of those *Phænomena*, as soon as we can determine them at *Gresham*.

I have not had a Line from the *Literati* of *Tobinambou*, these three last Ordinaries.

A N D now, Sir, having dispatch'd what I had to say of Forms, or of Business, let me intreat, you will suffer me to proceed upon my Subject; and to pardon me, if I make no farther Use of the Epistolary Stile, till I come to conclude.

SECTION I

'T I S recorded of *Mahomet*, that upon a Visit he was going to pay in *Paradise*, he had an Offer of several Vehicles to conduct him upwards; as fiery Chariots, wing'd Horses, and celestial Sedans; but he refused them all, and would be born to Heaven upon nothing but his *Ass*. Now, this Inclination of *Mahomet*, as singular as it seems, hath been since taken up by a great Number of devout *Christians*; and doubtless, with very good Reason. For, since That *Arabian* is known to have borrowed a Moiety of his Religious System from the *Christian* Faith; it is but just he should pay Reprisals to such as would Challenge them; wherein the good People of *England*, to do them all Right, have not been backward. For, tho' there is not any other Nation in the World, so plentifully provided with Carriages for that Journey, either as to Safety or Ease; yet there are abundance of us, who will not be satisfied with any other Machine, beside this of *Mahomet*.

F O R my own part, I must confess to bear a very singular Respect to this Animal, by whom I take human Nature to be most admirably held forth in its Qualities as well as Operations: And therefore, whatever in my small Reading, occurs, concerning this our Fellow-Creature, I do never fail to set it down, by way of Common-place; and when I have occasion to write upon Human Reason, Politicks, Eloquence, or Knowledge; I lay my *Memorandums* before me, and insert them with a wonderful Facility of Application. However, among all the Qualifications, ascribed to this distinguish'd Brute, by Antient or Modern Authors; I cannot remember this Talent, of bearing his Rider to Heaven, has been recorded for a Part of his Character, except in the two Examples mentioned already; Therefore, I conceive the Methods of this Art, to be a Point of useful Knowledge in very few Hands, and which the Learned World would gladly be better informed in. This is what I have undertaken to perform in the following Discourse. For, towards the Operation already mentioned, many peculiar Properties are required, both in the *Rider* and the *Ass*; which I shall endeavour to set in as clear a Light as I can.

B U T, because I am resolved, by all means, to avoid giving Offence to any Party whatever; I will leave off discoursing so closely to the *Letter* as I have hitherto done, and go on for the future by way of Allegory, tho' in such a manner, that the judicious Reader, may without much straining, make his Applications as often as he shall think fit. Therefore, if you please from hence forward, instead of the Term, *Ass*, we shall make use of *Gifted*, or *enlightned Teacher*; And the Word *Rider*, we will exchange for that of *Fanatick Auditory*, or any other Denomination of the like Import. Having settled this weighty Point; the great Subject of Enquiry before us, is to examine, by what Methods this *Teacher* arrives at his *Gifts* or *Spirit*, or *Light*; and by what Intercourse between him and his Assembly, it is cultivated and supported.

I N all my Writings, I have had constant Regard to this great End, not to suit and apply them to particular Occasions and Circumstances of Time, of Place, or of Person; but to calculate them for universal Nature, and Mankind in general. And of such Catholick use, I esteem this present Disquisition: For I do not remember any other Temper of Body, or Quality of Mind, wherein all Nations and Ages of the World have so unanimously agreed, as That of a *Fanatick* Strain, or Tincture of *Enthusiasm*; which improved by certain Persons or Societies of Men, and by them practised upon the rest, has been able to produce Revolutions of the greatest Figure in History; as will soon appear to those who know any thing of *Arabia, Persia, India,* or *China,* of *Morocco* and *Peru*: Farther, it has possessed as great a Power in the Kingdom of Knowledge, where it is hard to assign one Art or Science, which has not annexed to it some *Fanatick* Branch: Such are the *Philosopher's Stone*; * *The Grand Elixir*; *The Planetary Worlds*; *The Squaring of the Circle*; *The Summum bonum*; Utopian *Common-* * Some Writers hold them for the same, others not. *wealths*; with some others of less or subordinate Note; which all serve for nothing else, but to employ or amuse this Grain of *Enthusiasm*, dealt into every Composition.

B U T, if this Plant has found a Root in the Fields of *Empire,* and of *Knowledge.* it has fixt deeper, and spread yet farther upon *Holy Ground.* Wherein, though it hath pass'd under the general Name of *Enthusiasm,* and perhaps arisen from the same Original, yet hath it produced certain Branches of a very different Nature, however often mistaken for each other. The Word in its universal Acceptation, may be defined, A *lifting up of the Soul or its Facul-*

ties above Matter. This Description will hold good in general; but I am only to understand it, as applied to *Religion;* wherein there are three general Ways of ejaculating the Soul, or transporting it beyond the Sphere of Matter. The first, is the immediate Act of God, and is called, *Prophecy* or *Inspiration.* The second, is the immediate Act of the Devil, and is termed *Possession.* The third, is the Product of natural Causes, the effect of strong Imagination, Spleen, violent Anger, Fear, Grief, Pain, and the like. These three have been abundantly treated on by Authors, and therefore shall not employ my Enquiry. But, the fourth Method of *Religious Enthusiasm,* or launching out of the Soul, as it is purely an Effect of Artifice and *Mechanick Operation,* has been sparingly handled, or not at all, by any Writer; because tho' it is an Art of great Antiquity, yet having been confined to few Persons, it long wanted those Advancements and Refinements, which it afterwards met with, since it has grown so Epidemick, and fallen into so many cultivating Hands.

I T is therefore upon this *Mechanical Operation of the Spirit,* that I mean to treat, as it is at present performed by our *British Workmen.* I shall deliver to the Reader the Result of many judicious Observations upon the Matter; tracing, as near as I can, the whole Course and Method of this *Trade,* producing parallel Instances, and relating certain Discoveries that have luckily fallen in my way.

I have said, that there is one Branch of *Religious Enthusiasm,* which is purely an Effect of Nature; whereas, the Part I mean to handle, is wholly an Effect of Art, which, however, is inclined to work upon certain Natures and Constitutions, more than others. Besides, there is many an Operation, which in its Original, was purely an Artifice, but through a long Succession of Ages, hath grown to be natural. *Hippocrates,* tells us, that among our Ancestors, the *Scythians,* there was a Nation call'd, * *Longheads,* which at first began by a Custom among Midwives and Nurses, of molding, and squeezing, and bracing up the Heads of Infants; by which means, Nature shut out at one Passage, was forc'd to seek another, and finding room above, shot upwards, in the Form of a Sugar-Loaf; and being diverted that way, for some Generations, at last found it out of her self, needing no Assistance from the Nurse's Hand. This was the Original of the *Scythian Long-heads,* and thus did Custom, from being a second Nature proceed to be a first. To all which, there is something very analogous among Us of this Nation, who are the undoubted Posterity of that refined People. For, in the Age of our Fathers, there arose a Generation of Men in this Island,

* *Macrocephali.*

call'd *Round-heads*, whose Race is now spread over three Kingdoms, yet in its Beginning, was meerly an Operation of Art, produced by a pair of Cizars, a Squeeze of the Face, and a black Cap. These Heads, thus formed into a perfect Sphere in all Assemblies, were most exposed to the view of the Female Sort, which did influence their Conceptions so effectually, that Nature, at last, took the Hint, and did it of her self; so that a *Round-head* has been ever since as familiar a Sight among Us, as a *Long-head* among the *Scythians*.

U P O N these Examples, and others easy to produce, I desire the curious Reader to distinguish, First between an Effect grown from *Art* into *Nature*, and one that is natural from its Beginning; Secondly, between an Effect wholly natural, and one which has only a natural Foundation, but where the Superstructure is entirely Artificial. For, the first and the last of these, I understand to come within the Districts of my Subject. And having obtained these allowances, they will serve to remove any objections that may be raised hereafter against what I shall advance.

T H E Practitioners of this famous Art, proceed in general upon the following Fundamental; That, *the Corruption of the Senses is the Generation of the Spirit*: Because the *Senses* in Men are so many Avenues to the Fort of *Reason*, which in this Operation is wholly block'd up. All Endeavours must be therefore used, either to divert, bind up, stupify, fluster, and amuse the *Senses*, or else to justle them out of their Stations; and while they are either absent, or otherwise employ'd or engaged in a Civil War against each other, the *Spirit* enters and performs its Part.

N O W, the usual Methods of managing the Senses upon such Conjunctures, are what I shall be very particular in delivering, as far as it is lawful for me to do; but having had the Honour to be Initiated into the Mysteries of every Society, I desire to be excused from divulging any Rites, wherein the *Profane* must have no Part.

BUT here, before I can proceed farther, a very dangerous Objection must, if possible, be removed: For, it is positively denied by certain Criticks, that the *Spirit* can by any means be introduced into an Assembly of Modern Saints, the Disparity being so great in many material Circumstances, between the Primitive Way of Inspiration, and that which is practised in the present Age. This they pretend to prove from the second Chapter of the *Acts*, where comparing both, it appears; First, that *the Apostles were gathered together with one accord in one place*; by which is meant, an universal Agreement in Opinion, and Form of Worship; a Harmony (say they) so far from being found between any two Conventicles among Us, that it is in vain to expect it between any two Heads in the same. Secondly, the *Spirit* instructed the Apostles in the Gift of speaking several Languages; a Knowledge so remote from our Dealers in this Art, that they neither understand Propriety of Words, or Phrases in their own. Lastly, (say these Objectors) The Modern Artists do utterly exclude all Approaches of the *Spirit*, and bar up its antient Way of entring, by covering themselves so close, and so industriously a top. For, they will needs have it as a Point clearly gained, that the *Cloven Tongues*[2] never sat upon the Apostles Heads, while their Hats were on.

N O W, the Force of these Objections, seems to consist in the different Acceptation of the Word, *Spirit*: which if it be understood for a supernatural Assistance, approaching from without, the Objectors have Reason, and their Assertions may be allowed; But the *Spirit* we treat of here, proceeding entirely from within, the Argument of these Adversaries is wholly eluded. And upon the same Account, our Modern Artificers, find it an Expedient of absolute Necessity, to cover their Heads as close as they can, in order to prevent Perspiration, than which nothing is observed to be a greater Spender of Mechanick Light, as we may, perhaps, farther shew in convenient Place.

T O proceed therefore upon the *Phænomenon* of *Spiritual Mechanism*, It is here to be noted, that in forming and working up the *Spirit*, the Assembly has a considerable Share, as well as the Preacher; The Method of this *Arcanum*, is as follows. They violently strain their Eye balls inward, half closing the Lids; Then, as they sit, they are in a perpetual Motion of *See-saw*, making long Hums at proper Periods, and continuing the Sound at equal Height, chusing their Time in those Intermissions, while the Preacher is at Ebb. Neither is this Practice, in any part of it, so singular or improbable, as not to be traced in distant Regions, from Reading and Observation.

* Bernier, Mem. de Mogol.   For first, the * *Jauguis*, or enlightened Saints of *India*, see all their Visions, by help of an acquired straining and pressure of the Eyes. Secondly, the Art of *See-saw* on an Beam, and swinging by Session upon a Cord, in order to raise artificial Extasies, hath been derived to Us, from our

† Guagnini Hist. Sarmat.   † *Scythian* Ancestors, where it is practised at this Day, among the Women. Lastly, the whole Proceeding, as I have here related it, is performed by the Natives of *Ireland*, with a considerable Improvement; And it is granted, that this noble Nation, hath of all others, admitted fewer Corruptions, and degenerated least from the Purity of the *Old Tartars*. Now it is usual for a Knot of *Irish*, Men and Women, to abstract themselves from Matter, bind up all their Senses, grow visionary and spiritual, by Influence of a short Pipe of Tobacco, handed

round the Company; each preserving the Smoak in his Mouth, till it comes again to his Turn to take in fresh: At the same Time, there is a Consort of a continued gentle Hum, repeated and renewed by Instinct, as Occasion requires, and they move their Bodies up and down, to a Degree, that sometimes their Heads and Points lie parallel to the Horison. Mean while, you may observe their Eyes turn'd up in the Posture of one, who endeavours to keep himself awake; by which, and many other Symptoms among them, it manifestly appears, that the Reasoning Faculties are all suspended and superseded, that Imagination hath usurped the Seat, scattering a thousand Deliriums over the Brain. Returning from this Digression, I shall describe the Methods, by which the *Spirit* approaches. The Eyes being disposed according to Art, at first, you can see nothing, but after a short pause, a small glimmering Light begins to appear, and dance before you. Then, by frequently moving your Body up and down, you perceive the Vapors to ascend very fast, till you are perfectly dosed and flustred like one who drinks too much in a Morning. Mean while, the Preacher is also at work; He begins a loud Hum, which pierces you quite thro'; This is immediately returned by the Audience, and you find your self prompted to imitate them, by a meer spontaneous Impulse, without knowing what you do. The *Interstitia* are duly filled up by the Preacher, to prevent too long a Pause, under which the *Spirit* would soon faint and grow languid.

T H I S is all I am allowed to discover about the Progress of the *Spirit*, with relation to that part, which is born by the *Assembly*; But in the Methods of the Preacher, to which I now proceed, I shall be more large and particular.

S E C T I O N   I I

Y O U will read it very gravely remarked in the Books of those illustrious and right eloquent Pen-men, the Modern Travellers; that the fundamental Difference in Point of Religion, between the wild *Indians* and Us, lies in this; that We worship *God*, and they worship the *Devil*. But, there are certain Criticks, who will by no means admit of this Distinction; rather believing, that all Nations whatsoever, adore the *true God*, because, they seem to intend their Devotions to some invisible Power, of greatest *Goodness* and *Ability* to help them, which perhaps will take in the brightest Attributes ascribed to the Divinity. Others, again, inform us, that those Idolaters adore two *Principles*; the *Principle* of *Good*, and That of *Evil*: Which indeed, I am apt to look upon as the most Universal Notion, that Mankind, by the meer Light of Nature, ever enter-

tained of Things Invisible. How this Idea hath been managed by
the *Indians* and Us, and with what Advantage to the Understandings of either, may well deserve to be examined. To me, the difference appears little more than this, That They are put oftener upon
their Knees by their *Fears*, and We by our *Desires*; That the former
set them a *Praying*, and Us a *Cursing*. What I applaud them for, is
their Discretion, in limiting their Devotions and their Deities to
their several Districts, nor ever suffering the Liturgy of the *white*
God, to cross or interfere with that of the *Black*. Not so with Us,
who pretending by the Lines and Measures of our Reason, to
extend the Dominion of one invisible Power, and contract that of
the other, have discovered a gross Ignorance in the Natures of Good
and Evil, and most horribly confounded the Frontiers of both.
After Men have lifted up the Throne of their Divinity to the *Cælum
Empyræum*, adorned with all such Qualities and Accomplishments, as themselves seem most to value and possess: After they
have sunk their *Principle* of *Evil* to the lowest Center, bound him
with Chains, loaded him with Curses, furnish'd him with viler Dispositions than any *Rake-hell* of the Town, accoutred him with Tail,
and Horns, and huge Claws, and Sawcer Eyes; I laugh aloud, to see
these Reasoners, at the same time, engaged in wise Dispute, about
certain Walks and Purlieus, whether they are in the Verge of God
or the Devil, seriously debating, whether such and such Influences
come into Mens Minds, from above or below, or whether certain
Passions and Affections are guided by the Evil Spirit or the Good.

> *Dum fas atque nefas exiguo fine libidinum*
> *Discernunt avidi* ———[3]

Thus do Men establish a Fellowship of *Christ* with *Belial*, and such
is the Analogy they make between *cloven Tongues*, and *cloven
Feet*. Of the like Nature is the Disquisition before us: It hath continued these hundred Years an even Debate, whether the Deportment and the Cant of our *English* Enthusiastick Preachers, were
Possession, or *Inspiration*, and a World of Argument has been
drained on either side, perhaps, to little Purpose. For, I think, it is
in *Life* as in *Tragedy*, where, it is held, a Conviction of great
Defect, both in Order and Invention, to interpose the Assistance of
preternatural Power, without an absolute and last Necessity. However, it is a Sketch of Human Vanity, for every Individual, to imagine the whole Universe is interess'd in his meanest Concern. If he
hath got cleanly over a Kennel, some Angel, unseen, descended on
purpose to help him by the Hand; if he hath knockt his Head
against a Post, it was the Devil, for his Sins, let loose from Hell, on
purpose to buffet him. Who, that sees a little paultry Mortal, droning, and dreaming, and drivelling to a Multitude, can think it agree-

able to common good Sense, that either Heaven or Hell should be put to the Trouble of Influence or Inspection upon what he is about? Therefore, I am resolved immediately, to weed this Error out of Mankind, by making it clear, that this Mystery, of vending⁴ spiritual Gifts is nothing but a *Trade*, acquired by as much Instruction, and mastered by equal Practice and Application as others are. This will best appear, by describing and deducing the whole Process of the Operation, as variously as it hath fallen under my Knowledge or Experience.

*   *   *   *   *   *   *   *   *   *   *   *

*   *   *   *   *   *   *   *   *Here the whole Scheme*
*   *   *   *   *   *   *   *   *of spiritual Mechanism*
                                             was deduced and explained,
*   *   *   *   *   *   *   *   *with an Appearance of*
                                             great reading and obser-
*   *   *   *   *   *   *   *   *vation; but it was thought*
*   *   *   *   *   *   *   *   *neither safe nor Convenient*
                                             to Print it.
*   *   *   *   *   *   *   *   *   *   *   *

H E R E it may not be amiss, to add a few Words upon the laudable Practice of wearing *quilted Caps*;⁵ which is not a Matter of meer Custom, Humor, or Fashion, as some would pretend, but an Institution of great Sagacity and Use; these, when moistned with Sweat, stop all Perspiration, and by reverberating the Heat, prevent the Spirit from evaporating any way, but at the Mouth; even as a skilful Housewife, that covers her Still with a wet Clout, for the same Reason, and finds the same Effect. For, it is the Opinion of Choice *Virtuosi*, that the Brain is only a Crowd of little Animals, but with Teeth and Claws extremely sharp, and therefore, cling together in the Contexture we behold, like the Picture of *Hobbes's Leviathan*, or like Bees in perpendicular swarm upon a Tree, or like a Carrion corrupted into Vermin, still preserving the Shape and Figure of the Mother Animal. That all Invention is formed by the Morsure⁶ of two or more of these Animals, upon certain capillary Nerves, which proceed from thence, whereof three Branches spread into the Tongue, and two into the right Hand. They hold also, that these Animals are of a Constitution extremely cold; that their Food is the Air we attract, their Excrement Phlegm; and that what we vulgarly call Rheums, and Colds, and Distillations, is nothing else but an Epidemical Looseness, to which that little Commonwealth is very subject, from the Climate it lyes under. Farther, that nothing less than a violent Heat, can disentangle these Creatures from their hamated⁷ Station of Life, or give them Vigor and Humor, to imprint the Marks of their little Teeth. That if the Morsure be Hexagonal, it produces Poetry; the Circular gives Eloquence; If the Bite hath been Conical, the Person, whose Nerve is so affected, shall be disposed to write upon the Politicks; and so of the rest.

I shall now Discourse briefly, by what kind of Practices the Voice is best governed, towards the Composition and Improvement of the *Spirit*; for, without a competent Skill in tuning and toning each Word, and Syllable, and Letter, to their due Cadence, the whole Operation is incompleat, misses entirely of its effect on the Hearers, and puts the Workman himself to continual Pains for new Supplies, without Success. For, it is to be understood, that in the Language of the Spirit, *Cant* and *Droning* supply the Place of *Sense* and *Reason*, in the Language of Men: Because, in Spiritual Harangues, the Disposition of the Words according to the Art of Grammar. hath not the least Use, but the Skill and Influence wholly lye in the Choice and Cadence of the Syllables; Even as a discreet *Composer*, who in setting a Song, changes the Words and Order so often, that he is forced to make it *Nonsense*, before he can make it *Musick*. For this Reason, it hath been held by some, that the Art of Canting is ever in greatest Perfection, when managed by *Ignorance*: Which is thought to be enigmatically meant by *Plutarch*, when he tells us, that the best Musical Instruments were made from the Bones of an *Ass*. And the profounder Cricks upon that Passage, are of Opinion, the Word in its genuine Signification, means no other than a *Jaw-bone*: tho' some rather think it to have been the *Os sacrum*; but in so nice a Case, I shall not take upon me to decide: The Curious are at Liberty, to *pick* from it whatever they please.

THE first Ingredient, towards the Art of Canting, is a competent Share of *Inward Light*: that is to say, a large Memory, plentifully fraught with Theological Polysyllables, and mysterious Texts from holy Writ, applied and digested by those Methods, and Mechanical Operations already related: The Bearers of this *Light*, resembling *Lanthorns*, compact of Leaves from old *Geneva* Bibles; Which Invention, *Sir H—mphry Edw—n*, during his Mayoralty, of happy Memory, highly approved and advanced; affirming, the Scripture to be now fulfilled, where it says, *Thy Word is a Lanthorn to my Feet, and a Light to my Paths*.

NOW, the Art of *Canting* consists in skilfully adapting the Voice, to whatever Words the Spirit delivers, that each may strike the Ears of the Audience, with its most significant Cadence. The Force, or Energy of this Eloquence, is not to be found, as among antient Orators, in the Disposition of Words to a Sentence, or the turning of long Periods; but agreeable to the Modern Refinements in Musick, is taken up wholly in dwelling, and dilating upon Syllables and Letters. Thus it is frequent for a single *Vowel* to draw Sighs from a Multitude; and for a whole Assembly of Saints to sob to the Musick of one solitary *Liquid*. But these are Trifles; when even Sounds inarticulate are observed to produce as forcible Effects. A Master Work-man shall *blow his Nose so powerfully*, as to pierce the Hearts of his People, who are disposed to receive the *Excrements* of his Brain with the same Reverence, as the *Issue* of it. Hawking, Spitting, and Belching, the Defects of other Mens Rhetorick, are the Flowers, and Figures, and Ornaments of his. For, the *Spirit* being the same in all, it is of no Import through what Vehicle it is convey'd.

IT is a Point of too much Difficulty, to draw the Principles of this famous Art within the Compass of certain adequate Rules. However, perhaps, I may one day, oblige the World with my Critical Essay upon the Art of *Canting, Philosophically, Physically, and Musically considered.*

BUT, among all Improvements of the *Spirit*, wherein the Voice hath born a Part, there is none to be compared with That of *conveying the Sound thro' the Nose*, which under the Denomination of * *Snuffling*, hath passed with so great Applause in the World. The Originals of this Institution are very dark; but having been initiated into the Mystery of it, and Leave being given me to publish it to the World, I shall deliver as direct a Relation as I can.

T H I S Art, like many other famous Inventions, owed its Birth, or at least, Improvement and Perfection, to an Effect of Chance, but was established upon solid Reasons, and hath flourished in this Island ever since, with great Lustre. All agree, that it first appeared upon the Decay and Discouragement of *Bag-Pipes*, which having long suffered under the Mortal Hatred of the *Brethren*, tottered for a Time, and at last fell with *Monarchy*. The Story is thus related.

AS yet, *Snuffling* was not; when the following Adventure happened to a *Banbury Saint*. Upon a certain Day, while he was far engaged among the Tabernacles of the *Wicked*, he felt the Outward Man put into odd Commotions, and strangely prick'd forward by the Inward: An Effect very usual among the Modern Inspired. For, some think, that the *Spirit* is apt to feed on the *Flesh*, like hungry Wines upon raw Beef. Others rather believe, there is a perpetual Game at *Leap-Frog* between both; and, sometimes, the *Flesh* is uppermost, and sometimes the *Spirit*; adding, that the former, while it is in the State of a *Rider*, wears huge *Rippon* Spurs, and when it comes to the Turn of being *Bearer*, is wonderfully headstrong, and hard-mouth'd. However it came about, the *Saint* felt his *Vessel* full *extended* in every Part (a very natural Effect of strong *Inspiration;*) and the Place and Time falling out so unluckily, that he could not have the Convenience of Evacuating upwards,

---

* *The* Snuffling *of Men, who have lost their Noses by lewd Courses, is said to have given Rise to that Tone, which our Dissenters did too much Affect.* W. Wotton.

by Repetition, Prayer, or Lecture; he was forced to open an inferior Vent. In short, he wrestled with the Flesh so long, that he at length subdued it, coming off with honourable Wounds, all *before*. The Surgeon had now cured the Parts, primarily affected; but the Disease driven from its Post, flew up into his Head; And, as a skilful General, valiantly attack'd in his Trenches, and beaten from the Field, by flying Marches withdraws to the Capital City, breaking down the Bridges to prevent Pursuit; So the Disease repell'd from its first Station, fled before the *Rod* of *Hermes*, to the upper Region, there fortifying it self; but, finding the Foe making Attacks at the *Nose*, broke down the *Bridge*, and retir'd to the *Head*-Quarters. Now, the Naturalists observe, that there is in human Noses, an *Idiosyncrasy*, by Virtue of which, the more the Passage is obstructed, the more our Speech delights to go through, as the Musick of a Flagelate is made by the *Stops*. By this Method, the Twang of the Nose, becomes perfectly to resemble the *Snuffle* of a Bag-pipe, and is found to be equally attractive of *British* Ears; whereof the Saint had sudden Experience, by practising his new Faculty with wonderful Success in the Operation of the *Spirit*: For, in a short Time, no Doctrine pass'd for Sound and Orthodox, unless it were delivered thro' the Nose. Strait, every Pastor copy'd after this Original; and those, who could not otherwise arrive to a Perfection, spirited by a noble Zeal, made use of the same Experiment to acquire it. So that, I think, it may be truly affirmed, the *Saints* owe their Empire to the *Snuffling* of one *Animal*, as *Darius* did his, to the *Neighing* of another; and both Stratagems were performed by the same Art; for we read, how the * *Persian Beast* acquired his Faculty, by *covering a Mare* the Day before.

* *Herodot.*

I should now have done, if I were not convinced, that whatever I have yet advanced upon this Subject, is liable to great Exception. For, allowing all I have said to be true, it may still be justly objected, that there is in the Commonwealth of *artificial Enthusiasm*, some real Foundation for Art to work upon in the Temper and Complexion of Individuals, which other Mortals seem to want. Observe, but the Gesture, the Motion, and the Countenance, of some choice Professors, tho' in their most familiar Actions, you will find them of a different Race from the rest of human Creatures. Remark your commonest Pretender to a Light *within*, how dark, and dirty, and gloomy he is *without*; As Lanthorns, which the more Light they bear in their Bodies, cast out so much the more Soot, and Smoak, and fuliginous Matter to adhere to the Sides. Listen, but to their ordinary Talk, and look on the Mouth that delivers it; you will imagine you are hearing some antient Oracle, and your Understanding will be *equally* informed. Upon these, and the like Reasons, certain Objectors pretend to put it beyond all Doubt, that there must be a sort of preternatural *Spirit*, possessing the Heads of the Modern Saints; And some will have it to be the *Heat* of Zeal, working upon the *Dregs* of Ignorance, as other *Spirits* are produced from *Lees*, by the Force of Fire. Some again think, that when our earthly Tabernacles are disordered and desolate, shaken and out of repair; the *Spirit* delights to dwell within them, as Houses are said to be haunted, when they are forsaken and gone to Decay.

T O set this Matter in as fair a Light as possible; I shall here, very briefly, deduce the History of *Fanaticism*, from the most early Ages to the present. And if we are able to fix upon any one material or fundamental Point, wherein the chief Professors have universally agreed, I think we may reasonably lay hold on That, and assign it for the great Seed or Principle of the *Spirit*.

* THE most early Traces we meet with, of *Fanaticks*, in antient Story, are among the *Ægyptians*, who instituted those Rites, known in *Greece* by the Names of *Orgya*, *Panegyres*, and *Dionysia*, whether introduced there by *Orpheus* or *Melampus*, we shall not dispute at present, nor in all likelihood, at any time for the future. These Feasts were   * *Diod. Sic.* L. I. *Plut. de* celebrated to the Honor of *Osyris*, whom   *Iside & Osyride.* the *Grecians* called *Dionysius*, and is the same with *Bacchus:* Which has betray'd some superficial Readers to imagine, that the whole Business was nothing more than a Set of roaring, scouring Companions, over-charg'd with Wine; but this is a scandalous Mistake foisted on the World, by a sort of Modern Authors, who have too *literal* an Understanding; and, because Antiquity is to be traced *backwards*, do therefore, like *Jews*, begin their Books at the wrong End, as if Learning were a sort of *Conjuring*. These are the Men, who pretend to understand a Book, by scouting thro' the *Index*, as if a Traveller should go about to describe a *Palace*, when he had seen nothing but the *Privy*; or like certain Fortune-tellers in *Northern America*, who have a Way of reading a Man's Destiny, by peeping in his *Breech*. For, at the Time of instituting these Mysteries, * there was not one Vine in all *Egypt*, the, Natives drinking nothing but   * *Herod.* L. 2. *Ale*; which Liquor seems to have been far more antient than Wine, and has the Honor of owing its Invention and Progress, not only to the † *Egyptian Osyris*, but to the *Grecian* *Bacchus*, who in their famous Expedition,   † *Diod. Sic.* L. 1. & 3. carried the Receipt of it along with them, and gave it to the Nations they visited or subdued. Besides, *Bacchus* himself was very seldom, or never Drunk: For, it is recorded of him, that he was the first ** Inventor of the *Mitre*, which he   ** *Id.* L. 4. wore continually on his Head (as the whole

Company of *Bacchanals* did) to prevent Vapors and the Head-ach, after hard Drinking. And for this Reason (say some) the *Scarlet Whore*, when she makes the Kings of the Earth drunk with her Cup of Abomination, is always sober her self, tho' she never balks the Glass in her Turn, being, it seems, kept upon her Legs by the Virtue of her *Triple Mitre*. * Now, these Feasts were instituted in imitation of the famous Expedition *Osyris* made thro' the World, and of the Company that attended him, whereof the *Bacchanalian* Ceremonies were so many Types and Symbols. From which Account, it is manifest, that the Fanatick Rites of these *Bacchanals*, cannot be imputed to Intoxications by Wine, but must needs have had a deeper Foundation. What this was, we may gather large Hints from certain Circumstances in the Course of their Mysteries. For, in the first Place, there was in their Processions, an entire *Mixture and Confusion of Sexes*; they affected to ramble about Hills and Desarts: Their Garlands were of *Ivy* and *Vine*, Emblems of Cleaving and Clinging; or of *Fir*, the Parent of *Turpentine*. It is added, that they imitated *Satyrs*, were attended by *Goats*, and rode upon *Asses*, all Companions of great Skill and Practice in Affairs of Gallantry. They bore for their Ensigns, certain curious Figures, perch'd upon long Poles, made into the Shape and Size of the *Virga genitalis*, with its *Appurtenances*, which were so many Shadows and Emblems of the whole Mystery, as well as Trophies set up by the Female Conquerors. Lastly, in a certain Town of Attica, the whole Solemnity * stript of all its Types, was performed in *puris naturalibus*, the Votaries, not flying in Coveys, but sorted into Couples. The same may be farther conjectured from the Death of Orpheus, one of the Institutors of these Mysteries, who was torn in Pieces by Women, because he refused to † *communicate his Orgyes* to them; which others explained, by telling us, he had *castrated* himself upon Grief, for the Loss of his Wife.

* See the Particulars in Diod. Sic. *L.* 1. & 3.

* Dionysia Brauronia.

† Vid. Photium in excerptis è Conone.

OMITTING many others of less Note, the next *Fanaticks* we meet with, of any Eminence, were the numerous Sects of *Hereticks* appearing in the five first Centuries of the *Christian Æra*, from *Simon Magus* and his Followers, to those of *Eutyches*. I have collected their Systems from infinite Reading, and comparing them with those of their Successors in the several Ages since, I find there are certain Bounds set even to the Irregularities of Human Thought, and those a great deal narrower than is commonly apprehended. For, as they all frequently interfere, even in their wildest Ravings; So there is one fundamental Point, wherein they are sure to meet, as Lines in a Center, and that is the *Community of Women*: Great were their Sollicitudes in this Matter, and they never fail'd of certain Articles in their Schemes of Worship, on purpose to establish it.

THE last *Fanaticks* of Note, were those which started up in *Germany*, a little after the *Reformation* of *Luther*; Springing, *as Mushrooms* do at the *End of a Harvest*; Such were *John of Leyden, David George*,[8] *Adam Neuster*,[9] and many others: whose Visions and Revelations, always terminated in *leading about half a dozen Sisters, apiece,* and making That Practice a fundamental Part of their System. For, Human Life is a continual Navigation, and, if we expect our *Vessels* to pass with Safety, thro' the Waves and Tempests of this fluctuating World, it is necessary to make a good Provision of the *Flesh,* as Sea-men lay in store of *Beef* for a long Voyage.

NOW from this brief Survey of some Principal Sects, among the *Fanaticks,* in all Ages (having omitted the *Mahometans* and others, who might also help to confirm the Argument I am about) to which I might add several among our selves, such as the *Family of Love, Sweet Singers of Israel,* and the like: And from reflecting upon that fundamental Point in their Doctrines, about *Women,* wherein they have so unanimously agreed; I am apt to imagine, that the Seed or Principle, which has ever put Men upon *Visions* in Things *Invisible,* is of a Corporeal Nature: For the profounder Chymists inform us, that the Strongest *Spirits* may be extracted from *Human Flesh.* Besides, the Spinal Marrow, being nothing else but a Continuation of the Brain, must needs create a very free Communication between the Superior Faculties and those below: And thus the *Thorn in the Flesh* serves for a *Spur* to the *Spirit.* I think, it is agreed among Physicians, that nothing affects the Head so much, as a tentiginous[10] Humor, repelled and elated to the upper Region, found by daily practice, to run frequently up into Madness. A very eminent Member of the Faculty, assured me, that when the *Quakers* first appeared, he seldom was without some Female Patients among them, for the *furor* ——— Persons of a visionary Devotion, either Men or Women, are in their Complexion, of all others, the most amorous: For, *Zeal* is frequently kindled from the same Spark with other Fires, and from inflaming Brotherly Love, will proceed to raise That of a Gallant. If we inspect into the usual Process of modern Courtship, we shall find it to consist in a devout Turn of the Eyes, called *Ogling*; an artificial Form of Canting and Whining by rote, every Interval, for want of other Matter, made up with a Shrug, or a Hum, a Sigh or a Groan; The Style compact of insignificant Words, Incoherences and Repetition. These, I take, to be the most accomplish'd Rules of Address to a

Mistress; and where are these performed with more Dexterity, than by the *Saints?* Nay, to bring this Argument yet closer, I have been informed by certain Sanguine Brethren of the first Class that in the Height and *Orgasmus* of their Spiritual exercise it has been frequent with them * * * * * ; immediately after which, they found the *Spirit* to relax and flag of a sudden with the Nerves, and they were forced to hasten to a Conclusion. This may be farther Strengthened, by observing, with Wonder, how unaccountably all Females are attracted by Visionary or Enthusiastick Preachers, tho' never so contemptible in their *outward Men*; which is usually supposed to be done upon Considerations, purely Spiritual, without any carnal Regards at all. But I have Reason to think, the *Sex* hath certain Characteristicks, by which they form a truer Judgment of Human Abilities and Performings, than we our selves can possibly do of each other. Let That be as it will, thus much is certain, that however Spiritual Intrigues begin, they generally conclude like all others; they may branch upwards towards Heaven, but the Root is in the Earth. Too intense a Contemplation is not the Business of Flesh and Blood; it must by the necessary Course of Things, in a little Time, let go its Hold, and fall into *Matter*. Lovers, for the sake of Celestial Converse, are but another sort of *Platonicks*, who pretend to see Stars and Heaven in Ladies Eyes, and to look or think no lower; but the same *Pit* is provided for both; and they seem a perfect Moral to the Story of that Philosopher, who, while his Thoughts and Eyes were fixed upon the *Constellations*, found himself seduced by his *lower Parts* into a *Ditch*.

I had somewhat more to say upon this Part of the Subject; but the Post is just going, which forces me in great Haste to conclude,

S I R,

Yours, &c.

Pray, burn this
Letter as soon
as it comes to
your Hands.

F I N I S

EDITORS' NOTES TO *A TALE OF A TUB, THE BATTEL OF THE BOOKS, AND A FRAGMENT*

Title page. Published together in 1704 and three more times during the next year, these three works were given their final form in the edition of 1710. In composing the fifth edition, Swift enlarged the whole, adding the "Apology" and the great wealth of footnotes; and it is this edition that is here reproduced. The few significant instances in which the present editors have preferred readings from the earlier editions are acknowledged in their notes.

A TALE OF A TUB

Title page. "*Diu multumque desideratum.*": "Desired long and greatly."
Title page. "*Basima . . . Iren. Lib.* I. C. 18.": See Swift's own note, p. 279.
Title page. "*Juvatque . . . Musae.*": "I love to pluck fresh flowers, and to seek a glorious garland for my head from fields whence the muses have never yet crowned any brows at all." Lucretius, *De Rerum Natura*, I, 928–931.
1. A street near Moorfields (renamed Milton Street) inhabited by hack writers; and an expression used in literary tradition to indicate all kinds of hack writing.
2. The "Apology" appeared for the first time in the edition of 1710.
3. Chiefly Wotton's *Observations upon The Tale of a Tub* (1705), from which Swift drew a number of his notes for the 1710 edition. He identified these notes by adding at the end of each "W. Wotton"—as, for example, on p. 279.
4. The occasional concern most closely associated with these three works is the long-drawn-out controversy over ancient and modern learning. The exchanges in the controversy most immediate to Swift's entry into it are described in "The Bookseller to the Reader" (pp. 373–374), which precedes the *Battel*. Both the *Tale* and the *Fragment* present and parody a variety of "modern" attitudes and, in the process, indicate the virtues of the "ancient" position; however, the *Battel* is the only one of these works centrally and continuously devoted to the controversy itself.
5. "You have never yet lacked for an external enemy." Lucan, *De Bello Civili*, I, 23.
6. Here Swift acknowledges his use in the *Tale* of the persona or mask, actually indicating, in the expression "other *Writers*" and in his examples, that his practice involves the use of several different masks. At any point in the *Tale*, then, we should be prepared to face not Swift but a professed author, a mask, whose arguments and attitudes differ from Swift's own; furthermore, the professed author detected at one point in the work may differ from the professed author detected at another point.
7. P. 300.
8. Here Swift disclaims or seems to disclaim, several years after having finished the *Tale* itself, the interpretations and deductions which the professed author insists, especially in Sections I and X, and the "Conclusion," that readers must strive for in order to comprehend his discourse. Swift's admission in the "Apology" that the story of the coats and the brothers is allegorical, on the other hand, substantiates this insistence.
9. This, like Swift's disclaimers of "*ill Meanings,*" is hard to comprehend. Nothing really seems obvious about the *Tale*; indeed, readers have always found it terribly puzzling, as Swift's affixing footnotes to the 1710 edition attests. Furthermore, Sections I, III, V, VII and X, and the "Conclusion," in every one of which the professed author devotes himself to the interlocking difficulties and problems of writing and of reading such a work as the *Tale*, strongly indicate that it was actually designed, at least to some extent, to puzzle its readers, to draw them into questionable and troubling interpretations. At any rate, whether the reader thinks of Swift as disingenuous here—or merely projecting another mask—he must obviously play the professed author's game of deep, interpretive reading simply in order to follow the discourse; he must do so even if this involves his countenancing some foolish or vicious meanings. On the other hand, the reader must exercise caution in his interpretations and must determine to judge both the sense in them and the apparent sensibility that conceived them.
10. The reader may usefully compare this passage with the actual exposition and interpretation of the machines in the "Introduction" (pp. 292–297).
11. This gives us a further clue to the reading of the *Tale*. Sometimes when Swift enunciates notions and beliefs that differ from his own, he does so by projecting a palpable intellectual presence that differs from himself, that is, a mask: in these cases the reader must judge not only a statement or an argument but also a type of sensibility. At other times Swift may deviate not in this dramatic way, but simply in tone, illuminating his actual ideas by artfully presenting ideas that are at some degree of variance with them: in such cases it is sufficient for the reader to consider and judge the statement. Generally speaking, the digressions are those sections in which a mask, an apparent intelligence, is most commonly

apprehensible; whereas the impression of a mask often fades in the sections devoted to the three brothers, that is, notably, Sections II, IV and VI.
12. William King's *Remarks on the Tale of a Tub* (1704).
13. Wotton's *Observations.*
14. Sir William Temple.
15. A captured Roman assassin told the Etruscan king Porsenna, "three hundred of us have sworn to make the same attempt."
16. *The Battel of the Books* describes this whole business; see esp. pp. 373–374.
17. A part of Whitefriars, on which see p. 273.
18. "The necessary changes having been made."
19. Min-ellius and Farnaby were classical scholars of the seventeenth century.
20. P. 339.
21. White-Fryars was a precinct of London; it enjoyed the privileges of sanctuary until 1697.
22. Edmund Curll; see pp. 588–590 for excerpts from his *"foolish Paper."*
23. Lord Sommers was a Whig statesman and a patron of learning.
24. James I, who inherited the throne of Scotland in 1567 from his mother, Mary, and that of England in 1603 from his cousin, Elizabeth.
25. The English Order of the Garter, from the time of the Tudor King Henry VII, had red and white roses around the collar; the Order of the Thistle, which originated in Scotland, had thistles around the collar.
26. "Glittering choler": black bile, which has a glittering appearance and was traditionally supposed to cause choler or irascibility. Horace, *Satires,* II, iii, 141.
27. Vergil, *Aeneid,* VI, 128–129. The translation in the footnote is from Dryden.
28. "So that, when they are old, they may retire in safe repose." Horace, *Satires,* I, i, 31.
29. The reader may refer to the illustration occupying p. 293, which appeared in the 1710 edition, for a pictorial representation of these machines.
30. The Scottish woods.
31. Puritans, among them William Prynne and John Bastwick, were pilloried and lost their ears as a punishment for sedition. Men could also address passers-by from the pillory and thus have an influence on ears. See Defoe's "Hymn to the Pillory," published the year before the *Tale* first appeared, the opening line of which reads, "Hail! Hi'roglyphick State *Machin."*
32. Lucretius, *De Rerum Natura,* IV, 526–527. The translation in the footnote is by Creech, whose work the reader will find described in *The Battel of the Books.*
33. In this and the next few paragraphs the professed author gives his reader an example of the deductions, or, as he will call them, the exantlations, of deep meanings which, he insists, are persistently present within his work. If one follows the author's example in studying his whole system of oratorial machines, he may exantlate the drop of sense from *that* and find it to be simply, "this is an amusing book." By comparing this small measure of meaning with the elaborate discourse in which it was hidden, the reader may test the validity of this discourse and judge the mind, the sensibility, that would compose and publish it.
34. An expression for Puritans and Dissenters, enunciated during this time in a variety of tones.
35. To conclude, especially, to conclude an oration.
36. Mine and yours.
37. The Royal Society met at Gresham College.
38. Intriguing.
39. Here the professed author is saying, as exantlation will discover, "this is really a very deep book." Having drawn forth this assertion, one may compare it with the exantlated sense of the oratorial machines.
40. Drawing out, as from a well.
41. This and the following examples, by which the professed author develops his understanding of literary depth, cry out to be tested against common sense: can we really believe *Tom Thumb, The Wise Men of Goatham,* or any work with such a title as *Tommy Potts* to be intellectually profound; can we seriously consider the mind which finds them so to be reliable? The professed author's description of these works intensifies the need for a common-sense judgment of his substance and realiability. His figurative representation of wisdom a few pages before this (pp. 298–299), in which he likened wisdom, among other things, to a cheese whereof to a judicious palate the maggots are the best, and to a nut which may repay your opening it with nothing but a worm, similarly demands the practice of common sense. The reader may wonder, for example, whether the epicure who relished maggots found in the cheese might not also relish a worm found in a nutshell; and whether he himself would relish either.
42. One who has learned the great secret of alchemy: how to convert base metals into gold. On the alchemical terms and references used in this paragraph and elsewhere, see Guthkelch and Nichol Smith, pp. 354–355.

43. Artephius' thousand years may be attributed to his having taken the alchemically composed *elixir vitæ*.

44. Spelled *Gotham* in the first three editions.

45. Dryden dedicated his translation of Vergil to three patrons: the *Eclogues* to Lord Clifford, the *Georgics* to the Earl of Chesterfield, and the *Aeneid* to the Marquis of Normanby.

46. Beneath the open sky.

47. An iron, so called because the handle of it is shaped like a goose's neck.

48. Referring to the temple of Jupiter on the summit of the Capitoline Hill in Rome. The Capitol was saved from the Gauls in 390 B.C. when the sacred geese roused its defenders.

49. The dark place under a tailor's shopboard into which he threw scraps of cloth —which were thereafter looked on as his perquisites.

50. A god of an inferior order.

51. Waved or watered silk or taffeta.

52. The doctrine of traduction maintained that a person's soul is transmitted to him from his parents, just as his body is.

53. Sometimes written *Kalendæ*: the first day of any month.

54. A thrust at pedantry: this abbreviation simply stands for the Latin expression in the margin, which, in turn, is merely equivalent to the English expression that is given in the footnote. Peter was giving the aura of esoteric learning to his assertion that *Calendæ* was sometimes written *Kalendæ*.

55. According to the paternal law.

56. "Deep silence." Vergil, *Aeneid*, X, 65.

57. In some measure adhere to the essence.

58. By word of mouth.

59. If the same thing is affirmed with regard to word-of-mouth proclamation, it is denied.

60. Many absurdities would follow.

61. Zoilus attacked Homer; Tigellius, Horace.

62. Slightly misquoted from Lucretius, *De Rerum Natura*, VI, 786–787: Swift has substituted "odore . . . retro" ("with an odor from the rear") for "odore . . . tætro" ("with a vile odor"). The translation in the footnote is from Creech.

63. Insurance companies.

64. Sprinkling.

65. "It spreads variegated . . . plumes and ends in a black fish." Horace, *Ars Poetica*, lines 1–5.

66. "With this throwing out of paltry dust." Vergil, *Georgics*, IV, 87.

67. "This persuades me to carry out any work whatever and induces me to spend tranquil nights in wakefulness." Lucretius, *De Rerum Natura*, I, 141–142 (slightly misquoted).

68. Sluggishness.

69. Profit and pleasure, the two widely acknowledged values of poetry: see Horace, *Ars Poetica*, lines 341–346.

70. Double boiler.

71. That is, in sufficient quantity.

72. The leavings and the residuum.

73. Flower cullings, i.e., anthologies.

74. "Homer comprehended everything pertaining to humanity in his poetry." Xenophon, *Convivium*, IV, 6.

75. The great work: that is, the conversion of base metals into gold.

76. An alchemist.

77. A German mystic.

78. The fire-formed sphere.

79. I can hardly believe that this author has ever heard the voice of fire.

80. A device for holding candle-ends so that they can be totally burned up.

81. Here Swift suggests a positive mode of conduct primarily, of course, in church reform. But the scope of the allegorical presentation—the tenor being institutional and the vehicle articulated in the actions of one man—and the very allegoricalness of it allow for translations into other spheres of human life, indeed, into all those in which a person or a society finds itself unable to begin afresh, but rather forced to proceed from conditions already in effect. There are many other positive indications in the *Tale*, although they are commonly wedged in—as Martin is wedged in between the flamboyant absurdities of Peter and of Jack—between prevailingly satiric and destructive utterances. One may notice, for instance, the professed author's recognition of "a sort of morose, detracting, ill-bred People" who, as he explains in Section VII, reject the "Modern Improvement of Digressions"; also his acknowledgement in the same section that "the Society of Writers would quickly be reduced to a very inconsiderable Number, if Men were put upon making Books, with the fatal Confinement of delivering nothing beyond

what is to the Purpose." Again, one may notice the brief passage in Section IX in which the professed author makes passing reference to "the Brain, in its natural Position"; and passing reference to "common Understanding, as well as common Sense," the rejection of which brings on the intellectual madness and folly which he devotes himself to explaining and exalting.

82. The mob; from *mobile vulgus*, that is, the changeable crowd.

83. "I touch all with a honeyed charm." Slightly misquoted—substituting *mellœo* for *musœo*—from Lucretius, *De Rerum Natura*, I, 934.

84. The reader may feel inclined to add a third category of literary works to the professed author's antithesis, namely, an *Iliad* itself, although the author, as it seems, would have no interest in and no regard for this category.

85. Changed to *Pudenda* in the 1710 edition.

86. But whose genitals were thick and reached all the way to their ankles.

87. May governing Fortune turn that far from us.

88. Worship or service.

89. They honor Boreas (the North Wind) most of all the Gods.

90. Out of the innermost recesses and innermost rooms.

91. The chameleon lived, according to popular belief, on air.

92. This division of subject matter may remind the reader that the professed author's favorite number is three and, further, that he has earlier given this numerical preference as cause for confining himself to three oratorial engines as a representation of the realm of literature (p. 294). Elsewhere, moreover, he has categorized three kinds of readers, three brothers, and three types of critics. As Swift may have been suggesting by this emphatically recurrent method of literary order and definition, a study of the professed author's categories and his categorical procedure can often help the reader understand the author and judge his performance. To begin with, one may notice that he commonly fails to handle his categories either equitably or consistently. In the present case, for example, the author's first effort to comprehend his subject matter under three headings expands, almost unnoticeably, to include not only madmen, but all intellectual beings. This expansion occurs, first, in the passage on the sympathetic vibration between the mad and their proselytes and, second, in the great paragraph which explicitly inaugurates the topic of proselytes. In this process of discursive expansion, the three-part division of the subject matter seems to have been replaced by a two-part division: intellectual beings are categorized into the mad and the credulous—or the "enlightened teacher" and the "fanatick auditory," as the two will be named in the *Fragment*. When one examines this new scheme he sees that it really relates to only two of the three categories of madness: the exemplary kings were not portrayed as infecting any "fanatick auditory," as the revolutionaries in philosophy and religion have been. The reader may also discover still deeper failures in this new and imperfectly articulated categorization of human intelligence. It may occur, for example, partly because of the elements by which this scheme is developed and partly because of one's own common sense, that these two categories do not actually comprehend all intellectual beings and that one must, as he has done before, make up the professed author's favorite number, three, adding the category of sensible men, in order to achieve a truly comprehensive scheme.

93. "Any other bodies." Lucretius, *De Rerum Natura*, IV, 1065.

94. "The body seeks that by which the mind has been wounded with love." Lucretius, *De Rerum Natura*, IV, 1048.

95. "He stretches toward that body from which the impulse has radiated, and desires to be sexually united with it." Lucretius, *De Rerum Natura*, IV, 1055.

96. "Woman is the most terrible cause of war." Horace, *Satires*, I, iii, 107–108. The first word of this quotation was cut from the 1710 edition.

97. According to the teachings of Epicurus and Lucretius, the fortuitous swerve of the atoms as they fall through the void, from which derives free will in living beings. See Lucretius, *De Rerum Natura*, II, 216–293.

98. Actually, charioteers. Cicero, *Familiar Epistles*, VII, 6.

99. "It should please you to have come to the very place in which anyone may seem wise." Cicero, *Familiar Epistles*, VII, 10.

100. Johann Bockholdt, a tailor of Leyden and an Anabaptist; he seized the city of Münster briefly during the religious struggles and made himself king, with the title "John of Leyden."

101. Here as elsewhere in the *Tale*, the professed author enunciates an area of argument which seems comprehensive but is not: in this case he has omitted a most obvious set of things, things present.

102. As in the preceding paragraph, the professed author confuses the scope and

divisions of his subject matter: he passingly acknowledges a third possible realm of experiential awareness, qualities that are drawn upon the surface of things, but he argues as if he recognizes only two realms, the inside and the outside of things. The matter is actually worse than usual in such cases in the *Tale* because the professed author confuses the actual look and feel of things—that is, the surface things naturally present to the senses—with the falsely decorated outside of things, claiming to uphold the first of these as the proper concern of human awareness (against the hidden inward of things) while actually upholding the second. If the reader corrects the definitions of *things* in the immediately preceding paragraph and in this one, he may establish in his own mind a third time and a third realm for the activity of human sense and reason: the unadorned impressions of the present moment. On the basis of this he may affirm his belief in a third type of intellectual being besides the two considered by the professed author: not only the deeply disturbed man who imposes splendid falsities on others and the gullible man who is imposed on by them, but also the man who depends for his understanding and his description of things on the unadorned realities of his own continually unfolding experience, on the real things he sees and touches minute by minute.

103. "A temper equal to public affairs." Tacitus, *Annals*, VI, 39, and XVI, 18 (imprecisely quoted).

104. Both Gresham College, at which the Royal Society met, and Grub Street were close to Bedlam.

105. The Royal College of Physicians was in Warwick Lane.

106. Bedlam stood in Moor Fields.

107. Cave-dwelling; that is, living away from the affairs of human life.

108. Another apparently comprehensive antithesis to which the reader may wish to add a third category: the professed author could have waked while others waked. The critical and conversational help a lively and balanced circle of acquaintance might have provided him would surely have prompted him to compose a more lucid and sensible system of argument.

109. From whose tears proceeds a moist substance, from whose laughter a lucid substance, from whose sorrow a solid substance, and from whose terror a movable substance.

110. Changed to *Nature* in the 1710 edition.

111. Changed to *Fortune* in the 1710 edition.

112. "Scoundrelly Proteus will nevertheless escape these fetters." Horace, *Satires*, II, iii, 71.

113. Changed to *Marks of Grace* in the 1710 edition. For the origin of this expression see Acts II, 3.

114. William Prynne, a Puritan, had his ears cut off for sedition in 1634 and the stumps of his ears cut off for the same offense in 1637. See note 31, above.

115. "Like a banqueter filled with life." Lucretius, *De Rerum Natura*, III, 938 (imprecisely quoted).

THE BATTEL OF THE BOOKS

1. The same, that is, as the one who wrote the *Tale*. The *Tale*, the *Battel*, and the *Fragment* were printed together in all the early editions.

2. Subsequent scholarship has approved Bentley's argument that the epistles of Phalaris and the fables of Aesop are relatively modern forgeries.

3. Bentley.

4. The moderns, because they are living when the world is aged, are really the ancients.

5. See the Odyssey edition of Bacon's essays (New York, 1937), pp. 198–206, 274–275, and 313, for illuminating analogues to this fable. Here, if nowhere else in the *Battel*, Swift transcends the details of the ancient-and-modern controversy. The fable objectifies a major division in the intellectual life of Western man, that between the empirical mode of conduct (the bee) and the rationalistic mode (the spider), which is of persistent importance.

6. *Light-Horse*: Poets. *Bowmen*: Philosophers. *Stink-Pot-Flingers*: Chemists. *Dragoons*: Students of medicine. *Heavy-armed Foot*: Historians. *Engineers*: Mathematicians. See Guthkelch and Nichol Smith, pp. 235–239, for a detailed identification of the opposing armies.

7. The hard calcareous structure in the stomach of a lobster, called "lady" from its resemblance in shape to a seated female figure.

8. Translator of Lucretius and Horace.

9. Translator of Homer and Vergil.

10. Cowley was famous for both his Pindaric odes and his love poems.

11. Black as ink; inky.

12. The brazen bull, a torture device in which the victims of Phalaris were roasted.
13. Dr. Atterbury, perhaps, who helped the youthful Boyle with his *Dr. Bentley's Dissertations ... Examined*, Boyle's rejoinder of 1698 to Bentley's first attack on the authenticity of Phalaris.

A FRAGMENT

1. The western coast of Australia, so called because the Dutch had been exploring it.
2. See Acts II, 3 for an explanation of this sign.
3. "Wild with passion, they distinguish right and wrong according only to the narrow scope of their own inclinations." Horace, *Odes*, I, xviii, 10–11 (inexactly quoted).
4. *Venting*, in the first three editions.
5. Associated with Puritans. See John Aubrey, *Brief Lives*, ed. Andrew Clark (Oxford, 1898), II, 174, on William Prynne's wearing of his cap. See also notes 31 and 114 to the *Tale*.
6. The act of biting; a bite.
7. Furnished with hooks.
8. A Dutch Anabaptist, founder of "The Family of Love."
9. A German Socinian, eventually converted to the Mohammedan faith.
10. Excited to lust; lecherous.

A Meditation upon a Broom-stick:

According to the Style and Manner of the Honourable *Robert Boyle's* Meditations[1]

WRITTEN IN THE YEAR 1703

THIS single Stick, which you now behold ingloriously lying in that neglected Corner, I once knew in a flourishing State in a Forest: It was full of Sap, full of Leaves, and full of Boughs: But now, in vain does the busy Art of Man pretend to vye with Nature, by tying that withered Bundle of Twigs to its sapless Trunk: It is now at best but the Reverse of what it was; a Tree turned upside down, the Branches on the Earth, and the Root in the Air: It is now handled by every dirty Wench, condemned to do her Drugery; and by a capricious Kind of Fate, destined to make other Things clean, and be nasty it self. At length, worn to the Stumps in the Service of the Maids, it is either thrown out of Doors, or condemned to its last Use of kindling a Fire. When I beheld this, I sighed, and said within my self SURELY MORTAL MAN IS A BROOMSTICK; Nature sent him into the World strong and lusty, in a thriving Condition, wearing his own Hair on his Head, the proper Branches of this reasoning Vegetable; till the Axe of Intemperance has lopped off his Green Boughs, and left him a withered Trunk: He then flies to Art, and puts on a *Perriwig*; valuing himself upon an unnatural Bundle of Hairs, all covered with Powder, that never grew on his Head: But now, should this our *Broom-stick* pretend to enter the Scene, proud of those *Birchen* Spoils it never bore, and all covered with Dust, though the Sweepings of the finest Lady's Chamber; we should be apt to ridicule and despise its Vanity. Partial Judges that we are of our own Excellencies, and other Mens Defaults!

BUT a *Broom-stick*, perhaps you will say, is an Emblem of a Tree standing on its Head; and pray what is Man but a topsy-turvy Creature? His Animal Faculties perpetually mounted on his Rational; his Head where his Heels should be, groveling on the Earth. And yet, with all his Faults, he sets up to be a universal Reformer and Correcter of Abuses; a Remover of Grievances; rakes into every

1. Swift is parodying Boyle's *Occasional Reflections upon Several Subjects* (1665), separate sections of which have such titles as "Upon his paring of a rare summer apple," "Upon the sight of some variously-coloured clouds," "Upon the sight of a fair milk-maid singing to her cow," and "Upon the sight of a paper-kite in a windy day." See p. 600 above for the circumstances of Swift's writing of the "Meditation."

Slut's Corner of Nature, bringing hidden Corruptions to the Light, and raiseth a mighty Dust where there was none before; sharing deeply all the while in the very same Pollutions he pretends to sweep away. His last Days are spent in Slavery to Women, and generally the least deserving; till worn to the Stumps, like his Brother *Bezom*,[2] he is either kicked out of Doors, or made use of to kindle Flames for others to warm themselves by.

A Tritical Essay upon the
Faculties of the Mind

1707

To — — — — — —

SIR,
BEING *so great a Lover of Antiquities, it was reasonable to suppose you would be very much obliged with any Thing that was new. I have been of late offended with many Writers of Essays and moral Discourses, for running into stale Topicks and thread-bare Quotations, and not handling their Subject fully and closely: All which Errors I have carefully avoided in the following Essay, which I have proposed as a Pattern for young Writers to imitate. The Thoughts and Observations being entirely new, the Quotations untouched by others, the Subject of mighty Importance, and treated with much Order and Perspicuity: It hath cost me a great deal of Time; and I desire you will accept and consider it as the utmost Effort of my Genius.*

A *Tritical* Essay, &c.

PHILOSOPHERS say, that Man is a Microcosm or little World, resembling in Miniature every Part of the great: And, in my Opinion, the Body Natural may be compared to the Body Politick: And if this be so, how can the *Epicureans* Opinion be true, that the Universe was formed by a fortuitous Concourse of Atoms, which I will no more believe, than that the accidental Jumbling of the Letters in the Alphabet, could fall by Chance into a most ingenious and learned Treatise of Philosophy, *Risum teneatis Amici*, HOR.[1] This false Opinion must needs create many more; it is like an Error in the first Concoction, which cannot be corrected in the second; the

2. A broom made of a bunch of twigs bound together round a handle.
1. Could you, my friends, hold back your laughter?

Foundation is weak, and whatever Superstructure you raise upon it, must of Necessity fall to the Ground. Thus Men are led from one Error to another, till with *Ixion* they embrace a Cloud instead of *Juno*; or, like the Dog in the Fable, lose the Substance in gaping at the Shadow. For such Opinions cannot cohere; but like the Iron and Clay in the Toes of *Nebuchadnezzar's* Image, must separate and break in Pieces. I have read in a certain Author, that *Alexander* wept because he had no more Worlds to conquer; which he need not have done, if the fortuitous Concourse of Atoms could create one: But this is an Opinion fitter for that many-headed Beast, the Vulgar, to entertain, than for so wise a Man as *Epicurus*; the corrupt Part of his Sect only borrowed his Name, as the Monkey did the Cat's Claw, to draw the Chesnut out of the Fire.

HOWEVER, the first Step to the Cure is to know the Disease; and although Truth may be difficult to find, because, as the Philosopher observes, she lives in the Bottom of a Well; yet we need not, like blind Men, grope in open Day-light. I hope, I may be allowed, among so many far more learned Men, to offer my Mite, since a Stander-by may sometimes, perhaps, see more of the Game than he that plays it. But I do not think a Philosopher obliged to account for every Phænomenon in Nature; or drown himself with *Aristotle*, for not being able to solve the Ebbing and Flowing of the Tide, in that fatal Sentence he passed upon himself, *Quia te non capio, tu capies me.*[2]

WHEREIN he was at once the Judge and the Criminal, the Accuser and Executioner. *Socrates*, on the other Hand, who said he knew nothing, was pronounced by the Oracle to be the wisest Man in the World.

BUT to return from this Digression; I think it as clear as any Demonstration in *Euclid*, that Nature does nothing in vain; if we were able to dive into her secret Recesses, we should find that the smallest Blade of Grass, or most contemptible Weed, has its particular Use; but she is chiefly admirable in her minutest Compositions, the least and most contemptible Insect most discovers the Art of Nature, if I may so call it; although Nature, which delights in Variety, will always triumph over Art: And as the Poet observes,

Naturam expellas furcâ licet, usque recurret. Hor.[3]

BUT the various Opinions of Philosophers, have scattered through the World as many Plagues of the Mind, as *Pandora's* Box did those of the Body; only with this Difference, that they have not left Hope at the Bottom. And if Truth be not fled with *Astræa*, she

2. "Because I do not take you in, you take me in." This apocryphal story traces back to Hellenistic times.
3. "You may drive out Nature with a pitchfork, but she will always hasten back." Horace, *Epistles*, I, x, 24 (imprecisely quoted). The following Latin quotations do little more than repeat the English sentiments immediately preceding them.

is certainly as hidden as the Source of *Nile,* and can be found only in *Utopia.* Not that I would reflect on those wise Sages, which would be a Sort of Ingratitude; and he that calls a Man ungrateful, sums up all the Evil that a Man can be guilty of.

Ingratum si dixeris, omnia dicis.

BUT what I blame the Philosophers for, (although some may think it a Paradox) is chiefly their Pride; nothing less than an *ipse dixit,* and you must pin your Faith on their Sleeve. And, although *Diogenes* lived in a Tub, there might be, for ought I know, as much Pride under his Rags, as in the fine spun Garment of the Divine *Plato.* It is reported of this *Diogenes,* that when *Alexander* came to see him, and promised to give him whatever he would ask; the *Cynick* only answered, *Take not from me, what thou canst not give me; but stand from between me and the Light;* which was almost as extravagant as the Philosopher that flung his Money into the Sea, with this remarkable Saying, ———

HOW different was this Man from the Usurer, who being told his Son would spend all he had got, replied, *He cannot take more Pleasure in spending, than I did in getting it.* These Men could see the Faults of each other, but not their own; those they flung into the Bag behind; *Non videmus id manticæ quod in tergo est.* I may, perhaps, be censured for my free Opinions, by those carping *Momus's,* whom Authors worship as the *Indians* do the Devil, for fear. They will endeavour to give my Reputation as many Wounds as the Man in the Almanack; but I value it not; and perhaps, like Flies, they may buz so often about the Candle, till they burn their Wings. They must pardon me, if I venture to give them this Advice, not to rail at what they cannot understand; it does but discover that self-tormenting Passion of Envy; than which, the greatest Tyrant never invented a more cruel Torment.

Invidia Siculi non invenere Tyranni
Tormentum majus.——— Juven.

I MUST be so bold, to tell my Criticks and Witlings, that they are no more Judges of this, than a Man that is born blind can have any true Idea of Colours. I have always observed, that your empty Vessels sound loudest: I value their Lashes as little, as the Sea did when *Xerxes* whipped it. The utmost Favour a Man can expect from them, is that which *Polyphemus* promised *Ulysses,* that he would devour him the last: They think to subdue a Writer, as *Cæsar* did his Enemy, with a *Veni, vidi, vici.* I confess, I value the Opinion of the judicious Few, a *Rymer,* a *Dennis,* or a *Walsh;* but for the rest, to give my Judgment at once; I think the long Dispute among the Philosophers about a *Vacuum,* may be determined in the Affirmative, that it is to be found in a Critick's Head. They are, at best, but the Drones of the learned World, who devour the Honey, and will not work themselves; and a Writer need no more regard them, than the Moon does the Barking of a little sensless Cur. For, in spight of their terrible Roaring, you may with half an Eye discover the *Ass* under the *Lyon's* Skin.

BUT to return to our Discourse: *Demosthenes* being asked, what was the first Part of an Orator, replied, *Action*: What was the Second, *Action*: What was the Third, *Action*: And so on *ad infinitum*. This may be true in Oratory; but Contemplation, in other Things, exceeds Action. And, therefore, a wise Man is never less alone, than when he is alone:

Nunquam minus solus, quàm cum solus.

AND *Archimedes*, the famous Mathematician, was so intent upon his Problems, that he never minded the Soldier who came to kill him. Therefore, not to detract from the just Praise which belongs to Orators; they ought to consider that Nature, which gave us two Eyes to see, and two Ears to hear, hath given us but one Tongue to speak; wherein, however, some do so abound; that the *Virtuosi*, who have been so long in Search for the perpetual Motion, may infallibly find it there.

SOME Men admire Republicks; because, Orators flourish there most, and are the great Enemies of Tyranny: But my Opinion is, that one Tryant is better than an Hundred. Besides, these Orators inflame the People, whose Anger is really but a short Fit of Madness.

Ira furor brevis est.——— Horat.

AFTER which, Laws are like Cobwebs, which may catch small Flies, but let Wasps and Hornets break through. But in Oratory, the greatest Art is to hide Art.

Artis est celare Artem.

BUT this must be the Work of Time; we must lay hold on all Opportunities, and let slip no Occasion, else we shall be forced to weave *Penelope's* Web; unravel in the Night what we spun in the Day. And, therefore, I have observed that Time is painted with a Lock before, and bald behind; signifying thereby, that we must take Time (as we say) by the Forelock; for when it is once past, there is no recalling it.

THE Mind of Man is, at first, (if you will pardon the Expression) like a *Tabula rasa*; or like Wax, which while it is soft, is capable of any Impression, until Time hath hardened it. And at length Death, that grim Tyrant, stops us in the Midst of our Career. The greatest Conquerors have at last been conquered by Death, which spares none from the Sceptre to the Spade.

Mors omnibus communis.

ALL Rivers go to the Sea, but none return from it. *Xerxes* wept when he beheld his Army; to consider that in less than an Hundred Years they would all be dead. *Anacreon* was choqued with a Grape-stone; and violent Joy kills as well as violent Grief. There is nothing in this World constant, but Inconstancy; yet *Plato* thought, that if Virtue would appear to the World in her own native Dress, all Men would be enamoured with her. But now, since Interest governs the World, and Men neglect the Golden Mean, *Jupiter* himself, if he came on the Earth, would be despised, unless it were as he did to *Danaæ*, in a golden Shower. For Men, now-a-days, worship the rising Sun, and not the setting.

Donec eris fœlix, multos numerabis amicos.

THUS have I, in Obedience to your Commands, ventured to expose my self to Censure in this Critical Age. Whether I have done Right to my Subject, must be left to the Judgment of the learned Reader: However, I cannot but hope, that my attempting of it may be an Encouragement for some able Pen to perform it with more Success.

Predictions for the Year 1708

Wherein the Month, and Day of the Month, are set down, the Persons named, and the great Actions and Events of next Year particularly related as they will come to pass

Written to prevent the People of England *from being farther imposed on by vulgar Almanack-Makers*

BY ISAAC BICKERSTAFF, ESQ.[1]

HAVING long considered the gross Abuse of Astrology in this Kingdom; upon debating the Matter with my self, I could not possibly lay the Fault upon the Art, but upon those gross Impostors, who

1. Published in January, 1707–8, this is the initial installment in Swift's assault on a contemporary quack, the astrologer John Partridge, whose annual almanac, *Merlinus Liberatus*—parodied here—had been appearing for some twenty-five years. The papers won immediate fame and so did Swift's persona, Isaac Bickerstaff, whose name was appropriated in 1709 by Richard Steele when he began publishing *The Tatler*, a periodical largely written by Steele himself but to which Swift was an occasional contributor (see pp. 448–452 for one such contribution).

set up to be the Artists. I know, several learned Men have contended, that the whole is a Cheat; that it is absurd and ridiculous to imagine, the Stars can have any Influence at all upon human Actions, Thoughts, or Inclinations: And whoever hath not bent his Studies that Way, may be excused for thinking so, when he sees in how wretched a Manner this noble Art is treated, by a few mean illiterate Traders between us and the Stars; who import a yearly Stock of Nonsense, Lies, Folly, and Impertinence, which they offer to the World as genuine from the Planets; although they descend from no greater a Height than their own Brains.

I INTEND, in a short Time, to publish a large and rational Defence of this Art; and, therefore, shall say no more in its Justification at present, than that it hath been in all Ages defended by many learned Men; and among the rest, by *Socrates* himself; whom I look upon as undoubtedly the wisest of uninspired Mortals: To which if we add, that those who have condemned this Art, although otherwise learned, having been such as either did not apply their Studies this Way; or at least did not succeed in their Applications; their Testimony will not be of much Weight to its Disadvantage, since they are liable to the common Objection of condemning what they did not understand.

NOR am I at all offended, or think it an Injury to the Art, when I see the common Dealers in it, the *Students in Astrology*, the *Philomaths*, and the rest of that Tribe, treated by wise Men with the utmost Scorn and Contempt: But I rather wonder, when I observe Gentlemen in the Country, rich enough to serve the Nation in Parliament, poring in *Partrige*'s Almanack, to find out the Events of the Year at Home and Abroad; not daring to propose a Hunting-Match, until *Gadbury*, or he, hath fixed the Weather.

I WILL allow either of the Two I have mentioned, or any other of the Fraternity, to be not only Astrologers, but Conjurers too; if I do not produce an Hundred Instances in all their Almanacks, to convince any reasonable Man, that they do not so much as understand Grammar and Syntax; that they are not able to spell any Word out of the usual Road; nor even in their Prefaces to write common Sense, or intelligible *English*. Then, for their Observations and Predictions, they are such as will equally suit any Age, or Country in the World. *This Month a certain great Person will be threatned with Death, or Sickness.* This the News-Paper will tell them; for there we find at the End of the Year, that no Month passes without the Death of some Person of Note; and it would be hard, if it should be otherwise, when there are at least two Thousand Persons of Note in this Kingdom, many of them old; and the Almanack-maker has the Liberty of chusing the sickliest Season of the Year, where he may fix his Prediction. Again, *This Month an eminent Clergyman will be preferred*; of which there may be some Hundreds, Half of them with one Foot in the Grave. Then, *Such a Planet in such a House shews great Machinations, Plots and Conspiracies, that may in Time be brought to Light*: After which, if we hear of any Discovery, the Astrologer gets the Honour; if not, his Prediction still stands good. And at last, *God preserve King* William *from all his open and secret Enemies, Amen*. When if the King should happen to have died, the Astrologer plainly foretold it; otherwise, it passeth but for the pious Ejaculation of a loyal Subject: Although it unluckily happened in some of their Almanacks, that poor King *William* was prayed for many Months after he was dead; because, it fell out that he died about the Beginning of the Year.

TO mention no more of their impertinent Predictions: What have we to do with their Advertisements about *Pills, and Drinks for the Venereal Disease*, or their mutual Quarrels in Verse and Prose of *Whig* and *Tory*? wherewith the Stars have little to do.

HAVING long observed and lamented these, and a hundred other Abuses of this Art, too tedious to repeat; I resolved to proceed in a new Way; which I doubt not will be to the general Satisfaction of the Kingdom. I can this Year produce but a Specimen of what I design for the future; having employed most Part of my Time in adjusting and correcting the Calculations I made for some Years past; because I would offer nothing to the World of which I am not as fully satisfied, as that I am now alive. For these two last Years I have not failed in above one or two Particulars, and those of no very great Moment. I exactly foretold the Miscarriage at *Toulon*, with all its Particulars; and the Loss of Admiral *Shovel*; although I was mistaken as to the Day, placing that Accident about thirty six Hours sooner than it happened; but upon reviewing my Schemes, I quickly found the Cause of that Error. I likewise foretold the Battle at *Almanza* to the very Day and Hour, with the Loss on both Sides, and the Consequences thereof. All which I shewed to some Friends many Months before they happened; that is, I gave them Papers sealed up, to open at such a Time, after which they were at liberty to read them; and there they found my Predictions true in every Article, except one or two, very minute.

AS for the few following Predictions I now offer the World, I forbore to publish them, till I had perused the several Almanacks for the Year we are now entered upon: I found them all in the usual Strain, and I beg the Reader will compare their Manner with mine: And here I make bold to tell the World, that I lay the whole Credit of my Art upon the Truth of these Predictions; and I will be content that *Partridge*, and the rest of his Clan, may hoot me for a Cheat and Impostor, if I fail in any single Particular of Moment. I believe any Man, who reads this Paper, will look upon me to be at least a Person of as much Honesty and Understanding, as a common Maker of Almanacks. I do not lurk in the Dark; I am not wholly unknown in the World: I have set my Name at length, to be a Mark of Infamy to Mankind, if they shall find I deceive them.

IN one Point I must desire to be forgiven; that I talk more sparingly of Home-Affairs. As it would be Imprudence to discover Secrets of State, so it might be dangerous to my Person: But in smaller Matters, and such as are not of publick Consequence, I shall be very free: And the Truth of my Conjectures will as much appear from these as the other. As for the most signal Events abroad in *France*, *Flanders*, *Italy* and *Spain*, I shall make no Scruple to predict them in plain Terms: Some of them are of Importance, and I hope, I shall seldom mistake the Day they will happen: Therefore, I think good to inform the Reader, that I all along make use of the *Old Stile* observed in *England*; which I desire he will compare with that of the News-Papers, at the Time they relate the Actions I mention.

I MUST add one Word more: I know it hath been the Opinion of several learned Persons, who think well enough of the true Art of Astrology, That the Stars do only *incline*, and not force the Actions or Wills of Men: And therefore, however I may proceed by right Rules, yet I cannot in Prudence so confidently assure that the Events will follow exactly as I predict them.

I HOPE, I have maturely considered this Objection, which in some Cases is of no little Weight. For Example: A Man may, by the Influence of an over-ruling Planet, be disposed or inclined to Lust, Rage, or Avarice; and yet by the Force of Reason overcome that evil Influence. And this was the Case of *Socrates*: But the great Events of the World usually depending upon Numbers of Men, it cannot be expected they should all unite to cross their Inclinations, from pursuing a general Design, wherein they unanimously agree. Besides, the Influence of the Stars reacheth to many Actions and Events, which are not any way in the Power of Reason; as Sickness, Death, and what we commonly call Accidents; with many more needless to repeat.

BUT now it is Time to proceed to my Predictions; which I have begun to calculate from the Time that the *Sun* enters into *Aries*. And this I take to be properly the Beginning of the natural Year. I pursue them to the Time that he enters *Libra*, or somewhat more, which is the busy Period of the Year. The Remainder I have not yet adjusted upon Account of several Impediments needless here to mention. Besides, I must remind the Reader again, that this is but a Specimen of what I design in succeeding Years to treat more at large, if I may have Liberty and Encouragement.

MY first Prediction is but a Trifle; yet I will mention it, to shew how ignorant those sottish Pretenders to Astrology are in their own Concerns: It relates to *Partrige* the Almanack-Maker; I have consulted the Star of his Nativity by my own Rules; and find he will infallibly die upon the 29th of *March*[2] next, about eleven at Night, of a raging Fever: Therefore I advise him to consider of it, and settle his Affairs in Time.

THE Month of APRIL will be observable for the Death of many great Persons. On the 4th will die the Cardinal *de Noailles*, Archbishop of *Paris*: On the 11th the young Prince of *Asturias*, Son to the Duke of *Anjou*: On the 14th a great Peer of this Realm will die at his Country-House: On the 19th an old *Layman* of great Fame for Learning: And on the 23rd an eminent Goldsmith in *Lombard Street*. I could mention others, both at home and abroad, if I did not consider such Events of very little Use or Instruction to the Reader, or to the World.

AS to publick Affairs: On the 7th of this Month, there will be an Insurrection in *Dauphine*, occasioned by the Oppressions of the People; which will not be quieted in some Months.

ON the 15th will be a violent Storm on the South-East Coast of *France*; which will destroy many of their Ships, and some in the very Harbour.

THE 19th will be famous for the Revolt of a whole Province or Kingdom, excepting one City; by which the Affairs of a certain Prince in the Alliance will take a better Face.

MAY, Against common Conjectures, will be no very busy Month in *Europe*; but very signal for the Death of the *Dauphine*, which will happen on the 7th, after a short Fit of Sickness, and grievous Torments with the Strangury. He dies less lamented by the Court than the Kingdom.

ON the 9th a *Mareschal* of *France* will break his Leg by a Fall from his Horse. I have not been able to discover whether he will then die or not.

ON the 11th will begin a most important Siege, which the Eyes of all *Europe* will be upon: I cannot be more particular; for in relating Affairs that so nearly concern the *Confederates*, and consequently this Kingdom; I am forced to confine myself, for several Reasons very obvious to the Reader.

ON the 15th News will arrive of a very *surprizing Event*, than which nothing could be more unexpected.

ON the 19th, three Noble Ladies of this Kingdom, will, against all Expectation, prove with Child, to the great Joy of their Husbands.

2. In the old-style calendar this would be just four days after the beginning of 1708.

ON the 23rd, a famous Buffoon of the Play-House will die a ridiculous Death, suitable to his Vocation.

JUNE. This Month will be distinguished at home, by the utter dispersing of those ridiculous deluded Enthusiasts, commonly called the *Prophets*; occasioned chiefly by seeing the Time come, when many of their Prophecies were to be fulfilled; and then finding themselves deceived by contrary Events. It is indeed to be admired how any Deceiver can be so weak to foretel Things near at hand; when a very few Months must of Necessity discover the Imposture to all the World: In this Point less prudent than common Almanack-Makers, who are so wise to wander in Generals, talk dubiously, and leave to the Reader the Business of interpreting.

ON the 1st of this Month a *French* General will be killed by a random Shot of a Cannon-Ball.

ON the 6th a Fire will break out in the Suburbs of *Paris*, which will destroy above a thousand Houses; and seems to be the Foreboding of what will happen, to the Surprize of all *Europe*, about the End of the following Month.

ON the 10th a great Battle will be fought, which will begin at four of the Clock in the Afternoon, and last till nine at Night with great Obstinacy, but no very decisive Event. I shall not name the Place, for the Reasons aforesaid; but the Commanders on each left Wing will be killed.——I see Bonfires and hear the Noise of Guns for a Victory.

ON the 14th there will be a false Report of the *French* King's Death.

ON the 20th Cardinal *Portocarero* will die of a Dissentery, with great Suspicion of Poison; but the Report of his Intention to revolt to King *Charles* will prove false.

JULY. The 6th of this Month a *certain General* will, by a glorious Action, recover the Reputation he lost by former Misfortunes.

ON the 12th a *great Commander* will die a Prisoner in the Hands of his Enemies.

ON the 14th a shameful Discovery will be made of a *French* Jesuit giving Poison to a great Foreign General; and when he is put to the Torture, will make wonderful Discoveries.

IN short, this will prove a Month of great Action, if I might have Liberty to relate the Particulars.

AT home, the Death of an old famous Senator will happen on the 15th at his Country-House, worn with Age and Diseases.

BUT that which will make this Month memorable to all Posterity, is the Death of the *French* King *Lewis* the Fourteenth, after a Week's Sickness at *Marli*; which will happen on the 29th, about six a-Clock in the Evening. It seems to be an Effect of the Gout in his Stomach, followed by a Flux. And in three Days after Monsieur

Chamillard will follow his Master, dying suddenly of an Apoplexy. IN this Month likewise an *Ambassador* will die in *London*; but I cannot assign the Day.

AUGUST. The affairs of *France* will seem to suffer no Change for a while under the Duke of *Burgundy*'s Administration. But the Genius that animated the whole Machine being gone, will be the Cause of mighty Turns and Revolutions in the following Year. The new King makes yet little Change either in the Army or the Ministry; but the Libels against his Grandfather, that fly about his very Court, give him Uneasiness.

I SEE an Express in mighty Haste, with Joy and Wonder in his Looks, arriving by the Break of Day, on the 26th of this Month, having travelled in three Days a prodigious Journey by Land and Sea. In the Evening I hear Bells and Guns, and see the Blazing of a Thousand Bonfires.

A YOUNG Admiral, of noble Birth, does likewise this Month gain immortal Honour, by a great Atchievement.

THE Affairs of *Poland* are this Month entirely settled: *Augustus* resigns his Pretensions, which he had again taken up for some Time: *Stanislaus* is peaceably possessed of the Throne; and the King of *Sweden* declares for the Emperor.

I CANNOT omit one particular Accident here at home; that near the End of this Month, much Mischief will be done at *Bartholomew* Fair, by the Fall of a Booth.

SEPTEMBER. This Month begins with a very surprizing Fit of frosty Weather, which will last near twelve Days.

THE Pope having long languished last Month; the Swellings in his Legs breaking, and the Flesh mortifying, will die on the 11th Instant: And in three Weeks Time, after a mighty Contest, be succeeded by a Cardinal of the *Imperial* Faction, but Native of *Tuscany*, who is now about Sixty-One Years old.

THE *French* Army acts now wholly on the Defensive, strongly fortified in their Trenches; and the young *French* King sends Overtures for a Treaty of Peace, by the Duke of *Mantua*; which, because it is a Matter of State that concerns us here at home, I shall speak no farther of it.

I SHALL add but one Prediction more, and that in mystical Terms, which shall be included in a Verse out of *Virgil*.

> *Alter erit jam Tethys, & altera quæ vehat Argo,*
> *Dilectos Heroas.*[3]

UPON the 25th Day of this Month, the fulfilling of this Prediction will be manifest to every Body.

---

3. "Now there will be another Tethys, and another Argo, which carries the beloved heroes." Vergil, *Eclogues*, IV, 34–35. Swift has substituted Tethys, an ocean goddess, for Tiphys, who was the Steersman of the Argo.

THIS is the farthest I have proceeded in my Calculations for the present Year. I do not pretend that these are all the great Events which will happen in this Period; but that those I have set down will infallibly come to pass. It may, perhaps, still be objected, why I have not spoke more particularly of Affairs at home; or of the Success of our Armies abroad, which I might, and could very largely have done. But those in Power have wisely discouraged Men from meddling in publick Concerns; and I was resolved, by no Means, to give the least Offense. This I will venture to say; that it will be a glorious Campaign for the Allies; wherein the *English* Forces, both by Sea and Land, will have their full Share of Honour: That Her Majesty Queen ANNE will continue in Health and Prosperity: And that no ill Accident will arrive to any in the chief Ministry.

AS to the particular Events I have mentioned, the Readers may judge by the fulfilling of them, whether I am of the Level with common Astrologers; who, with an old paultry Cant, and a few Pot-hooks for Planets to amuse the Vulgar, have, in my Opinion, too long been suffered to abuse the World. But an honest Physician ought not to be despised, because there are such Things as Mountebanks. I hope, I have some Share of Reputation, which I would not willingly forfeit for a Frolick, or Humour: And I believe no Gentleman, who reads this Paper, will look upon it to be of the same Cast, or Mold, with the common Scribbles that are every Day hawked about. My Fortune hath placed me above the little Regard of writing for a few Pence, which I neither value nor want: Therefore, let not wise Men too hastily condemn this Essay, intended for a good. Design, to cultivate and improve an antient Art, long in Disgrace by having fallen into mean unskilful Hands. A little Time will determine whether I have deceived others, or my self; and I think it is no very unreasonable Request, that Men would please to suspend their Judgments till then. I was once of the Opinion with those who despise all Predictions from the Stars, till in the Year 1686, a Man of Quality shewed me, written in his *Album*, that the most learned Astronomer Captain *Hally*, assured him, he would never believe any thing of the Stars Influence, if there were not a great Revolution in *England* in the Year 1688. Since that Time I began to have other Thoughts; and after Eighteen Years diligent Study and Application, I think I have no Reason to repent of my Pains. I shall detain the Reader no longer than to let him know, that the Account I design to give of next Year's Events, shall take in the principal Affairs that happen in *Europe*: And if I be denied the Liberty of offering it to my own Country, I shall appeal to the learned World, by publishing it in *Latin*, and giving Order to have it printed in *Holland*.[4]

4. Latin is evoked as the universal language, Holland as the ideal home of

The Accomplishment of the First of Mr. Bickerstaff's Predictions

Being an Account of the Death of Mr. *Partrige,* the Almanack-maker, upon the 29th Inst.

In a Letter to a Person of Honour[1]

My Lo r d,

IN Obedience to your Lordship's Commands, as well as to satisfy my own Curiosity, I have for some Days past enquired constantly after *Partrige* the Almanack-maker; of whom it was foretold in Mr. *Bickerstaff's* Predictions, published about a Month ago, that he should die the 29th Instant, about Eleven at Night, of a raging Fever. I had some Sort of Knowledge of him when I was employed in the Revenue; because he used every Year to present me with his Almanack, as he did other Gentlemen upon the score of some little Gratuity we gave him. I saw him accidentally once or twice about ten Days before he died; and observed he began very much to droop and languish, although I hear his Friends did not seem to apprehend him in any Danger. About two or three Days ago he grew ill; was confined first to his Chamber, and in a few Hours after to his Bed; where Dr. *Case* and Mrs. *Kirleus* * were sent for to visit, and to prescribe to him. Upon this Intelligence I sent thrice every Day one Servant or other to enquire after his Health; and Yesterday about four in the Afternoon, Word was brought me that he was past Hopes: Upon which I prevailed with my self to go and see him; partly out of Commiseration, and, I confess, partly out of Curiosity. He knew me very well, seemed surprized at my Condescension, and made me Compliments upon it as well as he could in the Condition he was. The People about him said, he had been for some Hours delirious; but when I saw him, he had his Understanding as well as ever I knew, and spoke strong and hearty, without any seeming Uneasiness or Constraint. After I had told him I was sorry to see him in those melancholly Circumstances, and said some other Civilities, suitable to the Occasion; I desired him to tell me

---

Partridgean prophecy. For Swift's attitude towards Holland, especially its liberal social and religious practices, see *Gulliver's Travels*, p. 128, note 2.
1. Published at the end of March, 1708, Swift's second installment was carefully timed to confirm Bickerstaff's original prediction of the death of Partridge.
* *Two famous Quacks at that Time in* London.

freely and ingenuously whether the Predictions Mr. *Bickerstaff* had published relating to his Death, had not too much affected and worked on his Imagination. He confessed he had often had it in his Head, but never with much Apprehension till about a Fortnight before; since which Time it had the perpetual Possession of his Mind and Thoughts; and he did verily believe was the true natural Cause of his present Distemper: For, said he, I am thoroughly persuaded, and I think I have very good Reasons, that Mr. *Bickerstaff* spoke altogether by guess, and knew no more what will happen this Year than I did my self. I told him his Discourse surprized me; and I would be glad he were in a State of Health to be able to tell me what Reason he had to be convinced of Mr. *Bickerstaff's* Ignorance. He replied, I am a poor ignorant Fellow, bred to a mean Trade; yet I have Sense enough to know, that all Pretences of foretelling by Astrology are Deceits; for this manifest Reason, because the Wise and Learned, who can only judge whether there be any Truth in this Science, do all unanimously agree to laugh at and despise it; and none but the poor ignorant Vulgar give it any Credit, and that only upon the Word of such silly Wretches as I and my Fellows, who can hardly write or read. I then asked him, why he had not calculated his own Nativity, to see whether it agreed with *Bickerstaff's* Predictions? At which he shook his Head, and said, O! Sir, this is no Time for jesting, but for repenting those Fooleries, as I do now from the very Bottom of my Heart. By what I can gather from you, said I, the Observations and Predictions you printed with your Almanacks were meer Impositions upon the People. He replied, if it were otherwise, I should have the less to answer for. We have a common Form for all those Things: As to foretelling the Weather, we never meddle with that, but leave it to the Printer, who takes it out of any old Almanack as he thinks fit: The rest was my own Invention to make my Almanack sell; having a Wife to maintain, and no other Way to get my Bread; for mending old Shoes is a poor Livelihood: And (added he, sighing) I wish I may not have done more Mischief by my Physick than my Astrology; although I had some good Receipts from my Grandmother, and my own Compositions were such, as I thought could at least do no Hurt.

I HAD some other Discourse with him, which now I cannot call to Mind; and I fear I have already tired your Lordship. I shall only add one Circumstance, That on his Death-Bed he declared himself a Nonconformist, and had a fanatick Preacher to be his spiritual Guide. After half an Hour's Conversation, I took my Leave, being almost stifled by the Closeness of the Room. I imagined he could not hold out long; and therefore withdrew to a little Coffee-House hard by, leaving a Servant at the House with Orders to come immediately, and tell me, as near as he could, the Minute when *Partrige* should expire, which was not above two Hours after; when looking upon my Watch, I found it to be above five Minutes after Seven: By which it is clear, that Mr. *Bickerstaff* was mistaken almost four Hours in his Calculation. In the other Circumstances he was exact enough. But whether he hath not been the Cause of this poor Man's Death, as well as the Predictor, may be very reasonably disputed. However, it must be confessed, the Matter is odd enough, whether we should endeavour to account for it by Chance or the Effect of Imagination: For my own Part, although I believe no Man hath less Faith in these Matters; yet I shall wait with some Impatience, and not without Expectation, the fulfilling of Mr. *Bickerstaff's* second Prediction; that the Cardinal *de Noailles* is to die upon the 4th of *April*; and if that should be verified as exactly as this of poor *Partrige*; I must own, I should be wholly surprized, and at a Loss; and should infallibly expect the Accomplishment of all the rest.

A Vindication of Isaac Bickerstaff, Esq;

Against What is objected to him by Mr. *Partrige*, in his Almanack for the present Year 1709.

By the said ISAAC BICKERSTAFF, Esq;[1]

MR. *Partrige* hath been lately pleased to treat me after a very rough Manner, in *that which is called*, His Almanack for the present Year: Such Usage is very undecent from *one Gentleman to another*, and doth not at all contribute to the Discovery of Truth; which ought to be the great End in all Disputes of the *Learned*. To call a Man *Fool* and *Villain*, and *impudent Fellow*, only for differing from him in a Point meerly speculative, is, in my humble Opinion, a very improper Stile for a Person of *his Education*. I appeal to the *learned World*, whether in my last Year's Predictions, I gave him the least Provocation for such unworthy Treatment. Philosophers have differed in all Ages, but the discreetest among them have always differed as became Philosophers. Scurrility and Passion, in a Controversy among *Scholars* is just so much of nothing to the Pur-

---

1. Hoping to have the last word, Partridge sent forth a public "Answer" to Bickerstaff which repudiated the latter's prophetic powers by insisting that he, Partridge, was still alive; it gave Swift the occasion for this final "Vindication." See Davis, II, for additional Bickerstaff material, including Partridge's "Answer."

pose; and, at best, a tacit Confession of a weak Cause: My Concern is not so much for my own Reputation, as that of the *Republick of Letters*, which Mr. *Partrige* hath endeavoured to wound through my Sides. If Men of publick Spirit must be superciliously treated for their ingenuous Attempts; how will true useful Knowledge be ever advanced? I wish Mr. *Partrige* knew the Thoughts which *foreign Universities* have conceived of his ungenerous Proceedings with me; but I am too tender of his Reputation to publish them to the World. That Spirit of Envy and Pride, which blasts so many rising Genius's in our Nation, is yet unknown among *Professors* abroad: The Necessity of justifying my self, will excuse my Vanity, when I tell the Reader, that I have near an Hundred *honorary* Letters from several Parts of *Europe*, (some as far as *Muscovy*) in Praise of my Performance. Besides several others, which, as I have been credibly informed, were opened in the Post-Office, and never sent me. * It is true, the *Inquisition* in *Portugal* was pleased to burn my Predictions, and condemn the Author and Readers of them; but, I hope, at the same Time, it will be considered in how deplorable a State *Learning* lies at present in that Kingdom: And with the profoundest Veneration for *crowned Heads*, I will presume to add; that it a little concerned *his Majesty of Portugal*, to interpose his Authority in Behalf of a *Scholar* and a *Gentleman*, the Subject of a Nation with which he is now in so strict an Alliance. But, the other Kingdoms and States of *Europe* have treated me with more Candour and Generosity. If I had leave to print the *Latin* Letters transmitted to me from foreign Parts, they would fill a Volume, and be a full Defence against all that Mr. *Partrige* or his Accomplices of the *Portugal Inquisition*, will be ever able to object; who, by the way, are the only Enemies my Predictions have ever met with at home or abroad. But, I hope, I know better what is due to the Honour of a *learned Correspondence*, in so tender a Point. Yet, some of those illustrious Persons will, perhaps, excuse me for transcribing a Passage or two in my own Vindication. The † most learned Monsieur *Leibnitz* thus addresseth to me his third Letter: *Illustrissimo Bickerstaffio Astrologiæ Instauratori*, &c. Monsieur *le Clerc* quoting my Predictions in a Treatise he published last Year, is pleased to say, *Ità nuperime Bickerstaffius magnum illud Angliæ sidus.* Another great Professor writing of me, has these Words: *Bickerstaffius, nobilis Anglus, Astrologorum hujusce Seculi facilè Princeps.* Signior *Magliabecchi*, the *Great Duke's* famous Library-keeper, spends almost his whole Letter in Compliments and Praises. It is true, the

---

* *This is Fact, as the Author was assured by Sir* Paul Methuen, *then Ambassador to that Crown.*
† *The Quotations here inserted, are in Imitation of Dr.* Bentley, *in some Part of the famous Controversy between him and* Charles Boyle, *Esq; afterwards Earl of* Orrery.

renowned *Professor* of Astronomy at *Utrecht*, seems to differ from me in one Article; but it is after the modest Manner that becomes a Philosopher; as, *Pace tanti viri dixerim:* And, *Page* 55, he seems to lay the Error upon the Printer, (as indeed it ought) and says, *vel forsan error Typographi, cum alioquin Bickerstaffius vir doctissimus,* &c.

IF Mr. *Partrige* had followed these Examples in the Controversy between us, he might have spared me the Trouble of justifying my self in so publick a Manner. I believe few Men are readier to own their Errors than I, or more thankful to those who will please to inform him of them. But it seems this Gentleman, instead of encouraging the Progress of his own Art, is pleased to look upon all Attempts of that Kind, as an Invasion of his Province. He hath been indeed so wise, to make no Objection against the Truth of my Predictions, except in one single Point, relating to himself: And to demonstrate how much Men are blinded by their own Partiality; I do solemnly assure the Reader, that he is the *only* Person from whom I ever heard that Objection offered; which Consideration alone, I think, will take off all its Weight.

WITH my utmost Endeavours, I have not been able to trace above two Objections ever made against the Truth of my last Year's Prophecies: The first is of a *French* Man, who was pleased to publish to the World, that *the Cardinal* de Noailles *was still alive, notwithstanding the pretended Prophecy of Monsieur* Biquerstaffe: But how far a *French* Man, a *Papist,* and an *Enemy* is to be believed, in his own Cause, against an *English Protestant,* who is *true to the Government,* I shall leave to the candid and impartial Reader.

THE other Objection, is the unhappy Occasion of this Discourse; and relates to an Article in my Predictions, which foretold the Death of Mr. *Partrige* to happen on *March* 29, 1708. This he is pleased to contradict absolutely in the Almanack he hath published for the present Year; and in that ungentlemanly Manner, (pardon the Expression) as I have above related. In that Work, he very roundly asserts, That he *is not only now alive, but was likewise alive upon that very 29th of* March, *when I had foretold he should die.* This is the Subject of the present Controversy between us; which I design to handle with all Brevity, Perspicuity, and Calmness: In this Dispute, I am sensible, the Eyes not only of *England,* but of all *Europe,* will be upon us: And the *Learned* in every Country will, I doubt not, take Part on that Side where they find most Appearance of Reason and Truth.

WITHOUT entering into Criticisms of *Chronology* about the Hour of his Death; I shall only prove, that Mr. *Partrige* is not alive.

And my first Argument is thus: Above a Thousand Gentlemen having bought his Almanacks for this Year, meerly to find what he said against me; at every Line they read, they would lift up their Eyes, and cry out, betwixt Rage and Laughter, *They were sure no Man* alive *ever writ such damned Stuff as this.* Neither did I ever hear that Opinion disputed: So that Mr. *Partrige* lies under a *Dilemma*, either of disowning his Almanack, or allowing himself to be no *Man alive.*

SECONDLY, Death is defined by all Philosophers, a Separation of the Soul and Body. Now it is certain, that the poor Woman who has best Reason to know, has gone about for some time to every Alley in the Neighbourhood, and swore to the Gossips, that *Her Husband had neither Life nor Soul in him.* Therefore, if an *uninformed* Carcass walks still about, and is pleased to call it self *Partrige*; Mr. *Bickerstaff* does not think himself any way answerable for that. Neither had the said Carcass any Right to beat the poor Boy, who happened to pass by it in the Street, crying, A *full and true Account of Dr.* Partrige's *Death*, &c.

THIRDLY, Mr. *Partrige* pretends to tell Fortunes, and recover stolen Goods; which all the Parish says he must do by conversing with the Devil, and other evil Spirits: And no wise Man will ever allow he could converse personally with either, till after he was dead.

FOURTHLY, I will plainly prove him to be dead, out of his own Almanack for this Year, and from the very Passage which produceth to make us think him alive. He there says, *He is not only now alive, but was also alive upon that very 29th of* March, *which I foretold* he *should die on*: By this, he declares his Opinion, that a Man may be alive *now*, who was not alive a Twelve-month ago. And, indeed, there lies the Sophistry of his Argument. He dares not assert, he was alive ever since the 29th of *March*, but that he *is now alive, and was so on that Day*: I grant the latter, for he did not die till Night, as appears by the printed Account of his Death, in a *Letter to a Lord*; and whether he be since revived, I leave the World to judge. This, indeed, is perfect cavilling, and I am ashamed to dwell any longer upon it.

FIFTHLY, I will appeal to Mr. *Partrige* himself, whether it be probable I could have been so indiscreet, to begin my Predictions with the *only* Falshood that ever was pretended to be in them; and this in an Affair at Home, where I had so many Opportunities to be exact; and must have given such Advantages against me to a Person of Mr. *Partrige's* Wit and Learning, who, if he could possibly have raised one single Objection more against the Truth of my Prophecies, would hardly have spared me.

AND here I must take Occasion to reprove the abovementioned Writer of the Relation of Mr. *Partrige's* Death, in a *Letter to a Lord*; who was pleased to tax me with a Mistake of *four whole Hours* in my Calculation of that Event. I must confess, this Censure, pronounced with an Air of Certainty, in a Matter that so nearly concerned me, and by a *grave judicious Author*, moved me not a little. But although I was at that Time out of Town, yet several of my Friends, whose Curiosity had led them to be exactly informed, (for as to my own Part, having no doubt at all in the Matter, I never once thought of it,) assured me I computed to something under half an Hour; which (I speak my private Opinion) is an Error of no very great Magnitude, that Men should raise Clamour about it. I shall only say, it would not be amiss, if that Author would henceforth be more tender of other Mens Reputation as well as his own. It is well there were no more Mistakes of that Kind; if there had, I presume he would have told of them with as little Ceremony.

THERE is one Objection against Mr. *Partrige's* Death, which I have sometimes met with, although indeed very slightly offered; That he still continues to write Almanacks. But this is no more than what is common to all of that Profession; *Gadbury, Poor Robin, Dove, Wing*, and several others, do yearly publish their Almanacks, although several of them have been dead since before the *Revolution*. Now the natural Reason of this I take to be, that whereas it is the Privilege of other Authors, *to live after their Deaths*; Almanack-makers are alone excluded; because their Dissertations treating only upon the Minutes as they pass, become useless as those go off. In consideration of which, *Time*, whose *Registers* they are, gives them a Lease in Reversion, to continue their Works after their Death: Or, perhaps a Name can *make* an Almanack, as well as it can *sell* one. And to strengthen this conjecture, I have heard the Booksellers affirm, That they have desired Mr. *Partrige* to spare himself further Trouble, and only lend them his Name, which could make Almanacks much better than himself.

I SHOULD not have given the Publick or my self the Trouble of this Vindication, if my Name had not been made use of by several Persons, to whom I never lent it; one of which, a few Days ago, was pleased to father on me a new Set of Predictions. But I think these are Things too serious to be trifled with. It grieved me to the Heart, when I saw my Labours, which had cost me so much Thought and Watching, bawled about by common Hawkers of Grubstreet which I only intended for the weighty Consideration of the gravest Persons. This prejudiced the World so much at first, that several of my Friends had the Assurance to ask me, Whether I were in jest? To which I only answered coldly, *That the Event will shew*. But it is the Talent of our Age and Nation, to turn Things of the greatest Importance into Ridicule. When the End of the Year had *verified all my Predictions*; out comes Mr. *Partrige's* Almanack, disputing the Point of his Death; so that I am employed, like the General who was forced to kill his Enemies twice over, whom a *Necromancer* had raised to Life. If Mr. *Partrige* hath practised the same Experiment upon himself, and be again alive; long may he continue so; but that doth not in the least contradict my Veracity: For I think I have clearly proved, by *invincible Demonstration*, that he died at farthest within half an Hour of the Time I foretold.

Journal to Stella

Letter VI[1]

London, Oct. 10, 1710.

SO, as I told you just now in the letter I sent half an hour ago, I dined with Mr. Harley[2] to-day, who presented me to the attorney-general sir Simon Harcourt, with much compliment on all sides, &c. Harley told me he had shown my memorial to the queen,[3] and seconded it very heartily; and he desires me to dine with him again on Sunday, when he promises to settle it with her majesty, before she names a governor;[4] and I protest I am in hopes it will be done, all but the forms, by that time; for he loves the church: this is a popular thing, and he would not have a governor share in it; and, besides, I am told by all hands, he has a mind to gain me over. But in the letter I writ last post (yesterday) to the archbishop,[5] I did not tell him a syllable of what Mr. Harley said to me last night, because he charged me to keep it secret; so I would not tell it to you, but that before this goes, I hope the secret will be over. I am now writing my poetical *Description of a Shower in London*, and will send it to the *Tatler*. This is the last sheet of a whole quire I

---

1. Swift's *Journal* was in fact a series of letters written between September, 1710, and June, 1711, relating his day-to-day activities in London for the benefit of Esther Johnson ("Stella") and her companion, Rebecca Dingley, both settled in Ireland. See also Swift's several poems commemorating Stella's birthday (pp. 525–533).
2. Tory statesman, Lord Treasurer to Queen Anne, 1710–14.
3. Swift, representing the Irish bishops, asked the Queen for the remission to the Irish Clergy of the First Fruits and Twentieth Parts.
4. A Lord Lieutenant of Ireland.
5. William King, Archbishop of Dublin.

have written since I came to town. Pray, now it comes into my head, will you, when you go to Mrs. Walls, contrive to know whether Mrs. Wesley be in town, and still at her brother's, and how she is in health, and whether she stays in town. I writ to her from Chester, to know what I should do with her note; and I believe the poor woman is afraid to write to me: so I must go to my business, &c.

11. To-day at last I dined with lord Montrath, and carried lord Mountjoy and sir Andrew Fountain with me; and was looking over them at ombre till eleven this evening like a fool: they played running ombre half crowns; and sir Andrew Fountain won eight guineas of Mr. Coote: so I am come home late, and will say but little to MD[6] this night. I have gotten half a bushel of coals, and Patrick, the extravagant whelp, had a fire ready for me; but I pickt off the coals before I went to-bed. It is a sign London is now an empty place, when it will not furnish me with matter for above five or six lines in a day. Did you smoak in my last how I told you the very day and the place you were playing at ombre? But I interlined and altered a little, after I had received a letter from Mr. Manley, that said you were at it in his house, while he was writing to me; but without his help I guess'd within one day. Your town is certainly much more sociable than ours. I have not seen your mother yet, &c.

12. I dined to-day with Dr. Garth and Mr. Addison, at the Devil tavern, by Temple-bar, and Garth treated; and 'tis well I dine every day, else I should be longer making out my letters: for we are yet in a very dull state, only enquiring every day after new elections, where the Tories carry it among the new members six to one. Mr. Addison's election[7] has passed easy and undisputed; and I believe, if he had a mind to be chosen king, he would hardly be refused. An odd accident has happened at Colchester: one captain Lavallin coming from Flanders or Spain, found his wife with child by a clerk of Doctors Commons, whose trade, you know, it is to prevent fornications: and this clerk was the very same fellow that made the discovery of Dyet's[8] counterfeiting the stamp paper. Lavallin has been this fortnight hunting after the clerk to kill him; but the fellow was constantly employed at the Treasury about the discovery he made: the wife had made a shift to patch up the business, alledging that the clerk had told her her husband was dead, and other excuses; but t'other day somebody told Lavallin his wife had intrigues before he married her: upon which he goes down in a rage, shoots his wife

6. My Dear or My Dears; that is, Stella and Rebecca Dingley.
7. Joseph Addison was a Member of Parliament from 1709 until his death.
8. A Commissioner of Stamped Papers; he was tried for felony in 1711.

through the head, then falls on his sword; and, to make the matter sure, at the same time discharges a pistol through his own head, and died on the spot, his wife surviving him about two hours; but in what circumstances of mind and body is terrible to imagine. I have finished my poem on the *Shower*, all but the beginning, and am going on with my *Tatler*. They have fixt about fifty things on me since I came: I have printed but three. One advantage I get by writing to you daily, or rather you get, is, that I shall remember not to write the same things twice; and yet I fear I have done it often already: but I'll mind and confine myself to the accidents of the day; and so get you gone to ombre, and be good girls, and save your money, and be rich against Presto[9] comes, and write to me now and then: I am thinking it would be a pretty thing to hear sometimes from sawcy MD; but don't hurt your eyes, Stella, I charge you.

13. O Lord, here's but a trifle of my letter written yet; what shall Presto do for prittle prattle to entertain MD? The talk now grows fresher of the duke of Ormond for Ireland, though Mr. Addison says he hears it will be in commission, and lord Gallaway one. These letters of mine are a sort of journal, where matters open by degrees; and, as I tell true or false, you will find by the event whether my intelligence be good; but I don't care two-pence whether it be or no.—At night. To-day I was all about St. Paul's, and up at the top like a fool, with sir Andrew Fountain and two more; and spent seven shillings for my dinner like a puppy: this is the second time he has served me so; but I'll never do it again, though all mankind should persuade me, unconsidering puppies! There's a young fellow here in town we are all fond of, and about a year or two come from the university, one Harrison, a little pretty fellow, with a great deal of wit, good sense, and good nature; has written some mighty pretty things, that in your 6th *Miscellanea*, about the *Sprig of an Orange*, is his: he has nothing to live on but being governor to one of the duke of Queensbury's sons for forty pounds a year. The fine fellows are always inviting him to the tavern, and make him pay his club. Henley is a great crony of his: they are often at the tavern at six or seven shillings reckoning, and always makes the poor lad pay his full share. A colonel and a lord were at him and me the same way to-night: I absolutely refused, and made Harrison lag behind, and persuaded him not to go to them. I tell you this, because I find all rich fellows have that humour of using all people without any consideration of their for-

9. Swift. See Williams' edition of the *Journal*, I, 325, for the origins of this expression.

tunes; but I'll see them rot before they shall serve me so. Lord Halifax is always teazing me to go down to his country house, which will cost me a guinea to his servants, and twelve shillings coach hire; and he shall be hanged first. Is not this a plaguy silly story? But I am vext at the heart; for I love the young fellow, and am resolved to stir up people to do something for him: he is a Whig, and I'll put him upon some of my cast Whigs; for I have done with them, and they have, I hope, done with this kingdom for our time. They were sure of the four members for London above all places, and they have lost three in the four. Sir Richard Onslow, we hear, has lost for Surry; and they are overthrown in most places. Lookee, gentlewoman, if I write long letters, I must write you news and stuff, unless I send you my verses; and some I dare not; and those on the *Shower in London* I have sent to the *Tatler*, and you may see them in Ireland. I fancy you'll smoak me in the *Tatler* I am going to write; for I believe I have told you the hint. I had a letter sent me to-night from sir Matthew Dudley, and found it on my table when I came in. Because it is extraordinary I will transcribe it from beginning to end. It is as follows [Is the Devil in you? Oct. 13, 1710.] I would have answered every particular passage in it, only I wanted time. Here's enough for to-night, such as it is, &c.

14. Is that tobacco at the top of the paper, or what? I don't remember I slobbered. Lord, I dreamt of Stella, &c. so confusedly last night, and that we saw dean Bolton and Sterne go into a shop; and she bid me call them to her, and they proved to be two parsons I know not; and I walked without till she was shifting, and such stuff, mixt with much melancholy and uneasiness, and things not as they should be, and I know not how: and it is now an ugly gloomy morning.—At night. Mr. Addison and I dined with Ned Southwell, and walkt in the Park; and at the Coffee-house I found a letter from the bishop of Clogher, and a pacquet from MD. I opened the bishop's letter; but put up MD's, and visited a lady just come to town, and am now got into bed, and going to open your little letter: and God send I may find MD well, and happy, and merry, and that they love Presto as they do fires. Oh, I won't open it yet! yes I will! no I won't; I am going; I can't stay till I turn over. What shall I do? My fingers itch; and I now have it in my left hand; and now I'll open it this very moment.—I have just got it, and am cracking the seal, and can't imagine what's in it; I fear only some letter from a bishop, and it comes too late: I shall employ nobody's credit but my own. Well, I see though—Pshaw, 'tis from sir Andrew Fountain: What, another! I fancy that is from Mrs. Barton; she told me she would write to me; but she writes a better hand than

this: I wish you would inquire; it must be at Dawson's office at the Castle. I fear this is from Patty Rolt, by the scrawl. Well, I'll read MD's letter. Ah, no; it is from poor lady Berkeley, to invite me to Berkeley-castle this winter; and now it grieves my heart: she says she hopes my lord is in a fair way of recovery; poor lady. Well, now I go to MD's letter: faith, 'tis all right; I hoped it was wrong. Your letter, N. 3, That I have now received, is dated Sept. 26, and Manley's letter, that I had five days ago, was dated Oct 3, that's a fortnight difference: I doubt it has lain in Steele's office,[1] and he forgot. Well, there's an end of that: he is turned out of his place; and you must desire those who send me pacquets, to inclose them in a paper directed to Mr. Addison, at St. James's Coffee-house: not common letters, but pacquets: the bishop of Clogher may mention it to the archbishop when he sees him. As for your letter, it makes me mad: slidikins, I have been the best boy in Christendom, and you come with your two eggs a penny.[2]—Well; but stay, I'll look over my book; adad, I think there was a *chasm* between my N. 2 and N. 3. Faith, I won't promise to write to you every week; but I'll write every night, and when it is full I will send it; that will be once in ten days, and that will be often enough: and if you begin to take up the way of writing to Presto, only because it is Tuesday, a Monday bedad, it will grow a task; but write when you have a mind.—No, no, no, no, no, no, no, no—Agad, agad, agad, agad, agad, agad; no, poor Stellakins. Slids, I would the horse were in your—chamber. Have not I ordered Parvisol to obey your directions about him? And han't I said in my former letters, that you may pickle him, and boil him, if you will? What do you trouble me about your horses for? Have I any thing to do with them?—Revolutions a hindrance to me in my business; Revolutions—to me in my business? If it were not for the revolutions, I could do nothing at all; and now I have all hopes possible, though one is certain of nothing; but to-morrow I am to have an answer, and am promised an effectual one. I suppose I have said enough in this and a former letter how I stand with new people; ten times better than ever I did with the old; forty times more caressed. I am to dine to-morrow at Mr. Harley's; and if he continues as he has begun, no man has been ever better treated by another. What you say about Stella's mother, I have spoken enough to it already. I believe she is not in town; for I have not yet seen her. My lampoon is cried up to the skies; but nobody suspects me for it, except sir Andrew Fountain: at least they say nothing of it to me. Did not I tell you of a great man who

1. Swift used the office of Richard Steele in the Cockpit as a London mailing address.
2. That is, a trifling story.

received me very coldly?[3] That's he; but say nothing; 'twas only a little revenge: I'll remember to bring it over. The bishop of Clogher has smoaked my *Tatler* about shortening of words, &c. But God so! &c.

15. I will write plainer if I can remember it; for Stella must not spoil her eyes, and Dingley can't read my hand very well; and I am afraid my letters are too long: then you must suppose one to be two, and read them at twice. I dined to-day with Mr. Harley: Mr. Prior dined with us. He has left my memorial with the queen, who has consented to give the First-Fruits and Twentieth Parts, and will, we hope, declare it to-morrow in the cabinet. But I beg you to tell it to no person alive; for so I am ordered, till in publick: and I hope to get something of greater value. After dinner came in lord Peterborow: we renewed our acquaintance, and he grew mightily fond of me. They began to talk of a paper of verses called *Sid Hamet*. Mr. Harley repeated part, and then pulled them out, and gave them to a gentleman at the table to read, though they had all read them often: lord Peterborow would let nobody read them but himself: so he did; and Mr. Harley bobbed me at every line to take notice of the beauties. Prior rallied lord Peterborow for author of them; and lord Peterborow said, he knew them to be his; and Prior then turned it upon me, and I on him. I am not guessed at all in town to be the author; yet so it is: but that is a secret only to you. Ten to one whether you see them in Ireland; yet here they run prodigiously. Harley presented me to lord president of Scotland, and Mr. Benson, lord of the treasury. Prior and I came away at nine, and sat at the Smyrna till eleven, receiving acquaintance.

16. This morning early I went in a chair, and Patrick before it, to Mr. Harley, to give him another copy of my memorial, as he desired; but he was full of business, going to the queen, and I could not see him; but he desired I would send up the paper, and excused himself upon his hurry. I was a little baulkt; but they tell me it is nothing. I shall judge by next visit. I tipt his porter with half a crown; and so I am well there for a time at least. I dined at Stratford's in the city, and had Burgundy and Tockay: came back afoot like a scoundrel; then went to Mr. Addison and supt with lord Mountjoy, which made me sick all night. I forgot that I bought six pound of chocolate for Stella, and a little wooden box: and I have a great piece of Brazil tobacco[4] for Dingley, and a bottle of palsy water for Stella: all which, with the two handkerchiefs that Mr. Sterne has bought, and you must pay him for, will be put in the

3. Sydney Godolphin, Lord Treasurer until 1710. Swift lampooned him anonymously, as he here reports, in "Sid Hamet the Magician's Rod," on the reception of which see Oct. 15, below, and also Letter VIII, Nov. 8 (Williams' edition of the *Journal*, I, 85–89).
4. To be used as snuff.

box directed to Mrs. Curry's, and sent by Dr. Hawkshaw, whom I have not seen; but Sterne has undertaken it. The chocolate is a present, madam, for Stella. Don't read this, you little rogue, with your little eyes; but give it to Dingley, pray now; and I'll write as plain as the skies: and let Dingley write Stella's part, and Stella dictate to her, when she apprehends her eyes, &c.

17. This letter should have gone this post, if I had not been taken up with business, and two nights being late out; so it must stay till Thursday. I dined to-day with your Mr. Sterne, by invitation, and drank Irish wine;[5] but, before we parted, there came in the prince of puppies, colonel Edgworth; so I went away. This day came out the *Tatler* made up wholly of my *Shower*, and a preface to it. They say 'tis the best thing I ever writ, and I think so too. I suppose the bishop of Clogher will shew it you. Pray tell me how you like it. Tooke is going on with my *Miscellany*. I'd give a penny the letter to the bishop of Kilaloe was in it: 'twould do him honour. Could not you contrive to say you hear they are printing my *Things* together; and that you wish the bookseller had that letter among the rest: but don't say any thing of it as from me. I forgot whether it was good or no; but only having heard it much commended, perhaps it may deserve it. Well, I have to-morrow to finish this letter in, and then I'll send it next day. I am so vext that you should write your third to me, when you had but my second, and I had written five, which now I hope you have all: and so I tell you, you are sawcy, little, pretty, dear rogues, &c.

18. To-day I dined, by invitation, with Stratford and others, at a young merchant's in the city, with Hermitage and Tockay, and staid till nine, and am now come home. And that dog Patrick is abroad, and drinking, and I can't get my night-gown. I have a mind to turn that puppy away: he has been drunk ten times in three weeks. But I han't time to say more; so good night, &c.

19. I am come home from dining in the city with Mr. Addison, at a merchant's; and just now, at the Coffee-house, we have notice that the duke of Ormond was this day declared lord lieutenant, at Hampton-court, in council. I have not seen Mr. Harley since; but hope the affair is done about First-Fruits. I will see him, if possible, tomorrow morning; but this goes to-night. I have sent a box to Mr. Sterne, to send to you by some friend: I have directed it for Mr. Curry, at his house; so you have warning when it comes, as I hope it will soon. The handkerchiefs will be put in some friend's pocket, not to pay custom. And so here ends my sixth, sent when I had but three of MD's: now I am beforehand, and will keep so; and God Almighty bless dearest MD, &c.

5. Claret.

The Tatler

Number CCXXX

THURSDAY, SEPTEMBER 28, 1710

FROM MY OWN APARTMENT, SEPT. 27

THE following Letter hath laid before me many great and manifest Evils, in the World of Letters which I had overlooked; but they
open to me a very busy Scene, and it will require no small Care and
Application to amend Errors which are become so universal. The
Affectation of Politeness, is exposed in this Epistle with a great deal
of Wit and Discernment; so that, whatever Discourses I may fall
into hereafter upon the Subjects the Writer treats of, I shall at present lay the Matter before the World, without the least Alteration
from the Words of my Correspondent.

To ISAAC BICKERSTAFF, *Esq;*

SIR,
*THERE are some Abuses among us of great Consequence, the
Reformation of which is properly your Province; although, as far as
I have been conversant in your Papers, you have not yet considered
them. These are the deplorable Ignorance that for some Years hath
reigned among our English Writers; the great Depravity of our
Taste; and the continual Corruption of our Style. I say nothing here
of those who handle particular Sciences, Divinity, Law, Physick,
and the like; I mean the Traders in History and Politicks, and the
Belles Lettres; together with those by whom Books are not translated, but (as the common Expressions are) Done out of French,
Latin, or other Language, and made English. I cannot but observe
to you, that until of late Years, a Grub-street Book was always
bound in Sheep-skin, with suitable Print and Paper; the Price never
above a Shilling; and taken off wholly by common Tradesmen, or
Country Pedlars. But now they appear in all Sizes and Shapes, and
in all Places: They are handed about from Lapfulls in every Coffee-house to Persons of Quality; are shewn in Westminster-Hall,
and the Court of Requests. You may see them gilt, and in Royal
Paper of five or six Hundred Pages, and rated accordingly. I would
engage to furnish you with a Catalogue of English Books published*

*within the Compass of seven Years past, which at the first Hand
would cost you an Hundred Pounds; wherein you shall not be able
to find ten Lines together of common Grammar, or common Sense.*

THESE *two Evils, Ignorance, and want of Taste, have produced
a Third; I mean the continual Corruption of our* English *Tongue;
which, without some timely Remedy, will suffer more by the false
Refinements of Twenty Years past, than it hath been improved in
the foregoing Hundred. And this is what I design chiefly to enlarge
upon; leaving the former Evils to your Animadversion.*

BUT, *instead of giving you a List of the late Refinements crept
into our Language; I here send you the Copy of a Letter I received
some Time ago from a most accomplished Person in this Way of
Writing; upon which I shall make some Remarks. It is in these
Terms*:

S I R,
'I *Cou'dn't* get the Things you sent for all *about* Town.——I
thot to *ha'* come down my self, and then *I'd ha' bro't um*; but I
ha'nt don't, and I believe I *can't do't*, that's *pozz*——Tom begins
to *gi'mself* Airs, because *he's* going with the *Plenipo's*.——'Tis said
the *French* King will *bamboozel us agen*, which *causes* many *Speculations*. The *Jacks*,[1] and others of that *Kidney*, are very *uppish*, and
alert upon't, as you may see by their *Phizz's*.——[2] *Will Hazard* has
got the *Hipps*,[3] having lost *to the Tune* of five Hundr'd Pound,
tho' he understands Play very well, *no Body better*. He has promis't
me upon *Rep*, to leavve off Play; but you know 'tis a Weakness *he's*
too apt to *give into, tho'* he has as much Wit as any Man, *no body
more*. He has lain *incog* ever since.——The *Mob's* very quiet with
us now.——I believe you *tho't* I *banter'd* you in my last like a
Country Put.[4]——*I shan't* leave Town this Month, *&c.'*

THIS Letter is in every Point an admirable Pattern of the present polite Way of Writing; nor is it of less Authority for being an
Epistle: You may gather every Flower of it, with a Thousand more
of equal Sweetness, from the Books, Pamphlets, and single Papers,
offered us every Day in the Coffee-houses: And these are the Beauties introduced to supply the Want of Wit, Sense, Humour and
Learning; which formerly were looked upon as Qualifications for a
Writer. If a Man of Wit, who died Forty Years ago, were to rise
from the Grave on Purpose; how would he be able to read this
Letter? And after he had got through that Difficulty, how would he
be able to understand it? The first Thing that strikes your Eye, is

1. Jacobites.
2. Physiognomies, countenances.
3. Hippish, low-spirited.
4. Country lout.

the *Breaks* at the End of almost every Sentence; of which I know not the Use, only that it is a Refinement, and very frequently practised. Then you will observe the Abbreviations and Elisions, by which Consonants of most obdurate Sound are joined together, without one softening Vowel to intervene: And all this only to make one Syllable of two, directly contrary to the Example of the *Greeks* and *Romans*; altogether of the *Gothick* Strain, and a natural Tendency towards relapsing into Barbarity, which delights in Monosyllables, and uniting of mute Consonants; as it is observable in all the *Northern* Languages. And this is still more visible in the next Refinement, which consisteth in pronouncing the first Syllable in a Word that hath many, and dismissing the rest; such as *Phizz, Hipps, Mobb, Pozz, Rep,* and many more; when we are already over-loaded with Monosyllables, which are the Disgrace of our Language. Thus we cram one Syllable, and cut off the rest; as the Owl fattened her Mice after she had bit off their Legs, to prevent them from running away; and if ours be the same Reason for maiming of Words, it will certainly answer the End, for I am sure no other Nation will desire to borrow them. Some Words are hitherto but fairly split; and therefore only in their Way to Perfection; as *Incog.* and *Plenipo's*: But in a short Time, it is to be hoped, they will be further docked to *Inc* and *Plen.* This Reflection has made me, of late Years, very impatient for a Peace; which I believe would save the Lives of many brave Words, as well as Men. The War hath introduced abundance of Polysyllables, which will never be able to live many more Campaigns. *Speculations, Operations, Preliminaries, Ambassadors, Pallisadoes, Communication, Circumvallation, Battallions,* as numerous as they are, if they attack us too frequently in our Coffee-houses, we shall certainly put them to Flight, and cut off the Rear.

THE third Refinement observeable in the Letter I send you, consisteth in the Choice of certain Words invented by some *pretty Fellows,* such as *Banter, Bamboozle, Country Put,* and *Kidney,* as it is there applied; some of which are now struggling for the Vogue, and others are in Possession of it. I have done my utmost for some Years past, to stop the Progress of *Mob* and *Banter;* but have been plainly born down by Numbers, and betrayed by those who promised to assist me.

IN the last Place, you are to take Notice of certain choice Phrases scattered through the Letter; some of them tolerable enough, till they were worn to Rags by servile Imitators. You might easily find them, although they were not in a different Print; and therefore I need not disturb them.

THESE are the false Refinements in our Style, which you ought to correct: First, by Arguments and fair Means; but if those fail, I think you are to make Use of your Authority as Censor, and by an annual *Index Expurgatorius*, expunge all Words and Phrases that are offensive to good Sense, and condemn those barbarous Mutilations of Vowels and Syllables. In this last Point, the usual Pretence is, that they spell as they speak: A noble Standard for Language! To depend upon the Caprice of every Coxcomb; who, because Words are the Cloathing of our Thoughts, cuts them out, and shapes them as he pleases, and changes them oftner than his Dress. I believe, all reasonable People would be content, that such Refiners were more sparing of their Words, and liberal in their Syllables. On this Head, I should be glad you would bestow some Advice upon several young Readers in our Churches; who coming up from the University, full fraught with Admiration of our Town Politeness, will needs correct the Style of their Prayer-Books. In reading the Absolution, they are very careful to say *Pardons* and *Absolves*; and in the Prayer for the Royal Family, it must be *endue'm, enrich'um, prosper'um,* and *bring'um*. Then, in their Sermons they use all the modern Terms of Art; *Sham, Banter, Mob, Bubble, Bully, Cutting, Shuffling,* and *Palming*: All which, and many more of the like Stamp, as I have heard them often in the Pulpit from some young Sophisters; so I have read them in some of *those Sermons that have made a great Noise of late.* The Design, it seems, is to avoid the dreadful Imputation of Pedantry; to shew us, that they *know the Town, understand Men and Manners,* and have not been poring upon old unfashionable Books in the University.

I SHOULD be glad to see you the Instrument of introducing into our Style, that Simplicity which is the best and truest Ornament of most Things in human Life, which the politer Ages always aimed at in their Building and Dress, (*Simplex munditiis*) as well as their Productions of Wit. It is manifest, that all new affected Modes of Speech, whether borrowed from the Court, the Town, or the Theatre, are the first perishing Parts in any Language; and, as I could prove by many Hundred Instances, have been so in ours. The Writings of *Hooker,* who was a Country Clergyman, and of *Parsons* the Jesuit, both in the Reign of Queen *Elizabeth;* are in a Style that, with very few Allowances, would not offend any present Reader; much more clear and intelligible than those of Sir *H. Wooton, Sir Robert Naunton, Osborn, Daniel* the Historian, and several others who writ later; but being Men of the Court, and affecting the Phrases then in Fashion; they are often either not to be understood, or appear perfectly ridiculous.

WHAT Remedies are to be applied to these Evils, I have not

Room to consider; having, I fear, already taken up most of your Paper. Besides, I think it is our Office only to represent Abuses, and yours to redress them. I am, with great Respect,

S I R,

Yours, &c.

The Examiner

NO. 14. THURSDAY, NOVEMBER 9, 1710

E quibus hi vacuas implent Sermonibus aures,
Hi narrata ferunt alio: mensuraque ficti
*   Crescit, & auditis aliquid novus adjicit autor,*
Illic Credulitas, illic temerarius Error,
Vanaque Lætitia est, consternatique Timores,
Seditioque recens, dubioque autore susurri.[1]

I A M prevailed on, through the Importunity of Friends, to inter-rupt the Scheme I had begun in my last Paper, by an Essay upon the Art of *Political Lying.* We are told, *The Devil is the Father of Lyes,* and *was a Lyar from the beginning;* so that, beyond Contra-diction, the Invention is old: And, which is more, his first Essay of it was purely *Political,* employed in undermining the Authority of his Prince, and seducing a third Part of the Subjects from their Obedience. For which he was driven down from Heaven, where (as *Milton* expresseth it) he had been VICEROY of a great *Western Province;* and forced to exercise his Talent in inferior Regions among *other fallen Spirits,* or *poor deluded Men,* whom he still daily tempts to *his own Sin,* and will ever do so till he be *chained in the bottomless Pit.*

B U T although the Devil be the Father of *Lyes,* he seems, like other great Inventors, to have lost much of his Reputation, by the continual Improvements that have been made upon him.

W H O first reduced *Lying* into an Art, and adapted it to *Poli-ticks,* is not so clear from History; although I have made some dili-gent Enquiries: I shall therefore consider it only according to the modern System, as it hath been cultivated these twenty Years past in the Southern Part of our own Island.

T H E Poets tell us, That after the Giants were overthrown by the Gods, the *Earth* in revenge produced her last Offspring, which was *Fame.* And the Fable is thus interpreted; That when Tumults

---

1. "Some of these fill their idle ears with conversations; others spread what is told; the story grows, and each new teller adds to what he has heard. Here is Credulity; here heedless Error, vain Joy and confounded Fear, quick Sedition and Whisperings of dubious authority." Ovid, *Metamorphoses,* XII, 56–61.

and Seditions are quieted, Rumours and false Reports are plentifully spread through a Nation. So that by this Account, *Lying* is the
last Relief of a *routed, earth-born, rebellious Party* in a State.
But here, the Moderns have made great Additions, applying this Art to
the gaining of Power, and preserving it, as well as revenging themselves after they have lost it: As the same Instruments are made use
of by Animals to feed themselves when they are hungry, and bite
those that tread upon them.

B U T the same Genealogy cannot always be admitted for *Political Lying*; I shall therefore desire to refine upon it, by adding some
Circumstances of its Birth and Parents. A *Political Lye* is sometimes born out of a discarded Statesman's Head, and thence delivered to be nursed and dandled by the *Mob*. Sometimes it is produced a Monster, and *licked* into Shape; at other Times it comes
into the World compleatly formed, and is spoiled in the *licking*. It
is often born an Infant in the regular Way, and requires Time to
mature it: And often it sees the Light in its full Growth, but dwin-
dles away by Degrees. Sometimes it is of noble Birth; and sometimes the Spawn of a *Stock-jobber. Here,* it screams aloud at opening the Womb; and *there*, it is delivered with a *Whisper*. I know a
Lye that now disturbs half the Kingdom with its Noise, which
although too proud and great at present to own its Parents, I can
remember in its *Whisper-hood*. To conclude the Nativity of this
Monster; when it comes into the World without a *Sting*, it is still-
born; and whenever it loses its *Sting*, it dies.

NO Wonder, if an Infant so miraculous in its Birth, should be
destined for great Adventures: And accordingly we see it hath been
the *Guardian Spirit* of a *prevailing Party* for almost twenty Years. It
can conquer Kingdoms without Fighting, and sometimes with the
Loss of a Battle: It gives and resumes Employments; can sink
a Mountain to a Mole hill, and raise a Mole-hill to a Mountain;
hath presided for many Years at Committees of Elections; can wash
a *Black-a-moor* white; make a Saint of an Atheist, and a Patriot of a
Profligate; can furnish *Foreign Ministers* with Intelligence; and raise
or let fall the Credit of the Nation. This Goddess flies with a huge
Looking-glass in her Hands to dazzle the Crowd, and make them
see, according as she turns it, their Ruin in their Interest, and their
Interest in their Ruin. In this Glass you will behold your best
Friends clad in Coats powdered with *Flower-de-Luce's* and *Triple
Crowns;* their Girdles hung round with *Chains*, and *Beads*, and
Wooden Shoes: And your worst Enemies adorned with the Ensigns
of *Liberty, Property, Indulgence, Moderation,* and a *Cornucopia* in
their Hands. Her large Wings, like those of a flying Fish, are of no
Use but while they are moist; she therefore dips them in *Mud*, and

soaring aloft scatters it in the Eyes of the Multitude, flying with great Swiftness; but at every Turn is forced to stoop in *dirty Ways* for new Supplies.

I H A V E been sometimes thinking, if a Man had the Art of the *Second Sight* for seeing *Lyes*, as they have in *Scotland* for seeing Spirits; how admirably he might entertain himself in this Town; to observe the different Shapes, Sizes and Colours, of those Swarms of *Lyes* which buz about the Heads of *some People*, like Flies about a Horse's Ears in Summer: Or those Legions hovering every Afternoon in *Exchange-Alley*, enough to darken the Air; or over a Club of discontented Grandees, and thence sent down in Cargoes to be scattered at Elections.

T H E R E is one essential Point wherein a *Political Lyar* differs from others of the Faculty; That he ought to have but a short Memory, which is necessary according to the various Occasions he meets with every Hour, of differing from himself, and swearing to both Sides of a Contradiction, as he finds the Persons disposed, with whom he hath to deal. In describing the Virtues and Vices of Mankind, it is convenient, upon every Article, to have some eminent Person in our Eye, from whence we copy our Description. I have strictly observed this Rule; and my Imagination this Minute represents before me a certain * *Great Man* famous for this Talent, to the constant Practice of which he owes his twenty Years Reputation of the most skilful Head in *England*, for the Management of nice Affairs. The Superiority of his Genius consists in nothing else but an inexhaustible Fund of *Political Lyes*, which he plentifully distributes every Minute he speaks, and by an unparallelled Generosity forgets, and consequently contradicts the next half Hour. He never yet considered whether any Proposition were True or False, but whether it were convenient for the present Minute or Company to affirm or deny it; so that if you think to refine upon him, by interpreting every Thing he says, as we do Dreams by the contrary, you are still to seek, and will find your self equally deceived, whether you believe or no: The only Remedy is to suppose that you have heard some inarticulate Sounds, without any Meaning at all. And besides, that will take off the Horror you might be apt to conceive at the Oaths wherewith he perpetually Tags both ends of every *Proposition:* Although at the same Time, I think, he cannot with any Justice be taxed for Perjury, when he invokes *God* and *Christ*; because he hath often fairly given publick Notice to the World, that he believes in neither.

S O M E People may think that such an Accomplishment as this, can be of no great Use to the Owner or his Party, after it hath been

* *The late Earl of* Wharton.

often practised, and is become notorious; but they are widely mistaken: Few *Lyes* carry the Inventor's Mark; and the most prostitute Enemy to Truth may spread a thousand without being known for the Author. Besides, as the vilest Writer hath his Readers, so the greatest *Lyar* hath his Believers; and it often happens, that if a *Lye* be believed only for an Hour, it hath done its Work, and there is no farther Occasion for it. *Falshood flies*, and *Truth* comes *limping* after it; so that when Men come to be undeceived, it is too late, the Jest is over, and the Tale has had its Effect: Like a Man who has thought of a good Repartee, when the Discourse is changed, or the Company parted: Or, like a Physician who hath found out an infallible Medicine after the Patient is dead.

CONSIDERING that natural Disposition in many Men to *Lye*, and in Multitudes to *Believe*; I have been perplexed what to do with that Maxim, so frequent in every Bodies Mouth, That *Truth will at last prevail*. Here, has this Island of ours, for the greatest Part of twenty Years lain under the Influence of such Counsels and Persons, whose Principle and Interest it was to corrupt our Manners, blind our Understandings, drain our Wealth, and in Time destroy our Constitution both in Church and State; and we at last were brought to the very Brink of Ruin; yet by the Means of perpetual Misrepresentations, have never been able to distinguish between our Enemies and Friends. We have seen a great Part of the Nation's Money got into the Hands of those, who by their Birth, Education and Merit, could pretend no higher than to wear our Liveries. While others, who by their Credit, Quality and Fortune, were only able to give Reputation and Success to the Revolution, were not only laid aside, as dangerous and useless; but loaden with the Scandal of *Jacobites*, Men of *Arbitrary Principles*, and *Pensioners* to *France*; while Truth, who is said to *lie in a Well*, seemed now to be buried there under a heap of Stones. But I remember it was a usual Complaint among the *Whigs*, that the Bulk of Landed-Men was not in their Interests, which some of the Wisest looked on as an ill Omen; and we saw it was with the utmost Difficulty that they could preserve a Majority, while the Court and Ministry were on their Side; till they had learned those admirable Expedients for deciding Elections, and influencing distant Boroughs, by *powerful Motives* from the City. But all this was meer Force and Constraint, however upheld by most dextrous Artifice and Management; until the People began to apprehend their *Properties*, their *Religion*, and the *Monarchy* itself in Danger; then we saw them greedily laying hold on the first Occasion to interpose. But of this mighty Change in the Dispositions of the People, I shall discourse more at large in some following Paper; wherein I shall endeavour to undeceive or discover those deluded or deluding Persons, who hope or pretend, it is only a short Madness in the Vulgar, from which they may soon recover. Whereas, I believe, it will appear, to be very different in its Causes, its Symptoms, and its Consequences; and prove a great Example to illustrate the Maxim I lately mentioned, That *Truth* (however sometimes late) *will at last prevail.*

The Tatler[1]

Number 5

—— *Laceratque, trahitque*
Molle pecus. ——   Vir.[2]

FROM TUESDAY JAN. 23, TO SATURDAY JAN. 27, 1711

AMONGST other Severities I have met with from some Criticks, the cruellest for an old Man is, that they will not let me be at quiet in my Bed, but pursue me to my very Dreams. I must not dream but when they please, nor upon long continued Subjects, however visionary in their own Nature; because there is a manifest Moral quite through them, which to produce as a Dream is improbable and unnatural. The Pain I might have had from this Objection, is prevented by considering they have missed another, against which I should have been at a Loss to defend my self. They might have asked me, whether the Dreams I publish can properly be called *Lucubrations*, which is the Name I have given to all my Papers, whether in Volumes or Half-sheets: So manifest a Contradiction *in Terminis*, that I wonder no Sophister ever thought of it: But the other is a Cavil. I remember when I was a Boy at School, I have often dreamed out the whole Passages of a Day; that I rode a Journey, baited, supped, went to Bed, and rose the next Morning: And I have known young Ladies who could dream a whole Contexture of Adventures in one Night, large enough to make a Novel. In Youth the Imagination is strong, not mixed with Cares, nor tinged with those Passions that most disturb and confound it; such as Avarice, Ambition, and many others. Now, as old Men are said to grow Children again, so in this Article of Dreaming, I am returned to my Childhood. My Imagination is at full Ease, without Care, Avarice

1. From Harrison's continuation of this journal.
2. "[The hungry lion] tears and snatches the delicate prey." Vergil, *Aeneid*, IX, 340–341. Swift has substituted "lacerat" ("tears") for "mandit" ("chews").

or Ambition, to clog it; by which, among many others, I have this
Advantage, of doubling the small Remainder of my Time, and
living four and twenty Hours in the Day. However, the Dream I
am now going to relate, is as wild as can well be imagined, and
adapted to please these Refiners upon Sleep, without any Moral
that I can discover.

IT happened that my Maid left on the Table in my Bed-Chamber, one of her Story-Books (as she calls them) which I took up,
and found full of strange Impertinence, fitted to her Taste and Condition; of poor Servants who came to be Ladies, and *Serving-Men of
low Degree*, who married Kings Daughters. Among other things, I
met this sage Observation; That a Lion would never hurt a true
Virgin. With this Medly of Nonsense in my Fancy I went to Bed,
and dreamed that a Friend waked me in the Morning, and proposed for Pastime to spend a few Hours in seeing the Parish Lions,
which he had not done since he came to Town; and because they
showed but once a Week, he would not miss the Opportunity. I
said I would humour him; although, to speak the Truth, I was not
fond of those cruel Spectacles; and if it were not so ancient a
Custom, founded, as I had heard, upon the wisest Maxims, I should
be apt to censure the Inhumanity of those who introduced it. All
this will be a Riddle to the waking Reader, until I discover the
Scene my Imagination had formed upon the Maxim, That a Lion
would never hurt a true Virgin. I dreamed, that by a Law of imme-
morial Time, a He-Lion was kept in every Parish at the common
Charge, and in a Place provided, adjoyning to the Church-yard:
That, before any one of the Fair Sex was married, if she affirmed
her self to be a Virgin, she must on her Wedding-Day, and in her
Wedding-Clothes, perform the Ceremony of going alone into the
Den, and stay an Hour with the Lion let loose, and kept fasting
four and twenty Hours on purpose. At a proper Height, above the
Den, were convenient Galleries for the Relations and Friends of the
young Couple, and open to all Spectators. No Maiden was forced to
offer her self to the Lion; but if she refused, it was a Disgrace to
marry her, and every one might have Liberty of calling her a
Whore. And methought it was as usual a Diversion to see the Parish-Lions, as with us to go to Play or an Opera. And it was
reckoned convenient to be near the Church, either for marrying the
Virgin if she escaped the Trial, or for burying her Bones when the
Lion had devoured the rest, as he constantly did.

TO go on therefore with the Dream: We called first (as I
remember) to see St. *Dunstan's* Lion, but we were told they did
not shew To-day: From thence we went to that of *Covent-Garden*,
which, to my great Surprize, we found as lean as a Skeleton, when I

expected quite the contrary; but the Keeper said it was no Wonder at all, because the poor Beast had not got an Ounce of Woman's Flesh since he came into the Parish. This amazed me more than the other, and I was forming to my self a mighty Veneration for the Ladies in that Quarter of the Town; when the Keeper went on, and said, he wondered the Parish would be at the Charge of maintaining a Lion for nothing. Friend, (said I) do you call it nothing, to justify the Virtue of so many Ladies, or hath your Lion lost his distinguishing Faculty? Can there be any thing more for the Honour of your Parish, than that all the Ladies married in your Church were pure Virgins? That is true, (said he) and the Doctor knows it to his Sorrow; for there hath not been a Couple married in our Church since his Worship came amongst us. The Virgins hereabouts are too wise to venture the Claws of the Lion; and because no body will marry them, have all entered into Vows of Virginity. So that in Proportion we have much the largest Nunnery in the whole Town. This Manner of Ladies entering into a Vow of *Virginity*, because they were not *Virgins*, I easily conceived; and my Dream told me, that the whole Kingdom was full of Nunneries, plentifully stocked from the same Reason.

WE went to see another Lion, where we found much Company met in the Gallery: The Keeper told us, we should see *Sport* enough, as he called it; and in a little time, we saw a young beautiful Lady put into the Den, who walked up towards the Lion with all imaginable Security in her Countenance, and looked smiling upon her Lover and Friends in the Gallery; which I thought nothing extraordinary, because it was never known that any Lion had been mistaken. But however, we were all disappointed; for the Lion lifted up his right Paw, which was the fatal Sign, and advancing forward, seized her by the Arm, and began to tear it: The poor Lady gave a terrible Shriek, and cryed out, *The Lion is just, I am no true Virgin!* Oh! *Sappho, Sappho.* She could say no more; for the Lion gave her the *Coup de Grace*, by a Squeeze in the Throat, and she expired at his Feet. The Keeper dragged away her Body to feed the Animal after the Company should be gone; for the Parish-Lions never used to eat in publick. After a little Pause, another Lady came on towards the Lion in the same Manner as the former: We observed the Beast smell her with great Diligence; he scratched both her Hands with lifting them to his Nose, and laying one of his Claws on her Bosom, drew Blood: However he let her go, and at the same time turned from her with a Sort of Contempt, at which she was not a little mortified, and retired with some Confusion to her Friends in the Gallery. Methought the whole Company immediately understood the Meaning of this; that the Easiness of the

Lady had suffered her to admit certain imprudent and dangerous Familiarities, bordering too much upon what is criminal; neither was it sure whether the Lover then present had not some Sharers with him in those Freedoms, of which a Lady can never be too sparing.

THIS happened to be an extraordinary Day; for a third Lady came into the Den, laughing loud, playing with her Fan, tossing her Head, and smiling round on the young Fellows in the Gallery. However, the Lion leaped on her with great Fury, and we gave her for gone; but on a sudden he let go his Hold, turned from her as if he were nauseated, then gave her a Lash with his Tail; after which she returned to the Gallery, not the least out of Countenance: And this, it seems, was the usual Treatment of Coquets.

I THOUGHT we had now seen enough; but my Friend would needs have us go and visit one or two Lions in the City. We called at two or three Dens where they happened not to shew; but we generally found half a Score young Girls, between Eight and Eleven Years old, playing with each Lion, sitting on his Back, and putting their Hands into his Mouth; some of them would now and then get a Scratch, but we always discovered, upon examining, that they had been hoydening with the young Apprentices. One of them was calling to a pretty Girl about twelve Years old, who stood by us in the Gallery, to come down to the Lion, and upon her Refusal, said, *Ah, Miss Betty, we could never get you to come near the Lion, since you played at Hoop and Hide with my Brother in the Garret.*

WE followed a Couple, with the Wedding Folks, going to the Church of St. *Mary Ax.* The Lady although well stricken in Years, extremely crooked and deformed, was dressed out beyond the Gaiety of Fifteen; having jumbled together, as I imagined, all the tawdry Remains of Aunts, Godmothers, and Grandmothers, for some Generations past: One of the Neighbours whispered me, that she was an old Maid, and had the clearest Reputation of any in the Parish. There is nothing strange in that, thought I, but was much surprized, when I observed afterwards that she went towards the Lion with Distrust and Concern. The Beast was lying down; but upon Sight of her, snuffed up his Nose two or three Times, and then giving the Sign of Death, proceeded instantly to Execution. In the Midst of her Agonies, she was heard to name the Words, *Italy* and *Artifices,* with the utmost Horror, and several repeated Execrations: And at last concluded, *Fool that I was, to put so much Confidence in the Toughness of my Skin.*

THE Keeper immediately set all in Order again for another Customer, which happened to be a famous Prude, whom her Parents after long Threatnings, and much Persuasion, had with the extremest Difficulty prevailed on to accept a young handsome Gold-smith, who might have pretended to five times her Fortune. The Fathers and Mothers in the Neighbourhood used to quote her for an Example to their Daughters. Her Elbows were rivitted to her Sides; and her whole Person so ordered as to inform every Body that she was afraid they should touch her. She only dreaded to approach the Lion, because it was a He One, and abhorred to think a Male Animal should presume to breathe on her. The Sight of a Man at twenty Yards Distance made her draw back her Head. She always sat upon the farther Corner of the Chair, although there were six Chairs between her and her Lover, and with the Door wide open, and her little Sister in the Room. She was never saluted but at the Tip of her Ear; and her Father had much ado to make her dine without her Gloves, when there was a Man at Table. She entered the Den with some Fear, which we took to proceed from the Height of her Modesty, offended at the Sight of so many Men in the Gallery. The Lion beholding her at a Distance, immediately gave the deadly Sign; at which the poor Creature (methinks I see her still) miscarried in a Fright before us all. The Lion seemed to be surprized as much as we, and gave her time to make her Confes-sion; *That she was five Months gone, by the Foreman of her Fath-er's Shop; that this was her third big Belly*; and when her Friends asked, why she would venture the Trial? She said, *her Nurse assured her, that a Lion would never hurt a Woman with Child.* Upon this I immediately awaked, and could not help wishing, that the Deputy-Censors[3] of my late Institution were indued with the same Instinct as these Parish-Lions.

An Argument

To prove, That the Abolishing of Christianity in *England*, May, as Things now Stand, be attended with some Inconveniencies, and perhaps, not produce those many good Effects proposed thereby

WRITTEN IN THE YEAR 1708

I AM very sensible what a Weakness and Presumption it is, to reason against the general Humour and Disposition of the World. I remember it was with great Justice, and a due Regard to the Free-

3. See *Tatler*, Number 2 of Harrison's continuation (Davis, II, 255–256), in which Isaac Bickerstaff instituted offices of Rural Censors.

dom both of the Publick and the Press, forbidden upon severe Penalties to write or discourse, or lay Wagers against the *Union*,[1] even before it was confirmed by Parliament: Because that was looked upon as a Design to oppose the Current of the People; which besides the Folly of it, is a manifest Breach of the Fundamental Law, that makes this Majority of Opinion the Voice of God. In like Manner, and for the very same Reasons, it may perhaps be neither safe nor prudent to argue against the Abolishing of Christianity, at a Juncture when all Parties appear so unanimously determined upon the Point; as we cannot but allow from their Actions, their Discourses, and their Writings. However, I know not how, whether from the Affectation of Singularity, or the Perverseness of human Nature; but so it unhappily falls out, that I cannot be entirely of this Opinion. Nay, although I were sure an Order were issued out for my immediate Prosecution by the Attorney-General; I should still confess, that in the present Posture of our Affairs at home or abroad, I do not yet see the absolute Necessity of extirpating the Christian Religion from among us.

THIS perhaps may appear too great a Paradox, even for our wise and paradoxical Age to endure: Therefore I shall handle it with all Tenderness, and with the utmost Deference to that great and profound Majority, which is of another Sentiment.

AND yet the Curious may please to observe, how much the Genius of a Nation is liable to alter in half an Age: I have heard it affirmed for certain by some very old People, that the contrary Opinion was even in their Memories as much in Vogue as the other is now; and, that a Project for the Abolishing of Christianity would then have appeared as singular, and been thought as absurd, as it would be at this Time to write or discourse in its Defence.

THEREFORE I freely own, that all Appearances are against me. The System of the Gospel, after the Fate of other Systems is generally antiquated and exploded; and the Mass or Body of the common People, among whom it seems to have had its latest Credit, are now grown as much ashamed of it as their Betters: Opinions, like Fashions always descending from those of Quality to the middle Sort, and thence to the Vulgar, where at length they are dropt and vanish.

BUT here I would not be mistaken; and must therefore be so bold as to borrow a Distinction from the Writers on the other Side, when they make a Difference between nominal and real *Trinitarians*. I hope, no Reader imagines me so weak to stand up in the Defence of *real* Christianity; such as used in primitive Times (if we may believe the Authors of those Ages) to have an Influence upon

1. The Act of Union of 1707 politically uniting England and Scotland.

Mens Belief and Actions: To offer at the Restoring of that, would indeed be a wild Project; it would be to dig up Foundations; to destroy at one Blow *all* the Wit, and *half* the Learning of the Kingdom; to break the entire Frame and Constitution of Things; to ruin Trade, extinguish Arts and Sciences with the Professors of them; in short, to turn our Courts, Exchanges and Shops into Desarts: And would be full as absurd as the Proposal of *Horace*, where he advises the *Romans*, all in a Body, to leave their City, and seek a new Seat in some remote Part of the World, by Way of Cure for the Corruption of their Manners.[2]

THEREFORE, I think this Caution was in it self altogether unnecessary, (which I have inserted only to prevent all Possibility of cavilling) since every candid Reader will easily understand my Discourse to be intended only in Defence of *nominal* Christianity; the other having been for some Time wholly laid aside by general Consent, as utterly inconsistent with our present Schemes of Wealth and Power.

BUT why we should therefore cast off the Name and Title of Christians, although the general Opinion and Resolution be so violent for it; I confess I cannot (with Submission) apprehend the Consequence necessary. However, since the Undertakers propose such wonderful Advantages to the Nation by this Project; and advance many plausible Objections against the System of Christianity; I shall briefly consider the Strength of both; fairly allow them their greatest Weight, and offer such Answers as I think most reasonable. After which I will beg leave to shew what Inconveniencies may possibly happen by such an Innovation, in the present Posture of our Affairs.

FIRST, ONE great Advantage proposed by the Abolishing of Christianity is, That it would very much enlarge and establish Liberty of Conscience, that great Bulwark of our Nation, and of the *Protestant* Religion, which is still too much limited by *Priest-Craft*, notwithstanding all the good Intentions of the Legislature; as we have lately found by a severe Instance. For it is confidently reported, that two young Gentlemen soldiers of great Hopes, bright Wit, and profound Judgment, who upon a thorough Examination of Causes and Effects, and by the meer Force of natural Abilities, without the least Tincture of Learning; having made a Discovery, that there was no God, and generously communicating their Thoughts for the Good of the Publick; were some Time ago, by an unparalleled Severity, and upon I know not what *obsolete* Law, broke *only* for *Blasphemy*. And as it hath been wisely observed; if

2. Horace, *Epodes*, XVI.

Persecution once begins, no Man alive knows how far it may reach, or where it will end.

IN Answer to all which, with Deference to wiser Judgments; I think this rather shews the Necessity of a *nominal* Religion among us. Great Wits love to be free with the highest Objects; and if they cannot be allowed a God to revile or renounce; they will *speak Evil of Dignities*, abuse the Government, and reflect upon the Ministry; which I am sure, few will deny to be of much more pernicious Consequence; according to the Saying of *Tiberius; Deorum offensa Diis curæ.*[3] As to the particular Fact related, I think it is not fair to argue from one Instance; perhaps another cannot be produced; yet (to the Comfort of all those, who may be apprehensive of Persecution; Blasphemy we know is freely spoke a Million of Times in every Coffee-House and Tavern, or where-ever else *good Company* meet. It must be allowed indeed, that to break an *English Freeborn* Officer only for Blasphemy, was, to speak the gentlest of such an Action, a very high Strain of absolute Power. Little can be said in Excuse for the General; perhaps he was afraid it might give Offence to the Allies, among whom, for ought I know, it may be the Custom of the Country to believe a God. But if he argued, as some have done, upon a mistaken Principle, that an Officer who is guilty of speaking Blasphemy, may, some Time or other, proceed so far as to raise a Mutiny; the Consequence is, by no Means, to be admitted: For, surely the Commander of an *English* Army is like to be but ill obeyed, whose Soldiers fear and reverence him as little as they do a Deity.

IT is further objected against the Gospel System, that it obliges Men to the Belief of Things too difficult for Free-Thinkers, and such who have shaken off the Prejudices that usually cling to a confined Education. To which I answer, that Men should be cautious how they raise Objections, which reflect upon the Wisdom of the Nation. Is not every Body freely allowed to believe whatever he pleaseth; and to publish his Belief to the World whenever he thinks fit; especially if it serve to strengthen the Party which is in the Right? Would any indifferent Foreigner, who should read the Trumpery lately written by *Asgill, Tindall, Toland, Coward,*[4] and Forty more, imagine the Gospel to be our Rule of Faith, and confirmed by Parliaments? Does any Man either believe, or say he believes, or desire to have it thought that he says he believes one

3. "An offense to the gods is the concern of the gods." Tacitus, *Annals*, I, 73. Swift has substituted "offensa" ("an offense") for "injurias" ("insults").
4. John Asgill, Matthew Tindall, John Toland, and William Coward were writers on theology whose works threatened Christian orthodoxy. Toland wrote *Christianity not Mysterious* (1696); Tindall wrote *The Rights of the Christian Church* (1706) and *Christianity as old as the Creation* (1730).

Syllable of the Matter? And is any Man worse received upon that Score; or does he find his Want of *Nominal* Faith a Disadvantage to him, in the Pursuit of any Civil, or Military Employment? What if there be an old dormant Statute or two against him?[5] Are they not now obsolete, to a Degree, that *Empson* and *Dudley* themselves,[6] if they were now alive, would find it impossible to put them in Execution?

IT is likewise urged, that there are, by Computation, in this Kingdom, above ten Thousand Parsons; whose Revenues added to those of my Lords the Bishops, would suffice to maintain, at least, two Hundred young Gentlemen of Wit and Pleasure, and Free-thinking; Enemies to Priest-craft, narrow Principles, Pedantry, and Prejudices; who might be an Ornament to the Court and Town: And then again, so great a Number of able (bodied) Divines might be a Recruit to our Fleet and Armies. This, indeed, appears to be a Consideration of some Weight: But then, on the other Side, several Things deserve to be considered likewise: As, First, Whether it may not be thought necessary, that in certain Tracts of Country, like what we call Parishes, there should be *one* Man at least, of Abilities to read and write. Then, it seems a wrong Computation, that the Revenues of the Church throughout this Island, would be large enough to maintain two Hundred young Gentlemen, or even Half that Number, after the present refined Way of Living; that is, to allow each of them such a Rent, as, in the modern Form of Speech, would make them *easy*. But still, there is in this Project a greater Mischief behind; and we ought to beware of the Woman's Folly, who killed the Hen, that every Morning laid her a Golden Egg. For, pray, what would become of the Race of Men in the next Age, if we had nothing to trust to, besides the scrophulous consumptive Productions furnished by our Men of Wit and Pleasure; when having squandered away their Vigour, Health, and Estates; they are forced, by some disagreeable Marriage, to piece up their broken Fortunes, and entail Rottenness and Politeness on their Posterity? Now, there are ten Thousand Persons reduced by the wise Regulations of *Henry* the Eighth, to the Necessity of a low Diet, and moderate Exercise, who are the only great Restorers of our Breed; without which, the Nation would, in an Age or two, become but one great Hospital.

ANOTHER Advantage proposed by the abolishing of Christianity, is, the clear Gain of one Day in Seven, which is now entirely

5. Apparently refers to the group of statutes known as the Test Acts, enacted in 1661 and after, which required all holders of public office to profess their active membership in the Church of England.
6. Agents of Henry VII, who revived obsolete statutes of taxation and extortion; both were beheaded in the reign of Henry VIII.

lost, and consequently the Kingdom one Seventh less considerable in Trade, Business and Pleasure; beside the Loss to the Publick of so many stately Structures now in the Hands of the Clergy; which might be converted into Theatres, Exchanges, Market-houses, common Dormitories, and other publick Edifices.

I HOPE I shall be forgiven a hard Word, if I call this a perfect Cavil. I readily own there hath been an old Custom, Time out of Mind, for People to assemble in the Churches every *Sunday*, and that Shops are still frequently shut; in order, as it is conceived, to preserve the Memory of that antient Practice; but how this can prove a Hindrance to Business, or Pleasure, is hard to imagine. What if the Men of Pleasure are forced, one Day in the Week, to game at home, instead of the *Chocolate-House?* Are not the *Taverns* and *Coffee-Houses* open? Can there be a more convenient Season for taking a Dose of Physick? Are fewer Claps got upon *Sundays* than other Days? Is not that the chief Day for Traders to sum up the Accounts of the Week; and for Lawyers to prepare their Briefs? But I would fain know how it can be pretended, that the Churches are misapplied. Where are more Appointments and Rendezvouzes of Gallantry? Where more Care to appear in the foremost Box with greater Advantage of Dress? Where more Meetings for Business? Where more Bargains driven of all Sorts? And where so many Conveniences, or Incitements to sleep?

THERE is one Advantage, greater than any of the foregoing, proposed by the abolishing of Christianity; that it will utterly extinguish Parties among us, by removing those factious Distinctions of High and Low Church, of *Whig* and *Tory*, *Presbyterian* and *Church-of-England*; which are now so many grievous Clogs upon publick Proceedings, and dispose Men to prefer the gratifying themselves, or depressing their Adversaries, before the most important Interest of the State.

I CONFESS, if it were certain that so great an Advantage would redound to the Nation by this Expedient, I would submit and be silent: But, will any Man say, that if the Words *Whoring, Drinking, Cheating, Lying, Stealing*, were, by Act of Parliament, ejected out of the *English* Tongue and Dictionaries; we should all awake next Morning chaste and temperate, honest and just, and Lovers of Truth. Is this a fair Consequence? Or if the Physicians would forbid us to pronounce the Words *Pox, Gout, Rheumatism*, and *Stone*; would that Expedient serve like so many *Talismans* to destroy the Diseases themselves? Are Party and Faction rooted in Mens Hearts no deeper than Phrases borrowed from Religion; or founded upon no firmer Principles? And is our Language so poor, that we cannot find other Terms to express them? Are Envy, Pride,

Avarice and Ambition, such ill Nomenclators, that they cannot furnish Appellations for their Owners? Will not *Heydukes* and *Mamalukes, Mandarins,* and *Potshaws,* or any other Words formed at Pleasure, serve to distinguish those who are in the *Ministry* from others, who *would be in* it *if they could?* What, for Instance, is easier than to vary the Form of Speech; and instead of the Word *Church,* make it a Question in Politicks, Whether the *Monument* be in Danger? Because Religion was nearest at Hand to furnish a few convenient Phrases; is our Invention so barren, we can find no others? Suppose, for Argument Sake, that the *Tories* favoured * *Margarita,* the *Whigs* Mrs. *Tofts,* and the *Trimmers Valentini;* would not *Margaritians, Toftians,* and *Valentinians,* be very tolerable Marks of Distinction? The *Prasini* and *Veneti,* two most virulent Factions in *Italy,* began (if I remember right) by a Distinction of Colours in Ribbonds; which we might do, with as good a Grace, about the Dignity of the *Blue* and the *Green;* and would serve as properly to divide the Court, the Parliament, and the Kingdom between them, as any Terms of Art whatsoever, borrowed from Religion. Therefore, I think there is little Force in this Objection against *Christianity;* or Prospect of so great an Advantage as is proposed in the Abolishing of it.

IT is again objected, as a very absurd, ridiculous Custom, that a Set of Men should be suffered, much less employed, and hired to bawl one Day in Seven, against the Lawfulness of those Methods most in Use towards the Pursuit of Greatness, Riches, and Pleasure; which are the constant Practice of all Men alive on the other Six. But this Objection is, I think, a little unworthy so refined an Age as ours. Let us argue this Matter calmly. I appeal to the Breast of any polite Free-Thinker, whether in the Pursuit of gratifying a predominant Passion, he hath not always felt a wonderful Incitement, by reflecting it was a Thing forbidden: And therefore we see, in order to cultivate this Taste, the Wisdom of the Nation hath taken special Care, that the Ladies should be furnished with prohibited Silks, and the Men with prohibited Wine: And, indeed, it were to be wished, that some other Prohibitions were promoted, in order to improve the Pleasures of the Town; which, for want of such Expedients, begin already, as I am told, to flag and grow languid; giving way daily to cruel Inroads from the Spleen.

IT is likewise proposed, as a great Advantage to the Publick, that if we once discard the System of the Gospel, all Religion will, of Course, be banished for ever; and consequently along with it, those grievous Prejudices of Education; which, under the Names of Virtue, Conscience, Honour, Justice, and the like, are so apt to dis-

* Italian *Singers then in Vogue.*

turb the Peace of human Minds; and the Notions whereof are so hard to be eradicated by right Reason, or Free-thinking, sometimes during the whole Course of our Lives.

HERE, first, I observe how difficult it is to get rid of a Phrase, which the World is once grown fond of, although the Occasion that first produced it, be entirely taken away. For several Years past, if a Man had but an ill-favoured Nose, the Deep-Thinkers of the Age would, some way or other, contrive to impute the Cause to the Prejudice of his Education. From this Fountain are said to be derived all our foolish Notions of Justice, Piety, Love of our Country; all our Opinions of God, or a future State, Heaven, Hell, and the like: And there might formerly, perhaps, have been some Pretence for this Charge. But so effectual Care hath been since taken, to remove those Prejudices by an entire Change in the Methods of Education; that (with Honour I mention it to our polite Innovators) the young Gentlemen, who are now on the Scene, seem to have not the least Tincture left of those Infusions, or String of those Weeds; and, by Consequence, the Reason for abolishing *Nominal* Christianity upon that Pretext, is wholly ceased.

FOR the rest, it may perhaps admit a Controversy, whether the Banishing all Notions of Religion whatsoever, would be convenient for the Vulgar. Not that I am in the least of Opinion with those, who hold Religion to have been the Invention of Politicians, to keep the lower Part of the World in Awe, by the Fear of invisible Powers; unless Mankind were then very different from what it is now: For I look upon the Mass, or Body of our People here in *England*, to be as Free-Thinkers, that is to say, as stanch Unbelievers, as any of the highest Rank. But I conceive some scattered Notions about a superior Power to be of singular Use for the common People, as furnishing excellent Materials to keep Children quiet, when they grow peevish; and providing Topicks of Amusement in a tedious Winter Night.

LASTLY, It is proposed as a singular Advantage, that the Abolishing of Christianity, will very much contribute to the uniting of *Protestants*, by enlarging the Terms of Communion, so as to take in all Sorts of *Dissenters*; who are now shut out of the Pale upon Account of a few Ceremonies, which all Sides confess to be Things indifferent: That this alone will effectually answer the great Ends of a Scheme for Comprehension, by opening a large noble Gate, at which all Bodies may enter; whereas the chaffering with *Dissenters*, and dodging about this or the other Ceremony, is but like opening a few Wickets, and leaving them at jar, by which no more than one can get in at a Time, and that not without stooping and sideling, and squeezing his Body.

TO all this I answer, That there is one darling Inclination of Mankind, which usually affects to be a Retainer to Religion, although she be neither its Parent, its Godmother, or its Friend; I mean the Spirit of Opposition, that lived long before Christianity, and can easily subsist without it. Let us, for Instance, examine wherein the Opposition of Sectaries among us consists; we shall find Christianity to have no Share in it at all. Does the Gospel any where prescribe a starched squeezed Countenance, a stiff formal Gait, a Singularity of Manners and Habit, or any affected Modes of Speech, different from the reasonable Part of Mankind? Yet, if Christianity did not lend its Name, to stand in the Gap, and to employ or divert these Humours, they must of Necessity be spent in Contraventions to the Laws of the Land, and Disturbance of the publick Peace. There is a Portion of Enthusiasm assigned to every Nation, which if it hath not proper Objects to work on, will burst out, and set all in a Flame. If the Quiet of a State can be bought by only flinging Men a few Ceremonies to devour, it is a Purchase no wise Man would refuse. Let the Mastiffs amuse themselves about a Sheep-skin stuffed with Hay, provided it will keep them from worrying the Flock. The Institution of Convents abroad, seems in one Point a Strain of great Wisdom; there being few Irregularities in human Passions, that may not have recourse to vent themselves in some of those Orders; which are so many Retreats for the Speculative, the Melancholy, the Proud, the Silent, the Politick and the Morose, to spend themselves, and evaporate the noxious Particles; for each of whom, we in this Island are forced to provide a several Sect of Religion, to keep them quiet. And whenever Christianity shall be abolished, the Legislature must find some other Expedient to employ and entertain them. For what imports it, how large a Gate you open, if there will be always left a Number, who place a Pride and a Merit in refusing to enter?

HAVING thus considered the most important Objections against Christianity, and the chief Advantages proposed by the Abolishing thereof; I shall now with equal Deference and Submission to wiser Judgments as before, proceed to mention a few Inconveniences that may happen, if the Gospel should be repealed; which perhaps the Projectors may not have sufficiently considered.

AND first, I am very sensible how much the Gentlemen of Wit and Pleasure are apt to murmur, and be choqued at the sight of so many daggled-tail Parsons, who happen to fall in their Way, and offend their Eyes: But at the same Time these wise Reformers do not consider what an Advantage and Felicity it is, for great Wits to be always provided with Objects of Scorn and Contempt, in order to exercise and improve their Talents, and divert their Spleen from falling on each other, or on themselves; especially when all this may be done without the least imaginable *Danger to their Persons*.

AND to urge another Argument of a parallel Nature: If Christianity were once abolished, how would the Free-Thinkers, the strong Reasoners, and the Men of profound Learning be able to find another Subject so calculated in all Points whereon to display their Abilities. What wonderful Productions of Wit should we be deprived of, from those whose Genius, by continual Practice hath been wholly turned upon Raillery and Invectives against Religion; and would therefore never be able to shine or distinguish themselves upon any other Subject. We are daily complaining of the great Decline of Wit among us; and would we take away the greatest, perhaps the only Topick we have left? Who would ever have suspected *Asgill* for a Wit, or *Toland* for a Philosopher, if the inexhaustible Stock of Christianity had not been at hand to provide them with Materials? What other Subject through all Art or Nature could have produced *Tindal* for a profound Author, or furnished him with Readers? It is the wise Choice of the Subject that alone adorns and distinguishes the Writer. For had an hundred such Pens as these been employed on the Side of Religion, they would have immediately sunk into Silence and Oblivion.

NOR do I think it wholly groundless, or my Fears altogether imaginary; that the Abolishing of Christianity may perhaps bring the Church in Danger; or at least put the Senate to the Trouble of another Securing Vote. I desire, I may not be mistaken; I am far from presuming to affirm or think, that the Church is in Danger at present, or as Things now stand; but we know not how soon it may be so, when the Christian Religion is repealed. As plausible as this Project seems, there may a dangerous Design lurk under it. Nothing can be more notorious, than that the *Atheists, Deists, Socinians, Anti-Trinitarians*, and other Subdivisions of Free-Thinkers, are Persons of little Zeal for the present Ecclesiastical Establishment: Their declared Opinion is for repealing the Sacramental Test;[7] they are very indifferent with regard to Ceremonies; nor do they hold the *Jus Divinum* of Episcopacy. Therefore this may be intended as one politick Step towards altering the Constitution of the Church Established, and setting up *Presbytery* in the stead; which I leave to be further considered by those at the Helm.

IN the last Place, I think nothing can be more plain, than that by this Expedient, we shall run into the Evil we chiefly pretend to avoid; and that the Abolishment of the Christian Religion, will be the readiest Course we can take to introduce Popery. And I am the

7. The Test Acts required, among other things, that a public officer receive the sacrament of the Lord's Supper according to the rites of the Church of England.

more inclined to this Opinion, because we know it hath been the constant Practice of the *Jesuits* to send over Emissaries, with Instructions to personate themselves Members of the several prevailing Sects amongst us. So it is recorded, that they have at sundry Times appeared in the Guise of *Presbyterians, Anabaptists, Independents,* and *Quakers,* according as any of these were most in Credit: So, since the Fashion hath been taken up of exploding Religion, the *Popish* Missionaries have not been wanting to mix with the Free-Thinkers; among whom, *Toland,* the great Oracle of the *Anti-Christians,* is an *Irish* Priest, the Son of an *Irish* Priest; and the most learned and ingenious Author[8] of a Book, called the *Rights of the Christian Church,* was, in a proper Juncture, reconciled to the *Romish* Faith; whose true Son, as appears by an Hundred Passages in his Treatise, he still continues. Perhaps I could add some others to the Number; but the Fact is beyond Dispute; and the Reasoning they proceed by, is right: For, supposing Christianity to be extinguished, the People will never be at Ease, till they find out some other Method of Worship; which will as infallibly produce Superstition, as this will end in *Popery.*

AND therefore, if, notwithstanding all I have said, it shall still be thought necessary to have a Bill brought in for repealing Christianity; I would humbly offer an Amendment, that instead of the Word *Christianity,* may be put *Religion* in general; which I conceive, will much better answer all the good Ends proposed by the Projectors of it. For, as long as we leave in Being a God, and his Providence, with all the necessary Consequences, which curious and inquisitive Men will be apt to draw from such Premises; we do not strike at the Root of the Evil, although we should ever so effectually annihilate the present Scheme of the Gospel. For, of what Use is Freedom of Thought, if it will not produce Freedom of Action; which is the sole End, how remote soever, in Appearance, of all Objections against Christianity? And therefore, the Free-Thinkers consider it as a Sort of Edifice, wherein all the Parts have such a mutual Dependance on each other, that if you happen to pull out one single Nail, the whole Fabrick must fall to the Ground. This was happily expressed by him, who had heard of a Text brought for Proof of the Trinity, which in an antient Manuscript was differently read; he thereupon immediately took the Hint, and by a sudden Deduction of a long *Sorites,* most logically concluded; Why, if it be as you say, I may safely whore and drink on, and defy the Parson. From which, and many the like Instances easy to be produced, I think nothing can be more manifest, than that the Quarrel is not against any particular Points of hard Digestion in the Christian System; but

8. Matthew Tindall.

against Religion in general; which, by laying Restraints on human Nature, is supposed the great Enemy to the Freedom of Thought and Action.

UPON the whole; if it shall still be thought for the Benefit of Church and State, that Christianity be abolished; I conceive, however, it may be more convenient to defer the Execution to a Time of Peace; and not venture in this Conjuncture to disoblige our Allies; who, as it falls out, are all Christians; and many of them, by the Prejudices of their Education, so bigotted, as to place a Sort of Pride in the Appellation. If, upon being rejected by them, we are to trust to an Alliance with the *Turk*, we shall find our selves much deceived: For, as he is too remote, and generally engaged in War with the *Persian* Emperor; so his People would be more scandalized at our Infidelity, than our Christian Neighbours. Because, the *Turks* are not only strict Observers of religious Worship; but, what is worse, believe a God; which is more than is required of us, even while we preserve the Name of Christians.

TO conclude: Whatever some may think of the great Advantages to Trade, by this favourite Scheme; I do very much apprehend, that in six Months Time, after the Act is past for the Extirpation of the Gospel, the Bank and *East-India* Stock may fall, at least, One *per Cent*. And, since that is Fifty Times more than ever the Wisdom of our Age thought fit to venture for the *Preservation* of Christianity, there is no Reason we should be at so great a Loss, meerly for the Sake of *destroying* it.

A Letter to a Young Gentleman,

Lately entered into Holy Orders[1]

By a Person of QUALITY[2]

January 9, 1720.

SIR,

ALTHOUGH it were against my Knowledge, or Advice, that you entered into Holy Orders, under the present Dispositions of Man-

---

1. The title page of the Dublin edition of 1720 reads "Designing for Holy Orders."
2. This essay was represented on the title page of the 1720 edition as "A Letter from a Lay-Patron" and was hence, like Swift's other separate essays, anonymous. However, the title page of the London edition of 1721 contained the following note: "It is certainly known, that the following Treatise was writ in Ireland by the Reverend Dr. Swift, Dean of St. Patrick's in that Kingdom." The initials at the end of this epistle appear in the editions of 1720 and 1721 but were cut from that of 1735.

kind towards the *Church*; yet, since it is now supposed too late to recede, (at least according to the general Practice and Opinion,) I cannot forbear offering my Thoughts to you upon this new Condition of Life you are engaged in.

I COULD heartily wish that the Circumstances of your Fortune had enabled you to have continued some Years longer in the University, at least, until you were ten Years standing; to have laid in a competent Stock of human Learning, and some Knowledge in Divinity, before you attempted to appear in the World: For I cannot but lament the common Course, which at least Nine in Ten of those, who enter into the Ministry, are obliged to run. When they have taken a Degree, and are consequently grown a Burden to their Friends, who now think themselves fully discharged; they get into Orders as soon as they can, (upon which I shall make no Remarks,) first sollicit a Readership, and if they be very fortunate, arrive in Time to a Curacy here in Town; or else are sent to be Assistants in the Country, where they probably continue several Years (many of them their whole Lives) with thirty or forty Pounds a Year for their Support, until some Bishop, who happens to be not over-stocked with Relations, or attached to Favourites, or is content to supply his Diocese without Colonies from *England*, bestows them some inconsiderable Benefice; when it is odds they are already encumbered with a numerous Family. I would be glad to know what Intervals of Life such Persons can possibly set apart for Improvement of their Minds; or which Way they could be furnished with Books; the Library they brought with them from their College being usually not the most numerous, or judiciously chosen. If such Gentlemen arrive to be great Scholars, it must, I think, be either by Means supernatural, or by a Method altogether out of any Road yet known to the Learned. But I conceive the Fact directly otherwise; and that many of them lose the greatest Part of the small Pittance they received at the University.

I TAKE it for granted, that you intend to pursue the beaten Track, and are already desirous to be seen in a Pulpit; only I hope you will think it proper to pass your Quarentine among some of the desolate Churches five Miles round this Town, where you may at least learn to *read* and to *speak*, before you venture to expose your Parts in a City-Congregation: Not that these are better Judges, but because if a Man must needs expose his Folly, it is more safe and discreet to do so, before few Witnesses, and in a scattered Neighbourhood. And you will do well, if you can prevail upon some intimate and judicious Friend to be your constant Hearer, and allow him with the utmost Freedom to give you Notice of whatever he shall find amiss either in your Voice or Gesture; for want of which early Warning, many Clergymen continue defective, and sometimes ridiculous, to the End of their Lives: Neither is it rare to observe among excellent and learned Divines, a certain ungracious Manner, or an unhappy Tone of Voice, which they never have been able to shake off.

I COULD likewise have been glad, if you had applied your self a little more to the Study of the *English* Language, than I fear you have done; the Neglect whereof is one of the most general Defects among the Scholars of this Kingdom, who seem to have not the least Conception of a Stile, but run on in a flat Kind of Phraseology, often mingled with barbarous Terms and Expressions, peculiar to the Nation: Neither do I perceive that any Person either finds or acknowledges his Wants upon this Head, or in the least desires to have them supplyed. Proper Words in proper Places, makes the true Definition of a Stile: But this would require too ample a Disquisition to be now dwelt on. However, I shall venture to name one or two Faults, which are easy to be remedied with a very small Portion of Abilities.

THE first, is the frequent Use of obscure Terms, which by the Women are called *hard Words*, and by the better Sort of Vulgar, *fine Language*; than which I do not know a more universal, inexcusable, and unnecessary Mistake among the Clergy of all Distinctions, but especially the younger Practitioners. I have been curious enough to take a List of several hundred Words in a Sermon of a new Beginner, which not one of his Hearers among a Hundred, could possibly understand: Neither can I easily call to Mind any Clergyman of my own Acquaintance who is wholly exempt from this Error; although many of them agree with me in the Dislike of the Thing. But I am apt to put my self in the Place of the Vulgar, and think many Words difficult or obscure, which the Preacher will not allow to be so, because those Words are obvious to Schollars. I believe the Method observed by the famous Lord *Falkland*, in some of his Writings, would not be an ill one for young Divines: I was assured by an old Person of Quality, who knew him well; that when he doubted whether a Word were perfectly intelligible or no, he used to consult one of his Lady's Chambermaids, (not the Waiting-woman, because it was possible she might be conversant in Romances,) and by her Judgment was guided, whether to receive or reject it. And if that great Person thought such a Caution necessary in Treatises offered to the learned World; it will be sure at least as proper in Sermons, where the meanest Hearer is supposed to be concerned; and where very often a Lady's Chambermaid may be allowed to equal half the Congregation, both as to Quality and Understanding. But I know not how it comes to pass, that Profes-

sors in most Arts and Sciences are generally the worst qualified to
explain their Meanings to those who are not of their Tribe: A
common Farmer shall make you understand in three Words, *that
his Foot is out of Joint, or his Collar-bone broken;* wherein a *Surgeon,* after a hundred Terms of Art, if you are not a Scholar, shall
leave you to seek. It is frequently the same Case in Law, Physick,
and even many of the meaner Arts.

AND upon this Account it is, that among *hard Words,* I number
likewise those which are peculiar to Divinity as it is a Science;
because I have observed several Clergymen, otherwise little fond of
obscure Terms, yet in their Sermons very liberal of those which they
find in Ecclesiastical Writers, as if it were our Duty to understand
them: Which I am sure it is not. And I defy the greatest Divine, to
produce any Law either of God or Man, which obliges me to comprehend the Meaning of *Omniscience, Omnipresence, Ubiquity,
Attribute, Beatifick Vision,* with a Thousand others so frequent in
Pulpits; any more than that of *Excentrick, Idiosyncracy, Entity,* and
the like. I believe, I may venture to insist further, that many Terms
used in Holy Writ, particularly by St. *Paul,* might with more Discretion be changed into plainer Speech, except when they are introduced as part of a Quotation.

I AM the more earnest in this Matter, because it is a general
Complaint, and the justest in the World. For a Divine hath nothing to say to the wisest Congregation of any Parish in this
Kingdom, which he may not express in a Manner to be understood
by the meanest among them. And this Assertion must be true, or
else God requires from us more than we are able to perform. However, not to contend whether a Logician might possibly put a Case
that would serve for an Exception; I will appeal to any Man of
Letters, whether at least nineteen in twenty of those perplexing
Words might not be changed into easy ones, such as naturally first
occur to ordinary Men, and probably did so at first to those very
Gentlemen, who are so fond of the former.

WE are often reproved by Divines from the Pulpits, on Account
of our Ignorance in Things sacred; and perhaps with Justice
enough: However, it is not very reasonable for them to expect, that
common Men should understand Expressions, which are never
made use of in *common Life.* No Gentleman thinks it safe or prudent to send a Servant with a Message, without repeating it more
than once, and endeavouring to put it into Terms brought down to
the Capacity of the Bearer: Yet after all this Care, it is frequent for
Servants to mistake, and sometimes occasion Misunderstandings
between Friends; although the common Domestics in some Gentle-

men's Families, may have more Opportunities of improving their Minds, then the ordinary Sort of Tradesmen.

IT is usual for Clergymen who are taxed with this learned Defect, to quote Dr. *Tillotson*, and other famous Divines in their defence; without considering the Difference between elaborate Discourses upon important Occasions, delivered to Princes or Parliaments, written with a View of being made publick; and a plain Sermon intended for the Middle or lower Size of People. Neither do they seem to remember the many Alterations, Additions, and Expungings made by great Authors, in those Treatises which they prepare for the Publick. Besides, that excellent Prelate above-mentioned, was known to preach after a much more popular Manner in the City Congregations: And if in those Parts of his Works, he be any where too obscure for the Understandings of many, who may be supposed to have been his Hearers; it ought to be numbered among his Omissions.

THE Fear of being thought Pedants hath been of pernicious Consequence to young Divines. This hath wholly taken many of them off from their severer Studies in the University; which they have exchanged for Plays, Poems, and Pamphlets, in order to qualify them for Tea-Tables and Coffee-Houses. This they usually call *Polite Conversation, knowing the World,* and *reading Men instead of Books.* These Accomplishments, when applied in the Pulpit, appear by a quaint, terse, florid Style, rounded into Periods and Cadencies, commonly without either Propriety or Meaning. I have listened with my utmost Attention for half an Hour to an Orator of this Species, without being able to understand, much less to carry away one single Sentence out of a whole Sermon. Others, to shew that their Studies have not been confined to Sciences, or ancient Authors, will talk in the Style of a gaming Ordinary, and *White Friars*; where I suppose the Hearers can be little edified by the Terms of *Palming, Shuffling, Biting, Bamboozling,* and the like, if they have not been sometimes conversant among Pick-pockets and Sharpers. And truly, as they say, a Man is known by his Company; so it should seem, that a Man's Company may be known by his Manner of expressing himself, either in publick Assemblies, or private Conversation.

IT would be endless to run over the several Defects of Style among us: I shall therefore say nothing of the *mean* and the *paultry,* (which are usually attended by the *fustian,*) much less of the *slovenly* or *indecent.* Two Things I will just warn you against: The first is, the Frequency of flat, unnecessary Epithets; and the other is, the Folly of using old thread-bare Phrases, which will often make you go out of your Way to find and apply them; are nauseous to rational Hearers, and will seldom express your Meaning as well as your own natural Words.

ALTHOUGH, as I have already observed, our *English* Tongue be too little cultivated in this Kingdom; yet the Faults are nine in ten owing to Affectation, and not to the want of Understanding. When a Man's Thoughts are clear, the properest Words will generally offer themselves first; and his own Judgment will direct him in what Order to place them, so as they may be best understood. Where Men err against this Method, it is usually on Purpose, and to shew their Learning, their Oratory, their Politeness, or their Knowledge of the World. In short, that Simplicity, without which no human Performance can arrive to any great Perfection, is no where more eminently useful than in this.

I HAVE been considering that Part of Oratory, which relates to the moving of the Passions: This, I observe, is in Esteem and Practice among some Church Divines, as well as among all the Preachers and Hearers of the *Fanatick* or *Enthusiastick* Strain. I will here deliver to you (perhaps with more Freedom than Prudence) my Opinion upon the Point.

THE two great Orators of *Greece* and *Rome*, *Demosthenes* and *Cicero*, although each of them a Leader (or, as the *Greeks* called it, a *Demagogue*) in a popular State; yet seem to differ in their Practice upon this Branch of their Art: The former, who had to deal with a People of much more Politeness, Learning, and Wit, laid the greatest Weight of his Oratory upon the Strength of his Arguments offered to their Understanding and Reason: Whereas, *Tully* considered the Dispositions of a fiercer, more ignorant, and less mercurial Nation, by dwelling almost entirely on the pathetick Part.

BUT the principal Thing to be remembered is, that the constant Design of both these Orators in all their Speeches, was to drive some one particular Point; either the Condemnation, or Acquittal of an accused Person; a persuasive to War, the enforcing of a Law, and the like; which was determined upon the Spot, according as the Orators on either Side prevailed. And here it was often found of absolute Necessity to enflame, or cool the Passions of the Audience; especially at *Rome*, where *Tully* spoke, and with whose Writings young Divines (I mean those among them who read old Authors) are more conversant than with those of *Demosthenes*; who, by many Degrees, excelled the other, at least as an Orator. But I do not see how this Talent of moving the Passions, can be of any great Use towards directing Christian Men in the Conduct of their Lives, at least in these *Northern* Climates; where, I am confident, the strongest Eloquence of that Kind will leave few Impressions upon any of our Spirits, deep enough to last till the next Morning, or rather to the next Meal.

BUT what hath chiefly put me out of conceit with this moving Manner of Preaching, is the frequent Disappointment it meets with. I know a Gentleman, who made it a Rule in Reading, to skip over all Sentences where he spied a Note of Admiration at the End. I believe, those Preachers who abound in *Epiphonemas*,[3] if they look about them, would find one Part of their Congregation out of Countenance, and the other asleep; except, perhaps, an old Female Beggar or two in the Isles, who (if they be sincere) may probably groan at the Sound.

NOR is it a Wonder that this Expedient should so often miscarry, which requires so much Art and Genius to arrive at any Perfection in it; as every Man will find, much sooner than learn, by consulting *Cicero* himself.

I THEREFORE entreat you to make use of this Faculty (if you be ever so unfortunate as to think you have it) as seldom, and with as much Caution as you can; else I may probably have Occasion to say of you, as a great Person said of another upon this very Subject. A Lady asked him, coming out of Church, whether it were not a very moving Discourse? *Yes,* said he, *I was extremely sorry, for the Man is my Friend.*

IF in Company you offer something for a Jest, and no body seconds you in your own Laughter, or seems to relish what you said; you may condemn their Taste, if you please, and appeal to better Judgments; but, in the mean Time, it must be agreed you make a very indifferent Figure: And it is, at least, equally ridiculous to be disappointed in endeavouring to make other Folks grieve, as to make them laugh.

A PLAIN convincing Reason may possibly operate upon the Mind both of a learned and ignorant Hearer, as long as they live; and will edify a Thousand Times more than the Art of wetting the Handkerchiefs of a whole Congregation, if you were sure to attain it.

IF your Arguments be strong, in God's Name offer them in as moving a Manner as the Nature of the Subject will properly admit; wherein Reason, and good Advice will be your safest Guides: But beware of letting the pathetick Part swallow up the rational: For, I suppose, *Philosophers* have long agreed, that Passion should never prevail over Reason.

AS I take it, the two principal Branches of Preaching, are first to tell the People what is their Duty; and then to convince them that

3. An exclamatory or otherwise striking statement used to give climactic punctuation to a discourse or a passage in a discourse.

it is so. The Topicks for both these, we know, are brought from *Scripture* and *Reason*. Upon the former, I wish it were oftner practised to instruct the Hearers in the Limits, Extent, and Compass of every Duty, which requires a good deal of Skill and Judgment: The other Branch is, I think, not so difficult. But what I would offer upon both, is this; that it seems to be in the Power of a reasonable Clergyman, if he will be at the Pains, to make the most ignorant Man comprehend what is his Duty; and to convince him by Arguments, drawn to the Level of his Understanding, that he ought to perform it.

BUT I must remember, that my Design in this *Paper* was not so much to instruct you in your Business, either as a Clergyman, or a Preacher, as to warn you against some Mistakes, which are obvious to the Generality of Mankind, as well as to me; and we, who are Hearers, may be allowed to have some Opportunities in the Quality of being Standers-by. Only, perhaps, I may now again transgress, by desiring you to express the Heads of your Divisions in as few and clear Words, as you possibly can; otherwise, I, and many Thousand others, will never be able to retain them, nor consequently to carry away a Syllable of the Sermon.

I SHALL now mention a Particular, wherein your whole Body will be certainly against me; and the Laity, almost to a Man, on my Side. However it came about, I cannot get over the Prejudice of taking some little Offence at the Clergy, for perpetually reading their Sermons; perhaps, my frequent hearing of Foreigners, who never make use of Notes, may have added to my Disgust. And I cannot but think, that whatever is read, differs as much from what is repeated without Book, as a Copy doth from an Original. At the same Time, I am highly sensible what an extreme Difficulty it would be upon you to alter this Method; and that, in such a Case, your Sermons would be much less valuable than they are, for want of Time to improve and correct them. I would therefore gladly come to a Compromise with you in this Matter. I knew a Clergyman of some Distinction, who appeared to deliver his Sermon without looking into his Notes; which, when I complimented him upon, he assured me, he could not repeat six Lines; but his Method was to write the whole Sermon in a large plain Hand, with all the Forms of Margin, Paragraph, marked Page, and the like; then on *Sunday* Morning, he took care to run it over five or six Times, which he could do in an Hour; and when he delivered it, by pretending to turn his Face from one Side to the other, he would (in his own Expression) pick up the Lines, and cheat his People, by making them believe he had it all by Heart. He farther added, that whenever he happened, by Neglect, to omit any of these Circumstances, the Vogue of the *Parish* was, *our Doctor gave us but an indifferent Sermon to-day*. Now among us, many Clergymen act so directly contrary to this Method; that from a Habit of saving *Time* and *Paper*, which they acquired at the University, they write in so diminutive a Manner, with such frequent Blots and Interlineations, that they are hardly able to go on without perpetual Hesitations, or extemporary Expletives: And I desire to know what can be more inexcusable than to see a Divine, and a Scholar, at a Loss in reading his own Compositions; which, it is supposed, he hath been preparing with much *Pains* and *Thought*, for the Instruction of his People. The Want of a little more Care in this Article, is the Cause of much ungraceful Behaviour. You will observe some Clergymen with their Heads held down from the Beginning to the End, within an Inch of the Cushion, to read what is hardly legible; which, besides the untoward Manner, hinders them from making the best Advantage of their Voice: Others, again, have a Trick of popping up and down every Moment, from their *Paper* to the Audience, like an idle School-Boy on a Repetition-Day.

LET me entreat you therefore, to add one Half-Crown a Year to the Article of *Paper*; to transcribe your Sermons in as large and plain a Manner as you can, and either make no Interlineations, or change the whole Leaf: For we, your Hearers, would rather you should be less correct, than perpetually stammering; which I take to be one of the worst *Solecisms* in *Rhetorick*. And lastly, read your Sermon once or twice, for a few Days before you preach it: To which you will probably answer some Years hence, *That it was but just finished when the last Bell rang to Church*; and I shall readily believe, but not excuse you.

I CANNOT forbear warning you, in the most earnest Manner, against endeavouring at Wit in your Sermons: Because, by the strictest Computation, it is very near a Million to One, that you have none; and because too many of your Calling, have consequently made themselves everlastingly ridiculous by attempting it. I remember several young Men in this Town, who could never leave the *Pulpit* under half a Dozen *Conceits*; and this Faculty adhered to those Gentlemen a longer or shorter Time, exactly in Proportion to their several Degrees of Dulness: Accordingly, I am told that some of them retain it to this Day. I heartily wish the Brood were at an End.

BEFORE you enter into the common unsufferable Cant, of taking all Occasions to disparage the Heathen *Philosophers*; I hope you will differ from some of your Brethren, by first enquiring what those *Philosophers* can say for themselves. The System of Morality to be gathered out of the Writings, or Sayings of those antient

Sages, falls undoubtedly very short of that delivered in the Gospel; and wants, besides, the Divine Sanction which our Saviour gave to his. Whatever is further related by the Evangelists, contains chiefly Matters of Fact, and consequently of Faith; such as the Birth of Christ, his being the Messiah, his Miracles, his Death, Resurrection, and Ascension: None of which can properly come under the Appellation of human Wisdom, being intended only to make us wise unto Salvation. And therefore in this Point, nothing can be justly laid to the Charge of the *Philosophers*; further, than that they were ignorant of certain Facts which happened long after their Death. But I am deceived, if a better Comment could be any where collected upon the moral Part of the Gospel, than from the Writings of those excellent Men. Even that divine Precept of loving our Enemies, is at large insisted on by *Plato*; who puts it, as I remember, into the Mouth of *Socrates*. And as to the Reproach of Heathenism, I doubt they had less of it than the corrupted *Jews*, in whose Time they lived. For it is a gross Piece of Ignorance among us, to conceive, that in those polite and learned Ages, even Persons of any tolerable Education, much less the wisest Philosophers, did acknowledge, or worship any more than one Almighty Power, under several Denominations, to whom they allowed all those Attributes we ascribe to the Divinity: And, as I take it, human Comprehension reacheth no further: Neither did our Saviour think it necessary to explain to us the Nature of God; because I suppose it would be impossible, without bestowing on us other Faculties than we possess at present. But the true Misery of the Heathen World, appears to be what I before mentioned, the Want of a Divine Sanction; without which, the Dictates of the Philosophers failed in the Point of Authority; and consequently the Bulk of Mankind lay, indeed, under a great Load of Ignorance, even in the Article of Morality; but the Philosophers themselves did not. Take the Matter in this Light, and it will afford Field enough for a Divine to enlarge on; by shewing the Advantages which the Christian World hath over the Heathen; and the absolute Necessity of Divine Revelation, to make the Knowledge of the true God, and the Practice of Virtue more universal in the World.

I AM not ignorant how much I differ in this Opinion from some ancient Fathers in the Church; who arguing against the Heathens, made it a principal Topick to decry their Philosophy as much as they could: Which, I hope, is not altogether our present Case. Besides, it is to be considered, that those Fathers lived in the Decline of *Literature*; and in my Judgment, (who should be unwilling to give the least Offence,) appear to be rather most excellent holy Persons, than of transcendent Genius and Learning. Their genuine

Writings (for many of them have extreamly suffered by spurious Additions) are of admirable Use for confirming the Truth of ancient Doctrines and Discipline; by shewing the State and Practice of the primitive Church. But among such of them, as have fallen in my Way, I do not remember any, whose Manner of arguing or exhorting I could heartily recommend to the Imitation of a young Divine, when he is to speak from the Pulpit. Perhaps I judge too hastily, there being several of them, in whose Writings I have made very little Progress, and in others none at all. For I perused only such as were recommended to me, at a Time when I had more Leisure, and a better Disposition to read, than have since fallen to my Share.

TO return then to the Heathen Philosophers: I hope you will not only give them Quarter, but make their Works a considerable Part of your Study. To these I will venture to add the principal Orators and Historians, and perhaps a few of the Poets: By the reading of which, you will soon discover your Mind and Thoughts to be enlarged, your Imagination extended and refined, your Judgment directed, your Admiration lessened, and your Fortitude increased. All which Advantages must needs be of excellent Use to a Divine, whose Duty it is to preach and practise the Contempt of human Things.

I WOULD say something concerning Quotations; wherein I think you cannot be too sparing, except from Scripture, and the primitive Writers of the Church. As to the former, when you offer a Text as a Proof or an Illustration, we your Hearers expect to be fairly used; and sometimes think we have Reason to complain, especially of you younger Divines; which makes us fear, that some of you conceive you have no more to do than to turn over a Concordance, and there having found the principal Word, introduce as much of the Verse as will serve your Turn, although in Reality it makes nothing for you. I do not altogether disapprove the Manner of interweaving Texts of Scripture through the Style of your Sermon; wherein, however, I have sometimes observed great Instances of Indiscretion and Impropriety; against which I therefore venture to give you a Caution.

AS to Quotations from antient Fathers, I think they are best brought in, to confirm some Opinion controverted by those who differ from us: In other Cases we give you full Power to adopt the Sentence for your own, rather than tell us, *as St. Austin excellently observes*: But to mention modern Writers by Name, or use the Phrase of *a late excellent Prelate of our Church*, and the like, is altogether intolerable; and, for what Reason I know not, makes every rational Hearer ashamed. Of no better a Stamp is your

Heathen Philosopher, and *famous Poet*, and *Roman Historian*; at least in common Congregations, who will rather believe you on your own Word, than on that of *Plato* or *Homer*.

I HAVE lived to see *Greek* and *Latin* almost entirely driven out of the Pulpit; for which I am heartily glad. The frequent Use of the latter was certainly a Remnant of Popery, which never admitted Scripture in the vulgar Language; and I wonder that Practice was never accordingly objected to us by the Fanaticks.

THE Mention of Quotations puts me in mind of Commonplace Books, which have been long in use by industrious young Divines, and, I hear, do still continue so; I know they are very beneficial to Lawyers and Physicians, because they are Collections of Facts or Cases, whereupon a great Part of their several Faculties depend: Of these I have seen several, but never yet any written by a Clergyman; only from what I am informed, they generally are Extracts of Theological and Moral Sentences, drawn from Ecclesiastical and other Authors, reduced under proper Heads; usually begun, and perhaps, finished, while the Collectors were young in the Church; as being intended for Materials, or Nurseries to stock future Sermons. You will observe the wise Editors of ancient Authors, when they meet a Sentence worthy of being distinguished, take special Care to have the first Word printed in Capital Letters, that you may not overlook it: Such, for Example, as the *Inconstancy of Fortune, the Goodness of Peace, the Excellency of Wisdom, the Certainty of Death; that Prosperity makes Men insolent, and Adversity humble*; and the like eternal Truths, which every Plowman knows well enough, although he never heard of *Aristotle* or *Plato*. If Theological Common-Place Books be no better filled, I think they had better be laid aside: And I could wish, that Men of tolerable Intellectuals would rather trust to their own natural Reason, improved by a general Conversation with Books, to enlarge on Points which they are supposed already to understand. If a rational Man reads an excellent Author with just Application, he shall find himself extremely improved, and perhaps insensibly led to imitate that Author's Perfections; although in a little Time he should not remember one Word in the Book, nor even the Subject it handled: For, Books give the same Turn to our Thoughts and Way of Reasoning, that good and ill Company do to our Behaviour and Conversation; without either loading our Memories, or making us even sensible of the Change. And particularly, I have observed in Preaching, that no Men succeed better than those, who trust entirely to the Stock or Fund of their own Reason; advanced, indeed, but not overlaid by Commerce with Books. Whoever only reads, in order to transcribe wise and shining Remarks, without entering into the Genius and Spirit of the

Author; as it is probable he will make no very judicious Extract, so he will be apt to trust to that Collection in all his Compositions; and be misled out of the regular Way of Thinking, in order to introduce those Materials which he hath been at the Pains to gather: And the Product of all this, will be found a manifest incoherent Piece of Patchwork.

SOME Gentlemen abourding in their University Erudition, are apt to fill their Sermons with philosophical Terms, and Notions of the metaphysical or abstracted Kind; which generally have one Advantage, to be equally understood by the Wise, the Vulgar, and the Preacher himself. I have been better entertained, and more informed by a Chapter in the *Pilgrim's Progress*, than by a long Discourse upon the *Will* and the *Intellect*, and *simple* or *complex Ideas*. Others again, are fond of dilating on *Matter* and *Motion*, talk of the *fortuitous Concourse of Atoms*, of *Theories*, and *Phænomena*; directly against the Advice of St. *Paul*, who yet appears to have been conversant enough in those Kinds of Studies.

I DO not find that you are any where directed in the Canons, or Articles, to attempt explaining the Mysteries of the Christian Religion. And, indeed, since Providence intended there should be Mysteries; I do not see how it can be agreeable to *Piety*, *Orthodoxy*, or good *Sense*, to go about such a Work. For, to me there seems to be a manifest Dilemma in the Case: If you explain them, they are Mysteries no longer; if you fail, you have laboured to no Purpose. What I should think most reasonable and safe for you to do, upon this Occasion, is upon solemn Days to deliver the Doctrine as the Church holds it, and confirm it by Scripture. For my Part, having considered the Matter impartially, I can see no great Reason which those Gentlemen, you call the *Free-Thinkers*, can have for their Clamour against Religious Mysteries; since it is plain, they were not invented by the Clergy, to whom they bring no Profit, nor acquire any Honour. For every Clergyman is ready, either to tell us the utmost he knows, or to confess that he doth not understand them: Neither is it strange, that there should be Mysteries in Divinity, as well as in the commonest Operations of Nature.

AND here I am at a Loss what to say, upon the frequent Custom of preaching against *Atheism*, *Deism*, *Free-Thinking*, and the like; as young Divines are particularly fond of doing, especially when they exercise their Talent in Churches, frequented by People of Quality; which, as it is but an ill Compliment to the Audience, so I am under some doubt whether it answers the End. Because, Persons under those Imputations are generally no great Frequenters of Churches, and so the Congregation is but little edified for the Sake of three or four Fools, who are past Grace. Neither do I think it any part of *Prudence*, to perplex the Minds of well-disposed People with Doubts, which probably would never have otherwise come into their Heads. But I am of Opinion, and dare be positive in it, that not one in a Hundred of those, who pretend to be *Free-Thinkers*, are really so in their Hearts. For there is one Observation which I never knew to fail, and I desire you will examine it in the Course of your Life; that no Gentleman of a liberal Education, and regular in his Morals, did ever profess himself a *Free-Thinker*: Where then are these Kind of People to be found? Amongst the worst Part of the Soldiery, made up of Pages, younger Brothers of obscure Families, and others of desperate Fortunes; or else among idle Town-Fops; and now and then a drunken 'Squire of the Country. Therefore, nothing can be plainer, than that Ignorance, and Vice, are two Ingredients absolutely necessary in the Composition of those you generally call *Free-Thinkers*; who, in Propriety of Speech, *are no Thinkers at all.* And, since I am in the way of it, pray consider one Thing farther: As young as you are, you cannot but have already observed, what a violent Run there is among too many weak People, against University Education: Be firmly assured, that the whole Cry is made up by those, who were either never sent to a College; or through their Irregularities and Stupidity, never made the least Improvement while they were there. I have above Forty of the latter now in my Eye; several of them in this Town, whose *Learning, Manners, Temperance, Probity, Good-nature,* and *Politicks,* are all of a-piece. Others of them in the Country, oppressing their Tenants, tyrannizing over the Neighbourhood, cheating the Vicar, talking Nonsense, and getting drunk at the Sessions. It is from such Seminaries as these, that the World is provided with the several Tribes and Denominations of *Free-Thinkers*; who, in my Judgment, are not to be reformed by Arguments offered to prove the Truth of the *Christian Religion*; because, *Reasoning* will never make a Man correct an ill Opinion, which by *Reasoning* he never acquired: For, in the Course of Things, Men always grow vicious before they become Unbelievers: But if you could once convince the Town or Country Profligate, by Topicks drawn from the View of their own *Quiet, Reputation, Health,* and *Advantage*; their *Infidelity* would soon drop off: This, I confess, is no easy Task; because it is almost in a literal Sense, to *fight with Beasts.* Now, to make it clear, that we are to look for no other Original of this *Infidelity,* whereof Divines so much complain; it is allowed on all Hands, that the People of *England* are more corrupt in their *Morals,* than any other Nation at this Day under the *Sun*: And this Corruption is manifestly owing to other Causes, both *numerous* and *obvious,* much more than to the Publication of irreligious

Books; which, indeed, are but the Consequence of the former. For, all the Writers against Christianity, since the Revolution, have been of the lowest Rank among Men, in regard to *Literature, Wit,* and good *Sense;* and upon that Account, wholly unqualified to propagate *Heresies,* unless among People already abandoned.

IN an Age where every Thing disliked by those, who think with the Majority, is called *Disaffection;* it may perhaps be ill interpreted, when I venture to tell you, that this universal Depravation of *Manners,* is owing to the perpetual bandying of *Factions* among us for Thirty Years past; when, without weighing the *Motives of Justice, Law, Conscience,* or *Honour,* every Man adjusts his *Principles* to those of the *Party* he hath chosen, and among whom he may best find his own Account: But, by reason of our frequent Vicissitudes, Men, who were impatient to be out of Play, have been forced to recant, or at least to reconcile their former Tenets with every new System of Administration. Add to this, that the old fundamental Custom of annual Parliaments being wholly laid aside, and Elections growing chargeable; since Gentlemen found that their Country *Seats* brought them in less than a *Seat* in the House; the Voters, *that is to say,* the Bulk of the common People, have been universally seduced into *Bribery, Perjury, Drunkenness, Malice,* and *Slander.*

NOT to be further tedious, or rather invidious; these are a few, among other Causes, which have contributed to the Ruin of our *Morals,* and consequently to the Contempt of *Religion.* For, imagine to your self, if you please, a landed Youth, whom his Mother would never suffer to look into a Book, for fear of spoiling his Eyes; got into Parliament, and observing all Enemies to the Clergy heard with the utmost Applause; what Notions he must imbibe; how readily he will join in the Cry; what an Esteem he will conceive of himself; and what a Contempt he must entertain, not only for his Vicar at home, but for the whole Order.

I THEREFORE again conclude, that the Trade of *Infidelity* hath been taken up only for an Expedient to keep in Countenance that universal Corruption of *Morals,* which many other Causes first contributed to introduce, and to cultivate. And thus, Mr. *Hobbes's* Saying upon Reason, may be much more properly applied to Religion: That, *if Religion will be against a Man, a Man will be against Religion.* Although, after all, I have heard a Profligate offer much stronger Arguments against paying his Debts, than ever he was known to do against *Christianity;* indeed, the Reason was, because in that Juncture he happened to be closer pressed by the *Bailiff* than the *Parson.*

IGNORANCE may, perhaps, be the *Mother* of *Superstition;* but

Experience hath not proved it to be so of *Devotion*: For *Christianity* always made the most easy and quickest Progress in civilized Countries. I mention this, because it is affirmed, that the Clergy are in most Credit where Ignorance prevails, (and surely this Kingdom would be called the *Paradise* of Clergymen, if that Opinion were true) for which they instance *England* in the Times of *Popery*. But whoever knoweth any Thing of three or four Centuries before the Reformation, will find, the little Learning then stirring, was more equally divided between the *English* Clergy and Laity, than it is at present. There were several famous Lawyers in that *Period*, whose Writings are still in the highest Repute; and some *Historians* and *Poets*, who were not of the *Church*. Whereas, now-a-days our Education is so corrupted, that you will hardly find a young Person of Quality with the least Tincture of Knowledge; at the same Time that many of the Clergy were never more learned, or so scurvily treated. Here among Us, at least, a Man of Letters, out of the three Professions, is almost a Prodigy. And those few who have preserved any Rudiments of Learning, are (except, perhaps, one or two Smatterers) the Clergy's Friends to a Man: For, I dare appeal to any Clergyman in this Kingdom, whether the greatest Dunce in his Parish be not always the most proud, wicked, fraudulent, and intractable of his Flock.

I THINK the Clergy have almost given over perplexing themselves and their Hearers, with abstruse Points of Predestination, Election, and the like; at least, it is time they should; and therefore, I shall not trouble you further upon this Head.

I HAVE now said all I could think convenient with relation to your Conduct in the Pulpit. Your Behaviour in the World is another Scene, upon which, I shall readily offer you my Thoughts, if you appear to desire them from me, by your Approbation of what I have here written; if not, I have already troubled you too much.

> *I am*, SIR,
> *Your affectionate*
> *Friend and Servant.*
> A.B.

JANUARY 9,
1720.

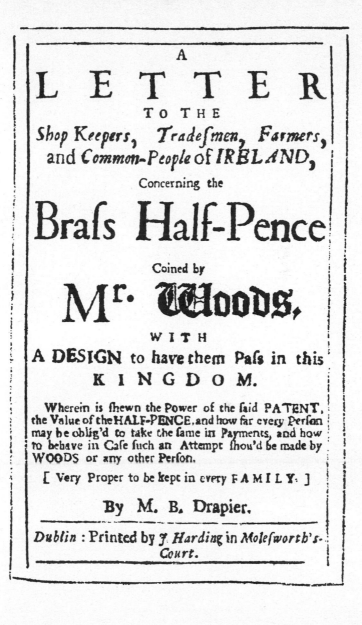

A
LETTER
TO THE

Shop Keepers, Tradesmen, Farmers,
and Common-People of IRELAND,

Concerning the

Braſs Half-Pence

Coined by

Mr. Woods,

WITH

A DESIGN to have them Paſs in this
KINGDOM.

Wherein is ſhewn the Power of the ſaid PATENT,
the Value of the HALF-PENCE, and how far every Perſon
may be oblig'd to take the ſame in Payments, and how
to behave in Caſe ſuch an Attempt ſhou'd be made by
WOODS or any other Perſon.

[Very Proper to be kept in every FAMILY.]

By M. B. Drapier.

Dublin : Printed by J. Harding in Moleſworth's-
Court.

To the *Tradesmen, Shop-Keepers, Farmers,* and *Common-People* in General, of the Kingdom of IRELAND. 1724[1]

Brethren, Friends, Countrymen, and *Fellow-Subjects*

WHAT I intend now to say to you, is, next to your Duty to God, and the Care of your Salvation, of the greatest Concern to your selves, and your Children; your *Bread* and *Cloathing,* and every common Necessary of Life entirely depend upon it. Therefore I do most earnestly exhort you as *Men,* as *Christians,* as *Parents,* and as *Lovers of your Country,* to read this Paper with the utmost Attention, or get it read to you by others; which that you may do at the less Expence, I have ordered the Printer to sell it at the lowest Rate.

IT is a great Fault among you, that when a Person writes with no other Intention than *to do you Good, you will not be at the Pains to read his Advices*: One Copy of this Paper may serve a Dozen of you, which will be less than a Farthing apiece. It is your Folly, that you have no common or general Interest in your View, not even the Wisest among you; neither do you know or enquire, or care who are your Friends, or who are your Enemies.

ABOUT four Years ago, a little Book was written to advise all People to wear the * *Manufactures of this our own Dear Country*: It had no other Design, said nothing against the *King* or *Parliament,* or *any* Person whatsoever, yet the Poor Printer[2] was prosecuted two Years, with the utmost Violence; and even some Weavers themselves, for whose Sake it was written, being upon the Jury, Found Him Guilty. This would be enough to discourage any Man from endeavouring to do you Good, when you will either neglect him, or fly in his Face for his Pains; and when he must expect

---

* Vide *one of the preceding Pamphlets, entitled, A Proposal for the Use of* Irish *Manufactures* [also by Swift—*Editors*].

1. Under the guise of M. B. Drapier, Swift composed a series of pamphlets defending Irish interests against English policy. His immediate provocation is set forth in this, the first, of the papers. For another version, from a later perspective, of the "plain story" the Drapier is about to render, see above, Book III of *Gulliver's Travels,* pp. 145–146. See too the related commentary in "Verses on the Death of Dr. Swift," lines 165–168, 339–354, 407–430, pp. 553–561.

2. Edward Waters, against whom the Chief Justice of Ireland, William Whitshed (d. 1727), attempted to force a jury to bring in a verdict.

only *Danger to himself*, and to be fined and imprisoned, perhaps to his Ruin.

HOWEVER, I cannot but warn you once more of the manifest Destruction before your Eyes, if you do not behave your selves as you ought.

I WILL therefore first tell you the *plain Story of the Fact*; and then I will lay before you, how you ought to act in common Prudence, and according to the *Laws of your Country*.

THE *Fact is thus*; It having been many Years since COPPER HALF-PENCE or FARTHINGS were last Coined in this *Kingdom*, they have been for some Time very scarce, and many *Counterfeits* passed about under the Name of RAPS: Several Applications were made to *England*, that we might have Liberty to *Coin New Ones*, as in former Times we did; but they did not succeed. At last one Mr. WOOD, *a mean ordinary Man, a Hard-Ware Dealer*, procured a *Patent* under His MAJESTY's BROAD SEAL, to coin 108000 *l.* in *Copper* for this *Kingdom*; which Patent however did not oblige any one here to take them, unless they pleased. Now you must know, that the HALF-PENCE and FARTHINGS in *England* pass for very little more than they are worth: And if you should beat them to Pieces, and sell them to the *Brazier*, you would not lose much above a Penny in a Shilling. But Mr. WOOD made his HALF-PENCE of such *Base Metal*, and so much smaller than the *English* ones, that the *Brazier* would hardly give you above a *Penny* of good Money for a *Shilling* of his; so that this sum of 108000 *l.* in good Gold and Silver, must be given for TRASH that will not be worth above *Eight* or *Nine Thousand Pounds* real Value. But this is not the Worst; for Mr. WOOD, when he pleases, may by Stealth send over *another* 108000 *l.* and buy *all our Goods for Eleven Parts in Twelve*, under the Value. For Example, if a *Hatter* sells a Dozen of *Hats* for *Five Shillings* a-piece, which amounts to *Three Pounds*, and receives the Payment in Mr. WOOD's Coin, he really receives only the Value of *Five Shillings*.

PERHAPS you will wonder how such an *ordinary Fellow* as this Mr. WOOD could have so much Interest as to get his MAJESTY's Broad Seal for so great a Sum of bad Money, to be sent to this poor Country; and that all the *Nobility* and *Gentry* here could not obtain the same Favour, and let us make our own HALF-PENCE, as we used to do. Now I will make that Matter very plain. We are at a great Distance from the *King's Court* and have no body there to solicit for us, although a great Number of *Lords* and *Squires*, whose Estates are here, and are our Countrymen, spend all their *Lives* and *Fortunes* there. But this same Mr. WOOD was able to attend constantly for his own Interest; he is an ENGLISHMAN and had GREAT FRIENDS, and it seems knew very well *where to give Money* to those that would speak to OTHERS that could speak to the KING, and would tell a FAIR STORY. And HIS MAJESTY, and perhaps the great Lord or Lords who advised him, might think it was for our *Country's Good*; and so, as the Lawyers express it, the KING was deceived in his Grant; which often happens in *all Reigns*. And I am sure if His MAJESTY knew that such a Patent, if it should take Effect according to the Desire of Mr. WOOD, would utterly ruin this Kingdom, which hath given such great Proofs of its *Loyalty*; he would immediately recall it, and perhaps shew his Displeasure to SOME BODY OR OTHER: *But a Word to the Wise is enough.* Most of you must have heard with what Anger our *Honourable House of Commons* received an Account of this WOOD'S PATENT. There were several *Fine Speeches* made upon it, and plain Proofs, that it was all a WICKED CHEAT from the *Bottom to the Top*; and several *smart Votes* were printed, which that same WOOD had the Assurance to answer likewise in *Print*, and in so confident a Way, as if he were *a better Man than our whole Parliament* put together.

THIS WOOD, as soon as his *Patent* was passed, or soon after, sends over a great many *Barrels of those* HALF-PENCE, to *Cork* and other *Sea-Port Towns*, and to get them off, offered an *Hundred Pounds* in his *Coin* for *Seventy* or *Eighty* in *Silver*: But the *Collectors* of the KING's Customs very honestly refused to take them, and so did almost every body else. And since the Parliament hath condemned them, and desired the KING that they might be stopped, all the *Kingdom* do abominate them.

BUT WOOD is still working *under hand* to force his HALF-PENCE upon us; and if he can by help of his *Friends* in *England* prevail so far as to get an Order that the *Commissioners* and *Collectors* of the King's Money shall receive them, and that the *Army* is to be paid with them, then he thinks *his Work shall be done*. And this is the Difficulty you will be under in such a *Case*: For the common Soldier when he goes to the *Market* or *Alehouse*, will offer this Money, and if it be refused, perhaps he will *swagger* and *hector*, and *threaten* to *beat* the *Butcher* or *Ale-wife*, or take the Goods by Force, and throw them the bad HALF-PENCE. In this and the like Cases, the *Shop-keeper*, or *Victualler*, or *any other Tradesman* has no more to do, than to demand ten times the Price of his Goods, if it is to be paid in WOOD's Money; for Example, Twenty Pence of that Money for a *Quart of Ale*, and so in all things else, and not part with his Goods till he gets the *Money*.

FOR suppose you go to an *Ale-house* with that base Money, and the *Landlord* gives you a Quart for Four of these HALF-

PENCE, what must the *Victualler* do? His *Brewer* will not be paid in that Coin, or if the *Brewer* should be such a Fool, the *Farmers* will not take it from them for their * *Bere*, because they are bound by their Leases to pay their Rents in Good and Lawful Money of *England*, which this is not, nor of *Ireland* neither, and the *Squire their Landlord* will never be so bewitched to take such *Trash* for his Land; so that it must certainly stop somewhere or other, and wherever it stops it is the same Thing, and we are all undone.

THE common Weight of these HALF-PENCE is between four and five to an *Ounce*; suppose five, then three Shillings and four Pence will weigh a Pound, and consequently *Twenty Shillings* will weigh *Six Pounds Butter Weight*. Now there are many hundred *Farmers* who pay Two hundred Pounds a Year Rent: Therefore when one of these *Farmers* comes with his Half-Year's Rent, which is One hundred Pound, it will be at least Six hundred Pound weight, which is Three Horses Load.

IF a *Squire* has a mind to come to Town to buy Cloaths and Wine and Spices for himself and Family, or perhaps to pass the Winter here; he must bring with him five or six Horses loaden with *Sacks* as the *Farmers* bring their Corn; and when his Lady comes in her Coach to our Shops, it must be followed by a Car loaded with Mr. WOOD's Money. And I hope we shall have the Grace to take it for no more than it is worth.

THEY say SQUIRE CONOLLY has *Sixteen Thousand Pounds a Year*; now if he sends for his *Rent* to Town, *as it is likely he does*, he must have *Two Hundred and Fifty Horses* to bring up his *Half Year's Rent*, and two or three great *Cellars* in his House for Stowage. But what the Bankers will do I cannot tell. For I am assured, that some great Bankers keep by them *Forty Thousand Pounds* in ready Cash to answer all Payments, which Sum in Mr. WOOD's Money, would require Twelve Hundred Horses to carry it.

FOR my own Part, I am already resolved what to do; I have a pretty good Shop of *Irish Stuffs* and *Silks*, and instead of taking Mr. W O O D's bad Copper, I intend to Truck with my Neighbours the *Butchers*, and *Bakers*, and *Brewers*, and the rest, *Goods for Goods*, and the little *Gold* and *Silver* I have, I will keep by me like my *Heart's Blood* till better Times, or until I am just ready to starve, and then I will buy Mr. WOOD's Money, as my Father did the Brass Money in King *James*'s Time; who could buy *Ten Pound* of it with a *Guinea*, and I hope to get as much for a *Pistole*, and so purchase *Bread* from those who will be such Fools as to sell it me.

THESE *Half-pence*, if they once pass, will soon be *Counterfeit*, because it may be cheaply done, the *Stuff* is so *Base*. The *Dutch*

* *A sort of Barley in Ireland.*

likewise will probably do the same thing, and send them over to us to pay for our *Goods*; and Mr. Wood will never be at rest, but coin on: So that in some Years we shall have at least five Times 108000 *l.* of this *Lumber.* Now the current Money of this Kingdom is not reckoned to be above Four Hundred Thousand Pounds in all; and while there is a *Silver* Six-Pence left, these *Blood-suckers* will never be quiet.

WHEN once the *Kingdom* is reduced to such a Condition, I will tell you what must be the End: The *Gentlemen of Estates* will all turn off their *Tenants* for want of Payment; because, as I told you before, the *Tenants* are obliged by their Leases to pay *Sterling,* which is Lawful Current Money of *England;* then they will turn their own *Farmers, as too many of them do already,* run *all* into *Sheep*[3] where they can, keeping only such other *Cattle* as are necessary; then they will be their own *Merchants,* and send their *Wool,* and *Butter,* and *Hides,* and *Linnen* beyond Sea for ready *Money,* and *Wine,* and *Spices,* and *Silks.* They will keep only a few miserable *Cottagers.* The *Farmers* must *Rob* or *Beg,* or leave their *Country.* The *Shop-keepers* in this and every other Town, must *Break* and *Starve:* For it is the *Landed-man* that maintains the *Merchant,* and *Shop-keeper,* and *Handicrafts-Man.*

BUT when the *Squire* turns *Farmer* and *Merchant* himself, all the good Money he gets from abroad, he will hoard up to send for *England,* and keep some poor *Taylor* or *Weaver,* and the like, in his own House, who will be glad to get Bread at any Rate.

I SHOULD never have done, if I were to tell you all the Miseries that we shall undergo, if we be so *Foolish* and *Wicked* as to take this *Cursed Coin.* It would be very hard, if all *Ireland* should be put into *One Scale,* and *this sorry Fellow* W o o D *into the other:* That Mr. W o o D should weigh down *this whole Kingdom,* by which *England* gets above a Million of good Money every Year clear into their *Pockets:* And that is more than the *English* do by *all the World besides.*

BUT your *great Comfort is,* that, as his Majesty's *Patent* doth not oblige you to take this *Money,* so the *Laws* have not given the *Crown* a Power of forcing the *Subjects* to take what *Money* the *King* pleases: For then by the same Reason we might be bound to take *Pebble-stones,* or *Cockle-shells,* or *stamped Leather* for *Current Coin;* if ever we should happen to live under an ill *Prince;* who might likewise by the same Power make a *Guinea* pass for Ten Pounds, a *Shilling* for Twenty Shillings, and so on; by which he would in a short Time get all the *Silver* and *Gold* of the *Kingdom* into his own Hands, and leave us nothing but *Brass* or *Leather,* or

3. Turn all arable land into sheep pastures.

what he pleased. Neither is any thing reckoned more *Cruel* or *Oppressive* in the *French Government*, than their common Practice of calling in all their Money after they have sunk it very low, and then coining it a-new at a much higher Value; which however is not the Thousandth Part so wicked as this *abominable Project* of Mr. *Wood*. For the *French* give their Subjects *Silver* for *Silver*, and *Gold* for *Gold*; but this *Fellow* will not so much as give us good *Brass* or *Copper* for our *Gold* and *Silver*, nor even a Twelfth Part of their Worth.

HAVING said this much, I will now go on to tell you the Judgments of some great *Lawyers* in this Matter; whom I fee'd on purpose for your Sakes, and got their *Opinions* under their *Hands*, that I might be sure I went upon good Grounds.

A *FAMOUS* Law-Book *called the* Mirrour of Justice,[4] *discoursing of the Charters (or Laws) ordained by our* Ancient Kings, *declares the* Law *to be as follows: It was ordained that no* King *of this Realm should* Change, *or* Impair *the* Money, *or make any other* Money *than of* Gold *or* Silver *without the Assent of all the Counties, that is,* as my Lord *Coke says, without the Assent of* Parliament.

THIS Book is very Ancient, and of great Authority for the Time in which it was wrote, and with that Character is often quoted by that great Lawyer my Lord *Coke*.[5] By the Laws of *England*, the several Metals are divided into *Lawful* or *true Metal* and *unlawful* or *false Metal*; the Former comprehends *Silver* or *Gold*, the Latter all *Baser Metals*: That the Former is only to pass in Payments, appears by an Act of *Parliament* made the Twentieth Year of *Edward* the *First*, called the *Statute concerning the passing of Pence*; which I give you here as I got it translated into *English*; For some of our *Laws* at that time were, as I am told, writ in *Latin*: Whoever in Buying or Selling presumeth to refuse an Half-penny or Farthing of Lawful Money, bearing the Stamp which it ought to have, let him be seized on as a Contemner of the King's Majesty, and cast into Prison.

BY this *Statute*, no Person is to be reckoned a *Contemner* of the *King's Majesty*, and for that Crime to be *committed to Prison*; but he who refuseth to accept the King's Coin made of *Lawful Metal*: by which as I observed before, *Silver* and *Gold* only are intended.

THAT this is the true *Construction* of the *Act*, appears not only from the plain Meaning of the Words, but from my Lord *Coke's* Observation upon it. By this Act (says he) it appears, that

4. Compiled by Andrew Horne; translated into English by William Hughes and published in London in 1646.
5. Sir Edward Coke, whose *Institutes of the Laws of England* (London, 1628–44) Swift here refers to.

no Subject can be forced to take in *Buying* or *Selling* or other *Payments*, any Money made but of lawful Metal; that is, of *Silver* or *Gold*.

THE Law of *England* gives the King all Mines of *Gold* and *Silver*, but not the Mines of other *Metals*; the Reason of which *Prerogative* or *Power*, as it is given by my Lord *Coke*, is because Money can be made of *Gold* and *Silver*; but not of other Metals.

PURSUANT to this Opinion, *Half-pence* and *Farthings* were anciently made of *Silver*, which is evident from the Act of *Parliament* of *Henry* the IVth. Chap. 4. whereby it is enacted as follows: *Item, for the great Scarcity that is at present within the Realm of* England *of Half-pence and Farthings of* Silver; *it is ordained and established, that the Third Part of all the Money of* Silver Plate *which shall be brought to the* Bullion, *shall be made in* Half-pence *and* Farthings. This shews that by the Words *Half-penny* and *Farthing* of Lawful Money in that Statute concerning the *passing of* Pence, is meant a small Coin in *Half-pence* and *Farthings* of *Silver*.

THIS is further manifest from the Statute of the Ninth Year of *Edward* the IIId. Chap. 3. which enacts, *That no sterling* Half-penny *or* Farthing *be Molten for to make* Vessels, *or any other thing by the Gold-smiths, nor others, upon* Foreiture *of the* Money *so molten* (or melted.)

BY another Act in this *King*'s Reign, *Black Money* was not to be current in *England*. And by an Act made in the Eleventh Year of his Reign, Chap. 5. *Galley Half-pence* were not to pass: What kind of *Coin* these were I do not know; but I presume they were made of *Base Metal*. And these Acts were no New *Laws*, but further Declarations of the old *Laws* relating to the *Coin*.

THUS the *Law* stands in Relation to *Coin*. Nor is there any Example to the contrary, except one in *Davis's Reports*; who tells us, that in the time of *Tyrone's* Rebellion, *Queen Elizabeth* ordered *Money* of *mixt Metal* to be coined in the Tower of *London*, and sent over hither for Payment of the *Army*; obliging all People to receive it; and Commanding, that all *Silver Money* should be taken only as *Bullion*, that is, for as much as it weighed. *Davis* tells us several Particulars in this Matter too long here to trouble you with, and that the *Privy Council* of this *Kingdom* obliged a *Merchant* in *England* to receive this *mixt Money* for Goods transmitted hither.

BUT this Proceeding is rejected by all the best Lawyers, as contrary to Law, the *Privy Council* here having no such legal Power. And besides it is to be considered, that the *Queen* was then under great Difficulties by a Rebellion in this *Kingdom* assisted from *Spain*. And, whatever is done in great Exigences and dangerous

Times, should never be an Example to proceed by in Seasons of *Peace* and *Quietness*.

I WILL now, my dear Friends, to save you the Trouble, set before you in short, what the *Law* obliges you to do; and what it does not oblige you to.

FIRST, you are obliged to take all Money in Payments which is coined by the *King*, and is of the *English* Standard or Weight; provided it be of *Gold* or *Silver*.

SECONDLY, you are not obliged to take any Money which is not of *Gold* or *Silver*; not only the *Half-pence* or *Farthings* of England, but of any other Country. And it is meerly for Convenience, or Ease, that you are content to take them; because the Custom of coining *Silver Half-pence* and *Farthings* hath long been left off; I suppose, on Account of their being subject to be lost.

THIRDLY, Much less are you obliged to take those *Vile Half-pence* of that same *Wood*, by which you must lose almost *Eleven-Pence* in every Shilling.

THEREFORE, my Friends, stand to it One and All: Refuse this *Filthy Trash*. It is no Treason to rebel against Mr. *Wood*. His *Majesty* in his Patent obliges no body to take these *Half-pence*: Our *Gracious Prince* hath no such ill Advisers about him; or if he had, yet you see the Laws have not left it in the *King*'s Power, to force us to take any Coin but what is Lawful, of right Standard, *Gold* and *Silver*. Therefore you have nothing to fear.

AND let me in the next Place apply my self particularly to you who are the poorer Sort of *Tradesmen*: Perhaps you may think you will not be so great Losers as the Rich, if these *Half-pence* should pass; because you seldom see any *Silver*, and your Customers come to your Shops or Stalls with nothing but *Brass*; which you likewise find hard to be got. But you may take my Word, whenever this Money gains Footing among you, you will be utterly undone. If you carry these *Half-pence* to a Shop for *Tobacco* or *Brandy*, or any other Thing you want; the Shop-keeper will advance his Goods accordingly, or else he must break and leave the *Key under the Door*. Do you think I will sell you a Yard of Ten-penny Stuff for Twenty of Mr. *Wood*'s *Half-pence*? No, not under Two Hundred at least; neither will I be at the Trouble of counting, but weigh them in a Lump. I will tell you one Thing further; that if Mr. *Wood*'s Project should take, it will ruin even our Beggars: For when I give a Beggar a Half-penny, it will quench his Thirst, or go a good Way to fill his Belly; but the Twelfth Part of a Half-penny will do him no more Service than if I should give him three Pins out of my Sleeve.

IN short; these *Half-pence* are like the *accursed Thing*, which, as the *Scripture* tells us, the *Children of Israel* were forbidden to touch. They will run about like the *Plague* and destroy every one who lays his Hands upon them. I have heard *Scholars* talk of a Man who told the King that he had invented a Way to torment People by putting them into a *Bull* of Brass with Fire under it: But the *Prince* put the *Projector* first into his own *Brazen Bull* to make the Experiment. This very much resembles the Project of Mr. *Wood*; and the like of this may possibly be Mr. *Wood's* Fate; that the *Brass* he contrived to torment this *Kingdom* with, may prove his own Torment, and his Destruction at last.

N. B. The Author of this Paper is informed by Persons who have made it their Business to be exact in their Observations on the true Value of these *Half-pence*; that any Person may expect to get a Quart of Two-penny Ale for Thirty Six of them.

I DESIRE that all Families may keep this Paper carefully by them to refresh their Memories whenever they shall have farther Notice of Mr. *Wood's* Half-pence, or any other the like Imposture.

A Short View of the State of Ireland

WRITTEN IN THE YEAR 1727

I AM assured, that it hath, for some Time, been practised as a Method of making Men's Court, when they are asked about the Rate of Lands, the Abilities of Tenants, the State of Trade and Manufacture in this Kingdom, and how their Rents are paid; to answer, that in their Neighbourhood, all Things are in a flourishing Condition, the Rent and Purchase of Land every Day encreasing. And if a Gentleman happen to be a little more sincere in his Representations; besides being looked on as not well affected, he is sure to have a Dozen Contradictors at his Elbow. I think it is no Manner of Secret why these Questions are so *cordially* asked, or so *obligingly* answered.

BUT since, with regard to the Affairs of this Kingdom, I have been using all Endeavours to subdue my Indignation; to which, indeed, I am not provoked by any personal Interest, being not the Owner of one Spot of Ground in the whole *Island*; I shall only enumerate by Rules generally known, and never contradicted, what are the true Causes of any Countries flourishing and growing rich; and then examine what Effects arise from those Causes in the Kingdom of *Ireland*.

THE first Cause of a Kingdom's thriving, is the Fruitfulness of the Soil, to produce the Necessaries and Conveniences of Life; not only sufficient for the Inhabitants, but for Exportation into other Countries.

THE Second, is the Industry of the People, in working up all their native Commodities, to the last Degree of Manufacture.

THE Third, is the Conveniency of safe Ports and Havens, to carry out their own Goods, as much manufactured, and bring in those of others, as little manufactured, as the Nature of mutual Commerce will allow.

THE Fourth is, that the Natives should, as much as possible, export and import their Goods in Vessels of their own Timber, made in their own Country.

THE Fifth, is the Priviledge of a free Trade in all foreign Countries, which will permit them; except to those who are in War with their own Prince or State.

THE Sixth, is, by being governed only by Laws made with their own Consent; for otherwise they are not a free People. And therefore, all Appeals for Justice, or Applications for Favour or Preferment, to another Country, are so many grievous Impoverishments.

THE Seventh is, by Improvement of Land, Encouragement of Agriculture, and thereby encreasing the Number of their People; without which, any Country, however blessed by Nature, must continue poor.

THE Eighth, is the Residence of the Prince, or chief Administrator of the Civil Power.

THE Ninth, is the Concourse of Foreigners for Education, Curiosity, or Pleasure; or as to a general Mart of Trade.

THE Tenth, is by disposing all Offices of Honour, Profit, or Trust, only to the Natives, or at least with very few Exceptions; where Strangers have long inhabited the Country, and are supposed to understand, and regard the Interest of it as their own.

THE Eleventh, is when the Rents of Lands, and Profits of Employments, are spent in the Country which produced them, and not in another; the former of which will certainly happen, where the Love of our native Country prevails.

THE Twelfth, is by the publick Revenues being all spent and employed at home; except on the Occasions of a foreign War.

THE Thirteenth is, where the People are not obliged, unless they find it for their own Interest or Conveniency, to receive any Monies, except of their own Coinage by a publick Mint, after the Manner of all civilized Nations.

THE Fourteenth, is a Disposition of the People of a Country to wear their own Manufactures, and import as few Incitements to

Luxury, either in Cloaths, Furniture, Food, or Drink, as they possibly can live conveniently without.

THERE are many other Causes of a Nation's thriving, which I cannot at present recollect; but without Advantage from at least some of these, after turning my Thoughts a long Time, I am not able to discover from whence our Wealth proceeds, and therefore would gladly be better informed. In the mean Time, I will here examine what Share falls to *Ireland* of these Causes, or of the Effects and Consequences.

IT is not my Intention to complain, but barely to relate Facts; and the Matter is not of small Importance. For it is allowed, that a Man who lives in a solitary House, far from Help, is not wise in endeavouring to acquire, in the Neighbourhood, the Reputation of being rich; because those who come for Gold, will go off with Pewter and Brass, rather than return empty: And in the common Practice of the World, those who possess most Wealth, make the least Parade; which they leave to others, who have nothing else to bear them out, in shewing their Faces on the *Exchange*.

AS to the first Cause of a Nation's Riches, being the Fertility of the Soil, as well as Temperature of Climate, we have no Reason to complain; for, although the Quantity of unprofitable Land in this Kingdom, reckoning Bogg, and Rock, and barren Mountain, be double in Proportion to what it is in *England*; yet the native Productions which both Kingdoms deal in, are very near on Equality in Point of Goodness; and might, with the same Encouragement, be as well manufactured. I except Mines and Minerals; in some of which, however, we are only defective in Point of Skill and Industry.

IN the Second, which is the Industry of the People; our Misfortune is not altogether owing to our own Fault, but to a Million of Discouragements.

THE Conveniency of Ports and Havens, which Nature hath bestowed so liberally on this Kingdom, is of no more Use to us, than a beautiful Prospect to a Man shut up in a Dungeon.

AS to Shipping of its own, *Ireland* is so utterly unprovided, that of all the excellent Timber cut down within these Fifty or Sixty Years, it can hardly be said, that the Nation hath received the Benefit of one valuable House to dwell in, or one Ship to trade with.

IRELAND is the only Kingdom I ever heard or read of, either in ancient or modern Story, which was denied the Liberty of exporting their native Commodities and Manufactures, wherever they pleased; except to Countries at War with their own Prince or State: Yet this Privilege, by the Superiority of meer Power, is refused us, in the most momentous Parts of Commerce; besides an Act of Navigation, to which we never consented, pinned down upon us, and rigorously executed; and a Thousand other unexampled Circumstances, as grievous, as they are invidious to mention. To go on to the rest.

IT is too well known, that we are forced to obey some Laws we never consented to; which is a Condition I must not call by its true uncontroverted Name, for fear of Lord Chief Justice *Whitshed's* Ghost, with his * *Libertas & natale Solum,* written as a Motto on his Coach, as it stood at the Door of the Court, while he was perjuring himself to betray both. Thus, we are in the Condition of Patients, who have Physick sent them by Doctors at a Distance, Strangers to their Constitution, and the Nature of their Disease: And thus, we are forced to pay five Hundred *per Cent.* to decide our Properties; in all which, we have likewise the Honour to be distinguished from the whole Race of Mankind.

AS to Improvement of Land; those few who attempt that, or Planting, through Covetousness, or Want of Skill, generally leave Things worse than they were; neither succeeding in Trees nor Hedges; and by running into the Fancy of Grazing, after the Manner of the *Scythians,* are every Day depopulating the Country.

WE are so far from having a King to reside among us, that even the Viceroy is generally absent four Fifths of his Time in the Government.

NO strangers from other Countries, make this a Part of their Travels; where they can expect to see nothing, but Scenes of Misery and Desolation.

THOSE who have the Misfortune to be born here, have the least Title to any considerable Employment; to which they are seldom preferred, but upon a political Consideration.

ONE third Part of the Rents of *Ireland,* is spent in *England;* which, with the Profit of Employments, Pensions, Appeals, Journeys of Pleasure or Health, Education at the *Inns* of Court, and both Universities, Remittances at Pleasure, the Pay of all Superior Officers in the Army, and other Incidents, will amount to a full half of the Income of the whole Kingdom, all clear Profit to *England.*

WE are denied the Libery of Coining Gold, Silver, or even Copper. In the Isle of *Man,* they coin their own *Silver;* every petty Prince, Vassal to the *Emperor,* can coin what Money he pleaseth. And in this, as in most of the Articles already mentioned, we are an Exception to all other States or Monarchies that were ever known in the World.

AS to the last, or Fourteenth Article, we take special Care to act diametrically contrary to it in the whole Course of our Lives. Both Sexes, but especially the Women, despise and abhor to wear any of

* Liberty and my native country.

their own Manufactures, even those which are better made than in other Countries; particularly a Sort of Silk Plad, through which the Workmen are forced to run a Sort of Gold Thread that it may pass for *Indian*. Even Ale and Potatoes are imported from *England*, as well as Corn: And our foreign Trade is little more than Importation of *French* Wine; for which I am told we pay ready Money.

NOW, if all this be true, upon which I could easily enlarge; I would be glad to know by what secret Method, it is, that we grow a rich and flourishing People, without *Liberty*, *Trade*, *Manufactures*, *Inhabitants*, *Money*, or the *Privilege of Coining*; without *Industry*, *Labour*, or *Improvement of Lands*, and with more than half the Rent and Profits of the whole *Kingdom*, annually exported; for which we receive not a single Farthing: And to make up all this, nothing worth mentioning, except the Linnen of the *North*, a Trade casual, corrupted, and at Mercy; and some Butter from *Cork*. If we do flourish, it must be against every Law of Nature and Reason; like the Thorn at *Glassenbury*, that blossoms in the Midst of Winter.

LET the worthy *Commissioners* who come from *England*, ride round the Kingdom, and observe the Face of Nature, or the Faces of the Natives; the Improvement of the Land; the thriving numerous Planations; the noble Woods; the Abundance and Vicinity of Country-Seats; the commodious Farmers Houses and Barns; the Towns and Villages, where every Body is busy, and thriving with all kind of Manufactures; the Shops full of Goods, wrought to Perfection, and filled with Customers; the comfortable Diet and Dress, and Dwellings of the People; the vast Numbers of Ships in our Harbours and Docks, and Ship-wrights in our Seaport-Towns; the Roads crouded with Carriers, laden with rich Manufactures; the perpetual Concourse to and fro of pompous Equipages.

WITH what Envy, and Admiration, would those Gentlemen return from so delightful a Progress? What glorious Reports would they make, when they went back to *England*?

BUT my Heart is too heavy to continue this Irony longer; for it is manifest, that whatever Stranger took such a Journey, would be apt to think himself travelling in *Lapland* or *Ysland*, rather than in a Country so favoured by Nature as ours, both in Fruitfulness of Soil, and Temperature of Climate. The miserable Dress, and Dyet, and Dwelling of the People. The general Desolation in most Parts of the Kingdom. The old Seats of the Nobility and Gentry all in Ruins, and no new ones in their Stead. The Families of Farmers, who pay great Rents, living in Filth and Nastiness upon Butter-milk and Potatoes, without a Shoe or Stocking to their Feet; or a House so convenient as an *English* Hog-sty, to receive them. These, indeed, may be comfortable Sights to an *English* Spectator; who comes for a short Time, only *to learn the Language*, and returns back to his own Country, whither he finds all our Wealth transmitted.

Nostrâ miseriâ magnus es.[1]

THERE is not one Argument used to prove the Riches of *Ireland*, which is not a logical Demonstration of its Poverty. The Rise of our Rents is squeezed out of the very Blood, and Vitals, and Cloaths, and Dwellings of the Tenants; who live worse than *English* Beggars. The Lowness of Interest, in all other Countries a Sign of Wealth, is in us a Proof of Misery; there being no Trade to employ any Borrower. Hence, alone, comes the Dearness of Land, since the Savers have no other Way to lay out their Money. Hence the Dearness of Necessaries for Life; because the Tenants cannot afford to pay such extravagant Rates for Land, (which they must take, or go a-begging) without raising the Price of Cattle, and of Corn, although themselves should live upon Chaff. Hence our encrease of Buildings in this City; because Workmen have nothing to do, but employ one another; and one Half of them are infallibly undone. Hence the daily Encrease of *Bankers*; who may be a necessary Evil in a trading Country, but so ruinous in ours; who, for their private Advantage, have sent away all our Silver, and one Third of our Gold; so that within three Years past, the running Cash of the Nation, which was about five Hundred Thousand Pounds, is now less than two; and must daily diminish, unless we have Liberty to coin, as well as that important Kingdom the Isle of *Man*; and the meanest Prince in the *German* Empire, as I before observed.

I HAVE sometimes thought, that this Paradox of the Kingdom growing rich, is chiefly owing to those worthy Gentlemen the BANKERS; who, except some Custom-house Officers, Birds of Passage, oppressive thrifty 'Squires, and a few others who shall be nameless, are the only thriving People among us: And I have often wished, that a Law were enacted to hang up half a Dozen *Bankers* every Year; and thereby interpose at least some short Delay, to the further Ruin of *Ireland*.

YE *are idle, ye are idle*, answered *Pharoah* to the *Israelites*, when they complained to *his Majesty*, that they were forced to make Bricks without Straw.

ENGLAND enjoys every one of those Advantages for enriching a Nation, which I have above enumerated; and, into the Bargain, a good Million returned to them every Year, without Labour or Hazard, or one Farthing Value received on our Side. But how long

1. You are great because of our misery.

we shall be able to continue the Payment, I am not under the least Concern. One Thing I know, that *when the Hen is starved to Death, there will be no more Golden Eggs.*

I THINK it a little unhospitable, and others may call it a subtil Piece of Malice; that, because there may be a Dozen Families in this Town, able to entertain their *English* Friends in a generous Manner at their Tables; their Guests, upon their Return to *England*, shall report, that we wallow in Riches and Luxury.

YET, I confess, I have known an Hospital, where all the House-hold-Officers grew rich; while the Poor, for whose Sake it was built, were almost starving for want of Food and Raiment.

TO conclude. If *Ireland* be a rich and flourishing Kingdom; its Wealth and Prosperity must be owing to certain Causes, that are yet concealed from the whole Race of Mankind; and the Effects are equally invisible. We need not wonder at Strangers, when they deliver such Paradoxes; but a Native and Inhabitant of this Kingdom, who gives the same verdict, must be either ignorant to Stupidity; or a Man-pleaser, at the Expence of all Honour, Conscience, and Truth.

A Modest Proposal

FOR *Preventing the Children of poor People in* Ireland, *from being a Burden to their Parents or Country; and for making them beneficial to the Publick*

WRITTEN IN THE YEAR 1729

IT is a melancholly Object to those, who walk through this great Town, or travel in the Country; when they see the *Streets*, the *Roads*, and *Cabbin-doors* crowded with *Beggars* of the Female Sex, followed by three, four, or six Children, *all in Rags*, and importuning every Passenger for an Alms. These *Mothers*, instead of being able to work for their honest Livelyhood, are forced to employ all their Time in stroling to beg Sustenance for their *helpless Infants;* who, as they grow up, either turn *Thieves* for want of Work; or leave their *dear Native Country, to fight for the Pretender*[1] *in* Spain, or sell themselves to the *Barbadoes.*

I THINK it is agreed by all Parties, that this prodigious Number

---

1. James Stuart, claimant to the throne lost by his father, James II, in 1688.

of Children in the Arms, or on the Backs, or at the *Heels* of their *Mothers*, and frequently of their *Fathers*, is *in the present deplorable State of the Kingdom*, a very great additional Grievance; and therefore, whoever could find out a fair, cheap, and easy Method of making these Children sound and useful Members of the Commonwealth, would deserve so well of the Publick, as to have his Statue set up for a Preserver of the Nation.

BUT my Intention is very far from being confined to provide only for the Children of *professed Beggars*: It is of a much greater Extent, and shall take in the whole Number of Infants at a certain Age, who are born of Parents, in effect as little able to support them, as those who demand our Charity in the Streets.

AS to my own Part, having turned my Thoughts for many Years, upon this important Subject, and maturely weighed the several *Schemes of other Projectors*, I have always found them grosly mistaken in their Computation. It is true a Child, *just dropt from its Dam*, may be supported by her Milk, for a Solar Year with little other Nourishment; at most not above the Value of two Shillings; which the Mother may certainly get, or the Value in *Scraps*, by her lawful Occupation of *Begging*: And, it is exactly at one Year old, that I propose to provide for them in such a Manner, as, instead of being a Charge upon their *Parents*, or the *Parish*, or *wanting Food and Raiment* for the rest of their Lives; they shall, on the contrary, contribute to the Feeding, and partly to the Cloathing, of many Thousands.

THERE is likewise another great Advantage in my *Scheme*, that it will prevent those *voluntary Abortions*, and that horrid Practice of *Women murdering their Bastard Children*; alas! too frequent among us; sacrificing the *poor innocent Babes*, I doubt, more to avoid the Expence than the Shame; which would move Tears and Pity in the most Savage and inhuman Breast.

THE Number of Souls in *Ireland* being usually reckoned one Million and a half; of these I calculate there may be about Two hundred Thousand Couple whose Wives are Breeders; from which Number I subtract thirty thousand Couples, who are able to maintain their own Children; although I apprehend there cannot be so many, under *the present Distresses of the Kingdom*; but this being granted, there will remain an Hundred and Seventy Thousand Breeders. I again subtract Fifty Thousand, for those Women who miscarry, or whose Children die by Accident, or Disease, within the Year. There only remain an Hundred and Twenty Thousand Children of poor Parents, annually born: The Question therefore is, How this Number shall be reared, and provided for? Which, as I have already said, under the present Situation of Affairs, is utterly impossible, by all the Methods hitherto proposed: For we can *neither employ them in Handicraft* or *Agriculture; we* neither build Houses, (I mean in the Country) nor cultivate Land: They can very seldom pick up a Livelyhood *by Stealing* until they arrive at six Years old; except where they are of towardly Parts; although, I confess, they learn the Rudiments much earlier; during which Time, they can, however, be properly looked upon only as *Probationers;* as I have been informed by a principal Gentleman in the County of *Cavan,* who protested to me, that he never knew above one or two Instances under the Age of six, even in a Part of the Kingdom *so renowned for the quickest Proficiency in that Art.*

I AM assured by our Merchants, that a Boy or a Girl before twelve Years old, is no saleable Commodity; and even when they come to this Age, they will not yield above Three Pounds, or Three Pounds and half a Crown at most, on the Exchange; which cannot turn to Account either to the Parents or the Kingdom; the Charge of Nutriment and Rags, having been at least four Times that Value.

I SHALL now therefore humbly propose my own Thoughts; which I hope will not be liable to the least Objection.

I HAVE been assured by a very knowing *American* of my Acquaintance in *London;* that a young healthy Child, well nursed, is, at a Year old, a most delicious, nourishing, and wholesome Food; whether *Stewed, Roasted, Baked,* or *Boiled;* and, I make no doubt, that it will equally serve in a *Fricasie,* or *Ragoust.*

I DO therefore humbly offer it to *publick Consideration,* that of the Hundred and Twenty Thousand Children, already computed, Twenty thousand may be reserved for Breed; whereof only one Fourth Part to be Males; which is more than we allow to *Sheep, black Cattle,* or *Swine;* and my Reason is, that these Children are seldom the Fruits of Marriage, *a Circumstance not much regarded by our Savages;* therefore, *one Male* will be sufficient to serve *four Females.* That the remaining Hundred thousand, may, at a Year old, be offered in Sale to the *Persons of Quality* and *Fortune,* through the Kingdom; always advising the Mother to let them suck plentifully in the last Month, so as to render them plump, and fat for a good Table. A Child will make two Dishes at an Entertainment for Friends; and when the Family dines alone, the fore or hind Quarter will make a reasonable Dish; and seasoned with a little Pepper or Salt, will be very good Boiled on the fourth Day, especially in *Winter.*

I HAVE reckoned upon a Medium, that a Child just born will weigh Twelve Pounds; and in a solar Year, if tolerably nursed, encreaseth to twenty eight Pounds.

I GRANT this Food will be somewhat dear, and therefore very

proper for Landlords; who, as they have already devoured most of the Parents, seem to have the best Title to the Children.

INFANTS Flesh will be in Season throughout the Year; but more plentiful in *March,* and a little before and after: For we are told by a grave * Author, an eminent *French* Physician, that *Fish being a prolifick Dyet,* there are more Children born in *Roman Catholick Countries* about Nine Months after *Lent,* than at any other Season: Therefore reckoning a Year after *Lent,* the Markets will be more glutted than usual; because the Number of *Popish Infants,* is, at least, three to one in this Kingdom; and therefore it will have one other Collateral Advantage, by lessening the Number of *Papists* among us.

I HAVE already computed the Charge of nursing a Beggar's Child (in which List I reckon all *Cottagers, Labourers,* and Four fifths of the *Farmers*) to be about two Shillings *per Annum,* Rags included; and I believe, no Gentleman would repine to give Ten Shillings for the *Carcase of a good fat Child;* which, as I have said, will make four Dishes of excellent nutritive Meat, when he hath only some particular Friend, or his own Family, to dine with him. Thus the Squire will learn to be a good Landlord, and grow popular among his Tenants; the Mother will have Eight Shillings net Profit, and be fit for Work until she produceth another Child.

THOSE who are more thrifty *(as I must confess the Times require)* may flay the Carcase; the Skin of which, artificially dressed, will make admirable *Gloves for Ladies,* and *Summer Boots for fine Gentlemen.*

AS to our City of *Dublin;* Shambles may be appointed for this Purpose, in the most convenient Parts of it; and Butchers we may be assured will not be wanting; although I rather recommend buying the Children alive, and dressing them hot from the Knife, as we do *roasting Pigs.*

A VERY worthy Person, *a true Lover of his Country,* and whose Virtues I highly esteem, was lately pleased, in discoursing on this Matter, to offer a Refinement upon my Scheme. He said, that many Gentlemen of this Kingdom, having of late destroyed their Deer; he conceived, that the Want of Venison might be well supplied by the Bodies of young Lads and Maidens, not exceeding fourteen Years of Age, nor under twelve; so great a Number of both Sexes in every County being now ready to starve, for Want of Work and Service: And these to be disposed of by their Parents, if alive, or otherwise by their nearest Relations. But with due Deference to so excellent a Friend, and so deserving a Patriot, I cannot be altogether in his Sentiments. For as to the Males, my *American* Acquaintance

* Rabelais.

assured me from frequent Experience, that their Flesh was generally tough and lean, like that of our School-boys, by continual Exercise, and their Taste disagreeable; and to fatten them would not answer the Charge. Then, as to the Females, it would, I think, with humble Submission, *be a Loss to the Publick*, because they soon would become Breeders themselves: And besides it is not improbable, that some scrupulous People might be apt to censure such a Practice (although indeed very unjustly) as a little bordering upon Cruelty; which, I confess, hath always been with me the strongest Objection against any Project, how well soever intended.

BUT in order to justify my Friend; he confessed, that this Expedient was put into his Head by the famous *Salmanazor*,[2] a Native of the Island *Formosa*, who came from thence to *London*, above twenty Years ago, and in Conversation told my Friend, that in his Country, when any young Person happened to be put to Death, the Executioner sold the Carcase to *Persons of Quality*, as a prime Dainty; and that, in his Time, the Body of a plump Girl of fifteen, who was crucified for an Attempt to poison the Emperor, was sold to his Imperial *Majesty's prime Minister of State*, and other great *Mandarins* of the Court, *in Joints from the Gibbet*, at Four hundred Crowns. Neither indeed can I deny, that if the same Use were made of several plump young girls in this Town, who, without one single Groat to their Fortunes, cannot stir Abroad without a Chair, and appear at the *Play-house*, and *Assemblies* in foreign Fineries, which they never will pay for; the Kingdom would not be the worse.

SOME Persons of a desponding Spirit are in great Concern about that vast Number of poor People, who are Aged, Diseased, or Maimed; and I have been desired to employ my Thoughts what Course may be taken, to ease the Nation of so grievous an Incumbrance. But I am not in the least Pain upon that Matter; because it is very well known, that they are every Day *dying*, and *rotting*, by Cold and *Famine*, and *Filth*, and *Vermin*, as fast as can be reasonably expected. And as to the younger Labourers, they are now in almost as hopeful a Condition: They cannot get Work, and consequently pine away for Want of Nourishment, to a Degree, that if at any Time they are accidentally hired to common Labour, they have not Strength to perform it; and thus the Country, and themselves, are in a fair Way of being soon delivered from the Evils to come.

I HAVE too long digressed; and therefore shall return to my Subject. I think the Advantages by the Proposal which I have made,

2. George Psalmanazar, the professed author of *An Historical and Geographical Description of Formosa* (London, 1704); a known imposter, he was French by birth, and not the Formosan he claimed to be.

are obvious, and many, as well as of the highest Importance.

FOR, *First*, as I have already observed, it would greatly lessen the *Number of Papists*, with whom we are yearly overrun; being the principal Breeders of the Nation, as well as our most dangerous Enemies; and who stay at home on Purpose, with a Design to *deliver the Kingdom to the Pretender;* hoping to take their Advantage by the Absence *of so many good Protestants*, who have chosen rather to leave their Country, than stay at home, and pay Tithes against their Conscience, to an idolatrous *Episcopal Curate.*

SECONDLY, The poorer Tenants will have something valuable of their own, which, by Law, may be made liable to Distress, and help to pay their Landlord's Rent; their Corn and Cattle being already seized, and *Money a Thing unknown.*

THIRDLY, Whereas the Maintenance of an Hundred Thousand Children, from two Years old, and upwards, cannot be computed at less than ten Shillings a Piece *per Annum*, the Nation's Stock will be thereby encreased Fifty Thousand Pounds *per Annum*; besides the Profit of a new Dish, introduced to the Tables of all *Gentlemen of Fortune* in the Kingdom, who have any Refinement in Taste; and the Money will circulate among ourselves, the Goods being entirely of our own Growth and Manufacture.

FOURTHLY, The constant Breeders, besides the Gain of Eight Shillings *Sterling per Annum*, by the Sale of their Children, will be rid of the Charge of maintaining them after the first Year.

FIFTHLY, This Food would likewise bring great *Custom to Taverns*, where the Vintners will certainly be so prudent, as to procure the best Receipts for dressing it to Perfection; and consequently, have their Houses frequented by all the *fine Gentlemen*, who justly value themselves upon their Knowledge in good Eating; and a skilful Cook, who understands how to oblige his Guests, will contrive to make it as expensive as they please.

SIXTHLY, This would be a great Inducement to Marriage, which all wise Nations have either encouraged by Rewards, or enforced by Laws and Penalties. It would encrease the Care and Tenderness of Mothers towards their Children, when they were sure of a Settlement for Life, to the poor Babes, provided in some Sort by the Publick, to their annual Profit instead of Expence. We should soon see an honest Emulation among the married Women, *which of them could bring the fattest Child to the Market.* Men would become as *fond* of their Wives, during the Time of their Pregnancy, as they are now of their *Mares* in Foal, their *Cows* in Calf, or *Sows* when they are ready to farrow; nor offer to beat or kick them, (as it is too *frequent* a Practice) for fear of a Miscarriage.

MANY other Advantages might be enumerated. For instance, the Addition of some Thousand Carcasses in our Exportation of barrelled Beef: The Propagation of *Swines Flesh*, and Improvement in the Art of making good *Bacon*; so much wanted among us by the great Destruction of *Pigs*, too frequent at our Tables, which are no way comparable in Taste, or Magnificence, to a well-grown fat yearling Child; which, roasted whole, will make a considerable Figure at a *Lord Mayor's Feast*, or any other publick Entertainment. But this, and many others, I omit; being studious of Brevity.

SUPPOSING that one Thousand Families in this City, would be constant Customers for Infants Flesh; besides others who might have it at *merry Meetings*, particularly *Weddings* and *Christenings*; I compute that *Dublin* would take off, annually, about Twenty Thousand Carcasses; and the rest of the Kingdom (where probably they will be sold somewhat cheaper) the remaining Eighty Thousand.

I CAN think of no one Objection, that will possibly be raised against this Proposal; unless it should be urged, that the Number of People will be thereby much lessened in the Kingdom. This I freely own; and it was indeed one principal Design in offering it to the World. I desire the Reader will observe, that I calculate my Remedy *for this one individual Kingdom of* IRELAND, *and for no other that ever was, is, or I think ever can be upon Earth.* Therefore, let no man talk to me of other Expedients:[3] *Of taxing our Absentees at five Shillings a Pound: Of using neither Cloaths, nor Houshold Furniture except what is of our own Growth and Manufacture: Of utterly rejecting the Materials and Instruments that promote foreign Luxury: Of curing the Expensiveness of Pride, Vanity, Idleness, and Gaming in our Women: Of introducing a Vein of Parsimony, Prudence and Temperance: Of learning to love our Country, wherein we differ even from* LAPLANDERS, *and the Inhabitants of* TOPINAMBOO: *Of quitting our Animosities, and Factions; nor act any longer like the Jews, who were murdering one another at the very Moment their City was taken: Of being a little cautious not to sell our Country and Consciences for nothing: Of teaching Landlords to have, at least, one Degree of Mercy towards their Tenants. Lastly, Of putting a Spirit of Honesty, Industry, and Skill into our Shop-keepers; who, if a Resolution could now be taken to buy only our native Goods, would immediately unite to cheat and exact upon us in the Price, the Measure, and the Goodness; nor could ever yet be brought to make one fair Proposal of just Dealing, though often and earnestly invited to it.*

THEREFORE I repeat, let no Man talk to me of these and the

3. These are in fact measures that Swift had proposed in such tracts as his *Proposal for the Universal Use of Irish Manufactures.*

like Expedients; till he hath, at least, a Glimpse of Hope, that there will ever be some hearty and sincere Attempt to put *them in Practice*.

BUT, as to my self; having been wearied out for many Years with offering vain, idle, visionary Thoughts; and at length utterly despairing of Success, I fortunately fell upon this Proposal; which, as it is wholly new, so it hath something *solid* and *real*, of no Expence, and little Trouble, full in our own Power; and whereby we can incur no Danger in *disobliging* ENGLAND: For, this Kind of Commodity will not bear Exportation; the Flesh being of too tender a Consistence, to admit a long Continuance in Salt; *although, perhaps, I could name a Country, which would be glad to eat up our whole Nation without it.*

AFTER all, I am not so violently bent upon my own Opinion, as to reject any Offer proposed by wise Men, which shall be found equally innocent, cheap, easy, and effectual. But before something of that Kind shall be advanced, in Contradiction to my Scheme, and offering a better; I desire the Author, or Authors, will be pleased maturely to consider two Points. *First*, As Things now stand, how they will be able to find Food and Raiment, for a Hundred Thousand useless Mouths and Backs? And *secondly*, There being a round Million of Creatures in human Figure, throughout this Kingdom; whose whole Subsistence, put into a common Stock, would leave them in Debt two Millions of Pounds *Sterling*; adding those, who are Beggars by Profession, to the Bulk of Farmers, Cottagers, and Labourers, with their Wives and Children, who are Beggars in Effect; I desire those Politicians, who dislike my Overture, and may perhaps be so bold to attempt an Answer, that they will first ask the Parents of these Mortals, Whether they would not, at this Day, think it a great Happiness to have been sold for Food at a Year old, in the Manner I prescribe; and thereby have avoided such a perpetual Scene of Misfortunes, as they have since gone through; by the *Oppression of Landlords*; the Impossibility of paying Rent, without Money or Trade; the Want of common Sustenance, with neither House nor Cloaths, to cover them from the Inclemencies of Weather, and the most inevitable Prospect of intailing the like, or greater Miseries upon their Breed for ever.

I PROFESS, in the Sincerity of my Heart, that I have not the least personal Interest, in endeavouring to promote this necessary Work; having no other Motive than the *publick Good of my Country, by advancing our Trade, providing for Infants, relieving the Poor, and giving some Pleasure to the Rich.* I have no Children, by which I can propose to get a single penny; the youngest being nine Years old, and my Wife past Child-bearing.

The Texts of
The Poems

Baucis and Philemon[1]

Imitated, From the Eighth Book of OVID[2]

1706–09

In antient Time, as Story tells
The Saints would often leave their Cells
And strole about, but hide their Quality,
To try the People's Hospitality.
It happen'd on a Winter's night,
As Authors of the Legend write
Two Brother-Hermits, Saints by Trade
Taking their Tour in Masquerade
Came to a Village hard by Rixham
Ragged, and not a Groat betwixt 'em.   10
It rain'd as hard as it could pour,
Yet they were forc't to walk an Hour
From House to House, wett to the Skin
Before one Soul would let 'em in.
They call'd at ev'ry Dore; good People,
My Comrade's Blind, and I'm a Creeple
Here we ly starving in the Street
'Twould grieve a Body's Heart to see't:
No Christian would turn out a Beast
In such a dreadfull Night at least;   20
Give us but Straw, and let us ly
In yonder Barn to keep us dry.
Thus in the Strolers usuall Cant
They beg'd Relief which none would grant;
No Creature valu'd what they se'd:
One Family was gone to Bed;
The Master bawl'd out half asleep
You Fellows, what a Noise you keep!
So many Beggers pass this way,
We can't be quiet Night nor Day;   30
We can not serve You every One,
Pray take your Answer and be gone.

1. The first 180 lines are those in Swift's autograph, printed by Williams in his edition of the *Poems*, pp. 90–95. These clearly are Swift's first and best thoughts, composed before he made the extensive revisions that, as he complained, Joseph Addison prompted. The last fifty lines, beginning "At Christnings well could act his Part," are taken from the printed version of the poem and were not, or so the autograph suggests, subjected to revision. For a complete account of the composition of the poem and for the printed version, see Williams, pp. 88–95 and 110–117.
2. Ovid, *Metamorphoses*, VIII, 611–724.

One swore he'd send 'em to the Stocks,
A third could not forbear his Mocks,
But bawl'd as loud as he could roar,
You're on the wrong side of the Door.
One surly Clown lookt out, and said,
I'll fling the P—— pot on your Head;
You sha'n't come here nor get a Sous
You look like Rogues would rob a House   40
Can't you go work, or serve the King?
You blind and lame! tis no such Thing
That's but a counterfeit sore Leg:
For shame! two sturdy Rascalls beg;
If I come down, I'll spoil your Trick
And cure You both with a good Stick.
    Our wand'ring Saints in wofull State,
Treated at this ungodly Rate
Having thro all the Village pass't,
To a small Cottage came at last   50
Where dwelt a poor old honest Yeman
Call'd thereabouts Goodman Philemon;
Who kindly did the Saints invite
In his poor House to pass the Night;
And then the hospitable Sire
Bade Goody Baucis mend the Fire
Whilst he from out the Chimny took
A Flitch of Bacon off the Hook,
And freely from the fattest Side
Cutt off large Slices to be fry'd;   60
Which tosst up in a Pan with Batter,
And serv'd up in an earthen Platter;
Quoth Baucis, this is wholsom Fare,
Eat, honest Friends, and never spare,
And if we find our Vittels fail
We can but make it out in Ale.
    To a small Kilderkin³ of Beer
Brew'd for the good Time of the Year
Philemon by his Wife's consent
Step't with a Jug, and made a Vent;   70
And having fill'd it to the Brink,
Invited both the Saints to Drink.
When they had took a second Draught,
Behold, a Miracle was wrought
For, Baucis with Amazement found
Although the Jug had twice gone round
It still was full up to the Top
As if they ne're had drunk a Drop.
You may be sure, so strange a Sight

3. Cask.

Put the old People in a Fright; 80
Philemon whisper'd to his Wife,
These Men are Saints I'll lay my Life
The Strangers overheard, and said,
You're in the right, but be'n't afraid
No Hurt shall come to You or Yours;
But for that Pack of churlish Boors
Not fitt to live on Christian Ground,
They and their Village shall be droun'd,
Whilst You shall see your Cottage rise,
And grow a Church before your Eyes. 90
    Scarce had they spoke when fair and soft
The Roof began to mount aloft
Aloft rose ev'ry Beam and Rafter,
The heavy Wall went clamb'ring after.
The Chimny widen'd and grew high'r,
Became a Steeple with a Spire:
The Kettle to the Top was hoist
And there stood fastned to a Joyst,
But with the upside doun to shew
It's Inclination for below; 100
In vain; for a superior Force
Apply'd at Bottom stops it's Course;
Doomd ever in Suspense to dwell,
Tis now no Kettle but a Bell.
The groaning Chair began to crawll
Like a huge Insect up the Wall,
There stuck, and to a Pulpitt grew,
But kept it's Matter and it's Hue,
And mindfull of it's antient State,
Still Groans while tatling Gossips prate. 110
    The Mortar onely chang'd it's Name,
In it's old Shape a Font became
    The Porrengers that in a Row
Hung high and made a glitt'ring Show
To a less noble Substance chang'd
Were now but leathern Buckets rang'd.
    The Ballads pasted round the Wall,
Of Chivy-chase, and English Mall,
Fair Rosamond, and Robin Hood,
The little Children in the Wood, 120
Enlarg'd in Picture, Size and Letter
And painted, lookt abundance better
And now the Heraldry describe
Of a Churchwarden or a Tribe.
    The wooden Jack[4] which had almost

4. Swift plays on two possible meanings of "Jack": a contrivance for turning a spit; a carved figure, usually of a man, that strikes the time on a tower bell. The "Fly'r," a wheel used for purposes of rotation, slows here to the pace of a clock.

Lost by Disuse the Art to roast
A sudden Alteration feels,
Encreas't by new intestin Wheels
But what adds to the Wonder more,
The Number made the Motion slower   130
The Fly'r, altho't had leaden Feet,
Would turn so quick you scarce could see't
But now stopt by some hidden Pow'rs
Moves round but twice in twice twelve Hours
While in the Station of a Jack
'Twas never known to turn its Back
A Friend in Turns and Windings try'd
Nor ever left the Chimny side.
The Chimny to a Steeple grown,
The Jack would not be left alone   140
But up against the Steeple rear'd,
Became a Clock, and still adher'd,
And still it's Love to Houshold Cares
By a shrill Voice at Noon declares,
Warning the Cook-maid not to burn
That Roast-meat which it cannot turn.
    A Bed-sted in the antique mode
Compos'd of Timber many a Load;
Such as our Grandfathers did use,
Was Metamorphos'd into Pews;   150
Which yet their former Virtue keep,
By lodging Folks dispos'd to sleep.
    The Cottage with such Feats as these
Grown to a Church by just Degrees,
The holy Men desir'd their Host
To ask for what he fancy'd most.
Philemon having paus'd a while
Reply'd in complementall Style:
Your Goodness more than my Desert
Makes you take all things in good Part: 160
You've rais'd a Church here in a Minute,
And I would fain continue in it;
I'm good for little at my Days;
Make me the Parson if you please.
He spoke. and presently he feels
His Grazier's Coat reach down his Heels,
The Sleeves new border'd with a List[5]
Widn'd and gatherd at his Wrist;
But being old continued just
As threadbare, and as full of Dust.   170
A shambling awkward Gate he took,
With a demure dejected Look.

5. Strip of cloth.

Talkt of his Off'rings, Tyths, and Dues,
Could smoak, and drink, and read the News;
Or sell a Goose at the next Toun
Decently hid beneath his Goun.
Contrivd to preach his Sermon next
Chang'd in the Preface and the Text:
Carry'd it to his Equalls high'r,
But most obsequious to the Squire.   180
At Christnings well could act his Part,
And had the Service all by Heart;
Wish'd Women might have Children fast,
And thought whose *Sow* had *farrow'd* last:
Against *Dissenters* wou'd repine,
And stood up firm for *Right Divine*:
Found his Head fill'd with many a System,
But Classick Authors—he ne'er miss'd 'em.
  Thus having furbish'd up a Parson,
Dame *Baucis* next, they play'd their Farce on: 190
Instead of Home-spun Coifs were seen,
Good Pinners edg'd with Colberteen:[6]
Her Petticoat transform'd apace,
Became Black Sattin, Flounc'd with Lace.
Plain *Goody* would no longer down,
'Twas *Madam*, in her Grogram Gown.
Philemon was in great Surprize,
And hardly could believe his Eyes,
Amaz'd to see her look so prim,
And she admir'd as much at him.   200
  Thus, happy in their Change of Life,
Were several Years this Man and Wife,
When on a Day, which prov'd their last,
Discoursing on old Stories past,
They went by chance, amidst their Talk,
To the Church-yard, to take a Walk;
When *Baucis* hastily cry'd out;
My Dear, I see your Forehead sprout:
Sprout, quoth the Man, What's this you tell us?
I hope you don't believe me Jealous: 210
But yet, methinks, I feel it true;
And re'ly, yours is budding too—
Nay,—now I cannot stir my Foot:
It feels as if 'twere taking Root.
  Description would but tire my Muse:
In short, they both were turn'd to *Yews*.
Old Good-man *Dobson* of the Green
Remembers he the Trees has seen;

6. Baucis' hood-like caps are transformed into more delicate lace-edged caps with
lappets.

He'll talk of them from Noon till Night,
And goes with Folks to shew the Sight: 220
On *Sundays*, after Ev'ning Prayer,
He gathers all the Parish there;
Points out the Place of either *Yew*;
Here *Baucis*, there *Philemon* grew.
Till once, a Parson of our Town,
To mend his Barn, cut *Baucis* down;
At which, 'tis hard to be believ'd,
How much the other Tree was griev'd,
Grew scrubby, dy'd a-top, was stunted:
So, the next Parson stub'd and burnt it.   230

A Description of the Morning

1709

Now hardly here and there an Hackney-Coach
Appearing, show'd the ruddy Morns Approach.
Now *Betty* from her Masters Bed had flown,
And softly stole to discompose her own.
The Slipshod Prentice from his Masters Door
Had par'd the Dirt, and sprinkled round the Floor.
Now *Moll* had whirl'd her Mop with dext'rous Airs,
Prepar'd to Scrub the Entry and the Stairs.
The Youth with broomy Stumps began to trace
The Kennel-Edge, where Wheels had worn the Place.   10
The Smallcoal-Man was heard with Cadence deep,
'Till drown'd in shriller Notes of Chimney-Sweep.
Duns at his Lordships Gate began to meet,
And Brickdust *Moll* had Scream'd through half the Street.
The Turnkey now his Flock returning sees,
Duly let out a Nights to steal for Fees.
The watchful Bailiffs take their silent Stands,
And School-Boys lag with Satchels in their Hands.

A Description of a City Shower

1710

Careful Observers may fortel the Hour
(By sure Prognosticks) when to dread a Show'r:
While Rain depends, the pensive Cat gives o'er

Her Frolicks, and purses her Tail no more.
Returning Home at Night, you'll find the Sink[1]
Strike your offended Sense with double Stink.
If you be wise, then go not far to dine,
You'll spend in Coach-hire more than save in Wine.
A coming Show'r your shooting Corns presage,
Old Aches throb, your hollow Tooth will rage.   10
Sauntring in Coffee-house is *Dulman* seen;
He damns the Climate, and complains of Spleen.
   Meanwhile the South rising with dabbled Wings,
A Sable Cloud a-thwart the Welkin flings,
That swill'd more Liquor than it could contain,
And like a Drunkard gives it up again.
Brisk *Susan* whips her Linen from the Rope,
While the first drizzling Show'r is born aslope,
Such is that Sprinkling which some careless Quean[2]
Flirts on you from her Mop, but not so clean.   20
You fly, invoke the Gods; then turning, stop
To rail; she singing, still whirls on her Mop.
Not yet the Dust had shun'd th' unequal Strife,
But aided by the Wind, fought still for Life;
And wafted with its Foe by violent Gust,
'Twas doubtful which was Rain, and which was Dust.
Ah! where must needy Poet seek for Aid,
When Dust and Rain at once his Coat invade;
His only Coat, where Dust confus'd with Rain,
Roughen the Nap, and leave a mingled Stain.   30
   Now in contiguous Drops the Flood comes down,
Threat'ning with Deluge this *devoted* Town.
To Shops in Crouds the dagged[3] Females fly,
Pretend to cheapen Goods, but nothing buy.
The Templer spruce, while ev'ry Spout's a-broach,
Stays till 'tis fair, yet seems to call a Coach.
The tuck'd-up Sempstress walks with hasty Strides,
While Streams run down her oil'd Umbrella's Sides.
Here various Kinds by various Fortunes led,
Commence Acquaintance underneath a Shed.   40
Triumphant Tories, and desponding Whigs,
Forget their Fewds, and join to save their Wigs.
Box'd in a Chair[4] the Beau impatient sits,
While Spouts run clatt'ring o'er the Roof by Fits;
And ever and anon with frightful Din
The Leather sounds, he trembles from within.
So when *Troy* Chair-men bore the Wooden Steed,
Pregnant with *Greeks*, impatient to be freed,

1. Sewer.
2. Slut.
3. Wet with drizzling rain.
4. Sedan chair, covered with leather.

(Those Bully *Greeks*, who, as the Moderns do,
Instead of paying Chair-men, run them thro')   50
Laoco'n struck the Outside with his Spear,
And each imprison'd Hero quak'd for Fear.
    Now from all Parts the swelling Kennels[5] flow,
And bear their Trophies with them as they go:
Filth of all Hues and Odours seem to tell
What Street they sail'd from, by their Sight and Smell.
They, as each Torrent drives, with rapid Force
From *Smithfield*, or St. *Pulchre*'s shape their Course,
And in huge Confluent join at *Snow-Hill* Ridge,
Fall from the *Conduit* prone to *Holborn-Bridge*.   60
Sweepings from Butchers Stalls, Dung, Guts, and Blood, ⎫
Drown'd Puppies, stinking Sprats, all drench'd in Mud, ⎬
Dead Cats and Turnip-Tops come tumbling down the Flood. ⎭

Phillis, or, the Progress of Love

1719

Desponding Phillis was endu'd
With ev'ry Talent of a Prude,
She trembled when a Man drew near;
Salute her, and she turn'd her Ear:
If o'er against her you were plac't
She durst not look above your Wast;
She'd rather take you to her Bed
Than let you see her dress her Head;
In Church you heard her thrô the Crowd
Repeat the Absolution loud;   10
In Church, secure behind her Fan
She durst behold that Monster, Man:
There practic'd how to place her Head,
And bit her Lips to make them red:
Or on the Matt devoutly kneeling
Would lift her Eyes up to the Ceeling,
And heave her Bosom unaware
For neighb'ring Beaux to see it bare.
    At length a lucky Lover came,
And found Admittance from the Dame.   20
Suppose all Partyes now agreed,
The Writings drawn, the Lawyer fee'd,
The Vicar and the Ring bespoke:

5. Street channels for the flow of refuse.

Guess how could such a Match be broke.
See then what Mortals place their Bliss in!
Next morn betimes the Bride was missing,
The Mother scream'd, the Father chid,
Where can this idle Wench be hid?
No news of Phil. The Bridegroom came,
And thought his Bride had sculk't for Shame,   30
Because her Father us'd to say
The Girl had such a bashfull Way.
  Now, John the Butler must be sent
To learn the Way that Phillis went;
The Groom was wisht to saddle Crop,
For John must neither light nor stop;
But find her where so'er she fled,
And bring her back, alive oi dead.
See here again the Dev'l to do;
For truly John was missing too: 40
The Horse and Pillion[1] both were gone
Phillis, it seems, was fled with John.
Old Madam who went up to find
What Papers Phil had left behind,
A Letter on the Toylet sees
To my much honor'd Father; These:
('Tis always done, Romances tell us,
When Daughters run away with Fellows)
Fill'd with the choicest Common-places,
By others us'd in the like Cases.   50
That, long ago a Fortune-teller
Exactly said what now befell her,
And in a Glass had made her see
A Serving-man of low Degree:
It was her Fate; must be forgiven;
For Marriages are made in Heaven:
His Pardon begg'd, but to be plain,
She'd do't if 'twere to do again.
Thank God, 'twas neither Shame nor Sin,
For John was come of honest Kin: 60
Love never thinks of Rich and Poor,
She'd beg with John from Door to Door:
Forgive her, if it be a Crime,
She'll never do't another Time,
She ne'r before in all her Life
Once disobey'd him, Maid nor Wife.
One Argument she summ'd up all in,
The Thing was done and past recalling:
And therefore hop'd she would recover
His Favor, when his Passion's over.   70

---

1. Cushioned or padded saddle designed for women.

She valued not what others thought her;
And was—His most obedient Daughter.
    Fair Maidens all attend the Muse
Who now the wandring Pair pursues:
Away they rode in homely Sort
Their Journy long, their Money short;
The loving Couple well bemir'd,
The Horse and both the Riders tir'd:
Their Vittells bad, their Lodging worse,
Phil cry'd, and John began to curse;   80
Phil wish't, that she had strained a Limb
When first she ventur'd out with him.
John wish't, that he had broke a Leg
When first for her he quitted Peg.
    But what Adventures more befell 'um
The Muse has now not time to tell 'um.
How Jonny wheadled, threatned, fawnd,
Till Phillis all her Trinkets pawn'd:
How oft she broke her marriage Vows
In Kindness to maintain her Spouse;   90
Till Swains unwholsome spoyld the Trade,
For now the Surgeon must be paid;
To whom those Perquisites are gone
In Christian Justice due to John.
    When Food and Rayment now grew scarce
Fate put a Period to the Farce;
And with exact Poetick Justice:
For John is Landlord, Phillis Hostess;
They keep at Stains the old blue Boar,
Are Cat and Dog, and Rogue and Whore.   100

The Progress of Beauty

1719

When first Diana[1] leaves her Bed
Vapors and Steams her Looks disgrace,
A frouzy dirty colour'd Red
Sits on her cloudy wrinckled Face.

But by Degrees when mounted high
Her artificiall Face appears
Down from her Window in the Sky,
Her Spots are gone, her Visage clears.

1. **Roman goddess one of whose associations was with the moon.**

'Twixt earthly Females and the Moon
All Parallells exactly run;
If Celia should appear too soon
Alas, the Nymph would be undone.

To see her from her Pillow rise
All reeking in a cloudy Steam,
Crackt Lips, foul Teeth, and gummy Eyes,
Poor Strephon, how would he blaspheme!

The Soot or Powder which was wont
To make her Hair look black as Jet,
Falls from her Tresses on her Front
A mingled Mass of Dirt and Sweat.

Three Colours, Black, and Red, and White,
So gracefull in their proper Place,
Remove them to a diff'rent Light
They form a frightfull hideous Face,

For instance; when the Lilly slipps
Into the Precincts of the Rose,
And takes Possession of the Lips,
Leaving the Purple to the Nose.

So Celia went entire to Bed,
All her Complexions safe and sound,
But when she rose, the Black and Red
Though still in Sight, had chang'd their Ground.

The Black, which would not be confin'd
A more inferior Station seeks
Leaving the fiery Red behind,
And mingles in her muddy Cheeks.

The Paint by Perspiration cracks,
And falls in Rivulets of Sweat,
On either Side you see the Tracks,
While at her Chin the Conflu'ents met.

A Skillfull Houswife thus her Thumb
With Spittle while she spins, anoints,
And thus the brown Meanders come
In trickling Streams betwixt her Joynts.

But Celia can with Ease reduce
By Help of Pencil, Paint and Brush
Each Colour to it's Place and Use,
And teach her Cheeks again to blush.

She knows her early self no more,
But fill'd with Admiration, stands,
As Other Painters oft adore
The Workmanship of their own Hands.

Thus after four important Hours
Celia's the Wonder of her Sex;
Say, which among the Heav'nly Pow'rs
Could cause such wonderfull Effects.

Venus, indulgent to her Kind
Gave Women all their Hearts could wish
When first she taught them where to find
White Lead, and Lusitanian Dish.[2]   60

Love with white Lead cements his Wings,
White Lead was sent us to repair
Two brightest, brittlest earthly Things
A Lady's Face, and China ware.

She ventures now to lift the Sash,
The Window is her proper Sphear;
Ah Lovely Nymph be not too rash,
Nor let the Beaux approach too near.

Take Pattern by your Sister Star,
Delude at once and bless our Sight,   70
When you are seen, be seen from far,
And chiefly chuse to shine by Night.

In the Pell-mell when passing by,
Keep up the Glasses of your Chair,
Then each transported Fop will cry,
G——d d——m me Jack, she's wondrous fair.

But, Art no longer can prevayl
When the Materialls all are gone,
The best mechanick Hand must fayl
Where Nothing's left to work upon.   80

Matter, as wise Logicians say,
Cannot without a Form subsist,
And Form, say I, as well as They,
Must fayl if Matter brings no Grist.

And this is fair Diana's Case
For, all Astrologers maintain
Each Night a Bit drops off her Face
When Mortals say she's in her Wain.

While Partridge wisely shews the Cause
Efficient of the Moon's Decay,   90
That Cancer with his pois'nous Claws
Attacks her in the milky Way:

But Gadbury[3] in Art profound
From her pale Cheeks pretends to show

2. Cosmetics dish of Portuguese design.
3. A contemporary astrologer, as was Partridge (line 89). See also Swift's
treatment of the astrological mode in his Bickerstaff papers (pp. 426–441).

That Swain Endymion[4] is not sound,
Or else, that Mercury's[5] her Foe.

But, let the Cause be what it will,
In half a Month she looks so thin
That Flamstead[6] can with all his Skill
See but her Forehead and her Chin.   100

Yet as she wasts, she grows discreet,
Till Midnight never shows her Head;
So rotting Celia stroles the Street
When sober Folks are all a-bed.

For sure if this be Luna's Fate,
Poor Celia, but of mortall Race
In vain expects a longer Date
To the Materialls of Her Face.

When Mercury her Tresses mows
To think of Oyl and Soot, is vain,   110
No Painting can restore a Nose,
Nor will her Teeth return again.

Two Balls of Glass may serve for Eyes,
White Lead can plaister up a Cleft,
But these alas, are poor Supplyes
If neither Cheeks, nor Lips be left.

Ye Pow'rs who over Love preside,
Since mortal Beautyes drop so soon,
If you would have us well supply'd,
Send us new Nymphs with each new Moon.   120

On Stella's Birth-day, 1719[1]

Stella this Day is thirty four,
(We won't dispute a Year or more)
However Stella, be not troubled,
Although thy Size and Years are doubled,
Since first I saw thee at sixteen
The brightest Virgin of the Green,
So little is thy Form declin'd

4. Beautiful youth in Greek legend with whom the moon fell in love.
5. Roman god of commerce and (in association with the Greek god Hermes) go-between for the other gods; the name also of a medicine used especially for syphilis: in the course of treatment, either from the disease or from the remedy, the subject's hair sometimes fell out, a fate suffered by Swift's heroine (line 109), whose damaged nose (line 111) is also suggestive of venereal infection.
6. John Flamsteed, first astronomer royal.
1. Stella's birthday fell on March 13, thus before the change of the year from 1718 to 1719 in the old-style calendar.

Made up so largly in thy Mind.
Oh, would it please the Gods to split
Thy Beauty, Size, and Years, and Wit,   10
No Age could furnish out a Pair
Of Nymphs so gracefull, wise and fair
With half the Lustre of your Eyes,
With half thy Wit, thy Years and Size:
And then before it grew too late,
How should I beg of gentle Fate,
(That either Nymph might have her Swain,)
To split my Worship too in twain.

The Progress of Poetry

1720

The Farmer's Goose, who in the Stubble,
Has fed without Restraint, or Trouble;
Grown fat with Corn and Sitting still,
Can scarce get o'er the Barn-door Sill:
And hardly waddles forth, to cool
Her Belly in the neighb'ring Pool:
Nor loudly cackles at the Door;
For Cackling shews the Goose is poor.
    But when she must be turn'd to graze,
And round the barren Common strays,   10
Hard Exercise, and harder Fare
Soon make my Dame grow lank and spare:
Her Body light, she tries her Wings,
And scorns the Ground, and upward springs,
While all the Parish, as she flies,
Hear Sounds harmonious from the Skies.
    Such is the Poet, fresh in Pay,
(The third Night's Profits of his Play;)[1]
His Morning-Draughts 'till Noon can swill,
Among his Brethren of the Quill: 20
With good Roast Beef his Belly full,
Grown lazy, foggy, fat, and dull:
Deep sunk in Plenty, and Delight,
What Poet e'er could take his Flight?
Or stuff'd with Phlegm[2] up to the Throat,
What Poet e'er could sing a Note?
Nor *Pegasus* could bear the Load,
Along the high celestial Road;

1. The performance the income from which was traditionally set aside for the author.
2. Lethargy.

The Steed, oppress'd, would break his Girth,
To raise the Lumber from the Earth.   30
　But, view him in another Scene,
When all his Drink is *Hippocrene*,[3]
His Money spent, his Patrons fail,
His Credit out for Cheese and Ale;
His Two-Year's Coat so smooth and bare,
Through ev'ry Thread it lets in Air;
With hungry Meals his Body pin'd,
His Guts and Belly full of Wind;
And, like a Jockey for a Race,
His Flesh brought down to Flying-case:[4]   40
Now his exalted Spirit loaths
Incumbrances of Food and Cloaths;
And up he rises like a Vapour,
Supported high on Wings of Paper;
He singing flies, and flying sings,
While from below all *Grub-street* rings.

Stella's Birth-day, 1721

All Travellers at first incline
Where'e'r they see the fairest Sign,
And if they find the Chambers neat,
And like the Liquor and the Meat
Will call again and recommend
The Angel-Inn to ev'ry Friend:
And though the Painting grows decayd
The House will never loose it's Trade;
Nay, though the treach'rous Rascal Thomas
Hangs a new Angel two doors from us   10
As fine as Dawbers Hands can make it
In hopes that Strangers may mistake it,
They think it both a Shame and Sin
To quit the true old Angel-Inn.
　Now, this is Stella's Case in Fact;
An Angel's Face, a little crack't;
(Could Poets or could Painters fix
How Angels look at thirty six)
This drew us in at first to find
In such a Form an Angel's Mind   20
And ev'ry Virtue now supplyes
The fainting Rays of Stella's Eyes:
See, at her Levee[1] crowding Swains

3. Legendary waters of inspiration, sacred to the muses.
4. Spare condition.
1. Occasion for receiving visitors and favor-seekers by persons of distinction.

Whom Stella freely entertains
With Breeding, Humor, Wit, and Sense,
And puts them to so small Expence,
Their Minds so plentifully fills,
And makes such reasonable Bills
So little gets for what she gives
We really wonder how she lives;   30
And, had her Stock been less, no doubt
She must have long ago run out.
    Then, who can think we'll quit the Place
When Doll hangs out a newer Face
Nail'd to her Window full in Sight
All Christian People to invite;
Or stop and light at Cloe's Head
With Scraps and Leavings to be fed.
    Then Cloe, still go on to prate
Of thirty six, and thirty eight;   40
Pursue thy Trade of Scandall picking,
Thy Hints that Stella is no Chickin,
Your Innuendo's when you tell us
That Stella loves to talk with Fellows
But let me warn thee to believe
A Truth for which thy Soul should grieve,
That, should you live to see the Day
When Stella's Locks must all be grey
When Age must print a furrow'd Trace
On ev'ry Feature of her Face;   50
Though you and all your senceless Tribe
Could Art or Time or Nature bribe
To make you look like Beauty's Queen
And hold for ever at fifteen.
No Bloom of Youth can ever blind
The Cracks and Wrinckles of your Mind,
All Men of Sense will pass your Dore
And crowd to Stella's at fourscore.

A Satirical Elegy On the
Death of a late Famous General[1]

1722

His Grace! impossible! what dead!
Of old Age too, and in his Bed!
And could that Mighty Warrior fall?

1. The Duke of Marlborough died June 16, 1722. Although written on this
occasion, Swift's poem was not published until 1764, nearly twenty years after his
own death.

And so inglorious, after all!
Well, since he's gone, no matter how,
The last loud Trump must wake him now:
And, trust me, as the Noise grows stronger,
He'd wish to sleep a little longer.
And could he be indeed so old
As by the News-papers we're told?   10
Threescore, I think, is pretty high;
'Twas time in Conscience he should die.
This World he cumber'd long enough;
He burnt his Candle to the Snuff;
And that's the Reason, some Folks think,
He left behind *so great a S - - - k.*
Behold his Funeral appears,
Nor Widow's Sighs, nor Orphan's Tears,
Wont at such Times each Heart to pierce,
Attend the Progress of his Herse.   20
But what of that, his Friends may say,
He had those Honours in his Day.
True to his Profit and his Pride,
He made them weep before he dy'd.
   Come hither, all ye empty Things,
Ye Bubbles rais'd by Breath of Kings;
Who float upon the Tide of State,
Come hither, and behold your Fate.
Let Pride be taught by this Rebuke,
How very mean a Thing's a Duke;   30
From all his ill-got Honours flung,
Turn'd to that Dirt from whence he sprung.

The Furniture of a Woman's Mind

1727

A Set of Phrases learn't by Rote;
A Passion for a Scarlet-Coat;
When at a Play to laugh, or cry,
Yet cannot tell the Reason why:
Never to hold her Tongue a Minute;
While all she prates has nothing in it.
Whole Hours can with a Coxcomb sit,
And take his Nonsense all for Wit:
Her Learning mounts to read a Song,
But, half the Words pronouncing wrong;   10
Has ev'ry Repartee in Store,
She spoke ten Thousand Times before.
Can ready Compliments supply

On all Occasions, cut and dry.
Such Hatred to a Parson's Gown,
The Sight will put her in a Swown.[1]
For Conversation well endu'd;
She calls it witty to be rude;
And, placing Raillery in Railing,
Will tell aloud your greatest Failing;   20
Nor makes a Scruple to expose
Your bandy Leg, or crooked Nose.
Can, at her Morning Tea, run o'er
The Scandal of the Day before.
Improving hourly in her Skill,
To cheat and wrangle at Quadrille.[2]
  In chusing Lace a Critick nice,
Knows to a Groat the lowest Price;
Can in her Female Clubs dispute
What Lining best the Silk will suit;   30
What Colours each Complexion match:
And where with Art to place a Patch.
  If chance a Mouse creeps in her Sight,
Can finely counterfeit a Fright;
So, sweetly screams if it comes near her,
She ravishes all Hearts to hear her.
Can dext'rously her Husband teize,
By taking Fits whene'er she please:
By frequent Practice learns the Trick
At proper Seasons to be sick;   40
Thinks nothing gives one Airs so pretty;
At once creating Love and Pity.
If *Molly* happens to be careless,
And but neglects to warm her Hair-Lace,
She gets a Cold as sure as Death;
And vows she scarce can fetch her Breath.
Admires how modest Women can
Be so *robustious* like a Man.
  In Party, furious to her Power;
A bitter Whig, or Tory sow'r;   50
Her Arguments directly tend
Against the Side she would defend:
Will prove herself a Tory plain,
From Principles the Whigs maintain;
And, to defend the Whiggish Cause,
Her Topicks from the Tories draws.
  O yes! If any Man can find
More virtues in a Woman's Mind,

1. Swoon.
2. Fashionable game of cards.

Let them be sent to Mrs. *Harding;*[3]
She'll pay the Charges to a Farthing: 60
Take Notice, she has my Commission
To add them in the next Edition;
They may out-sell a better Thing;
So, Holla Boys; God save the King.

Stella's Birth-day, 1727[1]

This Day, whate'er the Fates decree,
Shall still be kept with Joy by me:
This Day then, let us not be told,
That you are sick, and I grown old,
Nor think on our approaching Ills,
And talk of Spectacles and Pills;
To morrow will be Time enough
To hear such mortifying Stuff.
Yet, since from Reason may be brought
A better and more pleasing Thought,   10
Which can in spite of all Decays,
Support a few remaining Days:
From not the gravest of Divines,
Accept for once some serious Lines.
    Although we now can form no more
Long Schemes of Life, as heretofore;
Yet you, while Time is running fast,
Can look with Joy on what is past.
    Were future Happiness and Pain,
A mere Contrivance of the Brain,   20
As Atheists argue, to entice,
And fit their Proselytes for Vice;
(The only Comfort they propose,
To have Companions in their Woes.)
Grant this the Case, yet sure 'tis hard,
That Virtue, stil'd its own Reward,
And by all Sages understood
To be the chief of human Good,
Should acting, die, nor leave behind
Some lasting Pleasure in the Mind,   30
Which by Remembrance will assuage,

3. Widow of the Irish printer John Harding, whose issuance of Swift's *Drapier's Letters* (see p. 487) was followed by his arrest and, while in prison, his death.
1. Stella died on January 28, 1727–28.

Grief, Sickness, Poverty, and Age;
And strongly shoot a radiant Dart,
To shine through Life's declining Part.
  Say, *Stella*, feel you no Content,
Reflecting on a Life well spent?
Your skilful Hand employ'd to save
Despairing Wretches from the Grave;
And then supporting with your Store,
Those whom you dragg'd from Death before: 40
(So Providence on Mortals waits,
Preserving what it first creates)
Your gen'rous Boldness to defend
An innocent and absent Friend;
That Courage which can make you just,
To Merit humbled in the Dust:
The Detestation you express
For Vice in all its glitt'ring Dress:
That Patience under tort'ring Pain,
Where stubborn Stoicks would complain.   50
  Must these like empty Shadows pass,
Or Forms reflected from a Glass?
Or mere Chimæra's in the Mind,
That fly and leave no Marks behind?
Does not the Body thrive and grow
By Food of twenty Years ago?
And, had it not been still supply'd,
It must a thousand Times have dy'd.
Then, who with Reason can maintain,
That no Effects of Food remain?   60
And, is not Virtue in Mankind
The Nutriment that feeds the Mind?
Upheld by each good Action past,
And still continued by the last:
Then, who with Reason can pretend,
That all Effects of Virtue end?
  Believe me *Stella*, when you show
That true Contempt for Things below,
Nor prize your Life for other Ends
Than merely to oblige your Friends;   70
Your former Actions claim their Part,
And join to fortify your Heart.
For Virtue in her daily Race,
Like *Janus*, bears a double Face;
Looks back with Joy where she has gone,
And therefore goes with Courage on.
She at your sickly Couch will wait,
And guide you to a better State.
  O then, whatever Heav'n intends,

Take Pity on your pitying Friends;
Nor let your Ills affect your Mind,
To fancy they can be unkind.
Me, surely me, you ought to spare,
Who gladly would your Suff'rings share;
Or give my Scrap of Life to you,
And think it far beneath your Due;
You, to whose Care so oft I owe,
That I'm alive to tell you so.

A Pastoral Dialogue

1729

DERMOT, SHEELAH.

A Nymph and Swain, *Sheelah* and *Dermot* hight,
Who wont to weed the Court of *Gosford Knight*,
While each with stubbed Knife remov'd the Roots
That rais'd between the Stones their daily Shoots;
As at their Work they sate in counterview,
With mutual Beauty smit, their Passion grew.
Sing heavenly Muse in sweetly flowing Strain,
The soft Endearments of the Nymph and Swain.

DERMOT.

My Love to *Sheelah* is more firmly fixt
Than strongest Weeds that grow these Stones betwixt: 10
My Spud these Nettles from the Stones can part,
No Knife so keen to weed thee from my Heart.

SHEELAH.

My Love for gentle *Dermot* faster grows
Than yon tall Dock that rises to thy Nose.
Cut down the Dock, 'twill sprout again: but O!
Love rooted out, again will never grow.

DERMOT.

No more that Bry'r thy tender Leg shall rake:
(I spare the Thistle for Sir *Arthur*'s sake.)[1]

1. The setting of the poem is the estate in the North of Ireland of Sir Arthur
Acheson, who piqued himself on being a Scotsman.

Sharp are the Stones, take thou this rushy Matt;
The hardest Bum will bruise with sitting squat.   20

SHEELAH.

Thy Breeches torn behind, stand gaping wide;
This Petticoat shall save thy dear Back-side;
Nor need I blush, although you feel it wet;
Dermot, I vow, 'tis nothing else but Sweat.

DERMOT.

At an old stubborn Root I chanc'd to tug,
When the Dean threw me this Tobacco-plug:
A longer half-p'orth never did I see;
This, dearest Sheelah, thou shalt share with me.

SHEELAH.

In at the Pantry-door this Morn I slipt,
And from the Shelf a charming Crust I whipt: 30
Dennis was out, and I got hither safe;
And thou, my dear, shalt have the bigger half.

DERMOT.

When you saw Tady at Long-bullets play,[2]
You sat and lows'd him all the Sun-shine Day.
How could you, Sheelah, listen to his Tales,
Or crack such Lice as his betwixt your Nails?

SHEELAH.

When you with Oonah stood behind a Ditch,
I peept, and saw you kiss the dirty Bitch.
Dermot, how could you touch those nasty Sluts!
I almost wisht this Spud were in your Guts.   40

DERMOT.

If Oonah once I kiss'd, forbear to chide:
Her Aunt's my Gossip by my Father's Side:
But, if I ever touch her Lips again,
May I be doom'd for Life to weed in Rain.

2. A variety of ninepins.

SHEELAH.

Dermot, I swear, tho' *Tady*'s Locks could hold
Ten thousand Lice, and ev'ry Louse was gold,
Him on my Lap you never more should see;
Or may I lose my Weeding-knife—and Thee.

DERMOT.

O, could I earn for thee, my lovely Lass,
A pair of Brogues to bear thee dry to Mass!   50
But see, where *Norah* with the Sowins³ comes—
Then let us rise, and rest our weary Bums.

The Lady's Dressing Room

1730

Five Hours, (and who can do it less in?)
By haughty *Celia* spent in Dressing;
The Goddess from her Chamber issues,
Array'd in Lace, Brocades and Tissues.
    Strephon, who found the Room was void,
And *Betty* otherwise employ'd;
Stole in, and took a strict Survey,
Of all the Litter as it lay;
Whereof, to make the Matter clear,
An Inventory follows here.   10
    And first a dirty Smock appear'd,
Beneath the Arm-pits well besmear'd.
Strephon, the Rogue, display'd it wide,
And turn'd it round on every Side.
On such a Point few Words are best,
And *Strephon* bids us guess the rest;
But swears how damnably the Men lie,
In calling *Celia* sweet and cleanly.
Now listen while he next produces,
The various Combs for various Uses,   20
Fill'd up with Dirt so closely fixt,
No Brush could force a Way betwixt.
A Paste of Composition rare,

3. A food made of oatmeal.

Sweat, Dandriff, Powder, Lead and Hair;
A Forehead Cloth with Oyl upon't
To smooth the Wrinkles on her Front;
Here Allum Flower to stop the Steams,
Exhal'd from sour unsavoury Streams,
There Night-gloves made of *Tripsy*'s Hide,
Bequeath'd by *Tripsy* when she dy'd,   30
With Puppy Water, Beauty's Help
Distill'd from *Tripsy*'s darling Whelp;
Here Gallypots[1] and Vials plac'd,
Some fill'd with Washes, some with Paste,
Some with Pomatum, Paints and Slops,
And Ointments good for scabby Chops.
Hard by a filthy Bason stands,
Fowl'd with the Scouring of her Hands;
The Bason takes whatever comes
The Scrapings of her Teeth and Gums,   40
A nasty Compound of all Hues,
For here she spits, and here she spues.
But oh! it turn'd poor *Strephon*'s Bowels,
When he beheld and smelt the Towels,
Begumm'd, bematter'd, and beslim'd
With Dirt, and Sweat, and Ear-Wax grim'd.
No Object *Strephon*'s Eye escapes,
Here Pettycoats in frowzy Heaps;
Nor be the Handkerchiefs forgot
All varnish'd o'er with Snuff and Snot.   50
The Stockings, why shou'd I expose,
Stain'd with the Marks of stinking Toes;
Or greasy Coifs and Pinners[2] reeking,
Which *Celia* slept at least a Week in?
A Pair of Tweezers next he found
To pluck her Brows in Arches round,
Or Hairs that sink the Forehead low,
Or on her Chin like Bristles grow.
    The Virtues we must not let pass,
Of *Celia*'s magnifying Glass.[3]   60
When frighted *Strephon* cast his Eye on't
It shew'd the Visage of a Gyant.
A Glass that can to Sight disclose,
The smallest Worm in *Celia*'s Nose,
And faithfully direct her Nail
To squeeze it out from Head to Tail;
For catch it nicely by the Head,
It must come out alive or dead.
    Why *Strephon* will you tell the rest?

1. Earthenware.
2. Types of headwear.
3. See also the effects of magnification throughout Book II of *Gulliver's Travels*,
esp. pp. 85 and 90.

And must you needs describe the Chest?   70
That careless Wench! no Creature warn her
To move it out from yonder Corner;
But leave it standing full in Sight
For you to exercise your Spight.
In vain, the Workman shew'd his Wit
With Rings and Hinges counterfeit
To make it seem in this Disguise,
A Cabinet to vulgar Eyes;
For *Strephon* ventur'd to look in,
Resolv'd to go thro' thick and thin;   80
He lifts the Lid, there needs no more,
He smelt it all the Time before.
As from within *Pandora's* Box,
When *Epimetheus*[4] op'd the Locks,
A sudden universal Crew
Of humane Evils upwards flew;
He still was comforted to find
That *Hope* at last remain'd behind;
So *Strephon* lifting up the Lid,
To view what in the Chest was hid.   90
The Vapours flew from out the Vent,
But *Strephon* cautious never meant
The Bottom of the Pan to grope,
And fowl his Hands in Search of *Hope.*
O never may such vile Machine
Be once in *Celia's* Chamber seen!
O may she better learn to keep
Those "Secrets of the hoary Deep!"
    As Mutton Cutlets, Prime of Meat,
Which tho' with Art you salt and beat,   100
As Laws of Cookery require,
And toast them at the clearest Fire;
If from adown the hopeful Chops
The Fat upon a Cinder drops,
To stinking Smoak it turns the Flame
Pois'ning the Flesh from whence it came;
And up exhales a greasy Stench,
For which you curse the careless Wench;
So Things, which must not be exprest,
When plumpt into the reeking Chest;   110
Send up an excremental Smell
To taint the Parts from whence they fell.
The Pettycoats and Gown perfume,
Which waft a Stink round every Room.
    Thus finishing his grand Survey,

4. The brother of Prometheus, he accepted Zeus' creation, Pandora, who brought
with her a box which when opened let loose all manner of evils to afflict the earth;
"hope" alone remained at the bottom of the box, ever to be reached for.

Disgusted *Strephon* stole away
Repeating in his amorous Fits,
Oh! *Celia, Celia, Celia* shits!
   But Vengeance, Goddess never sleeping
Soon punish'd *Strephon* for his Peeping;   120
His foul Imagination links
Each Dame he sees with all her Stinks:
And, if unsav'ry Odours fly,
Conceives a Lady standing by:
All Women his Description fits,
And both Idea's jump like Wits:
By vicious Fancy coupled fast,
And still appearing in Contrast.
I pity wretched *Strephon* blind
To all the Charms of Female Kind;   130
Should I the Queen of Love refuse,
Because she rose from stinking Ooze?
To him that looks behind the Scene,
Satira's but some pocky Quean.
When *Celia* in her Glory shows,
If *Strephon* would but stop his Nose;
(Who now so impiously blasphemes
Her Ointments, Daubs, and Paints and Creams,
Her Washes, Slops, and every Clout,
With which he makes so foul a Rout;)   140
He soon would learn to think like me,
And bless his ravisht Sight to see
Such Order from Confusion sprung,
Such gaudy Tulips rais'd from Dung.

A Beautiful Young Nymph Going to Bed

1731

Corinna, Pride of *Drury-Lane*,
For whom no Shepherd sighs in vain;
Never did *Covent Garden* boast
So bright a batter'd, strolling Toast;
No drunken Rake to pick her up,
No Cellar where on Tick[1] to sup;
Returning at the Midnight Hour;
Four Stories climbing to her Bow'r;
Then, seated on a three-legg'd Chair,

1. Credit.

Takes off her artificial Hair: 10
Now, picking out a Crystal Eye,
She wipes it clean, and lays it by.
Her Eye-Brows from a Mouse's Hyde,
Stuck on with Art on either Side,
Pulls off with Care, and first displays 'em,
Then in a Play-Book smoothly lays 'em.
Now dextrously her Plumpers draws,
That serve to fill her hollow Jaws.
Untwists a Wire; and from her Gums
A Set of Teeth completely comes.   20
Pulls out the Rags contriv'd to prop
Her flabby Dugs and down they drop.
Proceeding on, the lovely Goddess
Unlaces next her Stccl-Rib'd Bodice;
Which by the Operator's Skill,
Press down the Lumps, the Hollows fill,
Up goes her Hand, and off she slips
The Bolsters that supply her Hips.
With gentlest Touch, she next explores
Her Shankers, Issues, running Sores,   30
Effects of many a sad Disaster;
And then to each applies a Plaister.
But must, before she goes to Bed,
Rub off the Dawbs of White and Red;
And smooth the Furrows in her Front,
With greasy Paper stuck upon't.
She takes a *Bolus* e'er she sleeps;
And then between two Blankets creeps.
With Pains of Love tormented lies;
Or if she chance to close her Eyes,   40
Of *Bridewell* and the *Compter*² dreams,
And feels the Lash, and faintly screams;
Or, by a faithless Bully drawn,
At some Hedge-Tavern lies in Pawn;
Or to *Jamaica* seems transported,
*Alone, and by no Planter courted;
Or, near *Fleet-Ditch*'s oozy Brinks,
Surrounded with a Hundred Stinks,
Belated, seems on watch to lye,
And snap some Cully³ passing by;   50
Or, struck with Fear, her Fancy runs
On Watchmen, Constables and Duns,
From whom she meets with frequent Rubs;

2. Compters were prisons, similar to Bridewell, for vagrants and harlots.
*————*Et longam incomitata videtur*
Ire viam ——— ["She seems to travel a long way alone." Inexactly quoted from
Vergil. *Aeneid.* IV, 467–68.—*Editors*]
3. Simpleton.

But, never from Religious Clubs;
Whose Favour she is sure to find,
Because she pays 'em all in Kind.
  Corinna wakes. A dreadful Sight!
Behold the Ruins of the Night!
A wicked Rat her Plaister stole,
Half eat, and dragg'd it to his Hole.   60
The Crystal Eye, alas, was miss't;
And *Puss* had on her Plumpers p - - - st.
A Pigeon pick'd her Issue-Peas;[4]
And *Shock* her Tresses fill'd with Fleas.
  The Nymph, tho' in this mangled Plight,
Must ev'ry Morn her Limbs unite.
But how shall I describe her Arts
To recollect the scatter'd Parts?
Or shew the Anguish, Toil, and Pain,
Of gath'ring up herself again?   70
The bashful Muse will never bear
In such a Scene to interfere.
Corinna in the Morning dizen'd,[5]
Who sees, will spew; who smells, be poison'd.

Strephon and Chloe

1731

Of *Chloe* all the Town has rung;
By ev'ry size of Poets sung:
So beautiful a Nymph appears
But once in Twenty Thousand Years.
By Nature form'd with nicest Care,
And, faultless to a single Hair.
Her graceful Mein, her Shape, and Face,
Confest her of no mortal Race:
And then, so nice, and so genteel;
Such Cleanliness from Head to Heel: 10
No Humours gross, or frowzy Steams,
No noisom Whiffs, or sweaty Streams,
Before, behind, above, below,
Could from her taintless Body flow.
Would so discreetly Things dispose,
None ever saw her pluck a Rose.

4. Peas or other small globular bodies put in surgical issues to keep up the effects
of irritation.
5. Dizened, i.e., dressed up.

Her dearest Comrades never caught her
Squat on her Hams, to make Maid's Water.
You'd swear, that so divine a Creature
Felt no Necessities of Nature.   20
In Summer had she walkt the Town,
Her Arm-pits would not stain her Gown:
At Country Dances, not a Nose
Could in the Dog-Days smell her Toes.
Her Milk-white Hands, both Palms and Backs,
Like Iv'ry dry, and soft as Wax.
Her Hands the softest ever felt,
*Tho' cold would burn, tho' dry would melt.
   Dear *Venus*, hide this wond'rous Maid,
Nor let her loose to spoil your Trade.   30
While she engrosseth ev'ry Swain,
You but o'er half the World can reign.
Think what a Case all Men are now in,
What ogling, sighing, toasting, vowing!
What powder'd Wigs! What Flames and Darts!
What Hampers full of bleeding Hearts!
What Sword-knots! What Poetic Strains!
What Billet-doux, and clouded Cains!
   But, *Strephon* sigh'd so loud and strong,
He blew a Settlement along: 40
And, bravely drove his Rivals down
With Coach and Six, and House in Town.
The bashful Nymph no more withstands,
Because her dear Papa commands.
The charming Couple now unites;
Proceed we to the Marriage Rites.
   Imprimis, at the Temple Porch
Stood *Hymen*[1] with a flaming Torch.
The smiling *Cyprian* Goddess brings
Her infant Loves with purple Wings;   50
And Pigeons billing, Sparrows treading,
Fair Emblems of a fruitful Wedding.
The Muses next in Order follow,
Conducted by their Squire, *Apollo:*
Then *Mercury* with Silver Tongue,
And *Hebe*, Goddess ever young.
Behold the Bridegroom and his Bride,
Walk Hand in Hand, and Side by Side;
She by the tender Graces drest,
But, he by *Mars*, in scarlet Vest.   60
The Nymph was cover'd with her †*Flammeum*,

* *Tho' deep, yet clear*, &c. DENHAM.
1. Greek god of marriage. Cyprian: Venus, here bearing her cupids.
† A Veil which the *Roman* Brides covered themselves with, when they were going
to be married.

And *Phœbus* sung th' *Epithalamium.*
And, last to make the Matter sure,
Dame *Juno* brought a Priest demure.
†*Luna* was absent on Pretence
Her Time was not till nine Months hence.
The Rites perform'd, the Parson paid,
In State return'd the grand Parade;
With loud Huzza's from all the Boys,
That now the Pair must *crown their Joys.*   70
But, still the hardest Part remains.
Strephon had long perplex'd his Brains,
How with so high a Nymph he might
Demean himself the Wedding-Night:
For, as he view'd his Person round,
Meer mortal Flesh was all he found:
His Hand, his Neck, his Mouth, and Feet
Were duly washt to keep 'em sweet;
(With other Parts that shall be nameless,
The Ladies else might think me shameless.)   80
The Weather and his Love were hot;
And should he struggle; I know what—
Why let it go, if I must tell it—
He'll sweat, and then the Nymph may smell it.
While she a Goddess dy'd in Grain
Was unsusceptible of Stain:
And, *Venus*-like, her fragrant Skin
Exhal'd *Ambrosia* from within:
Can such a Deity endure
A mortal human Touch impure?   90
How did the humbled Swain detest
His prickled Beard, and hairy Breast!
His Night-Cap border'd round with Lace
Could give no Softness to his Face.
Yet, if the Goddess could be kind,
What endless Raptures must he find!
And Goddesses have now and then
Come down to visit mortal Men:
To visit and to court them too;
A certain Goddess, God knows who,   100
(As in a Book he heard it read)
Took Col'nel *Peleus* to her Bed.[2]
But, what if he should lose his Life
By vent'ring *on* his heav'nly Wife?
For *Strephon* could remember well,
That, once he heard a School-boy tell,
How *Semele* of mortal Race,

---

† *Diana,* Goddess of Midwives.
2. The union of Peleus and the goddess Thetis produced Achilles, hero of the *Iliad.*

By Thunder dy'd in *Jove's* Embrace;[3]
And what if daring *Strephon* dies
By Lightning shot from *Chloe's* Eyes?   110
  While these Reflections fill'd his Head,
The Bride was put in Form to Bed;
He follow'd, stript, and in he crept,
But, awfully his Distance kept.
  Now *Ponder well ye Parents dear;*
Forbid your Daughters guzzling Beer;
And make them ev'ry Afternoon
Forbear their Tea, or drink it soon;
That, e'er to Bed they venture up,
They may discharge it ev'ry Sup;   120
If not; they must in evil Plight
Be often forc'd to risc at Night,
Keep them to wholsome Food confin'd,
Nor let them taste what causes Wind;
*('Tis this the Sage of *Samos* means,
Forbidding his Disciples Beans)
O, think what Evils must ensue;
Miss *Moll* the Jade will burn it blue:
And when she once has got the Art,
She cannot help it for her Heart;   130
But, out it flies, even when she meets
Her Bridegroom in the Wedding-Sheets.
†*Carminative* and ||*Diuretick,*
Will damp all Passion Sympathetick;
And, Love such Nicety requires,
One *Blast* will put out all his Fires.
Since Husbands get behind the Scene,
The Wife should study to be clean;
Nor give the smallest Room to guess
The Time when Wants of Nature press;   140
  But, after Marriage, practise more
Decorum than she did before;
To keep her Spouse deluded still,
And make him fancy what she will.
  In Bed we left the married Pair;
'Tis Time to shew how Things went there.
Strephon, who had been often told,
That Fortune still assists the bold,
Resolv'd to make his first Attack:
But, *Chloe* drove him fiercely back.   150
How could a Nymph so chaste as *Chloe,*
With Constitution cold and snowy,

---

3. Semele was consumed by Zeus' lightning; from her ashes Zeus retrieved the yet unborn Dionysus.
* A well known Precept of *Pythagoras,* not to eat Beans.
† Medicines to break Wind.
|| Medicines to provoke Urine.

Permit a brutish Man to touch her?
Ev'n Lambs by Instinct fly the Butcher.
Resistance on the Wedding-Night
Is what our Maidens claim by Right:
And, *Chloe*, 'tis by all agreed,
Was Maid in Thought, and Word, and Deed,
Yet, some assign a diff'rent Reason;
That *Strephon* chose no proper Season.   160
Say, fair Ones, must I make a Pause?
Or freely tell the secret Cause.
Twelve Cups of Tea, (with Grief I speak)
Had now constrain'd the Nymph to leak.
This Point must needs be settled first;
The Bride must either void or burst.
Then, see the dire Effect of Pease,
Think what can give the Colick Ease,
The Nymph opprest before, behind,
As Ships are toss't by Waves and Wind,   170
Steals out her Hand by Nature led,
And brings a Vessel into Bed:
Fair Utensil, as smooth and white
As *Chloe*'s Skin, almost as bright.
Strephon who heard the fuming Rill
As from a mossy Cliff distill;
Cry'd out, ye Gods, what Sound is this?
Can *Chloe*, heav'nly *Chloe* ———?
But, when he smelt a noysom Steam
Which oft attends that luke-warm Stream;   180
(*Salerno** both together joins
As sov'reign Med'cines for the Loins)
And, though contriv'd, we may suppose
To slip his Ears, yet struck his Nose:
He found her, while the Scent increas'd,
As *mortal* as himself at least.
But, soon with like Occasions prest,
He boldly sent his Hand in quest,
(Inspir'd with Courage from his Bride,)
To reach the Pot on t'other Side.   190
And as he fill'd the reeking Vase,
Let fly a Rouzer in her Face.
The little *Cupids* hov'ring round,
(As Pictures prove) with Garlands crown'd,
Abasht at what they saw and heard,
Flew off, nor evermore appear'd.
Adieu to ravishing Delights,
High Raptures, and romantick Flights;

---

* Vide Schol. *Salern. Rules of Health, written by the School of Salernum.*
Mingere cum bumbis res est saluberrima lumbis. ["To make water with sounds is
the most healthful thing for the loins."—*Editors*]

To Goddesses so heav'nly sweet,
Expiring Shepherds at their Feet;   200
To silver Meads, and shady Bow'rs,
Drest up with *Amaranthine*[4] Flow'rs.
    How great a Change! how quickly made!
They learn to call a Spade, a Spade.
They soon from all Constraint are freed;
Can see each other *do their Need.*
On Box of Cedar sits the Wife,
And makes it warm for *Dearest Life.*
And, by the beastly way of Thinking,
Find great Society in Stinking.   210
Now *Strephon* daily entertains
His *Chloe* in the homeli'st Strains;
And, *Chloe* more experienc'd grown,
With Int'rest pays him back his own.
No Maid at Court is less asham'd,
Howe'er for selling Bargains[5] fam'd,
Than she, to name her Parts behind,
Or when a-bed, to let out Wind.
    Fair *Decency*, celestial Maid,
Descend from Heav'n to Beauty's Aid;   220
Though Beauty may beget Desire,
'Tis thou must fan the Lover's Fire;
For, Beauty, like supreme Dominion,
Is best supported by Opinion;
If Decency brings no Supplies,
Opinion falls, and Beauty dies.
    To see some radiant Nymph appear
In all her glitt'ring Birth-day Gear,
You think some Goddess from the Sky
Descended, ready cut and dry: 230
But, e'er you sell your self to Laughter,
Consider well what may come after;
For fine Ideas vanish fast,
While all the gross and filthy last.
    O *Strephon*, e'er that fatal Day
When *Chloe* stole your Heart away,
Had you but through a Cranny spy'd
On House of Ease your future Bride,
In all the Postures of her Face,
Which Nature gives in such a Case;   240
Distortions, Groanings, Strainings, Heavings;
'Twere better you had lickt her Leavings,
Than from Experience find too late
Your Goddess grown a filthy Mate.
Your Fancy then had always dwelt

4. Never fading.
5. Answering innocent questions with coarse answers.

On what you saw, and what you smelt;
Would still the same Ideas give ye,
As when you spy'd her on the Privy.
And, spight of *Chloe*'s Charms divine,
Your Heart had been as whole as mine.   250
Authorities both old and recent
Direct that Women must be decent;
And, from the Spouse each Blemish hide
More than from all the World beside.
Unjustly all our Nymphs complain,
Their Empire holds so short a Reign;
Is after Marriage lost so soon,
It hardly holds the Honey-moon:
For, if they keep not what they caught,
It is entirely their own Fault.   260
They take Possession of the Crown,
And then throw all their Weapons down;
Though by the Politicians Scheme
Whoe'er arrives at Pow'r supreme,
Those Arts by which at first they gain it,
They still must practise to maintain it.
What various Ways our Females take,
To pass for Wits before a Rake!
And in the fruitless Search pursue
All other Methods but the true.   270
Some try to learn polite Behaviour,
By reading Books against their Saviour;
Some call it witty to reflect
On ev'ry natural Defect;
Some shew they never want explaining,
To comprehend a double Meaning.
But, sure a Tell-tale out of School
Is of all Wits the greatest Fool;
Whose rank Imagination fills,
Her Heart, and from her Lips distills;   280
You'd think she utter'd from behind,
Or at her Mouth was breaking Wind.
Why is a handsome Wife ador'd
By ev'ry Coxcomb, but her Lord?
From yonder Puppet-Man inquire,
Who wisely hides his Wood and Wire;
Shews *Sheba*'s Queen completely drest,
And *Solomon* in Royal Vest;
But, view them litter'd on the Floor,
Or strung on Pegs behind the Door;   290
Punch is exactly of a Piece
With *Lorraine*'s Duke, and Prince of *Greece*.
A prudent Builder should forecast
How long the Stuff is like to last;

And, carefully observe the Ground,
To build on some Foundation sound;
What House, when its Materials crumble,
Must not inevitably tumble?
What Edifice can long endure,
Rais'd on a Basis unsecure?   300
Rash Mortals, e'er you take a Wife,
Contrive your Pile to last for Life;
Since Beauty scarce endures a Day,
And Youth so swiftly glides away;
Why will you make yourself a Bubble
To build on Sand with Hay and Stubble?
  On Sense and Wit your Passion found,
By Decency cemented round;
Let Prudence with Good Nature strive,
To keep Esteem and Love alive.   310
Then come old Age whene'er it will,
Your Friendship shall continue still:
And thus a mutual gentle Fire,
Shall never but with Life expire.

Cassinus and Peter

A Tragical ELEGY

1731

Two College Sophs of *Cambridge* Growth,
Both special Wits, and Lovers both,
Conferring as they us'd to meet,
On Love and Books in Rapture sweet;
(Muse, find me Names to fix my Metre,
Cassinus this, and t'other *Peter*)
Friend *Peter* to *Cassinus* goes,
To chat a while, and warm his Nose:
But, such a Sight was never seen,
The Lad lay swallow'd up in Spleen;   10
He seem'd as just crept out of Bed;
One greasy Stocking round his Head,
The t'other he sat down to darn
With Threads of diff'rent colour'd Yarn.
His Breeches torn exposing wide
A ragged Shirt, and tawny Hyde.
Scorcht were his Shins, his Legs were bare,

But, well embrown'd with Dirt and Hair.
A Rug was o'er his Shoulders thrown;
A Rug; for Night-gown he had none.   20
His Jordan[1] stood in Manner fitting
Between his Legs, to spew or spit in.
His antient Pipe in Sable dy'd,
And half unsmoakt, lay by his Side.
  Him thus accoutred *Peter* found,
With Eyes in Smoak and Weeping drown'd:
The Leavings of his last Night's Pot
On Embers plac'd, to drink it hot.
  Why, *Cassy*, thou wilt doze thy Pate:
What makes thee lie a-bed so late?   30
The Finch, the Linnet and the Thrush,
Their Mattins chant in ev'ry Bush:
And, I have heard thee oft salute
Aurora with thy early Flute.
Heaven send thou hast not got the Hypps.[2]
How? Not a Word come from thy Lips?
  Then gave him some familiar Thumps,
A College Joke to cure the Dumps.
  The Swain at last, with Grief opprest,
Cry'd, *Cælia!* thrice, and sigh'd the rest.   40
  Dear *Cassy*, though to ask I dread,
Yet, ask I must. Is *Cælia* dead?
  How happy I, were that the worst?
But I was fated to be curs'd.
  Come, tell us, has she play'd the Whore?
  Oh *Peter*, wou'd it were no more!
  Why, Plague confound her sandy Locks:
Say, has the small or greater Pox
Sunk down her Nose, or seam'd her Face?
Be easy, 'tis a common Case.   50
  Oh *Peter!* Beauty's but a Varnish,
Which Time and Accidents will tarnish:
But, *Cæelia* has contriv'd to blast
Those Beauties that might ever last.
Nor can Imagination guess,
Nor Eloquence Divine express,
How that ungrateful charming Maid,
My purest Passion has betray'd.
Conceive the most invenom'd Dart,
To pierce an injur'd Lover's Heart.   60
  Why, hang her, though she seem'd so coy,
I know she loves the Barber's Boy.
  Friend *Peter*, this I could excuse;
For, ev'ry Nymph has Leave to chuse;

1. Chamber pot.
2. Depression (see p. 449).

Nor, have I Reason to complain:
She loves a more deserving Swain.
But, oh! how ill hast thou divin'd
A Crime that shocks all human Kind;
A Deed unknown to Female Race,
At which the Sun should hide his Face.   70
Advice in vain you would apply—
Then, leave me to despair and dye.
Yet, kind *Arcadians*,[3] on my Urn
These Elegies and Sonnets burn,
And on the Marble grave these Rhimes,
A Monument to after-Times:
"Here *Cassy* lies, by *Cælia* slain,
And dying, never told his Pain."
  Vain empty World farewel. But hark,
The loud *Cerberian*[4] triple Bark.   80
And there——behold *Alecto* stand,
A Whip of Scorpions in her Hand.
Lo, *Charon* from his leaky Wherry,
Beck'ning to waft me o'er the Ferry.
I come, I come,—*Medusa*, see,
Her Serpents hiss direct at me.
Begone; unhand me, hellish Fry;
*Avaunt—ye cannot say 'twas I.
  Dear *Cassy*, thou must purge and bleed;
I fear thou wilt be mad indeed.   90
But now, by Friendship's sacred Laws,
I here conjure thee, tell the Cause;
And *Cælia's* horrid Fact relate;
Thy Friend would gladly share thy Fate.
  To force it out my Heart must rend;
Yet, when conjur'd by such a Friend—
Think, *Peter*, how my Soul is rack'd.
These Eyes, these Eyes beheld the Fact.
Now, bend thine Ear; since out it must:
But, when thou seest me laid in Dust,   100
The Secret thou shalt ne'er impart;
Not to the Nymph that keeps thy Heart;
(How would her Virgin Soul bemoan
A Crime to all her Sex unknown!)
Nor whisper to the tattling Reeds,
The blackest of all Female Deeds.
Nor blab it on the lonely Rocks,
Where Echo sits, and list'ning mocks.

3. From Arcadia, i.e., pastoral, idealizing.
4. *Cerberus*: the three-headed watchdog of Hades. *Alecto*: one of the three Furies.
Charon: the ferryman who conveys the dead across the river Styx to Hades.
Medusa: one of the Gorgons; her hair was a tangle of serpents, her gaze would
turn the beholder to stone.
* See *Mackbeth*.

Nor let the Zephyr's treach'rous Gale
Through *Cambridge* waft the direful Tale.   110
Nor to the chatt'ring feather'd Race,
Discover *Cælia*'s foul Disgrace.
But, if you fail, my Spectre dread
Attending nightly round your Bed;
And yet, I dare confide in you;
So, take my Secret, and adieu.
　　Nor wonder how I lost my Wits;
Oh! *Cælia, Cælia Cælia* sh——.

Verses on the Death of Dr. Swift, D.S.P.D.

Occasioned by reading a Maxim in *Rochefoulcault*

Dans l'adversité de nos meilleurs amis nous trouvons quelque chose, qui
ne nous deplaist pas.
In the Adversity of our best Friends, we find something that doth not
displease us.

1731

As *Rochefoucault* his Maxims drew
From Nature, I believe 'em true:
They argue no corrupted Mind
In him; the Fault is in Mankind.
　　This Maxim more than all the rest
Is thought too base for human Breast;
"In all Distresses of our Friends
We first consult our private Ends,
While Nature kindly bent to ease us,
Points out some Circumstance to please us."   10
　　If this perhaps your Patience move
Let Reason and Experience prove.
　　We all behold with envious Eyes,
Our *Equal* rais'd above our *Size*;
Who wou'd not at a crowded Show,
Stand high himself, keep others low?
I love my Friend as well as you,
But would not have him stop my View;
Then let him have the higher Post;
I ask but for an Inch at most.   20
　　If in a Battle you should find,
One, whom you love of all Mankind,
Had some heroick Action done,
A Champion kill'd, or Trophy won;

Rather than thus be over-topt,
Would you not wish his Lawrels cropt?
   Dear honest *Ned* is in the Gout,
Lies rackt with Pain, and you without:
How patiently you hear him groan!
How glad the Case is not your own!   30
   What Poet would not grieve to see,
His Brethren write as well as he?
But rather than they should excel,
He'd wish his Rivals all in Hell.
   Her End when Emulation misses,
She turns to Envy, Stings and Hisses:
The strongest Friendship yields to Pride,
Unless the Odds be on our Side.
   Vain human Kind! Fantastick Race!
Thy various Follies, who can trace?   40
Self-love, Ambition, Envy, Pride,
Their Empire in our Hearts divide:
Give others Riches, Power, and Station,
'Tis all on me an Usurpation.
I have no Title to aspire;
Yet, when you sink, I seem the higher.
In *Pope,* I cannot read a Line,
But with a Sigh, I wish it mine:
When he can in one Couplet fix
More Sense than I can do in Six: 50
It gives me such a jealous Fit,
I cry, Pox take him, and his Wit.
   Why must I be outdone by *Gay,*
In my own hum'rous biting Way?
   Arbuthnot is no more my Friend,
Who dares to Irony pretend;
Which I was born to introduce,
Refin'd it first, and shew'd its Use.
   St. *John,* as well as *Pultney* knows,
That I had some repute for Prose;   60
And till they drove me out of Date,
Could Maul a Minister of State:
If they have mortify'd my Pride,
And made me throw my Pen aside;
If with such Talents Heav'n hath blest 'em
Have I not Reason to detest 'em?
   To all my Foes, dear Fortune, send
Thy Gifts, but never to my Friend:
I tamely can endure the first,
But, this with Envy makes me burst.   70
   Thus much may serve by way of Proem,
Proceed we therefore to our Poem.
   The Time is not remote, when I

Must by the Course of Nature dye:
When I foresee my special Friends,
Will try to find their private Ends:
Tho' it is hardly understood,
Which way my Death can do them good;
Yet, thus methinks, I hear 'em speak;
See, how the Dean begins to break: 80
Poor Gentleman, he droops apace,
You plainly find it in his Face:
That old Vertigo in his Head,
Will never leave him, till he's dead:
Besides, his Memory decays,
He recollects not what he says;
He cannot call his Friends to Mind;
Forgets the Place where last he din'd:
Plyes you with Stories o'er and o'er,
He told them fifty Times before.   90
How does he fancy we can sit,
To hear his out-of-fashion'd Wit?
But he takes up with younger Fokes,
Who for his Wine will bear his Jokes:
Faith, he must make his Stories shorter,
Or change his Comrades once a Quarter:
In half the Time, he talks them round;
There must another Sett be found.

    For Poetry, he's past his Prime,
He takes an Hour to find a Rhime: 100
His Fire is out, his Wit decay'd,
His Fancy sunk, his Muse a Jade.
I'd have him throw away his Pen;
But there's no talking to some Men.

    And, then their Tenderness appears,
By adding largely to my Years:
He's older than he would be reckon'd,
And well remembers *Charles* the Second.

    He hardly drinks a Pint of Wine;
And that, I doubt, is no good Sign.   110
His Stomach too begins to fail:
Last Year we thought him strong and hale;
But now, he's quite another Thing;
I wish he may hold out till Spring.

    Then hug themselves, and reason thus;
It is not yet so bad with us.

    In such a Case they talk in Tropes,
And, by their Fears express their Hopes:
Some great Misfortune to portend,
No Enemy can match a Friend;   120

With all the Kindness they profess,
The Merit of a lucky Guess,
(When daily Howd'y's come of Course,
And Servants answer; *Worse and Worse*)
Wou'd please 'em better than to tell,
That, GOD be prais'd, the Dean is well.
Then he who prophecy'd the best,
Approves his Foresight to the rest:
You know, I always fear'd the worst,
And often told you so at first: 130
He'd rather chuse that I should dye,
Than his Prediction prove a Lye.
Not one foretels I shall recover;
But, all agree, to give me over.

    Yet shou'd some Neighbour feel a Pain,
Just in the Parts, where I complain;
How many a Message would he send?
What hearty Prayers that I should mend?
Enquire what Regimen I kept;
What gave me Ease, and how I slept?   140
And more lament, when I was dead,
Than all the Sniv'llers round my Bed.

    My good Companions, never fear,
For though you may mistake a Year;
Though your Prognosticks run too fast,
They must be verify'd at last.

    Behold the fatal Day arrive!
How is the Dean? He's just alive.
Now the departing Prayer is read:
He hardly breathes. The Dean is dead.   150
Before the Passing-Bell begun,
The News thro' half the Town has run.
O, may we all for Death prepare!
What has he left? And who's his Heir?
I know no more than what the News is,
'Tis all bequeath'd to publick Uses.
To publick Use! A perfect Whim!
What had the Publick done for him!
Meer Envy, Avarice, and Pride!
He gave it all:—But first he dy'd.   160
And had the Dean, in all the Nation,
No worthy Friend, no poor Relation?
So ready to do Strangers good,
Forgetting his own Flesh and Blood?

    Now Grub-Street Wits are all employ'd;
With Elegies, the Town is cloy'd:
Some Paragraph in ev'ry Paper,

*To *curse* the *Dean,* or *bless* the *Drapier.*
The Doctors tender of their Fame,
Wisely on me lay all the Blame: 170
We must confess his Case was nice;
But he would never take Advice:
Had he been rul'd, for ought appears,
He might have liv'd these Twenty Years:
For when we open'd him we found,
That all his vital Parts were sound.
   From *Dublin* soon to *London* spread,
†'Tis told at Court, the Dean is dead.
   ‡Kind Lady *Suffolk* in the Spleen,
Runs laughing up to tell the Queen.   180
The Queen, so Gracious, Mild, and Good,
Cries, Is he gone? 'Tis time he shou'd.
He's dead you say; why let him rot;
**I'm glad the Medals were forgot.
I promis'd them, I own; but when?
I only was the Princess then;
But now as Consort of the King,
You know 'tis quite a different Thing.
   ‖Now, *Chartres* at Sir *Robert's* Levee,
Tells, with a Sneer, the Tidings heavy: 190
Why, is he dead without his Shoes?
§(Cries *Bob*) I'm Sorry for the News;

* *The Author imagines, that the Scriblers of the prevailing Party, which he always opposed, will libel him after his Death; but that others will remember him with Gratitude, who consider the Service he had done to* Ireland, *under the Name of M. B.* Drapier, *by utterly defeating the destructive Project of* Wood's *Half-pence, in five Letters to the People of* Ireland, *at that Time read universally, and convincing every Reader.*
† *The Dean supposeth himself to dye in* Ireland.
‡ *Mrs.* Howard, *afterwards Countess of* Suffolk, *then of the Bed-chamber to the Queen, professed much Friendship for the Dean. The Queen then Princess, sent a dozen times to the Dean (then in* London*) with her Command to attend her; which at last he did, by Advice of all his Friends. She often sent for him afterwards, and always treated him very Graciously. He taxed her with a Present worth Ten Pounds, which she promised before he should return to* Ireland, *but on his taking Leave, the Medals were not ready.*
** *The Medals were to be sent to the Dean in four Months, but she forgot them, or thought them too dear. The Dean, being in* Ireland, *sent Mrs.* Howard *a Piece of* Indian *Plad made in that Kingdom: which the Queen seeing took from her, and wore it herself, and sent to the Dean for as much as would cloath herself and Children, desiring he would send the Charge of it. He did the former. It cost thirty-five Pounds, but he said he would have nothing except the Medals. He was the Summer following in* England, *was treated as usual, and she being then Queen, the Dean was promised a Settlement in* England, *but returned as he went, and, instead of Favour or Medals, hath been ever since under her Majesty's Displeasure.*
‖ Chartres *is a most infamous, vile Scoundrel, grown from a Foot-Boy, or worse, to a prodigious Fortune both in* England *and* Scotland: *He had a Way of insinuating himself into all Ministers under every Change, either as Pimp, Flatterer, or Informer. He was Tryed at Seventy for a Rape, and came off by sacrificing a great Part of his Fortune (he is since dead, but this Poem still preserves the Scene and Time it was writ in.)*
§ Sir Robert Walpole, *Chief Minister of State, treated the* Dean *in* 1726, *with great Distinction, invited him to Dinner at* Chelsea, *with the* Dean's *Friends chosen on Purpose; appointed an Hour to talk with him of* Ireland, *to which*

Oh, were the Wretch but living still,
*And in his Place my good Friend *Will;*
Or, had a Mitre on his Head
†Provided *Bolingbroke* were dead.
‡Now *Curl* his Shop from Rubbish drains;
Three genuine Tomes of *Swift's* Remains.
And then to make them pass the glibber,
**Revis'd by *Tibbalds, Moore, and Cibber.*   200
He'll treat me as he does my Betters.
||Publish my Will, my Life, my Letters.
Revive the Libels born to dye;
Which *Pope* must bear, as well as I.
  Here shift the Scene, to represent
How those I love, my Death lament.
Poor *Pope* will grieve a Month; and *Gay*
A Week; and *Arbuthnot* a Day.
  St. John himself will scarce forbear,
To bite his Pen, and drop a Tear.   210
The rest will give a Shrug and cry,
I'm sorry; but we all must dye.
Indifference clad in Wisdom's Guise,
All Fortitude of Mind supplies:
For how can stony Bowels melt,
In those who never Pity felt;
When *We* are lash'd, *They* kiss the Rod;
Resigning to the Will of God.
  The Fools, my Juniors by a Year,
Are tortur'd with Suspence and Fear.   220

Kingdom *and* People *the* Dean *found him no great Friend; for he defended* Wood's
Project *of* Half-pence, *&c. The* Dean *would see him no more; and upon his next*
Year's *return to* England, Sir Robert *on an accidental Meeting, only made a civil
Compliment, and never invited him again.*
* *Mr.* William Pultney, *from being Mr.* Walpole's *intimate Friend, detesting his
Administration opposed his Measures, and joined with my* Lord Bolingbroke, *to
represent his conduct in an excellent Paper, called the* Craftsman, *which is still
continued.*
† Henry St. John, *Lord Viscount* Bolingbroke, *Secretary of State to* Queen Anne
of blessed Memory. He is reckoned the most Universal Genius in Europe; Walpole
dreading his Abilities, treated him most injuriously, working with King George,
*who forgot his Promise of restoring the said Lord, upon the restless Importunity
of* Walpole.
‡ Curl *hath been the most infamous Bookseller of any Age or Country: His
Character in Part may be found in Mr.* Pope's *Dunciad. He published three
Volumes all charged on the Dean, who never writ three Pages of them: He hath
used many of the Dean's Friends in almost as vile a Manner.*
** *Three stupid Verse Writers in* London, *the last to the Shame of the Court, and
the highest Disgrace to Wit and Learning, was made Laureat.* Moore, *commonly
called* Jemmy Moore, *Son of* Arthur Moore, *whose Father was Jaylor of* Monaghan
in Ireland. *See the Character of* Jemmy Moore, *and* Tibbalds, Theobald *in the
Dunciad.*
|| Curl *is notoriously infamous for publishing the Lives, Letters, and last Wills
and Testaments of the Nobility and Ministers of State, as well as of all the
Rogues, who are hanged at* Tyburn. *He hath been in Custody of the House of
Lords for publishing or forging the Letters of many Peers; which made the Lords
enter a Resolution in their Journal Book, that no Life or Writings of any Lord
should be published without the Consent of the next Heir at Law, or Licence from
their House.*

Who wisely thought my Age a Screen,
When Death approach'd, to stand between:
The Screen remov'd, their Hearts are trembling,
They mourn for me without dissembling.
My female Friends, whose tender Hearts
Have better learn'd to act their Parts.
Receive the News in *doleful Dumps*,
The Dean is dead, (*and what is Trumps?*)
Then Lord have Mercy on his Soul.
(Ladies I'll venture for the *Vole*.)   230
Six Deans they say must bear the Pall.
(I wish I knew what *King* to call.)
Madam, your Husband will attend
The Funeral of so good a Friend.
No Madam, 'tis a shocking Sight,
And he's engag'd To-morrow Night!
My Lady *Club* wou'd take it ill,
If he shou'd fail her at *Quadrill*.
He lov'd the Dean. (*I lead a Heart*.)
But dearest Friends, they say, must part.   240
His Time was come, he ran his Race;
We hope he's in a better Place.
    Why do we grieve that Friends should dye?
No Loss more easy to supply.
One Year is past; a different Scene;
No further mention of the Dean;
Who now, alas, no more is mist,
Than if he never did exist.
Where's now this Fav'rite of *Apollo?*
Departed; *and his Works must follow:*   250
Must undergo the common Fate;
His Kind of Wit is out of Date.
Some Country Squire to *Lintot goes,
Enquires for *Swift* in Verse and Prose:
Says *Lintot*, I have heard the Name:
He dy'd a Year ago. The same.
He searcheth all his Shop in vain;
Sir you may find them in †*Duck-lane*:
I sent them with a Load of Books,
Last *Monday* to the Pastry-cooks.   260
To fancy they cou'd live a Year!
I find you're but a Stranger here.
The Dean was famous in his Time;
And had a Kind of Knack at Rhyme:
His way of Writing now is past;

---

* Bernard Lintot, *a Bookseller in* London. *Vide Mr.* Pope's *Dunciad.*
† *A Place in* London *where old Books are sold.*

The Town hath got a better Taste:
I keep no antiquated Stuff;
But, spick and span I have enough.
Pray, do but give me leave to shew 'em;
Here's *Colley Cibber*'s Birth-day Poem.   270
This Ode you never yet have seen,
By *Stephen Duck*, upon the Queen.
Then, here's a Letter finely penn'd
Against the *Craftsman* and his Friend;
It clearly shews that all Reflection
On Ministers, is disaffection.
*Next, here's Sir *Robert*'s Vindication,
†And Mr. *Henly*'s last Oration:
The Hawkers have not got 'em yet,
Your Honour please to buy a Set?   280
  ‡Here's *Wolston*'s Tracts, the twelfth Edition;
'Tis read by ev'ry Politician:
The Country Members, when in Town,
To all their Boroughs send them down:
You never met a Thing so smart;
The Courtiers have them all by Heart:
Those Maids of Honour (who can read)
Are taught to use them for their Creed.
The Rev'rend Author's good Intention,
Hath been rewarded with a Pension: 290
He doth an Honour to his Gown,
By bravely running *Priest-craft* down:
He shews, as sure as GOD's in *Gloc'ster*,
That *Jesus* was a Grand Impostor:
That all his Miracles were Cheats,
Perform'd as Juglers do their Feats:
The Church had never such a Writer:
A Shame, he hath not got a Mitre!
  Suppose me dead; and then suppose
A Club assembled at the *Rose*;   300
Where from Discourse of this and that,
I grow the Subject of their Chat:
And, while they toss my Name about,

---

* Walpole *hires a Set of Party Scribers, who do nothing else but write in his Defence.*
† Henly *is a Clergyman who wanting both Merit and Luck to get Preferment, or even to keep his Curacy in the Established Church, formed a new Conventicle, which he calls an Oratory. There, at set Times, he delivereth strange Speeches compiled by himself and his Associates, who share the Profit with him: Every Hearer pays a Shilling each Day for Admittance. He is an absolute Dunce, but generally reputed crazy.*
‡ Wolston *was a Clergyman, but for want of Bread, hath in several Treatises, in the most blasphemous Manner, attempted to turn Our Saviour and his Miracles into Ridicule. He is much caressed by many great Courtiers, and by all the Infidels, and his Books read generally by the Court Ladies.*

With Favour some, and some without;
One quite indiff'rent in the Cause,
My Character impartial draws:
  The Dean, if we believe Report,
Was never ill receiv'd at Court:
As for his Works in Verse and Prose,
I own my self no Judge of those: 310
Nor, can I tell what Critics thought 'em;
But, this I know, all People bought 'em;
As with a moral View design'd
To cure the Vices of Mankind:
His Vein, ironically grave,
Expos'd the Fool, and lash'd the Knave:
To steal a Hint was never known,
But what he writ was all his own.
  He never thought an Honour done him,
Because a Duke was proud to own him: 320
Would rather slip aside, and chuse
To talk with Wits in dirty Shoes:
Despis'd the Fools with Stars and Garters,
So often seen caressing *Chartres:
He never courted Men in Station,
Nor Persons had in Admiration;
Of no Man's Greatness was afraid,
Because he sought for no Man's Aid.
Though trusted long in great Affairs,
He gave himself no haughty Airs: 330
Without regarding private Ends,
Spent all his Credit for his Friends:
And only chose the Wise and Good;
No Flatt'rers; no Allies in Blood;
But succour'd Virtue in Distress,
And seldom fail'd of good Success;
As Numbers in their Hearts must own,
Who, but for him, had been unknown.
  With Princes kept a due Decorum,
But never stood in Awe before 'em: 340
He follow'd David's Lesson just,
In Princes never put thy Trust.
And, would you make him truly sower;
Provoke him with a slave in Power:
The Irish Senate, if you nam'd,
With what Impatience he declaim'd!
Fair LIBERTY was all his Cry;
For her he stood prepar'd to die;
For her he boldly stood alone;
For her he oft expos'd his own.   350

* See the Notes before on Chartres.

*Two Kingdoms, just as Faction led,
Had set a Price upon his Head;
But, not a Traytor cou'd be found,
To sell him for Six Hundred Pound.

    Had he but spar'd his Tongue and Pen,
He might have rose like other Men:
But, Power was never in his Thought;
And, Wealth he valu'd not a Groat:
Ingratitude he often found,
And pity'd those who meant the Wound: 360
But, kept the Tenor of his Mind,
To merit well of human Kind:
Nor made a Sacrifice of those
Who still were true, to please his Foes.

†He labour'd many a fruitless Hour
To reconcile his Friends in Power;
Saw Mischief by a Faction brewing,
While they pursu'd each others Ruin.
But, finding vain was all his Care,
He left the Court in meer Despair.   370

    And, oh! how short are human Schemes!
Here ended all our golden Dreams.
What *St. John's* Skill in State Affairs,
What *Ormond's* Valour, *Oxford's* Cares,
To save their sinking Country lent,
Was all destroy'd by one Event.

‡Too soon that precious Life was ended,
On which alone, our Weal depended.

**When up a dangerous Faction starts,

---

* *In the Year* 1713, *the late Queen was prevailed with by an Address of the House of Lords in* England, *to publish a Proclamation, promising Three Hundred Pounds to whatever Person would discover the Author of a Pamphlet called,* The Publick Spirit of the Whiggs; *and in* Ireland, *in the Year* 1724, *my Lord* Carteret *at his first coming into the Government, was prevailed on to issue a Proclamation for promising the like Reward of Three Hundred Pounds, to any Person who could discover the Author of a Pamphlet called,* The Drapier's Fourth Letter, &c. *writ against that destructive Project of coining Half-pence for* Ireland; *but in neither Kingdoms was the Dean discovered.*

† *Queen* ANNE's *Ministry fell to Variance from the first Year after their Ministry began:* Harcourt *the Chancellor, and Lord* Bolingbroke *the Secretary, were discontented with the Treasurer* Oxford, *for his too much Mildness to the Whig Party; this Quarrel grew higher every Day till the Queen's Death: The Dean, who was the only Person that endeavoured to reconcile them, found it impossible; and thereupon retired to the Country about ten Weeks before that fatal Event: Upon which he returned to his Deanry in* Dublin, *where for many Years he was worried by the new People in Power, and had Hundreds of Libels writ against him in* England.

‡ *In the Height of the Quarrel between the Ministers, the Queen died.*

** *Upon Queen* ANNE's *Death the Whig Faction was restored to Power, which they exercised with the utmost Rage and Revenge; impeached and banished the Chief Leaders of the Church Party, and stripped all their Adherents of what Employments they had, after which* England *was never known to make so mean a Figure in* Europe. *The greatest Preferments in the Church in both Kingdoms were given to the most ignorant Men, Fanaticks were publickly caressed,* Ireland *utterly ruined and enslaved, only great Ministers heaping up Millions, and so Affairs continue until this present third Day of May,* 1732, *and are likely to go on in the same Manner.*

With Wrath and Vengeance in their Hearts: 380
By solemn League and Cov'nant bound,
To ruin, slaughter, and confound;
To turn Religion to a Fable,
And make the Government a *Babel:*
Pervert the Law, disgrace the Gown,
Corrupt the Senate, rob the Crown;
To sacrifice old *England's* Glory,
And make her infamous in Story.
When such a Tempest shook the Land,
How could unguarded Virtue stand?   390

    With Horror, Grief, Despair the Dean
Beheld the dire destructive Scene:
His Friends in Exile, or the Tower,
*Himself within the Frown of Power;
Pursu'd by base envenom'd Pens,
†Far to the Land of Slaves and Fens;
A servile Race in Folly nurs'd,
Who truckle most, when treated worst.

    By Innocence and Resolution,
He bore continual Persecution;   400
While Numbers to Preferment rose;
Whose Merits were, to be his Foes.
When, *ev'n his own familiar Friends*
Intent upon their private Ends;
Like Renegadoes now he feels,
Against him lifting up their Heels.

    The Dean did by his Pen defeat
‡An infamous destructive Cheat.
Taught Fools their Int'rest how to know;
And gave them Arms to ward the Blow.   410
Envy hath own'd it was his doing,
To save that helpless Land from Ruin,
While they who at the Steerage stood,
And reapt the Profit, sought his Blood.

    To save them from their evil Fate,
In him was held a Crime of State.
**A wicked Monster on the Bench,

* *Upon the Queen's Death, the Dean returned to live in* Dublin, *at his Deanry-House: Numberless Libels were writ against him in* England, *as a Jacobite; he was insulted in the Street, and at Nights was forced to be attended by his Servants armed.*
† *The Land of Slaves and Fens, is* Ireland.
‡ One Wood, *a Hardware-man from* England, *had a Patent for coining Copper Half-pence in* Ireland, *to the Sum of* 108,000 £ *which in the Consequence, must leave that Kingdom without Gold or Silver (See* Drapier's Letters.)
** One Whitshed *was then Chief Justice: He had some Years before prosecuted a Printer for a Pamphlet writ by the Dean, to perswade the People of* Ireland *to wear their own Manufactures.* Whitshed *sent the Jury down eleven Times, and kept them nine Hours, until they were forced to bring in a special Verdict. He sat as Judge afterwards on the Tryal of the Printer of the* Drapier's Fourth Letter; *but the Jury, against all he could say or swear, threw out the Bill: All the Kingdom took the* Drapier's *Part, except the Courtiers, or those who expected Places. The* Drapier *was celebrated in many Poems and Pamphlets: His Sign was set up in*

Whose Fury Blood could never quench;
As vile and profligate a Villain,
As modern *Scroggs*, or old *Tressilian*;   420
Who long all Justice had discarded,
Nor fear'd he GOD, nor Man regarded;
Vow'd on the Dean his Rage to vent,
And make him of his Zeal repent;
But Heav'n his Innocence defends,
The grateful People stand his Friends:
Not Strains of Law, nor Judges Frown,
Nor Topicks brought to please the Crown,
Nor Witness hir'd, nor Jury pick'd,
Prevail to bring him in convict.   430
†In Exile with a steady Heart,
He spent his Life's declining Part;
Where, Folly, Pride, and Faction sway,
‡Remote from *St. John, Pope*, and *Gay*.
**His Friendship there to few confin'd,
Were always of the midling Kind:
No Fools of Rank, a mungril Breed,
Who fain would pass for Lords indeed:
||Where Titles give no Right or Power,
And Peerage is a wither'd Flower,   440
He would have held it a Disgrace,
If such a Wretch had known his Face.
On Rural Squires, that Kingdom's Bane,
He vented oft his Wrath in vain:
§Biennial Squires, to Market brought;
Who sell their Souls and Votes for Naught;
The Nation stript go joyful back,
To rob the Church, their Tenants rack,
Go Snacks with Thieves and §§Rapparees,
And, keep the Peace, to pick up Fees: 450

---

most Streets of Dublin (*where many of them still continue*) *and in several Country Towns*.

* Scroggs *was Chief Justice under King* Charles *the Second: His Judgment always varied in State Tryals, according to Directions from Court*. Tressilian *was a wicked Judge, hanged above three hundred Years ago*.

† *In* Ireland, *which he had Reason to call a Place of Exile; to which Country nothing could have driven him, but the Queen's Death, who had determined to fix him in* England, *in Spight of the Dutchess of* Somerset, &c.

‡ Henry St. John, *Lord Viscount* Bolingbroke, *mentioned before*.

** *In* Ireland *the Dean was not acquainted with one single Lord Spiritual or Temporal. He only conversed with private Gentlemen of the Clergy or Laity, and but a small Number of either*.

|| *The Peers of* Ireland *lost a great Part of their Jurisdiction by one single Act, and tamely submitted to this infamous Mark of Slavery without the least Resentment, or Remonstrance*.

§ *The Parliament (as they call it) in* Ireland *meet but once in two Years; and, after giving five Times more than they can afford, return Home to reimburse themselves by all Country Jobs and Oppressions, of which some few only are here mentioned*.

§§ *The Highway-Men in* Ireland *are, since the late Wars there, usually called* Rapparees, *which was a Name given to those* Irish *Soldiers who in small Parties used, at that Time, to plunder the Protestants*.

In every Jobb to have a Share,
A Jayl or *Barrack to repair;
And turn the Tax for publick Roads
Commodious to their own Abodes.
   Perhaps I may allow, the Dean
Had too much Satyr in his Vein;
And seem'd determin'd not to starve it,
Because no Age could more deserve it.
Yet, Malice never was his Aim;
He lash'd the Vice but spar'd the Name.   460
No Individual could resent,
Where Thousands equally were meant.
His Satyr points at no Defect,
But what all Mortals may correct;
For he abhorr'd that senseless Tribe,
Who call it Humour when they jibe:
He spar'd a Hump or crooked Nose,
Whose Owners set not up for Beaux.
True genuine Dulness mov'd his Pity,
Unless it offer'd to be witty.   470
Those, who their Ignorance confess'd,
He ne'er offended with a Jest;
But laugh'd to hear an Idiot quote,
A Verse from *Horace*, learn'd by Rote.
   He knew an hundred pleasant Stories,
With all the Turns of *Whigs* and *Tories*:
Was cheerful to his dying Day,
And Friends would let him have his Way.
   He gave the little Wealth he had,
To build a House for Fools and Mad: 480
And shew'd by one satyric Touch,
No Nation wanted it so much:
†That Kingdom he hath left his Debtor,
I wish it soon may have a Better.

The Beasts' Confession to the Priest

1732–33

When Beasts could speak, (the Learned say
They still can do so every Day)
It seems, they had Religion then,
As much as now we find in Men.

---

* *The Army in* Ireland *is lodged in Barracks, the building and repairing whereof,
and other Charges, have cost a prodigious Sum to that unhappy Kingdom.*
† *Meaning* Ireland, *where he now lives, and probably may dye.*

It happen'd when a Plague broke out,
(Which therefore made them more devout)
The King of Brutes (to make it plain,
Of Quadrupeds I only mean)
By Proclamation gave Command,
That ev'ry Subject in the Land   10
Should to the Priest confess their Sins;
And, thus the pious Wolf begins:
  Good Father I must own with Shame,
That, often I have been to blame:
I must confess, on *Friday* last,
Wretch that I was, I broke my Fast:
But, I defy the basest Tongue
To prove I did my Neighbour wrong;
Or ever went to seek my Food
By Rapine, Theft, or Thirst of Blood.   20
  The Ass approaching next, confess'd,
That in his Heart he lov'd a Jest:
A Wag he was, he needs must own,
And could not let a Dunce alone:
Sometimes his Friend he would not spare,
And might perhaps be too severe:
But yet, the worst that could be said,
He was a *Wit* both born and bred;
And if it be a Sin or Shame,
Nature alone must bear the Blame: 30
One Fault he hath, is sorry for't,
His Ears are half a Foot too short;
Which could he to the Standard bring,
He'd shew his Face before the K——:
Then, for his Voice, there's none disputes
That he's the Nightingale of Brutes.
  The Swine with contrite Heart allow'd,
His Shape and Beauty made him proud:
In Dyet was perhaps too nice,
But Gluttony was ne'er his Vice: 40
In ev'ry Turn of Life content,
And meekly took what Fortune sent:
Inquire through all the Parish round
A better Neighbour ne'er was found:
His Vigilance might some displease;
'Tis true, he hated Sloth like Pease.
  The Mimick Ape began his Chatter,
How evil Tongues his Life bespatter:
Much of the cens'ring World complain'd,
Who said, his Gravity was feign'd: 50
Indeed, the Strictness of his Morals
Engag'd him in a hundred Quarrels:
He saw, and he was griev'd to see't,

His Zeal was sometimes indiscreet:
He found, his Virtues too severe
For our corrupted Times to bear;
Yet, such a lewd licentious Age
Might well excuse a Stoick's Rage.
The Goat advanc'd with decent Pace;
And, first excus'd his youthful Face;   60
Forgiveness begg'd, that he appear'd
('Twas Nature's Fault) without a Beard.
'Tis true, he was not much inclin'd
To Fondness for the Female Kind;
Not, as his Enemies object,
From Chance, or natural Defect
Not by his frigid Constitution;
But, through a pious Resolution;
For, he had made a holy Vow
Of Chastity, as Monks do now;   70
Which he resolv'd to keep for ever hence,
As strictly too; as doth *his Reverence.
Apply the Tale, and you shall find
How just it suits with human Kind.
Some Faults we own: But, can you guess?
Why?—Virtues carry'd to Excess;
Wherewith our Vanity endows us,
Though neither Foe nor Friend allows us.
The Lawyer swears, you may rely on't,
He never squeez'd a needy Clyent: 80
And, this he makes his constant Rule;
For which his Brethren call him Fool:
His Conscience always was so nice,
He freely gave the Poor Advice;
By which he lost, he may affirm,
A hundred Fees last *Easter* Term.
While others of the learned Robe
Would break the Patience of a *Job*,
No Pleader at the Bar could match
His Diligence and quick Dispatch;   90
Ne'er kept a Cause, he well may boast,
Above a Term or two at most.
The cringing Knave who seeks a Place
Without Success; thus tells his Case:
Why should he longer mince the Matter?
He fail'd, because he could not flatter:
He had not learn'd to turn his Coat,
Nor for a Party give his Vote:
His Crime he quickly understood;
Too zealous for the Nation's Good: 100

* *The Priest his Confessor.*

He found, the Ministers resent it,
Yet could not for his Heart repent it.
    The Chaplain vows, he cannot fawn,
Though it would raise him to the Lawn:[1]
He pass'd his Hours among his Books;
You find it in his meagre Looks:
He might, if he were worldly-wise,
Preferment get, and spare his Eyes:
But own'd, he had a stubborn Spirit
That made him trust alone in Merit: 110
Would rise by Merit to Promotion;
Alass! a meer Chymerick Notion.
    The Doctor, if you will believe him,
Confess'd a Sin, and God forgive him:
Call'd up at Mid-night, ran to save
A blind old Beggar from the Grave:
But, see how *Satan* spreads his Snares;
He quite forgot to say his Pray'rs.
He cannot help it for his Heart
Sometimes to act the Parson's Part: 120
Quotes from the Bible many a Sentence
That moves his Patients to Repentance:
And, when his Med'cines do no good,
Supports their Minds with heav'nly Food.
At which, however well intended,
He hears the Clergy are offended;
And grown so bold behind his Back
To call him Hypocrite and Quack.
In his own Church he keeps a Seat;
Says Grace before, and after Meat;   130
And calls, without affecting Airs,
His Houshold twice a Day to Pray'rs.
He shuns Apothecary's Shops;[2]
And hates to cram the Sick with Slops:
He scorns to make his Art a Trade;
Nor bribes my Lady's fav'rite Maid.
Old Nurse-keepers would never hire
To recommend him to the Squire;
Which others, whom he will not name,
Have often practis'd to their·Shame.   140
    The Statesman tells you with a *Sneer*,
His Fault is to be too *Sincere*;
And, having no sinister Ends,
Is apt to disoblige his Friends.
The Nation's Good, his Master's Glory,
Without Regard to *Whig* or *Tory*,

1. Bishopry.
2. Avoids the profitable practice of conspiring with apothecaries in the dispensing
of often useless drugs.

Were all the Schemes he had in View;
Yet he was seconded by few:
Though some had spread a thousand Lyes;
'Twas *He* defeated the EXCISE.   150
'Twas known, tho' he had born Aspersion;
That, *Standing Troops* were his Aversion:
His Practice was, in ev'ry Station
To serve the King, and please the Nation.
Though hard to find in ev'ry Case
The fittest Man to fill a Place:
His Promises he ne'er forgot,
But took Memorials on the Spot:
His Enemies, for want of Charity,
Said, he affected Popularity: 160
'Tis true, the People understood,
That all he did was for their Good;
Their kind Affections he has try'd;
No Love is lost on either Side.
He came to Court with Fortune clear,
Which now he runs out every Year;
Must, at the Rate that he goes on,
Inevitably be undone.
Oh! if his Majesty would please
To give him but a Writ of Ease,   170
Would grant him Licence to retire,
As it hath long been his Desire,
By fair Accounts it would be found
He's poorer by ten thousand Pound.
He owns, and hopes it is no Sin,
He ne'er was partial to his Kin;
He thought it base for Men in Stations,
To crowd the Court with their Relations:
His Country was his dearest Mother,
And ev'ry virtuous Man his Brother: 180
Through Modesty, or aukward Shame,
(For which he owns himself to blame)
He found the wisest Men he could,
Without Respect to Friends, or Blood,
Nor ever acts on private Views,
When he hath Liberty to chuse.
   The Sharper swore he hated Play,
Except to pass an Hour away:
And, well he might; for to his Cost,
By want of Skill, he always lost: 190
He heard, there was a Club of Cheats
Who had contriv'd a thousand Feats;
Could change the Stock, or cog a Dye,[3]

3. To manipulate the dice.

And thus deceive the sharpest Eye:
No Wonder how his Fortune sunk,
His Brothers fleece him when he's drunk.
I own, the Moral not exact;
Besides, the Tale is false in Fact;
And, so absurd, that could I raise up
From Fields *Elyzian*, fabling *Esop*;   200
I would accuse him to his Face
For libelling the *Four-foot* Race.
Creatures of ev'ry Kind but ours
Well comprehend their nat'ral Powers;
While We, whom *Reason* ought to sway,
Mistake our Talents ev'ry Day:
The Ass was never known so stupid
To act the Part of *Tray*, or *Cupid*;[4]
Nor leaps upon his Master's Lap,
There to be stroak'd and fed with Pap;   210
As *Esop* would the World perswade;
He better understands his Trade:
Nor comes whene'er his Lady whistles;
But, carries Loads, and feeds on Thistles;
Our Author's Meaning, I presume, is
A Creature *bipes et implumis*;
Wherein the Moralist design'd
A Compliment on Human-Kind:
For, here he owns, that now and then
†Beasts may *degen'rate* into Men.   220

On Poetry

A *Rapsody*

1733

All Human Race wou'd fain be *Wits*,
And Millions miss, for one that hits.
Young's universal Passion, *Pride*,[1]
Was never known to spread so wide.
Say *Britain*, cou'd you ever boast,——
Three *Poets* in an Age at most?

4. A pet dog.
* *A Definition of Man, disapproved by all Logicians. Homo est Animal bipes, im-plume, erecto vultu.*
† *Vide* Gulliver *in his Account of the* Houyhnhnms.
1. Edward Young, *The Universal Passion* (1725–28).

Our chilling Climate hardly bears
A *Sprig* of Bays in Fifty Years:
While ev'ry Fool his Claim alledges,
As if it grew in common Hedges.   10
What Reason can there be assign'd
For this Perverseness in the Mind?
Brutes find out where their Talents lie:
A *Bear* will not attempt to fly:
A founder'd *Horse* will oft debate,
Before he tries a five-barr'd Gate:
A Dog by Instinct turns aside,
Who sees the Ditch too deep and wide.
But *Man* we find the only Creature,
Who, led by *Folly*, fights with *Nature*;   20
Who, when *she* loudly cries, *Forbear*,
With Obstinacy fixes there;
And, where his *Genius* least inclines,
Absurdly bends his whole Designs.
   Not *Empire* to the Rising-Sun,
By Valour, Conduct, Fortune won;
Nor highest *Wisdom* in Debates
For framing Laws to govern States;
Nor Skill in Sciences profound,
So large to grasp the Circle round;   30
Such heavenly Influence require,
As how to strike the *Muses Lyre*.
   Not Beggar's Brat, on Bulk begot;
Nor Bastard of a Pedlar *Scot*;
Nor Boy brought up to cleaning Shoes,
The Spawn of *Bridewell*, or the Stews;
Nor Infants dropt, the spurious Pledges
Of *Gipsies* littering under Hedges,
Are so disqualified by Fate
To rise in *Church*, or *Law*, or *State*,   40
As he, whom *Phebus* in his Ire
Hath *blasted* with poetick Fire.
   What hope of Custom in the *Fair*,
While not a Soul demands your Ware?
Where you have nothing to produce
For private Life, or publick Use?
Court, City, Country want you not;
You cannot bribe, betray, or plot.
For Poets, Law makes no Provision:
The Wealthy have you in Derision.   50
Of State-Affairs you cannot smatter,
Are awkward when you try to flatter.
Your Portion, taking *Britain* round,
*Was just one annual Hundred Pound.

* Paid to the Poet Laureat, which Place was given to one *Cibber,* a Player.

Now not so much as in Remainder
Since *Cibber* brought in an Attainder;
For ever fixt by Right Divine,
(A Monarch's Right) on *Grubstreet* Line.
Poor starv'ling Bard, how small thy Gains!
How unproportion'd to thy Pains!   60
  And here a *Simile* comes Pat in:
Tho' *Chickens* take a Month to fatten,
The Guests in less than half an Hour
Will more than half a Score devour.
So, after toiling twenty Days,
To earn a Stock of Pence and Praise,
Thy Labours, grown the Critick's Prey,
Are swallow'd o'er a Dish of Tea;
Gone, to be never heard of more,
Gone, where the *Chickens* went before.   70
  How shall a new Attempter learn
Of diff'rent Spirits to discern,
And how distinguish, which is which,
The Poet's Vein, or scribling Itch?
Then hear an old experienc'd Sinner
Instructing thus a young Beginner.
  Consult yourself, and if you find
A powerful Impulse urge your Mind,
Impartial judge within your Breast
What Subject you can manage best;   80
Whether your Genius most inclines
To Satire, Praise, or hum'rous Lines;
To Elegies in mournful Tone,
Or Prologue sent from Hand unknown.
Then rising with *Aurora*'s Light,
The Muse invok'd, sit down to write;
Blot out, correct, insert, refine,
Enlarge, diminish, interline;
Be mindful, when Invention fails,
To scratch your Head, and bite your Nails.   90
  Your Poem finish'd, next your Care
Is needful, to transcribe it fair.
In modern Wit all printed Trash, is
Set off with num'rous *Breaks*——and *Dashes*——
  To Statesmen wou'd you give a Wipe,
You print it in *Italick Type*.
When Letters are in vulgar Shapes,
'Tis ten to one the Wit escapes;
But when in *Capitals* exprest,
The dullest Reader smoaks the Jest: 100
Or else perhaps he may invent
A better than the Poet meant,
As learned Commentators view

In *Homer* more than *Homer* knew.
Your Poem in its modish Dress,
Correctly fitted for the Press,
Convey by Penny-Post to *Lintot*,[2]
But let no Friend alive look into't.
If *Lintot* thinks 'twill quit the Cost,
You need not fear your Labour lost: 110
And, how agreeably surpriz'd
Are you to see it advertiz'd!
The Hawker shews you one in Print,
As fresh as Farthings from the Mint:
The Product of your Toil and Sweating;
A Bastard of your own begetting.
Be sure at *Will's* the following Day,
Lie Snug, and hear what Critics say.
And if you find the general Vogue
Pronounces you a stupid Rogue;   120
Damns all your Thoughts as low and little,
Sit still, and swallow down your Spittle.
Be silent as a Politician,
For talking may beget Suspicion:
Or praise the Judgment of the Town,
And help yourself to run it down.
Give up your fond paternal Pride,
Nor argue on the weaker Side;
For Poems read without a Name
We justly praise, or justly blame: 130
And Criticks have no partial Views,
Except they know whom they abuse.
And since you ne'er provok'd their Spight,
Depend upon't their Judgment's right:
But if you blab, you are undone;
Consider what a Risk you run.
You lose your Credit all at once;
The Town will mark you for a Dunce:
The vilest Doggrel *Grubstreet* sends,
Will pass for yours with Foes and Friends.   140
And you must bear the whole Disgrace,
'Till some fresh Blockhead takes your Place.
    Your Secret kept, your Poem sunk,
And sent in Quires to line a Trunk;
If still you be dispos'd to rhime,
Go try your Hand a second Time.
Again you fail, yet Safe's the Word,
Take Courage, and attempt a Third.
But first with Care imploy your Thoughts,
Where Criticks mark'd your former Faults.   150
The trivial Turns, the borrow'd Wit,

2. Bernard Lintot, a London bookseller.

The *Similes* that nothing fit;
The *Cant* which ev'ry Fool repeats,
Town-Jests, and Coffee-house Conceits;
Descriptions tedious, flat and dry,
And introduc'd the Lord knows why;
Or where we find your Fury set
Against the harmless Alphabet;
On A's and B's your Malice vent,
While Readers wonder whom you meant.　　160
A publick, or a private *Robber*;
A *Statesman*, or a South-Sea *Jobber*.
A *Prelate* who no God believes;
A———,[3] or Den of Thieves.
A Pick-purse at the Bar, or Bench;
A Duchess, or a Suburb-Wench.
Or oft when Epithets you link,
In gaping Lines to fill a Chink;
Like stepping Stones to save a Stride,
In Streets where Kennels are too wide:　　170
Or like a Heel-piece to support
A Cripple with one Foot too short:
Or like a Bridge that joins a Marish
To Moorlands of a diff'rent Parish.
So have I seen ill-coupled Hounds,
Drag diff'rent Ways in miry Grounds.
So Geographers in *Afric*-Maps
With Savage-Pictures fill their Gaps;
And o'er unhabitable Downs
Place Elephants for want of Towns.　　180
　　But tho' you miss your third Essay,
You need not throw your Pen away.
Lay now aside all Thoughts of Fame,
To spring more profitable Game.
From Party-Merit seek Support;
The vilest Verse thrives best at Court.
A Pamphlet in Sir *Rob*'s[4] Defence
Will never fail to bring in Pence;
Nor be concern'd about the Sale,
He pays his Workmen on the Nail.　　190
　　A Prince the Moment he is crown'd,
Inherits ev'ry Virtue round,
As Emblems of the sov'reign Pow'r,
Like other Bawbles of the Tow'r.
Is gen'rous, valiant, just and wise,
And so continues 'till he dies.
His humble *Senate* this professes,
In all their *Speeches, Votes, Addresses.*

3. A Parliament.
4. Robert Walpole, Prime Minister 1721–42, knighted in 1725.

But once you fix him in a Tomb,
His Virtues fade, his Vices bloom;   200
And each Perfection wrong imputed
Is Folly, at his Death confuted.
The Loads of Poems in his Praise,
Ascending make one Funeral-Blaze.
As soon as you can hear his Knell,
This God on Earth turns *Devil* in Hell.
And lo, his Ministers of State,
Transform'd to Imps, his Levee wait.
Where, in this Scene of endless Woe,
They play their former Arts below.   210
And as they sail in *Charon*'s Boat,
Contrive to bribe the Judge's Vote.
To *Cerberus* they give a Sop,
His triple-barking Mouth to Stop:
Or in the Iv'ry Gate of Dreams,
Project ***5 and ****   *** :6
Or hire their Party-Pamphleteers,
To set *Elysium* by the Ears.
    Then *Poet*, if you mean to thrive,
Employ your Muse on Kings alive;   220
With Prudence gath'ring up a Cluster
Of all the Virtues you can muster:
Which form'd into a Garland sweet,
Lay humbly at your Monarch's Feet;
Who, as the Odours reach his Throne,
Will smile, and think 'em all his own:
For *Law* and *Gospel* both determine
All Virtues lodge in royal Ermine.
(I mean the Oracles of Both,
Who shall depose it upon Oath.)   230
Your Garland in the following Reign,
Change but their Names will do again.
    But if you think this Trade too base,
(Which seldom is the Dunce's Case)
Put on the Critick's Brow, and sit
At *Wills* the puny Judge of Wit.
A Nod, a Shrug, a scornful Smile,
With Caution us'd, may serve a-while.
Proceed no further in your Part,
Before you learn the Terms of Art: 240
(For you may easy be too far gone,
In all our modern Critics Jargon.)
Then talk with more authentick Face,
Of *Unities, in Time and Place.*
Get Scraps of *Horace* from your Friends,

5. Excise.
6. South-Sea Schemes.

And have them at your Fingers Ends.
Learn *Aristotle's* Rules by Rote,
And at all Hazards boldly quote:
Judicious *Rymer* oft review:
Wise *Dennis*, and profound *Bossu*.   250
Read all the *Prefaces* of *Dryden*,
For these our Criticks much confide in,
(Tho' meerly writ at first for filling
To raise the Volume's Price, a Shilling.)
    A forward Critick often dupes us
With sham Quotations *Peri Hupsous:
And if we have not read *Longinus*,
Will magisterially out-shine us.
Then, lest with *Greek* he over-run ye,
Procure the Book for Love or Money,   260
Translated from *Boileau's* Translation,†
And quote *Quotation* on *Quotation*.
    At *Wills* you hear a Poem read,
Where *Battus*⁷ from the Table-head,
Reclining on his Elbow-chair,
Gives Judgment with decisive Air.
To whom the Tribe of circling Wits,
As to an Oracle submits.
He gives Directions to the Town,
To cry it up, or run it down.   270
(Like *Courtiers*, when they send a Note,
Instructing *Members* how to Vote.)
He sets the Stamp of Bad and Good,
Tho' not a Word be understood.
Your Lesson learnt, you'll be secure
To get the Name of *Conoisseur*.
And when your Merits once are known,
Procure Disciples of your own.
    Our Poets (you can never want 'em,
Spread thro' *Augusta Trinobantum*)⁸   280
Computing by their Pecks of Coals,
Amount to just Nine thousand Souls.
These o'er their proper Districts govern,
Of Wit and Humour, Judges sov'reign.
In ev'ry Street a City-bard
Rules, like an Alderman his Ward.
His indisputed Rights extend
Thro' all the Lane, from End to End.
The Neighbours round admire his *Shrewdness*,
For songs of *Loyalty* and *Lewdness*.   290

* A famous Treatise of *Longinus*.
† By Mr. *Welsted*.
7. Dryden.
8. London.

Out-done by none in Rhyming well,
Altho' he never learnt to spell.
Two bordering Wits contend for Glory;
And one is *Whig*, and one is *Tory*.
And this, for Epicks claims the Bays,
And that, for *Elegiack* Lays.
Some famed for Numbers soft and smooth,
By Lovers spoke in *Punch*'s Booth.
And some as justly Fame extols
For lofty Lines in *Smithfield* Drols.   300
Bavius in *Wapping* gains Renown,
And *Mævius*[9] reigns o'er *Kentish-Town*:
Tigellius[1] plac'd in *Phœbus*' Car,
From *Ludgate* shines to *Temple-bar*.
Harmonius *Cibber* entertains
The Court with annual Birth-day Strains;
Whence *Gay* was banish'd in Disgrace,
Where *Pope* will never show his Face;
Where Y- - - - - - -[2] must torture his Invention,
To flatter *Knaves*, or lose his *Pension*.   310
     But these are not a thousandth Part
Of Jobbers in the Poets Art,
Attending each his proper Station,
And all in due Subordination;
Thro' ev'ry Alley to be found,
In Garrets high, or under Ground:
And when they join their *Pericranies*,
Out skips a *Book of Miscellanies*.
Hobbes clearly proves that ev'ry Creature
Lives in a State of War by Nature.   320
The Greater for the Smallest watch,
But meddle seldom with their Match.
A Whale of moderate Size will draw
A Shole of Herrings down his Maw.
A Fox with Geese his Belly crams;
A Wolf destroys a thousand Lambs.
But search among the rhiming Race,
The Brave are worried by the Base.
If, on *Parnassus*' Top you sit,
You rarely bite, are always bit: 330
Each Poet of inferior Size
On you shall rail and criticize;
And strive to tear you Limb from Limb,
While others do as much for him.
     The Vermin only teaze and pinch

9. See Vergil, *Eclogues*, III, 90, for the proper contempt due to poets bearing such names as Bavius and Mævius.
1. See Horace, *Satires*, I, iii, 1–18, on this eccentric singer.
2. [Edward] Young.

Their Foes superior by an Inch.
So, Nat'ralists observe, a Flea
Hath smaller Fleas that on him prey,
And these have smaller Fleas to bite 'em,
And so proceed *ad infinitum*:   340
Thus ev'ry Poet in his Kind,
Is bit by him that comes behind;
Who, tho' too little to be seen,
Can teaze, and gall, and give the Spleen;
Call Dunces, Fools, and Sons of Whores,
Lay *Grubstreet* at each others Doors:
Extol the *Greek* and *Roman* Masters,
And curse our modern Poetasters.
Complain, as many an ancient Bard did,
How Genius is no more rewarded;   350
How wrong a Taste prevails among us;
How much our Ancestors out-sung us;
Can personate an awkward Scorn
For those who are not Poets born:
And all their Brother Dunces lash,
Who crowd the Press with hourly Trash.
   O, *Grubstreet!* how do I bemoan thee,
Whose graceless Children scorn to own thee!
Their filial Piety forgot,
Deny their Country like a Scot: 360
Tho' by their Idiom and Grimace
They soon betray their native Place:
Yet *thou* hast greater Cause to be
Asham'd of them, than they of thee.
Degenerate from their ancient Brood,
Since first the Court allow'd them Food.
   Remains a Difficulty still,
To purchase Fame by writing ill:
From *Flecknoe*[3] down to *Howard's*[4] Time,
How few have reach'd the *low Sublime?*   370
For when our high-born *Howard* dy'd,
Blackmore[5] alone his Place supply'd:
And least a Chasm should intervene,
When Death had finish'd *Blackmore's* Reign,
The *leaden Crown* devolv'd to thee,
Great *Poet of the *Hollow-Tree.*
But, oh, how unsecure thy Throne!
A thousand Bards thy Right disown:
They plot to turn in factious Zeal,

3. Richard Flecknoe, poet-priest, satirized by Dryden and Marvell.
4. One of two brothers, Robert and Edward; Robert collaborated with Dryden on
the heroic play *The Indian Queen.*
5. Sir Richard Blackmore, physician and heroic poet.
* Lord *G———*.[Lord Grimston, who in 1705 had published a play entitled *The
Lawyer's Fortune, or Love in a Hollow Tree.—Editors*]

Duncenia to a Common-weal;   380
And with rebellious Arms pretend
An equal Priv'lege to *descend.*

In Bulk there are not more Degrees,
From *Elephants* to *Mites* in Cheese,
Than what a curious Eye may trace
In Creatures of the rhiming Race.
From bad to worse, and worse they fall,
But, who can reach the Worst of all?
For, tho' in Nature Depth and Height
Are equally held infinite,   390
In Poetry the Height we know;
'Tis only infinite below.
For Instance: When you rashly *think,
No Rhymer can like W*elsted* sink.
His Merits ballanc'd you shall find,
That *Fielding* leaves him far behind.
Concannen, more aspiring Bard,
Climbs downwards, deeper by a Yard:
Smart *Jemmy Moor*[6] with Vigor drops,
The Rest pursue as thick as Hops: 400
With Heads to Points the Gulph they enter,
Linkt perpendicular to the Centre:
And as their Heels elated rise,
Their Heads attempt the nether Skies.

    O, what Indignity and Shame
To prostitute the Muse's Name,
By flatt'ring ———— whom Heaven design'd
The Plagues and Scourges of Mankind.
Bred up in Ignorance and Sloth,
And ev'ry Vice that nurses both.   410

    Fair *Britain* in thy Monarch blest,
Whose Virtues bear the strictest Test;
Whom never *Faction* cou'd bespatter,
Nor *Minister,* nor *Poet* flatter.
What Justice in rewarding Merit?
What Magnanimity of Spirit?
What Lineaments divine we trace
Thro' all the Features of his Face;
Tho' Peace with Olive bind his Hands,
Confest the conqu'ring Hero stands.   420
Hydaspes, Indus, and the *Ganges,*
Dread from his Hand impending Changes.
From him the *Tartar,* and *Chinese,*
Short by the Knees intreat for Peace.
The *Consort* of his Throne and Bed,

---

* *Vide* The Treatise on the *Profound,* and Mr. *Pope*'s *Dunciad.*
6. Leonard Welstead, Matthew Concannen, and James Moore Smythe were minor
literary figures of Swift's day.

A perfect Goddess born and bred.
Appointed sov'reign Judge to sit
On Learning, Eloquence and Wit.
Our eldest Hope, divine *Iülus*,[7]
(Late, very late, O, may he rule us.)   430
What early Manhood has he shown,
Before his downy Beard was grown!
Then think, what Wonders will be done
By going on as he begun;
An Heir for *Britain* to secure
As long as Sun and Moon endure.
   The Remnant of the royal Blood,
Comes pouring on me like a Flood.
Bright Goddesses, in Number five;[8]
Duke *William*,[9] sweetest Prince alive.   440
   Now sing the *Minister* of *State*,
Who shines alone, without a Mate.
Observe with what majestick Port
This *Atlas* stands to prop the Court:
Intent the Publick Debts to pay,
Like prudent *Fabius* by *Delay*.
Thou great Vicegerent of the King,
Thy Praises ev'ry Muse shall sing.
In all Affairs thou sole Director,
Of Wit and Learning chief Protector;   450
Tho' small the Time thou hast to spare,
The Church is thy peculiar Care.
Of pious Prelates what a Stock
You chuse to rule the Sable-flock.
You raise the Honour of the Peerage,
Proud to attend you at the Steerage.
You dignify the noble Race,
Content yourself with humbler Place.
Now Learning, Valour, Virtue, Sense,
To Titles give the sole Pretence.   460
St. George beheld thee with Delight,
Vouchsafe to be an azure Knight,
When on thy Breast and Sides *Herculean*,
He fixt the *Star* and *String Cerulean*.[1]
   Say, Poet, in what other Nation,
Shone ever such a Constellation.
Attend ye *Popes*, and *Youngs*, and *Gays*,
And tune your Harps, and strow your Bays.

7. Frederick Louis, Prince of Wales.
8. Queen Caroline had five daughters.
9. William Augustus, Duke of Cumberland.
* *Unus Homo nobis* Cunctando *restituit rem*. ["One man has retrieved our situation, by delaying."—*Editors*]
1. Walpole received the Order of the Garter, of which St. George is accounted the special patron, in 1726.

Your Panegyricks here provide,
You cannot err on Flatt'ry's Side.   470
Above the Stars exalt your Stile,
You still are low ten thousand Mile.
On *Lewis* all his Bards bestow'd,
Of Incense many a thousand Load;
But *Europe* mortify'd his Pride,
And swore the fawning Rascals ly'd:
Yet what the World refus'd to *Lewis*,
Apply'd to - - - - - - - -² exactly true is:
Exactly true! Invidious Poet!
'Tis fifty thousand Times below it.   480
    Translate me now some Lines, if you can,
From *Virgil, Martial, Ovid, Lucan;*
They could all Pow'r in Heaven divide,
And do no Wrong to either Side:
They'll teach you how to split a Hair,
*Give - - - - - - - -³ and *Jove* an equal Share.
Yet, why should we be lac'd so straight;
I'll give my * * * * *⁴ Butter-weight.⁵
And Reason good; for many a Year
- - - - -⁶ never intermeddl'd here: 490
Nor, tho' his Priests be duly paid,
Did ever we *desire* his Aid:
We now can better do without him,
Since *Woolston*⁷ gave us Arms to rout him.
***** *Cætera desiderantur* *****

The Day of Judgement

1732–33¹

With a Whirl of Thought oppress'd,
I sink from Reverie to Rest.
An horrid Vision seiz'd my Head,

---

2. George (George II).
* *Divisum Imperium cum* Jove Cæsar *habet.* ["Caesar has an equal power with Jove."—*Editors*]
3. George.
4. Monarch.
5. Butter-weight is eighteen ounces to the pound; figuratively, then, good measure.
6. Christ.
7. See "Verses on the Death," lines 281 ff., p. 557.
1. First published in 1773–74; neither the text of this poem nor its date of composition is entirely certain. The editors are indebted to Maurice Johnson, "Text, and Possible Occasion for Swift's 'Day of Judgment,'" *PMLA*, LXXVI (1971), 210–17.

I saw the Graves give up their Dead.
Jove, arm'd with Terrors, burst the Skies,
And Thunder roars, and Light'ning flies!
Amaz'd, confus'd, its Fate unknown,
The World stands trembling at his Throne.
While each pale Sinner hangs his Head,
Jove, nodding, shook the Heav'ns, and said,   10
Offending Race of Human Kind,
By Nature, Custom, Learning, blind;
You who thro' Frailty step'd aside,
And you who never fell—*thro' Pride*;
And you whom different Sects have shamm'd,
And come to see each other damn'd;
(So some Folks told you, but they knew
No more of Jove's Designs than you)
The World's mad Business now is o'er,
And I resent these Pranks no more.   20
I to such Blockheads set my Wit!
I damn such Fools!—Go, go, you're bit.

Backgrounds

CORRESPONDENCE

Swift to Charles Ford

Jan 19th, 1724

My greatest want here[1] is of somebody qualifyed to censure and correct what I write, I know not above two or three whose Judgment I would value, and they are lazy, negligent, and without any Opinion of my Abilityes. I have left the Country of Horses, and am in the flying Island, where I shall not stay long, and my two last Journyes will be soon over; so that if you come here this Summer you will find me returnd—adieu—

Aug 14th, 1725

I have finished my Travells, and I am now transcribing them; they are admirable Things, and will wonderfully mend the World.

Swift to the Rev. Thomas Sheridan

Sept, 11, 1725.[2]

If you are indeed a discarded Courtier, you have reason to complain, but none at all to wonder; you are too young for many Experiences to fall in your way, yet you have read enough to make

The correspondence of Swift in this section is reprinted from *The Correspondence of Jonathan Swift*, Vol. III. Oxford, England: The Clarendon Press. Reprinted by permission of the publisher.

1. Dublin, where, as Dean of St. Patrick's Cathedral, Swift had been in residence since 1714.

2. Swift's friend, Sheridan, through an indiscretion, had lost favor with the authorities in Ireland, and had lamented that loss to Swift, who here responds.

you know the Nature of Man. It is safer for a Man's Interest to blaspheme God, than to be of a Party out of Power, or even to be thought so. And since the last was the Case, how could you imagine that all Mouths would not be open when you were received, and in some manner prefer'd by the Government, tho' in a poor way? I tell you there is hardly a Whig in *Ireland* who would allow a Potato and Butter-milk to a reputed Tory. ... Therefore sit down and be quiet, and mind your Business as you should do, and contract your Friendships, and expect no more from Man than such an Animal is capable of, and you will every day find my Description of Yahoes more resembling.

Swift to Alexander Pope

Sep. 29. 1725

I have employd my time (besides ditching) in finishing correcting, amending, and Transcribing my Travells, in four parts Compleat newly Augmented, and intended for the press when the world shall deserve them, or rather when a Printer shall be found brave enough to venture his Eares. ... the chief end I propose to my self in all my labors is to vex the world rather then divert it, and if I could compass that designe without hurting my own person or Fortune I would be the most Indefatigable writer you have ever seen without reading I am exceedingly pleased that you have done with Translations Lord Treasurer Oxford often lamented that a rascaly World should lay you under a Necessity of Misemploying your Genius for so long a time.[3] But since you will now be so much better employd when you think of the World give it one lash the more at my Request. I have ever hated all Nations professions and Communityes and all my love is towards individualls for instance I hate the tribe of Lawyers, but I love Councellor such a one, Judge such a one for so with Physicians (I will not Speak of my own Trade) Soldiers, English, Scotch, French; and the rest but principally I hate and detest that animal called man, although I hartily love John,

---

[3] Pope had been occupied on and off for a decade with his translations of Homer.

Peter, Thomas and so forth. this is the system upon which I have governed my self many years (but do not tell) and so I shall go on till I have done with them I have got Materials Towards a Treatis proving the falsity of that Definition *animal rationale*; and to show it should be only *rationis capax.* Upon this great foundation of Misanthropy (though not Timons manner) The whole building of my Travells is erected: And I never will have peace of mind till all honest men are of my Opinion: by Consequence you are to embrace it immediately and procure that all who deserve my Esteem may do so too. The matter is so clear that it will admit little dispute. nay I will hold a hundred pounds that you and I agree in the Point. . . .

Mr Lewis sent me an Account of Dr Arbuthnett's Illness which is a very sensible Affliction to me, who by living so long out of the World have lost that hardness of Heart contracted by years and generall Conversation. I am daily loosing Friends, and neither seeking nor getting others. O, if the World had but a dozen Arbuthnetts in it I would burn my Travells but however he is not without Fault. There is a passage in Bede highly commending the Piety and learning of the Irish in that Age, where after abundance of praises he overthrows them all by lamenting that, Alas, they kept Easter at a wrong time of the Year. So our Doctor has every Quality and virtue that can make a man amiable or usefull, but alas he hath a sort of Slouch in his Walk. I pray god protect him for he is an excellant Christian tho not a Catholick and as fit a man either to dy or Live as ever I knew.

Swift to Alexander Pope

NOVR 26, 1725

Drown the World, I am not content with despising it, but I would anger it if I could with safety. I wish there were an Hospital built for it's despisers, where one might act with safety and it need not be a large Building, only I would have it well endowed. . . .

To hear Boys like you talk of Millimums and Tranquility I am older by thirty years. Lord Bol—by Twenty and you but by Ten then when we last were together and we should differ more then

ever. You coquetting a Maid of Honour. My Lord looking on to
see how the Gamesters play and I railing at you both. I desire you
and all my Friends will take a special care that my Affection to the
World may not be imputed to my Age, for I have Credible witnesses ready to depose that it hath never varyed from the Twenty
First to the f—ty-eighth year of my Life, (pray fill that Blank
Charitably) I tell you after all that I do not hate Mankind, it is
vous autres who hate them because you would have them reasonable Animals, and are Angry for being disappointed. I have always
rejected that Definition and made another of my own. I am no
more angry with —— Then I was with the Kite that last week flew
away with one of my Chickins and yet I was pleas'd when one of
my Servants Shot him two days after, This I say, because you are so
hardy as to tell me of your Intentions to write Maxims in Opposition to Rochfoucault who is my Favorite because I found my whole
character in him, however I will read him again because it is possible I may have since undergone some alterations.

John Arbuthnot to Swift

5 November 1726

I will make over all my profits to you, for the property of Gulliver's
Travells, which I believe, will have as great a Run as John Bunian.
Gulliver is a happy man that at his age can write such a merry
work.

I made my Lord ArchBishop's compliment to her R Highness
who returns his Grace her thanks. . . . when I had the honor to see
her She was Reading Gulliver, & was just come to the passage of
the Hobbling prince, which she laughed at. I tell yow freely the
part of the projectors is the least Brilliant. Lewis Grumbles a little
at it & says he wants the Key to it. . . .

Gulliver is in every body's Hands Lord Scarborow who is no
inventor of Storys told me that he fell in company with a Master
of a ship, who told him that he was very well acquainted with Gulliver, but that the printer had Mistaken, that he livd in Wapping,

& not in Rotherhith. I lent the Book to an old Gentleman, who went immediately to his Map to search for Lilly putt.

Alexander Pope to Swift

16 November 1726

I congratulate you first upon what you call your Couzen's wonderful Book, which is *publica trita manu* at present, and I prophecy will be in future the admiration of all men. That countenance with which it is received by some statesmen, is delightful; I wish I could tell you how every single man looks upon it, to observe which has been my whole diversion this fortnight. I've never been a night in London since you left me, till now for this very end, and indeed it has fully answered my expectations.

I find no considerable man very angry at the book: some indeed think it rather too bold, and too general a Satire: but none that I hear of accuse it of particular reflections (I mean no persons of consequence, or good judgment; the mob of Criticks, you know, always are desirous to apply Satire to those that they envy for being above them) so that you needed not to have been so secret upon this head. Motte receiv'd the copy (he tells me) he knew not from whence, nor from whom, dropp'd at his house in the dark, from a Hackney-coach: by computing the time, I found it was after you left England, so for my part, I suspend my judgment.[4]

John Gay to Swift

Nov. 17. 1726.

About ten days ago a Book was publish'd here of the Travels of one Gulliver, which hath been the conversation of the whole town

4.Benjamin Motte, the publisher in 1726 of *Gulliver's Travels*. Pope wittily alludes to the efforts made to conceal Swift's authorship.

ever since: The whole impression sold in a week; and nothing is more diverting than to hear the different opinions people give of it, though all agree in liking it extreamly. 'Tis generally said that you are the Author, but I am told, the Bookseller declares he knows not from what hand it came. From the highest to the lowest it is universally read, from the Cabinet-council to the Nursery. The Politicians to a man agree, that it is free from particular reflections, but that the Satire on general societies of men is too severe. Not but we now and then meet with people of greater perspicuity, who are in search for particular applications in every leaf; and it is highly probable we shall have keys published to give light into Gulliver's design. Your Lord [Bolingbroke] is the person who least approves it, blaming it as a design of evil consequence to depreciate human nature, at which it cannot be wondered that he takes most offence, being himself the most accomplish'd of his species, and so losing more than any other of that praise which is due both to the dignity and virtue of a man. Your friend, my Lord Harcourt, commends it very much, though he thinks in some places the matter too far carried. The Duchess Dowager of Marlborough is in raptures at it; she says she can dream of nothing else since she read it; she declares, that she hath now found out, that her whole life hath been lost in caressing the worst part of mankind, and treating the best as her foes; and that if she knew Gulliver, tho' he had been the worst enemy she ever had, she would give up all her present acquaintance for his friendship. You may see by this, that you are not much injur'd by being suppos'd the Author of this piece. If you are, you have disoblig'd us, and two or three of your best friends, in not giving us the least hint of it while you were with us; and in particular Dr. Arbuthnot, who says it is ten thousand pitys he had not known it, he could have added such abundance of things upon every subject. Among Lady-critics, some have found out that Mr. Gulliver had a particular malice to maids of honour. Those of them who frequent the Church, say, his design is impious, and that it is an insult on Providence, by depreciating the works of the Creator. Notwithstanding I am told the Princess hath read it with great pleasure. As to other Critics, they think the flying island is the least entertaining; and so great an opinion the town have of the impossibility of Gulliver's writing at all below himself, that 'tis agreed that Part was not writ by the same Hand, tho' this hath its defenders too. It hath pass'd Lords and Commons, *nemine contradicente*; and the whole town, men, women, and children are quite full of it.

Perhaps I may all this time be talking to you of a Book you have never seen, and which hath not yet reach'd Ireland; if it hath not, I believe what we have said will be sufficient to recommend it to your reading, and that you order me to send it to you. But it will be much better to come over your self, and read it here, where you will have the pleasure of variety of commentators, to explain the difficult passages to you.

Swift to Mrs. Howard

Novr 27th 1726[5]

When I received your Letter I thought it the most unaccountable one I ever saw in my Life, and was not able to comprehend three words of it together. The Perverseness of your lines astonished me, which tended downwards to the right on one Page, and upward in the two others. This I thought impossible to be done by any Person who did not squint with both Eyes; an Infirmity I never observed in you. However, one thing I was pleased with, that after you had writ me *down*; you repented, and writ me *up*. But I continued four days at a loss for your meaning, till a Bookseller sent me the Travells of one Capᵗⁿ Gulliver, who proved a very good Explainer, although at the same time, I thought it hard to be forced to read a Book of seven hundred Pages in order to understand a Letter of fifty lines; especially since those of our Faculty are already but too much pestered with Commentators. The Stuffs you require are making, because the Weaver piques himself upon having them in perfection, but he has read Gulliver's Book, and has no Conception of what you mean by returning Money, for he is become a Proselyte of the Houyhnhnms, whose great Principle (if I rightly remember) is Benevolence. And as to my self, I am

5. Henrietta Howard, Countess of Suffolk, was officially Bedchamber Woman to the Princess of Wales, and unofficially mistress to the Prince of Wales. She and Swift had a delightful exchange of letters in late 1726, full of playful allusions to the *Travels*; this is an excerpt from one of these.

rightly affronted with such a base Proposall, that I am determined to complain of you to her Royal Highness, that you are a mercenary Yahoo fond of shining Pebbles. What have I to do with you or your Court further than to show the Esteem I have for your Person, because you happen to deserve it, and my Gratitude to Her Royall Highness, who was pleased, a little to distinguish me; which, by the way is the greatest Compliment I ever made, and may probably be the last. For I am not such a prostitute Flatterer as Gulliver; whose chief Study is to extenuate the Vices, and magnify the Virtues, of Mankind, and perpetually dins our Ears with the Praises of his Country, in the midst of Corruptions, and for that Reason alone, hath found so many readers; and probably will have a Pension, which, I suppose, was his chief design in writing: As for his Compliments to the Ladyes, I can easily forgive him as a naturall Effect of that Devotion which our Sex always ought to pay to Yours.

Swift to Alexander Pope

Nov. [27] 1726

I am just come from answering a Letter of Mrs. Howard's writ in such mystical terms, that I should never have found out the meaning, if a Book had not been sent me called *Gulliver's Travellers*, of which you say so much in yours. I read the Book over, and in the second volume observe several passages which appear to be patched and altered, and the style of a different sort (unless I am much mistaken) Dr. Arbuthnot likes the Projectors least, others you tell me, the Flying island; some think it wrong to be so hard upon whole Bodies or Corporations, yet the general opinion is, that reflections on particular persons are most to be blamed: so that in these cases, I think the best method is to let censure and opinion take their course. A Bishop here said, that Book was full of improbable lies, and for his part, he hardly believed a word of it; and so much for Gulliver.

Swift to L'Abbé des Fontaines

July 1727[6]

We may concede that the taste of nations is not always the same. But we are inclined to believe that good taste is the same everywhere that there are people of wit, of judgment, and of learning. If, then, the writings of Gulliver were intended only for the British Isles, that traveller must be considered a very contemptible author. The same vices and the same follies reign everywhere; at least, in all the civilized countries of Europe: and the author who writes only for a city, a province, a kingdom, or even an age, warrants so little to be translated, that he deserves not even to be read.

The partisans of Gulliver—they number a good many amongst us—maintain that his book will endure as long as our language, because it draws its merit not from certain modes or manners of thought and speaking, but from a series of observations on the imperfections, the follies, and the vices of man. . . . you will no doubt be surprised to learn that [some] consider this ship's surgeon a solemn author, who never departs from seriousness, who never assumes a role, who never prides himself on possessing wit, and who is content to communicate to the public, in a simple and artless narrative, the adventures that have befallen him and the things that he has seen or heard during his voyages.

6. The Abbé des Fontaines had translated the *Travels* into French, dropping passages he thought inappropriate to France. What follows—Swift's reply to the omissions—is a translation of the French original.

WILLIAM WOTTON

Observations upon the *Tale of a Tub*

For, believe me, Sir, what concerns us,[1] is much the innocentest part of the Book, tending chiefly to make Men laugh for half an Hour, after which it leaves no farther Effects behind it. When Men are jested upon for what is in itself praiseworthy, the World will do them Justice: And on the other hand, if they deserve it, they ought to sit down quietly under it. Our Cause therefore we shall leave to the Public very willingly, there being no occasion to be concerned at any Man's Railery about it. But the rest of the Book which does not relate to us, is of so irreligious a nature, is so crude a Banter upon all that is esteemed as Sacred among all Sects and Religions among Men, that, having so fair an Opportunity, I thought it might be useful to many People who pretend they see no harm in it, to lay open the Mischief of the Ludicrous Allegory, and to shew what that drives at which has been so greedily bought up and read. In one Word, God and Religion, Truth and Moral Honesty, Learning and Industry are made a May-Game, and the most serious Things in the World are described as so many several Scenes in a *Tale of a Tub*.

That this is the true Design of that Book, will appear by these Particulars. The *Tale* in substance is this; "A Man had three Sons, all at a Birth, by one Wife; to whom when he died, because he had purchased no Estate, nor was born to any, he only provided to each of them a New Coat, which were to last them fresh and sound as long as they lived, and would lengthen and widen of themselves, so as to be always fit." By the Sequel of the *Tale* it appears, that by these three Sons, *Peter, Martin,* and *Jack; Popery,* the *Church of England,* and our *Protestant Dissenters* are designed. What can now be more infamous than such a *Tale?* The Father is *Jesus Christ,* who at his Death left his WILL or TESTAMENT to his Disciples, with a Promise of Happiness to them, and the Churches which they and their Successors should found for ever. So the Tale-teller's Father to his three Sons, "You will find in my WILL full

From *A Defense of the Reflections upon Ancient and Modern Learning, In Answer to the Objections of Sir W. Temple, and Others. With Observations upon the Tale of a Tub,* (1705).
1. Bentley and Wotton. [*Editors*]

Instructions in every Particular concerning the wearing and managing of your Coats; wherein you must be very exact, to avoid the Penalties I have appointed for every Transgression or Nelect, upon which your *Future Fortunes* will *entirely* depend." By his Coats which he gave his Sons, the Garments of the *Israelites* are exposed, which by the Miraculous Power of God waxed not old, nor were worn out for Forty Years together in the Wilderness. The number of these Sons born thus at one Birth, looks asquint at the TRIN-ITY, and one of the Books in our Author's Catalogue in the Off-page over-against the Title, is a Panegyric upon the Number THREE, which Word is the only one that is put in Capitals in that whole Page.

In the pursuit of his Allegory, we are entertain'd with the Lewd-ness of the Three Sparks. Their Mistresses are the *Dutchess d' Argent*, Madamoizelle *de Grands Titres*, and the Countess *d' Orgueil* i.e. *Covetousness, Ambition* and *Pride*, which were the Three great Vices that the Ancient Fathers inveighed against as the first Corrupters of Christianity. Their Coats having such an extraordinary Virtue of never wearing out, give him large Scope for his Mirth, which he employs in burlesquing *Religion, Moral Honesty* and *Conscience*, which are the strongest Ties by which Men can be tied to one another. *Is not Religion a Cloak, Honesty a Pair of Shoes worn out in the Dirt, Self-love a Surtout, Vanity a Shirt, and Conscience a Pair of Breeches?* Which last Allusion gives him an opportunity that he never misses of talking obscenely.

His Whim of Clothes is one of his chiefest Favourites. "Man, says he, is an Animal compounded of two *Dresses,* the *Natural* and the *Coelestial-Suit,* which were the Body and the Soul. And That the Soul was by daily Creation and Circumfusion they proved by Scripture, because *In them we live, and move, and have our Being.*" *In them* (i.e. *in the Clothes of the Body.*) Words applicable only to the Great God of Heaven and Earth, of whom they were first spoken by *St. Paul.* Thus he introduces his Tale; then that he might shelter himself the better from any Censure here in *England,* he falls most unmercifully upon *Peter* and *Jack, i.e.* upon *Popery* and *Fanaticism,* and gives *Martin,* who represents the *Church of England,* extream good Quarter. I confess, Sir, I abhor making Sport with any way of worshipping God, and he that diverts himself too much at the Expense of the *Roman Catholics* and the *Protestant Dissenters,* may lose his own Religion e're he is aware of it, at least the Power of it in his Heart. But to go on.

The first Part of the *Tale* is the *History of Peter.* Thereby *Popery* is exposed. Everybody knows the *Papists* have made great Additions to Christianity. That indeed is the great Exception which the

Church of *England* makes against them. Accordingly *Peter* begins his Pranks with *adding a Shoulderknot to his Coat*, "whereas his Father's Will was very precise, and it was the main Precept in it with the greatest Penalties annexed, not to add to, or diminish from their Coats one Thread, without a positive Command in the WILL." His Description of the Cloth of which the Coat was made, has a farther Meaning than the Words may seem to import. "The Coats their Father had left them were of very good Cloth, and besides so neatly sown, you would swear they were all of a Piece, but at the same time very plain, with little or no Ornament." This is the Distinguishing Character of the Christian Religion. *Christiana Religio absoluta & simplex*, was *Ammianus Marcellinus*'s Description of it, who was himself a Heathen. When the *Papists* cannot find any thing which they want in Scripture, they go to *Oral Tradition*: Thus *Peter* is introduced dissatisfied with the tedious Way of looking for all the Letters of any Word which he had occasion for in the *Will*, when neither the constituent Syllables, nor much less the whole Word were there *in Terminis*, and he expresses himself thus; "Brothers, if you remember, we heard a Fellow say when we were Boys, that he heard my Father's Man say, that he heard my Father say, that he would advise his Sons to get *Gold*-Lace on their Coats, as soon as ever they could procure Money to buy it." Which way of coming at any thing that was not expressly in his Father's W I L L, stood him afterwards in great stead.

The next Subject of our *Tale-Teller*'s Wit is the *Glosses* and *Interpretations of Scripture*, very many absurd ones of which kind are allow'd in the most Authentic Books of the Church of *Rome*: The Sparks wanted Silver Fringe to put upon their Coats. Why, says *Peter*, (seemingly perhaps to laugh at Dr. *Bentley* and his Criticisms); "I have found in a certain Author, which shall be nameless, that the same Word which in the Will is called *Fringe*, does also signifie a *Broomstick*, and doubtless ought to have the same Interpretation in this Paragraph." This affording great Diversion to one of the Brothers; "You speak, says *Peter*, very irreverently of a *Mystery*, which doubtless was very useful and significant, but ought not to be overcuriously pry'd into, or nicely reason'd upon." The Author, one would think, copies from Mr. *Toland*, who always raises a Laugh at the Word *Mystery*, the Word and Thing whereof he is known to believe to be no more than a *Tale of a Tub*.

Images in the Church of *Rome* give our *Tale-teller* but too fair a Handle. "The Brothers remembered but too well how their Father abhorred the Fashion of Embroidering their Clothes with *Indian* Figures of Men, Women and Children; that he made several Paragraphs on purpose, importing his utter Detestation of it, and bestowing his Everlasting Curse to his Sons, whenever they should wear it." The Allegory here is direct. The *Papists* formerly forbad the People the use of Scripture in a Vulgar Tongue; *Peter* therefore *locks up his Father's Will in a strong Box brought out of* Greece or Italy: Those Countries are named, because the *New Testament* is written in *Greek*; and the *Vulgar Latin*, which is the Authentic Edition of the Bible in the Church of *Rome*, is in the Language of Old *Italy*. The Popes in their *Decretals* and *Bulls* have given their Sanction to very many gainful Doctrines which are now receiv'd in the Church of *Rome*, that are not mentioned in Scripture, and are unknown to the Primitive Church. *Peter* accordingly pronounces *ex Cathedra*, that *Points tagged with Silver were absolutely Jure Paterno*, and so they wore them in great numbers. The Bishops of *Rome* enjoy'd their Privileges in *Rome* at first by the Favour of Emperors, whom at last they shut out of their own Capital City, and then forged a Donation from *Constantine the Great*, the better to justifie what they did. In imitation of this, *Peter*, "having run something behind hand with the World, obtained leave of a certain Lord to receive him into his House, and to teach his Children. A while after the Lord died, and he by long Practise upon his Father's Will, found the way of contriving a Deed of Conveyance of that House to himself and his Heirs: Upon which he took possession, turned the Young Squires out, and receiv'd his Brothers in their stead." *Pennance* and *Absolution* are plaid upon under the Notion of a Sovereign Remedy for the Worms, especially in the Spleen, which by observing of *Peter's* Prescriptions, would void insensibly by Perspiration ascending through the Brain. By his *Whispering Office* for the Relief of Eves-droppers, Physicians, Bawds and Privy-Councellors, he ridicules *Auricular Confession*, and the Priest who takes it is described by the Ass's Head. Holy-Water he calls an Universal Pickle, *to preserve Houses, Gardens, Towns, Men, Women, Children and Cattle, wherein he could preserve them as sound as Insects in Amber*; and because Holy-Water differs only in Consecration from Common Water, therefore our Tale-teller tells us that his Pickle by the Powder of *Pimperlimpimp* receives new Virtues, though it differs not in Sight nor Smell from the Common Pickle which preserves Beef, and Butter, and Herrings. The *Papal Bulls* are ridiculed by Name, so there we are at no loss for our *Tale-teller's* Meaning. *Absolution in Articulo Mortis*, and the *Taxa Camerae Apostolicae* are jested upon in Emperor *Peter's* Letter. The *Pope's Universal Monarchy*, and his *Triple Crown*, and *Key's* and *Fishers Ring* have their turns of being laughed at; nor does his Arrogant way of requiring Men to kiss his Slipper, escape Reflexion. The *Celibacy of the Romish Clergy* is struck at in *Peter's* turning his own and

Brothers Wives out of Doors. But nothing makes him so merry as *Transubstantiation*: *Peter* turns his Bread into Mutton, and according to the Popish Doctrine of Concomitance, his Wine too, which in his way he calls *pauming his damned Crust upon the Brothers for Mutton*. The ridiculous multiplying of the *Virgin Mary's Milk* among the Papists, he banters under the Allegory of a *Cow* which gave as much Milk at a Meal, as would fill Three thousand Churches: and the *Wood of the Cross* on which our Saviour suffered, is prophanely likened to an "Old Signpost that belonged to his Father, with Nails and Timber enough upon it to build Sixteen large Men of War": And when one talked to *Peter* of *Chinese* Waggons which were made so light as to sail over Mountains, he swears and curses four times in Eleven Lines, that the *Chapell* of *Loretto* had travelled Two Thousand *German* Leagues, though built with Lime and Stone, over Sea and Land.

But I expect, Sir, that you should tell me, that the *Tale-teller* falls here only upon the Ridiculous Inventions of Popery; that the Church of *Rome* intended by these things to gull silly Superstitious People; and to rook them of their Money; that the World had been but too long in Slavery; that our Ancestors gloriously redeemed us from that Yoak; that the Church of *Rome* therefore ought to be exposed, and that he deserves well of Mankind that does expose it.

All this, Sir, I own to be true: but then I would not so shoot at an Enemy, as to hurt my self at the same time. The Foundation of the Doctrines of the Church of *England* is right, and came from God: Upon this the Popes, and Councils called and confirmed by them, have built, as St. *Paul* speaks, *Hay and Stubble*, perishable and slight Materials, which when they are once consum'd, that the Foundation may appear, then we shall see what is faulty, and what is not. But our *Tale-teller* strikes at the very Root. 'Tis *all* with him *a Farce, and all a Ladle*, as a very facetious Poet says upon another occasion. The *Father*, and the W I L L, and his *Son Martin*, are part of the *Tale*, as well as *Peter* and *Jack*, and are all usher'd in with the Common Old Wives Introduction, *Once Upon a Time*. And the *main Body of the Will* we are told consisted in *certain admirable Rules about the wearing of* their Coats. So that let *Peter* be mad one way, and *Jack* another, and let *Martin* be sober, and spend his Time with Patience and Phlegm in picking the Embroidery off his Coat never so carefully, "firmly resolving to alter whatever was already amiss, and reduce all their future Measures to the strictest Obedience prescribed therein"; Yet still this is all part of a *Tale of a Tub*, it does but enhance the *Teller's* Guilt, and shews at the bottom his contemptible Opinion of every Thing which is called Christianity.

For pray, Sir, take notice that it is not saying he personates none but Papists or Fanatics, that will excuse him; for in other Places, where he speaks in his own Person, and imitates none but himself, he discovers an equal mixture of Lewdness and Irreligion. Would any Christian compare a *Mountebank's-Stage*, a *Pulpit*, and a *Ladder* together? A *Mountebank* is a profess'd Cheat, who turns it off when he is press'd, with the Common Jest, *Men must live*; and with this Man the Preacher of the Word of God is compared, and the Pulpit in which he preaches, is called *an Edifice* (or Castle) *in the Air*: This is not said by *Peter*, or *Jack*, but by the Author himself, who after he has gravely told us, that he has had Poxes ill cured by trusting to Bawds and Surgeons, reflects with "unspeakable Comfort, upon his having past a long Life with a *Conscience void of Offence towards God and towards Man*".

In his own Person, the Author speaks in one of his Digressions of "Books being not bound to Everlasting Chains of Darkness in a Library; but that when the Fulness of Time should come, they should happily undergo the Tryal of Purgatory, in order to ascend the Sky." In another Digression our Author describes one of his Madmen in *Bedlam*, who was distemper'd by the Loose Behaviour his Wife, to be like *Moses*: *Ecce Cornuta erat ejus Facies;* which is the rendring of the *Vulgar Latin* of that which in the *English* Bible is called *the shining of his Face* when he came down from the Mount. Our Author himself asserts, that the "Fumes issuing from a Jakes, will furnish as comely and useful a Vapor, as Incense from an Altar." And 'tis our Author in his own Capacity, who among many other Ludicrous Similes upon those that get their Learning out of *Indices*, which are commonly at the End of a Book, says, "Thus Human Life is best understood by the *Wise-man's* Rule of *regarding the End*." 'Tis in the *Fragment*, which has nothing to do with the *Tale*, that Sir *Humphrey Edwin* is made to apply the Words of the *Psalmist*, *Thy Word is a Lanthorn to my Feet, and a Light to my Paths*, to a Whimsical Dark Lanthorn of our Authors own contrivance; wherein he poorly alludes to *Hudibras's Dark-Lanthorn of the Spirit, which none see by those that bear it*. His whole VIIIth Section concerning the *Aeolists*, in which he banters Inspiration, is such a Mixture of Impiety and Immodesty, that I should have as little regard to you, Sir, as this Author has had to the Public, if I should barely repeat after him what is there. And it is somewhat surprising that the Citation out of *Irenaeus*, in the Title-Page, which seems to be all *Gibberish*, should be a Form of Initiation used anciently by the *Marcosian* Heretics. So great a delight has this Unhappy Writer, to play with what some part or other of Mankind have always esteemed as Sacred!

And therefore when he falls upon *Jack*, he deals as freely with him, and wounds Christianity through his Sides as much as he had done before through *Peter's*. The *Protestant Dissenters use Scripture-Phrases* in their Serious Discourses and Composures more than the Church of *England-men*. Accordingly *Jack* is introduced, making "his Common Talk and Conversation to run wholly in the Phrase of his W I L L, and circumscribing the utmost of his Eloquence within that compass, not daring to let slip a Syllable without Authority from thence." And because he could not of a sudden recollect *an Authentic Phrase*, for the Necessities of Nature, he would use no other: Can any thing be prophaner than this? Things compared, always shew the Esteem or Scorn of the Comparer. To ridicule Praedestination, *Jack* walks blindfold through the Streets; the Body of our Dissenters having till of late been *Calvinists* in the Questions concerning the *Five Points*. "It was ordained, said he, some few days *before* the Creation (*i.e.* immediately by God himself) that my Nose and this very Post should have a Rencounter; and therefore Providence thought fit to send us both into the World in the same Age, and to make us Country-men and Fellow Citizens." This is a direct Prophanation of the Majesty of God. "*Jack* would run Dog-mad at the Noise of Music, especially a Pair of Bagpipes." This is to expose our Dissenters Aversion to Instrumental Music in Churches. The Agreement of our Dissenters and the Papists, in that which Bishop *Stillingfleet* called the *Fanaticism of the Church of Rome*, is ludicriously described for several Pages together, by *Jack's* likeness to *Peter*, and their being often mistaken for each other, and their frequent meeting when they least intended it: In this, singly taken, there might possibly be little harm, if one did not see from what Principle the whole proceeded.

EDMUND CURLL

Some Annotations and Explanatory Notes upon the *Tale of a Tub*

A Preface of the *Bookseller* to the *Reader* before *the Battle of the Books* shews the Cause and Design of the whole Work, which

From *Some Annotations and Explanatory Notes upon the Tale of a Tub* (1710).

was perform'd by * a couple of young Clergymen in the Year 1697. who having been Domestick Chaplains to Sir *William Temple*, thought themselves oblig'd to take up his Quarrel in Relation to the Controversy then in Dispute between him and Mr. *Wotton* concerning *Ancient* and *Modern* Learning.

The † one of 'em began a *Defence* of Sir *William* under the Title of A *Tale of a Tub*, under which he intended to couch the General History of Christianity; shewing the Rise of all the Remarkable Errors of the *Roman Church* in the same order they enter'd, and how the Reformation endeavoured to root 'em out again, with the different Temper of *Luther* from *Calvin* (and those more violent Spirits) in the way of his Reforming: His aim is to Ridicule the stubborn Errors of the *Romish Church*, and the Humours of the *Fanatick Party*, and to shew that their Superstition has somewhat very fantastical in it, which is common to both of 'em, notwithstanding the Abhorrence they seem to have for one another.

The Author intended to have it very regular, and withal so particular, that he thought not to pass by the Rise of any one single Error or its Reformation: He design'd at last to shew the Purity of the Christian Church in the primitive Times, and consequently how weakly Mr. *Wotton* pass'd his Judgment, and how partially in preferring the *Modern* Divinity before the *Ancient*, with the Confutation of whose Book he intended to conclude. But when he had not yet gone half way, his || Companion borrowing the *Manuscript* to peruse, carried it with him to *Ireland*, and having kept it seven Years, at last publish'd it imperfect; for indeed he was not able to carry it on after the intended Method: because *Divinity* (tho it chanc'd to be his Profession) had been the least of his Study; However he added to it the *Battle of the Books*, wherein he effectually pursues the main Design of lashing Mr. *Wotton*, and having added a jocose Epistle Dedicatory to my Lord *Sommers*, and another to Prince *Posterity*, with a pleasant Preface, and interlarded with one *Digression* concerning *Criticks*, and another in the *Modern* kind, a *Third* in Praise of *Digressions*, and a Fourth in Praise of *Madness* (with which he was not unacquainted) concludes the Book with a *Fragment* which the first Author made, and intended should have come in about the middle of the *Tale*, as a Preliminary to *Jack's* Character.

---

* Generally (and not without sufficient Reason) said to be Dr. *Jonathan* and *Thomas Swift*; but since they don't think fit publickly to own it, wherever I mention their Names, 'tis not upon any other Affirmation than as they are the *Reputed Authors*.
† Thomas Swift.
|| Dr. *Jonathan Swift*.

Having thus shewn the Reasons of the little Order observ'd in the Book, and the Imperfectness of the *Tale*, 'tis so submitted to the Reader's Censure.

Thomas Swift is Grandson to Sir *William D'avenant*, *Jonathan Swift* is Cousin German to *Thomas Swift* both Retainers to Sir *William Temple*. The two Gentlemen as before hinted being the reputed Authors of the *Work*, the several Parts of the Book are thus attributed to 'em, *viz*.

The Dedication to my Lord *Sommers*, the Preface, Epistle to Prince *Posterity*, the four Digressions, *viz*. 1. Concerning *Criticks*. 2. In the Modern kind. 3. In Praise of *Digressions*. 4. In Praise of *Madness* and *the Battle of the Books* are assign'd to Dr. *Jonathan Swift*; and the *Tale of a Tub*, and the *Fragment* containing a Mechanical Account of the *Operation of the Spirit*, to *Thomas Swift*.

THOMAS SHERIDAN

[The Composition of "A Meditation upon a Broomstick"]

As Swift has been much censured for writing the "Meditation," on account of the ridicule contained in it of the style and manner of so great and pious a man as Mr. Boyle, it may not be improper here to relate an * anecdote which I had from undoubtedly good authority, with regard to the occasion of writing that piece, and which will in a great measure exonerate Swift from the charge brought against him on that account. In the yearly visits which he made to London, during his stay there, he passed much of his time at Lord Berkeley's, officiating as Chaplain to the family, and attending Lady Berkeley in her private devotions. After which the Doctor, by her desire, used to read to her some moral or religious discourse. The Countess had at this time taken a great liking to Mr. Boyle's Meditations, and was determined to go through them in that manner; but as Swift had by no means the same relish for that kind of writing which her Ladyship had, he soon grew weary of the task;

From Thomas Sheridan, *The Life of Swift* (1787).

* This anecdote came from Lady Betty Germaine, daughter of Lady Berkeley, and was communicated to me [Sheridan] by the late Lady Lambert, an intimate of Lady Betty's.

and a whim coming into his head, resolved to get rid of it in a way which might occasion some sport in the family; for which they had as high a relish as himself. The next time he was employed in reading one of these Meditations, he took an opportunity of conveying away the book, and dexterously inserted a leaf, on which he had written his own Meditation on a Broomstick; after which, he took care to have the book restored to its proper place, and in his next attendance on my Lady, when he was desired to proceed to the next Meditation, Swift opened upon the place where the leaf had been inserted, and with great composure of countenance read the title, "A Meditation on a Broom-stick." Lady Berkeley, a little surprised at the oddity of the title, stopped him, repeating the words, "A Meditation on a Broom-stick!" bless me, what a strange subject! But there is no knowing what useful lessons of instruction this wonderful man may draw, from things apparently the most trivial. Pray let us hear what he says upon it. Swift then, with an inflexible gravity of countenance, proceeded to read the Meditation, in the same solemn tone which he had used in delivering the former. Lady Berkeley, not at all suspecting a trick, in the fulness of her prepossession, was every now and then, during the reading of it, expressing her admiration of this extraordinary man, who could draw such fine oral reflections from so contemptible a subject; with which, though Swift must have been inwardly not a little tickled, yet he preserved a most perfect composure of features, so that she had not the least room to suspect any deceit. Soon after, some company coming in, Swift pretended business, and withdrew, foreseeing what was to follow. Lady Berkeley, full of the subject, soon entered upon the praises of those heavenly Meditations of Mr. Boyle. But, said she, the Doctor has been just reading one to me, which has surprised me more than all the rest. One of the company asked which of the Meditations she meant. She answered directly, in the simplicity of her heart, I mean that excellent Meditation on a Broom-stick. The company looked at each other with some surprise, and could scarce refrain from laughing. But they all agreed that they had never heard of such a Meditation before. Upon my word, said my Lady, there it is, look into that book, and convince yourselves. One of them opened the book, and found it there indeed, but in Swift's hand-writing; upon which a general burst of laughter ensued; and my Lady, when the first surprise was over, enjoyed the joke as much as any of them; saying, what a vile trick has that rogue played me! But it is his way, he never baulks his humour in any thing. The affair ended in a great deal of harmless mirth, and Swift, you may be sure, was not asked to proceed any farther in the Meditations. Thus we see that his original intention in writing this piece, was not to ridicule the great Robert Boyle, but only to furnish occasion for a great deal of innocent mirth on Lady Berkeley's enthusiasm, and simplicity of heart; and at the same time to get rid of the disagreeable task of reading to her writings which were not at all to his taste. And that it afterwards got out into the world, was owing to the eagerness of those who were acquainted with the Berkeley family, to procure copies of a piece of such exquisite humour.

ALEXANDER POPE

[Swift's Odd Blunt Way]

Dr. Swift has an odd blunt way, that is mistaken, by strangers, for ill-nature.—'Tis so odd that there's no describing it but by facts. —I'll tell you one that just comes into my head. One evening Gay and I went to see him: you know how intimately we were all acquainted. On our coming in; "Hey-day, gentlemen," says the Doctor, "what's the meaning of this visit? How come you to leave all the great lords, that you are so fond of, to come hither to see a poor Dean?"—Because we would rather see you than any of them. —"Ay, any one that did not know you so well as I do, might believe you. But, since you are come, I must get some supper for you, I suppose?"—No, Doctor, we have supped already.—"Supped already! that's impossible: why, 'tis not eight o'clock yet."—Indeed we have.—"That's very strange: but if you had not supped, I must have got something for you.—Let me see, what should I have had? a couple of lobsters? ay, that would have done very well;—two shillings: tarts; a shilling. But you will drink a glass of wine with me, though you supped so much before your usual time, only to spare my pocket?"—No, we had rather talk with you, than drink with you.—"But if you had supped with me, as in all reason you ought to have done, you must have drank with me.—A bottle of wine; two shillings.—Two and two, is four; and one is five: just two and sixpence a piece. There, Pope, there's half-a-crown for you; and there's another for you, sir: for I won't save any thing by you I am determined." This was all said and done with his usual seriousness on such occasions; and in spite of every thing we could say to the contrary, he actually obliged us to take the money.

From Joseph Spence, *Anecdotes, Observations, and Characters of Books and Men. Collected from the Conversation of Mr. Pope* (1820). This entry was recorded by Spence in May 1730.

ALEXANDER POPE

Mary Gulliver to Captain Lemuel Gulliver

ARGUMENT. *The Captain, some Time after his Return, being retired to Mr. Sympson's in the Country, Mrs. Gulliver, apprehending from his late Behaviour some Estrangement of his Affections, writes him the following expostulating, soothing, and tenderly-complaining Epistle.*

Welcome, thrice welcome to thy native Place!
—What, touch me not? what, shun a Wife's Embrace?
Have I for this thy tedious Absence born,
And wak'd and wish'd whole Nights for thy Return?
In five long Years I took no second Spouse;
What *Redriff* Wife so long hath kept her Vows?
Your Eyes, your Nose, Inconstancy betray;
Your Nose you stop, your Eyes you turn away.
'Tis said, that thou shouldst cleave unto thy Wife;
Once *thou* didst cleave, and *I* could cleave for Life.
Hear and relent! hark, how thy Children moan;
Be kind at least to these, they are thy own:
Behold, and count them all; secure to find
The honest Number that you left behind.
See how they pat thee with their pretty Paws:
Why start you? are they Snakes? or have they Claws?
Thy Christian Seed, our mutual Flesh and Bone:
Be kind at least to these, they are thy own.

  Biddel, like thee, might farthest *India* rove;
He chang'd his Country, but retain'd his Love.
There's Captain *Pennel*, absent half his Life,
Comes back, and is the kinder to his Wife.
Yet *Pennel's* Wife is brown, compar'd to me;
And Mistress *Biddel* sure is Fifty three.

  Not touch me! never Neighbour call'd me Slut!
Was *Flimnap's* Dame more sweet in *Lilliput?*
I've no red Hair to breathe an odious Fume;
At least thy Consort's cleaner than thy *Groom.*
Why then that dirty Stable-boy thy Care?
What mean those Visits to the *Sorrel Mare?*
Say, by what Witchcraft, or what Daemon led,
Preferr'st thou *Litter* to the Marriage Bed?

  Some say the Dev'l himself is in that *Mare:*
If so, our *Dean* shall drive him forth by Pray'r.
Some think you mad, some think you are possest

That *Bedlam* and clean Straw will suit you best:
Vain Means, alas, this Frenzy to appease!
That *Straw*, that *Straw* would heighten the Disease.

My Bed, (the Scene of all our former Joys,
Witness two lovely Girls, two lovely Boys)
Alone I press; in Dreams I call my Dear,
I stretch my Hand, no *Gulliver* is there!
I wake, I rise, and shiv'ring with the Frost,
Search all the House; my *Gulliver* is lost!
Forth in the Street I rush with frantick Cries:
The Windows open; all the Neighbours rise:
Where sleeps my Gulliver? *O tell me where?*
The Neighbours answer, *With the Sorrel Mare.*

At early Morn, I to the Market haste,
(Studious in ev'ry Thing to please thy Taste)
A curious *Fowl* and *Sparagrass* I chose,
(For I remember you were fond of those,)
Three Shillings cost the first, the last sev'n Groats;
Sullen you turn from both, and call for *Oats.*

Others bring Goods and Treasure to their Houses,
Something to deck their pretty Babes and Spouses;
My *only* Token was a Cup like Horn,
That's made of nothing but a Lady's *Corn.*
'Tis not for that I grieve; no, 'tis to see
The *Groom* and *Sorrel Mare* preferr'd to me!

These, for some Monuments when you deign to quit,
And (at due distance) sweet Discourse admit,
'Tis all my Pleasure thy past Toil to know,
For pleas'd Remembrance builds Delight on Woe.
At ev'ry Danger pants thy Consort's Breast,
And gaping Infants squawle to hear the rest.
How did I tremble, when by thousands bound
I saw thee stretch'd on *Lilliputian* Ground;
When scaling Armies climb'd up ev'ry Part,
Each Step they trod, I felt upon my Heart.
But when thy Torrent quench'd the dreadful **Blaze**,
King, Queen and Nation, staring with Amaze,
Full in my View how all my Husband came,
And what extinguish'd theirs, encreas'd my Flame.
Those *Spectacles*, ordain'd thine Eyes to save,
Were once my Present; *Love* that Armour gave.
How did I mourn at *Bolgolam's* Decree!
For when he sign'd thy Death, he sentenc'd me.

When folks might see thee all the Country round
For Six-pence, I'd have giv'n a thousand Pound.
Lord! when the *Giant-Babe* that Head of thine
Got in his Mouth, my Heart was up in mine!
When in the *Marrow-Bone* I see thee ramm'd;
Or on the House-top by the *Monkey* cramm'd;
The Piteous Images renew my Pain,
And all thy Dangers I weep o'er again!
But on the *Maiden's Nipple* when you rid,
Pray Heav'n, 'twas all a wanton Maiden did!
Glumdalclitch too!—with thee I mourn her Case.
Heav'n guard the gentle Girl from all Disgrace!
O may the King that one Neglect forgive,
And pardon her the Fault by which I live!
Was there no other Way to set him free?
My Life, alas! I fear prov'd Death to Thee!

O teach me, Dear, new Words to speak my Flame;
Teach me to wooe thee by thy best-lov'd Name!
Whether the Style of *Grildrig* please thee most,
So call'd on *Brobdingnag's* stupendous Coast,
When on the Monarch's ample Hand you sate,
And hollow'd in his Ear Intrigues of State:
Or *Quinbus Flestrin* more Endearment brings,
When like a Mountain you look'd down on Kings:
If Ducal *Nardac*, *Lilliputian* Peer,
Or *Glumglum's* humbler Title sooth thy Ear:
Nay, wou'd kind *Jove* my Organs so dispose,
To hymn harmonious *Houyhnhnm* thro' the Nose,
I'd call thee *Houyhnhnm*, that high sounding Name,
Thy Children's Noses all should twang the same.
So might I find my loving Spouse of course
Endu'd with all the *Virtues* of a *Horse*.

LAETITIA PILKINGTON

[Swift's Conduct as a Host]

"Well," says he, "I have brought you here [into the library] to shew you all the Money I got when I was in the Ministry, but do not steal any of it." "I will not indeed, Sir," says I; so he opened a

From Laetitia Pilkington, *Memoirs*, Vol. I (1749). The event reported here must have taken place around 1730.

Cabinet, and shewed me a whole Parcel of empty Drawers; "Bless me," says he, "the Money is flown!" He then opened his Bureau, wherein he had a great Number of curious Trinkets of various Kinds, some of which he told me, were presented to him by the Earl and Countess of *Oxford*; some by Lady *Masham*, and some by Lady *Betty Germain*; at last, coming to a Drawer filled with Medals, he bade me chuse two for myself; but he could not help smiling, when I began to poize them in my Hands, chusing them by Weight rather than Antiquity, of which indeed I was not then a Judge.

The Dean amused me in this Manner till we were summoned to Dinner, where his Behaviour was so humorous, that I cannot avoid relating some Part of it: He placed himself at the Head of the Table, opposite to a great Pier-Glass, under which was a Marble Side-board, so that he could see in the Glass whatever the Servants did at it. He was served entirely in Plate, and with great Elegance; but the Beef being over-roasted, put us all in Confusion; the Dean called for the Cook-maid, and ordered her to take it down Stairs, and do it less; the Maid answered, very innocently that she could not: "Why, what Sort of a Creature are you," says he, "to commit a Fault which cannot be amended?" And turning to me he said, very gravely, that he hoped, as the Cook was a Woman of Genius, he should, by this Manner of arguing, be able, in about a Year's Time, to convince her she had better send up the Meat too little than too much done; charging the Men Servants, whenever they imagined the Meat was ready, they should take it Spit and all, and bring it up by Force, promising to aid them, in case the Cook resisted. The Dean then turning his Eye on the Looking-glass, espied the Butler opening a Bottle of Ale, helping himself to the first Glass, and very kindly jumbling the rest together, that his Master and Guests might all fare alike. "Ha! Friend," says the Dean, "Sharp's the Word, I find; you drank my Ale, for which I stop two Shillings of your Board-Wages this Week, for I scorn to be out-done in any thing, even in cheating." Dinner at last was over, to my great Joy; for now I had Hope of a more agreeable Entertainment than what the squabbling with the Servants had afforded us.

The Dean thanked Mr. *Pilkington* for his Sermon: "I never," says he, "preached but twice in my Life, and then they were not Sermons, but Pamphlets." I asked him, What might be the Subject of them; he told me, they were against *Wood's* Half-pence. "Pray, Madam," says he, "do you smoke?" "No indeed, Sir," says I; "Nor your Husband?" "Neither, Sir," "It is a Sign," said he, "you were neither of you bred in the University of *Oxford*; for Drinking and

Smoking are the first Rudiments of Learning taught there; and in those two Arts no University in *Europe* can out-do them." "Pray Mrs. *Pilkington* tell me your Faults." "Indeed, Sir, I must beg to be excused, for if I can help it, you shall never find them out." "No," says he, "then Mr. *Pilkington* shall tell me." "I will, Sir," says he, "when I have discovered them." "Pray Mr. Dean," says Dr. *Delany*, why will you be so unpolite, as to suppose Mrs. *Pilkington* has any Faults?" "Why, I will tell you," replied the Dean; "whenever I see a Number of agreeable Qualities in any Person, I am always sure, they have bad ones sufficient to poize the Scale." I bowed, and told the Dean, he did me great Honour: And in this I copied Bishop *Berkley*, whom I have frequently heard declare, that when any Speech was made to him, which might be construed either into a Compliment, or an Affront, or that (to make use of his own Word) had two Handles, he was so meek and so mild, that he always took hold of the best.

The Dean then asked me, If I was a Queen, what I should chuse to have after Dinner? I answered, his Conversation. "Phooh!" says he, "I mean what Regale?" "A Dish of Coffee, Sir." "Why then I will so far make you as happy as a Queen, you shall have some in Perfection; for when I was Chaplain to the Earl of *Berkley*, who was in the Government here, I was so poor, I was obliged to keep a Coffee-house, and all the Nobility resorted to it to talk Treason." I could not help smiling at this Oddity, but I really had such an Awe on me, that I could not venture to ask him, as I longed to do, what it meant. The Bottle and Glasses being taken away, the Dean set about making the Coffee; but the Fire scorching his Hand, he called to me to reach him his Glove, and changing the Coffee-pot to his Left-hand, held out his Right one, ordered me to put his Glove on it, which accordingly I did; when taking up Part of his Gown to fan himself with, and acting in Character of a prudish Lady, he said, "Well, I do not know what to think; Women may be honest that do such Things, but, for my Part, I never could bear to touch any Man's Flesh—except my Husband's, whom perhaps," says he, "she wished at the Devil."

"Mr. *Pilkington*," says he, "you would not tell me your Wife's Faults; But I have found her out to be a d——ned, insolent, proud, unmannerly Slut." I now looked confounded, not knowing what Offence I had committed.—Says Mr. *Pilkington*, "Ay, Sir, I must confess she is a little saucy to me sometimes, but—what has she done now?" "Done! why nothing, but sat there quietly, and never once offered to interrupt me in making the Coffee; whereas had I had a Lady of modern good Breeding here, she would have struggled with me for the Coffee-pot till she had made me scald myself and her, and throw the Coffee in the Fire; or perhaps at her Head, rather than permit me to take so much trouble for her."

This raised my Spirits, and as I found the Dean always prefaced a Compliment with an Affront, I never afterwards was startled at the latter, (as too many have been, not entering into his peculiarly ironical Strain) but was modestly contented with the former, which was more than I deserved, and which the Surprize rendered doubly pleasing.

Criticism

NORMAN O. BROWN

The Excremental Vision

Any reader of Jonathan Swift knows that in his analysis of human nature there is an emphasis on, and attitude toward, the anal function that is unique in Western literature. In mere quantity of scatological imagery he may be equaled by Rabelais and Aristophanes; but whereas for Rabelais and Aristophanes the anal function is a part of the total human being which they make us love because it is part of life, for Swift it becomes the decisive weapon in his assault on the pretensions, the pride, even the self-respect of mankind. The most scandalous pieces of Swiftian scatology are three of his later poems—*The Lady's Dressing Room, Strephon and Chloe, Cassinus and Peter*—which are all variations on the theme:

> Oh! *Caelia, Caelia, Caelia* ———.

Aldous Huxley explicates, saying, "The monosyllabic verb, which the modesties of 1929 will not allow me to reprint, rhymes with 'wits' and 'fits.' "[1] But even more disturbing, because more comprehensively metaphysical, is Swift's vision of man as Yahoo, and Yahoo as excrementally filthy beyond all other animals, in the fourth part of *Gulliver's Travels*. Nor is the anal theme a new feature in Swift's mature or later period; it is already adumbrated in *A Tale of a Tub*, that intoxicated overflow of youthful genius and fountainhead of the entire Swiftian apocalypse. The understanding of Swift therefore begins with the recognition that Swift's anatomy of human nature, in its entirety and at the most profound and profoundly disturbing level, can be called "The Excremental Vision." "The Excremental Vision" is the title of a chapter in Middleton Murry's book (1954) on Jonathan Swift.[2] The credit for recognizing the central importance of the excremental theme in Swift belongs to Aldous Huxley. In an essay in *Do What You Will* (1929) he says, "Swift's greatness lies in the intensity, the almost insane violence of that 'hatred of the bowels' which is the essence

From *Life Against Death: The Psychoanalytical Meaning of History*, pp. 179–201. Middletown, Conn.: Wesleyan University Press, 1959; London: Routledge & Kegan Paul, Ltd., 1959. Copyright © 1959 by Wesleyan University and Routledge & Kegan Paul, Ltd. Reprinted by permission of the publishers.
1. A. Huxley, *Do What You Will* (London: Chatto & Windus, 1931), p. 94.
2. J. M. Murry, *Jonathan Swift: A Critical Biography* (London: Jonathan Cape, 1954), pp. 432–448.

of his misanthropy and which underlies the whole of his work."[3] Murry deserves credit for his arresting phrase, which redirects criticism to the central problem in Swift. Aldous Huxley's essay had no effect on Quintana's book *The Mind and Art of Jonathan Swift* (1936), which perfectly illustrates the poverty of criticism designed to domesticate and housebreak this tiger of English literature. Quintana buries what he calls the "noxious compositions" in a general discussion of Swift's last phase as a writer, saying, "From scatology one turns with relief to the capital verses entitled *Helter Skelter, or The Hue and Cry after the Attorneys going to ride the Circuit*, while developing the theme of bestiality. . . . Had part IV been excremental theme in the fourth part of *Gulliver's Travels* is dismissed as bad art (criticism here, as so often, functioning as a mask for moral prejudice): "The sensationalism into which Swift falls while developing the theme of bestiality. . . . Had part IV been toned down, *Gulliver's Travels* would have been a finer work of art."[4] It is reassuring to know that English literature is expounded at our leading universities by men who, like Bowdler, know how to improve the classics. The history of Swiftian criticism, like the history of psychoanalysis, shows that repression weighs more heavily on anality than on genitality. Psychoanalytical theorems on the genital function have become legitimate hypotheses in circles which will not listen to what Freud has to say about anality, or to what Swift had to say (and who yet write books on *The Mind and Art of Jonathan Swift*).

Even Huxley and Murry, though they face the problem, prove incapable of seeing what there is to see. After admitting into consciousness the unpleasant facts which previous criticism had repressed, they proceed to protect themselves and us against the disturbing impact of the excremental vision by systematic distortion, denunciation, and depreciation. It is a perfect example, in the field of literary criticism, of Freud's notion that the first way in which consciousness becomes conscious of a repressed idea is by emphatically denying it.[5] The basic device for repudiating the excremental vision is, of course, denunciation. Huxley adopts a stance of intellectual superiority—"the absurdity, the childish silliness, of this refusal to accept the universe as it is given."[6] Murry, echoing that paradoxically conservative philosopher of sexuality, D. H. Lawrence, adopts a stance of moral superiority—"so perverse, so unnatural, so men-

---

3. Huxley, p. 101.
4. R. Quintana, *The Mind and Art of Jonathan Swift* (New York: Oxford University Press, 1936), pp. 327, 360.
5. *Collected Papers*, ed. J. Riviere and J. Strachey, International Psycho-Analytical Library, no. 7–10, 37 (New York and London: The International Psycho-Analytical Press, 1924–50), V, 182. Hereafter cited as CP.
6. Huxley, p. 101.

tally diseased, so humanly *wrong*."[7] The transparently emotional character of their reaction to Swift is then masked as a psychoanalytical diagnosis; the excremental vision is a product of insanity. Huxley speaks of the "obsessive preoccupation with the visceral and excrementitious subjct," "to the verge of insanity," and suggests a connection between it and the "temperamental coldness" of Swift's relations to Stella and Vanessa, implying a disturbance in the genital function.[8]

Murry's attempt to transform Huxley's suggestions into a full-dress biography is a case study in perverted argumentation. The texts of the "noxious compositions" and the fourth part of *Gulliver* are crudely distorted, as we shall see later, so as to transform Swift's misanthropy into misogyny; then the entire excremental vision can be explained away as an attempt to justify his genital failure (with Varina, Vanessa, and Stella) by indicting the filthiness of the female sex. It is falsely insinuated that the excremental vision is restricted to Swift's latest phase. This insinuation not only has the advantage of suggesting that there is a Swiftian vision which is not excremental (on this point Huxley is more tough-minded than Murry); it has the further advantage of linking the excremental vision with Swift's final mental breakdown. The fact that the mental breakdown came ten years later (1742) will not stop anyone ignorant of psychopathology and determined to lobotomize Swift's scatology; the chronological gap is filled by an enthusiastic vision of Swift's mental breakdown as God's punishment for the scatology. The fact that the excremental theme is already prominent in the fourth part of *Gulliver* (1723) is explained away by a little psychoanalytical jargon buttressed by a little flight of historical imagination: "Evidently the whole complex was working in Swift's mind when he wrote the fourth part of *Gulliver*. . . . Its emergence at that moment may have been the outcome of a deep emotional upheaval caused by the death of Vanessa." The prominence of the same complex in the *Letter of Advice to a Young Poet* (1721), two years before the death of Vanessa, is ignored. Murry's amateur diagnosis finds the origin of the entire complex in Swift's rejection by Varina (1696). It is therefore essential to his thesis to regard *A Tale of a Tub* (1696–1698) as uninfected by the complex. Murry sustains this interpretation by averting his eyes from the prominence of anality in the *Tale* and by interpreting the whole book as wonderful tomfoolery which is not to be taken seriously—that is, by a notion of comedy which denies meaning to wit.[9]

7. Murry, p. 440; D. H. Lawrence, *Sex, Literature and Censorship* (New York: Twayne, 1953), p. 60.
8. Huxley, pp. 94, 104.
9. Murry, pp. 78–82, 86, 346–55, 432–48.

If the duty of criticism toward Jonathan Swift is to judge him insane, criticism should be turned over to the psychoanalysts. They have risen to the occasion and have shown that they can be counted on to issue a medical certificate of insanity against genius. Their general verdict is substantially the same as that of Huxley and Murry, with the addition of some handsome new terminology. Thus Ferenczi (1926): "From the psychoanalytical standpoint one would describe his neurotic behaviour as an inhibition of normal potency, with a lack of courage in relation to women of good character and perhaps with a lasting aggressive tendency towards women of a lower type. This insight into Swift's life surely justifies us who come after him in treating the phantasies in *Gulliver's Travels* exactly as we do the free associations of neurotic patients in analysis, especially when interpreting their dreams."[1] Karpman (1942): "It is submitted on the basis of such a study of *Gulliver's Travels* that Swift was a neurotic who exhibited psychosexual infantilism, with a particular showing of coprophilia, associated with misogyny, misanthropy, mysophilia and mysophobia."[2] Greenacre (1955): "One gets the impression that the anal fixation was intense and binding, and the genital demands so impaired or limited at best that there was a total retreat from genital sexuality in his early adult life, probably beginning with the unhappy relationship with Jane Waring, the first of the goddesses."[3]

In developing their diagnosis, the psychoanalysts, as might be expected, trace the origin of Swift's neurosis to his earliest childhood. If the psychoanalytical theory of the neuroses is correct, we must abandon Murry's attempt to isolate the excremental vision as a late excrescence; we must also abandon Murry's thesis (interconnected with his attempt to salvage part of Swift for respectability) that until he was rejected by her, Swift's love for Varina (Jane Waring) was "the healthy natural love of a naturally passionate, and naturally generous nature."[4] We shall have to return to Huxley's more tough-minded literary judgment that Swift *is* the excremental vision, and to his more tough-minded psychological judgment that Swift's sexuality was structurally abnormal from the start. And the biographical evidence, most carefully analyzed by Greenacre, supplies more than enough confirmation. Swift lost his father before he was born; was kidnaped from his mother by his nurse at

1. S. Ferenczi, *Final Contributions to the Problems and Methods of Psycho-Analysis*, ed. M. Balint, tr. E. Mosbacher and others (London: Hogarth Press and the Institute of Psycho-analysis, 1955), p. 59.
2. B. Karpman, "Neurotic Traits of Jonathan Swift," *Psychoanalytic Review*, XXIX (1942), 132.
3. P. Greenacre, "The Mutual Adventures of Jonathan Swift and Lemuel Gulliver," *Psychoanalytic Quarterly*, XXIV (1955), 60.
4. Murry, p. 60.

the age of one; was returned to his mother only three years later, only to be abandoned by his mother one month after his return to her at the psychoanalytically crucial Oedipal period.[5] By psychoanalytical standards such a succession of infantile traumata must establish more than a predisposition to lifelong neurosis.

The case, then, would appear to be closed. The psychoanalytical experts concur with the critics that Swift was mad and that his works should be read only as documents in a case history. Not just the fourth part of *Gulliver* and the "noxious compositions" but all of Swift. For if we cry "insane" to the objectionable parts of Swift, in all honesty we must hand the case over to the psychoanalysts. But after psychoanalytical scrutiny, there is nothing left of Swift that is not objectionable. We must not underestimate the ability of psychoanalysis to uncover the real meaning of symbols. For example, a psychoanalytical comment on Gulliver as a little man in a little boat on the island of Brobdingnag says that "the common symbolism of the man in the boat as the clitoris suggests the identification with the female phallus thought to be characteristic of the male transvestite." Similarly, psychoanalysis leaves the Dean's character without a shred of integrity. "Swift showed marked anal characteristics (his extreme personal immaculateness, secretiveness, intense ambition, pleasure in less obvious dirt [sc. satire], stubborn vengefulness in righteous causes) which indicate clearly that early control of the excretory function was achieved under great stress and perhaps too early."[6]

At this point common humanity revolts. If personal immaculateness, ambition, and the championship of righteous causes are neurotic traits, who shall 'scape whipping? And certainly no genius will escape if this kind of psychoanalysis is turned loose on literary texts. Common humanity makes us turn in revulsion against Huxley, Murry, and the psychoanalysts. By what right do they issue certificates of lunacy? By virtue of their own pre-eminent sanity? Judged for sanity and truthfulness, *Gulliver's Travels* will not suffer in comparison with the works of Murry and Huxley. Only Swift could do justice to the irony of Huxley condemning Swift for misanthropic distortion in a volume of essays devoted to destroying the integrity not only of Swift, but also of St. Francis and Pascal. Nor is the sanity of psychoanalysts—and their interpretations of what a man in a boat signifies—utterly beyond question. Only Swift could do justice to the irony of psychoanalysts, whose capacity for finding the anus in the most unlikely places is notorious, condemning Swift

5. Greenacre, pp. 21–22.
6. Greenacre, pp. 41, 56.

for obsessive preoccupation with anality. Fortunately Swift is not himself speechless in the face of these accusations of insanity:

> He gave the little Wealth he had
> To build a House for Fools and Mad.[7]

In Dr. Swift's mental hospital there is a room for Huxley and Murry; their religious eccentricities are prefigured under the name of Jack, the prototype of religious enthusiasm in *A Tale of a Tub*. For Huxley, as for Jack, it later came to pass that "it was for certain reported that he had run out of his Wits. In a short time after, he appeared abroad, and confirmed the Report by falling into the oddest Whimsies that ever a sick Brain conceived." Swift has also prepared a room for the psychoanalysts with their anal complex; for are they not prophetically announced as those "certain Fortune-tellers in Northern America, who have a Way of reading a Man's Destiny, by peeping in his Breech"?

The argument thus ends in a bedlamite babel filling the air with mutual accusations of madness. If we resist the temptation to stop our ears and run away, if we retain a psychiatric interest and a clinical detachment, we can only conclude that the accusations are all justified; they are all mad. And the crux of their madness is their proud insistence that everybody except themselves—Huxley, Murry, the psychoanalysts—are mad. We can only save ourselves from their madness by admitting that we are all mad. Psychoanalysis deserves the severest strictures, because it should have helped mankind to develop this kind of consciousness and this kind of humility. Freud saw psychoanalysis as the third great wound, comparable to the Newtonian and Darwinian revolutions, inflicted by science on human narcissism.[8] The Epigoni of Freud have set themselves up as a proud elect exempt from the general damnation. As we have argued elsewhere, the proper aim of psychoanalysis is the diagnosis of the universal neurosis of mankind, in which psychoanalysis is itself a symptom and a stage, like any other phase in the intellectual history of mankind.

If we reorient psychoanalysis in this direction, then a different method for the application of psychoanalysis to Swift (or any other literary figure) is in order. We no longer try to explain away Swift's literary achievements as mere epiphenomena on his individual neurosis. Rather we seek to appreciate his insight into the universal neurosis of mankind. Then psychoanalysis becomes a method not for explaining away but for explicating Swift. We are not disturbed by the fact that Swift had his individual version of the universal human neurosis; we are not even disturbed by the thought that his

---

7. *Verses on the Death of Dr. Swift*, lines 479–80.
8. CP, IV, 351–55.

individual neurosis may have been abnormally acute, or by the thought that his abnormality may be inseparable from his art.

Intense suffering may be necessary, though not sufficient, for the production of genius; and psychoanalysis has never thought through its position towards the age-old tradition of an affinity between genius and madness. Perhaps there is that "necessity of doctors and nurses *who themselves are sick*" of which Nietzsche spoke.[9] Psychoanalysis is then not less necessary for the study of Swift, but more so, though in a different way. It is necessary in order to sustain the requisite posture of humility—about ourselves, about mankind, and toward genius. It is also necessary in order to take seriously the Swiftian exploration of the universal neurosis of mankind. The thesis of this chapter is that if we are willing to listen to Swift we will find startling anticipations of Freudian theorems about anality, about sublimation, and about the universal neurosis of mankind. To anticipate objections, let me say that Swiftian psychoanalysis differs from the Freudian in that the vehicle for the exploration of the unconscious is not psychoanalysis but wit. But Freud himself recognized, in *Wit and the Unconscious*, that wit has its own way of exploring the universal neurosis of mankind.

Psychoanalysis is apparently necessary in order to explicate the "noxious compositions"; at least the unpsychoanalyzed neurotic appears to be incapable of correctly stating what these poems are about. These are the poems which provoke Murry to ecstasies of revulsion—"nonsensical and intolerable," "so perverse, so unnatural, so mentally diseased, so humanly *wrong*." What Murry is denouncing is the proposition that woman is abominable because she is guilty of physical evacuation. We need not consider whether the proposition deserves such denunciation, for the simple reason that it comes from Murry's imagination, not Swift's. Murry, like Strephon and the other unfortunate men in the poems, loses his wits when he discovers that Caelia ————, and thus unconsciously bears witness to the truth of Swift's psychological insight. Any mind that is at all open to the antiseptic wisdom of psychoanalysis will find nothing extraordinary about the poems, except perhaps the fact that they were written in the first half of the eighteenth century. For their real theme—quite obvious on a dispassionate reading—is the conflict between our animal body, appropriately epitomized in the anal function, and our pretentious sublimations, more specifically the pretensions of sublimated or romantic-Platonic love. In every case it is a "goddess," "so divine a Creature," "heavenly Chloe," who is exposed; or rather what is exposed is the illusion in the head of

9. F. W. Nietzsche, *The Philosophy of Nietzsche* (New York: Modern Library, 1927), p. 752.

the adoring male, the illusion that the goddess is all head and wings, with no bottom to betray her sublunary infirmities.

The peculiar Swiftian twist to the theme that Caelia ——— is the notion that there is some absolute contradiction between the state of being in love and an awareness of the excremental function of the beloved. Before we dismiss this idea as the fantasy of a diseased mind, we had better remember that Freud said the same thing. In an essay written in 1912 surveying the disorder in the sexual life of man, he finally concludes that the deepest trouble is an unresolved ambivalence in the human attitude toward anality:[1]

We know that at its beginning the sexual instinct is divided into a large number of components—or rather it develops from them—not all of which can be carried on into its final form; some have to be surpassed or turned to other uses before the final form results. Above all, the coprophilic elements in the instinct have proved incompatible with our aesthetic ideas, probably since the time when man developed an upright posture and so removed his organ of smell from the ground; further, a considerable proportion of the sadistic elements belonging to the erotic instinct have to be abandoned. All such developmental processes, however, relate only to the upper layers of the complicated structure. The fundamental processes which promote erotic excitation remain always the same. Excremental things are all too intimately and inseparably bound up with sexual things; the position of the genital organs—*inter urinas et faeces*—remains the decisive and unchangeable factor. The genitals themselves have not undergone the development of the rest of the human form in the direction of beauty; they have retained their animal cast; and so even today love, too, is in essence as animal as it ever was.

Again, in *Civilization and Its Discontents*, Freud pursues the thought that the deepest cause of sexual repression is an organic factor, a disbalance in the human organism between higher and lower functions:[2]

The whole of sexuality and not merely anal erotism is threatened with falling a victim to the organic repression consequent upon man's adoption of the erect posture and the lowering in value of the sense of smell; so that since that time the sexual function has been associated with a resistance not susceptible of further explanation, which puts obstacles in the way of full satisfaction and forces it away from its sexual aim towards sublimations and displacements of libido. . . . All neurotics, and many others too, take exception to the fact that "*inter urinas*

1. CP, IV, 215.
2. Tr. J. Riviere, International Psycho-Analytical Library, ed. E. Jones, no. 17 (London: Hogarth Press, 1930), 78n.

et faeces nascimur." . . . Thus we should find, as the deepest root of the sexual repression that marches with culture, the organic defense of the new form of life that began with the erect posture.

Those who, like Middleton Murry, anathematize Swift's excremental vision as unchristian might ponder the quotation from St. Augustine that Freud uses in both these passages.

That Swift's thought is running parallel with Freud's is demonstrated by the fact that a fuller explication of the poems would have to use the terms "repression" and "sublimation." It is of course not ignorance but repression of the anal factor that creates the romantic illusions of Strephon and Cassinus and makes the breakthrough of the truth so traumatic. And Swift's ultimate horror in these poems is at the thought that sublimation—that is to say, all civilized behavior—is a lie and cannot survive confrontation with the truth. In the first of his treatments of the theme (*The Lady's Dressing Room*, 1730), he reasons with Strephon that sublimation is still possible:

> Should I the Queen of Love refuse,
> Because she rose from stinking Ooze?

Strephon should reconcile himself to—

> Such Order from Confusion sprung,
> Such gaudy Tulips rais'd from Dung.

But in *Strephon and Chloe* (1731) sublimation and awareness of the excremental function are presented as mutually exclusive, and the conclusion is drawn that sublimation must be cultivated at all costs, even at the cost of repression:

> Authorities both old and recent
> Direct that Women must be decent:
> And, from the Spouse each Blemish hide
> More than from all the World beside . . .
> On Sense and Wit your Passion found,
> By Decency cemented round.

In *Cassinus and Peter*, the last of these poems, even this solution is exploded. The life of civilized sublimation, epitomized in the word "wit," is shattered because the excremental vision cannot be repressed. The poem tells of two undergraduates—

> Two College Sophs of *Cambridge* growth
> Both special Wits, and Lovers both—

and Cassinus explains the trauma which is killing him:

> Nor wonder how I lost my Wits;
> Oh! *Caelia, Caelia Caelia* sh——.

That blessed race of horses, the Houyhnhnms, are free from the illusions of romantic-Platonic love, or rather they are free from love. "Courtship, Love, Presents, Joyntures, Settlements, have no place in their thoughts; or Terms whereby to express them in their Language. The young Couple meet and are joined, merely because it is the Determination of their Parents and Friends: it is what they see done every Day; and they look upon it as one of the necessary Actions in a reasonable Being." If the Houyhnhnms represent a critique of the genital function and genital institutions of mankind, the Yahoos represent a critique of the anal function.

The Yahoos represent the raw core of human bestiality; but the essence of Swift's vision and Gulliver's redemption is the recognition that the civilized man of Western Europe not only remains Yahoo but is worse than Yahoo—"a sort of Animals to whose Share, by what Accident he could not conjecture, some small Pittance of *Reason* had fallen, whereof we made no other use than by its Assistance to aggravate our *natural* Corruptions, and to acquire new ones which Nature had not given us." And the essence of the Yahoo is filthiness, a filthiness distinguishing them not from Western European man but from all other animals: "Another Thing he wondered at in the *Yahoos*, was their strange Disposition to Nastiness and Dirt; whereas there appears to be a natural Love of Cleanliness in all other Animals." The Yahoo is physically endowed with a very rank smell—"the Stink was somewhat between a *Weasel* and a *Fox*"—which, heightened at mating time, is a positive attraction to the male of the species. The recognition of the rank odor of humanity stays with Gulliver after his return to England: "During the first Year I could not endure my Wife or Children in my Presence, the very Smell of them was intolerable"; when he walked the street, he kept his nose "well stopt with Rue, Lavender, or Tobacco-leaves." The Yahoo eating habits are equally filthy: "There was nothing that rendered the *Yahoos* more odious, than their undistinguishing Appetite to devour everything that came in their Way, whether Herbs, Roots, Berries, corrupted Flesh of Animals, or all mingled together."

But above all the Yahoos are distinguished from other animals by their attitude towards their own excrement. Excrement to the Yahoos is no mere waste product but a magic instrument for self-expression and aggression. This attitude begins in infancy: "While I held the odious Vermin in my Hands, it voided its filthy Excrements of a yellow liquid Substance, all over my Cloaths." It continues in adulthood: "Several of this cursed Brood getting hold of the Branches behind, leaped up into the Tree, from whence they began to discharge their Excrements on my Head." It is part of the

Yahoo ritual symbolizing the renewal of society: when the old leader of the herd is discarded, "his Successor, at the Head of all the *Yahoos* in that District, Young and Old, Male and Female, come in a Body, and discharge their Excrements upon him from Head to Foot." Consequently, in the Yahoo system of social infeudation, "this *Leader* had usually a Favourite as *like himself* as he could get, whose Employment was to *lick his Master's Feet and Posteriors, and drive the Female* Yahoos *to his Kennel.*" This recognition that the human animal is distinguished from others as the distinctively excremental animal stays with Gulliver after his return to England, so that he finds relief from the oppressive smell of mankind in the company of his groom: "For I feel my Spirits revived by the Smell he contracts in the Stable." Swift does not, as Huxley says he does, hate the bowels, but only the human use of the bowels

This demonic presentation of the excremental nature of humanity is the great stumbling block in *Gulliver's Travels*—an aesthetic lapse, crude sensationalism, says Quintana; a false libel on humanity, says Middleton Murry, "for even if we carry the process of stripping the human to the limit of imaginative possibility, we do not arrive at the Yahoo. We might arrive at his cruelty and malice; we should never arrive at his nastiness and filth. That is a gratuitous degradation of humanity; not a salutary, but a shocking one."[3] But if we measure Swift's correctness not by the conventional and complacent prejudices in favor of human pride which are back of Quintana's and Murry's strictures, but by the ruthless wisdom of psychoanalysis, then it is quite obvious that the excremental vision of the Yahoo is substantially identical with the psychoanalytical doctrine of the extensive role of anal erotism in the formation of human culture.

According to Freudian theory the human infant passes through a stage —the anal stage—as a result of which the libido, the life energy of the body, gets concentrated in the anal zone. This infantile stage of anal erotism takes the essential form of attaching symbolic meaning to the anal product. As a result of these symbolic equations the anal product acquires for the child the significance of being his own child or creation, which he may use either to obtain narcissistic pleasure in play, or to obtain love from another (feces as gift), or to assert independence from another (feces as property), or to commit aggression against another (feces as weapon). Thus some of the most important categories of social behavior (play, gift, property, weapon) originate in the anal stage of infantile sexuality and—what is more important—never lose their connection with it. When infantile sexuality comes to its cat-

3. Murry, p. 352; Quintana, p. 327.

astrophic end, non-bodily cultural objects inherit the symbolism originally attached to the anal product, but only as second-best substitutes for the original (sublimations). Sublimations are thus symbols of symbols. The category of property is not simply transferred from feces to money; on the contrary, money is feces, because the anal erotism continues in the unconscious. The anal erotism has not been renounced or abandoned but repressed.[4]

One of the central ambiguities in psychoanalytical theory is the question of whether the pregenital infantile organizations of the libido, including the anal organizations, are biologically determined. We have elsewhere taken the position that they are not biologically determined but are constructed by the human ego, or rather that they represent that distortion of the human body which *is* the human ego. If so, then psychoanalysis concurs with Swift's thesis that anal erotism—in Swift's language, "a strange Disposition to Nastiness and Dirt"—is a specifically human privilege; on the other hand, psychoanalysis would differ from Swift's implication that the strange Disposition to Nastiness and Dirt is biologically given. It comes to the same thing to say that Swift errs in giving the Yahoos no "Pittance of Reason" and in assigning to Reason only the transformation of the Yahoo into the civilized man of Western Europe. If anal organization is constructed by the human ego, then the strange Disposition to Nastiness and Dirt is a primal or infantile manifestation of human Reason. Swift also anticipates Freud in emphasizing the connection between anal erotism and human aggression. The Yahoos' filthiness is manifested primarily in excremental aggression: psychoanalytical theory stresses the interconnection between anal organization and human aggression to the point of labeling this phase of infantile sexuality the anal-sadistic phase. Defiance, mastery, will to power are attributes of human reason first developed in the symbolic manipulation of excrement and perpetuated in the symbolic manipulation of symbolic substitutes for excrement.

The psychoanalytical theory of anal erotism depends on the psychoanalytical theory of sublimation. If money etc. are not feces, there is not much reason for hypothesizing a strange human fascination with excrement. By the same token it is hard to see how Swift could have come by his anticipation of the doctrine of anal erotism if he did not also anticipate the doctrine of sublimation. But Swift did anticipate the doctrine of sublimation. Full credit for perceiving this goes to William Empson. Referring to *A Tale of a Tub* and

---

4. Cf. CP, II, 45–50, 164–71; E. Jones, *Papers on Psycho-Analysis* (London: Baillière, Tindal & Cox, 1918), pp. 664–88; K. Abraham, *Selected Papers on Psycho-Analysis*, tr. C. Bryan and A. Strachey (New York: Basic Books. 1953), pp. 370–92.

its appendix, *The Mechanical Operation of the Spirit,* Empson writes:[5]

It is the same machinery, in the fearful case of Swift, that betrays not consciousness of the audience but a doubt of which he may himself have been unconscious. "Everything spiritual and valuable has a gross and revolting parody, very similar to it, with the same name. Only unremitting judgment can distinguish between them"; he set out to simplify the work of judgement by giving a complete set of obscene puns for it. The conscious aim was the defense of the Established Church against the reformers' Inner Light; only the psychoanalyst can wholly applaud the result. Mixed with his statement, part of what he satirized by pretending (too convincingly) to believe, the source of his horror, was "everything spiritual is really material; Hobbes and the scientists have proved this; all religion is really a perversion of sexuality."

The source of Swift's horror, according to Empson, is the discovery of that relation between higher and lower, spiritual and physical, which psychoanalysis calls sublimation. Swift hit upon the doctrine of sublimation as a new method for the psychological analysis of religion, specifically religious enthusiasm. His new method sees religious enthusiasm as the effect of what he calls the "Mechanical Operation of the Spirit." At the outset he distinguishes his psychology of religion from traditional naturalistic psychology, which treats religious enthusiasm as "the Product of Natural Causes, the effect of strong Imagination, Spleen, violent Anger, Fear, Grief, Pain, and the like." If you want a distinctive label for Swift's new psychology of religion, it can only be called psychoanalysis. The first step is to define religious enthusiasm as "a lifting up of the Soul or its Faculties above Matter." Swift then proceeds to the fundamental proposition that "the Corruption of the Senses is the Generation of the Spirit." By corruption of the senses Swift means repression, as is quite clear from his explanation:

Because the Senses in Men are so many Avenues to the Fort of Reason, which in this Operation is wholly block'd up. All Endeavours must be therefore used, either to divert, bind up, stupify, fluster, and amuse the Senses, or else to justle them out of their Stations; and while they are either absent, or otherwise employ'd or engaged in a Civil War against each other, the Spirit enters and performs its Part.

The doctrine that repression is the cause of sublimation is vividly implied in the analogy which Swift sets up for the "Mechanical Operation of the Spirit":

5. W. Empson, *Some Versions of Pastoral* (London: Chatto & Windus, 1935), p. 60.

Among our Ancestors, the Scythians, there was a Nation, call'd Longheads, which at first began by a Custom among Midwives and Nurses, of molding, and squeezing, and bracing up the Heads of Infants; by which means, Nature shut out at one Passage, was forc'd to seek another, and finding room above, shot upwards, in the Form of a Sugar-Loaf.

Swift affirms not only that the spirit is generated by repression of bodily sensuousness, but also, as is implied by the analogy of the Scythian Longheads, that the basic structure of sublimation is, to use the psychoanalytical formula, displacement from below upward. Displacement from below upward, conferring on the upper region of the body a symbolic identity with the lower region of the body, is Swift's explanation for the Puritan cult of large ears: the ear is a symbolic penis. According to psychoanalysis, displacement of the genital function to another organ is the basic pattern in conversion hysteria "Conversion hysteria genitalizes those parts of the body at which the symptoms are manifested"; maidenly blushing, for example, is a mild case of conversion hysteria—that is, a mild erection of the entire head.[6] According to Swift's analysis of the Puritans, "The Proportion of largeness, was not only lookt upon as an Ornament of the Outward Man, but as a Type of Grace in the Inward. Besides, it is held by Naturalists, that if there be a Protuberancy of Parts in the *Superiour* Region of the Body, as in the Ears and Nose, there must be a Parity also in the *Inferior*." Hence, says Swift, the devouter Sisters "lookt upon all such extraordinary Dilatations of that Member, as Protrusions of Zeal, or spiritual Excrescencies" and also "in hopes of conceiving a suitable Offspring by such a Prospect." By this road Swift arrives at Freud's theorem on the identity of what is highest and lowest in human nature. In Freud's language: "Thus it is that what belongs to the lowest depths in the minds of each one of us is changed, through this formation of the ideal, into what we value highest in the human soul."[7] In Swift's language:

Whereas the mind of Man, when he gives the Spur and Bridle to his Thoughts, doth never stop, but naturally sallies out into both extreams of High and Low, of Good and Evil; His first Flight of Fancy, commonly transports Him to Ideas of what is most Perfect, finished and exalted; till having soared out of his own Reach and Sight, not well perceiving how near the Frontiers of Height and Depth, border upon each other; With the same Course and Wing, he falls down plum into the lowest Bottom of Things; like one

6. S. Ferenczi, *Further Contributions to the Theory and Technique of Psycho-analysis* (New York: Basic Books, 1952), p. 90; Ferenczi, *Thalassa: A Theory of Genitality* (New York: The Psycho-analytic Quarterly, 1938), p. 14.
7. *The Ego and the Id*, tr. J. Riviere, International Psycho-Analytical Library, no. 12 (London: Hogarth Press and The Institute of Psycho-Analysis, 1927), p. 48.

who travels the *East* into the *West;* or like a strait Line drawn by
its own Length into a Circle.

Such is the demonic energy with which Swift pursues his vision
that twice, once in A *Tale of a Tub* and once in *The Mechanical
Operation of the Spirit,* he arrives at the notion of the unity of
those opposites of all opposites, God and the Devil. Men, "pretending . . . to extend the Dominion of one Invisible Power, and contract that of the other, have discovered a gross Ignorance in the
Natures of Good and Evil, and most horribly confounded the Frontiers of both. After Men have lifted up the Throne of their Divinity
to the *Coelum Empyraeum;* . . . after they have sunk their *Principle
of Evil* to the lowest Center . . . I laugh aloud, to see these Reasoners, at the same time, engaged in wise Dispute, about certain walks
and Purlieus, whether they are in the Verge of God or the Devil,
seriously debating, whether such and such Influences come into
Men's Minds, from above or below, or whether certain Passions and
Affections are guided by the Evil Spirit or the Good. . . . Thus do
Men establish a Fellowship of Christ with Belial, and such is the
Analogy they make between *cloven Tongues,* and *cloven Feet.*"
Empson has shown how and by what law of irony the partially dis-
claimed thought is Swift's own thought.

As we have argued elsewhere, psychoanalysis finds far-reaching
resemblances between a sublimation and a neurotic symptom. Both
presuppose repression; both involve a displacement resulting from
the repression of libido from the primary erogenous zones. Thus the
psychoanalytic theory of sublimation leads on to the theory of the
universal neurosis of mankind. In the words of Freud:[8]

> The neuroses exhibit on the one hand striking and far-reaching
> points of agreement with . . . art, religion and philosophy. But
> on the other hand they seem like distortions of them. It might
> be maintained that a case of hysteria is a caricature of a work
> of art, that an obsessional neurosis is a caricature of religion and
> that a paranoic delusion is a caricature of a philosophical system.

Swift develops his doctrine of the universal neurosis of mankind
in the "Digression concerning the Original, the Use and Improvement of Madness in a Commonwealth," in A *Tale of a Tub.* Here
Swift attributes to Madness "the greatest Actions that have been
performed in the World, under the Influence of Single Men; which
are, *the Establishment of New Empires by Conquest: the Advance
and Progress of New Schemes in Philosophy; and the contriving, as
well as the propagating of New Religions.*" Psychoanalysis must

8. *The Standard Edition of the Complete Psychological Works of Sigmund Freud,*
ed. James Strachey, Anna Freud, Alix Strachey, and Alan Tyson (London:
Hogarth Press and the Institute of Psycho-Analysis, 1954), XIII, 73.

regret the omission of art, but applaud the addition of politics, to Freud's original list; Freud himself added politics in his later writings. And Swift deduces the universal neurosis of mankind from his notion of sublimation; in his words:

> For the *upper Region* of Man, is furnished like the *middle Region* of the Air; The Materials are formed from Causes of the widest Difference, yet produce at last the same Substance and Effect. Mists arise from the Earth, Steams from Dunghils, Exhalations from the Sea, and Smoak from Fire; yet all Clouds are the same in Composition, as well as Consequences: and the Fumes issuing from a Jakes, will furnish as comely and useful a Vapour, as Incense from an Altar. Thus far, I suppose, will easily be granted me; and then it will follow, that as the Face of Nature never produces Rain, but when it is overcast and disturbed, so Human Understanding, seated in the Brain, must be troubled and overspread by vapours, ascending from the lower Faculties, to water the Invention, and render it fruitful.

After a witty review of kings, philosophers, and religious fanatics Swift concludes: "If the *Moderns* mean by *Madness*, only a Disturbance or Transposition of the Brain, by force of certain *Vapours* issuing up from the lower Faculties; then has this *Madness* been the Parent of all these mighty Revolutions, that have happened in *Empire*, in *Philosophy*, and in *Religion*." And Swift ends the Digression on Madness with a humility and consistency psychoanalysis has never known, by applying his own doctrine to himself:

> Even I myself, the Author of these momentous Truths, am a Person, whose Imaginations are hard-mouthed, and exceedingly disposed to run away with his *Reason*, which I have observed from long Experience to be a very light Rider, and easily shook off; upon which account, my Friends will never trust me alone, without a solemn Promise, to vent my Speculations in this, or the like manner, for the universal Benefit of Human kind.

Swift, as we have seen, sees in sublimation, or at least certain kinds of sublimation, a displacement upward of the genital function. So much was implied in his attribution of genital significance to the Puritans' large ears. He makes a similar, only more elaborately obscene, derivation of the nasal twang of Puritan preachers. He also speaks of "certain Sanguine Brethren of the first Class," that "in the Height and *Orgasmus* of their Spiritual exercise it has been frequent with them *****; immediately after which they found the *Spirit* to relax and flag of a sudden with the Nerves, and they were forced to hasten to a Conclusion." Swift explains all these phenomena with his notion of sublimation:

> The Seed or Principle, which has ever put Men upon *Visions*

in Things *Invisible*, is of a corporeal Nature. . . . The Spinal Marrow, being nothing else but a Continuation of the Brain, must needs create a very free Communication between the Superior Faculties and those below: And thus the *Thorn in the Flesh* serves for a *Spur* to the *Spirit*.

Not only the genital function but also the anal function is displaced upward, according to Swift. The general theorem is already stated in the comparison of the upper Region of Man to the middle Region of the Air, in which "the Fumes issuing from a Jakes, will furnish as comely and useful a Vapour, as Incense from an Altar." The idea is developed in the image of religious enthusiasts as Aeolists, or worshipers of wind. Swift is here punning on the word "spirit," and as Empson says, "The language plays into his hands here, because the spiritual words are all derived from physical metaphors."[9] Psychoanalysis of course, must regard language as a repository of the psychic history of mankind, and the exploration of words, by wit or poetry or scientific etymology, as one of the avenues into the unconscious.[1] At any rate, Swift's wit, pursuing his "Physico-logical Scheme" for satirical anatomy, "dissecting the Carcass of Humane Nature," asks where all this windy preaching comes from, and his answer gives all the emphasis of obscenity to the anal factor:

At other times were to be seen several Hundreds link'd together in a circular Chain, with every Man a Pair of Bellows applied to his Neighbour's Breech, by which they blew up each other to the Shape and Size of a *Tun*; and for that Reason, with great Propriety of Speech, did usually call their Bodies, their *Vessels*. When by these and the like Performances, they were grown sufficiently replete, they would immediately depart, and disembogue for the Public Good, a plentiful Share of their Acquirements into their Disciples Chaps.

Another method of inspiration involves a Barrel instead of a Bellows:

Into this *Barrel*, upon Solemn Days, the Priest enters; where, having before duly prepared himself by the methods already described, a secret Funnel is also convey'd from his Posteriors, to the Bottom of the Barrel, which admits of new Supplies Inspiration from a *Northern* Chink or Crany. Whereupon, you behold him swell immediately to the Shape and Size of his *Vessel*. In this posture he disembogues whole Tempests upon his Auditory, as the Spirit from beneath gives him Utterance;

9. Empson, *op. cit.*, p. 60.
1. *A General Introduction to Psycho-Analysis*, tr. J. Riviere (New York: Perma Giants, 1953), pp. 166, 174–75; CP, IV, 184–91.

which issuing *ex adytis*, and *penetralibus*, is not performed without much Pain and Gripings.

Nor is Swift's vision of sublimated anality limited to religious preaching or A *Tale of a Tub*. In *Strephon and Chloe* the malicious gossip of women is so explained:

> You'd think she utter'd from behind
> Or at her Mouth were breaking Wind.

And more generally, as Greenacre observes, there is throughout Swift "a kind of linking of the written or printed word with the excretory functions."[2] When Swift writes in a letter to Arbuthnot, "Let my anger break out at the end of my pen,"[3] the psychoanalytically uninitiated may doubt the psychoanalytical interpretation. But Swift makes references to literary polemics (his own literary form) as dirt-throwing (compare the Yahoos). More generally he meditates that "mortal man is a broomstick," which "raiseth a mighty Dust where there was none before; sharing deeply all the while in the very same Pollutions he pretends to sweep away." In the *Letter of Advice to a Young Poet*, he advocates the concentration of writers in a Grub Street, so that the whole town be saved from becoming a sewer: "When writers of all sizes, like freemen of cities, are at liberty to throw out their filth and excrementitious productions, in every street as they please, what can the consequence be, but that the town must be poisoned and become such another jakes, as by report of great travellers, Edinburgh is at night." This train of thought is so characteristically Swift's that in the *Memoirs of Martinus Scriblerus*, now thought to have been written by Pope after talks with Arbuthnot and Swift, the story of Scriblerus' birth must be an inspiration of Swift's: "Nor was the birth of this great man unattended with prodigies: he himself has often told me, that on the night before he was born, Mrs. Scriblerus dreamed she was brought to bed of a huge ink-horn, out of which issued several large streams of ink, as it had been a fountain. This dream was by her husband thought to signify that the child should prove a very voluminous writer." Even the uninitiated will recognize the fantasy, discovered by psychoanalysis, of anal birth.

It would be wearisome to rehearse the parallels to Swift in psychoanalytical literature. The psychoanalysts, alas, think they can dispense with wit in the exploration of the unconscious. Fenichel in his encyclopedia of psychoanalytical orthodoxy refers to the "analerotic nature of speech" without intending to be funny.[4] Perhaps it

2. Greenacre, p. 56.
3. Cf. Greenacre, p. 56.
4. O. Fenichel, *The Psychoanalytic Theory of Neurosis* (New York: W. W. Norton, 1945), p. 312.

will suffice to quote from Ferenczi's essay on the proverb "Silence is golden" (for Ferenczi the proverb itself is one more piece of evidence on the anal character of speech):[5]

That there are certain connections between anal erotism and speech I had already learnt from Professor Freud, who told me of a stammerer all whose singularities of speech were to be traced to anal phantasies. Jones too has repeatedly indicated in his writings the displacement of libido from anal activities to phonation. Finally I too, in an earlier article ("On Obscene Words") was able to indicate the connection between musical voice-culture and anal erotism.

Altogether Ernest Jones' essay on "Anal-Erotic Character Traits"[6] leaves us with the impression that there is no aspect of higher culture uncontaminated by connections with anality. And Swift leaves us with the same impression. Swift even anticipates the psychoanalytical theorem that an anal sublimation can be decomposed into simple anality. He tells the story of a furious conqueror who left off his conquering career when "the Vapour or Spirit, which animated the Hero's Brain, being in perpetual Circulation, seized upon that Region of the Human Body, so renown'd for furnishing the Zibeta Occidentalis, and gathering there into a Tumor, left the rest of the World for that Time in Peace."

The anal character of civilization is a topic which requires sociological and historical as well as psychological treatment. Swift turns to the sociology and history of anality in a poem called A Panegyrick on the Dean. The poem is written as if by Lady Acheson, the lady of the house at Market Hill where Swift stayed in 1729–1730. In the form of ironic praise, it describes Swift's various roles at Market Hill, as Dean, as conversationalist with the ladies, as Butler fetching a bottle from the cellar, as Dairymaid churning Butter. But the Dean's greatest achievement at Market Hill was the construction of "Two Temples of magnifick Size," where—

In sep'rate Cells the He's and She's
Here pay their vows with bended Knees,

to the "gentle Goddess Cloacine." As he built the two outhouses, Swift seems to have meditated on the question of why we are ashamed of and repress the anal function:

Thee bounteous Goddess Cloacine,
To Temples why do we confine?

The answer he proposes is that shame and repression of anality did

5. Ferenczi, Further Contributions, p. 251.
6. See above, p. 612, note 4.

not exist in the age of innocence (here again we see how far wrong
Huxley's notion of Swift's "hatred of the bowels" is):

> When *Saturn* ruled the Skies alone
> That *golden* Age, to *Gold* unknown;
> This earthly Globe to thee assign'd
> Receiv'd the Gifts of all Mankind.

After the fall—the usurpation of Jove—came "*Gluttony* with greasy
Paws," with her offspring "lolling *Sloth*," "Pale *Dropsy*," "lordly
Gout," "wheezing *Asthma*," "voluptuous *Ease*, the Child of
Wealth"—

> This bloated Harpy sprung from Hell
> Confin'd Thee Goddess to a Cell.

The corruption of the human body corrupted the anal function and
alienated the natural Cloacine:

> . . . unsav'ry Vapours rose,
> Offensive to thy nicer Nose.

The correlative doctrine in psychoanalysis is of course the equation of money and feces. Swift is carried by the logic of the myth
(myth, like wit, reaches into the unconscious) to make the same
equation: the age of innocence, "the *golden* Age, *to Gold* unknown,"
had another kind of gold. The golden age still survives among the
Swains of Northern Ireland—

> Whose Off'rings plac't in golden Ranks,
> Adorn our Chrystal River's Banks.

But the perspectives now opening up are too vast for Swift, or for
us:

> But, stop ambitious Muse, in time;
> Nor dwell on Subjects too sublime.

SAMUEL HOLT MONK

The Pride of Lemuel Gulliver [1]

Gulliver's Travels is a complex book. It is, of course, a satire on four aspects of man: the physical, the political, the intellectual, and the moral. The last three are inseparable, and when Swift writes of one he always has in view the others. It is also a brilliant parody of travel literature; and it is at once science fiction and a witty parody of science fiction. It expresses savage indignation at the follies, vices, and stupidities of men, and everywhere implicit in the book as a whole is an awareness of man's tragic insufficiency. But at the same time it is a great comic masterpiece, a fact that solemn and too-sensitive readers often miss.

A friend once wrote me of having shocked an associate by remarking that he had laughed often on rereading *Gulliver's Travels.* 'What should I have done?' he asked me. 'Blown out my brains?' I am sure that Swift would have approved my friend's laughter. To conclude that *Gulliver's Travels* expresses despair or that its import is nihilistic is radically to misread the book. All of Swift's satire was written in anger, contempt, or disgust, but it was written to promote self-knowledge in the faith that self-knowledge will lead to right action. Nothing would have bewildered him more than to learn that he had led a reader to the desperate remedy of blowing out his brains. But the book is so often called morbid, so frequently have readers concluded that it is the work of an incipient madman, that I think it worth while to emphasize the gayety and comedy of the voyages as an indication of their author's essential intellectual and spiritual health. True, seventeen years after finishing *Gulliver's Travels,* Swift was officially declared *non compos mentis.* But his masterpiece was written at the height of his powers, and the comic animation of the book as a whole rules out the suspicion of morbidity and mental illness.

From *The Sewanee Review,* LXIII (1955), pp. 48-71. Sewanee, Tenn. Copyright © by The University of the South. Reprinted by permission of the author and the publisher.
1. Students of Swift will recognize my very great indebtedness to the work of other critics and scholars. It would be pedantic to acknowledge borrowings so numerous and so self-evident. I hope that it is sufficient here to acknowledge this general indebtedness and to express my gratitude to those who, over a period of twenty-five years, have helped me to better understand Jonathan Swift.

We laugh and were meant to laugh at the toy kingdom of the Lilliputians; at the acrobatic skill of the politicians and courtiers; at the absurd jealousy of the diminutive minister who suspects an adulterous relationship between his wife and the giant Gulliver. We laugh at the plight of Gulliver in Brobdingnag: one of the lords of creation, frightened by a puppy, rendered ludicrous by the tricks of a mischievous monkey, in awe of a dwarf; embarrassed by the lascivious antics of the maids of honor; and at last content to be tended like a baby by his girl-nurse. We laugh at the abstractness of the philosophers of Laputa, at the mad experimenters of Balnibarbi. And I am sure that we are right in at least smiling at the preposterous horses, the Houyhnhnms, so limited and so positive in their knowledge and opinions, so skilled in such improbable tasks as threading needles or carrying trays, so complacent in their assurance that they are 'the Perfection of Nature.' Much of the delight that we take in *Gulliver's Travels* is due to this gay, comic, fanciful inventiveness. Swift might well say in the words of Hamlet: 'Lay not that flattering unction to your soul/That not your trespass but my madness speaks.' Swift did not wish us to blow out our brains; he did wish us to laugh. But beyond the mirth and liveliness are gravity, anger, anxiety, frustration—and he meant us to experience them fully.

For there is an abyss below this fantastic world—the dizzying abyss of corrupt human nature. Swift is the great master of shock. With perfect control of tone and pace, with perfect timing, he startles us into an awareness of this abyss and its implications. We are forced to gaze into the stupid, evil, brutal heart of humanity, and when we do, the laughter that Swift has evoked is abruptly silenced. The surface of the book is comic, but at its center is tragedy, transformed through style and tone into icy irony. Soft minds have found Swift's irony unnerving and depressing and, in self-protection, have dismissed him as a repellent misanthrope. Stronger minds that prefer unpalatable truths to euphoric illusions have found this irony bracing and healthful.

Before I discuss the book itself it is necessary to speak of certain ideas and tendencies that were current in Swift's world. *Gulliver's Travels* was written at the height of that phase of European civilization which we know as the Enlightenment, and the Enlightenment was the first clearly defined manifestation of modernity—the modernity of which our age may be the catastrophic conclusion. Swift wrote always in opposition to the Enlightenment and as an enemy of 'modernism.' He detected with uncanny prescience the implications of such characteristic ideas as the following: (1) Rationalism, especially Cartesianism, with its radical tendency to abstract truth into purely intellectual concepts and its bold rejection of the experience and wisdom of the past. Swift doubted the capacity of human reason to attain metaphysical and theological truth. A safer guide in this life seemed to him to be what he called 'common forms,' the *consensus gentium*, the time-approved wisdom of the race. (2) Experimental and theoretical science, fathered by Bacon and Galileo, vindicated by Newton, and propagandized and nourished by the Royal Society. The science of Swift's day was predominantly concerned with physics and astronomy. Swift, I think, could not imaginatively relate to the moral—*i.e.*, the totally human —life of man the efforts of an astronomer to plot the trajectory of a comet or of a physicist to comprehend a universe that is 'really' no more than abstract mass, extension, and motion. Moreover science gave sanction to the idea of progress, deluding men with the promise of an ever-expanding and improving future, which to Swift seemed necessarily chimerical, man being limited as he is. And finally science unwittingly fostered the secularization of society and of human values, promising men mastery of nature and the abolition of all mysteries, and, by implication at least, of religion. Swift was a religious man. (3) The new conception of man, which was the result of both rationalism and science. It taught the essential goodness of human nature in a sentimental and optimistic tone of voice that irritated Swift and compelled him to reply with all his powers in *Gulliver's Travels*. (4) The new moneyed wealth of England, based upon trade and speculation and bolstering up the national importance of the middle class. Swift regarded this wealth and its owners as irresponsible and dangerous to the state. Divorced from land and the responsibilities implied in the ownership of land, it seemed to him abstract and at the same time frighteningly ambitious; and he had to look only to London and the Court to be assured that this new, vulgar, wealthy class was corrupting both the individual and the social and political institutions of England. (5) The increasing power of centralized government—in Swift's day a few ministers, the Crown, and the court. To Swift, such power seemed necessarily evil since it was divorced from concrete human needs.

Why was Swift inimical to these tendencies—all of which are familiar aspects of our world today? Very simply, I think, because he was a Christian and a humanist. As a Christian he believed that man's fallen nature could never transcend its own limitations and so fulfil the hopes of that optimistic age; as a humanist he was concerned for the preservation of those moral and spiritual qualities which distinguish men from beasts and for the health and continuity of fruitful tradition in church, state, and the sphere of the mind. As both Christian and humanist, he knew that men must be better than they are and that, though our institutions can never be perfect, they need not be corrupt. The 'savage indignation' which motivates all of Swift's satires arises from his anger at the difference between what men are and what they might be if they only would rise to the full height of their humanity. If he indulged no Utopian hopes, he also never gave way to cheap cynicism.

Two famous letters, written in the fall of 1725, the year before *Gulliver's Travels* was published, tell us much about Swift's state of mind at this time. In the first, to Pope, he writes:

> . . . when you think of the world, give it one lash the more at my Request. I have ever hated all Nations, Professions, and Communities; and all my love is towards Individuals; for Instance, I hate the Tribe of Lawyers, Physicians . . . Soldiers, English, Scotch, French, and the rest. But principally I hate and detest that animal called Man, although I heartily love John, Peter, Thomas, and so forth. This is the system upon which I have governed myself many Years . . . and so I shall go on until I have done with them. I have got Materials toward a Treatise, proving the falsity of that Definition, *Animal rationale* and to show that it should be only *rationis capax*. Upon this great foundation of Misanthropy (although not in Timon's Manner) the whole building of my travels is erected; and I will never have Peace of Mind until all honest Men are of my Opinion. . . .

This letter makes three important points.

(1) Swift's life and letters support his assertion that he could and did love individuals. His hatred was directed against abstract man, against men existing and acting within semi-human or dehumanized racial or professional groups. Apparently he felt that when men submerge their individual judgments and moral beings in such groups, they necessarily further corrupt their already corrupted natures. When for example an individual thinks or acts or feels not as a free moral agent responsible to God, but as a politician, a lawyer, a bishop, he abrogates to some degree his humanity. He becomes the instrument of a force that is larger than himself, but not so large as the moral law: and in so doing he becomes at least potentially evil. We hear a great deal today of group dynamics, group psychology, and mass communication. Swift would oppose these forces on the ground that they abridge the freedom which is necessary to the completely moral and responsible life.

(2) Swift dissociates his 'misanthropy' from that of Plutarch's Timon of Athens, the hero of Shakespeare's play, who withdrew in bitter disillusionment merely to rail in solitude against mankind. Swift knew how sterile such an attitude is. His own satire is seldom

merely invective. It is not paradoxical to say that it arises from philanthropy, not misanthropy, from idealism as to what man might be, not from despair at what he is.

(3) Swift rejects the definition of man as *animal rationale* in favor of the definition *animal capax rationis*. I think that he has Descartes in mind here, Descartes, who apparently had forgotten that God made man a little lower than the angels (pure intelligences) and consequently capable of only enough reason to order his world here and to find his way, with God's grace, to the next. The second letter, to Pope and Bolingbroke, amplifies this point.

I tell you after all I do not hate Mankind, it is *vous autres* who hate them, because you would have them reasonable Animals, and are angry at being disappointed: I have always rejected that Definition, and made another of my own. I am no more angry with — — — than I was with the Kite that last Week flew away with one of my Chickens; and yet I was pleased when one of my servants shot him two days after.

Swift argues that the man really in danger of becoming a misanthrope is he who holds an unrealistic view of the potentialities of human nature and who expects that men can somehow transcend their limitations and become, shall we say, angels. In the phrase *vous autres*, Swift includes all the secular, scientific, deistic, optimistic—in a word, liberal—thinkers of the Enlightenment; and he turns in anger from them. The philanthropist will not be angry when he has to recognize the corruptions and limitations of human nature; he will settle for a creature who is *capable* of reason and will do the best he can with him. The word *capable* is a positive concept, not a negative one. It imposes a sort of moral imperative on man to exploit his capability to its fullest. As Swift makes plain in *Gulliver's Travels*, this task is large enough to occupy the whole attention of man. It is fallacious and stupid to attribute to our race qualities that it can never possess. To do so is pride, the besetting sin of men and angels, the sin that disrupts the natural and supernatural order of God's creation. The theme of pride looms large in all four voyages.

Seven years after the publication of *Gulliver's Travels*, Pope published his well-known comment on the tragic duality of man:

> Placed on this isthmus of a middle state,
> A being darkly wise, and rudely great:
> With too much knowledge for the Sceptic side,
> With too much weakness for the Stoic's pride,
> He hangs between; in doubt to act, or rest;
> In doubt to deem himself a God, or Beast;
> In doubt his Mind or Body to prefer;

Born but to die, and reas'ning but to err;
Alike in ignorance, his reason such,
Whether he thinks too little, or too much:
Chaos of Thought and Passion, all confused:
Still by himself abused, or disabused;
Created half to rise, and half to fall;
Great lord of all things, yet a prey to all;
Sole judge of Truth, in endless Error hurl'd:
The glory, jest, and riddle of the world!

The idea that man occupies an anomalous, a middle, state in creation was a familiar one in Swift's day. The whole of living creation was conceived to be carefully ordered and subtly graded in one vast 'chain of being,' descending from God, through an almost infinite number of pure intelligences, to man, and thence through the lower animals to microscopic forms of life, which finally end in nothing. Man occupies the most uncomfortable position in this chain, since to a limited degree he shares the intelligence of higher creatures, and to an unlimited degree the sensuality of animals. He is the middle link because he is the transitional point between the purely intelligent and the purely sensual. With Pope, with Addison, and a number of other writers this image, for reasons which we shall not inquire into, became one of the chief supports of the optimism of the Enlightenment—optimism concerning God, nature, and man. To Pascal, in his moving 72nd *Pensée*, it had suggested tragic thoughts about the disproportion of man. Swift used it as an instrument of comedy, of irony, and of satire. In three of the four voyages, it plays an important role.

So much for background. Let us turn to the book. The first character to demand our attention is Gulliver himself. He is the narrator, the principal actor. We see through his eyes, feel his feelings, share his thoughts. We are in his company from first to last, and it is important that we come to know him as quickly as possible. What is he like and what is his role in the book? He is first of all a bit of a bore, for his mind is irritatingly circumstantial and unimaginative: observe the numerous insignificant biographical details which he gives us in the first pages of the book. Gradually, however, we come to like him and to enjoy his company. In all respects he is an average good man. He has had some university education both at Cambridge and at Leyden, where he studied medicine. He is observant (and we eventually come to be grateful for his gift of close observation and circumstantial reporting, once he has something worth observing and reporting), reasonably intelligent, thoroughly capable in an emergency, and both brave and hopeful. If he lacks imagination and inventiveness, so much the better; for we can be sure that what he tells us, no matter how strange, is true. He is simple, direct, uncomplicated. At the outset he is full of naive good will, and, though he grows less naive and more critical as a result of his voyaging among remote nations, he retains his benevolence throughout the first three voyages. It is a pity that so fine an example of the bluff, good-natured, honest Englishman should at last grow sick and morbid and should be driven mad—but that, I am afraid, is what befalls him.

All of this Gulliver is; but let us notice carefully what he is NOT. He is NOT Jonathan Swift. The meaning of the book is wholly distorted if we identify the Gulliver of the last voyage with his creator, and lay Gulliver's misanthropy at Swift's door. He is a fully rendered, objective, dramatic character, no more to be identified with Swift than Shylock is to be identified with Shakespeare. This character acts and is acted upon; he changes, he grows in the course of his adventures. Like King Lear, he begins in simplicity, grows into sophistication, and ends in madness. Unlike King Lear he is never cured.

The four voyages 'into several remote nations of the world' are so arranged as to attain a climactic intensification of tone as we travel through increasing darkness into the black heart of humanity. But the forward movement is interrupted by the third voyage, a macabre scherzo on science, politics, economics as they are practiced by madmen—Swift's term for those who misuse and abuse human reason. Observe that the tone of each voyage is established by the nature of the event that brings about the adventure: in the first voyage (the most benign and the gayest) accident, or at worst, the carelessness of the lookout, accounts for the shipwreck; in the second, much more savage in tone, Gulliver is left alone in a strange land, through the cowardice of his shipmates; in the third, he is captured and later abandoned by pirates (evil in action); in the fourth, his crew of cutthroats mutinies, seizes the ship, and leaves him to starve on a near-by island. Gulliver thus describes this crew to his Houyhnhnm master:

I said they were Fellows of desperate Fortunes, forced to fly from the Places of their Birth, on Account of their Poverty and their Crimes. Some were undone by Lawsuits; others spent all they had in Drinking, Whoring, and gaming; others fled for Treason; many for Murder, Theft, Poisoning, Robbery, Perjury, Forgery, Coining false Money; for committing Rapes and Sodomy; for flying from their Colours, or deserting to the Enemy; and most of them had broken Prison. . . .

The good ship *Adventure* was a little world which housed the whole of unregenerate human nature.

It is best to consider the first two voyages together and to notice how effectively Swift uses the idea of the great chain of being. Pascal, writing of man's disproportion, had asked: 'For in fact, what is man in nature? A nothing in comparison with the Infinite, an All in comparison with the Nothing, a mean between nothing and everything.' Swift transposes this theme into another key, and makes it the major instrument of his satire. In the first two voyages, Gulliver is made aware of his disproportion; placed on this isthmus of a middle state, in the voyage to Lilliput he looks down the chain of being and knows himself an awkward, if kindly, giant in that delicate kingdom; in the voyage to Brobdingnag he looks up the chain and discovers a race of 'superior beings,' among whom his pride shrivels through the humiliating knowledge of his own physical insignificance. The emphasis here is upon size, the physical; but it is none the less notable that Lilliputia calls into operation Gulliver's engaging kindliness and gentleness, and that Brobdingnag brings out his moral and physical courage. Though comically and tragically disproportioned, man has moral virtues which he can and does exercise.

But Swift's satire is a two-edged sword. What of the inhabitants of these strange lands? They too are disproportioned. From the start the Lilliputians win our interest and liking: these pigmies ingeniously capture the Hercules whom chance has cast on their shore; they humanely solve the problem of feeding him; their pretty land and their fascinating little city take our fancy. But in the end what do they prove to be? prideful, envious, rapacious, treacherous, cruel, vengeful, jealous, and hypocritical. Their primitive social and political systems have been corrupted; they are governed by an Emperor who is ambitious totally to destroy the neighboring kingdom, and by courtiers and ministers who are chosen not for their fitness for office, but for their skill in walking the tightrope, leaping over sticks or creeping under them. 'Climbing,' Swift once remarked, 'is performed in the same Posture with Creeping.' These little people, like Gulliver himself, are an instance of the disproportion of man. Their vices, their appetites, their ambitions, their passions are not commensurate with their tiny stature. They appear to Gulliver as he and his kind must appear to the higher orders of beings—as venomous and contemptibly petty.

In Brobdingnag we meet creatures ten times the size of Europeans, and we share Gulliver's anxiety lest their moral natures be as brutish as their bodies. But the reverse is true; and through a violent and effective shift of symbol, tone, and point of view, Gulliver, who seemed lovable and humane among the Lilliputians, appears an ignominious and morally insensitive being in contrast to the enlightened and benevolent Brobdingnagians. Since Gulliver represents us, his shame, insufficiency, and ludicrousness are ours.

When the peasants discover him, they feel both curiosity and repulsion: the farmer picks him up 'with the Caution of one who endeavours to lay hold on a small dangerous Animal in such a Manner that it shall not be able either to scratch or to bite him, . . .' Gulliver fears that his captor may dash him to the ground, 'as we usually do any little hateful Animal which we have a Mind to destroy.' The change in tone and intent is obvious.

Gulliver is submitted to one humiliation after another, but he is still capable of a fatuous blindness to the defects of European society, and when the King questions him about England he describes with uncritical enthusiasm its class system, its constitution, its laws, its military glory, and its history. In the questions which the king asks and which Gulliver meets with only an embarrassed silence, the voice of morality is heard condemning the institutions of the modern world. And the verdict of a moral being on European man is given in words as icy as controlled contempt can make them: 'But, by what I have gathered from your own Relation, and the Answers I have with much Pains wringed and extorted from you; I cannot but conclude the Bulk of your Natives to be the most pernicious Race of little odious Vermin that Nature ever suffered to crawl upon the Surface of the Earth.'

Such a conclusion is inevitable, for the King is high-minded, benevolent, and, in Swift's sense of the word, rational: i.e., he and his people think practically, not theoretically; concretely, not metaphysically; simply, not intricately. Brobdingnag is a Swiftian Utopia of common good sense and morality; and Gulliver, conditioned by the corrupt society from which he comes, appears naive, blind, and insensitive to moral values. His account of the history of England in the seventeenth century evokes the King's crushing retort:

. . . it was only an Heap of Conspiracies, Rebellions, Murders, Massacres, Revolutions, Banishments; the very worst Effects that Avarice, Faction, Hypocrisy, Perfidiousness, Cruelty, Rage, Madness, Hatred, Envy, Lust, Malice and Ambition could produce.

Notice the carefully arranged disorder of that list, the calculated avoidance of climax. This is a favorite device of Swift: the irrational, the appetitive, the evil nature of man *is* disorder.

The King is horrified when Gulliver offers him a way to complete dominion over his subjects by teaching him to make gunpowder. And Gulliver, speaking as a European, feels contemptuous surprise. 'A strange Effect of *narrow Principles* and *short Views!*' The King is baffled by the concept of political *science*—how can the *art* of government be reduced to a science?

He confined the knowledge of governing within very *narrow Bounds*; to common Sense and Reason, to Justice and Lenity, to the Speedy Determination of Civil and criminal Causes; with some other obvious Topicks which are not worth considering. And he gave it for his Opinion; that whoever could make two Ears of Corn, or two Blades of Grass to grow upon a Spot of Ground where only one grew before would deserve better of Mankind, and do more essential Service to his Country, than the whole Race of Politicians put together.

The learning of the Brobdingnagians is simple and practical, 'consisting only in Morality, History, Poetry, and Mathematicks.' Observe that Swift omits metaphysics, theoretical science, and theology from the category of useful knowledge.

Swift's attack on pride in the first two voyages is made more powerful because of his brilliant use of the chain of being. In so far as we recognize ourselves in the Lilliputians or in Gulliver in Brobdingnag, we become aware of our pettiness—of the disproportion of our race and of the shocking difference between what we profess and what we are. But Swift uses the good giants to strike an unexpected blow at human vanity and to introduce a motif which he employed with deadly effect in the last voyage. That motif is disgust, of which, as T. S. Eliot has remarked, he is the great master. Philosophers of the century were never tired of admiring the beautiful perfection of the human body, its intricateness, its perfect articulation, its happy appropriateness to the particular place that men occupy in the scheme of things. But how does this glorious body appear to lesser creatures—say to an insect? Swift forces us to answer by making us share Gulliver's disgust at the cancerous breasts and lousy bodies of the beggars; at the blotched color, the huge pores, the coarse hairs, and the nauseous odors of the maids of honor. Such is the skin, presumably, that the Brobdingnagians love to touch. Our beauty is only apparent; our disproportion is real.

The third voyage has always been considered the least successful; that may well be, but it is none the less interesting. Structurally it is loosely episodic, lacking unity of action and tone. Into it Swift seems to have put all the material that he could not work into the other three voyages. It is a fantasia on two themes which Swift treats under a single metaphor: the metaphor is science, the themes are politics and the abuse of reason. In short, the voyage is a digression on madness, on the divorce of man and good sense in the modern world.

At this point, I fear, it is necessary to defend Swift, since he will seem merely stupid and prejudiced to a generation that enjoys the blessings of television, the common cold, and the hydrogen bomb.

Moreover, to liberals he will appear an unenlightened political re-actionary. I have said earlier that in my opinion Swift distrusted science because it seemed irrelevant to the moral life of man. Though no scientist, he was not an ignoramus. He had read con-temporary science—Descartes, Newton, and the yearly *Transactions of the Royal Society*. The Flying Island is conceived on sound scientific principles; some of the mad experiments of the scientists of Balnibarbi are grotesque distortions of ideas actually advanced by members of the Royal Society. The philosophers of the Flying Island are lost in the abstractions of mathematics, music, and astronomy to the great neglect of all practical reality, including their wives. The very tailors measure Gulliver for clothes by abstruse mathematical processes and contrive a suit which fits him not at all. Swift lived before the age of applied science, but I do not think that he would be surprised to learn that modern citizens of his Flying Island con-trived the most significant event of the twentieth century—Hiroshima.

It is also necessary to apologize for Swift's political views. He was a Tory, a conservative—opprobrious terms today. In economics he was an agrarian; in politics a royalist; in religion a high churchman. He disapproved the founding of the National Bank; could make no sense of a national debt, a gadget invented in his time; he distrusted the new moneyed wealth, the ancestor of modern capitalism, which increased the political power and importance of the merchant class, and he found his distrust justified in 1720 by the disastrous collapse of South Sea stocks. Innovation and experimentation in politics he detested and fought. He would have hated the improvisations of the New Deal; he would have deplored the vast powers of our Federal Government; he would have loathed the whole program of the Labor Party in Britain. And were he alive, he would fight the ab-stract state of this century with every weapon within reach.

Too many liberals are unaware of the fact that a man may be a non-liberal without being illiberal; that he may distrust the abstract power of government, the theoretical formulae of economists, politi-cians, and social scientists and the like without ceasing to be actively and effectively concerned for human welfare. Swift was a Tory who fought valiantly and at times successfully for the oppressed. Living in Ireland, contemptuous of the Irish, detesting their Catholicism, he none the less became their champion against the oppression and exploitation of his adopted country by the English Court and Parlia-ment. He is one of the heroes of modern Ireland because he first gave effective expression to Irish nationalism. He earned the right to the last sentence of the epitaph which he composed for his own tombstone: *Abi Viator/ et imitare, si poteris/ Strenuum pro virili/ Libertatis Vindicatorem.*

The Flying Island is not only a trope for science; it is also a mordant image of the concentration of political power in the hands of a clique remote from human needs, motivated by pure theory, and given to experiment and improvisation. Laputa (perhaps, as has been suggested, Spanish *La Puta*, 'the whore') is a symbol of such government: it is controlled by madmen who govern scientifically, not morally; it is a *flying* island, and hence out of touch with subject territories, which it exploits and tyrannizes over by means of what we call today air power; it can withhold sun and rain as a punitive device, or can harass through bombing raids, or even tyrannously crush all opposition by settling its great weight upon the land below. One contrasts this form of government with that of the wise and good King of Brobdingnag.

When Gulliver visits the subject land of Balnibarbi, which is of course England, he sees the result of statism.

The People in the Streets walked fast, looked wild, their Eyes fixed, and were generally in Rags. We passed through one of the Town Gates, and went about three Miles into the Country, where I saw many Labourers working with several Sorts of Tools in the Ground, but was not able to conjecture what they were about; neither did I observe any Expectation either of Corn or Grass, although the Soil appeared to be excellent.

This is what comes of experimentation in government and of financial speculation. It strongly suggests the memories that some of us have of the great depression. A modern Tory used it effectively as the basis of an attack on the post-war Labor Government.

But there are other ills consequent to the abstract state. Too great a concentration of power leads to tyranny, tyranny breeds fear; fear breeds the obnoxious race of spies and informers. The abstract state becomes the police state.

I told him that in the Kingdom of *Tribnia* [Britain], by the Natives called *Langden* [England], where I had sojourned some time in my Travels, the Bulk of the People consist in a manner wholly of Discoverers, Witnesses, Informers, Accusers, Prosecutors, Evidences, Swearers; together with their several subservient and subaltern Intruments; all under Deputies. The Plots in that Kingdom are usually the Workmanship of those Persons who desire to raise their own Character of profound Politicians; to restore new Vigour to a crazy Administration; to stifle or divert general Discontents; to fill their Pockets with Forfeitures; and raise or sink the Opinion of publick Credit, as either shall best answer their private Advantage. It is first agreed and settled among them, what suspected Persons shall be accused of a Plot: then, effectual Care is taken to secure all their Letters and Papers, and put the Criminals in Chains. These Papers are delivered to a Set of Artists, very dexterous in finding out the mysterious Meanings of Words, Syllables, and Letters. For Instance, they can decypher a Close-stool to signify a Privy-Council; a Flock of Geese, a Senate; a lame Dog, an Invader; a Codshead, a [King]; the Plague, a Standing Army; a Buzzard, a Prime Minister; the Gout, a High Priest; a Gibbet, a Secretary of State; a Chamber Pot, a Committee of Grandees; a Sieve, a Court Lady; a Broom, a Revolution; a Mouse-trap, an Employment; a bottomless Pit, The Treasury; a Sink, the C[our]t; a Cap and Bells, a Favourite; a broken Reed, a Court of Justice; an empty Tun, a General; a running Sore, the Administration.

One cannot read that passage without thinking of certain testimony given of late years in Washington.

Such are the fruits of madness—of that pride which impels us to trust our reason beyond its proper scope and which suggests that we can build a heavenly city on earth on principles divorced from humanity and morality.

The climactic fourth voyage is the great section of *Gulliver's Travels*. It has provoked violent attacks on Swift and his book, entirely, I think, because it has been misunderstood. It has offended the unreflective and pious Christian, the sentimentalist, and the optimist. Thackeray, lecturing to the ladies in London in 1851, the year in which the Great Exhibition seemed to give the lie to every opinion that Swift held, may serve as an example, by no means unique, of the capacity of this voyage to shock. He advised his ladies not to read the last voyage, and to hoot the Dean. And the meaning that he found in it was 'that man is utterly wicked, desperate, and imbecile, and his passions are monstrous, and his boasted power mean, that he is and deserves to be the shame of brutes, and ignorance is better than his vaunted reason.' 'It is Yahoo language,' he continues, 'a monster gibbering shrieks and gnashing imprecations against mankind . . . filthy in word, filthy in thought, furious, raging, obscene.'

The legend of Swift as a savage, mad, embittered misanthrope largely rests upon this wrong-headed, sensational reading of the last voyage. In my opinion the work is that of a Christian-humanist and a moralist who no more blasphemes against the dignity of human nature than do St. Paul and some of the angrier prophets of the Old Testament. Swift has been misunderstood for several reasons.

1. The sheer intensity and violent rhetoric of the voyage are overwhelming and may well numb the critical sense of certain readers.

2. Gulliver in the frenzy of his mad misanthropy has been too facilely identified with Swift. Gulliver speaks for Gulliver and not for

his creator in the final pages of the book, and careful reading should reveal the plain fact that he becomes the victim of Swift's irony as he grows to hate the human race. The final pages of the book are grimly comic.

3. The primary symbols of the voyage have been totally misunderstood. The Houyhnhnms have been regarded as Swift's ideal for man, and the Yahoos have been identified as his representation of what men are. Neither of these opinions, I believe, is correct.

Let us begin with the Houyhnhnms and the Yahoos. In the first two voyages Gulliver is shown uncomfortably situated on the isthmus of a middle state between the very large and the very small. In this voyage he also stands on the isthmus, but now it is between the purely rational and the purely sensual—between Houyhnhnm and Yahoo. Neither of these symbols can stand for man, since Gulliver himself is the symbol of humanity. Unfortunately for poor Gulliver, he shares somehow in the nature of both extremes. Swift simply isolates the two elements that combine in the duality of man, the middle link, in order to allow Gulliver to contemplate each in its essence.

Does Swift recommend that Gulliver should strive to become a Houyhnhnm? We discover that in every sense Houyhnhnmland is a rationalistic Utopia. The Houyhnhnms are the embodiment of pure reason. They know neither love nor grief nor lust nor ambition. They cannot lie; indeed they have no word for lying and are hard put to it to understand the meaning of *opinion*. Their society is an aristocracy, resting upon the slave labor of the Yahoos and the work of an especially-bred servant class. With icy, stoical calm they face the processes of life—marriage, childbirth, accident, death. Their society is a planned society that has achieved the mild anarchy that many Utopian dreamers have aspired to. They practice eugenics, and since they know no lust, they control the size of their population; children are educated by the state; their agrarian economy is supervised by a democratic council; government is entirely conducted by periodic assemblies. The Houyhnhnms feel natural human affection for each other, but they love every one equally. It is all very admirable, but it is remote from the possibilities of human life.

Does Swift intend us to accept this as his ideal way of life? He who loved and hated and fought and bled internally through *saeva indignatio*? I think not. The Houyhnhnms resemble Cartesians and are clearly stoics. 'Neither is *Reason* among them a Point problematical as with us,' reports Gulliver, 'where Men can argue with Plausibility on both Sides of a Question; but strikes you with immediate Conviction; . . .' This is the Houyhnhnm version of Descartes' rational intuition of clear and distinct ideas. Now Swift was anti-Cartesian from his first published satire, for the simple reason that he held that Descartes was self-deluded and that man's reason was incapable of the feats that Descartes attributed to it. The Houyhnhnms are stoics, and Swift recorded his view of stoicism in *Thoughts on Various Subjects*: 'The Stoical Scheme of supplying our Wants, by lopping off our Desires, is like cutting off our Feet when we want Shoes.' It is Gulliver, not Swift, who is dazzled by the Houyhnhnms and who aspires to rise above the human condition and to become pure intelligence as these horses and the angels are.

The most powerful single symbol in all Swift is the Yahoos. They do not represent Swift's view of man, but rather of the bestial element in man—the unenlightened, unregenerate, irrational element in human nature. Hence the Houyhnhnms classify Gulliver with them; hence the female Yahoo wishes to couple with him; hence despite his instinctive recoiling from them, Gulliver has to admit with shame and horror that he is more like them than he is like the Houyhnhnms. This I think is clear. Because of his neglect or misuse of human reason, European man has sunk nearer to the Yahoo pole of his nature than he has risen toward the Houyhnhnm pole. The seeds of human society and of human depravity, as they exist in Europe, are clearly discerned in the society and conduct of the Yahoos. Gulliver looks into the obscene abyss of human nature unlighted by the frail light of reason and of morality, and the sight drives him mad.

Repelled by what he sees, he, not Swift, identifies the Yahoos with man; and he, not Swift, turns misanthrope. Since he will not be a Yahoo, he seeks to become, as nearly as possible, a Houyhnhnm. But he can do so only by denying his place in and responsibility to humanity, by aspiring above the middle link, which is man, to the next higher link, that of the purely rational. The wise Houyhnhnm, to whom he gives his terrifying account of European man and society, concludes that 'the corruption of reason' is worse than brutality itself, and that man is more dangerous than the Yahoo. This is profoundly true. But its effect on Gulliver is to awaken loathing of all that is human.

Lear, gazing on the naked, shivering Edgar, disguised as a Tom o' Bedlam, cries: 'Thou art the thing itself; unaccommodated man is no more but such a poor, bare, forked animal as thou art.' And in that intense moment, he goes mad. Something of the same thing befalls Gulliver. He thinks he has seen the thing itself. Though the Houyhnhnms never acknowledge that he is more than an unusually gifted Yahoo, he aspires to their rationality, stoicism, and simple wisdom; and persuaded that he has attained them, he feeds his growing misanthropy on pride, which alienates him not only from his remote kinsmen, the Yahoos, but eventually from his brothers, the human race. Looking back with nostalgia on his lost happiness in Houyhnhnmland, he recalls:

I enjoyed perfect Health of Body, and Tranquility of Mind; I did not feel the Treachery or Inconstancy of a Friend, nor the Injuries of a secret or open Enemy. I had no Occasion of bribing, flattering, or pimping, to procure the Favour of any great Man, or of his Minion. I wanted no Fence against Fraud or Oppression: Here was neither physician to destroy my Body, nor Lawyer to ruin my Fortune: No Informer to Watch my Words and Actions, or forge Accusations against me for Hire: Here were no Gibers, Censurers, Backbiters, Pickpockets, Highwaymen, Housebreakers, Attorneys, Bawds, Buffoons, Gamesters, Politicians, Wits, Spleneticks, Tedious Talkers, Controvertists, Ravishers, Murderers, Robbers, Virtuoso's; no Leaders or Followers of Party and Faction; no Encouragers to Vice, by Seducement or Examples: no Dungeon, Axes, Gibbets, Whippingposts, or Pillories; No cheating Shopkeepers or Mechanicks; No Pride, Vanity or Affection: No Fops, Bullies, Drunkards, strolling Whores, or Poxes: No ranting, lewd, expensive Wives: No stupid, proud Pedants: No importunate, over-bearing, quarrelsome, noisy, roaring, empty, conceited, swearing Companions: No Scoundrels raised from the Dust upon the Merit of their Vices; or Nobility thrown into it on account of their Virtues: No Lords, Fiddlers, Judges or Dancing-masters.

From the moment that the banished Gulliver despairingly sets sail from Houyhnhnmland, his pride, his misanthropy, his madness are apparent. Deluded by his worship of pure reason, he commits the error of the Houyhnhnms in equating human beings with the Yahoos. Captured by a Portuguese crew and forced to return from sullen solitude to humanity, he trembles between fear and hatred. The captain of the ship, Don Pedro de Mendez, like Gulliver himself, shares the nature of the Houyhnhnm and the Yahoo; and like the Gulliver of the first voyage he is tolerant, sympathetic, kindly, patient, and charitable; but Gulliver can no longer recognize these traits in a human being. With the myopic vision of the Houyhnhnms, he perceives only the Yahoo and is repelled by Don Pedro's clothes, food, and odor. Gradually, however, he is nursed back to partial health, and is forced to admit in the very accent of his admired horses, that his benefactor has a 'very good *human* Understanding.' But the Gulliver who writes this book is still under the control of his *idée fixe*, and when we last see him he prefers the smell and conversation of his two horses to the company of his wife and children. This is misanthropy in Timon's manner, not Swift's. In the brilliant and intricately ironic coda with which the book ends, Swift directs his savage, comic gaze straight at Gulliver and his insane pretensions.

My Reconcilement to the *Yahoo*-kind in general might not be so difficult, if they would be content with those Vices and Follies only which Nature hath entitled them to. I am not in the least provoked at the Sight of a Lawyer, a Pickpocket, a Colonel, a Fool, a Lord, a Gamester, a Politician, a Whoremunger, a Physician, an Evidence, a Suborner, an Attorney, a Traytor, or the like: This is all according to the due Course of Things: But when I behold a Lump of Deformity, and Diseases both of Body and Mind, smitten with *Pride*, it immediately breaks all the Measures of my Patience; neither shall I ever be able to comprehend how such an Animal and such a Vice could tally together.

The grim joke is that Gulliver himself is the supreme instance of a creature smitten with pride. His education has somehow failed. He has voyaged into several remote nations of the world, but the journeys were not long, because of course he has never moved outside the bounds of human nature. The countries he visited, like the Kingdom of Heaven, are all within us. The ultimate danger of these travels was precisely the one that destroyed Gulliver's humanity— the danger that in his explorations he would discover something that he was not strong enough to face. This befell him, and he took refuge in a sick and morbid pride that alienated him from his species and taught him the gratitude of the Pharisee—'Lord, I thank Thee that I am not as other men.'

Swift himself, in his personal conduct, displayed an arrogant pride. But he was never guilty of the angelic, dehumanizing pride of Gulliver, who writes in a letter to his Cousin Sympson:

I must freely confess, that since my last Return, some corruptions of my *Yahoo* Nature have revived in me by Conversing with a few of your Species, and particularly those of my own Family, by an unavoidable Necessity; else I should never have attempted so absurd a Project as that of reforming the *Yahoo* Race in this Kingdom; but, I have now done with all such visionary Schemes for ever.

Jonathan Swift was stronger and healthier than Lemuel Gulliver. He hated the stupidity and the sinfulness and the folly of mankind. He could not accept the optimistic view of human nature that the philosophers of the Enlightenment proposed. And so he could exclaim to his contemporaries: 'O wicked and perverse generation!' But, until he entered upon the darkness of his last years, he did not abandon his fellow man as hopeless or cease to announce, however indirectly, the dignity and worth of human kind.

ALLAN BLOOM

An Outline of *Gulliver's Travels*

Gulliver's Travels is an amazing rhetorical achievement.
It is the classic children's story and it is a rather obscene tale. Swift
was able to charm innocence and amuse corruption, and this is a
measure of his talent. I can think of no parallel: Hans Christian
Andersen for children, Boccaccio for adults. But, most of all, it is a
philosophic book presented in images of overwhelming power.
Swift had not only the judgment with which to arrive at a reasoned
view of the world, but the fancy by means of which he could recre-
ate that world in a form which teaches where argument fails and
which satisfies all while misleading none.

Gulliver's travel memoirs make abundantly clear that he is a
Yahoo in the decisive sense. He says "the thing which is not," or,
to put it into Yahoo language, he is a liar. This does not mean that
I do not believe he underwent the adventures he relates; but he
does have something to hide. A small bit of evidence can be
gleaned from his own defense of his conduct with a great Lilliputian lady, who had conceived a passion for his person. Gulliver
grounds his apology on the alleged fact that no one ever came to
see him secretly. But immediately afterward he tells of the secret
visit of a minister. We can only suppose the worst in the affair
between the lady and Gulliver. And we may further suppose that
Gulliver has certain hidden thoughts and intentions which are only
to be revealed by closely cross-examining him. He indicates this
himself at the close of his travels when he swears to his veracity.
He uses for this solemn occasion Sinon's treacherous oath to the
Trojans, by means of which that worthy managed to gain admittance for the horse and its concealed burden of Greeks.[1]

I should like to suggest that this book is also such a container,
filled with Greeks who are, once introduced, destined to conquer a
new Troy, or, translated into "the little language," destined to conquer Lilliput. In other words, I wish to contend that *Gulliver's
Travels* is one of the last explicit statements in the famous Quarrel
between the Ancients and Moderns and perhaps the greatest intervention in that notorious argument. By means of the appeal of its

From "An Outline of Gulliver's Travels" by Allan Bloom in *Ancients
and Moderns*, edited by Joseph Cropsey. New York. © 1964 by Basic
Books, Inc., Publishers, and reprinted with their permission.

1. Bk. IV, Ch. 12; cf. Vergil, *Aeneid*, II. 79–80.

myth, it keeps alive the classical vision in ages when even the importance of the quarrel is denied, not to speak of the importance of that classical viewpoint, which appears to have been swamped by history. The laughter evoked by *Gulliver's Travels* is authorized by a standard drawn from Homer and Plato. . . .

Gulliver's Travels is a discussion of human nature, particularly of political man, in the light of the great split. In general, the plan of the book is as follows: Book I, modern political practice, especially the politics of Britain and France; Book II, ancient political practice on something of a Roman or Spartan model; Book III, modern philosophy in its effect on political practice; Book IV, ancient utopian politics used as a standard for judging man understood as the moderns wished to understand him. By "ancient" Swift means belonging to Greece and Rome—Greece for philosophy and poetry, republican Rome for politics. For Swift, Thomas Aquinas is a modern.

There are many indications of both a substantial and a formal kind, which indicate the order of the parts. For example, Gulliver takes the same ship, the Adventure, to both Brobdingnag and the land of the Houyhnhnms. Books I and III are the only ones which are directly susceptible of an analysis appropriate to a *roman à cléf*: Lilliput is full of characters clearly identifiable as personages in British politics, and Laputa is peopled largely by modern philosophers and members of the Royal Academy. The only clearly identifiable modern elements in Brobdingnag or the land of the Houyhnhnms are those in England referred to by the travelling Gulliver. When he is in Lilliput and Laputa (notice the similarity of the names), he tells nothing of his world or native country. He need not, for the reader should recognize it; Gulliver is alien, and the interesting thing is the world seen through his eyes. His perspective is that of a man totally outside England; with the Brobdingnagians and the Houyhnhnms, he is all English, and they are usually foils used to bring out the weaknesses in his nature. In the former case, he is used as the standard for strictures against modern England; in the latter, the Houyhnhnms and Brobdingnagians are used as a standard in criticizing him in the role of a modern Englishman. In one sense the book is all about England, in another, it is all about antiquity. The formula is simply this: when he is good, the others are bad; when he is bad, they are good. The bad others are found in books I and III, which treat of the recognizably modern. The good others are in books II and IV, which are, at the least, removed from modernity. Parallel to this movement is Gulliver's sense of shame; in Book I he is shameless—he defecates in a temple and urinates on the palace; and in Lilliput, the people care. In Brobdingnag, where they could not care less, he is full of shame, will not allow himself to be seen performing these functions, and hides behind sorrel leaves. We can say that Gulliver is somehow in between—superior to the inferior and inferior to the superior, but never equal. He lacks something of perfection, but from a certain point of view he is superior to his contemporaries.

Gulliver informs us on his return from Brobdingnag that it was not necessary for him to visit Lilliput in order for him to see Englishmen as Lilliputians; it was only necessary for him to have been to Brobdingnag, for when he landed, he thought himself to be the size of a Brobdingnagian. This was not the case; but having shared their perspective, he could forget his real self and see his likes as he was seen by the giants. The English are truly pygmies. The lesson is that one must study Brobdingnag. Gulliver is as a giant in Lilliput because of what he has learned in Brobdingnag; when he is with the Brobdingnagians, however, he returns to his awareness of himself as a real Lilliputian. He recognizes his weaknesses, but he is great because of his self-consciousness or self-knowledge. He learns "how vain an attempt it is for a man to endeavor to do himself honor among those who are out of all degree of equality or comparison with him."

Swift's device in Lilliput and Brobdingnag is to take moral and intellectual differences and project them in physical dimensions. From this simple change everything else follows. In working this transformation, he pursues Aristotle's suggestion that nature intends the differences in men's souls to be reflected in their bodies and that men whose bodies are greatly superior, resembling the statues of gods, would readily be accepted as masters.[2] As a literary device, Swift's transformation works wonders; for literature lives on images and sensations, appealing to fancy and imagination, but there is no way that philosophy can make a direct appeal by means of the arts. When the imperceptible differences so suddenly become powerful sensual images, however, all becomes clear. Gulliver's attempts to take the physical beauty of the Lilliputians seriously, or the king of Brobdingnag's holding Gulliver in his hand and asking him if he is a Whig or a Tory, resume hundreds of pages of argument in an instant. And, moreover, the great majority of men cannot, for lack of experience, understand the great superiority of soul which is humanly possible. But when that power is seen in terms of size, all men, if only momentarily, know what superiority is and recognize the difficulties it produces for its possessor and those in its immediate vicinity. To tell men of the vanity of

2. Aristotle, *Politics* 1254^b 27–39.

human pretensions may be edifying, but what sermon has the force of the absurd claim that Lilliput is "the terror of the universe"?

Gulliver's adventures in Lilliput are largely an exposition of the problems faced by him and the Lilliputians because of his bigness. With the best of will, neither side can understand the concerns of the other. They do not belong together, but they are forced together, if only by their common humanity—a humanity stretched to its limits. He is imprisoned by them and needs them for his maintenance; they do not know how to get rid of him (if they were to kill him, the stench of his decaying body might sicken the atmosphere) and are torn between fear and distrust, on the one hand, and dazzling hopes for using him, on the other. Their problem is aggravated by their vision: The Lilliputians "see with great exactness but at no great distance." They suffer from a loss of perspective. It is not their fault; that is the way they are built.

What this entails is best revealed when we see giants through the eyes of our Cicerone: nothing could be more revolting than the description of the woman's breast. He sees things which are really there, but he no longer sees the object as a whole; a thing that from the human point of view should be beautiful and attractive becomes in his vision ugly and repulsive. Odors and tastes are distorted; Gulliver in Brobdingnag experiences the literally dirty underside of life. And thus we learn that the Lilliputians experienced him as he did the Brobdingnagians. One Lilliputian even had the audacity to complain of his smell on a hot day, although he was renowned for his cleanliness. They can never grasp him as he really is; the different parts seem ugly; the ugliness of nature, which disappears in the light of its unity, is their overwhelming impression. In them one can understand the maxim "no man is a hero to his valet; not because he is not a hero but because the valet is a valet." I think there can be little doubt that Swift believes the giant's perspective is ultimately proportionate to the true purpose of things; there is not a simple relativity. . . .

Gulliver's disaster in Lilliput occurs because he is too big for the Lilliputians; the specific charges against him are only corollaries of that fact. The outcome was inevitable. Civil society cannot endure such disproportionate greatness; it must either submit itself to the one best man or ostracize him. The condemnation of this comic Socrates is not to be blamed on the prejudices of the Lilliputians; it is a necessity that no amount of talk or education will do away with. The four major charges against Gulliver are as follows. (1) He urinated on the royal palace, even though there was a law against urinating within its confines. (2) He refused to subdue Blefuscu, to utterly destroy the Big-Endian exiles, to force the Blefuscudians to confess the Lilliputian religion, and to accept the Lilli-

ALLAN BLOOM

putian monarch. (3) He was friendly to the Blefuscudian ambassadors who came to treat for peace and helped them in their mission. (4) He had the intention of paying a visit to Blefuscu.

If we generalize these charges, they would read as follows. (1) He does not accept the judgments of the Lilliputians about what is noble and what is base. He does what is necessary to preserve the palace, using means indifferent in themselves but repulsive to the queen; from her point of view, of course, what was done was pretty disagreeable. Swift's humor in defense of the crown, which displeased Queen Anne, has been compared to the acts cited in this charge. It is also reminiscent of Aristophanes' Dung-beetle, who, because he goes low, can go high. But the chief thing to underline is the fact that, because of their different situations, Gulliver cannot have the same sentiments as the Lilliputians about what is fair and what is ugly. He identifies the fair or noble with the useful—a rational procedure, but one which can hardly be accepted by civil society which lives on the distinction between the two. (2) He does not share the religious prejudices of the nation and is unwilling to be inhuman for the sake of what can only appear as senseless dogma to him. He cannot see the importance of the faith or of the ambition of the king. Big end, small end—they all appear human to him. (3) He does not accept the distinction between friend and enemy defined by the limits of the nation. Once again, common humanity is what he sees. At the same time, from the Lilliputian standpoint, how can a foreigner who consorts with the enemy be trusted—especially a foreigner of such exceptional power? They can only attribute to him the motivations which they already know; they cannot see the interior workings of his soul, and, if they could, they would not understand them. By any canons, Gulliver's behavior is suspicious, no matter how innocent it may actually be. How can the Lilliputians see he has no ambition to subdue both kingdoms and make himself ruler of the known world? How could they believe that what seems so important to them is too petty to be even considered by Gulliver? (4) Gulliver is not satisfied in his new home; he thinks there is much to be learned elsewhere. He may find what pleases him more in another land. His loyalty is questionable; he has the dubious taste for being away from home.

Gulliver is condemned because the Lilliputians discovered in the palace fire that his moral taste was not the same as theirs. He did not behave as a good citizen; he did not identify what is good with what is Lilliputian. The court jealousies and hatreds were only predisposing factors in the ultimate crisis. Given the uses which could be made of him, he was bound to be an object of flattery and conspiracy, as he appeared to incline to one side or another. The proposal for resolving the Gulliver crisis is the standard for civil society's use of genius: he is to be blinded, for thus he would retain his power but could be used more easily by the civil authority. He is to be a blind giant—blind to the ends which he serves, adding only might to the means which are to achieve them. This is an intolerable solution for him, but the alternative would be for the Lilliputians to alter themselves to fit him. The disproportion is too great. Finally, the high hopes deceived, the kings of both Lilliput and Blefuscu are heartily glad to be rid of him. This is Swift's description of his own situation and that of other great men.

This interpretation of Lilliput depends, of course, on the information supplied by the voyage to Brobdingnag. Gulliver's superiority to the Lilliputians is as the Brobdingnagians' superiority to him. Against the background of Brobdingnag, Gulliver's moral perspective comes into focus. The Brobdingnagians are great because they are virtuous; they are, particularly, temperate. Political life is not a plaything of their lusts. There is neither faction nor Christian controversy (they are polytheists). Hence there is no war, for they have no neighbors and no civil strife—not because of the victory of one part of the body politic over the others, but because of the judicious blending of all three parts. They maintain themselves in a state of constant preparedness, simply for the sake of preserving the advantages stemming from military virtue. Theirs is entirely a citizen army. Their concentration is on obedience to law, not interpretation of it. Law is powerful so long as it is respected, and respect implies assent. The mind should not be used to reason away the clear bases of duty. No commentaries are allowed on the laws. There is no political science. Their learning is only such as will produce good citizens, or, put otherwise, their studies are made to produce not learning, but virtue. They know morality, history, poetry, and mathematics, and that is all.

The vices that Gulliver finds in the common people are at worst summed up in an excess of thrift, and most are simply a result of his peculiar perspective; he assumes ill-intention where there is probably only indifference or inattention. The Brobdingnagians are a simple, decent people whose state exists, not for the pursuit of knowledge or the cultivation of diversity, but for the sake of well-known, common-sense virtues. Brobdingnag is a sort of cross between Sparta and republican Rome; it concurs in almost all respects with the principles of Aristotle's *Ethics*. Swift was an enemy of the Enlightenment, its learning and its politics.

We can make only a short visit to Laputa.[3] Gulliver goes there, after having seen modern politics, to see modern science and its effects on life. He finds a theoretical preoccupation, which is abstracted from all human concerns and which did not start from the human dimension. On the flying island the men have one eye turned inward, the other toward the zenith; they are perfect Cartesians—one egotistical eye contemplating the self, one cosmological eye surveying the most distant things. The intermediate range, which previously was the center of concentration and which defined both the ego and the pattern for the study of the stars, is not within the Laputian purview. The only studies are astronomy and music, and the world is reduced to these two sciences. The men have no contact with objects of sensation; this is what permits them to remain content with their science. Communication with others is unnecessary, and the people require a beating to respond to them. Rather than making their mathematics follow the natural shapes of things, they change things so as to fit their mathematics; the food is cut into all sorts of geometrical figures. Their admiration for women, such as it is, is due to the resemblance of women's various parts to specific figures. Jealousy is unknown to them; their wives can commit adultery before their eyes without being noticed. Above all, they lack a sense for poetry. This is a touchstone for Gulliver; no mention is made of poetry in Lilliput and Laputa, although both the Brobdingnagians and the Houyhnhnms have excellent poetry, of a Homeric kind. Poetry expresses the rhythm of life, and its images capture the color of reality. Men without poetry are without a grasp of humanity, for the poetic is the human supplement to philosophy—not poetry in our more modern sense, but in that of the great epics which depict the heroes who are our models for emulation. Modern science cannot understand poetry, and hence it can never be a science of man.

3.For the interpretation of the details of the voyages to Laputa and Lagado, cf. Marjorie Nicolson, *Science and Imagination* (Ithaca: Cornell University Press, 1956), pp. 110–154; *Voyages to the Moon* (New York: Macmillan, 1948); with Nora Mohler, "The Scientific Background of Swift's Voyage to Laputa," *Annals of Science*, II (1937), 299–334; "Swift's Flying Island in the Voyage to Laputa," *ibid.*, pp. 405–430. The unifying theme of all of Swift's criticism of the new science is not the external absurdity of its propositions, or its impious character, or its newness, but its partialness and abstraction from what is known about human things. Modern science represented a complete break with classical principles and methods, and Swift believed that there was a whole range of phenomena it could not grasp but which it would distort. The commitment to it, if absolutized, would destroy the human orientation. This contention remains to be refuted.

Another peculiarity of these men is described by Gulliver as follows. "What I chiefly admired, and thought altogether unaccountable, was the strong disposition I observed in them towards news and politics, perpetually inquiring into public affairs, giving their judgments in matters of state, and passionately disputing every inch of a party opinion. I have indeed observed the same disposition among most of the mathematicians I have known in Europe, although I could never discover the least analogy between the two sciences." Gulliver, we see, has recovered his old superiority. On this theme of science and politics, so important today, Swift's perspicacity is astonishing. He not only recognizes the scientists' professional incapacity to understand politics, but also their eagerness to manipulate it, as well as their sense of special right to do so. The Laputians' political power rests on the new science. Their flying island is built on the principles of the new physics founded by Gilbert and Newton. Swift saw the possibility of great inventions that would open new avenues to political endeavor. This island allows the king and the nobles to live free from conspiracies by the people—in fact free from contact with them—while still making use of them and receiving the tribute which is necessary to the maintenance and leisure of the rulers. They can crush the terrestrial cities; their power is almost unlimited and their responsibilities nil. Power is concentrated in the hands of the rulers; hence they are not forced even by fear to develop a truly political intelligence. They require no virtue; everything runs itself, so there is no danger that their incompetence, indifference, or vice will harm them. Their island allows their characteristic deformity to grow to the point of monstrosity. Science, in freeing men, destroys the natural conditions which make them human. Here, for the first time in history, is the possibility of tyranny grounded not on ignorance, but on science. Science is no longer theoretical, but serves the wishes and hence the passions of men.

Gulliver is disgusted by this world; he represents common sense, and he is despised for it. This he finds disagreeable, and he seeks to return to earth, where he can be respected. But in Lagado he finds things even worse; everything is topsy-turvy because what works has been abandoned in favor of projects. Here Gulliver's critique, although funny, impresses us less than it does elsewhere. He seems to have seriously underestimated the possible success of the projects. But perhaps some of the reasons supporting this posture are still intelligible to us. The transformations planned by the projectors are direct deductions from the principles used in Laputa; they are willing to give up the old life and the virtues it engendered for the sake of a new life based only on wishes. If the new life succeeded it might produce some comforts; but they do not know what that way of life will do to them. This transformation and this incertitude induce Gulliver to be conservative. He distrusts the motives of the projectors and wonders if they do not represent a debasement of the noble purposes of contemplation. If Gulliver is not right in ridiculing the possibilities of applied science, he may nevertheless be right in doubting its desirability. At any rate, there is today in America a school of social criticism which is heavy-handedly saying the same thing. And as for education and politics, Gulliver looks as sound as ever when he ridicules substitutes for intelligence and study, or when he outlines Harold Lasswell's anal science of politics. Gulliver's attack on modern science and projecting foresaw the problem which has only recently struck the popular consciousness: what does the conquest of nature do to the conquerors?

The visit to Glubdubdribb allows Gulliver to see modern historical science as it really is, because he is able to evoke the shades of those with whom it deals. History is of particular importance, because from it one can understand what has been lost or gained and the direction in which one is going. We learn that this science is most inaccurate. It has embellished modern men and misunderstood the ancients; even our knowledge of the Greek language has decayed to the point of incomprehensibility. Gulliver most admires Homer, Aristotle, and the heroes who opposed tyranny. There is only one modern—Sir Thomas More—among these latter. All the later interpreters of the poets and the philosophers misunderstood and denatured them. An effort to recover them must be made; and the result of that study will be the recognition of the unqualified superiority of classical antiquity. "I desired that the senate of Rome might appear before me in one large chamber, and a modern representative, in counterview, in another. The first seemed an assembly of heroes and demigods; the other, a knot of pedlars, pick-pockets, highwaymen and bullies."

The fourth and last stop which we must make in the voyage to Laputa is Luggnag. Here Gulliver has his interlude on immortality. Death is feared in all other nations, but not in Luggnag, where immortality is constantly present in the form of the Struldbrugs. The desire for immortality, or the fear of death, leads men to all kinds of vain hopes and wishes. Gulliver is to some extent released from this anxiety by his experience with the Struldbrugs, who never die but grow ever older. They are repulsive and have no human traits. "They were not only opinionative, peevish, covetous, morose, and talkative, but incapable of friendship and dead to all natural affection. . . . Envy and impotent desires are their prevailing passions." They hate all that is young. No doubt, most men would prefer to be dead than to live this living death. However, it has often been remarked that to the extent one can imagine immortality, one can imagine perpetual youth. Gulliver himself imagines perpetual youth when he discovers the existence of the Struldbrugs and learns that they are not advisers at court, but are banished. He is surprised. These particular immortals grow old and decrepit; the criticism of man's desire for immortality applies only to those which do not include perpetual youth.

Now, why has Swift presented his case in this way? One might suggest that he was reflecting on the only example in our world of an institution that claims immortality, namely, the Church. I gather this from Gulliver's concluding remark about the Struldbrugs, who are not allowed to hold employment of public trust or to purchase lands:

I could not but agree that the laws of this kingdom relative to the Struldbrugs were founded upon the strongest reasons and such as any other country would be under necessity of enacting in the like circumstances. Otherwise, as avarice is the necessary consequent of old age, those immortals would in time become proprietors of the whole nation, and engross the civil power, which, for want of abilities to manage, must end in the ruin of the public.[4]

This merely echoes the views prevailing in England after the Reformation on the importance of limiting church lands, especially those of the Roman Catholic Church. Modern times are characterized by an immortal body inhabiting, but not truly part of, civil society—a decrepit body with a dangerous tendency to aggrandize itself. Death is preferable to the extension of life the Church offers; and civil society is safe only so long as that body is contained by law.

The voyage to the Houyhnhnms is of particular significance in our cross-examination of Lemuel Gulliver, for this was his last trip and the one that most affected him; it is under the influence of seeing Houyhnhnms contrasted with Yahoos that he wrote this book, which had as its explicit end the reform of all human vices. In Lilliput and Laputa he learned nothing and found nothing to admire; in Brobdingnag he admired; but among the Houyhnhnms he imitated. Any reform must be in the direction of their practices.

4. *Gulliver's Travels*, Bk. III, Ch. 10. Although Swift defended the property of the Church of Ireland, he did it only within severe limits and for the sake of preserving an important civil institution. He well knew the dangers of the higher clergy's possible avarice, and he also was perfectly aware of the political difficulties caused by the property and influence of the Roman Church prior to the Reformation.

The Houyhnhnms are not human beings; man's standard is now a nonhuman one. What Swift has done in the land of the Houyhnhnms is to elaborate a utopia, a utopia based on Plato's *Republic*; but it is a super *Republic*, for the problem which made the construction of the best city so difficult for Socrates has disappeared—the Houyhnhnms lack the passionate part of the soul. The whole difficulty in the *Republic* is to make the three orders take their proper role in relation to one another. Punishment and rhetoric are necessary; the book is full of the struggle between the rational and the appetitive; and the irascible or spirited, intended as reason's ally, shows a constant tendency to turn against it. The passionate and the spirited are in perfect natural harmony with the rational in the Houyhnhnms. Swift has taken everything that was connected with the passionate or erotic nature and made a kind of trash heap from it, which he calls the Yahoos. Or, in another and more adequate formulation, Swift has extrapolated the Houyhnhnms from man as depicted by Plato, and the Yahoos from man as depicted by Hobbes.

It is not correct to say that this section is a depreciation of man in general in favor of animals, for the animals are very particular animals, possessing certain human characteristics of a Platonic order, and the men are a very particular kind of passionate men. Man has a dual nature—part god, part beast; Swift has separated the two parts. In reality they are in tension with one another, and one must decide which is in the service of the other. Are the passions directed to the service of reason, or is reason the handmaiden of the passions? If the latter, then the Yahoo is the real man; if the former, then the Houyhnhnms represent man as he really is. The separation effected by Swift leads to clarity about the ends.

Nature is the standard, and the Houyhnhnms are "the perfection of nature," which is what the name means. Nature is Parmenidean; being *is*; the changeable has no meaning. The Houyhnhnms speak and speculate only about what is, for only what is can be said. There is not even a word for opinion, nor do the Houyhnhnms have those passions which partake of nonbeing. There is nothing in them that can take account of what is not or can partake of what is not; hence they cannot say what is not. They need not lie, for like Plato's gods, they need not deceive, nor do they have friends who need to be deceived. Virtue for them is knowledge. They see what must be done and do it; there is no need of moral habituation. They always reason like philosophers; when they recognize what a phenomenon is, they say so—otherwise they say nothing. This is why Gulliver is such a problem: is he a Yahoo or is he not? He is and he is not. This, by the way, perhaps indicates a weakness in the

Houyhnhnms' understanding; they cannot adequately grasp this composite being.

Gulliver, who in the first stages of his relationship with his master tried to obscure his Yahoo nature, is finally forced to undress himself. He makes a sort of girdle "to hide my nakedness," echoing Adam before the Lord. Gulliver again feels shame, as he did in Brobdingnag. The Houyhnhnms are shameless; no part of the body is any more or less beautiful than another. Gulliver feels shame because he is a lustful being and cannot control desires which he understands to be bad. He is a sinner and a repenter, whereas the Houyhnhnms are like Aristotle's gentleman who never blushes because he has nothing to be ashamed of. This is the indication which allows us to see the Yahoos as peculiarly modern man. They are a sort of cross between man as Augustine describes him and as Hobbes describes him. They have the uncontrollably corrupted nature of Augustinian man, with particular concentration on sexual lust. And the relation of Yahoos to one another is one of Hobbesean war. The Yahoos have infinite desires, and most of all they hate to see anyone else taking possession of anything at all. They are needy beings with a constant sense of scarcity. They hoard and have an unlimited desire for gold without any idea of what they want to use it for. They know of no natural limits, so they are never satisfied. They are strong, but fearful; and they set a leader over themselves to govern them. If one conceives of the real life of man as in the passions, this is the kind of picture one must have of him. There is absolutely no suggestion in Swift's view of the Houyhnhnms that a being who senses his own corruption and tries to improve himself, or who yearns for salvation, is desirable.

There can be little doubt that the land of the Houyhnhnms is a perfection of the *Republic*. A glance at the list of similarities is convincing; the changes are all based on the Houyhnhnms' superiority. There is hardly any need for politics, because the citizens are so orderly and accept their roles. The needs that cause war are absent. The rulers are free to converse. They are philosophers; in one example of their reasoning—the explanation of the origin of Yahoos—they reason exactly like pre-Socratic philosophers. At all events, this is a land ruled by philosophers.

The Houyhnhnms live simply, and their wants are provided by the community. There is no money. Because they live simply and naturally, there is no need for the arts of medicine or of forensic rhetoric. There is a class system, but one based entirely on natural differences. They do not fear death nor do they mourn those who depart. They regard the land as their first mother. They belong to the land as a whole and have no special, private interests.

To come to the paradoxes treated in Book V of the *Republic*, there is also among the Houyhnhnms equality of women and virtual community of wives and children. Marriages are arranged on grounds of reason; *eros* does not play a role. They separate into couples and have private houses, but when necessary they break up families, service one another, and switch children—all this in the name of the community as a whole. Friendship and benevolence are their virtues and the themes of their conversation. Their poetry, which has all the power of Homeric epics, supports their character. There is, therefore, no need for any of the elaborate devices mentioned in the *Republic* for the censorship of poetry or the destruction of the family interests. There is no distinction between public and private, between the good and one's own. They do not love their children; they take care of them for the sake of the common good.[5]

The contrast in Book IV is between Plato and Hobbes, between the perfected political animal and man in the state of nature. The Yahoos have tyrants; the Houyhnhnms are republicans who need no subordination because they have sufficient virtue to govern themselves. Swift took refuge in animals because nothing in the conception of man indicated the possibility of such a regime in state or soul. He conceived a hatred of the Yahoos; for only by this self-contempt could he cultivate that in himself which was akin to the Houyhnhnms.

It has been asked, Why, with all their virtues, do the Houyhnhnms have no god? But this clearly follows from their principle. They cannot say the thing which is not. They can see only the permanent, eternal, unchanging being. In England, Yahoos have a religion; their sacred issues cannot even be rendered in the Houyhnhnm language. These Trojan horses contain more than they appear to.

Gulliver's Travels has often been called a misanthropic book. Indeed, it does not present a very flattering picture of man. But we should ask ourselves what a misanthrope is. If anything, he is a hater of humanity—one who had great expectations of others and has been deceived. Above all—if we can believe Molière—he is a man who tries to live according to the highest standards of virtue and finds they are unacceptable in human society; he is a man who always tells the truth and acts according to principle. Rousseau, who left society to return to nature, was a misanthrope; and Kant taught the absolute morality of the misanthrope. Gulliver, in his letter to Sympson, doubtlessly speaks in the tones of a misanthrope.

5. *Ibid.*, Bk. IV, Ch. 8. Note the reference to Socrates and Plato at the beginning of this passage.

He has renounced all hopes of human reform, because he gave his countrymen six months since the publication of his book, which is surely more than sufficient, to improve—and they have not improved a bit.

But we also know that Gulliver is a liar and admires successful liars like Sinon. A liar can hardly be a misanthrope; he cares enough about his fellow men to respect their prejudices; noble lies are acts of generosity. They are based on the truth of becoming and the existence of opinion; they prove an understanding of this world, an understanding not possessed by Houyhnhnms. Finally, and above all, misanthropes are not funny; this world and morality are too serious for that. I do not know about Gulliver, but Swift is surely one of the funniest men who ever lived. His misanthropy is a joke; it is the greatest folly in the world to attempt to improve humanity. That is what it means to understand man. And, after all, perhaps we are not serious beings. In the jest, there is a truth; we glimpse the necessity of the distinction between what we are and what we ought to be. But this leaves us with a final impression of fond sympathy for poor mortals. To understand is to accept; *Gulliver's Travels* makes misanthropy ridiculous by showing us the complexity of our *nature* and thereby teaching us what we must accept.

NIGEL DENNIS

Swift and Defoe

Gulliver's Travels . . . begins with the will-power only partly roused and being employed with extreme grace, wit and subtlety; it ends with the will at its most vehement and monstrous, reflecting in this development the author's own march from his old self to his new one. It does not give the impression of having been planned as it stands from the start; on the contrary, it suggests that each part inspired its successor, and that the appetite grew with the feeding—a hunger for greater intensity and more powerful amplification being felt more and more strongly as the work proceeded. A

From *Jonathan Swift: A Short Character*, pp. 122–133. New York: The Macmillan Company and London: George Weidenfeld & Nicolson Ltd., 1964. Copyright © by The Macmillan Company, 1964. Reprinted by permission of the publishers.

great deal has been written about its originating in the ideas and table-talk of Swift and his London friends, but without questioning the correctness of this ascription, must we not also allow *Robinson Crusoe*, which appeared in 1719, some of the honor of having set it going? We cannot do so with any firmness, unfortunately, but we can certainly use the one book as a point of departure for the other; for the two, seen side by side, form a wonderful pair, representing two sorts of writing, two entirely disparate views of fiction and two superbly opposed authors. To describe *Gulliver's Travels* as Swift's deliberate retort to *Robinson Crusoe* would be unwarranted, but if we amuse ourselves by considering it as such, the result is as informative as it is entertaining. Moreover, we never see Swift more clearly than in relation to Defoe: each demands the presence of the other, in the sense that each side demands the presence of the other if we are to understand a battle, a Parliamentary conflict, a divided nation.

Defoe embodies everything that Swift hates: he is the other half of England that Swift struggled all his life to suppress or ignore and by which he was defeated and driven into isolation. Defoe, with his brickworks and bankruptcies, is the rising small businessman whom Swift saw very correctly as the man who would unseat his timocracy of landed gentlemen and substitute an economy of stocks and shares for one of estate and title. He is the Roundhead Dissenter to whom the Whigs run as an ally in their fight with the Tories of the Established Church—and, by turning to him, change what was formerly a private quarrel between Anglican landlords into a lasting division between regicide Puritan merchants and honorable county squires. Swift is the gentleman-author whose chosen home is society and the dignified sphere of the well-educated and well-born; Defoe is the born gander of Grub Street, the father of all that is noisiest and freest in modern journalism. Defoe is liberty in the form in which Swift detested it most: he is the rogue whom Swift loved best to "swinge," and his life is a constant, rapscallionly muddle, bursting with excitements and devoid of all dignity. Where Swift goes in danger of the Tower, Defoe's natural punishment is the pillory: the higher place is reserved for the treasonable gentleman, the lower for the provocative hack. The two men have only three things in common: the first is that they both took service under Harley, Swift as unpaid propagandist and Defoe as paid informer; the second is that they were both passionately in favor of the educating of women; and the third is that both were capable of satire. We expect satire from a Tory like Swift, but we are surprised and interested to find it in an enthusiastic Whig. Yet Defoe's *The Shortest Way with the Dissenters*, the satirical essay for which he was put in the pillory, anticipates exactly in tone and tendency Swift's *Modest Proposal* for dealing with surplus Irishmen: the only real difference between the two essays is that Defoe's makes its plea for the mutilating of Dissenters in rather a blunt way, whereas Swift's plea for eating babies is made with the refinement and gentility that we expect from a clergyman of the better class.

Of the two Defoe is by far the more sympathetic and agreeable man and fits most happily today into the excessively unaustere society that composes our democracy. He is the beginning of the social struggle of which we are the end, and he presses forward into modern times proportionately as Swift fights backwards into the time behind him. When we hold each man's masterpiece in our hands we hold the halves of one apple—the apple of discord that, in its wholeness, represents the England of the early eighteenth century.

Robinson Crusoe has been called aptly "the primary textbook of capitalism"—and who can resist the amusement of reading it as such? What author ever built such a warehouse or drew up a more satisfying inventory? Every page is a merchant's catalogue of hardware, woollens, leather goods and crockery, and from the fields outside the warehouse come the baaing of the good tradesman's flocks and the ripple of the breeze through his stalks of corn. All these goods, together with a snug house fenced and barricaded interminably against burglars, are available to the forceful capitalist, who, by diligent sowing of a little seed, builds his frugal investments into interest-bearing property. And how excitedly we labor with Crusoe, first for mere self-survival, later for a higher rate of interest and greater abundance of possessions! How we share his horrified terror when that most magical of all moments in fiction, the footprint in the sand, tells us brutally that some barbarous intruder threatens not only life but property! And how thankful we are to know that our heroic investor does not stand alone—that his marvels of free enterprise are noted and sanctioned by God Himself! For, certainly, there never was a book in which God's hand was busier—helping in the factory, making sound economical suggestions, keeping an eye on things generally and asking nothing in return but prayers—heart-felt prayers, of course; but who would *not* pray heartily to such a generous Father? No Puritan but Bunyan ever wrote a happier book; no merchant ever looked upon his gains and declared with greater self-satisfaction that the earth was the Lord's and the glory thereof.

At the time *Robinson Crusoe* appeared Swift was reading all the travel books he could find: they were all trash but a perfect antidote to the spleen, he assured Miss Vanhomrigh. Merely to imagine him reading *Robinson Crusoe* is enough to make one laugh, for it is pleasing to picture his contemptuous response to Defoe's unceasing power to declare, in all imaginable matters, his faith in all that Swift despised. Each author, to begin with, sets out upon his "Travels" with the intention of discovering only that which he already knows and erecting in a strange land that which he knows to have been built at home. Defoe turns a primitive island into a commercial enterprise: the only enemy to this sort of civilization is the naked savage—the terrifying cannibal whose primitive appetites threaten disaster to the God-fearing businessman. But Swift's islands are never menaced by barbarism: on the contrary, the only atrocities he finds are those of civilized, cultured persons who have degenerated grossly from the happier, natural state of man and have espoused reason only in order that "the corruption of that faculty might be worse than brutality itself." Where Defoe looks with horror at the naked footprint Swift looks with equal horror at the imprint of the court-shoe, and Gulliver, even after being wounded by savages, would still prefer "to trust myself among those barbarians, than live with European Yahoos." The Dissenting merchant and reformer never doubts that trade and colonization confer civilized benefits upon savage people: it is the Tory churchman who argues, with the modern radical, that colonists are no better than an "execrable crew of butchers" enjoying "a free license . . . to all acts of inhumanity and lust."

Man himself, as he walks the world, drives the two authors to opposite poles. Defoe will have no truck with the naked body; his excitements come from the fabricating of its garments out of the available raw materials and from its foodstuffs and implements. But the High Church Dean despises "the subject of . . . diet, wherewith other travellers fill their books," and where Defoe asks that we admire the fur hat and skin-breeches, Swift keeps pulling off these contemptible disguises and pressing our eyes and noses to the hairy warts and stenches of the flesh below. The Puritan is far too respectable even to mention the functions of the body, but the Dean's book abounds in hogsheads of urine and the voiding of excrement. This is why *Robinson Crusoe* is an essentially materialistic book and yet a wholly unphysical one, whereas *Gulliver's Travels* is only occasionally materialistic and always passionately physical.

The numerous other "opposites" in the two books are all very engaging and highly characteristic of their respective authors. Crusoe is a simple man of Defoe's own class; Gulliver, like Sir William Temple, is a graduate of Emmanuel College, Cambridge. Unlike Defoe's God, the Dean's is much too detached and Olympian to be involved in Gulliver's absurd affairs—and Gulliver himself is much too much an average gentleman to waste a moment in prayer. The Dissenter, once he has built himself a small realm abroad, delights in allowing "liberty of conscience throughout my dominions"; the Dean, however, does not lose the opportunity of requiring the monarch of Brobdingnag to assert that "a man may be allowed to keep poisons in his closet, but not to vend them about for cordials."

But the most entertaining contrast between the books, from a literary point of view, is in each author's declared intention. *Robinson Crusoe* is the work of a journalist; it is essentially what we would call a "documentary," or a blunt unpolished recital of the plain facts—yet it is of this documentary that Defoe says: "My story is a whole collection of wonders." *Gulliver's Travels*, on the other hand, *is* a whole collection of wonders—as much an imaginary creation as *Crusoe* is not and, for the most part, most admirably "turned" and polished. Yet Swift declares of it: "I could perhaps, like others, have astonished thee with strange, improbable tales, but I rather chose to relate plain matter of fact, in the simplest manner and style. . . ." Thus does each author indulge the perfectly excusable pretence that suits his book, the journalist seeking to elevate his facts into fancy, the wit to resolve pure fantasy into facts.

Robinson Crusoe, one may say, never gets off the ground at all: it is rarely touched by the imagination and asks nothing of the intellect. But *Gulliver's Travels* is a work of pure intellect, an act of unceasing invention. Defoe, patiently assembling material facts, needs forty pages of preliminaries to wreck his hero on a desert island; Swift, anxious to leave the factual world behind, carries Gulliver to Lilliput in little more than a page. Defoe, having retailed one fact, merely goes on to retail the next fact; but the chief purpose served by a fact in Swift is to be a spring-board into fantasy. And nothing about *Gulliver's Travels* is more interesting than to study the way in which this fantasy is anchored—to see why, even at its most fantastic moments, it does not lose its ties with the earth. To see how Swift does this, is to see what satire must always do if its angry fantasies are to be brought safely home.

Napoleon, discussing at St. Helena the innovations of the French Revolution, declared himself entirely in favor of the change made by the revolutionary intellectuals to the Metric System of weights and measures. But he pointed out that the mathematicians who arranged this change made a typical academic mistake: by throwing away the old *terms*, they turned weights and measurements into inhuman abstractions. The man who works with a terminology of *hands, feet,* and *ells* in effect bases all his calculations on the parts of his body: even when he speaks in terms of *poles* and *chains,* he is still speaking of what he regards as extensions of his own arms. But once he must calculate in *ares* and *meters,* he must lose his sense of physical conjunction with the world, and the loss of this sensuous tie, Napoleon believed, was precisely the sort of loss that always should be avoided in the modernizing of ancient systems.

In this spasm of light from a dying star we see clearly one of the great strengths of *Gulliver's Travels*—the anchoring of the high-flying mind to the physical body. This is not the book of an abstract "projector" calculating in a world apart; it is a book in which man *is* the measure of all things. We find this first, of course, in the simple matter of relative sizes in Lilliput and Brobdingnag, but it is the actual estimating of these proportions—the terms in which they are assessed—that is so unabstract and gives the book its fleshy solidity. Like Defoe, Swift will often tell us how small or large a thing was by giving its linear measurement; but, unlike Defoe, he prefers to lay a human limb alongside it, to make his comparison, and to press our eyes, noses and ears into the service of his imaginings. In the huge magnifications of Brobdingnag, the purring of a cat is not described in mere adjectival sonorities; instead, it is "like that of a dozen stocking-weavers at work." A gigantic infant's cry is "a squall that you might have heard from London Bridge to Chelsea"; and twenty wasps, "as large as partridges," sweep in at the window "humming louder than the drone of as many bagpipes." The Brobdingnagian queen can "craunch the wing of a lark, bones and all, between her teeth, although it were nine times as large as that of a full-grown turkey," and her table knives are "twice as long as a scythe." Each fly is of the greatness of "a Dunstable lark" and, as it walks, demonstrates its essential monstrousness to the eye of the tiny observer by leaving behind it a loathsome trail of excrement, spawn and "viscous matter." One paring from the Queen's thumbnail serves for the back of a horn comb, bladed with "stumps of the King's beard"; the corn on the toe of a royal maid-of-honor is of "about the bigness of a Kentish pippin"; sliced from its owner and carried home to England, it can be "hollowed into a cup, and set in silver." Waves of overpowering stench and scent are emitted by the naked bodies of those royal maids, and each charming mole that spots the skin stands "broad as a trencher, and hairs hanging from it thicker than packthreads." The thump on the scaffold floor of a murderer's decapitated head is such as to shake the ground for "at least half an English mile," while—most astonishing simile of all—the "veins and arteries [of the trunk] spouted up such a prodigious quantity of blood, and so high in the air, that the great *jet d'eau* at Versailles was not equal for the time it lasted." Reversed in their proportions to fit the world of Lilliput, the similes are more charming than gross, but they always retain their intense, familiar quality—tiny men ploughing through Gulliver's snuff-box "up to the mid-leg in a sort of dust" and sneezing dreadfully as they go; examining letters and diaries in which every character is "almost half as large as the palm of our hands"; discovering a pocket-watch, "which the emperor was very curious to see, and commanded two of his tallest yeomen of the guards to bear it on a pole upon their shoulders, as draymen in England do a barrel of ale." "I have been much pleased," says Gulliver, "with a cook pulling a lark, which was not so large as a common fly; and a young girl threading an invisible needle with invisible silk."

This intense proximity, this use of commonplaces to ground the imagination, has a curious effect. It is not noticed by the reader when he finds it pleasing: he merely smiles at the image without inquiring into the techniques that have made him smile. But when the simile is gross—when excrement and hairy moles replace invisible needles and snuff—he not only sees the technique but begins to wonder what sort of man the author was. Yet it should be plain that the same method is being used throughout and that there is a grand unity of treatment that covers in one way the nicest and nastiest things. For every grossness in Swift there is a corresponding delicacy—a point nicely made by Pope in his well-known lines on Swift. But whichever course, fine or gross, he chooses to take, an intensely personal intimacy lies at the core of it. The grand flights of his imagination are made plausible only by the point from which they take their departure, and this point is always the living human being and his familiar belongings, sensations and habits. Nor is there any limit to the use of this admirable art; it can be applied not only to the coarsest and most delicate things but also to the occasions when genius displays itself by listing details in the simplest way and then turning them, without the least change of expression, to irresistibly human account:

... Their manner of writing is very peculiar, being neither from the left to the right, like the Europeans; nor from the right to the left, like the Arabians; nor from up to down, like the Chinese; but aslant, from one corner of the paper to the other, like ladies in England.

The life we share with Robinson Crusoe has no place for such extraordinary felicities. It is, in the friendliest sense of the words, merely a life of gain, technical security, adventure and everyday ingenuity; it provides neither insight into human behavior nor interest in human thought. *Gulliver's Travels* begins where *Robinson Crusoe* ends; it inquires and reflects where the other rests content to act and possess. We see Crusoe naked only when he is afraid, but we see Gulliver in all his human weaknesses—in his fear, his vanity, his pride, his shame, his shivering little skin. Neither Gulliver nor Crusoe is of much interest as a principal character, but each is uninteresting for a different reason—Crusoe because his material possessions loom larger than he does, Gulliver because his story would have no solid center if he himself were made as dramatically extraordinary as the situations and persons he meets: in this respect we may compare him to the plain Martin in *A Tale of a Tub*. We ask that Gulliver be a bigger man only for one reason—we cannot forgive him for surrendering to the Houyhnhnms and recognizing in himself and us the beastly image of a Yahoo. And we do not forgive him for this because we shall never forgive Swift for it.

A good way to examine this matter is to compare good-humoredly the conclusions of *Robinson Crusoe* and *Gulliver's Travels*. In both books, the hero is carried safe back to Europe by a kindly ship's captain, a Portuguese in Gulliver's case, an Englishman in Crusoe's. We know the revulsion that the return to the world excites in Gulliver—how he shrinks from the touch of his own wife and children, how repugnant he finds the stench and character of the Yahoo. But we should remember, too, how different the world seems to Defoe's returning castaway. Crusoe finds that the world is good—indeed, that it is overflowing with probity and justice. The twenty-eight years of his absence have been devoted by his honest partners to the preservation and increase of his investments, and the totting up of the grand total, with the occasional pause for an *Ave Maria*, forms a most suitable conclusion to this best of mercantile books. Twelve hundred chests of sugar, 800 rolls of tobacco, thousands of golden Portuguese moidores, large Brazilian plantations worked assiduously by black slaves: it all amounts to "above £5,000 sterling" and a South American estate of "above £1,000 a year." And when we hear the chink of those moidores, do we not exclaim with Crusoe: "It is impossible to express the flutterings of my very heart when I looked over these letters and especially when I found all my wealth about me"? Do we not agree most heartily with him that "the latter end of Job was better than the beginning"? And are we at all surprised to find Job in that *galère?*

This is the happy end we all want—honest men, a banker-God, and accumulated interest. Defoe never denied it even to the worst of us: once Moll Flanders stopped being a whore and a thief and invested in probity and God, her income rose in due proportion with her piety, cementing the delights of capital to the forgiveness of sins. And because we feel that things *should* turn out like this in a novel—that money is what Job is being so patient about; that money is what Swift loses when Miss Vanhomrigh dies—we are profoundly offended when Gulliver shrinks from touching us, and his author, peeling us down to mere skin and claws, wipes us from his sight as stinking Yahoos. His terrible insult has survived two centuries unimpaired: it hurts us today even more than it hurt its first readers. Many, indeed, protest that no author who really believed in God could find it in his heart to condemn us so unkindly; others, more expert in the study of Swift, have turned the insult by tracing it to a psychological deformation in the author. All of which has one very amusing result—that we regard *Robinson Crusoe*, which is a documentary, as an acceptable piece of fiction, but dismiss *Gulliver's Travels*, which is a pure fiction, as a libellous piece of documentary. Yet this absurd conclusion suits both authors admirably, for Defoe, as has been noted, pretended to be a teller of wonders, while Swift pretended to be a reporter of facts. The journalist set out to please his public; the Dean intended to roast it. Both authors succeeded admirably in their intentions, and both are read still in the spirit in which they wrote. Both would be overjoyed to know it.

EDWARD W. ROSENHEIM, JR.

The Satiric Fiction

When the *Travels* is viewed simply as a tale, Gulliver seems a reasonable and convincing protagonist. His restlessness and curiosity lead him to travel; his understandable frailties precipitate

From Edward W. Rosenheim, Jr., *Swift and the Satirist's Art*, pp. 158–160; 166–167. Chicago: The University of Chicago Press, 1963. Copyright © 1963 by The University of Chicago Press. Reprinted by permission of the author and the publisher.

many of his dilemmas; his resourcefulness extricates him from them. He is benign enough to invite our sympathy, honest enough so that, once within the make-believe framework of his story, we are never tempted to accuse him of saying "the thing that is not." His deficiencies and rigidities are plausible, and plausible too are the consequences to which they lead within the plot. His character is, indeed, without peculiarity; whether as narrator, hero, or dupe (and he is variously all of these) he must be taken as one of ourselves.

Nor is there anything inconsistent in the satiric use which Swift makes of the character he has created. Gulliver is not a politician, a projector, a profiteer, pedant, lawyer, or lecher; the assaults upon these and other kinds of person and institution are achieved through what Gulliver sees and tells. He is, on the other hand, a travel-writer, an Englishman, a European, a human being, and where he is employed as surrogate-victim it is in one of these roles. Where he is truly a critic—where, that is, he literally offers judgments which essentially coincide with our own—it is at a level appropriate to his rather commonplace faculties; he is disgusted at whatever is grossly repellent, outraged by palpable cruelty or deceit, puzzled or amused by arrant folly. If, in very occasional passages, he displays an uncharacteristic cynicism, it seems engendered by a kind of blandly uncritical acceptance of evil as a fact of life. Thus, for example, his simple-minded astonishment at the political projectors of Lagado, who sought to instil notions of civic virtue into the conduct of government . . . reveals him as a sort of *faux ingénu*. His naïve dismissal of such reformers as mad, that is, expresses the bitter truth that it is hopeless to expect wisdom and honesty in government affairs. Although these sentiments are somewhat at odds with the glowing account of political appointment and preferment which Gulliver has earlier given to the Brobdingnagian king, they are not incompatible with his general character. The belief that governmental corruption is inevitable is a standard one in the doctrinal equipment of the ordinary man. (Indeed, great numbers of Americans today seem to accept, with a complacency equal to Gulliver's, the presumably inalterable venality and guile which operate within that political system they venerate above all others.)

Thus Gulliver in his several roles—as observer and reporter, as master and victim of circumstance—is a thoroughly flexible agent of Swift's many purposes yet preserves that consistency of character which renders him, wherever necessary, credible and sympathetic. With such a character there are few limits to what a writer like

Swift can do, and the *Travels* might well have gone on and on (or, for that matter, ceased earlier), leaving its readers with a rich miscellany of literary experiences, now satiric, now comic, now philosophic, untroubled by questions of unity, development, or total significance. This, in effect, is what is provided by such purely episodic but triumphantly satiric works as Lucian's *True History* or *Don Juan* or even, essentially, *Candide*. And it is, I believe, what is provided by the first three voyages of *Gulliver's Travels*. For despite the brilliant symmetry of conceit which links the first two books, it is Gulliver and what happens to him—rather than any unified satiric purpose or procedure, any coherence of imagery or idea, any singleness of philosophic vision—to which alone we look for organic continuity. What happens to Gulliver, moreover, is presented in a series of basically dissociated episodes, some with the magnitude and complexity of his disgrace, danger, and escape from Lilliput, others as short and simple as his Brobdingnagian encounters with the wasps, the monkey, and the rats. Among these episodes there are few relationships of antecedent and consequent. No character—not even the beloved Glumdalclitch—survives beyond one or two phases of Gulliver's adventures. Gulliver is confronted by no persistent problem, engaged in no compelling inquiry or search beyond the desire to return home (and even this plays little part in the second voyage). With the establishment of Gulliver's character and his propensity for travel, we are confronted with the possibilities for incident on whose substance and magnitude Swift's own wishes and talents impose the only limitation. This is, so to speak, a literary system of "occurrences," each to be relished for its own effect and in its own way, deriving credibility and intelligibility, to be sure, from the presence of a single character and the recurrent use of a voyage as the central activity of each book, but possessed of no further organic quality, whether of structure or of purpose.

All this is abruptly, even violently, changed with the voyage to the Houyhnhnms. This book, too, is above all a narrative, a series of happenings, yet happenings which are profound and startling, which are inseparably linked within the wholeness of a single myth, and which involve Gulliver in a sustained process of inquiry and discovery.

The belief or vision which Voyage IV presumably embodies has, quite understandably, commanded enormous attention. In our final chapter we shall attempt to discuss the philosophic ground from which this extraordinary fable proceeds, but at this moment we should recognize that the most obvious—and certainly a very crucial—way in which Book IV differs from its fellows is in the nature of its plot. However we may be tempted to attribute the singularity of the fourth book to the depth, intensity, or strangeness of its ultimate "meaning," we must also note that the "system of occurrences" by which the earlier books proceed has here yielded to an account of a single though complex experience. And that experience, fantastic though its form may be, is at heart one of the most shocking and powerful of which the human mind can conceive, for it is, in effect, a discovery so profound that a man's total view of life is violently and irrevocably altered. . . .

In the final analysis, our scrutiny of the *Travels* as a fictional narrative supplies the minimal unity which embraces the entire book, yet, perhaps paradoxically, forces us to recognize that, beyond this, no unifying artistic formula can be produced. As pure narrative and as philosophic myth, the Voyage to the Houyhnhnms is indeed climactic, but climactic largely by virtue of its contrast to, rather than its development from, the voyages which have preceded it. Against the shifting variety of the first three books, against their appearance of ebullient formlessness, the Fourth Voyage emerges with organic clarity as a magnificent finale. In its orderliness and magnitude, it is unanticipated and independent, and the more powerful for that fact. Yet it casts no retroactive magic over the pages which have preceded it. Their own freedom refuses to be embraced by a single concept of theme or belief, and they resist the boundaries imposed by a single satiric motive or a conventional literary formula. They are informed and sustained by invention; they are the product of a talent which, however varied the uses to which it is put, is unflaggingly and supremely imaginative.

A. E. DYSON

Swift: The Metamorphosis of Irony

In an age of few or shifting values irony becomes, very often, a tone of urbane amusement; assuming the right to be amused, but offering no very precise positives behind the right. It can degenerate into a mere gesture of superiority, superficially polished and civilized, but too morally irresponsible to be really so.

From *Essays and Studies*, 1958 (1959), pp. 53-67. London. Reprinted by permission of the author and the publisher, *The English Association*.

Eminent Victorians is an example of such irony which springs to mind. Lytton Strachey uses the tone of Gibbon in order to deflate the Victorians, but divorces the tone from any firm moral viewpoint, and so makes of it a negative and somewhat vicious instrument.

Irony can, also, become a mode of escape, as we have good cause to know in the twentieth century. To laugh at the terrors of life is in some sense to evade them. To laugh at oneself is to become less vulnerable to the scorn or indifference of others. An ironic attitude is, as we should all now agree, complex and un-predictable: fluctuating with mood and situation, and too subtle in its possibilities for any simple definition in terms of moral purpose or a "test of truth" to be generally applicable.

This is not, however, a state of affairs as new, or unusual, as we might be tempted to think. Even in that great age of moral irony, the eighteenth century, the technique is far from being simple. Irony is, in its very nature, the most ambivalent of modes, con-stantly changing colour and texture, and occasionally suffering a sea-change into something decidedly rich and strange. In the work of Swift, who will concern us here, we find, at characteristic mo-ments, that the irony takes a leap. It escapes from its supposed or apparent purpose, and does something not only entirely different from what it set out to do, but even diametrically opposite. Nor is this just a matter of lost artistic control or structural weakness. At the moments I have in mind the irony is at its most complex and memorable. It seems, in undergoing its metamorphosis, to bring us nearer to Swift's inner vision of man and the universe. It ceases to be a functional technique serving a moral purpose, and becomes the embodiment of an attitude to life. And just as Alice was forced, on consideration, to accept the metamorphosis of the Duchess's baby into a pig as an improvement ("it would have made a dread-fully ugly child: but it makes rather a handsome pig, I think"), so the readers of Swift will have to agree that the final impact of his irony, however disturbing, is more real, and therefore more worth while, than its continuation as simple moral satire would have been.

But this is to anticipate. We must begin by reminding ourselves that Swift *is* a satirist: and that satire, fiercer than comedy in its moral intentions, measures human conduct not against a norm but against an ideal. The intention is reformative. The satirist holds up for his readers to see a distorted image, and the reader is to be shocked into a realization that the image is his own. Exaggeration of the most extreme kind is central to the shock tactics. The reader must see himself as a monster, in order to learn how far he is from being a saint.

The Augustan age, as Professor Willey has most interestingly shown, was especially adapted to satiric writing. An age which does not really believe in sin, and which imagines that its most rational and enlightened ideals have been actualized as a norm, is bound to be aware also, at times, of a radical gulf between theory and practice.

. . . if you worship "Nature and Reason," you will be the more afflicted by human unreason; and perhaps only the effort to see man as the world's glory will reveal how far he is really its jest and riddle.

Economic and acquisitive motives were coming more and more into the open as mainsprings of individual and social action; Hobbes's sombre account of human nature in terms of competition and conflict was altogether too plausible on the practical level for the comfort of gentlemen philosophers who rejected it, as a theory, out of hand. The turning of Science, Britannia and The Moderns into idols was bound, in any case, to produce sooner or later some iconoclasm of the Swiftian kind. Satire thrives on moral extremes: and at this period, with Hobbes at hand to provide a view of man which was at once alarmingly possible and entirely opposite to the prevailing one, satire was bound to be very much at home.

It should follow from this, and to some extent really does, that Swift was a moralist, concerned, as he himself puts it, to "wonderfully mend the world," in accordance with the world's most ideal picture of itself. Gulliver's Travels is far more complex and elusive, however, than this intention would suggest. It is, indeed, a baffling work: I have been re-reading a number of excellent and stimulating commentaries on Book IV, and find that there are disagreements upon even the most fundamental points of interpretation. Clearly, we cannot arrive at Swift's "true" meaning merely by reversing what he actually says. The illusion that he is establishing important positives with fine, intellectual precision breaks down when we try to state what these positives are.

On the surface, at least, the irony does work in ways that can be precisely defined. Swift has a number of techniques which he is skilled in using either singly, or in powerful combination. At one moment he will make outrageously inhuman proposals, with a show of great reasonableness, and an affected certainty that we shall find them acceptable; at another, he will make soundly moral or Christian proposals, which are confidently held up for scorn. Again, we find him offering, with apparent sympathy and pride, an account of our actual doings, but in the presence of a virtuous outsider whose horrified reactions are sufficient index of their true worth.

Swift can, notoriously, shift from one technique to another with huge dexterity; setting his readers a problem in mental and moral gymnastics if they are to evade all of his traps. In Book III, for example, the Professors at Balnibarbi are presented as progressive scientists, of a kind whom the Augustan reader would instinctively be prepared to admire. We quickly find that they are devoid of all common sense; and that unless we are to approve of such extravagant projects as "softening marble for pincushions" we have to dissociate ourselves from them entirely. But when we do this, Swift is still ready for us. "In the school of political projectors," says Gulliver, "I was but ill entertained; the Professors appearing in my judgement wholly out of their senses" (a pleasant reassurance, this, that we have done well to come to a similar conclusion some time before). The crowning absurdity is that these "unhappy people were proposing schemes for persuading monarchs to choose favourites upon the score of their wisdom, capacity and virtue . . . of rewarding merit, great abilities and eminent services . . ." and so on. Dissociated from the Professors, we find ourselves, once more, in Swift's snare.

The technique is, of course, one of betrayal. A state of tension, not to say war, exists between Swift and his readers. The very tone in which he writes is turned into a weapon. It is the tone of polite conversation, friendly, and apparently dealing in commonplaces. Naturally our assent is captured, since the polite style, the guarantee of gentlemanly equality, is the last one in which we expect to be attacked or betrayed. But the propositions to which we find ourselves agreeing are in varying degrees monstrous, warped or absurd. The result is the distinctively satiric challenge: why, we have to ask, are we so easily trapped into thinking so? And is this, perhaps, the way we really do think, despite our normal professions to the contrary?

The technique of betrayal is made all the more insidious by Swift's masterly use of misdirection. No conjuror is more adept at making us look the wrong way. His use of the polite style for betrayal is matched by his use of the traveller's tale. The apparently factual and straightforward narrative with which *Gulliver's Travels* opens (the style of *Robinson Crusoe*), precludes suspicion. We readily accept Gulliver as a representative Englishman fallen into the hands of an absurd crew of midgets, and only gradually realize that the midgets, in fact, are ourselves, and Gulliver, in this instance, the outside observer. The same technique is used, I shall argue, in Book IV: though there, the misdirection is even more subtle, and the way to extricate ourselves from a disastrous committal to Gulliver's point of view far more difficult to discover.

So much, then, for the purpose of the irony, and its normal methods. It is, we notice, accomplished, full of surprises, and admirably adapted to the task of shocking the reader for his moral good. For a great part of the time, moreover, it functions as it is intended to. When Swift is satirizing bad lawyers, bad doctors, bad politicians and *id genus omne*, he is driven by a genuine humanity, and by a conviction that people ought not to act in this way, and need not act so. His tone of savage indignation is justified by the content, and relates directly to normal ideals of justice, honesty, kindness.

On looking closely, however, we find that his irony is by no means directed only against things which can be morally changed. Sometimes it is deflected, and turned upon states of mind which might, or might not, be alterable. Consider, for example, the Laputians. These people never, we are told, enjoy a moment's peace of mind, "and their disturbances proceed from causes which very little affect the rest of mortals." They are preoccupied with fears of cosmic disasters, and apprehensions that the world will come to an end. The ironic treatment pre-supposes that Swift is analysing a moral flaw, but it seems doubtful whether such fears can be regarded wholly a matter of culpable weakness, and even more doubtful whether ridicule could hope to effect a cure. The problem exists in a hinterland between the moral and the psychological, between sin and sickness. The Laputians are temperamentally prone to worry: and worry is not usually regarded, except by the most austerely stoical, as simply a moral weakness.

This dubious usage points the way to the real metamorphosis, which occurs when the irony is deflected again, and turned against states of mind, or existence, which cannot be changed at all. The irony intended to "wonderfully mend the world" transmutes itself into a savage exploration of the world's essential unmendability. It is turned against certain limitations, or defects (as Swift sees them), in the human predicament that are, by the nature of things, inevitable. When this happens, Swift seems to generate his fiercest intensity. The restless energy behind the style becomes a masochistic probing of wounds. The experience of reading him is peculiarly disturbing at such moments; and it is then that his tone of savage indignation deepens into that *disgust* which Mr. T. S. Eliot has called his distinctive characteristic.

In the first two books of *Gulliver* alterations of perspective usually precipitate this type of irony. The Lilliputians are ridiculous not only because they are immoral, but because they are small. The life of their court is as meaningless as it is unpleasant: their intrigues and battles a game, which Gulliver can manipulate like a child playing with toys, and as easily grow tired of. Gulliver himself becomes ridiculous when he is placed beside the Brobdingnagians; whose contempt for him, once again, is not wholly, or even primarily, a moral matter. The King, after hearing Gulliver prattling about his "beloved England," comments "how contemptible a thing was human grandeur, which could be mimicked by such diminutive insects," and continues

Yet I dare engage, these creatures have their titles and distinctions of honour; they contrive little nests and burrows, that they call houses and cities; they make a figure in dress and equipage; they love, they fight, they dispute, they cheat, they betray.

The force, here, is in "mimicked," "diminutive insects," "creatures," "little." The smallness of Gulliver and his kind makes anything they do equally contemptible, their loves as much as their battles, their construction of houses and cities as much as their destructiveness. The survey is Olympian; and the human setting, seen from this height, becomes, irrespective of moral evaluation, a tale of little meaning though the words are strong.

Likewise, the hugeness of the Brobdingnagians makes them potentially horrible. The sight of a huge cancer fills Gulliver with revulsion, as, too, does the sight of giant flies who "would sometimes alight on my victuals, and leave their loathsome excrement or spawn behind."

What do these alterations in perspective suggest? We are made to feel that perhaps all beauty or value is relative, and in the last resort of little worth. To be proud of human achievement is as absurd as to be proud of our sins. The insignificance of men in space suggests an inevitable parallel in time. Perhaps men really *are* no more than ants, playing out their fleeting tragicomedy to an uninterested or scornful void. The irony, now, is an awareness of possible cosmic insignificance. It is exploring a wound which no amount of moral reformation would be able to heal.

In Book IV of *Gulliver* the irony completes its transformation, and is turned upon human nature itself. Swift's intensity and disgust are nowhere more striking than here.[1] This is the classic

---

1. That striking *tour-de-force* 'A Modest Proposal' springs to mind as an exception. There, too, as Dr. Leavis has argued in his fine essay, the effect is almost wholly negative and destructive. The force of the irony is so savage that it robs its supposed positives of any power of asserting themselves. The ghastly imagery of the market and the slaughter-house ceases to sound like satiric exaggeration, and appals us with the sense of actuality. Man, we feel, really *is* as brutal and sordid as this. Theories that he

interpretative crux: and Aldous Huxley's remark, that Swift "could never forgive man for being a vertebrate mammal as well as an immortal soul" still seems to me to be the most seminal critical insight that has been offered.

The crux centres, of course, upon what we make of Swift's relationship to Gulliver. How far is Gulliver a satiric device, and how far (if at all), does he come to be a spokesman for Swift himself? The answer seems to me to be by no means clear. If we accept Gulliver as Swift's spokesman, we end in a state of despair. On this showing, it would seem that Swift has openly abandoned his positives, and that when he avows that he has "now done with all such visionary schemes" as trying to reform the Yahoos "for ever," he has passed from ironic exaggeration to sober truth. Few readers will be willing to take this view, especially when they reflect upon the dangers in store for those who identify themselves with Gulliver too readily. And yet, if we reject this, what is the alternative view to be? Swift leads us very skillfully to follow Gulliver step by step. If at some point we depart from his view of himself we have to depart also from the Houyhnhnms: who seem, however, to be an incarnation of Swift's actual positives, and the very standard against which the Yahoos are tried and found wanting. What happens in Book IV is that Gulliver is converted gradually to an admiration of the Houyhnhnms, and then to an acceptance of their judgements upon himself and his kind. The result of this enlightenment is that he comes to realize also the unattainability of such an ideal for himself. He sinks into bitterness and misanthropy, and ends, as a result of his contact with the ideal, far more unpleasant and unconstructive than he was before. At some stage, it seems, he has taken the wrong turning: but where has the mistake occurred?

The construction of the Book is of great interest. Gulliver first of all comes across the Yahoos, and is instantly repelled by them. "Upon the whole, I never beheld in all my travels so disagreeable an animal, or one against which I naturally conceived so strong an antipathy." Soon after this, he encounters the noble horses, and is equally strongly impressed, this time in their favour. Almost at

---

might be otherwise are merely an added torment, so energetically is his in-humanity realized, so impotent is the theoretic norm in the face of this reality.

A necessary conflict seems, too, to be exposed between our ideals of humanity and rational behaviour, and the actual motives of competition and self-interest which move society. Society can no more really be expected to change for the better than Yahoos can be expected to turn into Houyhnhnms. The law of love is absolutely incompatible with things as they are.

once, he starts to discover between himself and the Yahoos an appalling resemblance: "my horror and astonishment are not to be described, when I observed, in this abominable animal, a perfect human figure." At this stage, it is the physical resemblance which disturbs him. But later, as he falls under the influence of the Houyhnhnms, he comes also to accept a moral resemblance. And this is at the core of the satire.

The cleverness of Swift's technique is that at first the horses are only sketched in. They are clean, kindly, rational, but apart from seeing them through Gulliver's eyes we learn little in detail about them. Gulliver is first "amazed to see . . . in brute beasts . . . behaviour . . . so orderly and rational, so acute and judicious." But almost at once he finds that they regard *him* as the "brute beast," and with somewhat more justice "For they looked upon it as a prodigy, that a brute animal should discover such marks of a rational creature." From this moment, the Houyhnhnms start to insinuate into Gulliver's mind a vision of himself that becomes increasingly more repellent. They begin by rejecting his claim to be truly rational, speaking of "those appearances of reason" in him, and deciding that he has been taught to "imitate" a "rational creature." When they compare him with the Yahoos, Gulliver at first objects, acknowledging, "some resemblance," but insisting that he cannot account for "their degenerate and brutal nature." The Houyhnhnms will have none of this, however, deciding that if Gulliver does differ, he differs for the worse. "He said, I differed indeed from other Yahoos, being much more cleanly, and not altogether so deformed; but in point of real advantage, he thought I differed for the worse." The reason for this judgement—a reason which Gulliver himself comes to accept—is that his "appearance of reason" is a fraud; and that what seems reason in him is no more than a faculty which makes him *lower* than the Yahoos.

. . . when a creature pretending to reason, could be capable of such enormities, he dreaded, lest the corruption of that faculty, might be worse than brutality itself. He seemed therefore confident, that instead of reason, we were only possessed of some quality fitted to increase our natural vices.

Up to this point, the reader might feel fairly confident that he sees what is happening. The Houyhnhnms really are ideal, and Gulliver's conversion to their point of view is the lesson we should be learning. The contemptuous view of mankind formed by the Houyhnhnms is the main satiric charge. The view that man *is* a Yahoo and cannot become a Houyhnhnm is satiric exaggeration: near enough to the truth to shake us, but not intended to be taken literally. We shall be "betrayed" if we identify ourselves with Gulliver at the points where the horses scorn him, but safe enough if we accept his conversion at their hands.

This, I fancy, is what many readers are led to feel: and to my mind, in so leading them, Swift sets his most subtle trap of all. The real shock comes in the middle of Chapter VIII, when Gulliver turns, at long last, to give us a more detailed description of the horses. We have already been aware, perhaps, of certain limitations in them: they have a limited vocabulary, limited interests, and an attitude of life that seems wholly functional. But Gulliver has explained all these limitations as virtues, and persuaded us to see them as a sign of grace. No doubt, we feel, these horses *are* noble savages of some kind, and their simplicity a condition and a reward of natural harmony. It remains for the fuller account to show us two further truths about the horses: the first, that they are not human at all, so that their way of life is wholly irrelevant as a human ideal; and the second, that their supposedly rational way of life is so dull and impoverished that we should not wish to emulate them even if we could.

Their society, for instance, is stoic in appearance. They accept such inevitable calamities as death calmly; they eat, sleep and exercise wisely: they believe in universal benevolence as an ideal, and accordingly have no personal ties or attachments. The family is effectually abolished: marriage is arranged by friends as "one of the necessary actions in a reasonable being"; husband and wife like one another, and their children, just as much and as little as they like everyone else. Sex is accepted as normal, but only for the purpose of procreation. Like all other instincts, it is regarded as entirely functional, and has no relevance beyond the begetting of a standard number of offspring. They have no curiosity: their language, their arts and their sciences are purely functional, and restricted to the bare necessities of harmonious social existence. Life is lived "without jealousy, fondness, quarrelling or discontent"; and it is lived in tribal isolation, since they are "cut off from all commerce with other nations."

This impoverished and devitalized society is the one which Gulliver uncritically accepts as an ideal, and on the strength of which he sinks into a most negative and unedifying misanthropy. And yet, so plausibly does Swift offer this as the ideal of Reason and Nature which his own age believed in, so cunningly does he lead us to think that this is the positive against which a satiric account of the Yahoos is functioning, that the trick is hard to detect. Even the fact that Gulliver is in an escapist frame of mind is not immediately apparent, unless we are on the alert.[2] We see at once, it is true, that the Houyhnhnms are not *like* men: that physically Gulliver might be a monkey but is nothing like a horse, and that this physical placing is linked with a moral one. Yet we assume that this placing is only one more satiric technique: and it is with a distinct shock that we realize that it exists at a more fundamenal level than any *moral* amendment on the part of a man could resolve. The Houyhnhnms are literally not human: they are inaccessible to Gulliver not because they are morally superior, but because they are physically non-existent. They are mental abstractions disguised as animals: but they are no more animals, really, than the medieval angels were, and nothing like any human possibility, bad or good.

The horses have, in fact, no passions at all. Their "virtue" is not a triumph over impulse and temptation, but a total immunity from these things—and an immunity which is also, by its very nature, an absence of life and vitality. They have no compulsive sexual impulses, no sensuous pleasures, no capacity for any degree of human love. They have no wishes and fears, and scarcely any ideas. If they are incapable of human bestiality they are even less capable of human glory or sublimity; and it is only because Swift prevents us from thinking of humanity as anything other than a real or potential Yahoo that this is not at once immediately apparent.

What is the true force of Book IV, then? Swift seems to my mind, to have posed, in new form, and with appalling consequences, the old riddle of man's place as the microcosm. Instead of relating him to the angels and the beasts, he relates him to the Houyhnhnms and the Yahoos. The Houyhnhnm is as non-bodily and abstract, in its essential nature, as an angel, the Yahoo a beast seen in its most disgusting lights. As for man, represented by Gulliver, he is left in a disastrous microcosmic vacuum. Instead of having his own distinctive place, he has to *be* one or the other of the extremes. Swift drives a wedge between the intellectual and the emotional, makes one good, the other evil, and pushes them further apart, as moral opposites, than any except the most extreme Puritans have usually done. The result is the kind of tormenting and bitter dilemma which always lies in wait for those who do this and, to quote Huxley again (a writer temperamentally very similar

---

2. E.g. ". . . For, in such a solitude as I desired, I could at least enjoy my own thoughts, and reflect with delight on the virtues of those inimitable Houyhnhnms, without any opportunity of degenerating into the vices and corruptions of my own species." (Book IV, Chapter XI.)

to Swift himself), who cannot "forgive man for being a vertebrate mammal as well as an immortal soul." The ideal is unattainable, the vicious alternative inescapable, and both are so unattractive that one is at a loss to decide which one dislikes the more.

Once again, then, the irony intended for moral satire has undergone a metamorphosis: and starting as an attempt to improve man, ends by writing him off as incurable.

But how far did Swift intend this to be so? This is the question which now becomes relevant, and the answer cannot, I think, be a straightforward one. My own feeling is that we are faced with a split between conscious intention and emotional conviction, of a kind which modern criticism has familiarized us with in Milton. Perhaps Swift really did intend a simple moral purpose, and was not consciously betraying his reader into despair. And yet, the unpleasantness of the Yahoos is realized so powerfully, and any supposed alternative is so palpably non-existent, that he must have been to some degree aware of his dilemma. He must have known that men do, for better or worse, have bodily desires, and that the Houyhnhnms were therefore an impossible ideal. He must have known, too, being a man, that Houyhnhnms were both very limited and very unattractive. And in identifying Reason and Nature with them, he must have been aware that he was betraying his own positives and those of his age: leaving the Yahoos in triumphant possession of all the reality and the life, and removing the possibility of any human escape by way of Reason or Nature from their predicament.

As a satire, *Gulliver* can work normally only if we can accept the Houyhnhnms as a desirable human possibility: and this, I do not for a moment believe Swift thought we could. The very energy of the style is masochistic—a tormenting awareness of its own impotence to do, or change, anything. Swift is publicly torturing both himself and the species to which he belongs.[3] The irony, then, intended for moral reformation, has undergone a more or less conscious metamorphosis; and the total effect of Book IV, as Dr. Leavis has insisted, is largely negative.

3. We might feel, today, that in exploring the dangers of dissociating reason from emotion, and calling the one good, the other bad, Swift really did hit on the central weakness of his age: that Book IV is still valid, in fact, as a satire upon Augustanism itself. The Augustans, at their most characteristic, disapproved of strong emotions as necessarily disruptive, subordinated even those emotions they could not exile to the stern control of "Right Reason," and found no place for "feeling" in their search for "truth." This attitude, we might decide, is doomed to failure by the actual nature of man—and Swift, by driving reason and emotion to opposite poles (with the result that man can live happily by neither) reveals just *how* impossible it is.

There are, nevertheless, before this is finally asserted, one or two compensating factors to notice. The first, often surprisingly overlooked, is that Swift cannot really have supposed his readers to be Yahoos, if only because Yahoos could not have responded at all to *Gulliver's Travels*. The deliberate obtuseness with which Gulliver prattles of his "beloved England" will register only with a reader much less obtuse. The reader must not only be betrayed but see that he has been betrayed: and in order for this to happen he must have more intelligence and more moral sense than a Yahoo. Swift knew, in any case, that his readers *were* Augustan gentlemen with ideals of human decency that he had in common with them, and that however much a case against them could be both thought and felt, the ultimate *fact* of Augustan civilization—a fact embodied in his own style as much as anywhere—was not to be denied. *Gulliver's Travels* might leave us, then, with a wholly negative attitude, but the very fact of its being written at all is positive proof that Swift's own total attitude was not negative.

This may seem commonplace: but it leads on to another consideration, equally important, which most commentators upon *Gulliver* seem oddly afraid of: namely that Swift, writing for gentlemen, intended to give pleasure by what he wrote. When Gulliver says of the Yahoos (his readers), "I wrote for their amendment, and not their approbation," there is a general readiness to accept this at its face value, and to credit Swift with a similar sternness. Sooner or later most writers about *Gulliver* hit upon the word "exuberance," and then pause doubtfully, wondering whether, if Swift is so moral and so misanthropic as we think, such a word can have any place in describing him. Yet "exuberant" he certainly is, even in Book IV of *Gulliver*. The "vive la bagatelle," the flamboyant virtuosity of *A Tale of a Tub* is less central, but it is still to be detected, in the zest with which Gulliver describes bad lawyers, for example, and in the fantastic turns and contortions of the irony. Clearly, Swift enjoyed his control of irony: enjoyed its flexibility, its complex destructiveness, his own easy mastery of it. Clearly, too, he expects his readers to enjoy it. The irony is not *only* a battle, but a game: a civilized game, at that, since irony is by its very nature civilized, presupposing both intelligence, and at least some type of moral awareness. The "war" is a battle of wits: and if one confesses (as the present writer does) to finding *Gulliver* immensely enjoyable, need one think that Swift would really, irony apart, have been surprised or annoyed by such a reaction?

On a final balance, I fancy that we have to compromise: agreeing that *Gulliver* ends by destroying all its supposed positives, but deducing, from the exuberance of the style and the fact that it was written at all, that Swift did not really end in Gulliver's position. He was, at heart, humane, and his savage indignation against cruelty and hypocrisy in the straightforwardly satiric parts reflects a real moral concern. He was, also, iconoclastic, and disillusioned about the ultimate dignity of man at a deep level: and when his irony undergoes the type of metamorphosis that has been discussed here, it is as disturbing and uprooted as any we can find. But he always, at the same time, enjoyed the technique of irony itself, both as an intellectual game, and as a guarantee of at least some civilized reality. Very often, even at the most intense moments, we may feel that pleasure in the intellectual destructiveness of the wit is of more importance to him than the moral purpose, or the misanthropy, that is its supposed *raison d'être*. Irony, by its very nature, instructs by *pleasing:* and to ignore the pleasure, and its civilized implications, is inevitably to oversimplify, and falsify the total effect.

WILLIAM FROST

The Irony of Swift and Gibbon

. . . When one thinks of literature in . . . the light of relevant but extra-literary considerations, one is likely to think also of critics whose readership and influence transcends the company of literary teachers and scholars, and appropriately so since their own interests reach out into other areas, sociological or philosophic. I have in mind such critics as Yvor Winters in this country or F. R. Leavis in England, critics who function not only as estheticians but also as moralists, as perhaps the best literary critics, from Aristotle to Johnson and Arnold, have always done. Such men produce judgments, for example that the pastoral mode is 'easy, vulgar, and therefore disgusting', judgments which may partake of what our age is likely to label 'the affective fallacy' but which nonetheless are often remembered and valued because they vigorously postulate connections between writing and life.

A famous example of such vigour is Leavis's essay on Swift, first printed in *Scrutiny* in March, 1934, then republished as part of *The*

From *Essays in Criticism*, XVII (1967), pp. 41–47. Reprinted by permission of the publisher.

Common Pursuit in 1952, and still being read and studied with a care apparent in such essays as those on Swift and Gibbon in A. E. Dyson's *The Crazy Fabric* (1965). Leavis's treatment of Swift is vigorous and striking, certainly; but I think it is demonstrably wrong, wrong on its own premises, and in this paper I shall try briefly to show what is the matter with it.

According to Leavis, Swift is an egotist whose most intense effects occur when his egotism exerts itself as wholly destructive force. 'His intensities', says Leavis, 'are intensities of rejection and negation; his poetic juxtapositions are, characteristically, destructive in intention, and when they most seem creative of energy are most successful in spoiling, reducing, and destroying . . . the only thing in the nature of a positive that most readers will find convincingly present is self-assertion—*superbia*. Swift's way of demonstrating his superiority is to destroy, but he takes a positive delight in his power'. Elsewhere Leavis finds that Swift shows 'a complete incapacity even to guess what religious feeling might be', that he is animated by 'savagery' reinforced by 'insane egotism', when he supports the posture of kneeling during Communion; also, further, that his 'negative horror, at its most disturbing, becomes one with his disgust obsession: he cannot bear to be reminded that under the skin there is blood, mess, and entrails'; that he manifests with 'paradoxical vitality' a 'self-defeat of life'; that in him 'rejection is felt as self-assertion'; that we have in his writings 'probably the most remarkable expression of negative feelings and attitudes that literature can offer—the spectacle of creative powers . . . exhibited consistently in negation and rejection'; and finally that 'the actuality of presentiment for which Swift is notable, in prose as well as verse, always seems to owe its convincing "justness" to, at his least actively malicious, a coldly intense scrutiny, a potentially hostile attention'. I have been giving Leavis's very words in the order in which they occur in the essay; they are unqualified, and amount to a portrait of an evil genius, a literary Satan whose creative energies are perverted to destruction because his true nature is one of active malice.

With this Satan Leavis contrasts a kind of Messiah—the same contrast also occurs in Dyson, and by this time who knows where else?—a kind of Messiah in the person of another eighteenth-century prose ironist, to wit Gibbon. Though Gibbon's most notable irony may seem to be negative in that (unlike Swift's) it is directed against Christianity instead of being wielded in that religion's behalf, the fact is that, according to Leavis, Gibbon represents the positives—rationality, candour, politeness, elegance, humanity—of an eighteenth-century gentleman, positives also embodied in the Romans Gibbon admired but by no means embodied in Gibbon's targets, the Jews and early Christians whom Gibbon presents by contrast as 'ignorant fanatics, uncouth and probably dirty'. What Leavis likes about Gibbon as ironist is that, although he is obviously limited as a historian of Christianity, 'the positive standards by reference to which his irony works represent something impressively realized in eighteenth-century civilisation; impressively "there" too in the grand, assured and ordered elegance of his history'.

This is the essence of Leavis's argument; the body of the essay is devoted to sustained, detailed *explication de texte* of passages chosen to support the central point of view. This point of view, the Swift-Gibbon contrast, seems to me impressive and commensurate with any good reader's experience of Swift and Gibbon, except for two fatal flaws: a certain obtuseness in interpretation of some of Swift's effects, and a failure to ask basic questions about the kind of reader-author relation set up by each man and the order of values embodied therein.

To take the first point first, Leavis quotes, in the middle of a long series of comments on the passage of which it is a part, the well-known sentence from the madness digression in the *Tale of a Tub*: 'Last week I saw a woman flayed, and you would hardly believe how it altered her person for the worse'. He says the sentence induces in the reader 'repulsion intensified by the momentary co-presence . . . of incipient . . . acceptance', and I suppose this will do as a rough account of its psychology; but what seems to me notable is that in Leavis's entire essay the only point made concerning the *contents* of that sentence is that Swift (Leavis says) 'cannot bear to be reminded' that under the human skin 'there is blood, mess and entrails'. The fact that Swift alludes in the sentence to a well-known public sight visible in his London, the bloody back of a prostitute whipped at the end of a cart on the way to the Fleet Prison, this fact nowhere obtrudes itself into Leavis's discussion, in which it might, to be sure, constitute an incongruous footnote on the ordered and elegant eighteenth-century civilization so impressively present by implication in Gibbon. It might also, and this seems to me the crux of the matter, raise the question whether the preferable response to poignantly realized violence in literature— say, the description of the sacrifice of Iphigenia in Aeschylus's *Agamemnon*—is a comment on the author's psychology or the relevance of the passage to common human concerns—the presumed earlier practice of human sacrifice in Greek religion, or the widespread callousness to the sufferings of not very advantaged groups in Augustan England.

And this brings me to the main point. It seems to me absolutely true that, as Leavis puts it, 'Gibbon's irony . . . habituates and reassures, ministering to a kind of judicial certitude or complacency', while Swift's 'is essentially a matter of surprise and negation; its function is to defeat habit, to intimidate and to demoralize'. As an example of Gibbonian irony one might cite the language in which in the next-to-last paragraph of chapter XVI, the historian summarizes his statistical estimate of the number of Christians who died for their beliefs during the last persecutions, those of the emperors Galerius and Maximian: 'The whole might ... amount to about fifteen hundred, a number which, if it is equally divided between the ten years of the persecution, will allow an annual consumption of one hundred and fifty martyrs'.

I do not want to be too hard on Gibbon here. Part of the point of this whole discussion of numbers is that the pagan emperors at their worst were far more sparing of human life in ideological (politico religious) causes than were, a millennium later, certain heirs of the martyrs during the wars of the reformation; certainly, if institutionalized Christianity ever produced such inversions of the Sermon on the Mount as Gibbon cites from 16th-century Holland, then so much the worse for institutionalized Christianity, at any rate in that particular mutation. But, nevertheless, when all allowances have been made in favour of Gibbon's humanity, rationality, and hatred of bigotry, what about that phrase 'annual consumption of one hundred and fifty martyrs'—is there nothing in Swift of which it might be a reminder? Economic terminology applied to human life? I need only quote as Leavis himself does, from the *Modest Proposal*: 'It would increase the love and tenderness of Mothers towards their Children, when they were sure of a Settlement for Life, to the poor Babes, provided in some sort by the Publick, to their annual Profit instead of Expense; we should soon see an honest emulation among the married Women, *Which of them could bring the fattest child to the market*'. And I cannot improve on Leavis's immediate comment—'The implication is: "this, as you so obligingly demonstrate, is the only kind of argument that appeals to you; here are your actual faith and morals. How, on consideration, do you like the smell of them?"'

To summarize the argument so far: it is the function of Gibbon's irony to habituate and reassure; it is the function of Swift's to defeat habit, to intimidate and demoralize. It only remains, then, to ask two questions: first, which represents the greater achievement, in terms of literary difficulty, to confirm your readers in the existing patterns of their sensibilities or to reorient those patterns in unexpected ways; second, what *were* the habits, the complacencies, that Gibbon sought to reinforce and Swift to undermine? And I have in mind here not only the *Modest Proposal* but also such passages in Swift as one completely neglected by Leavis, apparently on the grounds that the main appeal of the first three books of *Gulliver* is

to children—the confrontation of Gulliver and the King of Brobdingnag on the subject of the discovery and employment of gun
powder.

C. J. RAWSON

Gulliver and the Gentle Reader

The book ends here, with Gulliver a monomaniac and his
last outburst a defiant, and silly, petulance. We are not, I am sure,
invited to share his attitudes literally, to accept as valid his fainting
at the touch of his wife (IV, xi) and his strange nostalgic preference for his horses. He has become insane or unbalanced, and I
have already suggested one reason why, in the whole design of the
work, this is appropriate: it makes his rant viable by dissociating
Swift from the taint of excess, without really undermining the
attack from Swift that the rant stands for. It is Gulliver's manner,
not Swift's, which is Timon's manner, as critics are fond of noting,
which means that he (like Lucian's or Plutarch's Timon), and not
Swift, is the raging recluse. But his are the final words, which produce the taste Swift chose to leave behind: it is no great comfort or
compliment to the reader to be assaulted with a mean hysteria that
he cannot shrug off because, when all is said, it tells what the
whole volume has insisted to be the truth.

It is wrong, I think, to take Gulliver as a novel-character who
suffers a tragic alienation, and for whom therefore we feel pity or
some kind of contempt, largely because we do not, as I suggested,
think of him as a "Character" at all in more than a very attenuated
sense: the emphasis is so preponderantly on what can be shown
through him (including what he says and thinks) than on his
person in its own right, that we are never allowed to accustom ourselves to him as a real personality despite all the rudimentary local
color about his early career, family life and professional doings. An
aspect of this are Swift's ironic exploitations of the Gulliver-figure,
which to the very end flout our most elementary expectations of
character consistency: the praise of English colonialism in the last
chapter, which startlingly returns to Gulliver's earlier boneheaded
manner, is an example. The treatment of Gulliver is essentially

From "Gulliver and the Gentle Reader" by C. J. Rawson in *Imagined
Worlds: Essays on Some English Novels and Novelists in Honour of John
Butt*, edited by M. Mack and I. Gregor. London: Methuen & Co., Ltd.,
1968. Reprinted by permission of the publisher.

external, as, according to Wyndham Lewis, satire ought to be. Nor is Gulliver sufficiently independent from Swift: he is not identical with Swift, nor even similar to him, but Swift's presence behind him is always too close to ignore. This is not because Swift approves or disapproves of what Gulliver says at any given time, but because Swift is always saying something *through* it.

Gulliver in his unbalanced state, then, seems less a character than (in a view which has much truth but needs qualifying) a protesting gesture of impotent rage, a satirist's stance of ultimate exasperation. Through him, as through the modest proposer (who once offered sensible and decent suggestions which were ignored), Swift is pointing, in a favorite irony, to the lonely madness of trying to mend the world, a visionary absurdity which, in more than a shallow rhetorical sense, Swift saw as his own. At the time of finishing *Gulliver*, Swift told Pope, in a wry joke, that he wished there were a "Hospital" for the world's despisers. (If Gulliver, incidentally, unlike the proposer, does not preach cannibalism, he does ask for clothes of Yahoo-skin — IV,iii — and uses this material for his boat and sails — IV,x.) But Gulliver does not quite project the noble rage or righteous pride of the outraged satirist. The exasperated petulance of the last speech keeps the quarrel on an altogether less majestic and more intimate footing, where it has, in my view, been all along. Common sense tells us that Swift would not talk like that in his own voice, but we know disturbingly (and there has been no strong competing voice) that this is the voice he chose to leave in our ears.

Still, Gulliver's view is out of touch with a daily reality about which Swift also knew, and which includes the good Portuguese Captain. Gulliver's response to the Captain is plainly unworthy, and we should note that he has not learnt such bad manners (or his later hysterical tone) from the Houyhnhnms' example. But we should also remember that the Captain is a rarity, who appears only briefly; that just before Gulliver meets him the horrible mutiny with which Book IV began is twice remembered (IV,x; IV,xi); that the first men Gulliver meets after leaving Houyhnhnmland are hostile savages (IV,xi); and that just after the excellent Portuguese sailors there is a hint of the Portuguese Inquisition (IV,xi). The Captain does have a function. As John Traugott says, he emphasizes Gulliver's alienation and "allows Gulliver to make Swift's point that even good Yahoos are Yahoos." But above all perhaps he serves as a reasonable concession to reality (as if Swift were saying there *are* some good men, but the case is unaltered), without which the onslaughts on mankind might be open to a too easy repudiation from the reader. In this respect, he complements the other disarming concessions, the humor and self-irony, the physical comicality of the Houyhnhnms, Gulliver's folly, and the rest.

Even if Swift is making a more moderate attack on mankind than Gulliver, Gulliver's view hovers damagingly over it all; in the same way that, though the book says we are better than the Yahoos, it does not allow us to be too sure of the fact. (The bad smell of the Portuguese Captain, or of Gulliver's wife, are presumably "objective" tokens of physical identity, like the She-Yahoo's sexual desire for Gulliver.) This indirection unsettles the reader, by denying him the solace of definite categories. It forbids the luxury of a well-defined stand, whether of resistance or of assent, and offers none of the comforts of that author-reader complicity on which much satiric rhetoric depends. It is an ironic procedure, mocking, elusive, immensely resourceful and agile, which talks at the reader with a unique quarrelsome intimacy, but which is so hedged with aggressive defenses that it is impossible for him to answer back.

Finally, a word about the Houyhnhnms. It is sometimes said that Swift is satirizing them as absurd or nasty embodiments of extreme rationalism. Apart from the element of humor, discussed earlier, with which they are presented, they are, it is said, conceited and obtuse in disbelieving the existence or the physical viability of the human creature. But, within the logic of the fiction, this disbelief seems natural enough. The Lilliputians also doubted the existence of men of Gulliver's size (I,iv), and Gulliver also needed explaining in Brobdingnag (II,iii). In both these cases the philosophers are characteristically silly, but everybody is intrigued, and we could hardly expect otherwise. Moreover, Gulliver tells Sympson that some human beings have doubted the existence of Houyhnhnms, which, within the terms of the story (if one is really going to take this sort of evidence solemnly), is just as arrogant. More important, the related Houyhnhnm doubt as to the anatomical viability or efficiency of the human shape (apart from being no more smug than some of Gulliver's complacencies *in favor* of mankind) turns to a biting sarcasm at man's, not at the Houyhnhnms', expense when, as we have seen, the Houyhnhnm master supposes that man is not capable of making war (IV,v).

The Houyhnhnms' proposal to castrate some younger Yahoos (IV,ix) has also shocked critics. But again this follows the simple narrative logic: it is no more than humans do to horses. Our shock should be no more than the "noble Resentment" of the Houyhnhnm master when he hears of the custom among us (IV,iv). To the extent that we *are* shocked, Swift seems to me to be meaning mildly to outrage our "healthy" sensibilities, as he does in the hoof-kissing episode. But in any event, the Houyhnhnms get the idea *from* Gulliver's account of what men do to horses, so that either way the force of the fable is not on man's side. The fiction throughout reverses the man-horse relationship: horses are degenerate in England (IV,xii), as men are in Houyhnhnmland. Again, I think man comes out of it badly both ways: the Yahoos of Houyhnhnmland make their obvious point, but the suggestion in reverse seems to be that English horses are poor specimens (though to Gulliver better than men) because they live in a bad human world. At least, a kind of irrational sense of guilt by association is generated. We need not suppose that Swift is endorsing Gulliver's preference of his horses to his family in order to feel offended about it. At many (sometimes indefinable) points on a complex scale of effects, Swift is getting at us.

The Houyhnhnms' expulsion of Gulliver belongs to the same group of objections. It seems to me that some of the sympathy showered on Gulliver by critics comes from a misfocused response to him as a full character in whom we are very involved as a person. The Houyhnhnm master and the sorrel nag are in fact very sorry to lose Gulliver, but the logic of the fable is inexorable: Gulliver is of the Yahoo kind, and his privileged position in Houyhnhnmland was offensive to some, while his rudiments of Reason threaten (not without plausibility, from all we learn of man's use of that faculty) to make him a danger to the state as leader of the wild Yahoos (IV,x). The expulsion of Gulliver is like Gulliver's treatment of Don Pedro: both episodes have been sentimentalized, but they are a harsh reminder that even good Yahoos are Yahoos.

The main charge is that the Houyhnhnms are cold, passionless, inhuman, unattractive to us and therefore an inappropriate positive model. The fact that we may not like them does not mean that Swift is disowning them: it is consistent with his whole style to nettle us with a positive we might find insulting and rebarbative. The older critics who disliked the Houyhnhnms but felt that Swift meant them as a positive were surely nearer the mark than some recent ones who translate their own dislikes into the meaning of the book. But one must agree that the Houyhnhnms, though they are a positive, are not a *model*, there being no question of our being able to imitate them. So far as it has not been grossly exaggerated, their "inhumanity" may well, like their literal *non*-humanity (which tells us that the only really rational animal is not man), be part of the satiric point: this is a matter of "passions."

They are, of course, not totally passionless. They treat Gulliver, in all personal contacts, with mildness, tenderness and friendly dignity (IV,i). Gulliver receives special gentleness and affection from his master, and still warmer tenderness from the sorrel nag (IV,xi).

Their language, which has no term for lying or opinion, "expressed the Passions very well," which may mean no more than "emotions" but does mean that they have them (IV,i). In contrast to the Laputans, who have no "Imagination, Fancy and Invention" (III,ii), but like the Brobdingnagians (II,vii), they excel in poetry (IV,ix), though their poems sound as if they might be rather unreadable and are certainly not enraptured effusions.

But their personal lives differ from ours in a kind of lofty tranquillity, and an absence of personal intimacy and emotional entanglement. In some aspects of this, they parallel Utopian Lilliput (I,vi), and when Gulliver is describing such things as their conversational habits ("Where there was no Interruption, Tediousness, Heat, or Difference of Sentiments"), a note of undisguised wishfulness comes into the writing (see the whole passage, IV,x). W. B. Carnochan has shown, in a well-taken point, that such freedom from the "tyrant-passions" corresponds to a genuine longing of Swift himself. I do not wish, and have no ability, to be psychoanalytical. But in a work which, in addition to much routine and sometimes rather self-conscious scatology (however "traditional"), contains the disturbing anatomy of Brobdingnagian ladies, the account of the Struldbrugs, the reeking sexuality of the Yahoos and the She-Yahoo's attempt on Gulliver, the horrible three-year-old Yahoo brat (IV,viii), the smell of Don Pedro and of Gulliver's family and Gulliver's strange relations with his wife, one might well expect to find aspirations for a society which practised eugenics and had an educational system in which personal and family intimacies were reduced to a minimum. Gulliver may be mocked, but the cumulative effect of these things is inescapable, and within the atmosphere of the work itself the longing for a world uncontaminated as far as possible by the vagaries of emotion might seem to us an unattractive, but is surely not a surprising, phenomenon.

But it is more important still to say that the Houyhnhnms are not a statement of what man ought to be so much as a statement of what he is not. Man thinks he is *animal rationale*, and the Houyhnhnms are a demonstration (which might, as we saw, be logically unacceptable, but is imaginatively powerful), for man to compare himself with, of what an *animal rationale* really is. R. S. Crane has shown that in the logic textbooks which commonly purveyed the old definition of man as a rational animal, the beast traditionally and most frequently named as a specific example of the opposite, the non-rational, was the horse. Thus Hudibras, who "was in logic a great critic," would

> undertake to prove by force
> Of argument, a man's no horse.

The choice of horses thus becomes an insulting exercise in "logical" refutation. The Yahoos are certainly an opposite extreme, and real man lies somewhere between them. But it is no simple comforting matter of a golden mean. Man is dramatically closer to the Yahoos in many ways, and with all manner of insistence. While the Houyhnhnms are an insulting impossibility, the Yahoos, though not a reality, are an equally insulting possibility. Swift's strategy of the undermining doubt is nowhere more evident than here, for though we are made to fear the worst, we are not given the comfort of knowing the worst. "The chief end I propose to my self in all my labors is to vex the world rather than divert it": and whatever grains of salt we may choose for our comfort to see in these words, "the world," gentle reader, includes *thee*.

KATHLEEN WILLIAMS

Giddy Circumstance

Of all Swift's mouthpieces, the "supposed author" of A *Tale of a Tub* is one of the least tangible. Gulliver, though changeable, is generally, except for particular uses, solid enough at a given moment, and the full extent and the precise nature of the satiric treatment he is to receive is only gradually revealed. But the Author of the *Tale* is from beginning to end a fantastic creature, a mere bundle of unrelated qualities. Though it is useful to speak of him so, it is not really possible to regard him as a person, when he is given such lines as these:

> In my Disposure of Employments of the Brain, I have thought fit to make Invention the Master, and give Method and Reason, the Office of its Lacquays. The Cause of this Distribution was, from observing it my peculiar Case, to be often under a Temptation of being Witty, upon Occasion, where I could be neither Wise nor Sound, nor any thing to the Matter in hand. And, I am too much a Servant of the Modern Way, to neglect any such Opportunities, whatever Pains or Improprieties I may be at, to introduce them.

The presentation of nonsense is, indeed, the Author's primary satiric function; fantasy, unreality, is what he is there to express. In a sense he is more simply conceived than Gulliver, being essentially a conglomeration of incompatible attitudes, all equally important,

From *Jonathan Swift and the Age of Compromise*, pp. 132–139. Lawrence: University of Kansas Press, 1958. Copyright © 1958 by the University of Kansas Press. Permission granted by the University Press of Kansas.

or unimportant, but in detail he works in a particularly elusive and shifting way. Swift's mouthpieces are one of his most flexible methods of indirection, of expressing his complicated meanings, but the Author of the *Tale* is least rigid of them all, for he has the special function of plunging us into chaos, confusion, self-deceit, a world of upheaval and destruction in which our own task, as readers, is to collect the scattered raw materials and rebuild our own attitudes to form a structure more firmly based upon reality.

In *A Tale of a Tub*, therefore, complexity is the rule, not, as in *The Battle of the Books*, an exception. The *Tale* is Swift's plunge into the chaos of mindless experience, "the unreality of the 'uncreating word'—the 'true No-meaning' which 'puzzles more than wit.' "[1] In it our mad world is parodied and heightened to a point where we can no longer believe it to be sane; every fragment of the broken truth is shattered into still smaller, scintillating pieces, and only the barest and most casually indirect hints are given to help us in the task of fitting them together into their proper shape. In all this activity Swift is, of course, far from irresponsible; the process is one of deliberate and purposeful destruction, and the simpler parts of the book, those which constitute the allegory of the three churches in the shape of the brothers Peter, Martin, and Jack, are a kind of key to the method and intention of those dazzling chapters which contain so much of the meaning and which are with wilful wrongheadedness described as "Digressions."

Apart from satiric hits at particular practices of the Roman Catholics and the Dissenters, and a good deal of incidental fun, the main theme of the allegory of the churches is of a gradual departure from given truth, a steady descent into self-deceit. Because they wish to do various things which under the terms of their father's will they are not permitted to do, the three brothers allow themselves to be deceived and become more and more adept at using their reason in the service of their passions until, by great ingenuity, they are able to find in the will permission to add whatever decorations they wish to their simple coats. The plain command "to wear no sort of Silver Fringe upon or about their said Coats" is evaded by a judicious use of mythological and allegorical senses; shoulder-knots are found to be permissible by the fitting together of separate letters in the will, a method invented by Peter: " 'Tis true, said he, there is nothing here in this Will, *totidem verbis*, making mention of Shoulder-knots, but I dare conjecture, we may find them *inclusivé*, or *totidem syllabis*." And having failed here: "Brothers, there

1. W. K. Wimsatt, "The Augustan Mode in English Poetry," *Journal of English Literary History*, XX, 9.

is yet Hopes; for tho' we cannot find them *totidem verbis*, nor *totidem syllabis*, I dare engage we shall make them out *tertio modo*, or *totidem literis*." Peter remains in this mad world of fantasy excused by a show of reason, but the other brothers, having been kicked out of doors, begin to reflect seriously upon their misfortune and its causes, and decide to return strictly to the terms of their father's will. Martin pulls off all the lace, fringe, and other decoration that he can, but stops when he finds that some of it is so tightly attached that he cannot remove it without tearing the coat itself, "resolving in no Case whatsoever, that the Substance of the Stuff should suffer Injury; which he thought the best Method for serving the true Intent and Meaning of his Father's Will." Jack, however, tears away decoration, coat, and all, ending in rags and tatters still ornamented by a few of Peter's most elaborate embroideries. In fact there is great danger in tearing away too drastically the deceits of our passions and desires; some of them may be, or may have become, an integral part of our nature. There are, as so often, two satiric standards: the will, by which all the churches, as all human-ity, stand condemned, and the compromise standard, the best that can practically be achieved by half-blind humanity, the conduct of the reformed Martin.[2]

The story of the three brothers has, in itself, less than Swift's usual power, and perhaps the lowering of intensity has the same cause here as in *The Battle of the Books*, that all is too plain; the work has been done for us. The compromise solution has been reached and exists before us in Martin. But though it is compara-tively low-powered if taken in isolation, the allegory of the churches has an essential part to play in the work as a whole, for the Digres-sions circle about a very similar theme. The Author of the *Tale* is himself an example of the very process through which Jack, the dis-senting brother, passes in the story which he himself recounts to us. He indulges in all the word-spinning which all three brothers use under the guidance of Peter, and with his wild theories and elabo-rate analogies, with his digression in praise of digressions, he is a perfect instance of the modern spider producing a cobwebby book out of his own entrails, just as the Dissenters initiated, according to Swift's sermon "Upon the Martyrdom," a "sect of religion that

2. No doubt Swift had in mind that "moderns" of various kinds, as well as the dissenters, were anxious to simplify religion. It was often the cloak for Deism and so was regarded with double suspicion. Fontenelle remarks with some regret, in *The History of Oracles:* "Meantime these Prejudices that have got into the true Religion are, as I may say, so closely interwoven with it, that they have attracted a Respect to themselves, which is only due to the true Religion; and we dare not censure the One for fear of attacking at the same time something that is sacred in the Other." This is precisely Martin's problem, and Swift himself has a worried comment on the question in his *Thoughts on Religion*.

grew out of their own bowels."[3] But though he is in fact so totally immersed in deceit that he can utter only nonsense, he considers himself to be a great reasoner, and a formidable enemy of "prejudice." Like Jack, and with as sorry results, he proposes to free himself from all such deceit, but he exists in the incoherent world of giddy circumstance that his whirling style and his proud presentation of nonsense so perfectly symbolize. Recognizing neither the weakness of reason nor the strength of deceit, he struggles, caught in his own cobweb but believing it to be a strong and rational structure; and in so nonsensical an atmosphere the difficulty for the reader is in determining, from the chaotic opinions of the supposed Author, what conclusions the true author intends us to reach.

From the outset we are aware that the Author is the object of satire, since this is established immediately by the use of parody; and from his opening words to Prince Posterity, self-importantly submitting "the Fruits of a very few leisure Hours, stollen from the short Intervals of a World of Business, and of an Employment quite alien from such Amusements as this," to the final promise to pause "till I find, by feeling the World's Pulse, and my own, that it will be of absolute Necessity for us both, to resume my Pen," he is clearly there to be laughed at. Having seen this, we assume that by reversing his values we will arrive at his creator's meaning; the Author, we feel complacently, may be astray in a fairyland of dreams, but we at least have our wits about us; we can see what is really intended. But this confidence is soon shaken by the intellectual pyrotechnics of Swift himself; we are continually pulled on to what seems to be firm ground, where we feel that we know just what is absurd in the remarks of the Author—and therefore, by implication, what is sensible—only to be pushed briskly off again into chaos. The experience is purely enjoyable; what we feel is a breathless exhilaration at being swept along in this lively mental activity, rather than a sense of loss and alarm. We share the true author's creative liberty, not the supposed Author's captivity in chaos. This, perhaps, is why the *Tale* has less power to disturb than *Gulliver's Travels*; in the later work we are faced by a frightening emptiness which forces us to the task of reconstruction, but here we can be content to enjoy, with Swift, the vigorous power of mind. And if there is less incentive, and less urgency, in working out meanings—as in Swift's satire we are always required to do—there is also more difficulty; because of the utter incoherence of the Author it is harder than usual to recognize where Swift is leading us.

In *Gulliver's Travels* and the shorter satiric pieces we have firm guidance from Swift; when once we are accustomed to his tone of

3. *Prose Works of Jonathan Swift*, ed. Herbert Davis (Basil Blackwell, 1937), IX, 226.

voice we can gauge with some accuracy what we should take seriously and what not. We are familiar with the apology for some
suggestion which everyone will think foolish, as in the paradox
timidly put forward by the author of *An Argument against Abolishing Christianity* that he does not yet see the absolute necessity of
extirpating the Christian religion; with the scorn for a point of
view, as in Gulliver's sneer at Brobdingnagian "Prejudices, and Narrowness of thinking"; with the grudging approval—"the least corrupted are the Brobdingnagians." We recognize Swift's guidance in
Gulliver's enthusiasm first for Britain and later for Houyhnhnmland, in his exaggerated complaints in his letter to his cousin Sympson, and in the exaggerated calm with which the writer of the
Modest Proposal puts forward his desperate remedy. But in *A Tale
of a Tub* all the opinions expressed appear equally ridiculous and
are expressed in the same fantastic style; the Author is himself a
style rather than a person, and his function is to display the madness of deceit and the greater madness of supposing that we are ever
free of it, this being the greatest deceit of all. Various philosophies
and particular philosophers are put forward as examples of the
modern Author's madness, again and again self-deceit masquerades
as reason, and in this atmosphere all value is negated. If we concentrate too exclusively on the fantastic Author as the object of the
satire, exact meanings are difficult to catch, for he can misunder-
stand, misrepresent, contradict his own findings, with the utmost
complacency, and he has no firm, even momentarily firm, opinion
which with Swift's guidance we can learn to disregard. The *Tale*
consists, so far as the Digressions are concerned, entirely of aberra-
tions from a norm which is barely suggested; in none of Swift's satires is positive value more indirectly expressed. This, presumably, is
why it has been called negative and destructive intellectual activity
designed to no end. Yet there are values in the *Tale*, though we
must shake off the supposed Author in order to see them, for he is
not, like Gulliver, a man of mistaken and changing values, which
we can allow for, but a man of no values at all, intended not so
much to express meaning as to nullify it.

It has been demonstrated in recent years that in several passages
of *A Tale of a Tub* Swift is specifically attacking certain modern
positions,[4] particularly those which are frankly materialist, like
"Epicureanism" and Hobbism, or those which so concentrate on
systematizing the physical world that the spiritual basis of that
world is forgotten. To Swift, of course, either materialism or a blind
pursuit of second causes is wrong, morally as well as intellectually,
since for him the world can only be properly interpreted in a con-

4. See Miriam K. Starkman, *Swift's Satire on Learning in "A Tale of a Tub"*
(Princeton, 1950).

text of moral truth enforced by divine authority. This firm positive standard is present throughout the allegorical part of the *Tale*, and in reading we do in fact carry over into the Digressions the standard we have absorbed from the story of the three brothers, comparing not only Peter and Jack but the Author and all the philosophies he jumbles together, with the sound and sensible Martin, and, behind him, with the supreme authority of *"Christiana Religio absoluta et simplex"* which he does his human best to embody. The flimsy uncertain world of the Digressions is seen against the certainty, solidity, and centrality of the Will and the three coats made of cloth "so neatly sown, you would swear they were all of a Piece." The two parts of the book are deliberately linked at several points; for instance, the satire on materialism in Section II, the description of the tailor idol and of his worshippers' belief in the micro-coat and macro-coat, takes the story of the three coats into the world of the Digressions, as the clear factual narrative style slips into the fantastic analogies and proudly produced false conclusions, so dear to the heart of the Author:

> What is that which some call Land, but a fine Coat faced with Green? or the Sea, but a Wastcoat of Water-Tabby? Proceed to the particular Works of the Creation, you will find how curious Journey-man Nature hath been, to trim up the vegetable Beaux....
> That the Soul was the outward, and the Body the inward Cloathing; that the latter was *ex traduce*; but the former of daily Creation and Circumfusion. This last they proved by Scripture, because in Them we Live, and Move, and have our Being: As likewise by Philosophy, because they are All in All, and All in every Part. Besides, said they, separate these two, and you will find the Body to be only a senseless unsavory Carcass. By all which it is manifest, that the outward Dress must needs be the Soul.

But the *Tale* is not primarily an attack on modern materialism as such. In his account of the doctrine "That the Soul was the outward, and the Body the inward Cloathing" Swift parodies not Hobbist but Scholastic terminology, for all such intricate reasonings move steadily away from reality; even when soul is not denied it is reasoned out of any useful existence, and with it morality, until religion is a cloak, honesty a pair of shoes worn out in the dirt, and a man can cry, "That Fellow has no Soul; where is his Shoulder-Knot?" Modern and ancient philosophies are attacked not so much in and for themselves but as illustrations of the spider-like reasoning which, because it disregards the firm outlines laid down by morality, tradition, and experience, moves into fantasy and leaves the mind spinning in a dead world, devoid of the true meaning which only "unrefined reason," the reasonable acceptance of revealed truth and morality, can find and which Martin approximately represents. Without the madness of uncontrolled reasoning and systematizing all mankind would be reduced to the "same Belief in Things Invisible." The world of fantasy presented in the Digressions is dead because it lacks the meaning which can be given to it only by a mind content to keep close to the known, to experience, and humbly depending upon the divine mind which alone can interpret its own creation. As so often in Swift, much is expressed by an accumulation of imagery, and the language of the *Tale* is full of images of lightness, shallowness, superficiality, and all that can suggest the meaningless. The Author is obsessed by surfaces and rinds and shells, by the footless Bird of Paradise which must fly up until it crashes to the ground, by "Edifices in the Air," by all that is "light enough to swim upon the surface for all Eternity," all that is "lofty and light" and soars above the earth. The pulpit of dissent is a symbol of the writings of the modern saints, "as they have spiritualized and refined them from the Dross and Grossness of Sense and Human Reason," because it is made of rotten wood, full of wormholes and shining in the dark, giving out the ghostly "Inward Light" of phosphorescence. Dead wood, rotten and treacherous and shining with an unreal light—the image sums up the whole world of madness, as does the Aeolist substitution of wind for spirit. The primary error of the Aeolists is that in their anxiety to escape from a world of sense into pure spirituality they have only sunk deeper into the power of the body, the passions, and the deceiving senses: and this happens to all who try to escape, whether by way of the spirit or by way of the reason. They end in a place of no-meaning, where revelation gives way to the Delphic oracle, where Saints and conquerors and philosophers are indiscriminately engendered and where a man may be a comparatively harmless Aeolist or an Alexander or a Descartes, doing infinite damage. For in this state, no moral standards exist.

MARTIN PRICE

Swift's Rhetorical Art

In A *Tale of a Tub* Swift dramatizes the corruptions of religion and learning in two ways: the allegory embodies in the career of

From *Swift's Rhetorical Art: A Study in Structure and Meaning*, pp. 78–82. New Haven: Yale University Press, 1953. Reprinted by permission of the author.

typical Restoration fops the history of the church in the world, and the prefaces and digressions embody in a continuous dramatic monologue the bathos and pretentious folly of the modern spirit. The monologue includes numerous symbolic accounts of the corruption of learning; they are presented as a panegyric upon the moderns, but they are written in the language of a man so obtuse and uncritical that he unwittingly betrays his case at every turn. Since Swift is concerned with the misuse of religion to serve "schemes of wealth and power," his allegory treats religion on the level of manners, as one more means of achieving self-aggrandizement or domination at the expense of reason. True religion can survive only if man serves God; when man serves himself and seeks "sublunary happiness" as an end in itself, as Swift frequently points out, he may use *nominal* Christianity as an instrument, but he has already discarded true Christianity. The three brothers of the allegory slay "certain Dragons" but soon come to the town, the *grand monde* or world of fashion. They cease, in short, to redeem the time but live for it instead, and fashion becomes Swift's principal symbol of this absorption in the world.

Much of the *Tale* is built around the contrast of the temporal or fashionable and the permanent or timeless. The Epistle to Prince Posterity first shows the inevitable conflict of Time and the ambitions of a time-bound generation. The moderns seek distinction rather than truth, and they seek it by novelty and singularity, by ignoring the universal or enduring. Though they seek to reach Posterity by evading the judgment of Time, their works vanish before they can so much as offer them. In seeking distinction, the moderns wish to *conquer* the past. "I here think fit," says the Tale Teller, "to lay hold on that great and honourable Privilege of being the *Last Writer*; I claim an absolute Authority in Right, as the *freshest Modern*, which gives me a Despotick Power over all Authors before me." The result of this view is self-indulgence—private meaning, "tender wit," ephemeral achievement. The Tale Teller's demonstration of his own age's greatness collapses, and he is finally left clinging to the specious present: "what I am going to say is literally true this Minute I am writing."

What is ephemeral, however, may be praised all the more as fashionable, and Swift uses clothes symbolism to present this inversion. The three coats of the brothers (the simple and plain truths of doctrine) become, in their misuse, the instruments of pride and worldly ambition. The Tale Teller is ready to systematize this, and he presents us with an inverted theology to support inverted practices and institutions. The God of the clothes philosophy is the tailor, who "daily create[s] Men, by a kind of Manufactory Operation." His creatures, which "the World calls improperly *Suits of Cloaths*," are "in Reality the most refined Species of Animals"—in fact, "Rational Creatures, or Men." The soul of man is really his celestial or outer suit, daily created anew, and its faculties are parts of dress:

> *Embroidery,* was *Sheer wit; Gold Fringe* was *agreeable Conversation,* Gold Lace was Repartee, a huge long *Periwig* was *Humour,* and a *Coat full of Powder* was very good *Raillery:* All which required abundance of *Finesse* and *Delicatesse* to manage with Advantage, as well as strict Observance after Times and Fashions.

The implications are clear: when the end of man is self-love and distinction and his means singularity or fashion, he has no standards which endure, no integrity. In a sense, he has ceased to have a soul at all, for when religion and the soul cease to be regulatory and moral they have become lackeys rather than masters and no longer deserve their original names: "Is not Religion a *Cloak,* Honesty a *Pair of Shoes,* worn out in the Dirt, Self-love a *Surtout,* Vanity a *Shirt,* and Conscience a *Pair of Breeches,* which, tho' a Cover for Lewdness as well as Nastiness, is easily slipt down for the Service of both."

Elsewhere, Swift deals at length with the instability of happiness as a human end. The pagan philosophers, never able to agree about the *summum bonum,* either became cynical skeptics or, for lack of any solid faith, were inclined "to fall into the vulgar pursuits of common men, to hunt after greatness and riches, to make their court, and to serve occasions." The world offers no stable end; only heavenly wisdom ("a daily vision of God") can provide it.[1] To return to the words of the *Tale,* "as human Happiness is of a very short Duration, so in those Days were human Fashions, upon which it entirely depends." The very nature of fashion makes every victory a necessary defeat. The pattern of natural man for Swift, as for Hobbes, shows him endlessly acquisitive and endlessly unsatisfied.[2] Such limited self-love involves the need for superiority or pre-eminence; at best it retains the spirit of opposition, the love of party or sect. Reason seeks victory instead of truth and becomes sophistry in the process. Knowledge gives way to an imagination which can frame a gratifying image of the world. The soul itself becomes a mere image of the fashions of the day, an ever-changing garment of the body whose needs it now serves. Over all this, as

1. *On the Wisdom of This World,* in *The Prose Writings of Jonathan Swift,* ed. Herbert Davis (Oxford, 1939), IX, 244, 248. Hereafter cited as HD.
2. "For learning, like all true merit, is easily satisfied; while the false and counterfeit is perpetually craving, and never thinks it has enough." *The Prose Works of Jonathan Swift,* ed. Temple Scott (London, 1907–1908), XI, 20. Hereafter cited as TS.

Swift wrote elsewhere, hovers the threat of Time, the instrument of
judgment: "Principles, as the world goes, are little more than fashion; and the apostle tells us, that 'the fashion of this world passeth
away.' "[3]

The *Tale* points throughout to a middle way that lies between
opposed forms of corruption. Reason is always a balance between
extremes of refinement and superficiality or, as we might put it, idle
curiosity and naive credulity. Refinement takes the form of theoriz-
ing, of finding at any expense meanings which can be built into a
system. It is the typical seventeenth-century crime of wresting Scriptures carried into the realms of criticism, science, and philosophy.
The piety of the Tale Teller requires that the hacks of Grub Street
be revealed as "*Grubaean* Sages," their works as "Vehicles of Types
and Fables" containing the "most finished and refined Systems of
all Science and Arts." But the systems can only be revealed by
"Untwisting or Unwinding"; much industry is required to force
impressive meaning from trivialities.

The systems themselves are either built, like "Edifices in the Air"
out of sight and hearing, completely beyond empirical test, or they
may be turned into "Oratorial Machines," devices for raising dema-
gogues to a position from which they may dominate the crowd. So,
too, the three ladies who lead the brothers away from simplicity are
"at the very Top of the Fashion." In both cases height is the departure from the common forms which confers distinction and authority. Each system builder seeks to conquer all of nature, as do the
moderns all of literature, and thereby to overthrow all rival systems.
The Tale Teller boasts of an essay on the number three: "I have by
most convincing Proofs, not only reduced the *Senses* and the *Elements* under its Banner, but brought over several Deserters from its
two great Rivals *SEVEN* and *NINE*." The system builder becomes,
in short, the hero in the universe of fashion. Swift places together all
revolutions "in empire, philosophy, and religion." Each is achieved
by the conqueror's reduction of "Multitudes to his own *Power*, his
Reasons or his *Visions*." The patterns of conqueror, bully, and
tyrant all contribute to the archetype by which proselytizing and
system building are to be understood. In his account of Bedlam
Swift finally shows the fundamental standard of this inverted world;
madness is only heroism out of fashion.

The story of the three brothers is itself one of the typical modern
systems, a reductive allegory of the history of the church from its
primitive simplicity to its division and further corruption under the
pretense of reformation and counterreformation. The story, how-

3. "Advertisement to the Reader," *Memoirs of Captain John Creichton*, TS,
XI, 167. Cf. I Corinthians 7:31.

ever, is more than allegory; it provides a causal explanation of these corruptions in terms of personal morality. It allows Swift to study the individual motives which underlie the decay of religion, while the Tale Teller presents specious rationalization for a comparable decay in learning. Swift reduces the behavior of the churches to that of fops and gallants, while the Tale Teller refines foppery and gallantry into mock religion.

The culmination of Swift's satiric point comes with the reduction of man to mechanism. Swift once noted that "climbing is performed in the same Posture with Creeping."[4] In the same way pretension which seeks to lift man above reason can also reduce him to the mechanism of physical causation. Man loses freedom when he surrenders the power of *rational* choice, and his visions have a way of turning out to be irrational compulsions. This is best illustrated in the fate of words: as sound replaces meaning and words are "spiritualized and refined . . . from the Dross and Grossness of Sense and Human Reason," their operation may be described in "physico-logical" terms. Words become weapons rather than symbols; they are "Bodies of much Weight and Gravity, as it is manifest from those deep *Impressions* they make and leave upon us; and therefore must be delivered from a due Altitude, or else they will neither carry a good Aim, nor fall down with a sufficient Force." When words are reduced to mere forceful sound, all sound becomes operative. The uncritical audience which abandons a standard of rational communication treasures all forms of expression or stimulation. "For, the *Spirit* being the same in all, it is of no Import through what Vehicle it is convey'd." And Swift, in *The Mechanical Operation of the Spirit*, provides a picture of that preromantic personality, the evangelistic preacher of the Puritans: "A Master Work-man shall *blow his Nose so powerfully*, as to pierce the Hearts of his People, who are disposed to receive the *Excrements* of his Brain with the same Reverence, as the *Issue* of it. Hawking, Spitting, and Belching, the Defects of other Mens Rhetorick, are the Flowers, and Figures, and Ornaments of his."

Again, the Tale Teller readily systematizes the doctrine of the Aeolists, who value inspiration and take all eccentricity to be divine possession. Their "inspiration" is literalized to the point where they affirm "the Gift of BELCHING to be the noblest Act of a Rational Creature." The Aeolists do not disclaim rationality but simply invert its meaning, just as the moderns do not dismiss religion but turn it into the worship of fashion. Swift makes Aeolism a substitution both of the physical for the truly rational and of self-induced

4. *Thoughts on Various Subjects*, HD, I, 245 (TS, I, 277).

disease for normal health. His scheme may be reduced to a matrix somewhat as follows:

CORRUPTION		DECENCY	
Principle	Expression	Expression	Principle
passion	flatulency	health	reason
display	belching	speech	communication
imagination	cant	meaning	thought
domination	sound	argument	persuasion

This scheme could be extended in several ways—for example, the kinds of effect achieved in each case, conviction or ecstasy, comprehension or titillation.[5]

Reason may be neglected by the bestial Aeolists or transcended by the sophistical system builders. Swift brings the two groups together in his digression on madness. The vapors of the brain are fed by the lower parts of the body: "Mists arise from the Earth, Steams from Dunghills, Exhalations from the Sea, and Smoak from Fire; yet all Clouds are the same in Composition, as well as Consequences: and the Fumes issuing from a Jakes, will furnish as comely and useful a Vapor, as Incense from an Altar . . . [The vapors may be repressed sexuality, the rains a bursting storm of conquest.] The same Spirits, which in their superior Progress would conquer a Kingdom, descending upon the *Anus*, conclude in a *Fistula*." Higher and lower become transposed terms in this inverted world; the physical expression is at least less harmful than the spiritual. Both forms of expression are escapes from rational control, and all their issue in human conduct is an inversion of rational order, whether social or religious, poetic or rhetorical. In place of order man enjoys the endless whirl of fashion and the endless competition for distinction and power.

5. For the use of a matrix, see Scott Buchanan, *Symbolic Distance in Relation to Analogy and Fiction* (London, Psyche Miniatures, 1932).

ROBERT M. ADAMS

Satiric Incongruity and the Inner Defeat of the Mind

Although the world of satire is traditionally a world of disorganization and dislocation, it is typically seen by an eye which knows something better and which can emphasize the disorder by contrast-

From *Strains of Discord: Studies in Literary Openness*, pp. 146–157. Ithaca, New York: Cornell University Press, 1958. Copyright © 1958 by Cornell University. Used by permission of Cornell University Press.

ing it with an understood or remembered order, a standard of excellence somehow known or implied. For this reason, mock heroic is one of the natural modes of satire. It has sometimes been observed, however, that the effect of constant mock-heroic juxtaposition is to exalt Dullness, or Duplicity, into a heroic quality. It has not so often been emphasized that satire may also dissolve the order which ostensibly serves as a foil for disorder, leaving the author and reader bewildered amid a glare of glittering, cutting incongruities. An example of such satire, many-faceted and sharp-edged, is Jonathan Swift's *Tale of a Tub*, with its appendages *The Battle of the Books* and *A Discourse Concerning the Mechanical Operation of the Spirit*. It is a bold, hard, angular engine, which still cannot be carelessly handled without danger of a slash.

Swift's hydra headed satire is in many respects a work peculiar to its time. The ancients-versus-moderns controversy, around which much of the satire is grouped, was strictly ephemeral. The sort of reading which Swift's book implies (like that which it attacks) was already outmoded; important objects of his satire, the fanatic preachers, were essentially creatures of the dying century. The very manner of the book which is shapeless, rhapsodic, stuffed with learning and authorial crotchets, clearly derives from that wonderful, crazy century which had produced *The Anatomy of Melancholy* and William Prynne, *Pseudodoxia Epidemica* and the Fifth Monarchy Men—not to mention *Don Quixote*. Thus, the "corruptions in Religion and Learning" against which the author leveled his lance were in outward form at least those of a bygone or bygoing day. But *A Tale of a Tub* is not to be understood as a mechanical derivation from the social circumstances of the time, much less as a collection of intellectual factors piled together in a basket of "moral realism." If there is one thing clear about Swift, it is the high tension at which his mind operated, its impatient energy, its tendency to dominate and use intellectual material. His prose, even when polished to a high gloss, is always muscular; and its muscles are always at work. His jokes, his games, his private languages and little societies, his paradoxes, and all the dramatic contrasts of his life, which furnish such rich material for the biographer, the dramatist, and the purveyor of avowed or unavowed fiction, are also evidence of an emotional and intellectual turbulence which made him the theater of an endless struggle. He did not develop placidly, one more chain-linked bacillus on a neo-Stoic string; his mind was torn by agonies of conflict before he possessed the ideological framework to explain or the symbolic dress in which to clothe it; and his book is the expression quite as much of a temperament as of an era. One illustration of this fact derives from a contrast between *A Tale of a*

Tub and *Gulliver's Travels*. Gulliver is much the more polished performance; it has a clarity of outline and concept which is scarcely broken, and a steady progression of symbols. The ragged edges of Swift's fury have been buried within a deliberately smooth, deceptive surface, like broken glass set in concrete. A *Tale of a Tub*, on the other hand, is all hard, raw, self-assured, and fantastic in its angled bravado. It lacks a good deal in scheme and symbols, in shape and structure—not that the book fails to exploit its own lacks in these regards; because it is committed to so little, it makes all the more capital of its freedom to mock structure as well as lack of structure—but for this very reason it exposes more nakedly the bare bones and quivering nerves of Swift's logical and emotional conflicts. One cannot help feeling that in A *Tale of a Tub* Swift was reaching into the deepest, and most immediate, background of frustrations, which were partly psychological and partly philosophical but which determined and involved his whole existence as an individual. If his reading, as he declared, was all fresh in his head, so also were his angers and humiliations; and out of the two he created a work altogether original—one which he flung on the counters of a shopkeeping nation with the rage of a man who finds he has been handed a counterfeit coin.

One of the key scenes of A *Tale of a Tub*, which gave contemporary opinion one of its rudest shocks, shows Peter establishing for his brothers the doctrine of transubstantiation. He carves them a couple of pieces of bread and pretends that it is mutton. After some discussion:

> "What, then, My Lord," replied the first, "it seems this is a shoulder of mutton all this while." "Pray, sir," says Peter, "eat your vittles and leave off your impertinence, if you please, for I am not disposed to relish it at present." But the other could not forbear, being overprovoked at the affected seriousness of Peter's countenance. "By G——, My Lord," said he, "I can only say that to my eyes and fingers and teeth and nose it seems to be nothing but a crust of bread." Upon which, the second put in his word: "I never saw a piece of mutton in my life so nearly resembling a slice from a twelve-penny loaf." "Look ye, gentlemen," cries Peter in a rage, "to convince you what a couple of blind, positive, ignorant, wilful puppies you are, I will use but this plain argument: By G——, it is true, good, natural mutton as any in Leaden-Hall market, and G—— confound you both eternally, if you offer to believe otherwise."

Peter's outburst of hysterical rage is in the dominant key of A *Tale of a Tub*; like the weaver of the Preface, he speaks in the thick, choked accents of violent fury—a fury which at once perpetrates and exposes a gross, outrageous fraud. If we suppose one of the central concerns of the book to be the discovery and rejection of fraud, it will appear as the expression of a temperament and a function only secondarily determined by social circumstance and prudential motives. Swift denounces in A Tale of a Tub the two forms of fraud and corruption that time and circumstance had rendered most obnoxious. But the relish with which he goes about his denunciations and the lengths to which he carries them express a purely personal need. So much intense and peculiar pleasure seemed to lie in the uprooting of deceit and corruption that truth and health, even if found, could only have appeared as a disappointment.

But this denunciation of fraud, while an overriding concern of the author, is not the principle on which A Tale of a Tub is organized. Neither can the book be wholly described as an exposé of the innocent who pretends to be its author, important as this theme doubtless is. Although its surface is flauntingly and defiantly incoherent, A Tale of a Tub is, I think, chiefly held together by a pair of images which achieve explicit statement only in a fragment never fully incorporated in the book itself, though constantly associated with it. A Discourse Concerning the Mechanical Operation of the Spirit places in opposition two concepts, the machine and the spirit, which had been deeply involved in the history of the seventeenth century and in the experience of Jonathan Swift. These two concepts are also, and singularly, themes common to the story of Jack, Peter, and Martin, to the digressions, and to the (no less than five) comments prefatory to A Tale of a Tub. The wind and the machine are of central, summary importance to Swift, his book, and his time; he is equally hostile to both, and, though he generally uses one to mock the other, he sometimes plays audaciously at identifying them.

The "spirit" for which Swift feels such antipathy is a quality that takes many forms; in one of his formal moments the author distinguishes manifestations of the spirit according to their origin, as the products of divine inspiration, diabolic possession, inner motives (imagination, anger, fear, grief, pain, etc.), or mechanical manipulation. But the spirit shows itself in all sorts of ways which cannot be so strictly catalogued: in self-importance (the greedy importunity of the bookseller, the lofty airs of the starving author, the alleged delusions of Descartes); in dogmatic ignorance; in esoteric doctrines, numerology, and elaborate word spinnings; in the deliberate vagaries of digression counterdigressed by digression; in the pretensions of the modern age over the ancients; in the interpretive triumph of the three brothers over their father's will; in military conquests; in the lucky victory of the madman over the sane.

What precisely is the spirit? It is agitated air, "a redundancy of vapors," whether denominated enthusiasm, hysteria, or inspiration; its exponents are the learned Aeolists, a set of inflated gapers after air; it is the effective cause of conquests and systems, of faction and madness. Its normal seat is in the lungs, the belly, and the genitals; denied adequate expression here, it may rise to the brain and afflict that organ with a vapor. What the difference is between overt, acknowledged madness and those forms of undeclared madness which are socially rewarded Swift half offers to make clear; but the explanation dissolves into a *Hiatus in MS*, and the satiric edge of his wit is turned against all forms of wind, because all make, or are capable of making, man turbulent and fantastic.

> For the brain in its natural position and state of serenity disposeth its owner to pass his life in the common forms, without any thought of subduing multitudes to his own power, his reasons, or his visions; and the more he shapes his understanding by the pattern of human learning, the less he is inclined to form parties after his particular notions, because that instructs him in his private infirmities, as well as in the stubborn ignorance of the people. But when a man's fancy gets astride on his reason, when imagination is at cuffs with the senses, and common understanding as well as common sense is kickt out of doors, the first proselyte he makes is himself, and when that is once compass'd the difficulty is not so great in bringing over others—a strong delusion always operating from without as vigorously as from within.

The function and title of the book are themselves involved in the image of the spirit as an explosive "redundancy of vapors"; the wits of the age having been found to threaten the church and state, a project for diverting their energies was sought; and as whales are given a tub to play with in order to divert them from attacking a ship, so *A Tale of a Tub* was produced to divert the wits who, puffed up with modern presumption and armed with sharp weapons from Hobbes's *Leviathan*, were becoming dangerous. Thus the mechanical excitement and mechanical manipulation of wind into one social form or another become the predominant images of Swift's satire; and while no more precise definitions are made of the sort of wind or the sort of social form satirized, the nature of the wind or spirit particularly is pretty clear. The weight of Swift's attack lies against the private spirit, the irrational personal conviction of logical rightness, physical authority, or spiritual justification.

How heavy that weight lies may be realized when one notes the vast arsenal of satiric weapons with which Swift assaults the spirit and its manifestations. He persistently implies that all forms of inspiration are of the two lower varieties—neither divine nor diabolic in origin, but the product of imaginative self-indulgence or of deliberate mechanical manipulation, of lust, filth, greed, or folly. Thus he explains an imperial conquest as the effect of an unsatisfied erection, imputes pulpit eloquence to sexual excitement, and bitterly derogates all forms of enthusiasm by equating the winds which puff them up.

> Mists arise from the earth, steams from dunghills, exhalations from the sea, and smoke from fire; yet all clouds are the same in composition as well as consequences, and the fumes issuing from a jakes will furnish as comely and useful a vapor as incense from an altar.

All clouds are the same, in composition as well as consequences; that is to say, all clouds and vapors are degrading to human nature. Sex and excrement are the unremitting associates of spiritual inspiration, the mechanical foundations on which enthusiasms are founded and to which they inevitably revert. No more terrible and degrading association is open to Swift's imagination. The preacher whose canting reaches its height in an act of physical orgasm; the prince whose urge to conquest derives from unexpended semen; the Aeolists, who worship in circles "with every man a pair of bellows applied to his neighbor's breech"; the female priests, ancient and modern, "whose organs were understood to be better disposed for the admission of those oracular gusts"; the Aeolian admiration for belching (especially, by a fine touch of art, through the nose) and for the ancient institution of barrels, from which air is introduced, through funnels, to the breech—all bespeak an aversion which, for Swift, amounted almost to phobia. The similarity that Swift affects to discover between Jack and Peter, the church of Geneva and that of Rome, is found upon their mutual susceptibility to wind, "the phrenzy and the spleen of both having the same foundation." And for Swift no more repulsive view of the human species is conceivable than that of the inflated and presumptuous Aeolist.

But though the primary edge of the *Tale of a Tub* is directed against the windy Aeolists and their most picturesque exemplars, the fanatic sectarians, the book's emotional structure is not that of an author secure in his possession of "that natural position and state of security" which enables a man "to pass his life in the common forms." One could look for no better example of the placid, adjusted man than Swift's great enemy William Wotton, whose reaction to the *Tale of a Tub* was one of unqualified horror. Although Swift's theological blasphemies may have been exaggerated, his raging contempt for the whole race of moderns can scarcely be overstated; and surely this implies, on the face of it, a considerable contempt for the "common forms." Indeed, a treatise so fantastic, sardonic, and derisive as A *Tale of a Tub* could scarcely

culminate in a calm conformity; the expenditure of so much nerv-
ous ingenuity merely to endorse the "common forms" would be at
the least a paradox, akin to that by which the fourth book of *Gulliver* may be read as the most passionate denunciation of passion
ever penned. Undoubtedly *A Tale of a Tub* partakes of this paradoxical character; and Swift (or at least his author-mask) is explicit
in his recognition of the fact:

> Even I myself, the author of these momentous truths, am a per-
> son whose imaginations are hard-mouthed, and exceedingly dis-
> posed to run away with his reason, which I have observed from
> long experience to be a very light rider, and easily shook off.

But there is a further complexity to *A Tale of a Tub*; the problem
is not simply that the satiric attack includes, in some measure, as its
object the author himself; it is that the point of view from which
one satire is launched is itself the object of a second attack, and the
"common forms" into which the sane and ordinary mind placidly
fits are ridiculed under the aspect of a machine.

The story of Jack, Peter, and Martin, the Calvinist, Roman Catholic, and Lutheran churches, is ostensibly a story in which the reasonable *via media* of the church of England is upheld against the
superstition of Rome and the crude, violent inspirations of the
sects. The satire upon the philosophers of wind, likewise, tends to
support the reasonable, common-sense judgment of the enlightened,
unprejudiced few. But Martin's placid responses to Jack are ridiculed as the tricky devices of a cunning debater; and the three
machines, of ladder, pulpit, and stage itinerant, are presented as the
types of all modern authorship—grotesque devices of elevation to
facilitate the puffing of air into a multitude. Here once more the
author introduces himself and his own book within the framework
of the satire, describing his present production as a work of the
stage itinerant; and indeed, there is no evident principle (save
obiter dictum) by which any work or author could be exempted
from the satire. Swift's hatred of the moderns (which is a principle
more vital to him than love of the ancients) seems to allow no
room for exceptions, no escape from primitive presumption and
mechanical craft.

Not only is the machine a frequent device for controlling the
escape of redundant vapor (as most schemes of religion and government resemble tubs in being "hollow and dry and empty and noisy
and wooden and given to rotation"); machines may also be used to
excite the more pretentious and windy spiritual activities. Under the
cover of spiritual aims, carnal energies are gratified; by mechanical
devices, excess spiritual wind is diverted into useful channels. The

relation of wind and machine is reciprocal; schemes and projects are the mere complements of fanaticism and enthusiasm. This of course is the history of Protestant sectarianism in a nutshell; the energy of the saints, diverted to secular projects and mechanical improvements, gave rise to that eighteenth-century outlook for which philosophy and religion are both in different ways too exalted names but which is very adequately described as Franklinism. The application of religious zeal to business ends is the essence of Franklinism, as of the "modern spirit" which Swift hated. Because his Tory principles involved a deep-seated preference for the slow, traditional forms of a landed aristocracy over the sharper, more competitive, turbulent, and individualist ways of the money men, Swift despised all Getting Ahead; and he hated individual passion or appetite more even than wind and machines because it was the determining agent of both.

Standing apart from "discipline-directed" as from "system-directed" man, Swift saw, I think, a good deal deeper into the human dilemma of the day than any of the formal philosophers of his time. Shaftesbury and Mandeville, for example, disagreed as to the motive power of the social machine; did benevolence or greed make it tick? But neither dreamed of repudiating the view that society at its best is a clockwork which absorbs and makes use of the various motives of men. While Locke was rendering Christianity reasonable in terms of a mechanical philosophy and while Berkeley was quietly gathering the spiritual principle into a defiant solipsism, Swift, instead of trying to reconcile the alternatives of spirit and matter or to choose between them, made it his concern to repudiate them both. He figures, then, as a man utterly deprived of those usual philosophical supports and props of belief with which the average man surrounds himself. Swift's pride is a particularly brilliant, because partly inadequate, substitute for a system; had it been more formalized, he would never have defied with such savage success his own prescriptions against scribbling. Standing apart from his society, and with special horror from those who had rebelled against it, Swift achieved at bitter expense an especially acute and individual insight into it. If his performance seems sometimes to partake of levitation or puppetry because he gets along with so much less positive, constructive belief than his contemporaries found decent, a modern eye may find in that fact at least one measure of his achievement.

JAY ARNOLD LEVINE

The Design of A *Tale of a Tub*

The allegory of the *Tale* is not the center, or kernel but the enveloping shell; within that shell is the Worm, the Self, the Nothingness (all suggestively satanic in implication) of the digressions. The meaning of the *Tale* resides precisely in its emptiness, in its dose of wormwood.

We can now chart the pattern imposed by the purpose of the work; the design produced by the design. In the Critic's movement towards the assertion of Nothingness, the allegorical narrative and the commentaries drift apart, or *digress*, from each other, with the allegory eventually disappearing and the digressions assuming the primary position. This movement is related to, or even a reflection of, the *digression* (in the root sense of the word) of the three brothers, who swerve from the truth in their separate directions.

The first chapter of religious allegory, Section II, is almost entirely devoted to the sacred criticism practiced by Peter (the "Learned Brother," the "best Scholar") in his exegetical and linguistic analysis of the Will. The digression immediately following ("Concerning *Criticks*," appropriately) shows our Author and Commentator doing exactly what Peter does, and exactly what Bentley was famous for (as Wotton was the first to observe). Moreover, all the resources of verbal criticism are directed at Criticism *itself*, as the Critic examines the documents relating to the genealogy of Criticism. Here, as throughout the *Tale*, Criticism turns upon itself, exhibiting the egocentric folly of its Goddess ("Her Eyes turned inward, as if she lookt only upon herself").

The connection between Sections II and III, then, is *close*, in that the Critic recapitulates the manner of Peter, but highly *ironic*, in that our Critic is presumably the champion of Martin.

Section IV, the second installment of the parable, presents Peter as Projector, devising the doctrines and offices of the Roman Church. In like manner, the accompanying "Digression in the Modern Kind"—*Modern* being the Swiftian equivalent of *projecting*—presents the Critic as a Bentleyan projector: (after praising

From *ELH*, XXXIII, 2 (1966), 214–17. Baltimore: The Johns Hopkins Press. Copyright © 1966 by The Johns Hopkins Press. Reprinted by permission of the publisher.

Bentley for his overthrow of the Ancients) "I cannot but bewail, that no famous *Modern* hath yet attempted an universal System in a small portable Volume, of all Things that are to be Known, or Believed, or Imagined, or Practised in Life." That is, precisely that Bible for the Moderns which our Critic is in fact writing in the book before us; a parody of that book "within whose sacred context all wisdome is infolded" (according to Milton), or which, as Anthony Collins was to complain (in Swift's paraphrase), "requires a thorow Knowledge in Natural, Civil, Ecclesiastical History, Law, Husbandry, Sailing, Physick, Pharmacy, Mathematicks, Metaphysicks, Ethicks, and everything else that can be named."

Once more, the relationship between allegory and digression is firm but perverse; once more, the Critic imitates the corrupt method of Peter, this time in projecting a new Bible, a new system of belief and knowledge.

In the next pairing, Sections VI and VII, the formal breakdown commences. The tale proper, describing the reforms of Jack and Martin, is followed by the "Digression in Praise of Digressions," signalling that the critical eye is beginning to turn completely inwards. The digression, or critical act, is now valued for itself, without even a token attempt to relate the commentary to the allegory (except insofar as the imagery of the tale underscores the shift in emphasis from the "coat" to the "embroidery").

This digression on digressions is the crucial break in the *apparent* design of the *Tale*—the connection between parable and commentary, maintained precariously in the first two units (II and III, IV and V), dissolves entirely. Section VIII should bring us back to the narrative, since the even-numbered chapters, with the running title "Tale of a Tub," contain the religious allegory. But the eighth chapter is actually *another* digression, on the Aeolist sect. A comparable digression earlier, on "Sartorism" in Section II, was at least contained *within* the narrative; in Section VIII, the biblical narrative re-appears only in the last two paragraphs. The commentary, then, has not only become an end in itself, but is beginning to poach on the actual territory of the parable.

The true climax of the work, which is fast disintegrating under the stress of the Critic's disordered manner and personality, occurs in the next section (IX), forthrightly called "A Digression on Madness." Our Author concludes this disquisition by confirming our suspicion that we have been listening to a tale told by an idiot: "I my self, the Author of these momentous Truths, am a Person, whose Imaginations are hard-mouth'd, and exceedingly disposed to run away with his *Reason*, which I have observed from long Experience, to be a very light Rider, and easily shook off." All has blown up; the rest of the book is deliberate anti-climax (on Swift's part). The work fades in a raggedy collection of odds-and-ends, in mounting subjectivity, and in the final inversion of the formal pattern.

In considering Section X, we can again profit from the testimony of contemporary readers—but this time from their mistakes. In some modern editions of the *Tale*, this even-numbered section, which in the scheme of the work should be a continuation of the religious allegory and so labelled "Tale of a Tub," bears the titles "The Author's Compliment to the Readers &c," and "A Further Digression." Neither heading, however, is Swift's. The first was invented by the editors of the unauthorized edition of 1720, and the second by Hawkesworth in 1755. In devising those headings, Swift's editors were properly responding to the actual nature of the chapter, which is indeed digressive, but in altering the title they obscured Swift's point. Section X, called "Tale of a Tub," *should be* allegorical narrative and not digression, but, following the total collapse of the work in Section IX, it *is* in fact digressive. The mistake is the "Author's," not Swift's. The commentary has entirely overthrown the tale, usurping the place reserved for the allegory, which is supposed to be the kernel of our nut. The allegory does make a fitful final appearance, but in Section XI, in the place designed for the commentary, and there in atomistic form. We close our reading of the *Tale* not with a narrative conclusion, but with a transcription of note-cards that the Critic—like the rest of us —could not bear to file away unused. The apparent design of the work has thus been totally subverted; the final coupling confirms our judgment that for the Critic the true focus of interest is the commentary, not the parable. In the last pages the ascendant Critic is left writing upon Nothing—that is, quite frankly spinning the words out of his inner void.

Swift's work is indeed a "Tale of a Tub," but not exactly in the sense proposed by the Critic. Intended to divert enemies of religion from attacks on the Church, it is itself a ludicrous and dangerous "defense," very much in the manner of the "Argument against Abolishing Christianity." It is the rant of an egocentric scholiast, not an acceptable Anglican apology; like the "Argument," it is medicinal *in spite* of its author's prescriptions. And, in accordance with the Bentleyan Critic's confusion and perversion of the relationship between soul and body, spirit and letter, inner and outer (as displayed in his "Sartorism" and by his language), the allegory— the presumed essence (or kernel) of the work—is displaced by the peripheral commentary, the shell. In the manner of Peter and Jack, the weight of personal idiosyncrasy (or rampant subjectivity) destroys the Critic's own Bible, leaving the nothingness of his Self as the ultimate subject of the *Tale.* . . .

Bibliography

STUDIES OF SWIFT

Ricardo Quintana's *The Mind and Art of Jonathan Swift* (New York, 1936; reissued Gloucester, Mass., 1953) remains the best general introduction to Swift and his work, though it should be supplemented by the same author's *Swift: An Introduction* (New York, 1955), and, more recently, by Kathleen Williams' *Jonathan Swift and the Age of Compromise* (Lawrence, Kans., 1958) and Denis Donoghue's *Jonathan Swift: A Critical Introduction* (New York, 1969).

Though still in progress, Irvin Ehrenpreis' *Swift: The Man, His Works, and the Age* (Cambridge, Mass.: vol. I, 1962; vol. II, 1967) promises through its comprehensiveness to be the definitive modern biography. Henry Craik's two-volume *Life of Swift* (1882; rev. ed. 1894) is the best of the nineteenth-century biographies; still useful are Leslie Stephen's *Swift* (1882) and J. Churton Collins' *Jonathan Swift* (1893). The essays in Ehrenpreis' earlier *The Personality of Jonathan Swift* (Cambridge, Mass., 1958) are biographical and critical in emphasis. J. Middleton Murry's *Jonathan Swift: A Critical Biography* (London, 1954) is often suggestive, but persistently marred by a recklessness of interpretation; more extreme is Phyllis Greenacre's ingeniously earnest *Swift and Carroll: A Psychoanalytic Study of Two Lives* (New York, 1955). Designed for the general reader, Nigel Dennis' *Jonathan Swift: A Short Character* (New York, 1964) provides a lively, if hurried, assessment. Swift as cleric is studied by R. W. Jackson, *Jonathan Swift: Dean and Pastor* (New York, 1939) and by Louis A. Landa, *Swift and the Church of Ireland* (New York, 1954). Swift's public standing is surveyed in Donald Berwick's *The Reputation of Jonathan Swift, 1781–1882* (1941; reissued New York, 1969); of related interest are Harold Williams' commentary on "Swift's Early Biographers," in *Pope and His Contemporaries: Essays Presented to George Sherburn*, ed. J. L. Clifford and Louis A. Landa (New York, 1949), and Kathleen Williams' collection, largely of early criticisms of Swift, in *Swift and the Critical Heritage* (New York, 1970).

Swift's satirical methods are analyzed from varying perspectives by John M. Bullitt, *Jonathan Swift and the Anatomy of Satire* (Cambridge, Mass., 1953); Martin Price, *Swift's Rhetorical Art: A Study in Structure and Meaning* (New Haven, 1953); and Edward W. Rosenheim, *Swift and the Satirist's Art* (Chicago, 1963). Herbert Davis' *The Satire of Jonathan Swift* (New York, 1947) consists of three essays on Swift's literary, political, and moral satire. The various guises and points of view assumed by Swift in his writings receive close attention in William B. Ewald's *The Masks of Swift* (Cambridge, Mass., 1954). C. A. Beaumont's *Swift's Classical Rhetoric* (Athens, Ga., 1961) demonstrates Swift's use of formal rhetorical modes in certain of the shorter prose pieces; though differently emphasized, a similar rhetorical concern is to be found in Richard Cook's *Jonathan Swift as a Tory Pamphleteer* (Seattle, 1967). See also the substantial sections on Swift in Robert C. Elliott, *The Power of Satire* (Princeton, 1960); Martin Price, *To the Palace of Wisdom* (New York, 1964); and Ronald Paulson, *The Fictions of Satire* (Baltimore, 1967). For Swift's poetry, see Maurice Johnson, *The Sin of Wit: Jonathan Swift as a Poet* (Syracuse, 1950).

The tercentenary of Swift's birth brought forth several collections of miscellaneous essays: *Fair Liberty Was All His Cry*, ed. A Norman Jeffares (New York, 1967); *Jonathan Swift, 1667–1967*, ed. Roger McHugh and Philip Edwards (Chester Springs, Pa., 1968); and, of particular note, *The World of Jonathan Swift*, ed. Brian Vickers (Cambridge, Mass., 1968).

The standard bibliography, *Jonathan Swift: A List of Critical Studies Published from 1895 to 1945*, ed. Louis A. Landa and James E. Tobin (New York, 1945), has been extended in time by the separate publication of *A Bibliogra-*

718

BIBLIOGRAPHY

phy of Swift Studies, 1945–1965, ed. James J. Stathis (Nashville, 1967). Complementary to both listings is Milton Voigt's *Swift and the Twentieth Century* (Detroit, 1964), which provides a selective but cogent review of modern scholarship.

STUDIES OF *Gulliver's Travels*

Barroll, J. Leeds. "Gulliver and the Struldbrugs." *PMLA*, LXXIII (March 1958), 43–50. Relates the Struldbrugs to a lengthy literary tradition in which old age, fear of death, and desire for immortality are typical subjects of satire and reflection.

Carnochan, W. B. *Lemuel Gulliver's Mirror for Man*. Berkeley and Los Angeles, 1968. Related essays with emphasis on the *Travels* in relation to modes of Augustan satire.

Case, Arthur E. *Four Essays on "Gulliver's Travels."* Princeton, 1945. The four essays deal with textual matters (defending the authority of the 1727 edition); matters of chronology and geography; personal and political references; and the general significance of the *Travels*.

Clubb, Merrel D. "The Criticism of Gulliver's 'Voyage to the Houyhnhnms,' 1726–1914." *Stanford Studies in Language and Literature* (1941), 203–232. A revealing survey of responses to Book IV, and of the images of Swift that accompanied them.

Dircks, Richard J. "Gulliver's Tragic Rationalism." *Criticism*, II (Spring 1960), 134–149. Gulliver in Book IV exemplifies the excesses of eighteenth-century rationalism.

Eddy, W. A. *Gulliver's Travels: A Critical Study*. Princeton, 1923. Though by no means exhaustive in its listings or treatment, this early study gives many of Swift's sources and indicates somewhat his manner of adapting them.

Ehrenpreis, Irvin. "The Meaning of Gulliver's Last Voyage." *A Review of English Literature*, III (July 1962), 18–38. Swift's satire, in pressing the reader to reassess his definition of man, relates back to seventeenth-century efforts to define the nature of man.

Elliott, Robert C. "Gulliver as Literary Artist." *A Journal of English Literary History*, XIX (March 1952), 49–63. This close analysis of point of view tests the premise that the *Travels* are the memoirs of a misanthropic sea captain, and implicitly raises the problem of whether the book can, in fact, be read as a novel.

Frye, Roland M. "Swift's Yahoos and the Christian Symbols for Sin." *Journal of the History of Ideas*, XV (April 1954), 201–217. The description of the Yahoos includes many of the physical traits associated with sin and depravity by religious writers of the sixteenth and seventeenth centuries.

Halewood, William H. and Marvin Levich. "Houyhnhnm Est Animal Rationale." *Journal of the History of Ideas*, XXVI (1965), 273–278. The Houyhnhnms represent "perfect and essential" man and therefore the sole "realistic" norm for evaluating human behavior.

Kallich, Martin. *The Other End of the Egg: Religious Satire in Gulliver's Travels*. Bridgeport, 1970. Argues the presence of religious satire in each of the four voyages.

Kelling, Harold D. "*Gulliver's Travels:* A Comedy of Humours." *University of Toronto Quarterly*, XXI (July 1952), 362–375. Explores the ironic effects of Gulliver's partial point of view.

Moore, John B. "The Role of Gulliver." *Modern Philology*, XXV (May 1928), 469–480. An early but still useful exposition of Gulliver's character and its development through the four voyages.

Nicolson, Marjorie and Nora Mohler. "The Scientific Background of Swift's *Voyage to Laputa*." *Annals of Science*, II (July 1937), 299–334; reprinted in Nicolson, *Science and Imagination*, Ithaca, 1956. A detailed study of Swift's use of the *Transactions* of the Royal Society for his satire on science.

———. "Swift's 'Flying Island' in the *Voyage to Laputa*." *Annals of Science*, II (October 1937), 405–430. Swift's sources and his use of them.

Reichert, John F. "Plato, Swift, and the Houyhnhnms." *Philological Quarterly*, XLVII (April 1968), 179–192. A detailed comparison of *The Republic* and Book IV of the *Travels*.

Ross, John F. "The Final Comedy of Lemuel Gulliver." *Studies in the Comic*, University of California Publications in English, 1941, VIII, No. 2, 175–196. One of the earliest of modern studies to argue that Swift did not share Gulliver's final misanthropic view of man.

Sherburn, George. "Errors Concerning the Houyhnhnms." *Modern Philology*, LVI (November 1958), 92–97. An important counter statement to recent interpretations of Book IV which stress the limitations of the Houyhnhnms.

Stone, Edward. "Swift and the Horses: Misanthropy or Comedy?" *Modern*

Language Quarterly, X (September 1949), 367–376. Book IV is essentially comic in vision, not misanthropic.

Suits, Conrad. "The Role of the Horses in 'A Voyage to the Houyhnhnms.' " *University of Toronto Quarterly*, XXXIV (January 1965), 118–132. Gulliver is entirely sane; mankind, not the Houyhnhnms, is the object of satire.

Sutherland, John N. "A Reconsideration of Gulliver's Third Voyage." *Studies in Philology*, LIV (January 1957), 45–52. Book III has an inner unity and also is integral to the total pattern of the *Travels*.

Taylor, Aline Mackenzie. "Sights and Monsters and Gulliver's *Voyage to Brobdingnag*." *Tulane Studies in English*, VII (1957), 28–82. Important for what it suggests of Swift's use of contemporary material—in this instance, eighteenth-century equivalents of the freak show.

Taylor, Dick. "Gulliver's Pleasing Visions: Self-Deception as a Major Theme in *Gulliver's Travels*." *Tulane Studies in English*, XII (1962), 7–61. A detailing of Gulliver's capacity for self-deception.

Tilton, John W. "*Gulliver's Travels* as a Work of Art." *Bucknell Review*, VIII (December 1959), 246–259. Affirms the *Travels* on three accounts: its structure is coherent, its point of view consistent, and its hero psychologically convincing.

Traugott, John. "A Voyage to Nowhere with Thomas More and Jonathan Swift: *Utopia* and *The Voyage to the Houyhnhnms*." *The Sewanee Review*, LXIX (Autumn 1961), 534–565. To the extent that they ironically apprehended their Utopias, Swift and More could inhabit their "city of the mind" and yet participate in its corrupt counterpart.

Tuveson, Ernest. "Swift: The Dean as Satirist." *University of Toronto Quarterly*, XXII (July 1953), 368–375. Considering his religious commitment, Swift could not have offered the Houyhnhnms as his ideal.

Tyne, James L. "Gulliver's Maker and Gullibility." *Criticism*, VII (Spring 1965), 151–167. Relates the gullibility motif of the *Travels* to Swift's use of the same motif in his poetry.

Wedel, T. O. "On the Philosophical Background of *Gulliver's Travels*." *Studies in Philology*, XXIII (October 1926), 434–450. The religious and philosophical context governing the *Travels*.

Williams, Harold. *The Text of Gulliver's Travels*. Cambridge, England, 1952. Written to justify the authority of the 1735 text (cf. A. E. Case above), this brief study brings together valuable information on the writing, publication, and revision of the *Travels*.

Williams, Kathleen. "Gulliver's Voyage to the Houyhnhnms." *A Journal of English Literary History*, XVIII (December 1951), 275–286. The Houyhnhnms represent an extreme impossible to emulate, and thus are an unlikely model for man.

Wilson, James R. "Swift's Alazon." *Studia Neophilologica*, XXX (1958), 153–164. Gulliver as imposter.

STUDIES OF *A Tale of a Tub*, OTHER PROSE, AND POETRY

Adams, Robert Martin. "Jonathan Swift, Thomas Swift and the Authorship of *A Tale of a Tub*." *Modern Philology*, LXIV (February 1967), 198–232. Argues dual authorship of the *Tale*. For a response, see Dipak Nandy, *Modern Philology*, LXVI (May 1969), 333–337.

Andreasen, J. C. "Swift's Satire on the Occult in *A Tale of a Tub*." *Texas Studies in Literature and Language*, V (Autumn 1963), 410–421. Relates Swift's parody of occultism to the central theme of madness.

Brown, Lloyd W. "The Person of Quality in the Eighteenth Century: Aspects of Swift's Satire." *Dalhousie Review*, XLVIII (Summer 1968), 171–184. Swift's use of the type as satiric persona in *Abolishing Christianity* and the *Letter to a Young Gentleman*.

Chiasson, Elias J. "Swift's Clothes Philosophy in the *Tale* and Hooker's Concept of Law." *Studies in Philology*, LIX (January 1962), 64–82. The close, if ironic, affinities between Swift's clothes philosophy and the concept of law formulated in Hooker's *Ecclesiastical Polity*.

Clark, John R. *Form and Frenzy in Swift's "Tale of a Tub*." Ithaca, 1970. Emphasizes the artistic, as opposed to the rhetorical, quality of the *Tale*.

England, A. B. "World without Order: Some Thoughts on the Poetry of Swift." *Essays in Criticism*, XVI (January 1966), 32–43. Swift's pictorial and structural indecisiveness reflects one aspect of his reaction to his world.

Garrod, H. W. "Phalaris and Phalarism." *Seventeenth Century Studies Presented to Sir Herbert Grierson*. Oxford, 1938. Pp. 360–371. A good account of the Bentley-Boyle hostilities.

Goodwin, A. "Wood's Halfpence." *English Historical Review*, LI (October 1936), 647–674. Examines the Irish opposition to Wood's patent and its significance in the history of Anglo-Irish relations.

Greene, Donald. "On Swift's 'Scatalogical' Poems." *Sewanee Review*, LXXV
   (Autumn 1967), 672–689. Urges the antiromantic, as opposed to excremental, vision of these poems.
Harth, Philip. *Swift and Anglican Rationalism: The Religious Background of
   "A Tale of a Tub."* Chicago, 1961. A close study of one important strand in
   the *Tale's* web of literary influence and allusion.
Hopkins, Robert H. "The Personation of Hobbism in Swift's *Tale of a Tub*
   and *Mechanical Operation of the Spirit*." *Philological Quarterly*, XLV (April
   1966), 372–378. Discusses Swift's allusions to *Leviathan* and his parody of
   elements of Hobbes' teaching.
Johnson, Maurice. "Text and Possible Occasion for Swift's 'Day of Judgment.'" *PMLA*, LXXXVI (March 1971), 210–217. Argues convincingly that
   the poem was written in 1732–33 on the occasion of a new attempt by dissenters to repeal the Sacramental Test Act.
————. "'Verses on the Death of Dr. Swift.'" *Notes & Queries*, CIC (November 1954), 473–474. Swift implies a middle ground of truth between the
   self-abuse of the first half of the poem and the self-praise at the end.
Jones, Richard Foster. *Ancients and Moderns: A Study of the Background of
   "The Battle of the Books."* St. Louis, 1936. Discusses Swift's sympathy for
   the ancients. For a further refinement, see Philip Pinkus, "Swift and the
   Ancients-Moderns Controversy," *University of Toronto Quarterly*, XXIX
   (1959–60), 46–58.
Kelling, Harold. "Reason in Madness: *A Tale of a Tub*." *PMLA*, LXIX
   (March 1954), 198–222. Especially good on the religious atmosphere in
   which the *Tale* was conceived and on the teaching of "sense and reason" by
   contemporary Anglican clergy.
Kulisheck, Clarence L. "Swift's Octosyllabics and the Hudibrastic Tradition."
   Journal of English and Germanic Philology, LIII (July 1954), 361–368.
   Demonstrates the greater precision of Swift's couplet and its adaptability to
   larger structural patterns.
Leavis, F. R. "The Irony of Swift," in *The Common Pursuit*. New York, 1952.
   Pp. 73–87. See William Frost, "The Irony of Swift and Gibbon," reprinted
   herein (pp. 684–687), for a summary of Leavis' argument.
O'Hehir, Brendan. "Meaning in Swift's 'Description of a City Shower.'" *A
   Journal of English Literary History*, XXVII (September 1960), 194–207.
   Swift's allusions to Vergil, Dryden, and the Scriptures enforce his "denuncia-
   tion of cathartic doom upon the corruption of the city."
Paulson, Ronald. "Swift, Stella and Permanence." *A Journal of English Liter-
   ary History*, XXVII (December 1960), 298–314. Swift's "Verses on the
   Death" resolve his persistent concern, on the one hand, with the mutability
   of physical life, on the other, with the permanence of human virtue.
————. *Theme and Structure in Swift's "Tale of a Tub."* New Haven, 1960. A
   valuable study of the *Tale*, reaching toward a unified view of it by elucidat-
   ing a number of its major themes.
Quinlan, Maurice J. "Swift's Use of Literalization as a Rhetorical Device."
   PMLA, LXXXII (December 1967), 516–521. A good discussion of one of
   Swift's rhetorical techniques.
Roscelli, William John. "*A Tale of a Tub* and the 'Cavils of the Sour.'" *Jour-
   nal of English and Germanic Philology*, LXIV (January 1965), 41–56.
   Swift's attempt to expose corrupt theological beliefs without undermining
   the foundations of Christian faith proved an impossible task.
San Juan, E., Jr. "The Anti-Poetry of Jonathan Swift." *Philological Quarterly*,
   XLIV (July 1965), 387–396. Swift's highly charged language conveys the
   "deidealizing" meaning of facts.
Slepian, Barry. "The Ironic Intention of Swift's Verses on his own Death."
   Review of English Studies, XIV (August 1963), 249–256. In the "apologia"
   which ends the "Verses" Swift is capping the argument that all men are vain
   by proving himself vain. For a response, see Marshall Waingrow, "'Verses
   on the Death of Dr. Swift,'" *Studies in English Literature*, V (Summer
   1965), 513–518.
Smith, Curtis C. "Metaphor Structure in Swift's *A Tale of a Tub*." *Thoth*, V
   (1964), 22–41. The meaphor structure becomes unmanageable for the hack,
   who uses metaphors inconsistently and therefore against himself.
Smith, Frederik N. "Dramatic Elements in Swift's *Journal to Stella*." *Eighteenth-Century Studies*, I (June 1968), 332–352. Swift intentionally developed
   dramatic elements in composing the *Journal*.
Starkman, Miriam K. "Swift's Rhetoric: The 'Overfraught Pinnace'?" *South
   Atlantic Quarterly*, LXVIII (Spring 1969), 188–197. Questions the concentration on rhetorical techniques in recent Swift criticism and stresses his pre-
   eminence in generic prose satire.

————. *Swift's Satire on Learning in "A Tale of a Tub."* Princeton, 1950. Studies important elements in the intellectual background of the *Tale* and shows the nature of their integration in the work; concerned chiefly with the digressions.

Stephens, Lamarr. " 'A Digression in Praise of Digressions' as a Classical Oration: Rhetorical Satire in Section VII of Swift's *A Tale of a Tub.*" *Tulane Studies in English*, XIII (1963), 41–49. Swift satirizes the rhetorical deficiencies of modern wits by making this digression all that the persona says their digressions are not.

Stout, Gardner D., Jr. "Speaker and Satiric Vision in Swift's *Tale of a Tub.*" *Eighteenth-Century Studies*, III (Winter 1969), 175–199. Considers the speaker to be Swift himself, practicing "shifting ironies" and in the process discovering his own face as well as everyone else's in the satiric glass of the *Tale*.

Thomas. W. K. "The Bickerstaff Caper." *Dalhousie Review*, XLIX (Autumn 1969), 346–360. Emphasizes Swift's attack on Partridge's false learning and hostility to the Church of England.

Williams, Kathleen. "Restoration Themes in the Major Satires of Swift." *Review of English Studies*, XVI (August 1965), 258–271. Describes the Author's practices in the *Tale* of debasing words, of taking metaphors literally, and of reasoning by means of them.